Mistletoe Path
Sorrel Path
Sedge Path
Heath Path
Eglantine Path
Lupine Path
Mimosa Path
Yarrow Path
Green Brier Path
ELM AVENUE
SPRUCE AVENUE
PINE AVENUE
CENTRAL AVENUE
Snowberry Path
FOREST POND
Narcissus Path
Linden Path
Indian Ridge Path
Primrose Path
GARDEN POND
Lilac Path
GARDEN
D1560606

Urban Life and Urban Landscape Series

Silent City on a Hill

Forest Pond at Mount Auburn, engraving by William H. Bartlett, ca. 1845.

Blanche Linden-Ward

Landscapes of Memory and Boston's Mount Auburn Cemetery

OHIO STATE UNIVERSITY PRESS : COLUMBUS

LIBRARY OF CONGRESS

Library of Congress Cataloging-in-Publication Data

Linden-Ward, Blanche, 1946–

Silent city on a hill : landscapes of memory and Boston's Mount Auburn Cemetery / Blanche Linden-Ward.

p. cm. — (Urban life and urban landscape series)

Bibliography: p.

Includes index.

ISBN 0–8142–0469–4

1. Mount Auburn Cemetery (Boston, Mass.) 2. Cemeteries—Massachusetts—Boston—Landscape architecture. 3. Boston (Mass.)—Buildings, structures, etc. I. Title. II. Series.

F73.61.M8L56 1989

974.4′61—dc19 88–22577

CIP

The paper in this book meets the guidelines for permanence and durability of the Committee on Production Guidelines for Book Longevity of the Council on Library Resources.

Printed in the U.S.A.

9 8 7 6 5 4 3 2 1

In memory of my maternal grandparents

Anna Blanche Techoires Cate

(1902–1977)

and

Frank Brinton Cate

(1889–1957)

Contents

Acknowledgments

I HAVE INCURRED MANY DEBTS of thanks in the research, writing, illustration, and completion of this book. First and foremost, I am grateful to Alan Ward, my friend, partner, husband, and collaborator. Beyond the usual moral support and domestic assistance provided by an author's spouse, he was the catalyst for my research into cemeteries in the first place. When we were both graduate students at Harvard in 1977, he urged me to write a brief history of cemetery design to accompany his photo essay on garden cemeteries; but, for me, the project expanded into much more. Over the years since, he has helped with my research, served as copyeditor and proofreader, provided a landscape architect's perspective on design, and, most importantly, produced much of the visual documentation in this book. We have spent countless wonderful days together in the field, "reading" landscapes, searching for documentary views of English gardens, Père Lachaise, Mount Auburn, other graveyards, cemeteries, and monuments. Alan contributed hours, days, and weekends in the darkroom doing copy photographs of historic images and printing them along with his own images. We both owe thanks to the Hubbard Educational Trust for a generous grant that permitted us to purchase or produce much of the important visual component of this book.

My first teachers in graduate school, Henry D. Shapiro and Zane Miller, laid the groundwork in intellectual and urban history for my approach to this subject and taught me the love of history that has sustained this project to its completion. They have continued to be mentors, encouraging my writing of this and related papers, essays, and projects, especially in their positions as co-directors of the Center for Neighborhood and Community Studies in the History Department of the University of Cincinnati. Their rigorous criticisms of my ideas in their various incarnations over the past decade have been invaluable. Any flaws in the finished product are probably in places where I failed to heed their advice.

Saul Benison, Albert Fein, Barbara Rosenkrantz, Jack Salzman, Howard Segal, Anne Whiston Spirn, and Morris Vogel have read parts of this manuscript or related writings and have offered opinions that I value greatly. Conversations with a number of friends and acquaintances have raised or answered important questions pertinent to this book; and I would like to thank especially Charlotte Lindgren and Donald Winslow, Henry Deeks, Greer Hardwicke, John Lowe, Barbara Ramusak, Barbara Rotundo, David Sloane, and Frederick Voss. Daniel Aaron was also early to encourage me to pursue this interdisciplinary research for my Harvard doctoral thesis in History of American Civilization, and three Radcliffe Grants (now administered by the Bunting Institute) made my work possible at that stage.

Many librarians and archivists have provided invaluable assistance. The staffs of the Massachusetts Historical Society, the New York Public Library, the Philadelphia Free Public Library, the Watertown Free Public Library, Harvard University Archives, and the Houghton Library at Harvard responded promptly and generously to requests to use their manuscript or visual collections. Special help came from Richard Wolfe at Harvard's Countway Library of Medicine; Barbara Puorro Galasso of the George Eastman House International Museum of Photography; Ellie Reichlin and Lorna Condon at the Archives of the Society for the Preservation of New England Antiquities; Mary Grenci, Roberta Zonghi, Eugene Zepp, and Dr. Laura V. Monti in the Rare Books Room of the Boston Public Library; Georgia Barnhill at the American Antiquarian Society, Worcester; and Walter Punch of the Massachusetts Horticultural Society.

The officers, trustees, and staff of Mount Auburn Cemetery have been most supportive of my work since its inception. Presidents Alan D. Chesney and William Clendaniel, Superintendent Duncan W. Munro, and Assistant Superintendent Roger Kindred have granted me ready access to all of the records of the cemetery, have answered all sorts of questions, and have provided helpful advice. Gordon Abbott, Jr., James M. Storey, and Malcolm D. Perkins, trustees on the Book Committee, have steadfastly and patiently encouraged this publication despite repeated but unavoidable delays; the entire Board made publication of such a heavily illustrated volume possible through a generous subvention to the press. The recommendation of Sam Bass Warner, Jr., that extensive illustration of my manuscript was necessary also helped make this book possible in its present form.

Emerson College has given me a supportive group of colleagues, a Faculty Research Grant, and assistance in production of the final draft. John M. Kittross and Jacqueline Liebergott granted me access to the typing services of Brian McCarthy and Mary Ellen Horne, who took great care of my work, despite repeated revisions. Gregory Conti, Elliot Shapiro, and Jaime Triplett were conscientious research assistants and proofreaders. And through it all, a network of friends, especially Joanne Jacobson, Patricia Palmieri, Lois Rudnick, Nancy Shapiro, Jennifer Tebbe, and members of the New England American Studies Association Council, have offered professional advice and moral support.

My oldest debt is to my mother, Lauretta Cate Gemrose, who took me to France many times when I was growing up, thus introducing me to different landscapes of memory, and who then sent me to college. Finally, although they may protest that they did not have a part in this book, I owe many thanks to my children, Julie and Marc, who have grown to adolescence in the process of its completion. They have consistently displayed patience, understanding, and cooperation that made it possible for me to concentrate on my work even when I did not have the proverbial "room of one's own"; and they have been of relatively good humor the many times I have conned them into field trips to cemeteries.

Blanche Linden-Ward
Watertown, Massachusetts, 1989

Abbreviations

AAS	American Antiquarian Society, Worcester, Massachusetts.
BPL	Boston Public Library Rare Books and Archives, Boston.
CLMH	Countway Library of Medicine, Harvard University, Boston
HLH	Houghton Library, Harvard University, Cambridge.
HUA	Harvard University Archives, Cambridge.
MHIS	Massachusetts Historical Society, Boston.
MHOR	Massachusetts Horticultural Society, Boston.
MTA	Mount Auburn Cemetery, Cambridge.
NYPL	New York Public Library, New York City.
SPNEA	Society for the Preservation of New England Antiquities, Boston.

Introduction

ঌ

If we were able to go back to the elements of states and to examine the oldest monuments of their history, I doubt not that we should discover in them the primal causes of . . . the habits, the ruling passions, and, in short, all that constitutes what is called the national character.

—Alexis de Tocqueville,
Democracy in America (1832)

TOCQUEVILLE, LIKE MANY OF HIS ERA, believed in the possibility of reinventing the state in republican form and in the necessity for building monuments to epitomize and preserve civic virtue, to shape the character of the citizenry, and to stabilize society in order to forestall inevitable decline and ruin. In new republics, the art of the painter, sculptor, architect, or landscape gardener would augment and perpetuate the work of statecraft. Art would function by redefining a history in secular terms compatible with political ideals and ideology and their preservation.[1]

During his travels in America in the fall and spring of 1831–32, Tocqueville found that the beliefs about the importance of material commemoration of many of the young nation's cultural leaders were similar to his own. They, after all, knew the debates of the French revolutionary era on the importance of creating a "cult of ancestors" as a way to redefine history and culture, an especially pressing necessity in the wake of their iconoclastic rejection of the Old Order, the forms and traditions of Church and sovereign. Americans and the French drew heavily on the Whiggish aesthetics and philosophy that inspired development of eighteenth-century English gardens as landscapes of memory—but memory newly fabricated as an alternative to the medieval, ecclesiastical, and monarchical past.

For six years before Tocqueville's visit, Bostonians had been planning a new funerary institution and landscape for display of commemorative monuments of the sort that had become fashionable as well as politically functional in England and France. Mount Auburn Cemetery, coincidentally dedicated in the autumn of Tocqueville's visit, was designed to reflect republican taste, ideology, and a new post-revolutionary definition of history. Its founders' motivations were more idealistic than practical, although in the process of forming America's first "rural" cemetery they also reformed local burial practices at a time of rising urban land costs, fear of church control of burials, and suggestions that burials in the city might endanger public health. If Tocqueville had arrived a year or so later, his hosts undoubtedly would have given him a tour of the cemetery run by an innovative, nonsectarian, nonprofit corporation, because Mount Auburn illustrated many of the characteristics that the political philosopher considered distinctly American. It exemplified their ability to work through voluntary associations to create institutions to stabilize society and raise the level of culture. Bostonians proudly presented Mount Auburn to visitors as their chief tourist attraction and evidence of local and national worth.[2]

This book is an inquiry into the intellectual and aesthetic origins of Mount Auburn Cemetery and an analysis of its development from the initial formative period through the 1860s, when the aesthetics of the picturesque and notions about its role as an agent of history still remained intact. The founding of Mount Auburn cannot be fully understood without analysis of the origins and ideological meanings attached to elements of its design idiom derived from eighteenth-century English landscaped gardens and subsequently applied in an exemplary fashion by the French, intent on funerary as well as cultural reform. This book traces the rise through the eighteenth century and demise in the mid-nineteenth—the age of revolutions—of a Whiggish historical consciousness, shaped by a conjunction of larger religious, political, intellectual, and aesthetic trends, all of which contributed to the design of these landscapes of memory.

Concepts of a linear, unchanging sacred past in which God intervened in the lives of men through dramatic, cataclysmic events gave way by the eighteenth century to an emphasis on Nature and its cycles as operative principles behind the course of history as well as metaphors for it. Providence might still intervene, but man became empowered to change the course of history by making a dramatic break with the past, with traditions, or with established law, thereby challenging religious authorities who labeled such action sin and sacrilege. Rediscovery of both Nature and the classics became subversive to Christian orthodoxy, and both provided vocabularies for redefining the past and man's relationship to it. The "enlightened" believed in the *revolutionary* possibility of hastening the inexorable forces of Nature in cyclical history, swinging the pendulum of Time back to a Golden Age, an Arcadian new beginning. Thereafter, they would reinterpret history in secular terms with celebration of the founding events and individuals who epitomized civic virtue and moral philosophy, aspects of the natural law and basis for the new republican state.

Philosophers, aestheticians, and politicians recommended institutionalization of ideology through commemorative monuments and landscapes of memory. Wordsworth believed that landscape gardening, in particular, was a liberal art like poetry and painting, capable of moving "the affections under the control of reason." By melding classicism and naturalism, the designer could teach lessons of moral philosophy and natural law, contributing to development of a "cult of melancholy" or a "cult of ancestors," to convey messages about Man's relationship to God and Nature just as surely as any form of literature.[3]

The quest to reattain a simpler, more natural state of society free from the corruptions associated with the traditions of Church and State relates to the revolutionary attempts of Calvinists to "purify" Christianity, thereby earning the epithet "Puritan." Historicism aided assertion of a radical Protestantism. Historicism involves making new interpretations and uses of history when orthodox versions of the past are judged unacceptable; it may involve the mimicking of forms and patterns previously used, but in very different ways, or application of selected "lessons" of the past to new circumstances. Given a radical discontinuity with a former, familiar past rejected as corrupt, historicism is a way of starting over by reasserting an intellectual continuity between the present and remote historical periods. Self-conscious and selective copying of ancient styles with the intent to *make* history anew produced the common elements of design used in eighteenth- and nineteenth-century landscapes of memory—picturesque English gardens, French landscape gardens and cemeteries in the English fashion, patriotic monuments of the young American republic, and Mount Auburn and other "rural" cemeteries copied after its example.

The historical consciousness shared through that long period by many members of new elites on both sides of the Atlantic involved a cyclical view of the fate of nations. The Italian philosopher Giambattista Vico (1669–1744) propounded a theory of history in which stages of growth, maturation, and decay are intrinsically connected. Only Providence could forestall the inevitable cataclysms and keep the course of history progressing to higher levels. Although Vico's personal influence was minor, he expressed pessimistic ideas shared by many of his contemporaries, forestalling the general acceptance of an unqualifiedly linear concept of history as constant progress. Jefferson reflected such beliefs in asserting that each generation might have its own revolution. The Reverend William B. O. Peabody told an audience of Bostonians in 1831, "in the mighty system of the universe, not a single step of the destroyer, Time, is not made subservient to some ulterior purpose of reproduction; and the circle of creation and destruction is eternal." As late as 1861, the Bostonian Wilson Flagg still believed that "revolution after revolution is destined to pass over us."[4]

Until 1789, the term "revolution" signified a return to a previous state rather than a leap to the future; for many, it had positive connotations. It provided a second chance for re-forming civilization, rid of the corruptions of the immediate past, by starting over at the beginning, returning to a simpler, primitive, and idealized beginning epoch, regaining Eden or Arcadia. Such was the significance of the term "Glorious Revolution," applied in 1688 to Britain's new political beginning with a new royal family.[5]

The cyclical concept of history ran counter to the orthodoxy of the Old Order, premised on the tyranny of tradition or political and theological stasis. It provided justification in naturalistic terms for the rejection of established Church and sovereign by distinct sectarian and political factions, usually Dissenters and Whigs, generally comprised of coalitions of new elites—professionals, merchants, bankers, occasionally artisans, members of the gentry, and lesser nobility. Its proponents had a personal stake in ignoring their recent past and inventing a new one compatible with starting the processes of civilization anew to forestall the forces of decline, corruption, and death, which seemed all too inevitable. Otherwise, death would be the ultimate revolutionary.

The new ideology necessitated reevaluation of traditional deathways and eventually burial reform. Chapter 1 considers the *status quo,* the unpleasant conditions in the deliberately urbanized, Church-controlled places of death of most of western Europe from the fifth into the eighteenth centuries. Decrees that burials be tightly regulated under ecclesiastical auspices had theological as well as administrative motivations. Medieval ecclesiastics held that after Adam's ejection from Eden, the Devil and other evil spirits, including the gods and demigods of folklore and classical myth, frequented rural places, waiting to lead to evil, paganism, or pantheism the faithful who strayed from the sacred center of the city, literally and figuratively from the fold of the Church, its law, and civilization. Those who died in the Church's good graces were incorporated into the body of the Church via the anonymous cemetery, where, in most cases, earthly identity was lost in exchange for assurances of salvation. The institutionalization of death served as an agent of social and political control.

The first major challenge to this traditional order came from seventeenth-century Calvinists, who called for a return to the simpler forms of primitive Christianity, including reform of burial practices. Later, High Church historians would call Cal-

Fig. I.1. Monument of Demetria and Pamphile, two sisters, and tombs of Greek Worthies, Ceramicus outside of Athens' Dipylon Gate, stereographic photograph by Underwood and Underwood, ca. 1880.

vinism's antiritualism a radical cultural "breach with the past," just as surely showing "contempt invoked upon the whole of the past" as the French Revolution.[6] Calvinists insisted on secularizing burials as part of their larger agenda. Calvin's Geneva liturgy stipulated: "The Corps is reuerently brought to the graue, accompanied by the congregation, with owte any further ceremonies, which beying buriede, the minister goeth to the churche, if it be not farre of, and maketh some comfortable exhortacion to the people, towchyng deathe, and the resurrection." There would be no extreme unction, funeral mass, or prayers for the soul of the deceased. Calvinists refused to consecrate the simple "burial ground" or "graveyard" as sacred space; they also removed it, whenever possible, from proximity to the church, itself simply called a "meetinghouse." They intended "to avoid any recurrence of prayers offered to the dead or on their behalf" by shunning use of the cross, traditionally placed in cemeteries for that reason. When Calvinists insisted on rejecting "superstition" in funeral practices, they referred to papist rather than pagan forms.[7]

Still, Calvinists, like many of their Catholic predecessors, generally believed that God concealed the order of death deliberately to teach man to remain constantly prepared for the unknown future and the hereafter. Unlike the Catholics, however, they could not count on the sacraments of the Church to take care of their postmortem fate. The doctrine of Predestination made both uncertainty and confusion central to the Calvinist mind, and the material forms of their burial places epitomized the harshness of their theology. The chaos and barrenness of New England's colonial graveyards suggested the fate of the unregenerate; their two-dimensional, gray slate stones graphically represented the ideological dualism that divided mankind into good and evil, saved and damned. Yet unlike traditional Catholic cemeteries, these burials were not all anonymous. When substantial numbers of permanent gravestones began to appear in Puritan burial grounds in the 1660s, however, their ritualized messages of *memento mori* urged passersby to remember the finality of death, the pastness and insignificance of the earthly past, rather than the lives of particular individuals or the sense of a common history made by individuals shaping their fate through works. Cut off from sacramental assurances of salvation and confronted with the stark reality of death, many people agonized about their personal future. The Reverend Edward Young observed: "Few ages have been deeper in dispute about religion than this. . . . I think it may be reduced to this single question: Is man immortal, or is he not?"[8]

Some Protestants bypassed such disturbing philosophical questions by focusing on simpler spiritual lessons drawn from the natural world and the significance of man's journey through it. Allegory, unrelated to Scripture or theology, became possible. The taste for a metaphoric landscape was suggested by the widely read *Pilgrim's Progress,* first published in 1678. John Bunyan, a Baptist preacher, wrote the pious tract while jailed by Charles II, the Catholic king. It presents an account of the arduous travels of Everyman along the long and winding road from the City of Destruction to the Celestial City "upon a mighty hill." Protestants identified with the quest of the individual traveler through the landscape, punctuated, like life, by challenges and hazards—the Hill of Difficulty, the Valley of Humility, the Valley of the Shadow of Death, the Delectable Mountains, the Slough of Despond, Mount Marvel, Mount Innocent, and Mount Charity, as well as the River of Death. Those who read *Pilgrim's Progress,* which rivaled the Bible as a best-seller well into the nineteenth century, were inspired to look for symbolism in the material world and even to design landscapes to epitomize their ideas and values. The placing into landscape of forms of a metaphoric journey of life or pilgrimage of the soul, questing for the eternal, influenced even those who did not share Bunyan's evangelical faith, those who preferred to think in even more secular terms of the questing travels of Aeneas or other classical heroes. The circuit walk of newly invented eighteenth-century English landscaped gardens and of nineteenth-century "rural" cemeteries modeled after them presented a sequence of programmed spiritual experiences that gave a physical dimension to abstract ideas in a way that had particular significance to those familiar with Bunyan.[9]

The metaphor for travel as an experience of learning and growth had its real-life component as increasing numbers of people made the Grand Tour of Italy and Greece in search of the "picturesque." Through the eighteenth century, the quest for pastoral scenes with classical antiquities and other ruins, melancholy monuments to the heights of civilization achieved in a distant past, led visitors to a variety of historical and mythical sites like Lake Avernus, site of the grotto of the Cumaean sibyl, where Aeneas supposedly began his descent into the underworld in search of his father. Travelers were particularly attracted to ancient funerary landscapes, which seemed so much more appealing than their own. English and French visitors flocked to the Ceramicus, the ancient cemetery outside the gates of Athens where Plato met with his students in the Academy. (Fig. I.1.) They walked among the linear, extramural burials of the Appian Way and Pompeii. (Figs. I.2, 3.) In England, they sought out sites like the ruins of Tintern Abbey. Eventually, they even made their way to more ancient sites in Egypt, to Palmyra, and to Baalbec. Such "picturesque" places testified to the resurgence of Nature, triumphant after the fall of civilization, a message that appealed to those critical of their own immediate past. The experience was sobering as well as inspirational.

The itinerary of Joseph Addison, Whig editor of the *Spectator,* kept him abroad from 1701–1703. On his return to England, Addison proselytized the taste for picturesque landscapes of distant vistas and woods framing ancient monuments and architectural fragments, relics of a distant past, scenes like those painted by Salvador Rosa, Nicolas Poussin, and Claude Lorrain. Richard Boyle, Third Lord Burlington, similarly returned from Italy in 1719 determined to recreate such scenes in his own gardens at Chiswick. The French poet Jacques Delille credited travelers' discovery of the ancients in the naturalistic landscape of Italy with feeding the modern taste for landscape gardening that drew upon allegorical and historicist themes. Gardens designed to cater to these tastes wended the visitor's steps along a sinuous path called a "tour" past structures fabricated to stir philosophical or literary associations, from areas of sunlight into the darkness of grottoes suggestive of death, and to

Fig. I.2. Tombs on Appian Way, albumen print photograph by Giorgio Sommer (Italian), ca. 1875.

Fig. I.3. Burials along road outside of Pompeii, albumen print photograph by Giorgio Sommer (Italian), ca. 1875.

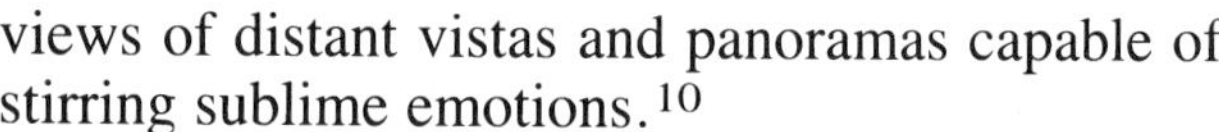

views of distant vistas and panoramas capable of stirring sublime emotions.[10]

Chapter 2 traces some of the philosophical and political currents that premised invention of the form and formula of the English landscaped garden in the eighteenth century. English Nonconformists and Whigs were the first and chief champions of developing their own "picturesque" landscapes imbued with allegory and historicism. Whiggish philosophers particularly celebrated political liberties governed by natural law and reason. Most often, they used "liberty" in the Lockean sense of freedom to enjoy property without interference, a particular concern of those ambitious to build estates, to enclose property, and to win more power in Parliament free from royal interference. Their reverence for the "rural" had associations of retreat from the political corruptions of the court to one's own estate in the country, asserting personal independence and the natural claim of the landowner to political power. Whigs decried the political decadence of Toryism and chose to retreat from it whenever possible. Rejection of the older taste in gardening for French formalism, associated with the ecclesiastical and monarchical establishment, became a matter of ideology preached by Addison and other Whigs. The "modern" style of landscape gardening contrasted dramatically with the highly controlled linearity of the French garden *à la* Le Nôtre.[11]

Horace Walpole likened naturalistic gardens to the English constitution; other theorists suggested that the sinuous paths represented traditional English liberties. In these gardens Whigs enshrined references to an ancient Anglo-Saxon history of constitutionalism and defense of individual liberties, values they also found represented in classical architecture drawn from the republics of Greece and Rome. Many gardens incorporated memories of legendary ancestors—King Alfred and Aeneas. Some made material reference to ancient Druids as exemplars of natural law. So great was the quest for alternatives to the immediate but rejected past that some gardens displayed Egyptian structures, intended to imply an even older and purer source of law and civilization. Forms drawn from Nature itself referred not only to natural law but to the inexorable processes of Nature in the cyclical view of history. Elevation of "taste" through exposure of all of these elements, so philosophers argued, would raise the moral and ethical character of a new class of citizens able to govern themselves. It would create a "natural aristocracy" and stabilize civilization in radically new ways.[12]

Themes of longing for an Arcadian past, philosophical allegory, and commemoration of heroes–

ancient and modern–shaped the English style of landscape gardening. Elements of design permitted an imaginary recovery of a lost past. The taste for the picturesque had certain nostalgic motivations, representing an attempt to compensate through deliberately designed irregularities for the disappearance of truly natural wildness. English garden landscapes conveyed, according to Arthur O. Lovejoy, "a sense of the transitoriness of all natural beauty and human glory." They were akin to *memento mori,* reminders of inexorable change and the cycles of Nature and history. They provided natural sites for location of commemorative monuments bearing similar messages, and even for relocation of burials of those who would not accept burial by the Church. These gardens became, therefore, intensely personal, meditative places designed to permit solitary indulgence in the "pleasures of melancholy," a philosophical exercise recommended to heighten introspection and retrospection in a way that appealed more to the growing romantic sensibilities of the era than to the proponents of Reason. Such gardens were true "Muse-aeums," places where one might consult a variety of Muses.[13]

Trends in "affective individualism" can also be found in English gardens, as well as in the funerary landscapes they would later inspire. Lawrence Stone finds that trends in affective individualism accompanied "massive shifts in world views and value systems" to become "perhaps the most important change in *mentalité* to have occurred in the Early Modern period, indeed possibly in the last thousand years of Western history." Affective individualism was a cluster of changing values away "from distance, deference, and patriarchy" of the traditional, open-lineage family to increasingly emotional relationships between spouses as well as between parents and children (and one might add friends), including new ideas about child rearing and remembrance of "loved ones" after death. Stone argues that this dramatic rise in sentiment is traceable from the late seventeenth century on, appearing first among the upper classes, professionals, and gentry. It premised Whiggish sentimentality and the cluster of philosophical and political ideas about "life, liberty, and the pursuit of happiness" propounded first in England but most successfully in the United States.[14]

Affective individualism certainly appeared in France as well, as did admiration for the style and significance of the *jardin anglais*. Chapter 3 traces the process of adaptation by the French elite of English landscaped garden taste for their own estates, but especially for creation of an unprecedented funerary landscape that would permit a display of affective individualism and patriotic commemoration unprecedented in modern times. French philosophers, reformers, and revolutionaries, like the poet Delille, praised and shared "the *sublime melancholy* of the English nation"; many of them adapted elements of Whiggish culture and thought as alternatives to their Old Order. But they took elements of naturalistic landscape design further than the English by applying them to proposals for burial reform and for creation of a "cult of ancestors" to counteract the iconoclastic excesses of their Revolution. Eventually, that design precedent resulted in creation of Père Lachaise Cemetery on the outskirts of Paris in 1804.[15]

Chapter 4, "The Necessity for Monuments," describes development of the impulse to commemorate a new, secular, and civil past in material terms in America in the first decades of the nineteenth century. Americans had a particular affinity for the Whiggish adulation of an Edenic period as return to a new political and cultural beginning; and millennialism from several strands of American Protestantism contributed additional symbolic meaning to the Revolution and the new republic that necessitated monuments to mark the fortuitous beginning. Furthermore, as Gordon Wood observes, Americans imbibed radical Whiggism in the late colonial period and shared its belief in the efficacy of mnemonic monuments to convey lessons of moral philosophy and civic virtue. Both John Adams and Thomas Jefferson in the correspondence of their declining years used Whiggish arguments to debate the pros and cons, the potential uses and hazards, of art in a republic; however, it was not until the coming of age of the second generation after the Revolution that Americans began to work in earnest to create material representations of patriotism, history, and republicanism that could sustain their "experiment" in government through many generations. Around the time of the semicentennial of independence, Americans began to build upon, adapt, and reinterpret commemorative design precedents from abroad. They heeded Wordsworth's call for memory and imagination "to enshrine the spirit of the past / For future restoration." They believed that monuments and historic places could be imbued with patriotic meaning to last in the popular imagination. The search for a usable past, the quest for national identity, and the deep psychological need for anchors of stability—especially felt by urban elites at a time of disturbing, escalating change in traditional patterns of life—spurred on these efforts and made the time one of renaissance, a creative recycling of classical and naturalistic forms. American Whigs, the cultural and economic elite, shared the political philosophy of their English cousins as well as their tastes. They claimed a Saxon lineage and avidly read Addison, Pope, Locke, Bacon, and Wordsworth. They believed in the abilities of Art and Nature to stabilize the new nation.[16]

Similarly, Americans shared trends in affective individualism; with the growth of romanticism, their commemorative urge took on private as well as public dimensions in the half-century following the Revolution. Chapter 5 surveys the American sensibility to melancholy, including the growing desire to commemorate individuals through reform of traditional burial places. Manifestations of American melancholy ranged from the domestic production of mourning pictures in memory of family members to the literary celebration of the beauty of death in harmony with nature. In the process, Americans pioneered in burial reform, creating a corporate and landscape structure to ensure family burials in perpetuity at New Haven's Burial Ground years before the French created Père Lachaise.

Sensitivity closely accompanied sensibility on both sides of the Atlantic and especially among the urban elite. A genteel repulsion for foul smells and imposition of new standards of public cleanliness were only occasionally rationalized in the name of public health. More often, new standards were simply a matter of taste, but they developed with enough force to impel all sorts of reform in the urban environment.[17] Hence, motivations for burial reform involved more than the ideals of commemoration, the spread of affective individualism, and a simple copying of design precedents from abroad. They were complicated by the texture of social and cultural change experienced by urbanites through the first half of the nineteenth century. They involved pragmatic considerations as well as ideals and fears. Because of particular conditions endemic to their urban area, Bostonians responded early to perceived needs for public as well as private commemoration, for the building of patriotic monuments as well as the creation of a new cemetery.

The search for order and history, evident in the building of public monuments and eventually in creation of Mount Auburn Cemetery, came at a time of chaotic, unprecedented change in New England and its "metropolis" following the War of 1812. Boston experienced the sort of urban explosion that transformed the size, shape, and nature of many American cities in the first quarter of the nineteenth century. Its population jumped from 33,250 to 43,290 between 1810 and 1820, and to 70,000 in the next decade, triple its revolutionary-era population. Boston was no longer the homogeneous, traditional New England town it had been through the seventeenth century or even the stagnating port it became through the second half of the eighteenth; the great waves of immigration that would transform it even more were yet to come. In 1822, Boston formally became a city, putting aside government by selectmen for that by mayor, aldermen, and common council.[18]

The social shape of Boston changed dramatically as well in this period. The North End, economically and socially mixed in the late colonial era, was left to the lower and middling classes with a few retail businesses by the 1820s. The elite either moved to new residences on Beacon Hill or to country estates in Cambridge, Dorchester, Brookline, or Roxbury, where they could enjoy fresh air, forego fears of epidemic disease, and engage in gentlemanly horticultural experimentation. Quite unlike the "outlivers" in colonial times, rejecting and rejected by the town, these first suburbanites were the city's leaders. The prosperous in peripheral areas looked to Boston for urban life and institutions. A new metropolitan consciousness developed, expanding the constituency that favored improving the city and its amenities. Not all "Bostonians" lived within city limits, nor were all amenities for the city assumed to be contained within the bounds of the Shawmut Peninsula.

Yet growth did not represent progress for many Yankees; indeed, other events predisposed Yankees to thoughts of the past and of death, giving a particular timeliness to the taste for melancholy that permeated western romanticisms. Massachusetts lost Maine in 1820; and the General Court, the state legislature, hotly debated religious disestablishment after several decades of escalating sectarian fragmentation and growing theological uncertainties fomented by the Unitarian Controversy, which factionalized congregation after congregation, town after town. The Panic of 1819 inaugurated a long depression, the most severe economic crisis to date in the nation's young history. Countless citizens lost their homes, farms, businesses, and property. Economic paralysis persisted through the early 1820s; and the psychological, political, legal, and institutional ramifications of the depression continued for over a decade.

Such extremes in the economic cycle created an atmosphere of chronic insecurity and pessimism, especially among the elite. In 1823, Harrison Gray Otis wrote, "Two years ago our sun had sunk never to rise again"; recovery came quickly but temporarily. By 1830, some Boston boosters determined that the only way to save the prosperity of their city and region was to assume a posture of dogged optimism. Thomas G. Fessenden, an editor, cautioned, "the cry of *decline* is one of the causes of decline. Many hear this cry and hearing no answer to it, take it to be true." Commerce was indeed depressed, but Fessenden reasoned, "Where, in the world, at this moment, is it not depressed?" Temporary setbacks were not signs of the imminent demise of city and state, he suggested, especially if Yankees would fall back on civic virtue and stewardship of wealth. After all, he asked, "to what portion of the earth is one to go to find more general comfort and natural thrift than in New England?"[19]

Bostonians in the 1820s and 1830s still cherished a sense of their own exemplary importance. They updated John Winthrop's missive to form "a City upon a Hill." Bronson Alcott articulated the region's self-confident self-consciousness in 1828, declaring: "There is a city in our world upon which the light of the sun of righteousness has risen. There is a sun which beams in its full meridian splendour upon it. Its influences are quickening and invigorating the souls which dwell within it. It is the same from which every pure stream of thought and purpose and performance emanates. It is the city that is set on high. . . . It is Boston!" A number of urban cultural leaders harkened to such calls, believing that through public-spirited efforts they could carry on the principles upon which their city and nation had been founded, forestalling the demise of both.[20] (Fig. I.4.)

Yet Boston's leaders' fears that they were not keeping pace with changes and improvements made in competing commercial cities along the Atlantic seaboard exacerbated their insecurities and motivated them to plan additional projects to improve their culture and environment. Hastening not to be outdone by Southern competitors in Baltimore, Boston's civic leaders created one of the first voluntary associations in America to build a historical monument proclaiming the centrality of their role in the Revolution, choosing the site of the Battle of Bunker Hill for erection of a structure inspired by classical and, more recently, English and French precedents but so ambitious in scale that it would take two decades to complete. Boston's cultural elite reinterpreted the traditional, Puritan sense of mission to form a particularly militant historical consciousness vying with interpretations of the past being promoted by Southerners and Democrats. Boston's literati especially reacted to British criticism of the apparent lack of American history and civilization and to predictions of dire consequences for independence and the republican experiment because of absence of traditional forms of status, theology, and a sense of the past. Whiggish Bostonians grew more uneasy because they were already fearful of growing democratic tendencies in the nation.

Boston cultural leaders responded to warnings about the precariousness of their civilization by translating and updating the old Puritan assurance of the divinely sanctioned role of their Common-

Fig. I.4. Boston and Bunker Hill, view across the Mystic River from the east, engraving by William H. Bartlett, 1839.

wealth in the vanguard of human history. They would assert their central role in the American Revolution and make their city the "Athens of America," a cultural capital with hegemony ensured by creation of literary journals and clubs, institutions meant to preserve and foster knowledge and the arts, places modeled on European precedents but reshaped to meet contemporaneous American needs. They began to compete not only with New York, Philadelphia, and Baltimore but to look to recent urban improvements in London, Liverpool, Edinburgh, and Paris.

Boston's second mayor, Josiah Quincy, tackled many problems associated with the rapid growth of the city; he made burial reform a major issue in his administration's crusade to eliminate urban filth, to make Boston competitive with and as attractive as other prosperous seacoast cities. Yet public controversy over crypt burials in new churches preoccupied many Bostonians in 1823 and revealed that burial reform was not simply a matter of cleaning up the city or fostering public health. General Henry A. S. Dearborn observed, "We cannot speak confidently with respect to the dangers to health which arise from such practices. It has probably been over-rated, if, indeed, it exists at all." Chapter 6 considers the dimensions of the controversy over burials in Boston churches and the first proposals for creation of an extramural cemetery.[21]

Debate over the propriety of burials in urban churches took on the rhetoric of other social and political concerns of the era, especially the anti-elitism of the mechanic class (artisans, skilled workers, small shopkeepers) in resistance to attempts by the elite to invent new forms and places indicative of social status. The Boston burial controversy also involved reinterpretations of the old Puritan rejection of forms associated with papist or High Church practices. Certainly, burials in existing graveyards surrounded by urban activity clashed with new sensitivities to smell and unsightly nuisances as well as with enlightened attitudes toward death. Bostonians wanted to change their burial practices as much for aesthetic as for practical reasons; they sought to do so in a way acceptable to various factions in the metropolitan area and in a way that would solve several problems, cultural as well as practical, at once.

Mayor Quincy's proposal of an extramural burial place—one large cemetery symbolic of the city itself—was an important contribution to a series of plans for new institutions required by a modernizing, cosmopolitan, commercial city that were developed during his administration; however, the municipality was unprepared to implement his plan. Burial reform in Boston would require voluntary, private initiative, and a number of cultural leaders were ready and willing to take on the project.

Bostonians were among the most active of American urbanites in forming voluntary associations for various purposes. By the nineteenth century, prosperous merchants, early industrialists, bankers, real estate speculators, and new professionals supplanted the old colonial elite, many of whom had left with the British after the Revolution. Many of Boston's new leaders of the 1820s had relatively humble origins in provincial New England towns. They identified themselves more with the new republican order than with the colonial past. Sons of ministers, farmers, and sea captains found their way to the "Metropolis of New England" and into prominent positions in the first quarter of the century. A new upper class coalesced through bonds of marriage, kinship, friendship, and institutional affiliation—particularly bonds formed during Harvard College years—and it sought ways to define gentility and to form new traditions in regional as well as national terms.[22]

One such individual was the young doctor Jacob Bigelow, who stepped forward in 1825 to propose to a circle of his friends, all influential Bostonians, the idea of forming a voluntary association to procure land and found a "rural" cemetery. Chapter 7, "The Cemetery Idea and Founding of Mount Auburn," traces development of Bigelow's proposal through the founding of Mount Auburn Cemetery in 1831 under the auspices of the Massachusetts Horticultural Society. Good economic times in the late 1820s facilitated creation of new institutions like Mount Auburn that required an outlay of capital as well as the cooperative efforts of an established voluntary association. The cemetery project meshed well with the intentions and ambitions of founders of the new Horticultural Society, who sought to develop a better stock of American plant materials in order to strengthen the economy of the region and of the nation and to improve their urban and rural environments through a greater diversity of plantings and better landscape design. Articles in the *New England Farmer* by these horticulturists and cemetery founders reflect a rational response to nature, considered as source of unlimited potential, real and symbolic, not at all in conflict with trends of urbanization and industrialization. Individuals like Bigelow, Dearborn, and their friends Zebedee Cook, Jr., and Joseph Story were confident that through "rural" taste they could develop a harmony between cities and the New England countryside—between the future, present, and past. In founding Mount Auburn, these Bostonians attempted to solve a variety of problems and to develop an American culture, in all senses of the word. As Alexander Everett noted of the similarities between Père Lachaise and Mount Auburn: "While they tend to promote the salubrity of cities, they connect agreeable images with the recollections of the past, and the anticipation of the future; and strip the idea of death of a part of the horrors with which superstition and the weakness of our nature have unnecessarily invested it."[23]

Chapter 8, "Cemetery and Garden: Landscape Design and Conflicting Institutional Purposes," assigns responsibility for initial design of Mount Auburn's picturesque landscape to General Dearborn, assisted by Bigelow and other members of the Garden and Cemetery Committee of the Horticultural Society. It describes the reasons for the reincorporation of the cemetery in 1835 as an independent institution. Over the next two decades, as seen in Chapter 9, "Art and Nature Balanced," little change was made in the naturalistic landscape that Dearborn had initially shaped on the site; however, Yankees increasingly displayed their new commemorative consciousness—public and private—at the cemetery, creating "a marble history in the forest cemetery." Addition of major structures in various architectural styles to "embellish the picturesque" in a fashion reminiscent of English landscaped gardens is the subject of Chapter 10. During the cemetery's first fifty years, founders and proprietors expressed definite ideas about which forms derived from antiquity would be appropriate for their funerary landscape, which was intended to represent their city, region, nation, and past. Issues of taste as well as shifting cultural priorities both inside the institution and outside in the culture at large conspired to make even these contributions of art and architecture controversial.

Eventually even the attempts by Whiggish Bostonians to cultivate a historical consciousness as a socially stabilizing force to counteract the dangerous potential of rampant change failed. In the 1820s, Daniel Webster, newly arrived in Boston from New Hampshire, won public acclaim as a vocal advocate of fostering awareness of the republican past rooted in moral philosophy and a long regional history dating back to the landing of the Pilgrims at Plymouth two hundred years before. But by mid-century, only a few elite Bostonians, labeled Brahmins by Oliver Wendell Holmes, clung to such ambitions. By then, most New Englanders wanted to think in more recent and personal terms. Presentism and individualism triumphed over advocacy of a usable past. Development of sentimentalism, sometimes described as the "domestication of death," a private celebration of affective individualism and the duration of family ties beyond the grave, was certainly one factor contributing to creation of Mount Auburn Cemetery; by mid-century, it had emerged as a dominant cultural force that transformed the cemetery landscape through a proliferation of structures objectifying sentimentalism rather than historicism.[24]

Through its first four decades, Mount Auburn attracted national and international recognition. Visitors from abroad made the cemetery a major stop on itineraries that included a barge ride on the Erie Canal, a look at the sublime wonder of Niagara Falls, and inspection of booming frontier cities like Cincinnati. Tourists' positive responses to Mount Auburn vindicated Bostonians' pride in their city's cultural accomplishments. But area residents also flocked to Mount Auburn, using it as a "pleasure ground" for active rather than passive recreation. The place served as more than the morally refreshing, genteel "asylum" that its founders intended. Chapter 11 describes this "rage" for Mount Auburn and the consequential conflicts over whether the place was to be set aside as a sacred site or left open to be used in more democratic ways as a secular, public park.

Civic leaders from other American cities visited Mount Auburn and went home determined to create similar institutions and landscapes for themselves. Mount Auburn served as catalyst for the "rural" cemetery movement as city after city, large and small, created similar multifunctional landscapes in the antebellum decades. Before the founding of public parks and art museums, these cemeteries were urban amenities that provided green open space for display of fine commemorative sculpture and architecture. By mid-century, these picturesque cemeteries were commonplace, even copied on smaller scale by towns and villages as far west as American settlement extended.

Mount Auburn also inspired the first proposals for public parks. Andrew Jackson Downing wrote to President Millard Fillmore advocating conversion of Washington's Mall into a picturesque landscape like Mount Auburn. Downing urged that "a national park like this, laid out and planted in a thorough manner, would *exercise as much influence on public taste* as Mount Auburn Cemetery near Boston had done. Though only twenty years have elapsed since that spot was laid out, the lesson there taught has been so largely influential that at the present moment the United States, while they have no public parks, are acknowledged to possess the finest rural cemeteries in the world." Although the Mall would not be laid out in a picturesque fashion for years to come, Downing did not hesitate to crusade for other public parks following its example; indeed, he can be credited with achieving public funding for New York's Central Park before his early death.[25]

The New York art critic Clarence Cook, son of Zebedee Cook, Jr., of Boston and New York, who had been influential in the formative years of both Mount Auburn and Green-Wood cemeteries, recognized the influence of "rural" cemeteries on formation of public parks in the second half of the century. The younger Cook wrote in 1869, "These cemeteries . . . became famous over the whole country and thousands of people visited them annually. They were among the chief attractions of the cities to which they belonged. No stranger visited . . . these cities for pleasure or observation who was not taken to the cemeteries, nor was it long before the smaller cities, and even towns and villages began to set aside land and to lay it out for the double purpose of burying-ground and pleasure-ground." Cook concluded, "These cemeteries were all the rage, and so deeply was the want felt which they supplied, and so truly beautiful were they in themselves, that it was not to be wondered at if people were slow to perceive that there was a certain incongruity between a graveyard and a place of recreation." Cook recognized that people simply "were glad to get fresh air, and a sight of grass and trees and flowers with, now and then, a pretty piece of sculpture, to say nothing of the drive to all this beauty, and back again, without considering too deeply whether it might not be better to have it all without the graves and funeral processions."[26]

The historical consciousness that premised creation of Mount Auburn Cemetery was ephemeral and limited to a particular social class that celebrated its primary role in having shaped the national past. The notion of the pastness of the past itself became a precondition for the belief in progress, shifting attention to the future in an entirely new way during the second half of the nineteenth century. Americans put behind them cataclysmic and cyclical concepts of history. Faith in science and optimism replaced the older belief that only examples from the past, the lessons of history, and inspiration drawn from the lives of Great Men could stabilize the republic into the uncertain future. Romantic notions associating nature and history turned into Victorian sentimentalism and unabashed nostalgia. Ironically, when Americans put their past under grass at the cemetery, equating history and death, they made the past no longer usable. Tastes changed along with the mind of the times; well before the end of the century, Mount Auburn and other cemeteries fashioned after its example had lost their primary purpose as historical institutions, although they continued to be used for burials. Still, they retain material evidence for the historiographer intent on discovering how Americans attempted to define a relatively new past in both public and private terms a century and a half ago.

1

Grim Graveyards and Common Pits: Death Banal, the Past Forgotten

If *Beauty* could the beautiful defend
From Death's dominion, then fair *Absalom*
Had not been brought to such a shameful end:
But fair and foul unto the Grave must come.
—Michael Wigglesworth, "A Song of Emptiness, To Fill Up the Empty Pages Following, Vanity of Vanities" (1660s)

THE UGLINESS AND INEVITABILITY of death were institutionalized in the Old Order that dated from the fifth century and generally persisted into the eighteenth throughout western civilization, extending even into New England as it had to Old. For over a millennium in Latin Christendom, the past was reduced to the toll taken by death in terms of pure mortality. Historical consciousness was minimal, limited to tales of the divine right of kings, heroes defending a sacred cause, and saints interceding for the living. Secular memory was suspect. Details of the lifetime accomplishments of notables were reduced, at best, to the simplicity of myth transmitted through oral tradition and were given little or no material commemoration. Although the fifteenth-century advent of humanism and rediscovery of classical civilizations were harbingers of eventual change, the medieval system remained firmly entrenched in much of western Europe; the lessons, rituals, and places of death remained ecclesiastical monopolies.[1]

No cemetery could exist apart from the Church, literally or figuratively; burials *ad sanctos,* in consecrated ground either in or adjacent to a church, within the city or town, became the new rule, in contrast to the Roman Law of the Twelve Tablets and the Theodosian Code, which had relegated the dead to areas uninhabited by the living. Older Gallo-Roman, Barbarian, and Merovingian cemeteries in open fields were abandoned rather than consecrated for continued use. In Carolingian Germany, an area forcibly converted to Christianity, ecclesiastics decreed abandonment of pagan cemeteries. In the vicinity of many old Roman cities, however, Christian martyrs had been buried with pagans in "suburban" locations; their graves became cult objects. Even though these burial grounds were beyond city walls, ecclesiastics frequently chose to build churches atop the sites as a way to accommodate large numbers of pilgrims at masses held over the martyrs' bones and to control the growing cult of saints. The churches of Saint-Marcel, Saint-Germain, Saint-Martin, and Sainte-Geneviève in present-day Paris, as well as Saint-Seurin in Bordeaux and Saint-Victor in Marseilles, were built over Merovingian burial places and became centers of population growth that expanded beyond urban limits. Many of them remained extramural until the eleventh century. From about the fifth to the eleventh centuries, however, Church leaders encouraged urbanization as a means of exerting religious control. Churchmen refused to let Christian Saxons keep their old, rural burial places. Cemeteries predating the Christian era, therefore, were preserved only if they had been used for burial of those canonized as saints and if they remained in close proximity to the city.[2]

Denial of burial in consecrated earth was the harshest ecclesiastical punishment. Medieval man did not think in terms of occupying an individual grave in a fixed place *in aeternum;* he cared only that the Church accept his body, disposing of it as it pleased but within sacred grounds, thus including himself in the regular prayers said for the dead collectively. Extramural sites for burial unaffiliated with the Church were used only for suicides, the excommunicated, the executed, and occasionally members of their families; often, the bodies of such pariahs were merely discarded in refuse dumps, exposed to the elements, to beasts of prey, and to the jaded glances of travelers. When such corpses were not prominently displayed on gibbets, they were left to rot under the gibbet or simply cast by the wayside without even the covering of earth provided by a shallow grave. Only in time of dire necessity were victims of plague consigned to pits hastily dug beyond town walls where they were protected neither spiritually by the relics of a saint nor physically from predators by cemetery walls.

The words *ecclesia* and *cimeterium* became nearly synonymous, although use of the later latinized Greek word remained limited to clerical scholarly language even in French until the seventeenth century; it did not enter English usage until two centuries later. Terms for burial space adjacent to the church or chapel remained purely architectural—*aître* (atrium), *charnier* (chancel), or ossuary (the covered cloister or gallery in which old bones were stacked after removal from the grave).

The Church deliberately undid many heathen practices associated with burial by instituting this new system and by insisting on urbanization of burials. The process was more difficult in western Europe, where Germanic, Romantic, Celtic, and Slavic peoples had a rich, pantheistic folklore that persisted, mixing paganism with Christian beliefs long after the conversions of the fourth to eighth centuries. In Celtic religion, for instance, wells, rivers, ponds, and sacred trees, especially the oak, had patron gods and goddesses, served as objects of veneration, and marked choice sites for burials. According to Teutonic belief, certain trees were capable of capturing the spirits of the dead. To demonstrate the superiority of Christianity over paganism in the fifth century, Saint Boniface deliberately cut down the sacred oak reputed to contain the spirit of Donar, a Germanic god who whispered his messages to the living from its branches.

In the myths of many northern Europeans, settings of the afterlife resembled the Greek concept of Elysium, a pastoral or gardenlike setting, and may have had common roots in ancient Indo-European tradition. The undoing of such deeply entrenched pagan funerary practices and beliefs drawn from ancient, "natural" religions required the force of Church law. Early efforts included prohibition by Saint Ambrose, fourth-century Bishop of Milan, of the practice of consuming bread and wine at the graves of saints as had formerly been the custom over the burials of heroes.

From the ninth century, many ecclesiastics refused permission for burial of prosperous landowners and their kin *in agris suis,* in one's own fields, or *in quaedam solitaria loca,* in any solitary location, even if the propertied elite paid for the privilege or promised to create a private sacred ground by acquiring a martyr's relic and erecting a chapel. Burial for the faithful could only be *in locum publicum et ecclesiasticum,* in an urban location owned by the Church. As late as the seventeenth century in England, according to a Calvinist historian, "No corpse could be carried away from home for burial; and, if such burial took place, the body was required to be exhumed and returned to its own parish cemetery for final interment." In 1682, the Bishop of Rennes ruled that no one in his diocese could be buried away from the parish church without specific provision in an approved will. Elsewhere, only organizations of heretics like Waldensians and Hussites managed to avoid the Church-controlled burial system and to found their own graveyards.[3]

Urbanization of burial places involved more than institutionalization of burials by the Church. Medieval Christians considered nature evil, the tainted vestiges of Eden lost in Adam's Fall or the wilderness outside the sacred walled Garden into which God thrust Man in punishment for original sin; even the tamed Nature of the walled garden seems inappropriate for the burial place and the lessons about death it was meant to objectify. By refusing to permit burials in rural locations, the Church did more than assert control over funerary rites; it made cemeteries into material manifestations of Christian theology. Death was incomprehensible chaos, to be accepted with resignation on the basis of faith alone. Cemeteries displayed the fearful lessons of sin that forced individual expectation of death with the hortatory message *memento mori*—"remember death"—ever visible in the very center of towns. Many cemeteries remained focal points even at night because of the "lantern of the dead," the flame lit atop a small tower commonly placed in the middle of the burial area. The inevitable cross, also at the center of the cemetery, glimpsed over high walls or atop the locked lych-gate, was meant to "solicit" a prayer from the passerby for the souls of the deceased. Those who had not the status to be buried to the east of the church, nearest the altar, willed burial south or west of the church so that their graves would be visible and often passed by those attending church, who might then be more inclined to pray for the dead. So often was this location chosen "that it was difficult to prevent other portions of the churchyard from becoming actually disused."[4] (Figs. 1.1, 2.)

Calvinists later labeled these objects and symbols of the churchyard, especially the cross, superstitious relics intended to make the common man "enter into a bondage of fear with reference to spirits of evil, which he would be taught to conceive of as roaming in malicious throngs invisibly through space, on mischief to men intent." Solicitation at the cemetery of prayers from passersby was akin to the corruption of selling indulgences, Calvinists thought, for it created a system "falsely pretending to people that they had delivered their dead friends from purgatory and neutralizing all civil and ecclesiastical discipline." The Church, on the other hand, intended to impose social control, to make men proceed on in life after passing the cemetery, sobered by realization of the inevitability of their own demise and their dependence on the Church as sole source of salvation.[5]

Despite the medieval institutionalization of a cult of the dead, cemeteries remained primarily functional places for the disposal of corpses. Only the relics of select saints, kings, knights, and leading ecclesiastics were preserved and enshrined with perpetuity in mind. (Fig. 1.3.) Now and then, aristocrats could purchase postmortem commemoration by patronage of the Church. The *very* elite might be entombed in the sanctuary, but members of lesser noble families and confraternities had vaults in the nave. Most other bodies were consigned to the grave—large or small—for only as long as it took flesh to decompose. After a few years, as a matter of course, bones were removed to the ossuary for drying and then to the charnel house, where, in most cases, they would be mixed indiscriminately with other anonymous remains of humanity. Charnel houses or ossuaries were usually under or adjacent to churches and cemeteries. As early as the thirteenth century, even small-town churches in France "sat on beds of human bones" that accumulated over the years.[6]

Figs. 1.1., 1.2. Melrose Abbey, England, views from the east with burials positioned for proximity to the altar and from the southwest with graves placed to elicit prayers from those entering the church for services. Photographs, ca. 1891.

Fig. 1.3. Interior of the Cathedral of Saint-Denis with tombs of royalty, engraving by Frederick Nash, 1823.

While most western Christians considered rapid dissolution of the body desirable as well as inevitable, they did not dispose of the dead by the sort of exposure to wild animals and birds of prey used by some other cultures. Some northern European barbarians had followed such practices, but even they were careful to place bodies high in trees, limiting access to carrion-seeking birds. Thus they prevented the packs of wolves roaming the countryside from drawing sustenance from their dead, increasing in numbers, and endangering the living. The wolf population increased dramatically, they knew, following epidemics and famines. In very cold winters, wolves were even so bold as to enter cities to disinter corpses from churchyard common pits, especially those near the urban periphery like Saint-Germain-des-Près, surrounded by fields southwest of the center of Paris, the Ile-de-la-Cité.

The ubiquitous European wolf had a greater impact on landscape and design of towns than has previously been acknowledged. It was to keep out such animals as well as men with bad intentions that a French edict in 1695 required that all cemeteries be enclosed by solid walls with locked gates. In addition, city walls on the Continent were defensive, whereas those in England were often only administrative. In England, in contrast to France or Germany, the great medieval cathedrals as well as simple parish churches were frequently built at the edge of towns rather than immediately at the centers; many graveyards were truly rural. In Great

Figs. 1.4., 1.5. Engravings of English country churchyards from the *Gentleman's Quarterly,* ca. 1810.

Britain, one Frenchman enviously observed in 1779, wolves had been eliminated six centuries before; they still ravaged French cities, however, even entering fortified gates to kill children well into the eighteenth century, although by that time they had been largely confined to Eastern European forests. A single explanation like the absence of wolves, however, does not suffice to account for the prevalence of rural churchyards in England in contrast to the Continent, but wolves must be acknowledged as one factor influencing differences in the built environments of death.[7] (Figs. 1.4, 5.)

If cultural patterns alone could explain the differences between English and French deathways, then Puritan towns in New England would have followed the freer spatial arrangement of English towns. Rather, the close clustering of houses in Massachusetts towns not only epitomized peculiar ideals of community but also was defensive, more so against wolves than against Indians. Wolves preyed upon stray cattle, and many Massachusetts towns constructed palisades to protect livestock. The systematic offering of bounties for wolf heads and pelts finally eliminated the beasts in the middle of the eighteenth century. At the same time as Puritans spatially separated burial grounds from meetinghouses, deliberately to avoid the "papist superstition" of burial *ad sanctos,* they located their graves at the centers of towns to keep the bodies of the dead out of easy reach of roaming wolves. (Fig. 1.6). Because even this relatively protected location did not suffice to keep wolves from the dead, recalled a local resident in the 1840s, "it is a well established fact that it was the custom of our ancestors, in many localities, to fill up the grave after interment with stones that the remains might thus be protected from wolves."[8]

Removal of burial places from rural locations did not account for their becoming barren, unsightly places, however. Certainly the necessity of using and reusing almost every inch of the small property allotted for the dead among the living precluded, for functional reasons, ornamental plantings of many trees and shrubs. Still, through the Middle Ages, a few isolated trees—only one or two, at best—appeared in graveyards and retained traditional funerary significance. These varied from one region to another. The cypress was favored in burial grounds across southern Europe and in Muslim countries; in France, it appeared only on the graves of the elite, not on those of plebians. Myth held that Apollo turned Cyparissus into a cypress, making that tree symbolic of death. The walnut was the funerary tree in Poitou; the rowan, said to have been sacred to Druids, in Wales; and elms, in parts of northern Europe. Rose trees had appeared in English burial grounds since Roman times. Rosemary, grown to the height of a hedge, was "the most highly esteemed of all flowers for the dead," even considered "effective in retarding putrefaction," a quality primarily favored by the elite who could afford or merit private tombs to separate the remains of their dead from those of the vulgar masses and who, especially from the fifteenth century on, began to aspire to postmortem preservation.[9]

Along with rank weeds and miscellaneous grasses, the most common vegetation in English, Scottish, and Irish churchyards was the "unlucky" yew, "planted in almost every church-yard throughout the kingdom." (Fig. 1.7.) Some large and famous yews of the eighteenth century reputedly dated from the fourth and fifth. According to lore, souls spent time in purgatory perched in yew branches, and yew roots were supposed to find and quiet the dead mouth. Like the ivy, the yew had symbolized immortality since pagan times because it is evergreen. The growing of trees, especially those with superstitious associations, in burial places often had to be rationalized as in the benefit of the Church to be permitted at all; and ecclesiastics sometimes tolerated trees in graveyards by ignoring the lore or by co-opting it. Some English parishes, for instance, grew a few trees in churchyards to provide lumber for church repairs; the growth of yews was particularly favored as a source of pliable wood ideal for longbows needed to arm the militia. In the tenth century, priests dedicated Holy Yew trees to various saints. One historian explains the acceptability of yews to priests: "their branches meet the ecclesiastical necessities of Palm-Sunday and its ceremonies."

Fig. 1.6. Plan of Old Cambridge, Massachusetts, ca. 1742.

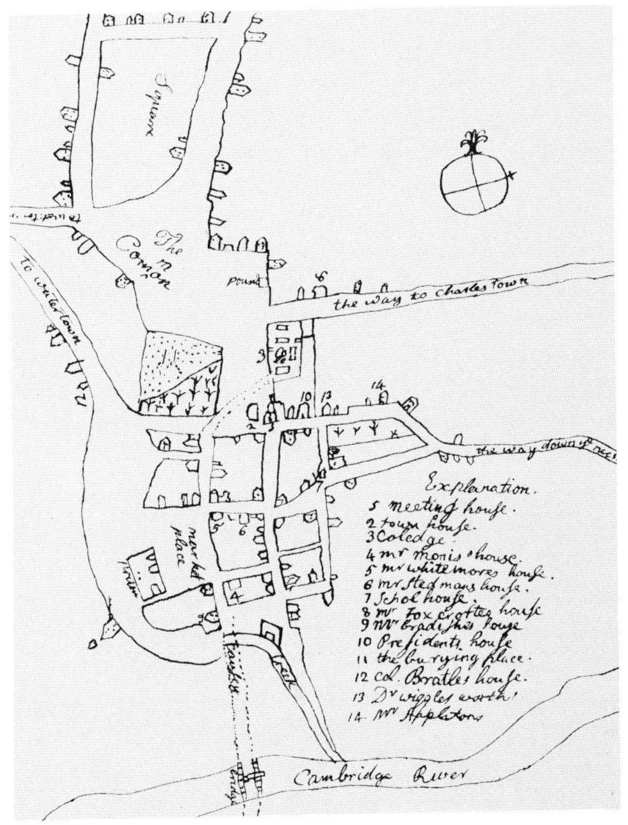

Fig. 1.7. Ancient yews in English country churchyard, Wiltshire, photograph by Alan Ward, 1985.

Most churchmen, however, considered the yew an unwelcoming plant that would not seduce the faithful back to pantheistic paganism, for few would choose to sit "Beneath a gloomy Yews unhealthy Shade / Whose noxious Covert's shunn'd by Bird and Beast." Therefore, the yew could be grown in many churchyards as one of the few "safe" plants that would not symbolize a sacred Nature.[10]

Accounts of trees with traditional funerary significance in churchyards and cemeteries before the eighteenth century are misleading, however. Even engravings of rural burial grounds in English villages in the modern period reveal the same sort of wilderness in microcosm that existed in burial grounds in the hearts of London, Paris, and other European cities. Churchmen shunned plantings just as they rejected the image of heaven as garden. It was precisely the superstitious valuation of various plants persisting from paganism that prompted leaders of the Counter-Reformation formally to ban use of plants in cemeteries in the period after the Council of Trent in 1563. Extending the Council's work in defining sacraments and dogma, especially those related to death such as extreme unction, purgatory, and the veneration of relics, Charles Borromeo, later canonized a saint, declared in 1577 the Church's formal ban on planting trees, shrubs, vines, flowers, and grasses in cemeteries. Various local Post-Tridentine councils extended the Catholic fight against vestiges of paganism and rustic folk practices with similar bans. The Bishop of Rennes ordered elimination of yew trees in cemeteries; they were heathen relics as well as impediments to grave digging and to circulation of air. Peasants supposedly made "evil use of them," and priests who tried to carry out the order for their uprooting encountered violent popular resistance. The Church attempted to combat pantheistic tendencies in many existing European folk practices of ancient origin, but it did not always succeed.[11]

Many Protestants, following the letter of Scripture and rejecting Catholic traditions dictated by the Counter-Reformation hierarchy, turned back to older folkways not explicitly banned in the Bible. In turn, the Church excluded Protestants from burial in hallowed ground of Roman Catholic cemeteries. Bishop Henri de Sponde addressed Huguenots with sardonic remarks published in Bordeaux in 1598: "Where in the Gospel [since the Gospel is *all* you believe in] does it say that a person cannot be buried privately in his woods, or his field, or his house, as was Abraham . . . and as was done almost universally by the ancients, both Jew and Gentile alike? . . . Therefore, search, if you will, in other cemeteries than those [of the Catholic Church] to which you no longer have any right, either by nature or by humanity [one can bury the dead anywhere] or by religion."[12]

Evidence of new notions about death as well as a reformation of practices and places associated with it related directly to the rise of Protestantism and Calvinism in particular. Seeds of John Calvin's theology were planted in France, flowered in Switzerland, and took best root in England and her colonies. Calvinist rejection of papist culture reflected theological change, necessitated iconoclasm, and premised creation of new and alternative cultural forms. Places of "Publique Buriall" were to be secular and civil, and the funeral liturgy was abolished. Calvin personally, but unsuccessfully, ordered that the precise site of his grave not be marked so that followers would not turn his remains into relics. Other Calvinists deliberately created "burying grounds" or "graveyards" without spatial proximity to meetinghouses, which were unconsecrated structures no longer called "churches." They eschewed the terms "churchyard" and "cemetery," which were associated with Church control. Because of the doctrine of Predestination, they considered presumptuous the expectation that all bodies interred were destined to "the resurrection to eternal life." Such matters were beyond man's ability to influence through works in life or prayers thereafter.[13]

Institutionalization of secular, nonsacred burial places was most successful in England and her colonies, persisting even after overthrow of Cromwell's Commonwealth and restoration of the Stuart monarchy, which reestablished Anglican control over all burials in England. The Church could again arbitrarily refuse burial in consecrated ground to the excommunicated, the unbaptized, suicides, lunatics, and those found guilty of capital crimes. After passage of the Act of Uniformity forced Puritans, Quakers, Presbyterians, and other Independents into formal "nonconformity," such Dissenters suffered the same postmortem fate. On the other hand, Puritans and other new Protestant sectarians in England were equally loath to associate the remains of their dead with the "popish" or to pay burial fees to Church of England coffers. Still, in 1611, Calvin had allowed "that in the burial of the dead we must use some honest shew." In 1665, Dissenters petitioned the Corporation of the City of London for land north of the Moorgate for their own burial ground and received approval to create a small graveyard at Bunhill Fields, a block-square site used for the dead outside Church auspices since Elizabethan times. Edward Seymour, Duke of Somerset, first used the place, reputed to be an ancient site of a Saxon tumulus, for burial in 1547. He reinterred a thousand cartloads of bones there from the charnel house of Saint Paul's Cathedral; henceforth, the grounds were called "Bone Hill." It was used as a common cemetery during the plague; such use was haphazard, however, until Non-conformists received permission to enclose the site with a brick wall and gate.[14]

There, across the City Road from John Wesley's house, Puritans, Baptists, Methodists, Presbyterians, Quakers, Swedenborgians, Independents, and other Non-Conformists established their new cult of tombs, erecting monuments to religious, intellectual, and political leaders. Called the Dissenters' Westminster Abbey or

Campo Santo, by virtue only of the number of notable burials, this repository accumulated the cenotaph of Isaac Watts near graves of Daniel Defoe; Susannah Wesley, mother of the leaders of Methodism; George Fox, founder of the Society of Friends; and many of Cromwell's associates. (Fig. 1.8) The precise location of William Blake's burial there was unmarked and forgotten; the grave of John Bunyan, however, served as a focal point, ironically revered much like the relics of a saint placed under an altar to sanctify Catholic church and churchyard, the very forms rejected by the Non-Conformists. (Fig. 1.9) One observer wrote as late as 1819, "so numerous have been and still are the dying requests of his idolaters to be buried as near as possible" to the grave of the author of the very popular *Pilgrim's Progress* "that it is not now possible to obtain a grave near him, the whole surrounding earth being entirely preoccupied by dead bodies."[15]

Fig. 1.9. John Bunyan's new monument in Bunhill Fields, ca. 1865, photograph by Dundall Downes, frontispiece of *The Pilgrim's Progress* (London: T. Nelson & Sons, 1865).

Dissenters considered Bunhill Fields a common cemetery for all of London. It was nondenominational, in that anyone who could not or would not be buried under High Church auspices could find a place there for a price. Freeholds for rare space were sold in perpetuity until land ran out in 1832. By 1852, when the last burials were made, the grounds had received an estimated 124,000 bodies. Over six thousand vaults and tombs sank seven or more feet below the surface, which, like older churchyards, had few plantings. Simply the sale of graves in perpetuity was innovative and signaled new motivations to keep the body of the dead intact in the first place of "rest" that could be identified and used to keep memory alive. Bunhill Fields also provided facilities for commoners in the form of a central trench, later covered by a paved walk, into which coffins were stacked. Bunhill Fields provided nothing new in terms of landscape design (or lack thereof). The narrow spaces between its crowded stones were just as full of weeds and barren earth as any existing Anglican churchyard. One visitor wrote that in the 1840s it was "choke-full of graves in a state of neglect, and so far as disorderly arrangement and want of care were concerned, made a painful impression." Still, its creation signaled the nascent impulse among radical Protestants to make

Fig. 1.8. Tomb of Dr. Isaac Watts, Bunhill Fields Burial Ground, London, half of a stereographic photograph by William Miller, ca. 1860.

Fig. 1.10. Old Burying Ground, Marblehead, Massachusetts, photograph by Alan Ward, 1979.

new sorts of burial places and to use gravestones for lasting commemorative purposes indicative of valuation of memory of individual and communal history independent of Church or State.[16]

Seventeenth-century New England graveyards reflect the same urge to secularize burials as was evident in the making of Bunhill Fields. The symbolic importance of structuring burial space away from the Church was not lost on English authorities. After the Catholic King James II revoked the Massachusetts Bay Company charter and established administrative control through the Dominion of New England, his hated governor, Sir Edmund Andros, dug up part of Boston's first burying ground in May of 1688, displacing graves of the colony's founding fathers to plant the Anglican King's Chapel on the site. Andros's motivations were multiple. His small group of local Anglicans needed their own church because

Bostonians begrudged their use of the Old South Meetinghouse. Moreover, Andros personally wanted to sanctify the burying ground where he had laid his wife, the Lady Marie, the previous February. But there were larger, symbolic reasons for the action. Conversion of the originally secular burial ground to a churchyard represented forcible imposition of royal political and religious control over the Puritan Commonwealth. For Tories, the act may have served as a ritualized retaliation for the Puritan Cromwell's destruction of High Church property in England three decades before. But Bostonians resented the loss of political autonomy and the "very grievous" introduction of "idolatrous," papist forms like the closing of schools and shops on Christmas even more than the violation of the graves of Isaac Johnson and the town's first settlers, the precise locations of which had long been forgotten.[17]

Indeed, seventeenth-century New England ministers preached a new Puritan rationale for continuing to disregard the dead. Increase Mather declared that "to praise the dead is to praise corruptible flesh . . . to praise memory is to worship the dead." Zealous Puritans cautioned against making their dead saintlike. Ministers counseled their congregations to use burial grounds to aid in realization of the common inevitability of death. William Cooper urged, "Look into the grave, and see a dead body, that has been buried there but a month or two, all covered with darkness and corruption, and say whether it is suitable for one to have high thoughts of himself." Gazing into graves, an activity that became almost unavoidable as urban life expanded around poorly kept burying grounds, was meant to mortify pride, to squelch individualism, rather than to raise ambitions to live and accomplish worldly goals by following examples offered by lives lived in the past.[18]

No burial landscapes were structured to facilitate public access, however, let alone meditation. No paths guided visitors' steps between the graves, and family tombs were tightly clustered together to utilize virtually every bit of space. (Figs. 1.10, 11.) Through the eighteenth century, New Englanders considered their graveyards more common areas, not unlike other functional pieces of land reserved to serve the practical needs of the town. Most often burial grounds doubled for the grazing of cattle because of their well-fertilized and highly nutritious grasses, more desirable than the ordinary grass of the town's central common. The burial ground provided an especially safe enclosure to keep cattle from straying onto other property. In 1703, the town of Boston charged George Ripley with watering the bulls kept "by night in the burrying [*sic*] place" later called the Granary. Likewise, in 1713, James Williams convinced the Selectmen "to Lett unto him the grass of Ye South burying place" for forty shillings. For the privilege, he agreed to pay for any damage "wch may happen to the graves by reason of his Cows going there." In 1718, William Young paid only fifteen shillings "for his Cow^s^ grazeing [*sic*] in the Old Burying place the Last Summer." In 1758, John Ramstead spent three pounds, six shillings, and eight pence for the "Herbage" in the South (Granary) graveyard. Similar practices existed even in more rural towns around Boston. In 1654, Roxbury selectmen re-

Fig. 1.11. "Old Burial Hill," Plymouth, Massachusetts, half of a stereographic photograph by William S. Robbins, ca. 1860.

Fig. 1.12. Death's-head iconography on Hannah Tuckerman stone, Old Granary Burial Ground, Boston, photograph by Alan Ward, 1980.

Fig. 1.13. Death's-head on Rachel Procter stone, Old Granary Burial Ground, Boston, photograph by Alan Ward, 1987.

corded that after "a voat consarning the burying place Mr John Alcok was granted liberty to fed the burying place he keping the sayd burying place in good and sufficyent fenc and a gate with a locke and two kieas." A century later, Roxbury town fathers again voted to "Lett as Usual the Herbage" in the graveyard. The practice was not questioned until the early nineteenth century, when new notions developed about what should and should not happen in a city and concerns arose about issues of sanitation if not public health involved in keeping animals in overused burial grounds.[19]

Certainly, under these conditions, gravestones were not placed over every burial; to date, gravestone scholars have yet to determine precisely who merited markers in Puritan New England. One wonders whether it was simply a matter of the deceased's having family or friends with financial means to commission the stone or ready availability of markers from local carvers. Some stones indicate only the name of the first burial or that of the patriarch and were placed over family tombs sunken as inconspicuous, vertical brick and masonry shafts below ground level. Well through the eighteenth century, these stones objectified the persistence of the medieval dualism of good and evil, although recently scholars have tended to interpret the ubiquitous death's-head as a spirit portrait or sign representing the soul of the deceased. (Figs. 1.12, 13.) Still, the two-dimensional stones, usually of gray slate with graven letters often painted black, emphasize the message of *memento mori,* the reminder that each individual must die; they preach the grim lessons of Calvinistic Predestination. Memory of individual lives lived and mundane accomplishments had no place in New England graveyards.[20]

Even in Massachusetts towns surrounded by plenty of rural land, burial grounds were small plots of land sandwiched in among the living. The crowding became a particular problem in Boston. As early as the 1730s, the town's three original burial places—King's Chapel, Copp's Hill, and the Old Granary—had so little remaining space that new burials were often made four-deep or in small, common trenches. (Fig. 1.14.) A fourth graveyard was opened on the south end of the Common in 1756; tradition holds that it was the first used by blacks. There, during the Revolution, the British buried common soldiers who died in combat or of disease. Since it was farthest from the market center of town, Bostonians considered it the least desirable, indicating an unwillingness at that time even to consider the possibility of creating more commodious burial places in a more removed location. A tradition of burial close to home persisted even among those who rejected other burial practices established over the centuries by the Church.

Persistent use of small cemeteries over the

course of many centuries posed far greater problems of crowding and filth in the burial grounds of London and Paris than in those of Boston or other New England towns. Even newer London cemeteries like Saint Margaret's and Saint George's were unpleasant places well into the nineteenth century. One Englishman observed, "Many a time have I shudderingly passed by the old graveyards of London. I have one of them now in my mind's eye—it is situated in one of the most densely populated portions of the metropolis, between Fleet Street and Holborn, surrounded by high, dark dwellings, whose smokey walls frown upon the small patch of mortality. Not a blade of grass cheers that lonely charnel-house, but its black, uneven surface lies bare to the sun whenever that luminary can pierce the mass of fog and mist which envelopes the overgrown city. The few stones which lie here and there, bearing frail records of scarcely more enduring love, are broken and defaced, and 'seem tottering to their fall.' One miserable, stunted tree, with blackened trunk and leafless boughs, remains—a horrible libel upon vegetation."[21]

Use of small plots of urban land for burials was extended in London by an efficient system for re-

Fig. 1.14. King's Chapel Burying Ground, April 19, 1840, daguerreotype by Samuel Bemis, courtesy of the George Eastman House.

Fig. 1.15. Church and Cemetery of the Innocents, engraving, ca. 1780.

Fig. 1.16. Saint-Innocents Cemetery, Paris, engraving, ca. 1780.

Fig. 1.17. Ossuaries walling in Saint-Innocents Cemetery, Paris, engraving by Bernier, 1786.

cycling space and disposing of exhumed bones. As late as 1819, one Englishman observed, "Many tons of human bones every year are sent from London to the north, where they are crushed in mills contrived for the purpose and used as manure." Demand for such fertilizer was even greater than could be met by the periodic emptying of urban graves. According to one Lincolnshire resident, "The eagerness of English agriculturists to obtain this manure (human bones) and the cupidity of foreigners in supplying it, is such as to induce the latter to rob the tombs of their forefathers. Bones of all descriptions are imported, and pieces of half-decayed coffin attire are found among them." The extent of the commerce in human remains to English fertilizer mills is still unknown, as are its international dimensions. Use of human remains for fertilizer was such a sordid business that few records or accounts of the practice exist, but knowledge of it appeared even in America. One young Bostonian observed in 1832, "In some places, so little is the respect for the dead, that the mouldering bodies have been bartered to nourish vegetation."[22]

Parisians had not developed such a system to ease the gross crowding of their cemeteries. Criticisms of burial places in the French capital, therefore, appeared decades before reformers' scrutiny of London cemeteries. The Saint-Innocents, the oldest, most conspicuous, and notorious of Parisian cemeteries, attracted attention first. When founded in the tenth century, the Saint-Innocents or des Champeaux ("Little Fields") was located next to the small Merovingian church of Saint-Germain-l'Auxerrois northeast of the city walls. In 1186, Philippe Auguste enlarged the urban enclosure to encompass it and built high walls around the trapezoidal cemetery itself, secured at night by a locked gate. Reputed to be the most notorious and fearsome of all European burial places, the Innocents was, by the seventeenth century, a walled wilderness in the heart of the city's most active market quarter. Fourteenth-century cloisters surrounded a barren, earthen area approximately two hundred by four hundred feet in size. One wall bore a mural of thirty panels depicting the *danse macabre* of skeletal Death confronting the living of all social stations. Images of the place suggested purgatory, at best. (Figs. 1.15, 16, 17.)

By the mid-eighteenth century, the Innocents served twenty-two parishes in addition to receiving dead from the Hôtel-Dieu and epidemic victims. In eight centuries, it received over two million Parisians. Most went into the trenches or *fosses communes*. Some pits sank twenty feet deep and ranged from six to eight feet in width; others were thirty feet deep and twenty feet square. They remained open, covered only by crude planks, until filled to capacity and above with bodies sewn into shrouds. Only then did sextons cover the anonymous pit with a thin layer of dirt, and then only for a brief time. Soil in parts of the Innocents was mounded eight feet above street level when pits were full. The standard two years of burial was usually too short to permit complete decomposition of bodies before bones were removed for the pit's reuse. Still tales persisted that earth at the Innocents had powers to consume flesh in twenty-four hours to nine days, depending on the account.

Practices at the Innocents were not unique in Paris or elsewhere in Europe. Only about 5 to 7 percent of the dead escaped the common trench. Smaller pits might contain only about 150 bodies; however, even newer and smaller Parisian cemeteries like the Sainte-Marguerite, created in 1634, contained trenches almost twelve feet deep. Such was the rule rather than the exception in most Catholic countries. Burial of the great mass of the people was simply a matter of disposal, at best in hallowed ground. Even the bodies of notables—the likes of Mozart, La Fontaine, and Molière—were consigned to common pits. Madame de Pompadour willed to escape the fate of mixing with the masses after death by use of a leaden coffin buried near the central cross in the Innocents; but even that permanent container was exhumed, reburied, dug up again, and eventually lost. Only an elite minority could purchase the privilege of a family tomb or perhaps a small memorial tablet temporarily to counteract the anonymity of the system and to prolong memory at the burial place.

Through the centuries, complaints by the common people about treatment of the dead, per se, were few or went unrecorded and unheeded. One Frenchman reflected his countrymen's resignation, writing in 1685, "Among our people it makes no difference whether we are buried in a cemetery or in a place where asses are flayed." John

Sheffield Buckingham's 1701 translation of the French poem "The Temple of Death" describes a characteristically barren burial place crowded with gaping pits and graves, where "Poisons are all the Plants the Soil will bear, / And Winter is the only Season there." French cemeteries, in particular, remained but "a Collection of the Ruins of many Ages, and the Rubbish of Twenty Generations." Louis-Sebastien Mercier, writer of bourgeois dramas and follower of Rousseau, observed, "He who wishes to be mourned after death should not die in Paris." Indeed, the number of wills stipulating a desired place of burial declined through the eighteenth century, indicating not so much a disregard of grave location as an indifference grounded in the lack of options and a resignation to the equal terribleness of any choices that might be made.[23]

By the mid-eighteenth century, however, escalating urbanization and rise of a bourgeoisie accentuated perceptions of and complaints about social inequities of the sepulchral system. New ambitions for postmortem remembrance arose among the newly prosperous, who found it increasingly difficult and painful to bury their dead anonymously with the masses or to anticipate with requisite selfless humility their own burial under such conditions. Many members of the bourgeoisie readily questioned Church sanctions and traditions even if they did not formally convert to Protestantism; they were particularly concerned with issues impinging on personal self-interest and individuality. The "affective individualism" that historians now identify as transforming familial relationships escalated through the eighteenth century and had ramifications on attitudes toward burial.[24]

Complaints stemming from newly sensitized tastes and increasingly sentimental family relationships among the bourgeoisie and lesser nobility became empassioned. In the words of the architect Pierre Patte, cemeteries were "veritable refuse dumps." As he gazed in the 1790s into the gaping common pits containing the remains of fathers, brothers, spouses, kin, and friends, the public prosecutor Nicher-Cerisy, otherwise a cold-blooded revolutionary, wondered how his supposedly enlightened generation could tolerate such a profanation of Man. His perspective would be rearticulated again and again by reformers in the decades to follow. Marchant de Beaumont complained that under the old system, "the remains of the vulgar masses went incessantly to stuff the vast common pits—putrid miasmas struck neighborhoods with epidemics as if to punish the living for lack of respect for the dead." The old cemeteries were "narrow, hideous, fetid places where the sun hardly shone; they buried the remains of the poor by the hundreds in large, deep pits kept open for months on end. Thousands of bones torn from the earth before being reduced to dust added to the horror of these awful places, where the poor hardly dared place a foot during the burial of their dear ones—the middle class had no more advantages." The bourgeoisie considered cemeteries even more

Fig. 1.18. Locked gates of the Clamart Cemetery, Paris, engraving by Regnier, April 5, 1804.

offensive than slaughterhouses, prisons, insane asylums, and hospitals where the terminally ill went to die; and all of these institutions were considered ripe for reform by removal from proximity to urban life. The French began to consider ways to distance these nuisances from their capital city in the early eighteenth century.[25]

Responding to numerous complaints, increasingly made by persons of influence, the Parlement of Paris charged physicians in 1734 to investigate the sanitary conditions of cemeteries. Charges of public health dangers joined more purely aesthetic complaints to hasten the reform movement; the resulting report, however, only called for better maintenance. Even a few Church officials, newly sensitized to stench and squalor and urged on by prosperous parishioners, called for burial reform. New sensitivities to foul smells such as those produced by rotting corpses added to the momentum for change. Such foul odors could no longer be rationalized as sacred or simply ignored; they became suspect as evil, in the mundane sense of engendering disease, if not in the supernatural sense as well. At the Clamart cemetery, adjacent to the royal botanical gardens, investigations in 1713 by Marc-Réné D'Argenson, Lieutenant-General of the Paris Police, responded to complaints of polluted air and led to discovery of two pits containing over thirteen thousand and eighteen thousand bodies each; the pits were intended for only ten thousand each. D'Argenson demanded that quicklime be added to these trenches and that they be mounded over with four hundred cartloads of dirt. He issued new regulations limiting the size of mass burials. Each pit could thereafter be no larger than ten feet deep, nine feet wide, and forty-eight feet long to accommodate a maximum of five hundred bodies deposited in a maximum of six or seven orderly layers. No regulatory agency existed, however, and the order proved unenforceable.[26] (Fig. 1.18.)

Criticisms of burial places, which paralleled demands for secularization if not complete disestablishment of Church control, escalated through the second half of the eighteenth century. Both France and England paid considerable attention to theories and proposals set forth in the other country. Even before the Revolution, French secular authorities determined to have a say in burial practices administered for all by the Church. A report from the king's procurator general to the Parlement of Paris in an inquisition lasting from 1763 to 1765 declared burial grounds in the capital glutted. The Parlement ordered them closed in 1765, but with no effect. Years passed until, on March 10, 1776, King Louis XVI confirmed the order but exempted the Innocents, the worst of the lot. The royal decree authorized municipalities to purchase land outside their limits to create new, secular cemeteries. Each parish, according to the plan, could have a walled enclosure of consecrated ground containing common pits, but small areas of private grave space would also be made available. The grounds, however, would still be devoid of monuments or plantings, landscape amenities that were, after all, unprecedented; nor would they be readily accessible to visitors. This plan, too, went unrealized, although as a result of the mandate single cemeteries such as the Innocents began to be used by several parishes. With this pattern of use of cemeteries often quite distant from the home of the deceased, mourners often ceased to accompany the body beyond the church.

When civil decrees, to say nothing of sentiment and taste, proved ineffective in changing the Church-run burial system, would-be funerary reformers resorted increasingly to arguments of public health dangers of urban cemeteries. The prominent physician Félix Vicq-d'Azyr followed this tack in the 1778 publication of his *Essay on Burial Places and Dangers,* borrowing many ideas from an Italian treatise that postulated that noxious effluvia from mass graves might engender disease.

Still, without cooperation from ecclesiastical authorities, no action could be taken to reform burial places in Paris or in any other cities controlled by the Roman Catholic or Anglican churches. Theories, studies, complaints, and even decrees with the force of law were of no avail until 1780, when several basements of houses bordering on the Innocents caved in under the weight of two thousand cadavers in a grave fifty feet deep. The incident precipitated a decisive report on the ill effects of the old burial system by Cadet de Vaux, Inspecteur Général des Objets de Salubrité, read before the Royal Academy of Science in 1783. Finally, in

Fig. 1.19. Paris Catacombs in old limestone quarries beyond the city limits, engraving by Frederick Nash, 1820.

Fig. 1.20 Passageway in the Paris Catacombs, engraving by Frederick Nash, 1820.

Fig. 1.21. Chapel in the Paris Catacombs, engraving by Cloquet from Héricart de Thury, *Déscription des Catacombes de Paris,* 1815.

turn, the Council of State, on November 9, 1785, ordered the cemetery to be destroyed and replaced by a public market. But more than a civil decree was necessary to accomplish the dismantling of the Innocents. Under intense pressure by 1786, Monseigneur Leclerc de Juigné, the Archbishop of Paris, reluctantly lent the Church's authority to the move, ordering final suppression of the cemetery. Supervised by a committee of the Royal Society of Medicine, the earth of the Innocents was broken to a depth of five feet and sifted to locate as many bones as possible. These were transported to subterranean limestone quarries west of the city, consecrated as an ossuary. (Fig. 1.19.) The Church renamed the site the Catacombs in reference to the secret labyrinth under Rome used by the early Christians for burial as well as worship. The architect, Héricast de Thury, supervised artistic rearrangement of the bones in the corridors and rooms carved out of the quarries. (Figs. 1.20, 21.) The spectacle created by moving the contents of the old cemetery to the Catacombs at Montrouge on the urban periphery continued even by night by torchlight for two years; it served as a mild prelude to the public spectacles of death witnessed in Paris in the next decade under the Reign of Terror.

Criticism of and even change in burial places controlled by the Church occurred through the seventeenth and eighteenth centuries, first among radical Protestants and then among secular authorities; but, with the exception of New England, secularization of burial grounds was rare. The growing impulse toward reform, however, involved far more than "de-Christianization." It drew upon trends in tastes and sentiments that permeated the cultures of new classes of literate artisans, merchants, and professionals in France as well as Old and New England. Clearly, a new international consensus was developing, demanding and then shaping the design of alternative, pastoral places for commemoration of lives lived, in private as well as public terms. When William Wordsworth repeated the old complaints of "the unsightly manner in which our monuments are crowded together in the busy, noisy, unclean, and almost grassless church-yard of a large town," he went one step further than most previous critics by providing a vision of a new sort of place to reintegrate Death in Nature, to create a funerary setting that would be a landscape of memory, not a place for forgetting the dead or for heeding the lessons of theological authority. Secular memory—whether personal and inspired by affective individualism or communal in the new name of patriotism—could be enshrined in material terms with monuments with funerary associations placed in the sort of naturalistic landscape long proscribed by the Church for burials. The first models for such places appeared with development of eighteenth-century English landscaped gardens.[27]

2

English Gardens: Models of Melancholy, Nature, and Design

God Almightie first planted a garden.
—Francis Bacon, *Of Gardens* (1625)

Gardening is more antique and nearer God's work than poetry.
—Charles Bridgeman (1725)

NATURE WAS NOT AS FEARSOME for the English in the seventeenth and eighteenth centuries as it was for other Europeans, and rural places served as particularly attractive retreats for those with various new religious, philosophic, and political propensities. Their taste for nature had revolutionary implications, involving first the effort of individuals to find a proper place for melancholy contemplation of divine Providence outside the auspices of the established Church and later the desire of the literate elite to create places representative of a tangle of new notions of "natural law," national history, and the relationship between civic virtue and cultural forms—material as well as literary. The melding of a new commemorative sensibility with neoclassical forms set in picturesque places occurred in the design of formulaic English "landscaped gardens," which subsequently inspired emulation on the Continent and in America.

The appearance of a commemorative sensibility among the rising educated classes must be understood in the context of changing sensibilities as well as tastes beginning in the seventeenth century, and even earlier among the elite. Some historians find trends in the history of mentalities underlying the dawning desire for memoralization. Philippe Ariès attributes it to a major alteration in the "collective unconscious." Lawrence Stone finds that from the sixteenth century "the art of dying was replaced by the art of living"; emotions formerly put off until the day of death were "spread out over the whole space of a lifetime," affecting every day with "a melancholy sense of the brevity of life." At least for the liberal, intellectual elite, by the eighteenth century, the notion of death was "replaced by the idea of mortality in general" and thus "lost its intensity."[1] Sentiments of melancholy, newly valued as virtuous rather than pathological, gave to daily life the merit formerly associated with dying a good death. Naturalistic landscapes, designed to stir melancholy and provide appropriate places for structures commemorating ordinary individuals as well as notables, appealed to this new mentality.

The taste for melancholy, or pleasure drawn from subtle sadness cultivated in a naturalistic setting, grew as a variation on and an outgrowth of Calvinist theology of Election; it was evident also in the notion of innate excellence articulated by many eighteenth-century philosophers. The word "sentimental" similarly achieved currency in the first decades of the century. According to the literary historian John Draper, a sentimentalist is nothing more than "a Calvinist who believes himself saved" and finds signs of personal grace through meditation.[2] Louis Cazamian also observed that in England "midnight thoughts, the obsession of the grave, the effusions of intimate grief and the pleasure of shedding tears, are directly connected through their innermost origins with the renascence of the Puritan spirit, which is favored by the rise of the middle class."[3] England's graveyard poetry and evidence of the cult of the melancholy in landscaped garden design were natural outgrowths and adaptations of trends originating in seventeenth-century Protestantism and shaped by subsequent trends in rationalism, deism, and finally romanticism.

By being made a matter of frequent contemplation, death could no longer remain banal, an inevitability to be accepted on the basis of faith alone. Calvinists emphasized logic rather than simple faith or Revelation, but eventually they came to value sentiment as a means of achieving a desired state of mind in which the individual would determine to follow the paths of virtue. As early as the 1630s, Calvinists described the ideal place for contemplation of death as amid nature, precisely the sort of place that post-Tridentine Catholic ecclesiastics decried as pantheistic. The eighteenth- and nineteenth-century cults of melancholy that flourished in literature, art, and landscape in various western nations drew impetus from this aspect of Calvinism.

John Milton played a major role in furthering the taste for melancholy by rejecting the notion that it was a sign of sickness, an older interpretation of the emotion. In his poem *Il Penseroso* (ca. 1635), Milton describes the meditative mood of the person who likes to be alone at night "or who by day courts the brown shadows in the close coverts of a wood by the brook." The poet postulates a protoromantic landscape especially suited for melancholy, advising retreat:

> To arched walks of twilight groves,
> And shadows brown, that Sylvan loves.
> Of pine or monumental oak,
> Where the rude ax with heaved stroke
> Was never heard the nymphs to daunt,
> Or fright them from their hallowed haunt.

Such a landscape became a magical place capable of bewitching a person with "the cherub of Contemplation" or with Sleep. The spirits of this wooded wilderness were benign, no longer the demons of tradition. Milton envisioned the perfect garden as re-creation of Eden. In contrast to the "loathed Melancholy" despised by the active man of the world in Milton's poem *L'Allegro* (1632), a "divinest Melancholy" with implications of holiness, sensibility, wisdom, beauty, and positive uses of leisure was fostered in this naturalistic landscape.[4] In secularized terms, this version of wooded wilderness came into vogue in England in the last decades of the seventeenth century.

Melancholy was fashionable in the Commonwealth and with Dissenters thereafter. Even Anglican culture, exemplified by John Evelyn's writings, at times lauded a "religious melancholy or pious sadness." Samuel Clarke, ecclesiastic, rationalist, and author of *A Discourse Concerning the Unchangeable Obligations of Natural Re-*

ligion (1706), considered the "most overt proof of Election a longing for death and a delight in musing upon it." The Dissenting minister George Cokayne urged his congregation in 1691 "To walk amongst the Tombs while we are here; that Death might not be a surprise."[5] Nonconformist hymn writer Isaac Watts counseled melancholy meditation in *Reliquiae Iuveniles* [*sic*] (1742) and suggested the burial ground as an ideal place for such thoughts. Yet verbal pictures painted by Watts were those of the old, unintelligible, chaotic death rather than inventions of inviting places of nature conducive to quiet, melancholy sentiments.[6]

Memory and melancholy found a place even before the end of the seventeenth century in New England as well. The earliest surviving grave marker in Massachusetts is the rough-hewn boulder marked simply E. L. and dated 1647 in the common burying ground of Ipswich, but quantities of what would become the conventional slate gravestone of the region did not appear until the 1660s and 1670s. The urge for postmortem remembrance of individuals lagged in New England several decades behind the trend that was increasingly shared by members of the growing middle class in England through the first decades of the seventeenth century. A new sense of individuality, although not so named, accompanied the rise of commercial classes or a bourgeoisie in both England and Western Europe. Members of the gentry and even the artisan classes joined this group in aspiring to individual postmortem recognition and other trappings of status formerly reserved for the aristocracy, clergy, and high bourgeoisie.[7]

The growing desire for status and commemoration inspired the royalist physician Sir Thomas Browne (1605–82) to write *Hydriotaphia: Urne-Buriall, or A Discourse of the Sepulchrall Urnes Lately Found in Norfolk* (1658). Based on the examples of the ancient burials, Browne warned his readers of the futility of wishing "to extend our memories by monuments." The identities of ancients interred with such intentions had long ago been forgotten. Browne tried to discourage new ambitions for remembrance. "To hope for eternity by enigmatical epithets or first names given us like mummies, are cold consolations unto students of perpetuity," Browne concluded, for "the iniquity of oblivion blindly deals with the memory of men without distinction to merit of perpetuity. The greater part must be content to be as though they had not been: to be found in the register of God, not in the record of man." Browne considered, "Diurturnity [*sic*], is a dream and folly of expectation. In vain do individuals hope for immortality, or any patent from oblivion. There is nothing strictly immortal but immortality."[8] Browne's tract failed to slow the growing commemorative impulse in England or elsewhere, however, and other intellectual and cultural forces only further hastened its ascendancy.

The cult of memory or of melancholy remembrance, which I refer to simply as the cult of melancholy because of its generalized literary and aesthetic dimensions, first flourished in England and stirred aesthetic criticisms of existing burial practices. John Evelyn's celebration of rural taste dates from his self-imposed exile on his estate at Watton in Surrey from the outbreak of the Civil War in 1641 until the restoration in 1660 and his return to prominence. Evelyn remained an Anglican and a royalist. A taste for the classical informed Evelyn's recommendations for landscape solutions to burial reform. In his book *Silva; or, A Discourse of Forest-Trees* (1664), Evelyn recounts the history of "divine, as well as civil uses" of groves consecrated as by the ancients "to the Gentile Deities and Heroes." Oak groves or "Arboreus Temples" provided sublime and sacred sites for worship. Plato planted trees over sepulchers "to obumbrate [*sic*] the departed," and the "Saviour chose a garden as a place of Sepulchre." Evelyn concluded that "for many weighty causes, there are no places more fit to bury our dead in than our gardens and groves, or airy fields, *sub dio,* where our beds may be decked and carpeted with verdant and fragrant flowers, trees, and perennial plants, the most natural and instructive hieroglyphics of our expected resurrection and immortality; besides what they might conduce from dwelling too intently upon more vain and sensual objects."[9]

Evelyn recommended planting various profitable trees imported from around the world in both gardens and cemeteries to build up the nation's depleted timber resources. Trees would be useful as well as ornamental. He liked the "architectonial qualities" of trees and considered them among the most stable elements in a landscape. His essay "The Sacredness and Use of Standing Groves" points to the emotional benefits to be derived from a wooded setting.[10] Trees in a burial landscape would be didactic as well as practical. Even if the English were slow to create such cemeteries, many landscape gardeners in the following century heeded Evelyn's advice in the making of private estates that developed timber reserves at the same time that they created places of melancholy contemplation.

After the plague of 1665 and the Great Fire of London the following year, Evelyn crusaded unsuccessfully for creation of linear, extramural cemeteries following the example of the Ceramicus outside Athens or Rome's Appian Way. Evelyn's specific suggestions for wooded cemeteries, however, were far different aesthetically from the picturesque landscape designs eventually developed in eighteenth-century English gardens and nineteenth-century cemeteries. The writer proposed a "universal cemetery to all the parishes" of London on a mile-long, linear strip of land north of the city walls. There, visitors could stroll through "ample walks of trees, the walls adorned with monuments, inscriptions and titles, apt for contemplation and the memory of the defunct." Despite reference to the design as a "funeral grove," the description suggests a huge, out-of-doors, walled nave displaying funerary tablets like those found in English churches.[11]

Sir Christopher Wren (1632–1723), who along with Evelyn planned the reconstruction of London, proposed similar cemeteries as potential sites for display of monuments by architects and sculptors. Wren desired discontinuation of both churchyards and burials in church crypts, which he feared might endanger the salubrity of the city. The burial grounds proposed by both Evelyn and Wren would not differentiate according to sect or parish but would serve all of London. The writings of Evelyn and Wren reflect the increasing desire, even among Anglicans, for a more widespread postmortem commemoration not possible under England's Church-controlled burial system.[12]

Nevertheless, the rejection of traditional forms of authority of church and state premised the making of landscapes celebrating Nature as sacred and providing appropriate settings for material reinterpretation of an idealized past to be usable in an age of changing ideology or mentality. Philosophers and designers began to share ideas on how material forms could foster both a public and a private cult of ancestors or cult of heroes. Cultivation of melancholy could make better citizens through lessons of moral philosophy gleaned by the individual contemplating mortality and the inexorable processes of time. A new frame of mind, sometimes associated with Whiggish ideology, pantheism, deism, rationalism, and eventually romanticism, contributed to the design of and taste for eighteenth-century pastoral gardens, to the building of monuments tastefully placed in green open spaces, and eventually to the creation of "rural" cemeteries in France, America, and England—in that chronological order. Anglicans and Catholics considered Whigs deists and even atheists, and the Whiggish taste for secularized commemoration only contributed to such suspicions.

"Taste"—which meant perception or appreciation for quality, especially in reference to landscape, as defined by Addison, Swift, and Pope—came into fashion in England in the first decades of the eighteenth century. Milton, Congreve, and Addison used the word "taste" in reference to a discerning sense of the appropriate, harmonious, beautiful, and excellent. Taste would, they thought, be a catalyst for the good, the virtuous, and the moral. Hence, the word took on ideological and spiritual connotations. Styles favored by the taste of the literati bore complex associations meant to stir emotions and impart lessons of civic and secular virtue.

Taste, therefore, had religious dimensions. Despite persistent use of a grim iconography of death and stern warnings of man's postmortem fate, Puritanism in Old and New England contained seeds of a more benign view of death than that of medieval Christianity. The Puritans constantly scrutinized their daily lives, souls, and environment for evidence of the designs of Providence for themselves and their communities. They urged each individual's intellectual confrontation of mortality; and as early as the 1630s, they described the ideal place for contemplation of death as amid nature. The eighteenth-century cult of the melancholy that flourished in literature and landscape had origins in this aspect of radical Protestantism.

As religious orthodoxy declined at the turn of the eighteenth century, a philosophical void remained to be filled by reason and recognition of "natural" rather than divine law. Sacred space was secularized and reshaped in more natural forms. Religious liberals, even more than their Calvinist forebears, favored meditative, pastoral environments conducive to melancholy thoughts of the passage of time—past, present, and future—and the place of the individual in the great, inexorable system of nature. Poets and theorists replaced ministers in prescribing proper spiritual places. They favored natural landscapes with mnemonic ruins or monuments, describing the sort of landscape that would later take the form of the English garden with all the proper elements—cenotaphs, mausoleums, temples, grottoes, reflective bodies of water or gently flowing streams, meandering paths through cool and gloomy woods, and clearings that highlighted distant perspectives and panoramas. Memory replaced *memento mori* on inscriptions on monuments framed in such natural settings. Recollection of the life and deeds of the individual as part of ongoing, nonrecurring historical processes supplanted stern warnings of the commonality of the four last things—death, judgment, heaven, and hell. Or, in absence of references to real people and events, allegorical figures and mythological events drawn from classical literature represented moral and philosophic lessons. Ideally, in such a landscape, the visitor would achieve a personal understanding of the relationship of the self to the universe, of man to Nature.

John Evelyn's writings reveal these nascent trends, expressing increasing interest in melancholy and encouraging creation of naturalistic places to foster meditation. Evelyn wrote his friend Browne in 1675 of his intention "to show how the air and genius of gardens operate upon the human spirits towards virtue and sanctity. . . How caves, grots, mounts, and irregular ornaments of gardens do contribute to contemplative and philosophical enthusiasm; how *elysium, antrum, nemus, paradysus, hortus, locus, etc.*, signify all of them *rem sacrum et divinam;* for these expedients do influence the soul and spirits of men and prepare them to converse with good angels." Evelyn adapted Robert Burton's theories from *The Anatomy of Melancholy* (1621), which held that a pensive, sad state of mind could be induced by a stroll "amongst orchards, gardens, bowers, mounts, and arbours, artificial wilderness, green thickets, arches, groves, lawns, rivulets, fountains, and such like pleasant places."[13]

The theme of death in a pastoral setting also recurred in art, following the example of Nicolas Poussin's painting *Et in Arcadia Ego* (1635–36), depicting shepherds contemplating an ancient funerary monument. The painting marked, according to Erwin Panofsky, "a radical break with the mediaeval, moralizing tradition."[14] Such images, copied by Richard Wilson, Welsh founder of the English school of landscape painting, in his *Ego fui in Arcadia* (1755), and by Sir Joshua Reynolds in his *Et in Arcadia Ego* (1769), recurred repeatedly in verse and in actual landscapes shaped to cultivate philosophy if not fantasy in the visitor's mind. From multiple sources in art, literature, and philosophy, naturalistic, contemplative environments emerged as a composite of specific landscape elements to revolutionize English garden aesthetics and eventually to provide a prototype for a new sort of burial place.

After the death of Charles II in 1685, English funeral elegies idealized naturalistic landscapes conducive to contemplation of death. Edmund Arwaker's ode on that occasion presents a literary description of a place fit for melancholy:

> Behold a *Grove,* whose *Melancholy* shade
> Appear'd for *Sorrow's* last retirement made,
> Where in confus'd disorder grew,
> Bidding Defiance to the Sun's bright Eye
> The *Mournful* Cypress and *Unlucky* Yew:
>   So closely interwov'n they were,
>   His Mid-day Beams were Strangers There.

On the same occasion, a poet identified only as "J. H. Esq." depicted a setting where "the melancholy Muse" overcome by "the horror of the Dismal News" of the king's death languishes "Beneath a Doting Willow's Shade." Here was one of the first references to the willow as site and symbol of mourning the dead. Another Cavalier ode, by "Sir F. F., Knight of Bath," carried grief to a spot among "*Ruins,* that to Religion Sacred were of *yore.*"[15] These verses suggest specific landscape elements later to characterize the English garden and the stylized images of mourning pictures.

Philosophical trends contributed greatly to development of English gardens as meditative places. Notions of the essential goodness of natural man and of individual freedom premised the growing taste for nature. The writings of the Cambridge Platonists, academics educated by Puritans but derisively labeled Unitarians by Calvinists, emphasized a natural and rational moral sense. Creation of landscaped gardens coincided with a period of relatively free religious expression and the heights of Deism from 1685 to 1742. Given the central role accorded the senses—especially the visual—in Lockean epistemology, it seems only inevitable that those thinkers who rejected the Church as the prime place for instilling or fostering spiritual values would try to create alternative, sensually rich, naturalistic environments for the purposes of moral philosophy—places much different from existing, formally structured, geometric gardens.

Perhaps the first English philosopher to do this was Anthony Ashley Cooper, Third Earl of Shaftesbury (1671–1713) and grandson of the founder of Whiggism, educated by John Locke to become a leading Deist and Whig politician. He considered taste a kind of civic virtue. Aesthetics and ethics were so closely related as to be virtually the same. Shaftesbury thought of the "moral sense" as a "natural virtue" and as the ability to distinguish beauty from ugliness rather than simply good from evil. Equating the sense of beauty with the moral sense, he found both inherent in the mind when associated with emotions activated by elements of a natural environment. The solitude of groves and sense of the sacred in nature appealed to both emotion and intellect among a growing number of those of like mind with Shaftesbury, enamored with beauty in the "romantick way."[16] For them, a country seat with naturalistic gardens became an asylum and place of healing leisure from the profane sphere of commerce and politics. Shaftesbury invoked the Genius of Place, "Ye fields and Woods, my Refuge from the toilsome World of Business . . . receive me in your quiet Sanctuarys." In his *Characteristicks of Men, Manners, Opinions, Times* (1711), Shaftesbury deified and personified Nature as "Wise Substitute of Providence!" Nature became "All loving and All-lovely," and "Rural Meditations," sacred.[17] Shaftesbury's writings in turn influenced English literati and many on the Continent who read him in Diderot's translation.

Similarly, the Scottish philosopher Francis Hutcheson reflected Shaftesbury's ideas about the relationship of the moral sense to other internal and external senses. His advocacy of the "natural garden" appeared in his *Inquiry into the Origins of Our Ideas of Beauty and Virtue* (1725). But Shaftesbury's most immediate impact on shaping landscaped garden design came through his influence on the work of the poet and aesthetic theorist Alexander Pope (1688–1744).

In his *Moral Essays* and other writings, Pope built upon Shaftesbury's suggestions of the moral powers of nature. Pope propounded human capabilities to shape a naturalistic environment deliberately to stir certain emotions and associations. Pope believed in Art's ability to improve Nature, an idea expressed by Aristotle and by the first-century Greek philosopher Longinus. Blending classical and contemporary philosophy, literature, and art to form the underpinnings for the rising vogue in landscape gardening, Pope laid down rules for garden design and detailed the functions of many recommended garden elements. For instance, statuary in gardens has "moral utility," especially when bearing instructive messages from the past to become commemorative monuments. Like Horace, Pope considered the death of an individual, unknown and unwept, an unfortunate fate; he proposed both poetry and material commemoration in a garden setting as remedies for the failure of memory. Pope's *Essay on Man* describes the ethical usefulness of memory perpetuating both fame and infamy.

Pope's guidelines for garden design were followed by many estate proprietors ambitious to make their own gardens. In a poetic epistle to Richard Boyle, Earl of Burlington, Pope cautions his friend not to forget the Goddess Nature in laying out his suburban land at Chiswick between 1730 and 1736. In number IV of the *Moral Essays,* published in 1731, Pope advises Burlington and all prospective garden designers:

Consult the Genius of Place in all:
That tells the Water or to rise or fall;
Or helps the ambitious hill the heav'ns to scale,
Or scoops in circling theatres the Vale;
Calls in the Country, catches op'ning glades,
Joins willing woods, and varies shades from
shades;
Now breaks, or now directs, th' intending Lines;
Paints, as you plant, and, as you work, designs.

With "good sense," a sensitivity to natural topography and indigenous plants, and a flexibility of design able to take advantage of "spontaneous beauties" arising "from Chance," the estate owner would be able to create an aesthetic unity in gardens in which "Parts answ'ring parts shall slide into a whole." Pope promises, "Nature shall join you; time shall make it grow." Such naturalistic gardening contrasted dramatically with the formal style borrowed from the French, which required an architect, intensive labor of teams of gardeners, and considerable expense, to say nothing of maintenance costs.[18]

Pope's was only one of many poetic prescriptions for "modern" landscaped gardens that made the task of creating a picturesque estate relatively easy for a well-read proprietor even if he lacked a gardener's design services. Another such account was an anonymous letter in verse to Charles Lord Viscount Irwin, in which the author virtually paraphrases Pope:

O study Nature! and with thought profound,
Previous to laying out with taste your ground;
O mark her beauties as they striking rise,
Bid all her adventitious charms surprise!
Eye all her shining, all her shadowy grace,
And to conceal them every blemish trace:
Yet there's a happiness that baffles Art,
In showing Nature *great* in every part,
Which chiefly flows from mingled lights and
shades,
In lawns, and woods, hills, rivers, rocks and
glades;
For only happy's that assemblage made,
Where force of light contends with force of
shade.[19]

Instead of the old medieval dualism of good and evil, contending forces in the English garden would be light and shadow, voids and solids, stirring both cheerful and melancholy associations, but ever shifting in new dynamic relationships in three-dimensional space representative of a new worldview. Such gardens forged a compromise with Milton's *L'Allegro* and *Il Penseroso.*

Following Pope's lead, this anonymous poet "improved" Nature with monuments and structures intended to focus the various happy and sad associations stirred in the garden. He counseled placing "spiry temples" on hills and "sculptur'd obelisks with statues crown'd" as focal points for perspectives. A major fixture in the English garden was the grotto, a secluded, sheltered, dark and damp, private spot, usually fashioned of rustic rock and located near a "weeping rill." The term "grotto" appropriately comes from the Latin "crypta," meaning a vault or place in which to hide but also suggesting death. Since ancient Greece, grottoes were considered sacred places especially fit for meditation. According to Pope:

Here widow'd love, pale woe may rest their
head,
Or, with the suddening Spring soft sorrows shed;
Here meditation may pursue her theme,
And of celestial joys enraptur'd dream.

This landscape where "weeping willows kiss the *watry glades,* / And rills still murmur thro' the pensive shades," where "horrid rocks," architectural ruins "moulder'd by Time," and mausoleums on "pine-crown'd hills" marked perspectives was definitely intended to stir the spirit of melancholy.[20] Narrow, winding paths, wide enough for only one person, provided for solitary contemplation. Such literary descriptions served

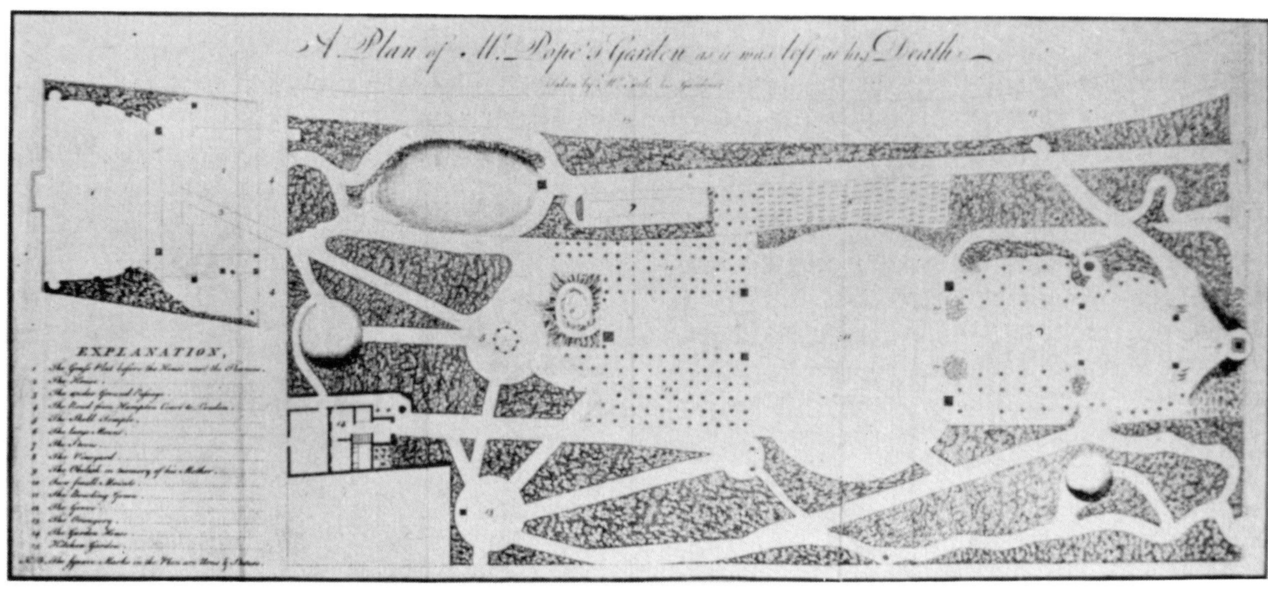

Fig. 2.1. "A Plan of Mr. Pope's Garden as it was left at His Death," Twickenham, engraved by John Serle, his gardener, 1745.

as inspiration for the "amateur" who wished for his own English garden, articulating and developing a taste for a new poetics of space.

Pope practiced what he preached. His small, five-acre rented estate at Twickenham in Middlesex was a "poetical villa" just west of London on the banks of the Thames and near Horace Walpole's Strawberry Hill. (Fig. 2.1.) It was composed of a sequence of spaces, alternately light and dark, open and closed, through which the visitor passed before reaching the focal point of the garden, nestled in a grove of mournful cypresses: the tomb of the poet's mother. Pope erected a commemorative obelisk on the spot in 1719; William Kent (1684–1748), Pope's close friend, described a picture the poet had of himself "in a mourning gown with a strange view of the garden to shew the obelisk as in memory of his mother's Death." Pope made his garden a "Musaeum," or, according to John Dixon Hunt, "a place where his muses communicated with his best self"; but Pope's muses were highly melancholy. Pope combined his personally commemorative theme with a classical one, applying his studies of Roman antiquities from Georg Graevius's *Thesaurus* and Pieter Schenk's *Romae Novae Delineatio;* reminiscence of the Roman soothsayer Egeria was woven into his garden with marble fragments imported by a friend from Egeria's grotto near the Appian Way. Pope worked closely with Kent and encouraged his transition from painter to architect and maker of naturalistic garden compositions fit for philosophy and melancholy. Both realized that the creation of picturesque landscapes depended on combination of a poetic and a painterly sensibility, one that could be cultivated or acquired by the well-read.[21]

A number of other major writers joined Pope in shaping landscape gardening tastes. Many contemporaries judged the poet James Thomson (1700–1748) as having equal influence with Milton and Pope. Thomson, called the "English Virgil," a member of the popular Graveyard School of poets, specialized in patriotic eulogies; but it was his long poem, *The Seasons,* published in four parts between 1726 and 1730, that foreshadowed romanticism and celebrated nature's melancholy potentials. William Kent designed plates showing neoclassical temples and monuments in picturesque, rural landscapes for the 1730 edition. Thomson praised the "Sacred Influence" of nature when it "inflames Imagination" and "Philosophic Melancholy." He yearned to meditate in "twilight groves and visionary values," in "weeping grottoes and prophetic

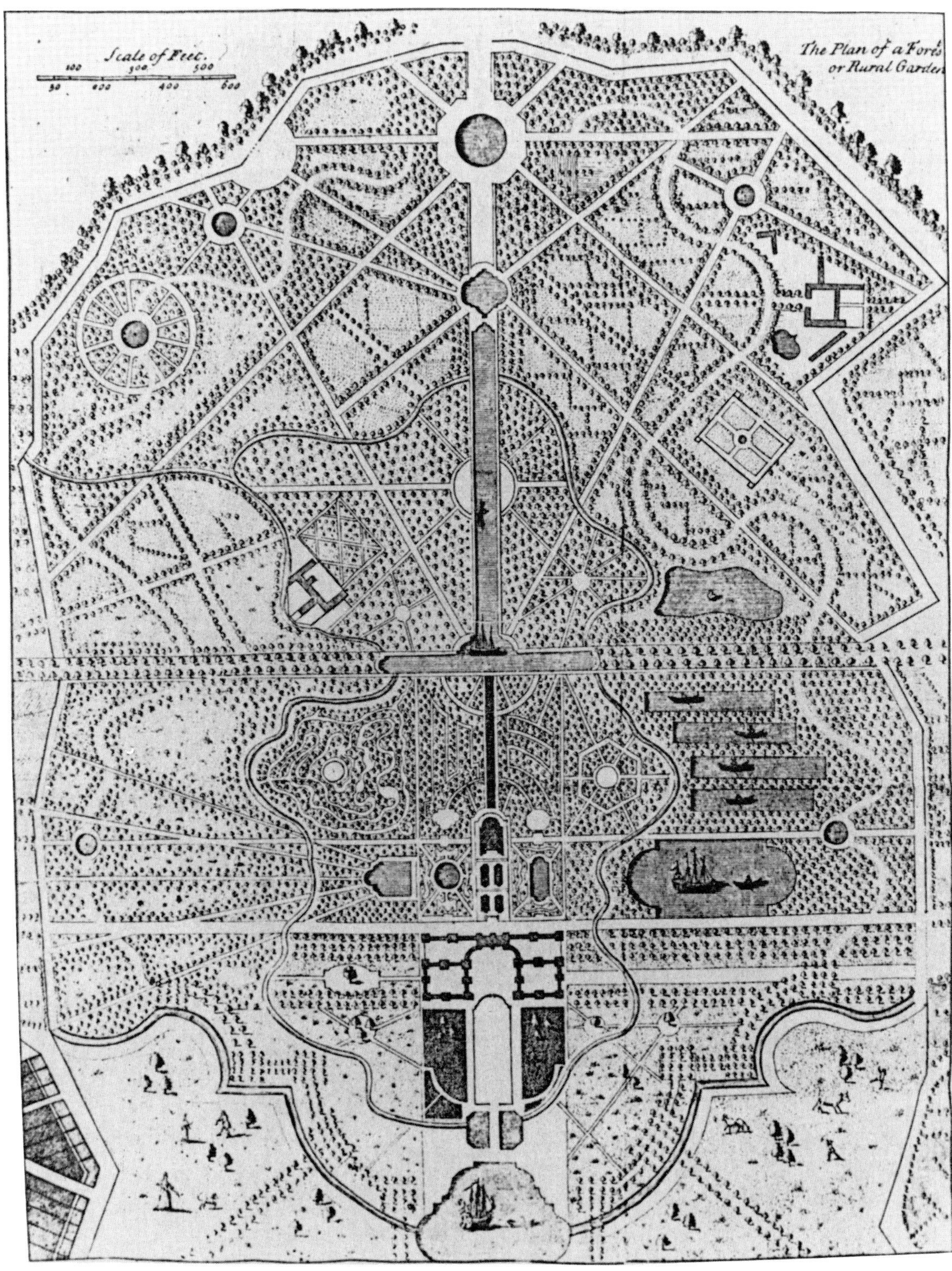

Fig. 2.2. Stephen Switzer, "The Manour of Paxton Divided and Planted into Rural Gardens," engraving from *Ichnographia Rustica* (London, 1742).

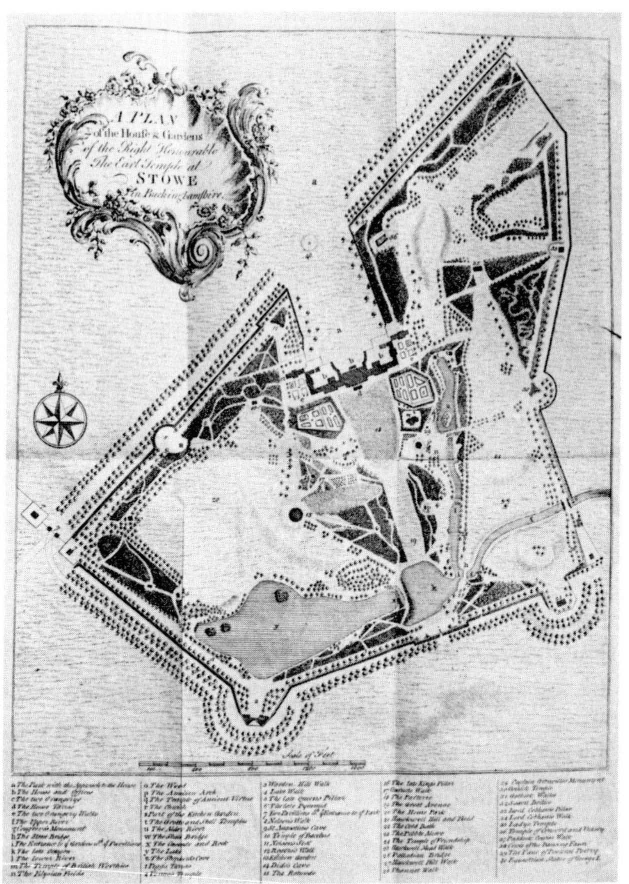

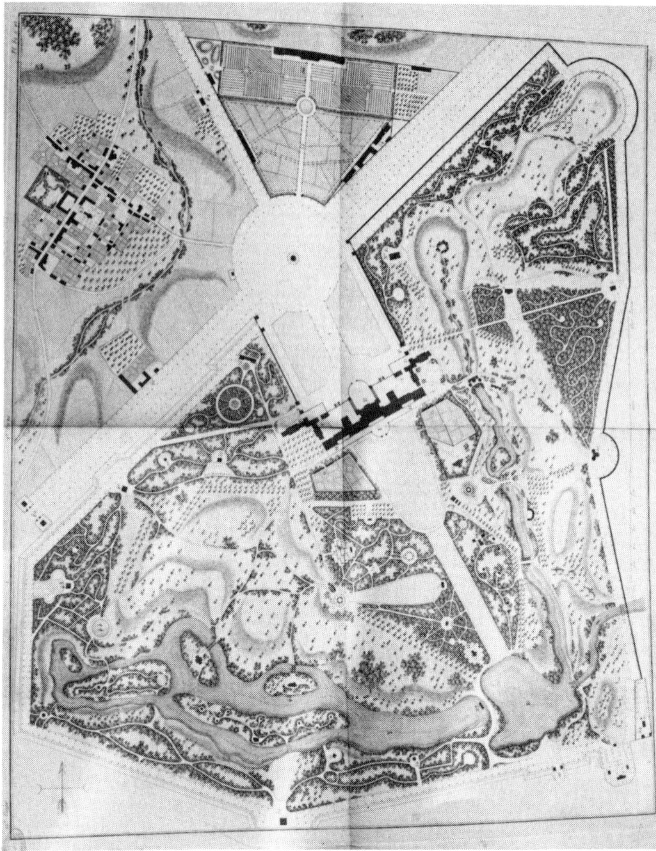

Fig. 2.3. (*Above*) Stowe, Buckinghamshire, 1774, engraved plan from LeRouge, 1776.

Fig. 2.4. (*Above, right*) Stowe, engraved plan by Jean Charles Krafft, 1810.

Fig. 2.5. (*Right*) Temple of British Worthies designed by William Kent, ca. 1735, with busts by Rysbrack and Scheemakers, across the artificial water called the River Styx at Stowe, photograph by Alan Ward, 1985.

glooms." Thomson echoed Shaftesbury and Pope in his belief that nature could inspire a beneficial state of mind.[22] Other poets of his school—Robert Blair, Thomas Gray, Henry Kirke White, and Edward Young—also helped spread the taste for pastoralism and melancholy through their verses.

Joseph Addison (1672–1719), along with Richard Steele, disseminated similar ideas to a wide, international audience through articles in the *Spectator*. The journal, reaching about 10,000 originally and more in reprints, popularized the liberal philosophy of the likes of Newton and Voltaire, bridging the gap between theology, science, and taste. Addison was the first, in 1711, to attack publicly the artificial, linear formality in garden design borrowed from the French, at the same time as he praised the new style of naturalistic gardens fashioned as Elysia.[23]

Stephen Switzer, with his prestigious position as royal gardener, similarly promoted tastes for the "Rural or Forest Garden" in his three-volume *Ichnographia Rustica; or, the Nobleman, Gentleman, and Gardener's Recreation* (1718). (Fig. 2.2.) Switzer drew from Milton a regret for Eden lost, and his garden designs were meant to temper the burdens of the Fall from God's grace. Nature would compensate for the consequence of death; the visitor would imbibe lessons from it on solitary walks along narrow paths. Yet Switzer required Art in his gardens to shape and augment Nature. He admired classical gardens, where "the ancient Attick and Roman Worthies erected magnificent Statues, and decreed Annual Honours to be paid to their Rural and Hortensial Deities." He considered statues "one of the noblest Ornaments of our best Gardens and Plantations," artifacts where visitors "hieroglyphically find the great Ideas and Valour and Renown, that particularly distinguished those Ancients above the rest of their Fellow Creatures, and is of continual Use and Amusement to the serious Beholders! 'tis there . . . we read true Lineaments of Heroism and Virtue, and other Attributes which deified those never-dying Heroes." But although Switzer preached pantheism and pastoralism, his gardens remained predominantly linear, although asymmetrical and lacking the systematic order of French gardens in the fashion of Le Nôtre. Only a few sections had the sinuous paths that would come to characterize the English garden. Still, Switzer's "natural" garden theory made clear equations between Whiggish notions of liberty and the informal style of gardening, although the sources of the landscape movement remained more philosophical, emotional, and aesthetic than political.[24]

Another fashionable writer ranting against formal parterres and topiary was Batty Langley (1696–1751), whose *New Principles of Gardening* (1728) urged estate proprietors to make "a beautiful rural garden" of their land, precisely at a time when the ranks of estate owners were swelling with new wealth from trade and with land produced by Enclosure Acts. Langley, like many other garden theorists of his day, urged proprietors to place structures in their gardens to stir emotions. Langley and other writers called naturalistic gardens Arcadias, versions of a primordial idealized countryside. Ironically, they favored them at precisely the time when the traditional relationship of the peasantry to the land was undergoing upheaval. Creation of many important landscaped gardens was premised on recent historical disjunctures. The land itself held nostalgic associations of families and towns that were no more. Indeed, the taste for arcadian pleasure grounds hastened displacement of some agrarian communities, formally lamented by few until Oliver Goldsmith wrote his "The Deserted Village" (1770) about a fictional town, Sweet Auburn, in Ireland, then recently destroyed by estate building.[25]

The historic sensibility evident in English gardens was more often ancient than modern in focus. Arcadian gardens were meant to be allegorical places with complex spiritual and commemorative associations, usually of ancient origin. According to Peter Gay, enlightened Englishmen sought "discovery of their true ancestors" in pagan antiquity.[26] Langley and the others revived Palladio's interest in classical literature and art, especially because the style stirred in the mind the melancholy sense of the inexorable passage of time; they also shared Palladio's taste for ruins.

A number of prominent landowners used these literary sources to create their own landscape compositions. The second quarter of the eighteenth

Fig. 2.6 (*Above*) Temple of Ancient Virtue and Roman rostral column to memory of Captain Thomas Grenville (1747), topped by allegorical figure of Heroic Poetry pointing to scroll with Latin inscription "None but Heroic Deeds I Sing," and facing the Temple of British Worthies. Kent designed the Temple of Ancient Virtue, ca. 1734. Photograph by Alan Ward, 1985.

Fig. 2.7. (*Above*) Grotto on the River Styx at Stowe, engraving by T. Medland from J. Seeley, 1797.

Fig. 2.8. "The Serpentine River [Styx] and Grotto in Stow [*sic*] Gardens," engraving, ca. 1760.

century marked the heyday of English garden design, amalgamating the philosophic, political, and patriotic themes of the era. In many cases, highly literate proprietors played major roles in making gardens that objectified poetics of place drawn from classical tales as well as from writers of their own era. These gardens promoted the sort of melancholy contemplation described and prescribed since Milton. Despite poetic assurances that the task of garden-making would be simple, these man-made landscapes in the "natural" manner were often artfully contrived and arduously constructed environments. The ambitious garden-maker had only tastefully to place "fabriques"—monuments, buildings, ruins, or other architectural features, often with commemorative significance—in spaces formed in a naturalistic fashion. The term fabrique was used in reference to such structures common in compositions of landscape paintings. Hence, fabriques were elements necessary to compose or embellish the "picturesque."

Aaron Hill (1685–1750), a poet and dramatist (who adapted Voltaire's *Zaïre* for the English stage) and friend of Pope, created a small "Moral Garden" at Petty France, Westminster, in 1735. Its grottoes, cave, winding paths, and statues of virtues and vices were meant to inspire moral qualities in visitors. Sometimes, estate owners enlisted the aid of William Kent or even Pope in the effort to create didactic, evocative landscapes; however, many other gardens were constructed by their proprietors alone. The theme of melancholy and nostalgia for the past—either classical, familiar, or political—permeated these landscapes. Eventually, demand for "picturesque" gardens grew so great that it contributed to the rise of professionalized landscape gardeners. Professionalization eventually led to imposition of quite different landscape aesthetics, the "beautiful," often associated with Lancelot "Capability" Brown, devoid of many of the complex philosophic and literary underpinnings of the garden taste prevalent through mid-century and resurgent at the end.

Fig. 2.9. (*Above*) Monument to William Congreve, designed by William Kent, 1736, Stowe, photograph by Alan Ward, 1985.

Fig. 2.10. (*Below*) Monument to Queen Caroline by Rysbrack, ca. 1730, Stowe, photograph by Alan Ward, 1985.

Fig. 2.11. Octagon Pond in the Vale of Venus with statue of Pan, Rousham, Oxfordshire, photograph by Alan Ward, 1985.

Fig. 2.12. Praeneste Terrace by William Kent, Rousham, photograph by Alan Ward, 1985.

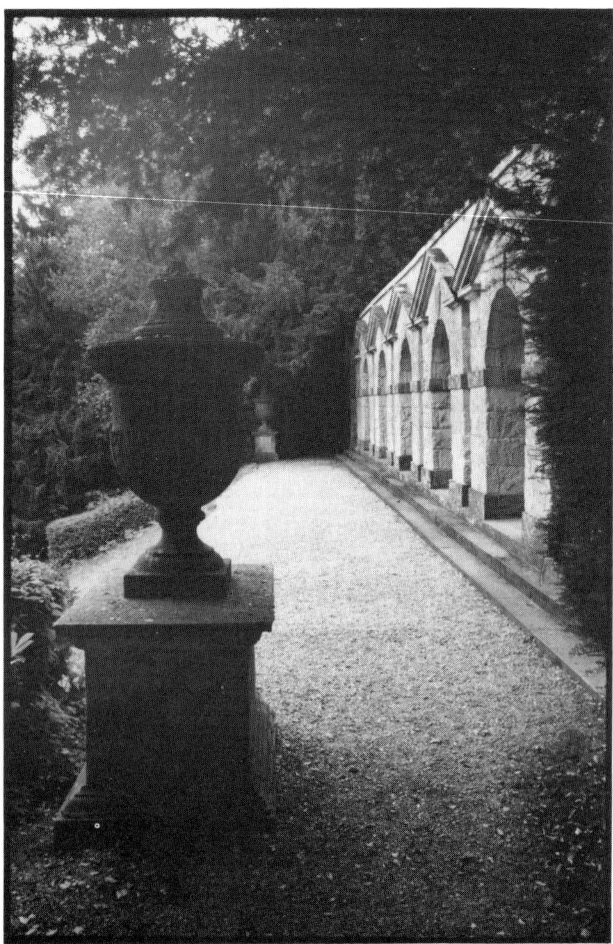

Yet it was the "picturesque" garden of the second quarter of the century that gained international currency as *le jardin anglais*. Of all English gardens of this period, Stowe in Buckinghamshire was the most celebrated in its day and remains so today. Its proprietor, Sir Richard Temple, had been raised by George I to the peerage as Lord Viscount Cobham in 1718 because of his role under Marlborough in the War of Spanish Succession. Cobham settled down on his own estate the next year and hired the architect Charles Bridgeman to begin a garden composition. As early as 1731, Cobham's close friend Pope recognized Stowe's aesthetic excellence and acclaimed it in his "Epistle to Burlington" as the epitome of gardening art. Pope's was only the first of many literary notices taken of the allegorical landscape developed at Stowe over the next several decades.[27] (Figs. 2.3, 4.)

Kent deserves prime responsibility for designing major portions of Stowe's landscape in a manner appealing to the complex literary associations in an era of high symbolic and antiquarian consciousness, and particularly representative of Cobham's notions of Protestant Whiggery, including subtle criticism of the then-current political corruption of Sir Robert Walpole. The gardens contained a semi-circular stone exedra, designed in 1735 by Kent as the Temple of British Worthies to contain sixteen busts by Rysbrack and Scheemakers of kings, queens, and writers, including Shakespeare, Milton, Bacon, Newton, Locke, Pitt, Penn, and Pope himself. (Fig. 2.5.) An inscription from *The Aeneid,* minus original reference to priests, proclaims the passage of spirits of the Good across the River Styx to the Elysian Fields, the name given to an area of the grounds designed by Kent in the 1730s on the opposite bank of the small stream, site of Kent's Temple of Ancient Virtue, but with more ancient reference to the pastoral haunt of mortals made immortal by divine favor. (Figs. 2.6, 2.7, 2.8.) Kent also designed temples of Venus and of Contemplation for the grounds, which included a 115-foot, octagonal tower designed by James Gibbs, topped by a portrait statue, and dedicated by Lady Cobham in 1749 in memory of her recently deceased husband. Richard Grenville, Earl Temple, continued work

Fig. 2.13. Temple of Echo by Kent and Townsend, Rousham, photograph by Alan Ward, 1985.

on the grounds, following the fashions of the times, after the death of his uncle Cobham.[28]

Stowe, frequently called the "national Valhalla," evidenced a new English commemorative consciousness. (Figs. 2.9, 10.) Madame du Boccage, visiting from France, praised the way the English "immortalize their great men: the statues erected to their honour are, like seed, capable of producing others to all eternity." Another visitor in 1744 described the garden with "buildings dedicated to Patriots, Heroes, Lawgivers and Poets, men of ingenuity and invention, they receive a dignity from the persons to whom they are consecrated. Others that are sacred to imaginary powers, raise pleasing enthusiasm in the mind." The visitor concluded, "At Stowe you walk amidst Heroes and Deities, powers and persons whom we have been taught to honour, who have embellished the world with arts, or instructed it in Science, defended their country and improved." The landscape celebrated an aristocracy of merit of particular appeal to Whigs.[29]

Most of the garden architecture that accumulated through the century served as "allusion to patterns of cultural heritage." A column erected in 1747 and topped by the allegorical figure of Heroic Poetry commemorates Captain Thomas Grenville, who died in a naval battle with the French. The Grecian Temple of Concord and Victory, thought

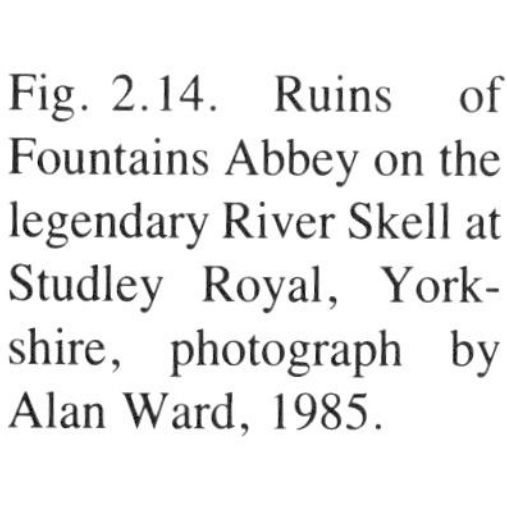

Fig. 2.14. Ruins of Fountains Abbey on the legendary River Skell at Studley Royal, Yorkshire, photograph by Alan Ward, 1985.

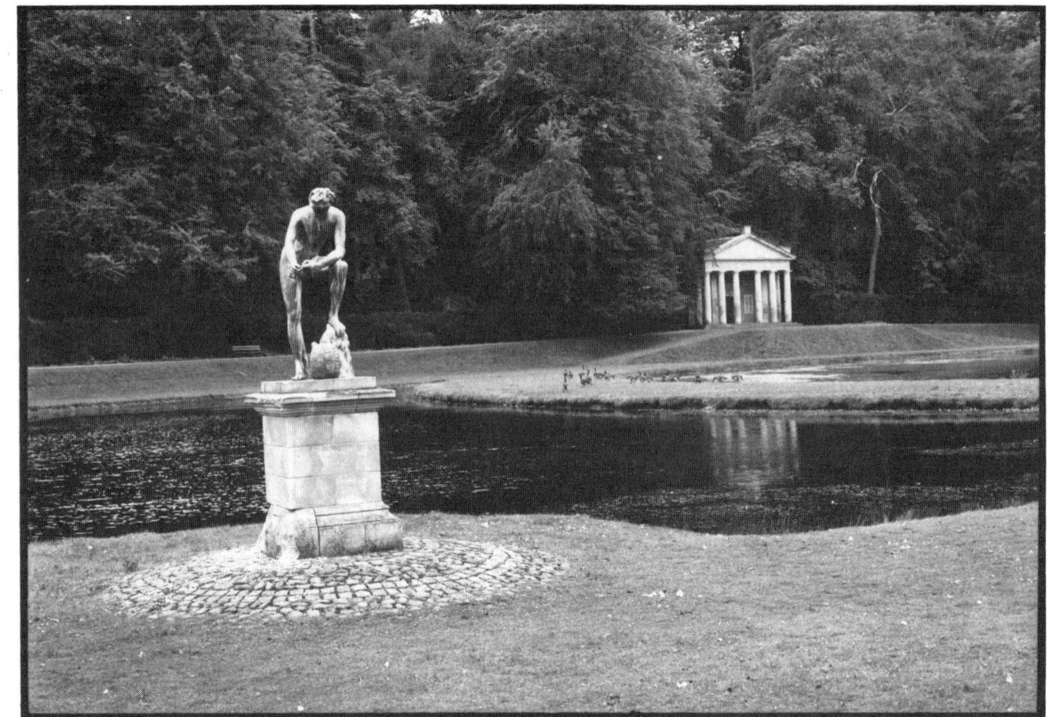

Fig. 2.15. Temple of Filial Piety erected by William Aislabie in memory of his father at Studley Royal, photograph by Alan Ward, 1985.

to have been designed by Lord Cobham himself in 1747, was rededicated in 1763 in honor of the end of the Seven Years War. The low relief on its pediment is of Britannia receiving homage. A monument of Captain Cook dates from 1778 and once included a globe of the world, later replaced by a classical sarcophagus. An obelisk to General Wolfe's death in Canada also celebrates Empire. Commemorative nationalism permeated the spirit of Stowe and other English gardens.

Capability Brown succeeded Bridgeman, Kent, and Gibbs in contributing to Stowe's landscape composition. Brown assisted with erection of a 117-foot obelisk commemorating General Wolfe in 1747. Brown's work there, as at many other English gardens, however, was more subtractive than contributive to a sense of intimate melancholy, accessible to the individual on a mediative stroll through the grounds. Brown's landscape gardens were meant to be seen from a distance, panoramically, from the windows of the house or from a commanding vantage point. Indeed, they were more landscape than garden. Brown left Stowe in 1751 after softening some of Bridgeman's formalities but before he could obliterate the human scale of Kent's symbolic landscape by imposing spaces and vistas on the grand scale characteristic of most of his work.

General James Dormer, Cobham's close friend, undoubtedly drew inspiration from the first phase of Stowe's development for his creation of a landscaped garden at Rousham in Oxfordshire between 1720 and 1725. After completing his major work at Stowe, William Kent contributed to Rousham's composition from 1738 to 1741, making an Elysium, a commemorative place, rather than simply a bucolic arcadia. Kent built temples and other neoclassical structures on a diminutive scale, dispersed through the grounds to emphasize a sense of intimacy when the visitor was close and an illusion of monumentality and exaggerated distance when viewed from another point in the garden. The grounds contain a glade dedicated to Venus with a central memorial to the owner's favorite dog, long deceased (Fig. 2.11.) Rousham's classic interpretation of the picturesque style sometimes termed Kentian has pleasure walks confined by trees, yews in a deciduous woods, and a winding, romantic river. Its mount provides panoramic views over a spreading agrarian landscape; the visitor walks through a varied terrain in order to experience a sequence of sensual extremes of sun and shade, light and shadow, metaphoric of the vicissitudes of life. Rousham is a prime example of the landscaped walking garden with programmed sequences of multi-sensory experience structured in an informal series of naturalistic scenes intended to stir emotions and associations referenced to classical and contemporary literature. Alexander Pope was a frequent visitor at Rousham and may even have contributed to its design. (Figs. 2.12, 13.)

At about the same time, John Aislabie, former chancellor of the Exchequer, laid out most of his own northern estate at Studley Royal, Yorkshire, where he went into self-imposed exile after sponsoring in 1720 an ill-fated financial venture for investing in the lucrative slave trade and subsequent assumption of England's national debt, the speculative mania of the South Sea Bubble. In the darkly wooded valley of the River Skell, with its ancient associations with Robin Hood, Aislabie spent the next two decades creating his melancholy garden incorporating many of the ingredients of topography, plantings, and architecture seen at Stowe and Rousham. After John Aislabie's death, his son William completed the garden composition by building a neoclassical temple to filial piety; in 1768, William acquired adjacent land and the monumental monastic ruins of Fountains Abbey to terminate a major vista along the river from the garden's heights. (Figs. 2.14, 15.) Medieval ruins were particularly favored garden elements, reminders of the transitoriness of life, the toll taken by time, and the nation's long history.

Other proprietors similarly undertook garden-

Fig. 2.16. Pantheon by Henry Flitcroft, 1753–54, and bridge inspired by Palladio's original at Vicenza; Stourhead, Wiltshire, photograph by Alan Ward, 1985.

Fig. 2.17. Temple of Apollo by Henry Flitcroft, 1765, based on archaeological drawings by Robert Woods, Stourhead, photograph by Alan Ward, 1985.

making as a ritualistic act of melancholy in response to a personal tragedy. At Hagley, Worcestershire, George, First Baron Lyttelton (1709–73), Secretary to the Prince of Wales, Cobham's cousin, and another of Pope's friends, composed a garden around a ruined castle to assuage his grief after the deaths of his wife in childbirth in 1747, of his friend, the poet James Thomson, the next year, and of his father in 1751. Lyttelton also commemorated Pope with an urn. The English garden remained essentially a personal, introspective place until Capability Brown's design reform in the second half of the century. Earlier gardens epitomize the idea of elysium as personal retreat. They are human-scaled, walking gardens of winding paths through sheltered, inward-turning spaces, punctuated for contrast with perspectives and panoramic views to remind the pensive that they must return to the larger world after their spiritual exercise in the controlled, naturalistic environment.

Beginning in the 1740s, visitors regularly marveled at Stowe and similar gardens. A host of poems, articles, and guidebooks invited travelers to discover the wonders of estates that were not purely private.[30] Stourhead attracted visitors from its inception and through its construction from 1744 to 1770. By the 1760s, so many travelers went to see the estate that an inn was built to accommodate them. Henry Hoare the younger (1705–85), a member of the rising financial elite, inherited his estate on the death of his widowed mother in 1741. It already had melancholy associations derived from its creation in 1717 by Hoare, Senior, on remains of a royalist, Catholic estate sacked and seized by Cromwell's Parliamentary troops during the Civil War. But for Hoare, it held more personal significance because of a series of bereavements. Two of his children died in 1735 and 1740 and his mother in 1741. Hoare's wife died in 1743, leaving him a widower, never to remarry, with three children, only one of whom survived to adulthood. Hoare directed his melancholy into the design of his garden, a task that took almost four decades and helped assuage his grief.

Hoare created a place reminiscent of Virgil's *Aeneid*, the epic of Rome's founding, but also representative of his own insistence on founding a family estate despite death's toll. Like Virgil's Elysium, the site had "cool meadows" watered by streams. Hoare built an allegorical landscape even more explicit than that at Stowe. By damming a small river, Hoare created a reflective, rambling water body that he thought of as Lake Avernus, crossed by Aeneas to reach Hades. In 1748, the architect Henry Flitcroft placed a rough-hewn rock arch over the spot called the entrance to the netherworld, marked with the Latin quote "Easy is the Descent to Avernus!" A visit to the grotto, first descending along a path into the cool, dark enclosure, and then reemerging into the light, represented death and rebirth. The grotto on the lake, designed as a solitary, contemplative place, was a standard fixture in English gardens. (Fig. 2.16.)

In 1744, Flitcroft, protégé of Lord Burlington and close associate of William Kent, built Stourhead's first garden structure, a Roman Doric Temple of Flora, containing an altar and marble busts of Marcus Aurelius and Alexander the Great, and inscribed with Sibyl's words before she led Aeneas through the underworld in search of his father, Anchises. Hoare added a Corinthian Pantheon in 1753 to shelter other statues of classical figures, including the moral hero Hercules, by Michael Rysbrack; 1765 saw completion of Flitcroft's Temple of Apollo, modeled after a round structure excavated at Baalbec and illustrated by Robert Wood in a book Hoare purchased in 1757. (Fig. 2.17.)

Allegorical themes in the garden functioned for redefinition of the national past as well as for indulgence of personal melancholy. The search of Aeneas for his father parallels the search for British history, which, indeed, some traced back to Aeneas, following the often-repeated story originating with the twelfth-century chronicler Geoffrey of Monmouth that the British race was founded by Brutus the Trojan, great-grandson of Aeneas. Other historical references appeared when Hoare erected an imposing brick tower in 1769 designed by Flitcroft and dedicated to King Alfred. Hoare also acquired in 1765 the early fifteenth-century High Cross, commemorating eight royal patrons of the city of Bristol, for his garden, a cross that residents of the city had discarded as a "ruinous and superstitious Relick." Added to this melancholy historicism are the remains of an old village, its church and churchyard, burial place of the Hoare family, all incorporated within Stourhead. Stourhead was a collage of mnemonic forms representative of a symbolic and mythological past. On visiting Stourhead in 1765, Horace Walpole judged that "the whole composes one of the most picturesque scenes in the world." Stourhead was second only to Stowe in attracting international recognition and emulation.[31]

William Shenstone's (1714–63) moralistic poetry and idyllic garden at the Leasowes in Shropshire were even more elegaic, shaped by melancholy following his mother's death in 1743. The Leasowes, built on a hilly site near Lyttelton's romantic garden at Hagley and commanding panoramic views into distant Worcestershire, was built between 1745 and 1763; there, Shenstone promulgated his ideas of "landskip or picturesque-gardening," expressed in his *Unconnected Thoughts on Gardening,* a guidebook and treatise on taste published posthumously in 1764 and illustrated with an engraving of one of the funerary urns set in the dense woods of Leasowes. A circuit walk at the Leasowes took visitors past a sequence of compositions or pictures such as a ruined, ivy-draped gothic priory and assorted urns, seats, and other memorials to literary friends, living and deceased, including James Thomson, George Lyttelton, and William Somerville. There, Shenstone placed an urn inscribed to his love, Maria Dolman, who died at age twenty-two of smallpox. The Leasowes was a personal garden of remembrance or "consecrated groves" reached by serpentine paths through darkened valleys—the ideal elements of place to inspire melancholy. Shenstone designed one small, deep valley crossed by a mossy stream and hemmed in by thickly overgrown banks as "Virgil's Grove." There, nearly hidden amid ancient oaks, he erected an obelisk as a cenotaph to the ancient philosopher.

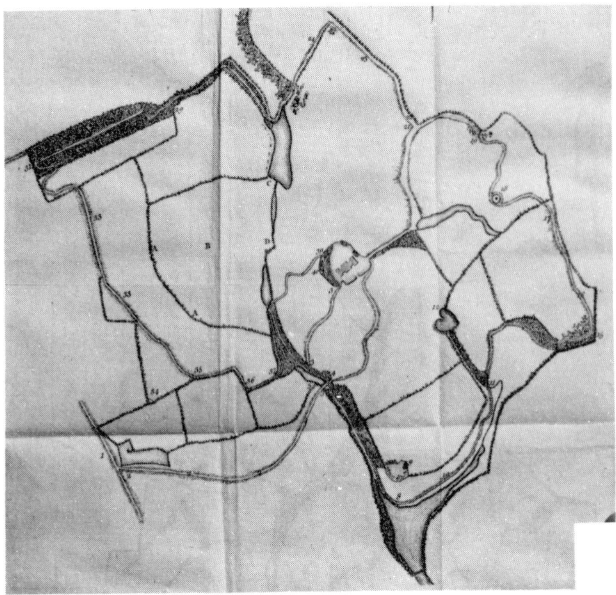

Fig. 2.18. William Shenstone's estate, The Leasowes, plan engraved by Shenstone, 1764.

He intended the place to stir visitors' sentiments, to elicit nostalgia, and to refresh spirits wearied by business and the bustle of London life. Although Shenstone advocated turning sites associated with history into gardens, he realized that if actual historical associations did not exist, a sense of the past could be created in a garden through use of commemorative monuments. (Figs. 2.18, 19.)

Fig. 2.19. Engraving from posthumous edition of Shenstone's "Elegy," 1764.

Visitors to the Leasowes and to similar gardens often left with the ambition to create similar places for themselves. Samuel Johnson and James Boswell visited the Leasowes in 1774 and recommended it to their friends. James Luckock, a Birmingham gem merchant, toured the Leasowes in 1820 and went home to make his own garden, marked by a sarcophagus inscribed "To the creative and amiable qualities of Shenstone." Indeed, the Leasowes became a place of pilgrimage for the Whiggish intelligentsia—Oliver Goldsmith, Edmund Burke, Adam Smith, and others. Parties including the Grenvilles, the Pitts, the Lytteltons, and the Reverend Richard Jago frequented the place. Robert and James Dodsley's 1761 account of the Leasowes was widely read and influenced the nascent romanticism of the likes of Sir Walter Scott. Only John Wesley criticized the dangers of such gardens, warning that they preoccupied owners and visitors to the point of pantheistic idolatry.

The popularity of naturalistic gardens among the liberal, intellectual elite conditioned and reflected the fascination of English poets and essayists for such places for spiritual renewal and philosophic inspiration. Shortly before her own death, the "bluestocking" Mrs. Elizabeth Rowe (1674–1737) wrote of the pleasure she found in solitary, "mournful" meditation on mortality in such a natural setting:

While drooping winds among the branches sigh,
And sluggish waters heavily roll by.
Here to my fatal sorrows let me give
The short remaining hours I have to live.[32]

Similarly, Thomas Warton celebrated such places in his blank verse poem "The Pleasures of Melancholy," written in 1745 and published two years later. Nature tamed by human hands produced sacred places or asylums to which one repaired, like Voltaire's Candide retreating from the vicissitudes of the world to his garden, for stoical meditations on life and fate.

Thomas Gray expressed a similar melancholy spirit in his *Elegy Written in a Country Church-Yard* (1751). Gray found a positive usefulness in the site of graves of humble, rural Englishmen. Shifting focus from the dead to the living, following the pattern observed by Philippe Ariès, Gray was concerned with how conducive a landscape was to contemplation of death; therefore, he favored old rural burial places where such ancient folk customs as planting flowers and trees on graves marked by rude markers persisted despite High Church opposition to the practice. Gray advocated cultivating a tender, sweetened response to death, a soothing state of mind to relieve the world-weary. His brand of melancholy suggests return to Arcadia's lost rhythms; many garden designers harkened to the message. Images reminiscent of the *Elegy* recurred in places like Stowe.[33]

Gray advised his friends to visit landscaped gardens as well as rural churchyards to find reminders of "transcience and decay." He particularly favored Charles Hamilton's Painshill in Surrey, developed between 1738 and 1773 with a "narrow gloomy path" that revealed picturesque scenes along a "broad, sinuous, island-studded river apparently without beginning or end." One major area focused on a Roman mausoleum.[34]

Landscaped gardens appealed to many Englishmen as appropriate new sites for burials. Stephen Switzer, the royal landscape gardener, ends his *Ichnographia Rustica* (1718) with the wish to be buried in a country garden "Cover'd with flowers, free from noise and pain." Switzer exclaimed:

> Let ever-greens the turfy tomb adorn,
> And roscid dews, the glory of the morn,
> My carpet deck; then let my soul possess
> The happier scenes of an eternal bliss.[35]

The garden would be an Eden, as before Adam's Fall, where the dead could rest in paradise, rather than in a place metaphoric of hell. The poet Paul Whitehead requested that his heart be kept in a marble urn at West Wycombe; others with poetic sensibilities began to dream of similar resting places. Melancholy monuments, especially urns and obelisks, already allegorical or commemorative fixtures in landscaped gardens, increasingly took on renewed connotations.

The demand for such monuments was so great that Batty Langley placed a notice in the *Daily Advertiser* in 1731 that he would provide sculptured "bustos of gentlemen and ladies, living or dead, at five guineas each," as well as vases, urns, columns, obelisks, temples, and other garden ornaments, many commemorative "of all the most eminent emperors, kings, generals, admirals, ministers of state, philosophers, mathematicians, architects, poets, and painters."[36] An urn erected by Copleston Warre Banpfylde at Hestercombe near Taunton honors Henry Hoare, depicting him as Virgil because of his accomplishments at Stourhead. A major feature at Hawkstone in Shropshire, the picturesque seat of Sir Rowland Hill, is a 112-foot Tuscan column topped by a statue of the family founder, the first Protestant Lord Mayor of London, holding the Magna Carta. Lyttelton's estate at Hagley has an urn dedicated to the memory of Pope and a half-octagonal building to James Thomson: "*Ingenio Immortali, Jaboi Thomson, Poetae Sublimis, Viri Boni, Aediculam hanc, in secessu quam virus dilexit, Post mortem ejus constructam, Dicat dedicatque, Georgius Lyttelton.*" These are only a few of many examples. So great was the desire for such monuments that proprietors often fashioned them of wood painted to resemble stone. (Fig. 2.20.) Such structures were the ideal sort of cenotaphs favored by Leone Battista Alberti (1401–72), whose *Ten Books of Architecture* was first published in English in 1726 and influenced many theorists of the "modern" style in gardening.

The most ambitious estate owners combined many commemorative features in their gardens. Castle Howard's park contained an obelisk to William Lord Howard erected by his son, another dedicated in 1714 to the Duke of Marlborough, and a pyramid built in 1728 to honor the female ancestor whose marriage had united a series of properties to make the founding of the estate possible. Commemorative elements accumulated in Castle Howard's landscape, displaying a sort of secular ancestor worship. Lady Ann Irwin, daughter of Charles Howard, third Earl of Carlisle (1669–1738), proprietor of the Yorkshire estate, praised her family's idealized landscape in neoclassical terms:

> Buildings the proper points of view adorn
> Of Grecian, Roman and Egyptian form
> Interspersed with woods and verdant plains
> Such as possess'd of old th' Arcadian swains.[37]

Fig. 2.20. Churchill's commemorative pillar and weeping tree, engraving from the *Gentleman's Magazine*, ca. 1800.

The focal point of Castle Howard's park was a family mausoleum designed by Nicholas Hawksmore to replace the local parish churchyard, destroyed by consolidation of the estate. Constructed in 1742, the domed classical mausoleum rivaled the proportions of the castle's central section and was the first funeral structure standing free of a church to be built in England since ancient times. The Castle Howard mausoleum inspired poetic description:

How rich the columns—and how light the dome!
A Temple worthy of immortal Rome!
O'er the Mosaic floor O lightly tread,
Beneath's the sacred mansion of the dead;
Where with his race th' illustrious founder lies.[38]

Horace Walpole thought the palatial mausoleum "would tempt one to be buried alive." Following this example, mausoleums became standard fixtures in English gardens. (Fig. 2.21.)

The rejection of traditional Anglican burials by members of the elite, for one reason or another, contributed to make the last decades of the eighteenth century "the great age of mausolea," according to art historian Nicholas Penny.[39] Dozens of mausoleums, literally and figuratively unconnected with the Church, were erected in the English countryside. Neoclassical architects produced hundreds of designs for similar structures never executed. The family mausoleum at Park Place, Oxfordshire, home of Henry Seymour Conway, close friend of Thomas Gray and Horace Walpole, took the form of a pyramid atop a square base with low relief of a sarcophagus surrounded by some of England's first Lombardy poplars. The Duke of Oldenburg built a family tomb in the form of a small Grecian temple outside of an old churchyard near his estate. The Marquis of Stafford constructed an imposing family tomb opposite his property's entrance. At West Wycombe, the mausoleum of the Dashwood family serves as an eyecatcher perched on an adjacent hill. Robert Adam designed a gothic mausoleum for a prominent hilltop in the Claremont gardens. The structure was dedicated to Princess Charlotte, who died in childbirth in 1817; stained-glass windows cast a melancholy light on the bust of the princess inside. The litany of examples of funerary structures and cenotaphs in landscaped gardens goes on and on.

Often mausoleums remained cenotaphs, used merely as garden ornaments to shelter commemorative sculpture, urns, or other monuments and to suggest death and the past. Stowe had a sixty-foot-tall pyramid by the architect Vanbrugh, which was dedicated to Cobham but demolished in the 1770s, having received no burials. The Rockingham mausoleum constructed in Wentworth Park in Yorkshire between 1785 and 1791 is a similar case. It contains busts of eight of Rockingham's Whig friends, supporters of the prime minister's political opposition to the Stamp Act and Britain's war against the American Rebellion. A long inscription by Edmund Burke states its purpose "to instruct the mind" and invokes the English to "Remember. Resemble. Preserve." This neoclassical structure inspired the Temple of Liberty at Woburn, with busts of another leading Whig, Charles Fox, and his allies, who like Burke supported the American cause but opposed the French Revolution.

Based on these examples alone, it is no wonder that the distinct ideological implications of the English garden were recognized internationally; the likes of Franklin, Adams, and Jefferson and Americans of subsequent generations discovered in such gardens justification for an anglophilia that did not conflict with their new republicanism.[40]

Architectural eclecticism associated with melancholy structures in English gardens even influenced styles of funerary monuments placed in existing churchyards and churches. An article in a 1755 issue of the *Connoisseur* criticizes neoclassical iconography. "Taste has introduced the heathen mythology into our gardens." The author predicts that use of pagan forms and allegorical figures points to trends in taste that would soon favor Egyptian hieroglyphics and Chinese forms.[41] The writer was indeed prescient.

Whiggish aesthetic theorists helped spread the taste for English gardens through writings on aesthetics and philosophy. One of the most influential was Edmund Burke (1727–97), whose *Philosophical Inquiry into the Origin of our Ideas of the Sublime and the Beautiful* (1756) crystallized ideas and design formulae developed in the picturesque gardens of his nation over preceding decades. Burke emphasizes the link between philosophy, politics, and poetics, and his theory that all emotion is sensation expands on Lockean epistemology. The sublime results from either a pastoral landscape or classical architecture giving the eye, and hence the imagination, no boundaries on which to rest. Melancholy associations are particularly important, according to Burke, who traces them to classical precedents. Sensations stirred by the sublime, "melancholy as they are," give pleasure, accord-

Fig. 2.21. Castle Howard mausoleum by Nicholas Hawksmoor, begun 1731, photograph by Alan Ward, 1985.

ing to Burke, who quotes Homer to prove his case:

> Still in the short intervals of *pleasing woe,*
> Regardful of the friendly dues I owe,
> I to the glorious dead, for ever dead,
> *Indulge* the tribute of a *grateful* tear.[42]

Like many of his contemporaries, Burke considers solitude and contemplation of mortality sublime, and he favors creation of environments to foster melancholy. Burke believes that spreading such a refined taste would be socially beneficial, counteracting the baser motives of the "rabble."

In his "Introduction to Taste" in *A Philosophical Inquiry,* Burke argues the relativity of taste to human sensations and emotions. His emphasis on the pleasure derived from sympathy with pain, or ideas of pain when pain is not actually present, relates directly to the celebration of melancholy. Burke describes the capacity of the "affecting" arts to graft "a delight on wretchedness, misery, and death itself," even to the "dark, uncertain, confused, terrible, and sublime to the last degree," the Death referred to by Milton.[43] Hence, for Burke, an aesthetically ideal landscape incorporates ideas of death, explicitly and implicitly, with elements such as actual burials, cenotaphs, mausoleums, places of solitude, winding paths leading directly from sunny lawns through areas of cool dark woods, damp grottoes reminiscent of the tomb, dark and reflective water bodies, flowing streams, material evidence of the ravages of nature such as blasted tree trunks or of deciduous plants displaying nature's inexorable cycle of symbolic seasons, and vistas of great distance, height, or depths—all considered sublime.

The taste for melancholy grew even more toward the end of the eighteenth century. Encouraged by theorists of the picturesque style, a wilder, untamed version of nature was favored by those who rejected the mid-century vogue of Capability Brown's vast, sweeping lawns. The Whig Parliamentarian Sir Uvedale Price (1747–1829) and the architect Sir William Chambers (1723–96) developed an aesthetics of the "picturesque," considered a greater catalyst for serious emotions than the more carefully tended "beautiful." (Figs. 2.22, 23.) Price described the picturesque as having "the two qualities of roughness and of sudden variation, joined to that of irregularity." Drawing on experience on his own estate at Foxley, he proclaimed the picturesque within the practical reach of any gentleman competent to undertake his own landscape "improvements"; and with such encouragement, members of the elite began to study horticulture. Chambers, in his *Dissertation on Oriental Gardening* (1772), introduced the English to another precedent in the form of Chinese gardens "especially laid out for the purpose of evoking a mood of agreeable melancholy and the sense of the transitoriness of all natural beauty and human glory."[44]

Chambers particularly favored landscapes that would display the "vicissitudes of seasons" through varied plantings. He prescribed adding plants that in autumn "afford in their decline a rich variegated colouring" representative of impending mortality. The most resplendent colors of autumn, such as those seen in New England, would be particularly desirable for the sense of melancholy that they suggest. Ideal garden structures, according to Chambers, would also "indicate decay, being intended as mementos . . . the tombs of predecessors, who lie buried around them; others are ruins of castles, palaces, temples . . . or half-buried triumphal arches and mausoleums, with mutilated inscriptions, that once commemorated the heroes of antient [*sic*] times; or they are sepulchres of their ancestors, catacombs and cemeteries of their favorite domestic animals; or whatever else may serve to indicate the debility, the disappointments, and the dissolution of humanity; which . . . fill the mind with melancholy and incline it to serious reflections." Chambers's ideal landscape, a sequence of "surprising" or "supernatural" scenes, was "calculated to excite in the mind of the spectator quick successions of opposite and violent sensations." The garden itself would take control of the visitor's thoughts and actions. "Sometimes the passenger is hurried by steep descending paths to subterraneous vaults. . . . Sometimes the traveller, after having wandered in the dusk of the forest, finds himself on the edge of precipices, in the glare of day-light . . . or at the foot of impending rocks, in gloomy valleys, overhung with woods; or on the banks of dull moving rivers, whose shores are covered with

Fig. 2.22 (*Above*) "The Picturesque," engraving by Hearne and Pouncy from Richard Payne Knight, *The Landscape,* 1794.

Fig. 2.23. (*Below*) "The Beautiful," engraving by Hearne and Pouncy from Richard Payne Knight, *The Landscape,* 1794.

sepulchral monuments, under the shade of willow, laurel, and other plants sacred to . . . the Genius of Sorrow." For Chambers, variety in landscape and artifice combined to accentuate the sense of the melancholy.[45] Chambers summarizes the elements of landscape found in many eighteenth-century English gardens, but his description of one ideal landscape would not be realized until the creation of America's first "rural" cemetery, outside of Boston at Mount Auburn in 1831.

Advocacy of such landscapes grew through the last decades of the eighteenth century. In his *Essays on the Nature and Principles of Taste* (1790), the philosopher-aesthetician the Reverend Archibald Alison (1757–1839) formulates a theory that further rationalized the form of the English garden and influenced designers on both sides of the Atlantic. Alison drew on studies in natural history and Scottish philosophical pragmatism, such as that of Francis Hutcheson, a disciple of Shaftesbury, to develop his theory of associationism, which held that beautiful things trigger a series of mental suggestions of divine power and love. Both the beautiful and the sublime sparked moral emotions and religious sentiment perceived by the individual through the "Emotion of Taste." Alison favored the form and associations of the English garden, yet he considered even these tamed landscapes sublime if tending by the hand of man was not too evident. Alison notes that "in the vegetable kingdom, the form of trees are [*sic*] sublime. . . . Nothing is more sublime than the form of rocks, which seem to be coeval with creation, and which all the convulsions of nature have not been able to destroy. The sublimest of all the mechanical arts is architecture, principally from the durableness of its productions; and these productions are in themselves sublime, in proportion to their antiquity, or the extent of their duration." Alison acknowledges that "the form of temples, although very different as forms, have [*sic*] in all ages been accounted sublime. . . . The forms of all those things . . . which are employed in the burial of the dead are strikingly sublime." And, of course, the sublime was the most potent aesthetic force in stirring salutary emotions and instilling lessons of moral philosophy. Alison systematically defines and praises the standard elements of the English garden as sublime; he considers such a landscape sacred. Americans knew Alison's theories either directly from his book, reprinted in Edinburgh in 1811 and in Boston the next year, or in condensed form from Francis Jeffrey's article on Beauty in the 1816 *Encyclopaedia Britannica Supplement*.[46]

The second and third generations of romantic gardeners and proprietors did more than carry on a taste; they proselytized. Sir William Stanhope, who bought Pope's Twickenham estate, sent numerous cuttings of the willow under which the philosopher sat as mementos to friends across England and abroad before the parent tree died in 1801. Sir Horace Walpole predicted to a friend in 1775, "Some American will . . . revive the true taste in gardening. . . . I love to skip into futurity and imagine what will be done on the grand scale of a new hemisphere."[47] So many were the advocates of landscaped garden taste by the end of the century that Walpole was bound to be right.

Sir Walter Scott applied Price's aesthetic principles to transform an old gravel pit into a bower on property he acquired at Abbotsford in 1813. He planted thousands of trees—weeping birches, poplars, firs, horse chestnuts, elms—and he confessed in correspondence "how deeply" he was bitten "with the madness of the picturesque." According to the art historian A. A. Tait, "Scott shared with [Sir Humphrey] Repton an almost evangelical enthusiasm for landscape" evident in the gardens he planned for others in the 1820s and in the crusading zeal evident in his correspondence.[48] Scott bragged of how easy it was for the ordinary gentleman to lay out and plant his own grounds. Scott's enthusiasm for landscape gardening helped spread the taste in Scotland and even to America through his writings in the *Quarterly Review* (1828) and international correspondence. The picturesque appealed particularly to the strain of melancholy retrospection in Scott's celebration of his Caledonian past, represented in ruins, monuments, and the persistence of wild Nature in the land. As an honorary member of the Massachusetts Horticultural Society, he undoubtedly influenced Bostonians like Dr. Jacob Bigelow and General Henry A. S. Dearborn as they, in turn, became some of the first arbiters of "rural" landscape taste in America in the 1830s.

Throughout his writings, Wordsworth (1770–1850) preaches the values of "musing in solitude" in a romantic setting; his "Essay on Epitaphs" (1810), in particular, plays upon rural tastes fostered by the English garden. Wordsworth proposes relegating all burials to the country. He criticizes "the unsightly manner in which our monuments are crowded together in the busy, noisy, unclean, and almost grassless church-yard of a large town." Gravestones with epitaphs along country roads, following the Roman examples, would present lessons to travelers, functioning like ruins in the English garden and eliciting beneficial emotions, according to Wordsworth. They would take the traveler's mind away from the present, sending it into the past and teaching lessons of moral philosophy. Wordsworth updates Evelyn's criticisms of urban burials: "We, in modern times, have lost much of these advantages [the hortatory functions of funerary monuments]. . . . Even were it not true that tombs lose their monitory virtue when obtruded upon the notice of men occupied with the cares of the world, and too often sullied and defiled by those cares, yet still, when death is in our thoughts, nothing can make amends for the want of the soothing influences of nature, and for the absence of those types of renovation and decay, which the fields and woods offer to the notice of the serious and contemplative mind." Wordsworth recommends as an alternative "the still seclusion of a Turkish cemetery, in some remote place; and yet further sanctified by the grove of cypress in which it is embosomed."[49] He summarizes the concerns and commemorative trends that grew through the eighteenth century and articulates a desire for burial reform that was expressed with increasing frequency in urban areas at the turn of the nineteenth century. His major objection to old burial ways was primarily aesthetic and spiritual, however, shaped by changing notions of death and nature rather than by practical concerns for urban real estate values or public health. In western civilizations, changing mentality and tastes and a growing commemorative impulse, rather than urbanization or medical theories, underlay the demand for creation of new burial places based in naturalistic aesthetics.

English landscape gardens inspired countless copies on the Continent and even in America as visitors brought home memories of their form and elements or ordered books and engravings presenting detailed views of the picturesque. Part of a larger vogue for English culture or *anglomanie,* literary descriptions and poetical formulae for landscape composition helped enlightened proprietors beyond the British Isles prepare their own grounds as contemplative places suitable for commemoration and objectification of new definitions of the past—public and private. Across the Continent, *le jardin pittoresque et sentimental, le bosquet melancholique, le jardin anglais, il giardino inglese,* or *der englische Garten* inspired philosophical and political liberals in search of new aesthetic forms capable of representing the transition from rationalism to romanticism, from the Old Order to the New. (Figs. 2.24, 25, 26, 27.) Plans for a memorial temple to King Gustav III set in a picturesque landscape appeared at Droftningholm in Sweden in 1798; a Dutch book of plans of commemorative structures in a romantic landscape was published less than a decade later. English landscaped gardens, including the use of cenotaphs, mausoleums, and other melancholy monuments, appeared in Ireland, Scotland, Italy, Germany, Hungary, and Poland. From 1773 to 1784, Prince Frederick of Norway and Denmark created a garden at Jaegerspris near Copenhagen commemorative of national heroes, ancient and modern, including a number of burials and life-sized portrait statues. Even before the end of the eighteenth century, one resident of Princeton, New Jersey, attempted to recreate Pope's Twickenham garden on his property; Samuel Vaughan laid out the grounds of Gray's Inn on the Schuylkill River near Philadelphia in the English fashion. Exiled to America after the Battle of Waterloo, Joseph Napoleon Bonaparte (1768–1844), former king of Spain and elder brother of the emperor, built a picturesque landscape at Point Breeze near Bordentown, New Jersey.[50]

The international influence of the English landscape garden persisted well into the nineteenth century because of its strong literary foundation and the formation of societies in major cities following the example of the Royal Horticultural Society, established in 1804 and chartered in 1809.

Fig. 2.24. (*Above*) Engraved view of fictional English landscaped garden from G. Van Laar (Rotterdam, 1802).

Fig. 2.25. (*Below*) Urn and weeping tree, engraving by G. Van Laar, 1802.

Fig. 2.26. (*Above, right*) Plan of picturesque avenues and paths, engraving by G. Van Laar, 1802.

Fig. 2.27. (*Right*) Engraving of funerary monuments for English gardens by G. Van Laar, 1802.

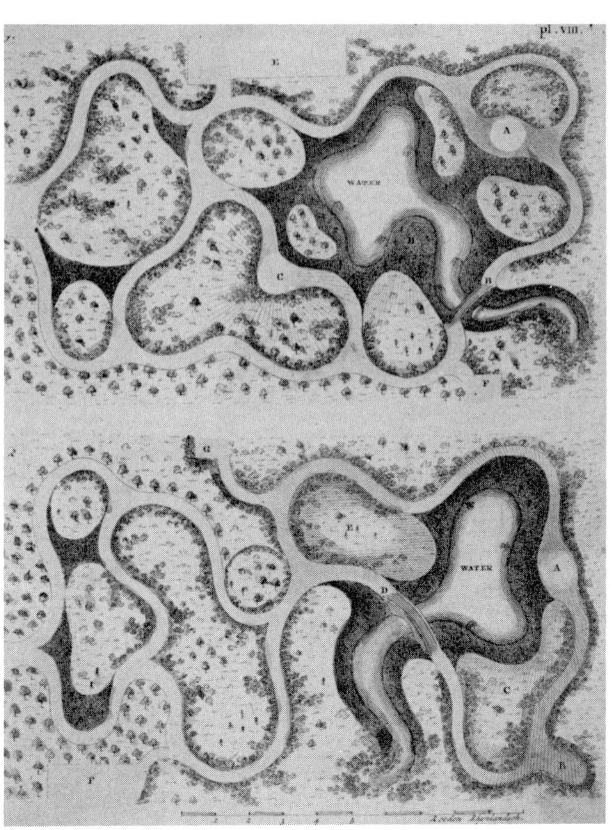

By 1824, it had almost 2,200 members, many living outside of Britain. Americans associated the English garden form with the best of their colonial heritage and even with their own independence. According to Daniel Webster in 1825, "A chief distinction of the present day is a community of opinions and knowledge amongst men in various nations. . . . The whole world is becoming a common field for intellect to act in. . . . A great chord of sentiment and feeling runs through two continents and vibrates over both. . . . There is a vast commerce of ideas."[51] Webster's observation applied particularly to development of a taste for Nature and for the spread of English garden aesthetics. (Fig. 2.28.)

The *furor hortensis* or pastoral gardening rage extended to France and the United States; however, revolutions intervened to prevent creation of as many picturesque gardens on private estates there as in England. The British socio-political system continued to permit preservation of landscape gardens on estates handed down in families intact, many to the present day, given the persistence of aristocracy and the preservationist influence of the National Trust. In France and America, however, with only a few exceptions, similar picturesque grounds were from their inception rationalized in the form of cemeteries, with space sold to families who could not or would not establish their own private burial grounds on suburban property. By the nineteenth century, the legacy of the English garden, with emphasis on *le genre sombre,* the melancholy components in the landscape, lay primarily in providing precedents for new pastoral cemeteries, the prime examples of which were founded outside Paris at Père Lachaise in 1804 and outside Boston at Mount Auburn in 1831.

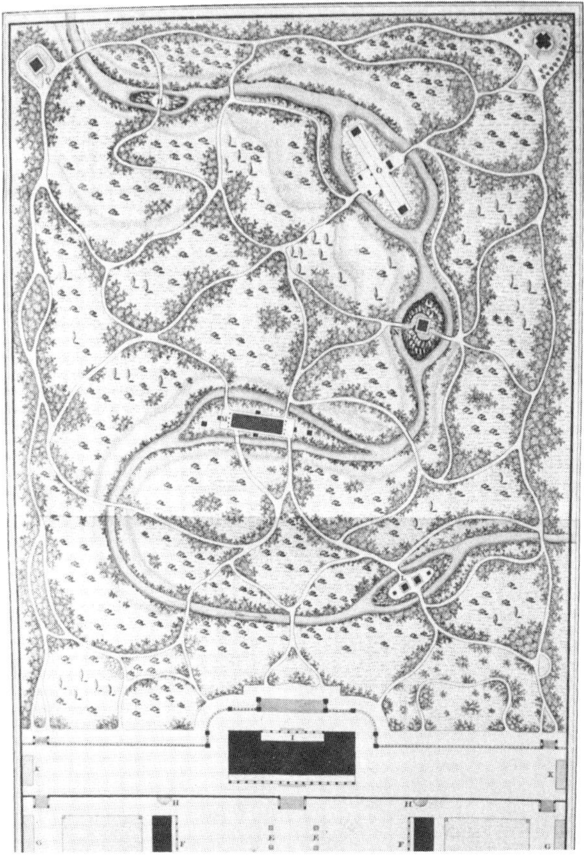

Fig. 2.28. Plan of *jardin anglo-chinois,* based on Mandarin estate forty-five leagues from Peking, designed by M. Stornberg, gardener, engraving from J. C. Krafft, 1810.

3

The French Cult of Ancestors and Père Lachaise Cemetery

And finally philosophy
Teaches you to despise the horrors of the tomb
And the terrors of the afterlife
—Voltaire, "Epître à Uranie" (1732)

Come here, all you whose meditative hearts
Love the sad joys that melancholy imparts.
Behold this tombstone where the bending birch
Like the Chinese willow, but more solemnly
With its long branches and sad falling leaves
And hanging arms weeps upon the grave. . . .
In the peaceful fields, place my humble tomb.
—Abbé Jacques Delille, *Des Jardins* (1782)

Funerary institutions are one of the first needs of civilization.
—Nicholas-Thérèse-Bénoist Frochot, Prefect of the Department of the Seine (1800)

THE ENGLISH LANDSCAPE GARDEN MOVEMENT extended to the Continent along with romantic tastes and the cult of the melancholy in the second half of the eighteenth century.* A growing body of literature—philosophy, aesthetic theory, descriptive poetry and prose—made possible the repetition and reinterpretation of trends in English pastoral melancholy as well as monument and garden design. Given the revolutionary intellectual and political climate in France, only a few private commemorative gardens were formed in the English fashion. Rather, French writers and designers gradually translated and reinterpreted the naturalistic and neoclassical elements of the *jardin anglais* to create an entirely new institution to function as ritualistic focal point for a new "cult of ancestors," to become a material manifestion of a secularized historical consciousness with both public and private dimensions. The ideas underlying this dramatically new public policy were formulated even before the Revolution as a way to bind citizens to the nation through burial reform. The Cemetery of Père Lachaise, founded outside of Paris in 1804, would be the result.

Postéromanie, or the vogue for celebrating "the virtuous fathers of families whose achievements lived on in their well-brought-up children, the cit-

*Unless otherwise indicated, translations from the French are by Linden-Ward.

izens of the future," grew among the new bourgeoisie through the eighteenth century, to the dismay of ecclesiastics and members of the old elite. Although Claude-Adrien Hélvetius (1715–71), host of *philosophes,* preferred to celebrate the present rather than a past defined in terms of patriarchs and nobles, other writers insisted upon creating a cult of posthumous memory. Abbé Remi, in his poem *Les Jours,* a corrective and rejection of Young's *Night,* asserted that death held no dominion over fathers of families who spawned progeny and endowed them with property. Such men thus "journey on through the centuries under the auspices of Nature." One problem remained—the creation of a mechanism for transmission of such memory through new landscapes, cultural practices, and monuments.[1]

The *philosophes* were first to turn to English culture in search of alternatives to the forms of the traditional order. After returning from a three-year exile in England from 1726 to 1729, Voltaire wrote that "it is not the tombs of kings that one admires, but the monuments that the recognition of the nation has erected to the greatest men who contributed to its glory; you see their statues as in Athens one saw those of Sophocles and Plato; . . . just the sight of these glorious monuments has excited more than one soul and has formed more than one great man."[2] Voltaire (1694–1788) favored the social uses of commemoration of exemplary individuals; following the examples of many of his English friends, he advocated creation of new heroes to replace saints, kings, and nobles. Neoclassicism provided Voltaire and others of like mind with a new vocabulary for commemoration, and the English style of landscape gardening offered an aesthetic alternative to royalist formalism.

Like many of his English friends, Voltaire aimed to dispel images of death institutionalized by the Church at the same time as he postulated creation of new commemorative forms. He relied heavily on classical references, particularly those to the condemnation of the fear of death in *De rerum natura* by Titus Lucretius Carus. Voltaire saw himself as a new Lucretius, teaching his contemporaries to "despise the horrors of the tomb and the terrors of another life." Voltaire liked to paraphrase the Epicurean, "This dread and darkness of mind, therefore, require not the rays of the sun . . . only knowledge of nature's form dispels them."[3] Voltaire and other readers of Lucretius saw contemporary epitomes of such ancient wisdom in funerary elements in English gardens.

In his essay "Enterrement" ("Burial"), written shortly before his death, Voltaire argued that traditional canon law bans on burial within churches had been perverted over time by "some bourgeois with the vanity to change temples into charnel houses so they could rot there in a distinguished manner."[4] He cited the better example of ancient Rome, governed by the laws of the Twelve Tablets, where few families had the privilege of burial within the city walls. How much more rational was the Roman practice, in which cadavers polluted neither sacred places nor any part of the secular city, Voltaire wondered.

Jean d'Alembert proposed creation of a large extramural cemetery in his essay in *L'Encyclopédie.* Entries in that compendium of Enlightenment knowledge, published between 1750 and 1781, blamed the Church for feeding and perpetuating fears of death and obscuring death's natural "narcotic sweetness." D'Alembert, like Montesquieu and Voltaire, agreed with Bolingbroke and other English philosophers that the idea of history could be reinterpreted and rehabilitated in secular and intellectual terms. D'Alembert postulated that history, framed as a compendium of good and great lives in the fashion of Plutarch, could have a socially beneficial moral and didactic function. Like Voltaire, d'Alembert reflected trends in the consciousness of the eighteenth-century French philosophical elite, recently described by George Armstrong Kelly as "Mortal Politics," a period in which "questions of death and immortality affected historical understanding." It was an era "focused more fixedly on the memory of deeds than on a metaphysics of the unchanging. Memory suggested perpetuating the human chronicle, and that chronicle is what we call history." Voltaire, d'Alembert and their fellow *philosophes* advocated fostering a laicized funerary cult in the name of immortality and history; their followers chose a vocabulary of style associated with English landscaped gardens and romantic poetry as well as classical sources.[5]

Fig. 3.1. Pastoral scene, engraved frontispiece from Gessner, *Oeuvres*, 1797.

Many writers of the period suggested to French literati creation of their own elegaic, pastoral landscapes. The popular tales and verse of Swiss poet Salomon Gessner won international acclaim and a wide readership with the appearance of his *Idyllen* in 1756 and its subsequent translations and sequel, although the popular poet Abbé Jacques Delille (1738–1813) felt "one must be a good heathen to relish" these pastorals. The frontispiece to the 1797 edition of Gessner's *Oeuvres* depicts a tomb in a pastoral landscape. (Fig. 3.1.) Gessner advocated burial customs not to celebrate national heroes but to perpetuate domestic sentiment, parental virtue, and affection transcending death. His poetry both reflected and increased the sentimentality associated with the rising tide of affective individualism.[6] Gessner's writing and accompanying illustrations presented rural landscapes as proper places for cultivation of salutary emotions, melancholy in particular. So, too, did publication of *Cahiers* (1776–85) by LeRouge, which included drawings of Stowe and other "*jardins anglo-chinois à la mode*."[7]

With his *Essai sur les jardins* in 1774, Claude-Henri Watelet introduced French literati to ideas from Joseph Addison, Thomas Whately, and other English garden theorists and furthered the vogue for the *paysage humanisé,* an alternative to the formality of classic French gardens. Denis Diderot translated Shaftesbury in the 1740s and assured his influence on French landscapes. A translation of Thompson's *Seasons* appeared in 1760; Delille, translator of Virgil and Milton, further popularized "the *sublime melancholy* of the English Nation" evident in picturesque landscape design and the ideas Whately expressed in his *Observations on Modern Gardening* (1770). Delille helped to shape a French cult of the melancholy and to spread an ideal of individual burials with symbolic as well as utilitarian value. In his extended poem *Les Jardins* (1782), he listed diverse trees, shrubs, and grasses to be imported from around the world to make his cemetery a horticulturist's delight. Plants of different shades and textures would form rugs of ground cover over earthen graves.[8]

The greatest voice of romanticism in pre-revolutionary France was Delille's friend Jean-Jacques Rousseau (1712–78). His view of death was shaped by a new valuation of nature, tempered by a Calvinist childhood in Geneva and subsequent conversion to Catholicism. Rousseau, like many of his philosophical contemporaries, was resigned, although pessimistically, to the belief that the natural system of birth, growth, degeneration, and death governed both the life of man and that of

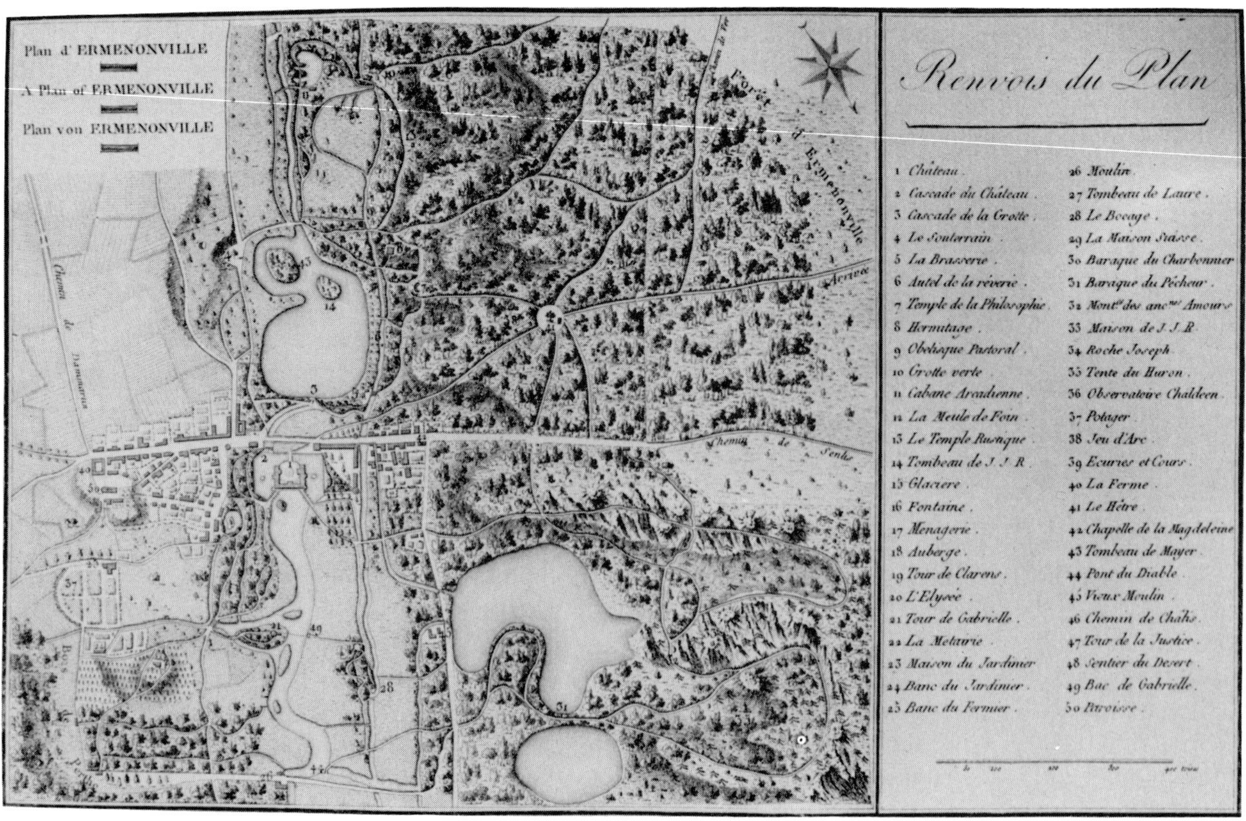

Fig. 3.2. Plan of Ermenonville gardens, engraving by Laborde, 1808.

societies and polities. Calmly contemplating his approaching death in *Les Rêveries du promeneur solitaire,* Rousseau found consolation in nature and the lonely melancholy or "savage solitude" he enjoyed in the last six weeks of his life in 1778 at Ermenonville, a landscape thirty miles or fifty kilometers northeast of Paris in the countryside of the Ile de France (Oise). The 2,100-acre (850-hectare) property, dotted with lakes and traversed by picturesque rivers, the Nonette and the Laurette, perfectly reflected Rousseau's naturalistic aesthetic, as if created by his Julie in *La Nouvelle Héloise* (1761).[9] (Fig. 3.2.)

Ermenonville's owner and designer, Réné Louis Marquis de Girardin (1735–1808), was the leading authority on the English garden style in France because of his extensive travels prior to 1766 and friendship with proprietors of English estates. The poet William Shenstone, owner-designer of internationally famous gardens at the Leasowes, and the landscape painter Jean-Marie Morel (1728–1810) gave the marquis advice on the design of his grounds. Girardin intended his "jardin paysager" to make the visitor meditate on antiquity, mortality, nature, and philosophy. Following the example of William Kent, Girardin planted dead trees in his garden to inspire melancholy and philosophy. Girardin's *De la composition des paysages sur le terrain, ou des moyens d'embellir la nature (On the Composition of Landscape on the Terrain, or Some Ways to Embellish Nature),* published in Geneva in 1777 and translated into English as *An Essay on Landscape* in 1783, adapted English garden elements to evoke melancholy worthy of a French philosopher. The landscapes intentionally reflected the secular and natural spirituality of the Age of Reason.[10]

Rousseau's death shortly after his arrival at Ermenonville and Girardin's awareness of the conventional placing of mausoleums, graves, and cenotaphs in English gardens led to the decision to bury the philosopher right there. From the start of his garden-making, Girardin intended to make a funerary monument the focal point; initially, he had considered an urn containing the ashes of two faithful lovers. Rousseau's death provided an even more romantic object. Moreover, burial of the philosopher on the spot solved a potential problem in disposition of the body. Girardin knew that Voltaire, who had died only days before, had been damned as an atheist and denied church burial by the Paris clergy. Voltaire was quietly but defiantly entombed by relatives at a small Cistercian abbey near Romilly-sur-Seine. Girardin's insistence on burying Rousseau at Ermenonville may have been premised on the knowledge that the Church would likewise deny burial to Rousseau. Therefore, on July 4, 1778, by torchlight at midnight, the time prescribed for burials of Dissenters, a small group accompanied the embalmed body of the philosopher to a tomb newly made on a picturesque island in a rambling lake.

Rousseau's grave was initially marked by a temporary, neoclassical monument topped by an urn, perhaps the one intended for the anonymous lovers; but this was quickly replaced by a marble sarcophagus designed by Hubert Robert in 1780 and bearing the inscription "Here rests the man of Nature and Truth." (Figs. 3.3, 4, 5, 6.) A bas-relief by Jacques Philippe Lesueur included allegorical female figures of maternal virtue and a scene of natural child rearing, inspired by Rousseau's *Emile,* that depicted unswaddled babies and mothers praying to the goddess Nature. Rousseau's philosophy glorified Nature even more than did the best English landscape gardeners.

Rousseau's tomb on the Isle of Poplars, called the Elysium, became part of a collage of ruins, broken columns, urns, cenotaphs, and other commemorative structures set in the bucolic landscape. The rustic, tomblike, rock dolmen was a prehistoric grotto that had served as an ossuary in the sixteenth century. The marquis dedicated a grotto to the English poet Thomson and erected a memorial to his friend Shenstone. There were busts of Lycurgus, Socrates, Homer, and Epaminondas elsewhere on the grounds. Beside a serpentine stream, Girardin placed a small, red-brick pyramid in memory of Theocritus, Virgil, and the contemporary poets Saint-Lambert and Gessner, his favorite authors. (Fig. 3.7.) A poem by Voltaire about the value of thought and love inspired the construction of the Altar of Dreams.

A Temple of Philosophy nestled amid tall Scotch pines was dedicated to Montaigne and bore a verse from Virgil declaring in Latin, "Happy is

Fig. 3.3. *(Above)* Rousseau's first tomb on the Isle of Poplars, Ermenonville, engraving by J.-M. Moreau le Jeune, 1778, from C. C. L. Hirschfeld, 1780.

Fig. 3.4. *(Above)* Rousseau's second tomb by Hubert Robert on the Isle of Poplars, Ermenonville, engraving by Donnet, 1824.

Fig. 3.5. Rousseau's second tomb by Hubert Robert with low relief of mother and children, scene inspired by Rousseau's *Emile*, engraving from Hirschfeld, 1780.

he who would know the cause of things." The structure was meant to appear as though still under construction rather than in ruins. Its columns celebrate theories of Descartes, the "enlightening" discoveries of Newton, the humanitarianism of William Penn's "Holy Experiment" in Pennsylvania, Montesquieu's defense of justice, Voltaire's use of ridicule to fight prejudice and superstition, and Rousseau's celebration of Nature. Girardin left space for future additions, intending to commemorate Benjamin Franklin, Joseph Priestley, and others. An inscription of Descartes's wisdom, "there is no void in Nature," expressed the significance of the garden itself. (Fig. 3.8.)

Eventually the marquis added two other graves to the park. In 1779, the Alsatian landscape painter Georges-Frédéric Mayer (Meier) died while a guest at Ermenonville, and he was interred on a second small island near Rousseau's tomb. An unidentified thirty-year-old "neurasthenic" committed suicide in the park in June of 1791, leaving a note signed "a victim of love." Girardin seized the romantic opportunity to bury the man on the spot, marking the grave with a stone inscribed to "an unhappy, melancholy dreamer." (Fig. 3.9.) Three years later, Girardin added a cenotaph to the painter Gandat, who died of apoplexy at Ermenonville but was buried elsewhere. Another tombstone in the garden honored an unnamed mother and child. It bore the grieving words "To my son, to my wife / I lived to love them / I survive to weep them." Girardin also told visitors that one antique urn contained the ashes of two faithful lovers, but that was probably only his melancholy fantasy. Finally, in 1810, after Girardin's own death, admirers constructed a monument to his memory on the estate.[11]

Ermenonville's didactic landscape was meant to be visited, and Girardin's brother even wrote a guidebook.[12] Benjamin Franklin, Sweden's King Gustav III, Austria's Emperor Joseph II, Louis XVI, and Marie Antoinette, as well as Delille, Mirabeau, Saint-Just, Danton, Robespierre, and

Fig. 3.6. Visitors to Rousseau's grave at Ermenonville, engraving by Rouargues frères, ca. 1800.

Fig. 3.7. (*Above*) Parc d'Ermenonville, the Philosophers' Pyramid, engraving by Constantin Bourgeois from Laborde, 1808.

Fig. 3.8. Parc d'Ermenonville, Temple of Philosophy, engraving after the drawing of S. Gobelin by Bullura, ca. 1800.

Napoleon, made pilgrimage to Ermenonville. Rousseau's tomb provided a model of taste and a secular shrine for the old elite as well as for future revolutionaries. But revolutionary vandalism forced closing of the gardens to the public in 1788, and six years later the philosopher's body was moved to the Panthéon in the heart of the heavily urbanized Left Bank of Paris, an unlikely tomb for the "Apostle of Nature." Still, the site of Rousseau's first tomb remains the focal point of the old picturesque gardens of Ermenonville.

Landscapes reflecting Rousseau's romanticism spread in France in the last quarter of the eighteenth century as the pantheistic celebration of Nature replaced old religious orthodoxy among some members of the elite. After visiting Ermenonville, Marie Antoinette determined to make a similar naturalistic retreat at Versailles beyond Le Nôtre's linear waters and geometrical parterres, although the queen's gardens were less melancholy or philosophic and more playfully fanciful, omitting the ruins and commemorative monuments conventional in English gardens. (Figs. 3.10, 11, 12.) Louis XVI, however, was not reluctant to include mock funerary monuments as focal points in the English park that he added to the gardens of Rambouillet. (Figs. 3.13, 14.) His associates followed suit. The Comte de Vaudreuil, the Comte d'Albon, and even the Comte d'Artois, the King's brother, shaped their own estates as *jardins anglais* with melancholy elements. At

Fig. 3.9. Parc D'Ermenonville, Tomb of the Stranger, engraving by Constantin Bourgeois from Laborde, 1808.

Maupertuis, Alexandre-Théodore Brongniart, student of Boullée, designed an Elysium in 1780 for Anne-Pierre marquis de Montesquiou, with a cenotaph to the Protestant martyr of the 1572 Saint Bartholomew's Day Massacre, Admiral Gaspard de Coligny. (Fig. 3.15.) Hubert Robert (1733–1808) designed and documented in paintings and engravings other monuments in naturalistic gardens built in France, thus contributing to the growing taste for them under the reign of Louis XVI.[13]

The writer and designer Louis Corrogis de Carmontelle drew the picturesque plan for the forty-six-acre Monceau Park northwest of Paris for the Duke of Chartres. (Fig. 3.16.) It contained a rustic pyramid, a Roman temple in ruins, medieval relics, and other eclectic architecture. The fantasy landscape created among thick and varied plantings focused on a *bois des tombeaux* or woods with

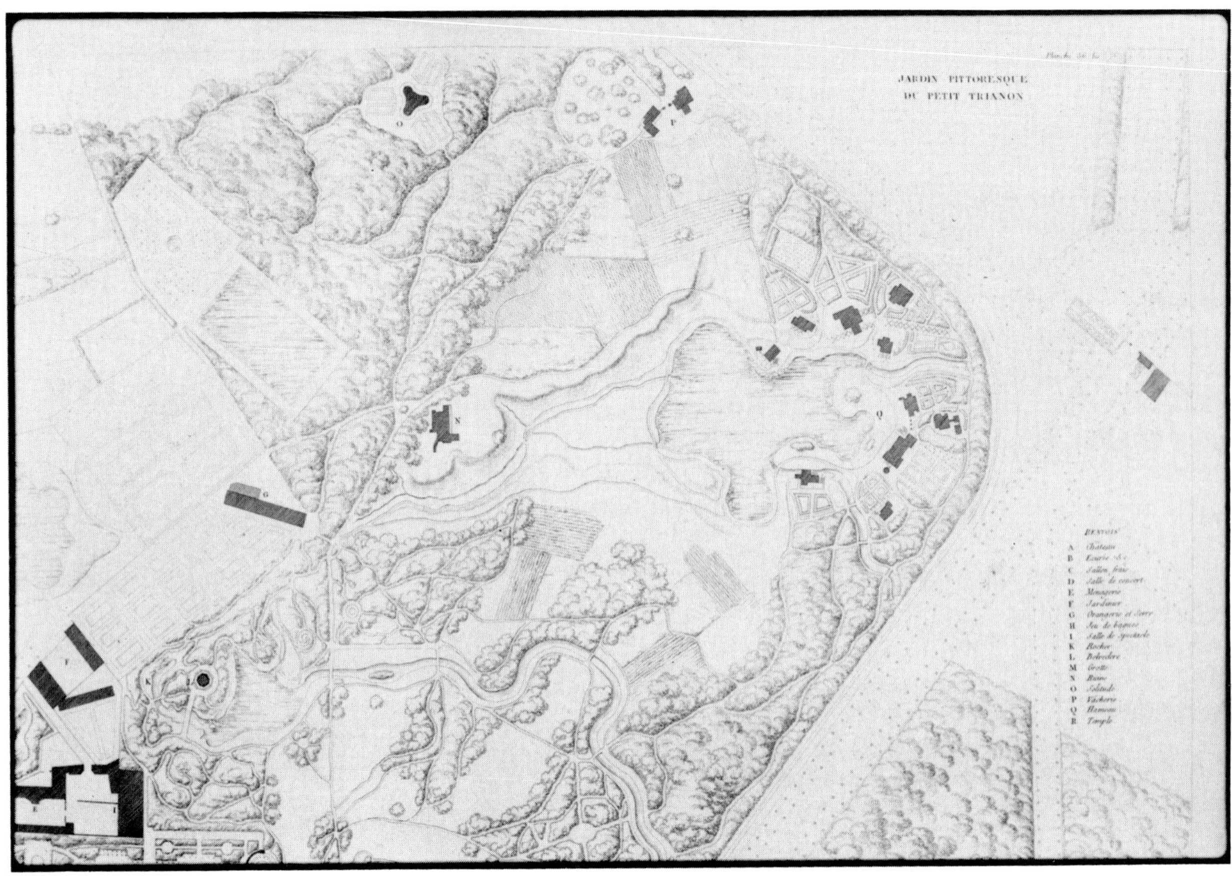

Fig. 3.10. (*Below*) Jardin pittoresque du Petit Trianon, Versailles, from LeRouge, 1776.

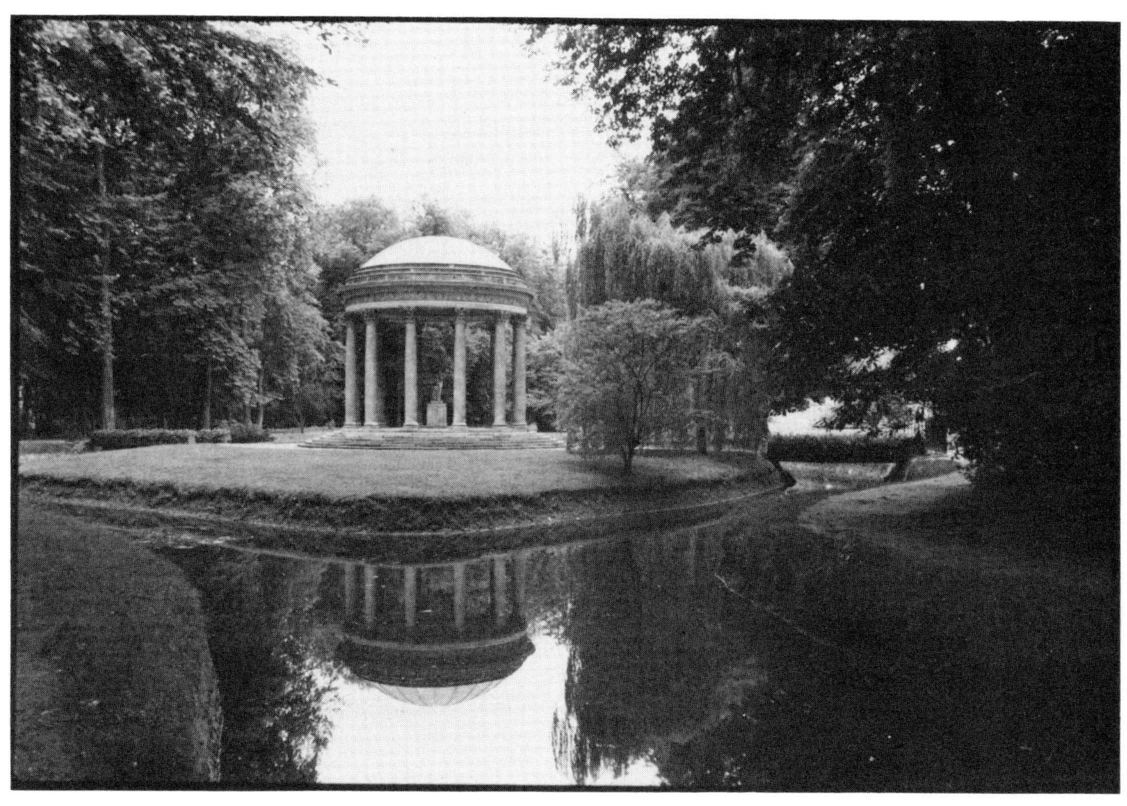

Fig. 3.11. (*Above*) Temple d'Amour in *jardin anglais,* Versailles, photograph by Alan Ward, 1985.

Fig. 3.12. (*Below*) Hermitage and grotto in *jardin anglais,* Versailles, photograph by Alan Ward, 1985.

Figs. 3.13., 3.14. Classical tombs by the architect Famin in the wooded Park of Rambouillet, engraving from Laborde, 1808.

tombs, where statues, severed columns, obelisks, and memorial stones elicited visitors' melancholy emotions. (Figs. 3.17, 18.) Monceau soon became a favored promenade for the elite. Architectural drawings of Monceau by Hubert Robert emphasized the fashionable melancholia, the taste for ruins, and the importance of funerary monuments in a picturesque garden.

The vogue for such melancholy scenes brought Robert a number of commissions for monument designs to embellish picturesque landscapes. In the 1780s, the court banker Jean-Joseph, Duc de Laborde, transformed his estate at Méréville near Etampes, seventeen leagues from Paris on the plains of Beauce, into a *jardin anglais* complete with funerary structures by Robert set in a diversified terrain traversed by a sinuous river dotted by islands. Two prominent eye-catchers were a temple commemorative of Captain Cook and a simple column in memory of the proprietor's two sons, shipwrecked near California in 1786. (Figs. 3.19, 20, 21.)

Robert contributed structures to the gardens of the château at Betz for the Princess of Monaco, focused on a "valley of tombs" approached on an avenue lined by symbolic funerary trees—cypress, sycamore, poplar, and arbor-vitae. At the center were the pulpit moved from the Saint-Innocents Cemetery in Paris and an urn-topped monument encouraging prayer and meditation. Other mnemonic structures eclectic in style included an obelisk from the Innocents; an authentic stele gravestone guarded by allegorical figures of Faith, Hope, and Charity; modern tombs by sculptor Mezières for the legendary crusader Thibaut de Nanteuil, killed in 1182, and for his wife, who died of a broken heart; ruins of an ancient castle; a Druid temple; and an obelisk proclaiming American independence. Betz was a historical museum as well as a place to enjoy the pleasures of melancholy. (Fig. 3.22.)

By the last quarter of the eighteenth century, many elite Frenchmen and women had discovered such gardens as commemorative places that could stir their emotions even better than the romantic literature coming into vogue. In addition, as in England, such gardens offered a desirable alternative to Church-controlled cemeteries, even to non-Protestants. Abbé Chaulieu, Chateaubriand,

Fig. 3.15. (*Above*) Pyramid to the memory of Admiral Coligny and Cenotaph to Rousseau in the Elysium of Maupertuis, gardens of the Marquis de Montesquiou, engraving by Constantin Bourgeois from Laborde, 1808.

Fig. 3.16. (*Below*) Parc Monceau of the Duc de Chartres, engraved plan from Carmontelle, ca. 1779.

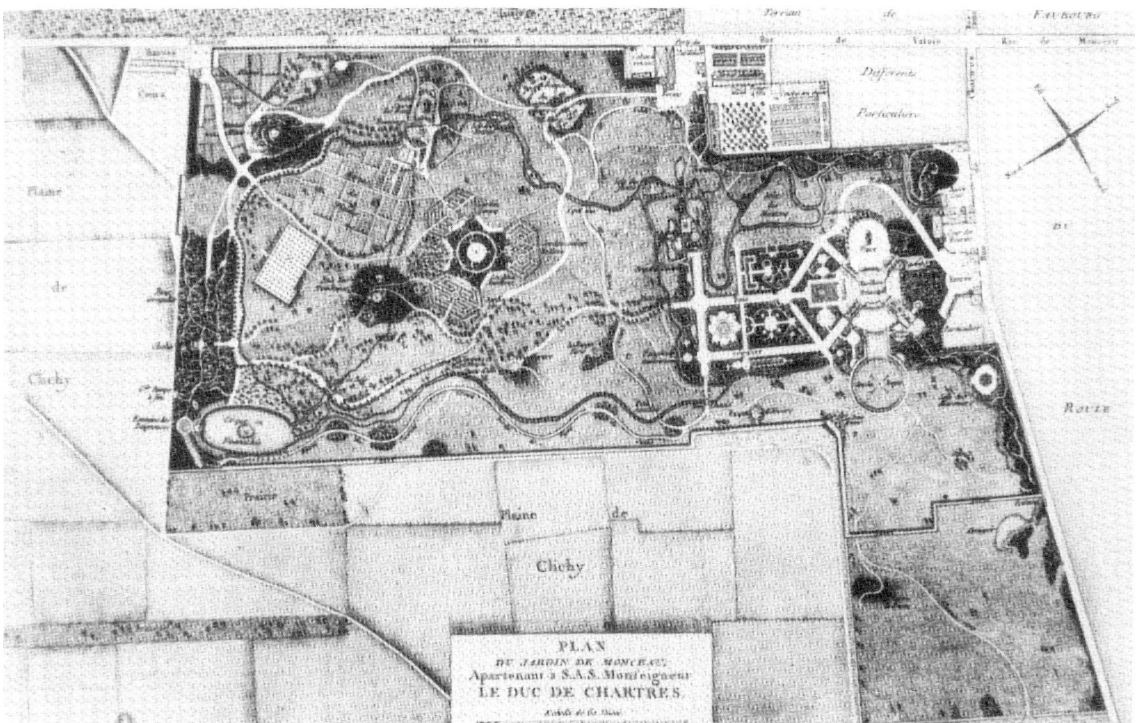

Fig. 3.17. Visitors to the Bois des Tombeaux in the Parc Monceau, engraving by Carmontelle, 1779.

Fig. 3.18. Rustic pyramid in the Bois des Tombeaux, Monceau, photograph by Alan Ward, 1985.

Madame Necker, and the Prince de Ligne described their ideal burial place in a grove under a majestic tree—now more often deciduous than evergreen. A simple tomb marked by neoclassical monuments and surrounded by an iron fence was a focal point in the wooded garden at Le Plessis-Chamant. (Fig. 3.23.) Le Péletier, president of the Parlement of Paris, placed a black marble tomb in a picturesque setting at the center of his *jardin anglais* at Morfontaine in 1770. (Fig. 3.24.) A cenotaph with bust of Carolus Linnaeus was placed in the Jardin des Plantes, the king's botanical gardens, in 1790; and the actual grave of naturalist Louis Daubenton became a focal point in those grounds in 1800. (Fig. 3.25.) Michel-Barthélemy Hazon, Brongniart's father-in-law, composed detailed plans for an idyllic funerary grove on his own Normandy estate. Hazon invited friends to choose burial places on his property near the central earthen pyramid under which he and his wife

Fig. 3.19. (*Above, left*) Sarcophagus (cenotaph) of Captain Cook, white marble with low-relief bust, surrounded by "a great number of forest trees" that "seem to reproduce the savage and remote country which contains the real tomb of that illustrious voyager." Gardens of Méréville, engraving by Constantin Bourgeois from Laborde, 1808.

Fig. 3.20. (*Above*) Rostral column in memory of the two Laborde brothers lost at sea while following the navigator La Pérouse to the Pacific. Monument of "fine turkey-blue marble rostrated with bronze," Méréville, engraving by Constantin Bourgeois from Laborde, 1808.

Fig. 3.21. (*Left*) Monument "au Genie des Arts," Méréville, engraving by Constantin Bourgeois from Laborde, 1808.

Fig. 3.22. (*Left*) Temple of Friendship by Hubert Robert in the Park at Betz, engraving by Constantin Bourgeois from Laborde, 1808.

Fig. 3.23. (*Above*) Tomb of the proprietor's wife, "distinguished by her goodness and virtues," mourned by daughters and husband, gardens of Le Plessis-Chamant, engraving by Constantin Bourgeois from Laborde, 1808.

Fig. 3.24. (*Below*) Tomb of black marble sheltered by tuyas, larch, and evergreens in the little Park of Morfontaine, engraving by Constantin Bourgeois from Laborde, 1808.

intended to lie. (Fig. 3.26.) So great was the vogue that the Comte de Laborde, despite his taste for the English style of gardening, lamented "those tombs of parade and fashion which some people take a pleasure in multiplying in gardens through a puerile affecting of sentiment and melancholy."[14]

Despite these aesthetic trends, the French did not consider pastoral funerary landscapes possible on a large scale until after scientific theories emerged to prove that plants actually cleansed the air of pollutants by "imbibing the phlogistic matter." Joseph Priestley, a British Unitarian minister encouraged in scientific studies by Franklin, read a paper in 1772 to the Royal Society of London suggesting that plants create "dephlogisticated air," which Lavoisier later renamed oxygen. By 1779, Jan Ingenhousz, a London physician, validated this theory by publishing his discovery of photosynthesis. As early as 1777, Girardin advocated that "it is without the gates that tombs and sepulchres should always be placed. It was certainly a sublime idea to deposit the ashes of great

Fig. 3.25. Grave of the horticulturist Daubenton in the Jardin des Plantes, Paris, photograph by Alan Ward, 1985.

men in some beautiful situation, as was the custom of the ancients; it recalled the memory of them in a very interesting manner, instead of that repugnance which is produced by dismal burying grounds; those masses of rottenness and corruption, which placed in the midst of cities, become infectuous to the living."[15] From the late 1770s on, French cemetery reformers felt free, because of these discoveries, to formulate ideas for burial places in rural or garden settings.

Theoretical plans for wooded cemeteries proliferated in France after the 1770s. In 1784, the famous writer and *philosophe* Jacques-Henri Bernardin de Saint-Pierre (1737–1814), one of Rousseau's only enduring friends to the end, published the most detailed description of a funerary garden or pastoral cemetery produced in his century. His plan was purely verbal, however; he drew nothing. This landscape would contain a variety of readable ideas in material form meant to elicit particular emotional and intellectual responses based on Lockean theories that all ideas are acquired directly from visual or other sensory experience. Bernardin thought rural settings in particular inculcated republican virtues and other noble sentiments. He delighted in the emotion of "gentle melancholy," considered "the most voluptuous of affections of the soul," simultaneously gratifying man's feelings of both misery and excellence.

Bernardin's cemetery would be a compendium of the nation's social and cultural history in secular terms. It would contain monuments honoring those who made major contributions to the nation—botanists, inventors, explorers, dignitaries, and women who anonymously maintained family order. Merit alone would dictate tomb location, with the "most venerable"—writers, generals, and virtuous women—buried toward the center. Bernardin suggested all sorts of monument shapes indicative of different merit—obelisks, columns, pyramids, urns, bas-reliefs, medallions, statues, pedestals, peristyles, and domes. They would not be "packed together as in a store or warehouse, but distributed with taste." Sculpture would be of var-

Fig. 3.26. (*Below*) Bosquet religieux ("religious bosk") funerary site of Michel-Barthélemy Hazon and his wife, pyramid of earth and turf topped by a tree in his park at Cantiers, Normandy, engraving, ca. 1800.

Fig. 3.27. Monument in melancholy, moonlit landscape, engraving from Hirschfeld, 1780.

Fig. 3.28. Funerary urn in forest, engraving from Hirschfeld, 1780.

ied materials, not all white marble from the same quarry. Objects would remind visitors of the physical images of the deceased during life rather than in the grave; however, the philosopher discouraged decorative bronzes and gilding, associated with baroque ostentation that would detract from the monuments' visual and psychological impact. "The more simple" the monuments are, declared Bernardin, "the more energy they communicate to the sentiment of melancholy. They produce a more powerful effect when poor rather than rich, antique rather than modern, detailed with misfortunes rather than with attributes of power."[16] Personal and private monuments, therefore, would have as much or more importance in such a place as the monuments erected to public figures.

Bernardin de Saint-Pierre called a tomb "a monument erected on the frontier between two worlds," the symbolic frontier between those of the living and the dead and, in the scheme of his cemetery plan, between those of the city and the country. His cemetery would be a "Middle Landscape," to use Leo Marx's term; most important, it would be a hierophany, as later described by Mircea Eliade, an *axis mundi* or sacred space linking the sphere of man with that of God. Modeled as a horticultural park with a wide variety of indigenous and imported trees, shrubs, and grasses, Bernardin de Saint-Pierre's ideal cemetery would have none of the symmetry and manicured lawns and shrubs of Le Nôtre's formal gardens; it would contrast dramatically with existing barren burial grounds that included no indications of Eden before Adam's Fall.[17]

Bernardin recommended locating a cemetery or Elysium on an island planted with poplars in the Seine in the suburbs of Paris. The river would serve as moat to isolate burials from the population, preserving public health and eliminating the necessity for high walls, which would mar the pastoral effect; it would also function as a transportation route for funeral barges and boats bearing visitors. Occasional views of distant vistas from the cemetery would elicit a realization of infinity and cause the visitor to muse on the distance between past and present, the vicissitudes of human affairs, man's fleeting existence, his relative smallness, and, above all, his immortality. Bernardin expanded on English garden theories by describing design principles applied specifically to a rural cemetery; his essay entitled "On the Pleasure of Tombs" was widely read even in nineteenth-century America.[18]

Of similar influence was Christian Cayus L. Hirschfeld's *Theorie der Gartenkunst,* published in Leipzig in five volumes from 1779 to 1785 and immediately translated into French.[19] Hirschfeld praised Stowe and urged addition of real tombs and family burials to similar gardens in place of simple cenotaphs. Hirschfeld's quarto volumes contained copperplate engravings of commemorative monuments in picturesque settings, and he gave a descriptive model for a cemetery where a variety of trees purified the air and intensified a sense of melancholy by the varied hues of their foliage. (Figs. 3.27, 28, 29, 30.) Many German, French, and American landscape gardeners used Hirschfeld as major text well into the nineteenth century.

French plans for wooded cemeteries proliferated in the last decades of the century. The architect François-Joseph Bélanger sketched a funerary scene highly reminiscent of Rousseau's tomb, and Jean Lecointe proposed a cemetery with a minimum of architecture other than monuments, mausoleums, and a ceremonial entrance gate. Lecointe wanted a heavily planted landscape that would blend into the countryside and not reduce arable land near the city. As advocated by John Evelyn, fruit trees and aromatic plants, some producing materia medica, would maximize the usefulness of the land. These theories developed independent of the growing criticism of the conditions of burials that remained under Church control. Many would-be funerary reformers simply wanted to eliminate burials from the city or to free them from ecclesiastical auspices and failed to present substantial proposals for new landscapes of death.

Fig. 3.29. Grotto with willow tree and urn, Méréville, engraving from Hirschfeld, 1780.

Fig. 3.30. Contemplation of ruins with severed column, engraving from Hirschfeld, 1780.

The revolutionary policy to desecrate or de-Christianize all cemeteries, not only the tombs of the privileged, fueled discussion of creation of new deathways as well as new forms of commemoration of notables. The iconoclasm of the French Revolution far surpassed that of the English Civil War, creating a "problem of the past," which some arbiters of culture eventually considered solvable through erection of monuments marking and defining the start of a new national history and by creation of innovative commemorative places incorporating secularized and romantic notions of death and nature to celebrate the lives of new sorts of heroes. Joseph Fouché, Jacobin deputy to the Convention and close associate of Robespierre, ordered a statue of Sleep to replace the central cross in the Lyons cemetery; he placed the motto "Death is Eternal Sleep" at entrances to all burial grounds in the Department of Nièvre. Also symbolically, Fouché ordered the planting of shade trees. Fouché wanted cemeteries to represent the new reign of secular reason. Inspired by the example of Ermenonville, he rejected use of cypresses or other dark evergreens, funerary plantings associated with sadness, and favored poplars. Everything would be calculated to inspire "sweet, agreeable, and touching ideas, like the virtue that made men respectable," Fouché decreed. The funerary landscape he proposed would convey patriotic pride and even a sort of pleasure in survivors for having had a virtuous friend or relative "worthy of his equals and of the Republic." Nothing would remind visitors of hell or purgatory, "invented to make priests indispensable" through their efforts to "eternalize sadness." Fouché determined to banish the bare bones, death's-heads, and other medieval iconography. His cemetery would objectify "the sweet repose that the dead enjoy"; in it he implemented Robespierre's declaration that death is "the beginning of immortality."[20]

On 28 vendémiaire, year II (October 19, 1793), Pierre-Gaspard Chaumette, radical anti-Girondin Procureur-Syndic of the Paris Commune, ordered that funerary honors be the same for all classes. Chaumette wanted cemeteries to reflect the classical concept of Elysian Fields, with odoriferous, deciduous trees planted instead of traditional cypresses. Graves surrounded with flowers would permit the average citizen to "breathe the soul of his father in the rose." This secularized ideal of death, adapted from Fouché, represented an official rejection of old forms of fear and mourning and a desire to develop a commemorative consciousness; the same ideal was also expressed on the banners Jacobins bore at the head of their funerary processions—"The just man never dies; he lives in the memory of his fellow citizens." Following Fouché's example Chaumette ordered the Commission of Public Works to remove from cemeteries crosses and any other forms that radical revolutionaries considered somber and repelling, the traditional iconography of death.[21]

The next day, the Commune of Arts and Commissioner Jean-Baptiste Avril's Administration of Public Works petitioned the National Convention to move cemeteries of all major cities "to the four corners of their circumference" and to establish Temples of Liberty and Humanity, surrounded by "humble and respectable tombs of heroes, friends of the fatherland, on which one will read touching inscriptions" while strolling "under the lugubrious shadow" of black cypresses. Avril proposed surrounding his cemeteries with low hedges and a large, grass-lined ditch, a soft border or "ha-ha" characteristic of the English garden, rather than the foreboding walls of old cemeteries. A lawn would cover the entire site, in contrast to the arid expanse of dirt seen in parish burial grounds. Only a few notables would merit perpetual burials in this proposal, which perpetuated the old pattern of burial near a sacred place. The egalitarian and anticlerical Chaumette opposed Avril's plan for that reason. The Convention responded by ordering four new cemeteries on "simple, rustic, isolated" sites outside of Paris, but it left implementation of the decree to the Commune.[22] Before any new extramural sites could be created, however, the mass executions of the Reign of Terror forced the city to open new cemeteries inside Paris. One open pit a few blocks north of the guillotine received the headless bodies of Louis XVI and Marie-Antoinette. (Fig. 3.31.) Chaumette himself joined many *sans-culottes* in a common grave. The bodies of Danton, Robespierre, and their partisans were placed in the Monceau Park, but no burial reform resulted from the social chaos of the period.

Moderate theorists feared the potentially destructive influence of the devaluation of life and the centrality of death under the Terror on public morale and on basic civilized behavior. They advocated creation of a "cult of tombs," not just functional burial reform, to educate posterity in duties to a Supreme Being and society. Memory of the goals and lives of the nation's forebears would accomplish this. Delille stressed the necessity of the funerary in any new "*cultes domestiques.*" In his 1794 poem "L'Imagination," Delille urged government sanctions of ceremonies and places permitting ordinary families to honor their dead. François-Valentin Mulot (1749–1804) agreed: "Thus a society of families, of which the large part of human society is formed, will extend the limits of life into the hereafter and will perpetuate the stay of the dead. Delicious ideas! How consoling you are!"[23] Having descended to the brink of chaos, having experienced anarchy and demagoguery, the French recoiled from iconoclasm and tried to reassemble pieces of a shattered culture.

Revolutionaries eventually became reformers, and they realized that a change in public sensibilities could not be decreed or legislated but would have to be instilled as a new vogue. Mulot observed, "No, the law cannot oblige me to employ what faculties I have to honor those who were dear to me. In the closed garden, in the open field where I will have placed my father's, wife's, or son's body, if there remains to me the means to obtain the help of able artist, I must have constructed on their bodies a monument which retraces their virtues for me."[24] It was time to reaffirm certain rights of property, even if it meant permitting privileges of wealth and class. Theorists began to consider institutionalization of postmortem property in the privatized grave and agreed that "proper" burial should reflect both a citizen's spiritual and material worth.

Fig. 3.31. Cimetière de la Madeleine, site of the common pit used for victims of the guillotine during the Terror, engraving, ca. 1810, showing new plantings.

According to Pierre Doliver, a cult of ancestors would "resurrect public morale, almost extinguished in all hearts, or rather give it a new existence, better conceived and worthy." The professor of history continued, "What is more powerful than funeral religion? The honors rendered to mortal remains are a homage addressed to the party that survives and the cult of tombs is a tie between the living and the dead. The development of a cult of the dead would be one of the most powerful ties to attach men to the Nation, the most effective way to instill duty, to praise great virtues and talents, and the last duty of the country to its citizens."[25]

Public prosecutor Nicher-Cérisy noted that Egyptian legislators found nothing contributed more to social stability than solemn, public burial of the dead. Herodotus said such customs assured religious observance and payment of debts. Nicher-Cérisy declared that "it is among funeral monuments that man comes to study his heart and tie the knots that attach him to the fatherland and humanity. . . . It is among tombs that he appreciates the past and foresees life to come."[26] If the graves of average Frenchmen were considered sacred, how much more so would be those of political and cultural leaders? Planning creation of rites and burial places based on the classical traditions of Greece and Rome and a heritage traced to the Gauls, the French made certain to honor national heroes. They created a repository for notables on the Left Bank in Paris in the former church of Sainte Geneviève, renamed the Panthéon, and reinterred Rousseau there in 1794, arousing controversy from those who favored the original pastoral site of Ermenonville as more appropriate. In considering creation of new cemeteries, however, most theorists postulated commemorative natural landscapes in the English fashion rather than grand architectural structures at the center of the urban fabric.

Classes at the Lycée des Arts studied the topic of burial reform in 1796 following a call by the National Institute of Sciences and Arts for papers on the creation of cults. On 15 messidor, year IV (1796), the National Institute held a public meeting on the social uses of celebrating deaths; in 1798, it obliged all its members to attend the funerals of their confreres. Under official mandate from Minister of the Interior P.-C.-L. Baudin, the Institute offered a prize for the best essay on funeral ceremonies and new sepulchral sites. Baudin declared that "the first principles of morals, of medicine, and of social science demand prompt reform of the state of inhumations."[27] Forty essays by architects, writers, teachers, government workers, and ordinary citizens were judged on 14 vendémiaire, year IX (1801). Some entries included detailed plans and instructions for new, rigid systems, whereas others were more general conceptual essays. Two men, Duval and Mulot, shared the prize.

Amaury Duval, antiquarian scholar and former ambassador to Naples, thought that all cemeteries should be outside city limits following the example of the ancients, for tombs near dwellings inspired public fear and disgust. Only national heroes deserved urban burials. A reading of Bernardin informed Duval's own observations of Italian burial places, especially his praise for the ancient Roman cemetery, the "Champs-Elysées," on the "smiling hill" overlooking the river near the old city of Messina. High poplars and ruined tombs garlanded with vines created a picturesque atmosphere inviting melancholy meditation. Yet Duval wanted to avoid the elite ostentation of old Roman tombs, and he decried the Egyptian funerary style designed for king and aristocracy at the people's expense. He warned that "moderns will fall into the same excesses as the ancients," that "the rich and distinguished will always be buried magnificently" while the bourgeois will continue to ruin himself financially "to be interred with almost equal pomp." He considered that without government regulations "the poor and the proletariat will again be thrown into the gutter." To eliminate class jealousies stirred by "theatricals" in public cemeteries, Duval advocated laws to forbid tombs of stone, symbols of rank and "foolish ambition." Members of all religions would lie side by side in this "asylum of peace," helping to diminish factionalism detrimental to national unity. He would permit only graves of earth and grass in small, private cemeteries on stretches of lawn where families could install plantings and small stones over their dead. Duval favored epitaphs, especially expressing domestic sentiments; he advocated listing the faults as well as the virtues of the deceased, however, to educate youth to "profit from [their] errors." He frowned on displaying titles and accomplishments.[28]

Duval wanted his own grave, like Rousseau's, to be under poplars by a small stream. It would be an idyllic spot, near his hometown, planted with lilacs and violets, and attracting his frequent visits in life to picnic and meditate on mortality. He wrote, "There several times each year, I will conduct my friends. . . . I will tell them, soon one of us will be cold and insensible under this earth. Since we can remain together for so little time, let's put hatred and enmity away. Only death can separate us. . . . And we will renew this vow always to remain united." Duval considered such sentiments the basis of social stability; law took over only in its absence. Each body would rest in its own grave, marked by a modest monument erected by family or friends, for a generously prescribed time—about three years—to assure decomposition with addition of quicklime before removal of bones to an ossuary. In this way the poor would develop closer ties to the nation and the cemetery would be "almost property for those who have none." Duval felt that "If the world was populated with loving and sensible souls, there would be no need to order respect for the dead."[29] On the other hand, sensibilities would have to be cultivated rather than legislated. Such was the major concern of members of the National Institute.

Duval recommended two sorts of burial places. He preferred burial on private property after Roman custom as the most personal form to foster sentiments and strengthen individual ties to family and the state. For those without private property, Duval proposed public cemeteries in infertile fields at opposite ends of the city. The social role of citizens would not end at death, since bodies buried would help "to fertilize the soil so that trees and vegetables to nourish their posterity will use their substance." Duval countered charges that any cemeteries located near cities wasted good land: "a graveyard planted with trees and covered with grass will not be lost to the living." Useful plants would provide produce as payment to gardeners and other workers, making the space self-supporting. Pure air, free of "pestilential miasmas," would be maintained by avoiding concentration and size in cemetery design. Duval proposed surrounding his "field of death" with ditches and "a hedge of sad evergreens," following the fashion of the English garden.[30]

Abbé Mulot's essay closely resembled Duval's. Mulot agreed that burials should be left to private initiative for families with land outside of the city. For yeoman farmers, such sepulchers would become personal sanctuaries. Mulot observed, "How happy is he who, in the garden he saw his father plant, can deposit the precious remains of that dear parent, who can go to the simple mound that covers him to render respectful and flattering homage of the heart that makes him live again, to recall the lessons of childhood and to receive new ones." For those without land, the government would establish "places of rest," where "simple but noble" family tombs would be the rule even for the poor and laboring classes, "where all have the right to be received without distinctions." There would be no "terrible" anonymous mass graves "Where a friend will seek in vain his friend! Where the son will not be able to find his father! Where the thankful nation will not be able to distinguish the remains of its benefactor when the law finally permits it to render him honors and to pay him the tribute of its gratitude!" Mulot hoped to prevent return of the days when birth or benevolence of kings allowed certain individuals to raise themselves to a superior rank with magnificent tombs, "marble imposters"; yet he hoped that more modest monuments would still encourage patronage of art.[31]

Whereas Duval proposed a lawn cemetery with occasional, optional plantings, Mulot described a heavily wooded terrain, where rugs of ferns covered graves and the picturesque landscape elicited melancholy. Dark cypresses, lilacs, and roses would be "living emblems," making the "place of sadness" naturally consoling. The grounds would be planted with indigenous trees guaranteed to thrive in the soil nourished by human remains, hastening sanitary decomposition and setting a melancholy mood. Although air in this natural environment would remain unpolluted, Mulot stipulated that it be located at least a half-kilometer from the city.[32]

Other essays to the National Institute presented variations on the cemetery proposals of Duval and Mulot. (Figs. 3.32, 33.) Pommereul, Prefect of Indre-et-Loire, envisioned making several fields of rest, of two hectares each and located at least one kilometer from the city. Locating them on elevated terrain would clear the air of pollutants and hasten decomposition of corpses. Owners of family burial space would be responsible for construction and upkeep of their graves, decorating them according to their means and taste and enclosing the property with a fence or grille. There, only individuals bearing the family surname, however, could be buried. If no heir survived, the plot would revert to ownership of the Commune, although existing graves would remain inviolate in perpetuity. Only the poor would be buried at public expense in small mass graves (with a maximum of a hundred bodies each) in the "silent shade of the woods." The central square in Pommereul's plan would be a place of national apotheosis, the "field of honor," where individuals distinguished for private virtue and designated by the state would be buried at public expense. At the very center would be a white marble statue of the Genie of Life extinguishing the flame of his torch. Plantings, mainly dwarf cypress, would be maintained by horticulturists from the botanical gardens, the Jardin des Plantes.[33]

With only one exception, all essayists in the National Institute contest suggested burial in a garden setting. Everyone seemed to agree with Athanase-Charles Détournelle that future ordering of cemeteries would correct excesses of both the social inequalities of the *ancien régime* and the revolutionary leveling of citizens' status. Détournelle proposed twelve cemeteries around the periphery of Paris. Although an architect, he frowned on creation of mausoleums or other formal burial structures, declaring, "only the state of nature should surround the simple, rustic places destined to become the asylum of tombs." He concluded, "the most solitary and most silent place charms sorrow and is most fitting for sad reflection."[34]

Détournelle and Jacques-Michel Coupé both speculated that cemeteries would become useful places—socially, psychologically, and in a practical sense. In Détournelle's plan, fruit trees would assure continued productivity of the land, and eventually earthen pyramids over the graves would be covered with grains and hay. Similarly, Coupé proposed six Parisian cemeteries to serve as models of decency and grandeur, as well as to produce fruit and wine. Coupé envisioned other French and foreign cities emulating such a plan.[35]

Essayist Joseph Girard summarized the desire of many of his contemporaries to create a "religion of memory" based more on personal ties than on creation of national heroes. Family graves on private property would bind citizens "to the soil that gave them birth." Girard declared, "He who cherishes his father's land is more attached to his country by that simple bond than the proud philosopher." Property and melancholy were "the elements of which true love of country is composed." The landscape would contain all of the elements of the

SÉPULTURES

PUBLIQUES ET PARTICULIÈRES.

La Piété naturelle commande le respect pour les Morts; un Gouvernement sage le garantit.

PAR AUTORISATION DU MINISTRE DE L'INTÉRIEUR.

AN IX.

DES FUNÉRAILLES.

Par le C DÉTOURNELLE, architecte.

Mémoire qui a concouru pour le prix de l'Institut, en vendémiaire an 9.

Non toti morimur; vivit post funera virtus.

PARIS,

A la Librairie, rue des Prêtres-Saint-Germain-l'Auxerrois, n°. 44, vis-à-vis l'église.

AN IX

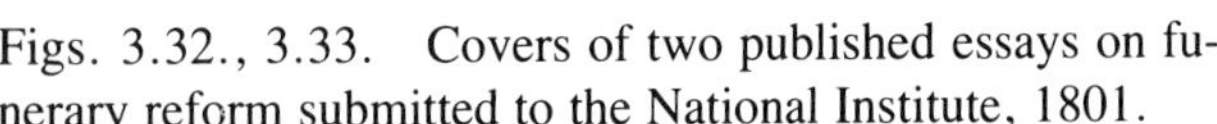

Figs. 3.32., 3.33. Covers of two published essays on funerary reform submitted to the National Institute, 1801.

Elysium or *jardin anglais*—hills, streams, and paths for melancholy promenades. Burial would be under an oak's shade in one's own field or under symbolic aspens, cypresses, or weeping willows.[36]

A similar argument was presented to the Council of Five Hundred on 9 fructidor, year V (1797) by J.-B. Leclerc, representative from Maine-et-Loire. Leclerc advocated civil institutions like marriage, public education, national holidays, and funeral practices to ensure stability and social order. He declared, "Respect for elders, memory of relatives and friends, veneration commended by the memory of those who were notable by actions dear to the fatherland are too useful sentiments for public morale, for religious principles, to be abandoned exclusively at random by the legislator." Through cults, the French could establish "a chain of sociability in which factions join in the hands of the government and keep the unity on which reposes the survival and internal peace of the State." Leclerc warned, "Break that unity, show the citizens that they only have transitory, earthly ties between each other, continually put before their eyes the image of eternal separation, and you considerably contribute to the natural tendency of sects to segregate themselves one from the other. . . . Instead of one big family, you will have numerous jealousies one against another." Summarizing many of the essays received by the National Institute, Leclerc counseled fellow legislators to foster new burial practices to promote political as well as social stability. In his "Report on Institutions Related to the Civil State of Citizens," delivered 16 brumaire, year VI (1798), he proposed to the Corps Législatif that public cemetery plots be allotted to families for that reason.[37]

Shortly thereafter, in 1799, Administrator Jacques Cambry recommended that the Department of the Seine construct the circular, pastoral funerary landscape designed by Jacques Molinos, architect and inspector of civil buildings. Cambry proposed use of a relatively flat site in the old Montmartre quarries north of the city; the Molinos design permitted sinking of elaborate private crypts on the site and construction of common, catacomb-like ossuaries. On the surface, however, the cemetery would have picturesque plantings of various trees and be crisscrossed by serpentine paths. A monumental, pyramidal temple, symbolic of the sacred mount or tomb and containing a crematory and columbarium, would occupy the center of the cemetery. Molinos rationalized that the rich would use their monuments for artistic patronage, serving an additional cultural function. (Fig. 3.34.) Cambry's long essay on funerary reform accompanied the design and echoed many of the ideas expressed in the National Institute contest.[38] Molinos and Cambry were not simply public-spirited reformers, however, but

Fig. 3.34. *Champs de repos,* design for picturesque, circular cemetery by Jacques Molinos, 1799.

Fig. 3.35. View of Alexander Lenoir's Museum of French Monuments, engraving by Sir John Carr, 1803.

members of a commercial company intent on developing and managing with a thirty-year monopoly a new municipal cemetery equipped with a crematory. The French, however, unlike the English and some Americans, would not turn funerary reform over to entrepreneurs.

Proposals for creation of a "cult of ancestors" through the design of pastoral cemeteries also responded to a contemporaneous debate over preservation and reinterpretation of a historical consciousness through artifacts of the past. Abbé Henri Grégoire, Bishop of Blois and deputy to the convention from Loir-et-Cher, issued in 1794 one of the most forceful pleas to undo some of the damage of the "vandalism" of antidespotic patriots during the Terror. Grégoire proposed a museum to assemble, preserve, and display artifacts as well as archival records from all periods of French history, even those distasteful to revolutionaries, in order to foster nationalism and moral improvement of the citizenry in a didactic way.[39]

Antoine-Chrysostome Quatremère de Quincy delivered another report in 1800 with an impassioned plea for restoration of old monuments in any new cemetery project. The architectural theoretician criticized the perversion of aesthetics by iconoclasm: "Sophisticated ignorants, stop finding pleasure in ruins! Yes, those made by time are respectable, those of barbarism are horrors. Ruins of time, monuments to human fragility, are a lesson to man, the other are a shame." The report advised, "tombs without sculpture and graves without epitaphs say nothing." Without patriotic shrines, France would "present a terrible example to Europe after peace." Establishment of grand cemeteries for the capital would be one part of the government's attempts to revive commerce and the arts, to secure confidence of citizens and family heads in the nation, and to win respect of the rest of the world.[40]

Fortunately, a wealth of France's past cultural glory had escaped the campaigns of spoliation to be preserved and displayed as the Museum of French Antiquities and Monuments, a "veritable cemetery of the arts," incorporated under the auspices of the Louvre in 1796. It was the creation of the painter and architect Alexandre Lenoir, who began in 1791 by supervising a warehouse of architectural ruins placed in the Château d'Anet, formerly a Petits-Augustins convent. (Fig. 3.35.) Lenoir saved many large tombs and ecclesiastical relics from the Church of Saint-Denis and elsewhere. He reassembled miscellaneous fragments to make monuments to Turenne, Molière, Descartes, Boileau, La Fontaine, Abélard and Héloïse, and others. Lenoir displayed them as cenotaphs, like *fabriques* or ornaments in the small picturesque garden he laid out around the Museum as an Elysium. (Figs. 3.36, 37.) Some visitors to the Museum praised its creation of "cult of heroes," and others, like the young Jules Michelet, found in its chronological arrangement of artifacts from successive historical eras the epitome of "the true order of the ages." It was precisely this revolutionary interpretion of history that attracted powerful foes for the Museum, especially Quatremère de Quincy, and led to its eventual closing in 1817. By then, however, a better site had

Fig. 3.36. Lenoir's Elysium gardens at the Museum of French Monuments, engraving by Hubert Robert, ca. 1800.

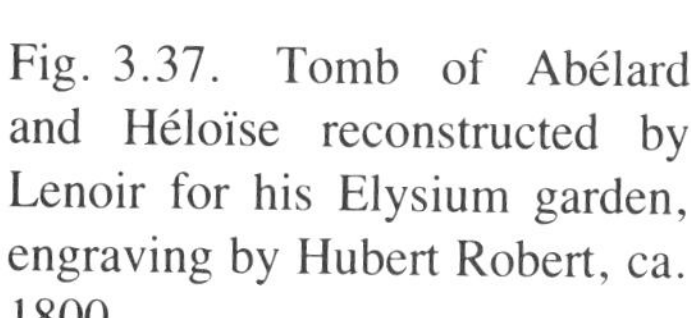

Fig. 3.37. Tomb of Abélard and Héloïse reconstructed by Lenoir for his Elysium garden, engraving by Hubert Robert, ca. 1800.

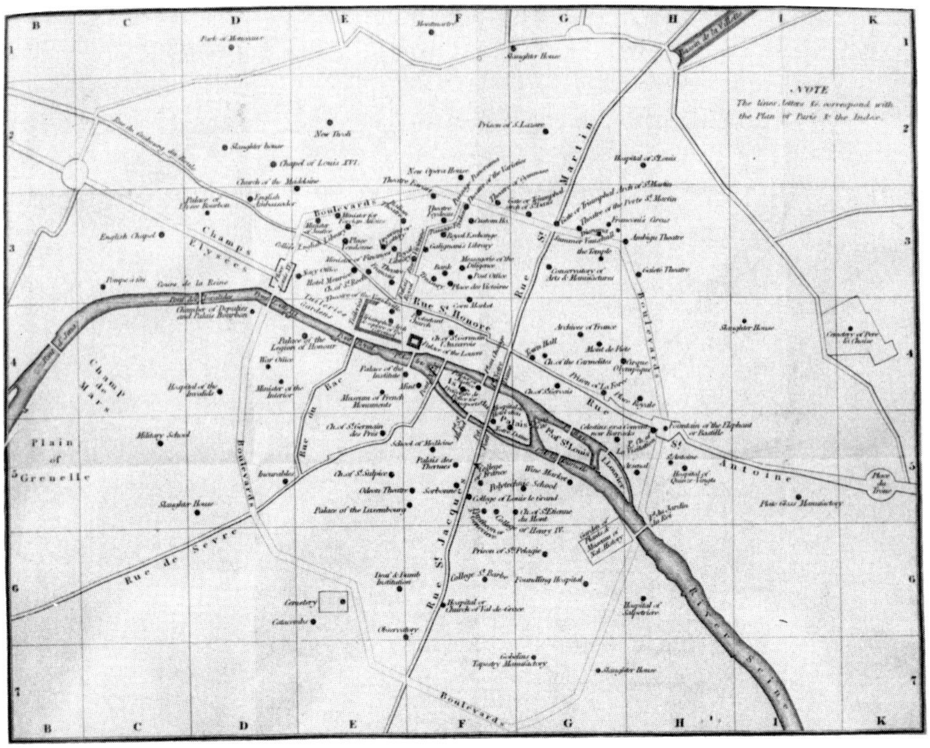

Fig. 3.38. Guide to the Principal Objects of Curiosity in Paris, map showing location of Père Lachaise Cemetery and other urban institutions and asylums, from Edward Planta, *A New Picture of Paris; or, the Stranger's Guide to the French Metropolis* (London, 1819).

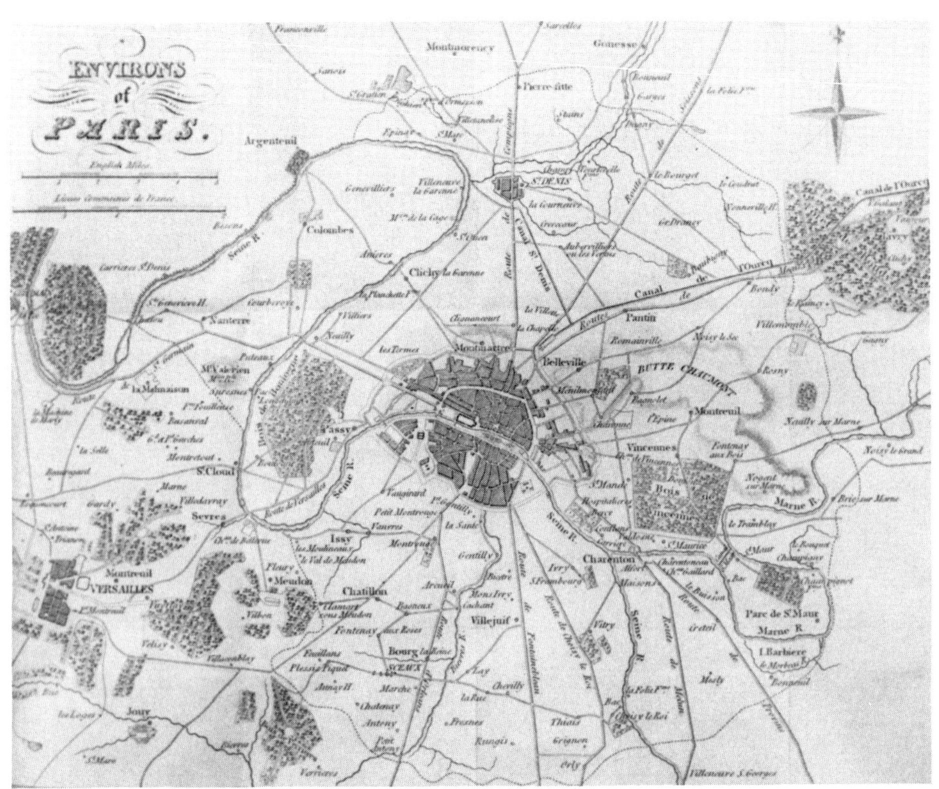

Fig. 3.39. Map of Paris showing Père Lachaise and other areas of green open space in the urban region, from Planta, 1819.

been invented for display of the new monuments to an older past.[41]

On 7 germinal, year IX (1801), the legislature set up procedural mechanisms by which communes might purchase land outside their legal boundaries for public cemeteries. On 21 ventôse (March 12), the Paris Prefect of Police ordered establishment of three cemeteries one mile beyond city walls; that winter the legislature allocated public monies for the purpose. The Department of the Seine, headed by Prefect and Minister of General Police Nicholas-Thérèse-Benoist Frochot, created the office of health commissioner (Conseil d'Hygiène) in 1802 to oversee sanitary inspection of cemeteries; on 17 floréal, year XI (1803), Frochot won authorization to purchase land for cemeteries for the commune.[42]

Frochot unsuccessfully tried to acquire the Monceau Park for one cemetery. He finally purchased another tract of land east of Paris on the slopes and ridge of a twenty-seven-meter hill, an escarpment called the Butte Saint-Chaumont. (Figs. 3.38, 39.) It had been a Jesuit country seat called La Folie-Regnault until Louis XIV authorized his confessor, Père François d'Aix de la Chaize [*sic*], to rename it Mont Louis. The property commanded views over Belleville, Montmartre, and Ménilmontant to the north with vistas to Bicêtre and Meudon on the southern horizon and to the fertile banks of the Marne in the east. Visitors preferred the panorama of Paris to the southwest. Although near the rapidly growing city, the site remained rural in character; Mont Louis was still bordered by arable land, although its gardens had fallen into disrepair. No site of such compact size presented more picturesque and varied views or had more interesting topography. The soil was ideal for burials, with a thick, sandy layer covering a deep, chalky mass, perfectly constituted to aid rapid decomposition of bodies without allowing escape of gaseous exhalations to pollute the city's air. Besides, the location assured that prevailing winds would carry any effluvia away from Paris. The old estate conformed to Napoleon's decree on 23 prairial, year XI (June 12, 1804), that each municipality establish a nondenominational cemetery of at least thirty-five to forty square meters on the most elevated site possible, preferably exposed to the north; acquisition of the land permitted the closing of several old urban burial grounds, including the Clamart.[43] (Fig. 3.40.)

Frochot appointed the prominent neo-antique

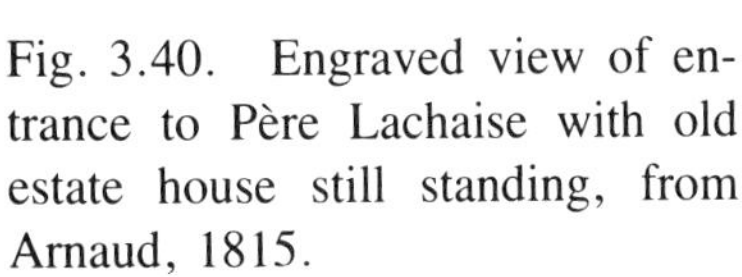

Fig. 3.40. Engraved view of entrance to Père Lachaise with old estate house still standing, from Arnaud, 1815.

architect of the Department of the Seine, Brongniart, to design this cemetery. Brongniart had experience designing French estates as *jardins anglais,* although he said he modeled his design of the Cemetery of the East on the Ceramicus, the site just beyond the Dipylon gates of Athens where the Greeks buried their heroes. Frochot participated actively in the design process, urging the architect to plan a funeral chapel as a focal point to elicit a spiritual yet secular melancholy. Literally and fig-

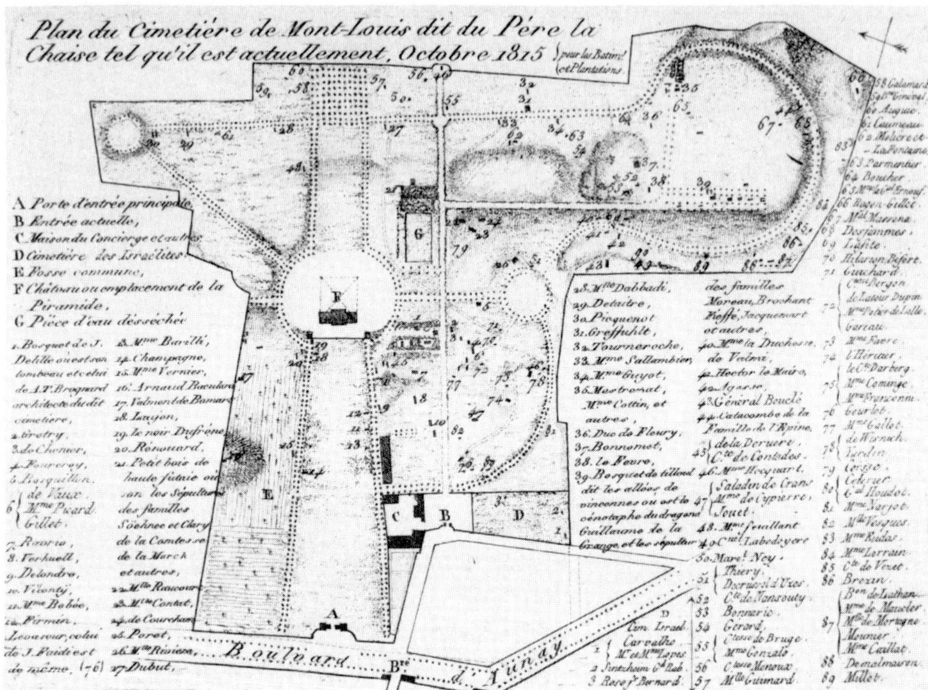

Fig. 3.41. Plan du Cimetière de Mont-Louis dit du Père Lachaise, Arnaud, 1815.

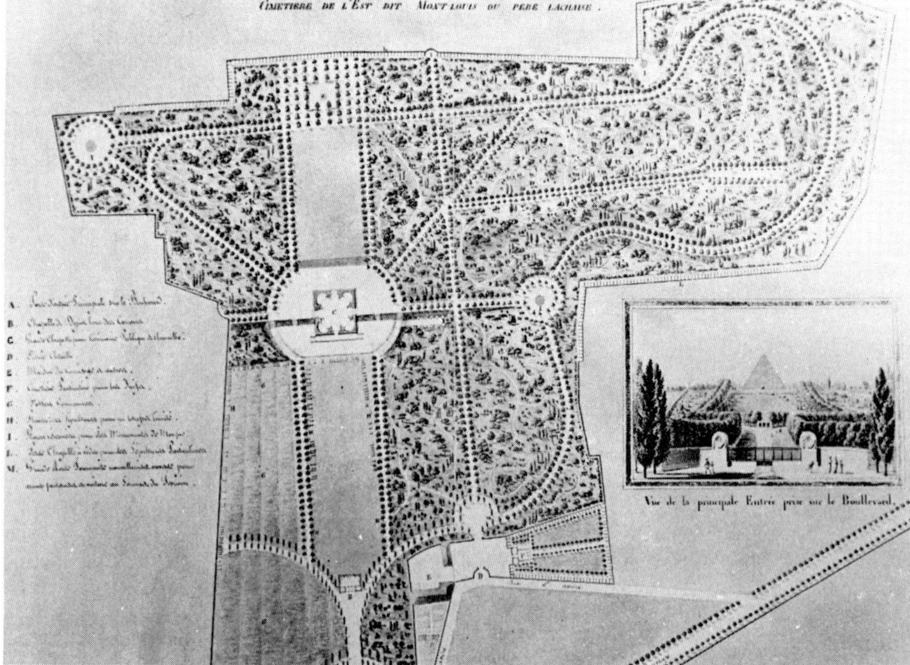

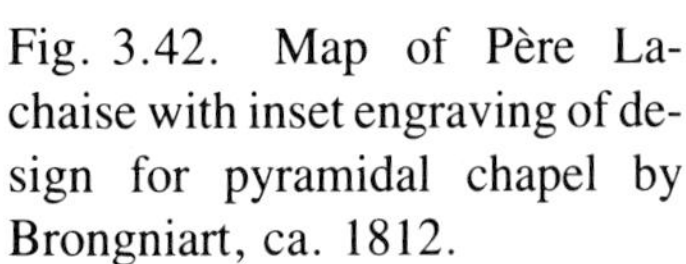

Fig. 3.42. Map of Père Lachaise with inset engraving of design for pyramidal chapel by Brongniart, ca. 1812.

uratively central to Brongniart's landscape design was a two-hundred-foot-high pyramidal chapel to be visible from the entire city below. (Figs. 3.41, 42.) It would recall in modified scale the monumental funerary structures of Brongniart's teacher, Boullée, but Brongniart's design emphasized landscape rather than heroic architecture. The chapel would be like the eye-catchers or *fabriques* of English gardens. Napoleon heartily approved of the Egyptian chapel but had to postpone construction due to the wars that raged through the next decade.

Brongniart's plans for the cemetery entrance were relatively modest. At first, he wanted to build a gate composed of heaps of false ruins scattered as if by chance on half-destroyed pillars, but friends criticized the design as too poetical. Perhaps some of the Emperor's advisers also considered it negatively prescient. So Brongniart drew a simpler, more austere plan for the gate that stood through the cemetery's first two decades. The grilled entry was set into a high, pillared wall adorned with wreathes and flaming torches and defining a semicircular exterior space.

Inside Mont Louis, Brongniart laid out winding footpaths separate from straight and sinuous carriage avenues through the irregular terrain. He preserved some of the gardens of the old estate, and the central axis lined the slope under the estate house with old chestnut trees. Poplar-lined roads and acacia-shaded paths followed the curve of the hill to the summit, where another straight road stretched behind the house to the east, defined by more ancient chestnuts. This combination of picturesque footpaths with a formal, central axis and linear avenues had precedents in the English "forest or rural garden" and the design for the Manor at Paxton published in Stephen Switzer's *Ichnographia Rustica* in 1718, an early description of the "modern" style of landscape gardening. Brongniart's design for the Cemetery of the East similarly placed major monuments at terminal points of varied views defined along avenues. He augmented the vestiges of the old garden's plants, neglected for half a century, by adding fruit trees, plane trees, lindens, sycamores, and symbolic cypresses and weeping willows. The cemetery remained pastoral and picturesque for at least a decade after its consecration on the first day of spring, premier prairial, 1804, although the site lacked the conventional romantic, symbolic streams or ponds of English gardens, Ermenonville, or naturalistic cemeteries designed in the next few decades.

Most of the burials remained five- and ten-year leaseholds on flat ground just to the left of the central alley. A temporary marker was allowed on each single burial until its disinterment. Gone were the traditional mass graves. This area of "public graves" for the masses, however, lacked the scenic seclusion of lots purchased in perpetuity on more varied, elevated terrain. (Fig. 3.43.) Brongniart's plan slowly took shape, and the enthusiasm of the monied classes was not quick in coming. Yet until 1824, innovative perpetual freehold concessions, the best category of burial, costing 250 francs for two meters of land, existed exclusively at the Cemetery of the East or Père Lachaise, as the people affectionately called the place in reference to the former, Jesuit owner. For the first ten years, most monuments were temporary stone markers or wooden crosses in the section of common graves. (Fig. 3.44.) Observers have speculated that the slow acceptance of Père Lachaise for perpetual burials resulted from the post-revolutionary disruption of social values; however, the common people immediately loved the cemetery as a drastic improvement over the old system of common pits anonymously containing thousands of bodies. One French engineer lauded the cemetery in 1821 as evidence of a new, happy era produced by simple, affectionate sentiments combined with the "desire for immortality" and reacting against the "horror of nothingness."[44] Still, the bourgeoisie, many of whom could still bury their dead on private estates, required several decades to acquire the means and taste to participate in the new cult of tombs and to make Père Lachaise the most fashionable cemetery for the capital.

Officials attempted to hasten the popularity of the Cemetery of the East among the new middle class in 1817 by moving from the Museum of French Monuments the so-called tomb of Abélard and Héloïse newly constructed of twelfth-century Gothic fragments by Lenoir. (Fig. 3.45.) Under other modern cenotaphs fashioned in ancient style, they pretended to reinter the remains of La Fontaine and Molière, although the greater writers'

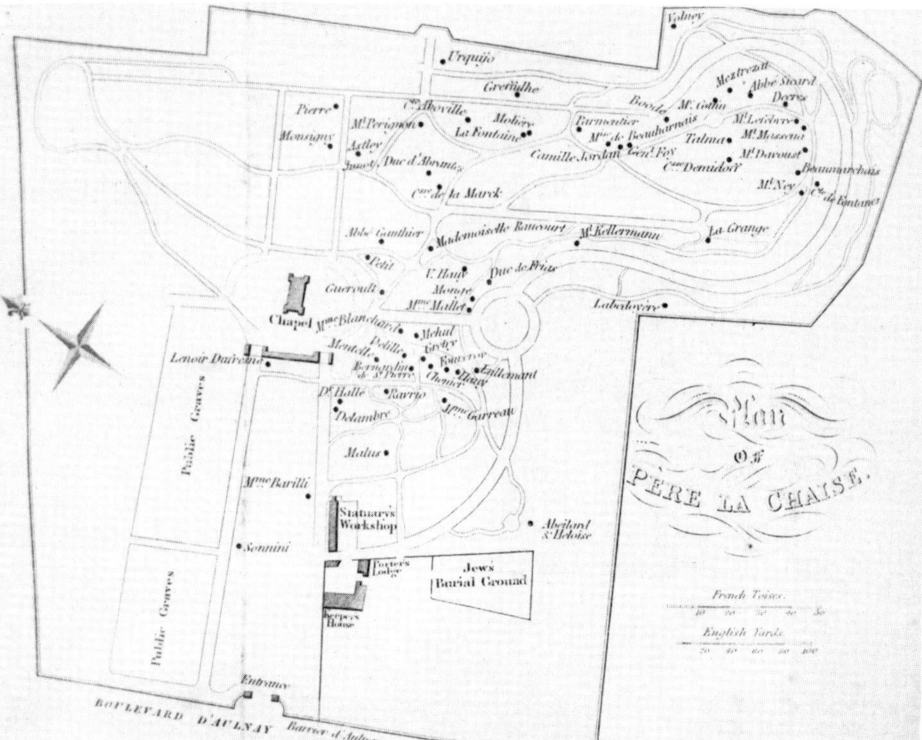

Fig. 3.43. Map of Père Lachaise, engraving by Samuel Leigh showing locations of notable burials, from Planta, 1819.

Fig. 3.44. "View of the Cemetery of Père Lachaise Taken from the Entrance," by Courvoisier, ca. 1817.

bodies had long since been lost in common graves. (Fig. 3.46.) Soon, however, new notables joined the old to increase the prestige of the place. Chopin and Géricault lay near Napoleon's heroic marshalls. The deaths of popular figures—the poet Delille, Marshall Ney, and General Foy—fostered a patriotic melancholy; their elaborate funerals set the fashion for national obsequies attended by thousands of all classes. (Figs. 3.47, 48, 49, 50.) These events served a dual purpose, creating a national "cult of heroes" and popularizing the new cemetery.[45]

The author of an 1820 guide to Père Lachaise, Marchant de Beaumont, felt this sort of publicity alone would be insufficient to make the new, secularized burial landscape acceptable to the Catholic French without a general change in public sensibilities concerning death. The cemetery was slow

Fig. 3.45. Monument of Abélard and Héloïse moved to Père Lachaise, engraving by Frederick Nash, 1822.

to find favor, he explained, because "public opinion, which submits everything to its laws, had not yet attributed a number of essential virtues in families: respect for the ashes and memories of their kin." Furthermore, the necessary shift in mentality responded first to larger political and economic fortunes of the nation. During the heyday of the Empire, "people drunk with glory and victory proud ignored sad subjects, anything that would remind them of the fragility of happiness." Marchant de Beaumont observed that "the dead are soon forgotten during days of prosperity."[46]

Indeed, only seventy-two permanent monuments were erected in the cemetery's first four years. But as the Napoleonic wars progressed and France suffered defeat, death became again a more vivid reality. As an index of the shift in attitudes toward commemoration during this period, the speed with which private monuments were added annually to Père Lachaise escalated from 51 in 1808, to 113 in 1812, 242 in 1813, 509 in 1814, and 635 in 1815, the year of Waterloo. The government encouraged personal memorials by providing those who could afford them the services of a marble sculptor on the cemetery's premises; the concierge sold wrought-iron fences "for the protection" of monuments and plants on private plots. By the 1820s, a new local funerary industry had grown in the neighborhood of the cemetery, with

Fig. 3.46. Monuments to La Fontaine and Molière moved to Père Lachaise, engraving by Frederick Nash, 1822.

Fig. 3.47. Tomb of the poet Delille, engraving by Jolimont, 1821.

twenty marble cutters, an ironworker making decorative fences, florists, and architects catering to proprietors of perpetual plots. Drawings of grand monuments by Brongniart and other architects indicate promotion of an even more ambitious architectural scale than actually characterized Père Lachaise after a quarter-century. (Figs. 3.51–58.)

In a manner representative of French taste, the appearance of the cemetery changed dramatically, rapidly, and eventually for the worst. Delille once admitted, "we enclosed where it is not necessary, we crowd our buildings upon one another, and fritter every thing into small parts." By 1830, over 31,000 monuments were in place, and the original look of the picturesque was nearly obliterated. Prosperous Parisians rejected the simplicity of earthen graves for elaborate funerary structures built to occupy the entire space of family plots; the layout of lots allowed no interim spaces or margins to be preserved as green borders or open space. The taste for the English garden had been merely a passing vogue in France, quickly superceded by the grandiose Second Empire style. Mausoleums fronted directly on the avenues and paths and nearly touched one another, resembling buildings on the city streets. After only fifteen years, an Englishman observed, "many of the best and costliest monuments are fallen to pieces, having like so many other things in that country been made for display and not for duration." So many vandals and thieves preyed on the stones that large guard dogs patrolled the grounds to prevent removal of bronze and gilt copper.[47]

Other circumstances intervened to prevent realization of major features of Brongniart's original design. Both the architect and the administrator, Brongniart and Frochot, died in 1813. Brongniart was buried in his relatively modest family lot near the tomb he designed for his friend, the poet Delille, the "French Virgil," who had preceded him with a grand public funeral to the site by only a

Fig. 3.48. Monument to General Maximilien-Sébastien Foy, whose funeral in 1825 drew over 100,000 persons, engraving by Augustus Pugin, 1829.

Fig. 3.49. (*Above*) Monument to Maréchal Massena by M. Vincent, architect, and M. Jacques, sculptor, erected in 1817, engraving by Frederick Nash, 1822.

Fig. 3.50. (*Below*) Monuments to Massena, Lefevre, and other military heroes, engraving by Augustus Pugin, 1829.

Fig. 3.51. Grave of Cottin, engraving by Jolimont, 1821.

Fig. 3.52. Grave of Demoiselle Contat, engraving by Jolimont, 1821.

Fig. 3.53. Monument to Craufurt, engraving by Jolimont, 1821.

Fig. 3.54. Monument to the Comtesse Demidoff, engraving by Jolimont, 1821.

Fig. 3.55. Monument to Alexandre Tremaire, 1813, engraving by Arnaud, 1817.

Fig. 3.56. Monument to Jean Louis Lefevre, 1812, engraving by Arnaud, 1817.

Fig. 3.57. Monument to Pierre Bernard Nardot and his daughter, engraving by Arnaud, 1817.

Fig. 3.58. Monument to Damme Marie Anne de Cetto, 1811, engraving by Arnaud, 1817.

Fig. 3.59. Brongniart family lot. Monument to the architect is at the right in the front row. Photograph by Alan Ward, 1985.

month. (Fig. 3.59.) By the end of the war, Napoleon was in exile and the plan for a central pyramid was abandoned. The old estate house, demolished in 1822, made way for a simple, classical, Doric granite chapel designed by Etienne-Hippolyte Goddé and completed in 1824. (Fig. 3.60.) The following year, Goddé built a new gate for the cemetery, overturning Brongniart's plan.

By 1814 the vogue for Père Lachaise as public open space caught on, and it began to function as an urban park. Balzac loved to walk there and used it as the setting for a particularly dramatic moment in his novel *Le Père Goriot* (1819). One English visitor exclaimed, "Burial grounds *à la pittoresque,* laid out for a promenade. . . . This invention is indeed original in the people of Paris." Failing to anticipate movements to found similar cemeteries outside of the British capital in the 1830s, he declared that "it would hardly happen in London that we should have a Guide to the burying-grounds, as a fashionable promenade; that parties would be made to visit them . . . that taverns and drinking-houses should be established close beside them for the accommodation not only of these parties of pleasure but for mourners also!"

Fig. 3.60. Design for Doric chapel by Etienne-Hippolyte Goddé, engraving by Jolimont, 1821.

Fig. 3.61. Funeral at Père Lachaise with panorama of Paris, engraving by Rouargues frères, ca. 1825.

Augustus Charles Pugin, ignoring the design origins of the place in the *jardin anglais,* asked, "What Englishman will undertake either to condemn or entirely approve it, unless he could enter completely into the minds of the French themselves?" Indeed, at that time, no other city in a western nation managed burial reform and the spatial handling of death in quite the same aesthetically innovative manner. Numerous guidebooks spread the popularity of the cemetery among non-Parisians, many of whom returned home with the idea of creating such a place for their cities.[48] (Figs. 3.61, 62.)

Marchant de Beaumont, one of the most poetic of the publicists of Père Lachaise, told visitors from abroad that they could find scenes "shaded by the leaves of eternally green trees," tombs "surrounded with flowers and decorated with wreathes that seem to make reign in this abode a continual spring." There, "the charms of nature enjoy the power to banish grief, sadness, and melancholy from the soul, where one breathes pure air, where under a magnificent sky the soul soars to its most sublime thoughts, where one feels at home in an Elysium conversing freely with the new residents of the celestial regions."[49] Such a place had international appeal, especially at a time of budding romanticism.

By 1830, a dozen Americans were buried in Père Lachaise, and articles in various American periodicals spread the fame of the place. The *Atlantic Souvenir,* published in Philadelphia in 1826, lauded the French cemetery's "appearance of a wide and variegated garden. . . . where trees and shrubs conceal and disclose wild romantic beauty, tombs and temples."[50] The French had institutionalized the cult of the melancholy, and Americans admired this first attempt at both creating a public place objectifying the sentimental pastoralism of romantic literature and solving urban burial problems.

The French had made a major advance in landscape design, adapting a garden style formerly associated with essentially private environments for use in a public funerary institution meant as much for the living as for the dead. Marchant de Beaumont recognized the importance of the arrangement of space, which literally conducted the visitor and his eye through a programmed landscape intended to teach certain lessons of history and moral philosophy and to rouse emotions, following and expanding upon principles articulated by

English design theoreticians and aesthetic philosophers. Space became dynamic, "now rising into an amphitheater on the crest of the plateau, now hidden by the ondulations of the irregular terrain." The landscape was the active agent leading the visitor on passive promenade. Serpentine paths, a variety of rocky and smooth roads and paths, the rising and falling topography all directed the visitor through the grounds as a "variety of sights and vistas incessantly struck the eye to keep the heart from saddening." New "pleasures of melancholy" counterbalanced the old response to death.[51] Père Lachaise explicitly contrasted the realm of the living and the dead, the city and the rural cemetery, the present and past, especially in the panoramic view over Paris from the highest point in the grounds. (Figs. 3.63, 64.)

Fig. 3.62. Panorama of Paris from the General Foy monument, engraving, ca. 1825.

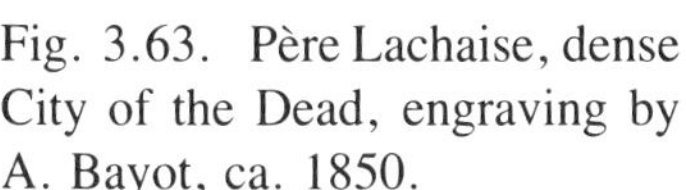

Fig. 3.63. Père Lachaise, dense City of the Dead, engraving by A. Bayot, ca. 1850.

Just as the Gothic cathedral functioned as encyclopedia for medieval man, preaching lessons in visual terms, Père Lachaise offered a complex compendium of similar, albeit secularized, messages for modern man. Like the Gothic cathedral, it invited emulation. In such a cemetery, according to Marchant de Beaumont, "All the lessons of contemporary history are inscribed for all ages, for all classes." There, "Each tomb would without doubt offer some special lessons" to visitors. The cemetery succeeded in creating a usable past for a republic without immediate precedent, and it presented new heroes to its citizens. The dead "were not all virtuous, without doubt"; at Père Lachaise, however, "all become useful," providing "vivid lessons" and "great examples that did not exist in previous cemeteries nor in church crypts." Marchant de Beaumont concluded, "The reunion of the majority of memories of a vast city within the same wall is in this manner the most powerful stimulant to live well in that city."[52] The cemetery would teach lessons of civic virtue.

Parisians were justly proud. Père Lachaise attracted international attention, and it formed the model for many similar multifunctional funerary landscapes in cities of another republic attempting to create a sense of history and social order in the wake of its own revolution. Bostonians referred frequently to Père Lachaise as inspiration and point of comparison for creation of their own Mount Auburn Cemetery. Although the landscapes of Père Lachaise and Mount Auburn subsequently developed to reflect the differences between French and American material culture, the two cemeteries were both responses to many of the same problems and were originally designed as commemorative landscapes borrowing elements from the English garden.[53]

Fig. 3.64. Panorama of Paris from Père Lachaise, engraving by Augustus Pugin, 1829.

4

The Necessity for Monuments: Art and Public Commemoration in the Young Republic

And You! ye bright ascended Dead,
  Who scorned the bigot's yoke,
Come, round this place your influence shed;
  Your spirits I invoke.
  —Charles Sprague, "An ode Pronounced before the Inhabitants of Boston . . . at the Centennial Celebration of the Settlement of the City" (1830)

ALTHOUGH THEIR REVOLUTION did not leave social and cultural chaos in its wake as did that in France, Americans still faced the problem of creating a republican civilization and finding forms to redefine history in new terms. The dual impulse for public and private commemoration grew through the first half-century of independence as a solution to the problem of defining a common, national past separate from that of the mother country. As in France, those intent on creating high culture as a unifying and stabilizing force turned to the building of monuments and the cultivation of a taste for melancholy to provide retrospective forms for both communities and families and to diminish the dangers of divisive factionalism—religious, political, social, or regional. A cataclysmic view of the inexorable processes of history and the fragility of governmental order premised their response; the optimistic idea of progress as an operative force in their civilization had yet to dominate the American mind. Monuments would be material manifestations of a new civic religion—patriotism. The necessity for monuments and commemorative landscapes, however, became a major concern only after the War of 1812, when the Treaty of Ghent assured Americans that their experiment in republican government could succeed if properly bolstered culturally. Eventually, creation of public monuments and pastoral cemetery landscapes revealed Americans' ability to adapt borrowed aesthetic forms to create their own usable past through self-commemoration.

New Englanders in particular wanted to lay claim to national history through commemorative literary and material forms. They drew upon a historical consciousness rooted in their Puritan past, its rejection of established Anglican culture, and the belief that their mission in the New World was determined by Providence in the founding of an exemplary commonwealth, "a city on a hill," a major event in the history of mankind. They retained their forefathers' belief that their own history could be a conservative social force. They updated William Bradford's concern to counteract dispersion and declension of consensus by invoking a commemorative consciousness. They particularly harkened to Bradford's lament;

> O New England, thou canst not boast;
> Thy former glory thou hast lost.
> When Hooker, Winthrop, Cotton died,
> And many precious ones beside,
> And still doth languish more away.

Celebrations of the bicentennials of the planting of Plimouth Plantation in 1620 and the establishment of the Massachusetts Bay Commonwealth in 1630 added a distinctly regional focus to their uses of retrospection. Yankees sought the perspectives of their own historians' interpretations of the sense of mission of the past, intending to recycle it for the needs of their own era. They read William Hubbard, first historian of the Massachusetts Bay Colony, who from the early vantage point of the 1650s referred to the founding decade as a "golden age," a time of God's special grace. Similarly, Nathaniel Morton and Edward Johnson recorded the deeds of the founding generation just as it was dying. The zeal for defining a common Puritan past only began to grow as Calvinist orthodoxy declined by the eighteenth century.[1]

For generations, Puritans and their heirs had built no monuments as material equivalents of written histories. Their iconophobia, rejection of ostentation, and emphasis on practicality in developing settlements provide only partial explanations. Although New Englanders erected many gravestones, these markers remained *memento mori,* exhortations to remember death, more often than records of exemplary individual lives; they were not considered "monuments" until the mid-nineteenth century, when people began to read them as historic documents. Meanwhile, both Governor John Winthrop's tomb in Boston's first graveyard and that of the Mather dynasty on Copp's Hill were barely marked. (Fig. 4.1.) Leaders of the colonial period received scant commemorative recognition in the burial place. Nor were there monuments to mark events in the founding of the colony. The Plymouth Rock was not made a monument until 1820.[2] (Fig. 4.2.)

Fig. 4.1. Mather family tomb, Copp's Hill Burial Ground, Boston, engraving from Moses King, *Hand-Book of Boston,* 1878.

Still, some nineteenth-century Yankees realized that a commemorative impulse began among American Puritans, as among the English, with discussion of the beneficial effects of mourning certain deaths. Architectural metaphors were used. Samuel Willard counseled his flock in 1683, "When a Saint *Dies* there is manifold ground of mourning; there is then a Pillar pluckt out of the Building, a Foundation Stone taken out of the Wall." Willard advised his congregation to "embalm the memory of the Saints with the sweet smelling Spices that grew in their own Graves withal . . . [to] remember and make mention of them with honourable thoughts and words." Many Puritan ministers realized as the founding generation died that remembrance of the lives of early leaders would stabilize society and perpetuate their principles. On Thomas Savage's death, Willard wondered in significantly symbolic terms, "When the Pillars are gone, how shall the building stand? . . . When the Wall is pluckt down, and the hedge removed, who shall keep out the Bore of the Wilderness."[3] Memory of a past shaped by virtuous individuals and their accomplishments would forestall lawlessness and destruction of the social order. Such views struck a chord of agreement with Yankees in the 1820s, who keenly felt the passing of time with the deaths of their Founding Fathers.

Despite his metaphors, Willard certainly was not urging creation of commemorative gardens, which the English had yet to do; rather, he was echoing Milton's yearning for new material forms of remembrance capable of inspiring retrospection and resolve. Puritans generally favored literary over material remembrance, however. "Every other monument will become old, and grow over with the Moss of time and their Titles, though cut in Brass, will be Canker-eaten and illegible," Willard wrote. Only the memory of virtuous lives of the community's elect, those predestined to salvation, would endure "when Marble itself shall be turned into common dust."[4] New Englanders would build no monuments of marble or brass until a century later, nor had they any grand buildings of their own with pillars and cornerstones, symbolic of their commonwealth, from which to draw symbols. Yet Willard was ahead of many of his fellow Englishmen in referring in metaphor to commemorative forms in encouraging his community to perpetuate the examples of visible saints. The term "saints" took on new meaning in reference to individuals with civic prominence and church membership. Willard urged commemoration through histories and biographies. Increasingly, ministers like Willard prescribed a formal, ritualized response to death combining the growing desire for remembrance of notable individuals with proscription of excessive grief and moderation of emotion characteristic of Puritanism in general and of the Yankee culture that followed. Memory of the exemplary individual—the "Saint" or later the secular "Great Man"—functioned in the same didactic way as Winthrop's concept of the "city on a hill,"

Fig. 4.2. Plymouth Rock, dedicated 1820, stereographic photograph of first cast-iron enclosure, taken by Kilburn Brothers, ca. 1860.

Fig. 4.3. "La Destruction de la Statue Royale à Nouvelle Yorck," anonymous engraving of patriots destroying statue of George III, Library of Congress.

to perpetuate notions of community ordained by Providence and based on divine law followed religiously by his chosen people.

Material evidence of a historical or commemorative consciousness was equally absent in colonies outside New England. Americans did not develop an appreciation of monuments until they *became* Americans after their Revolution. As part of the rebellion, New York patriots and their slaves pulled down a statue of King George III that stood in the Bowling Green, but even the British had erected few monuments in the colonies against which patriots could vent revolutionary sentiments. (Fig. 4.3.) The war did, however, produce many heroes for Americans with names and stories ready to be invoked as independence created the need for defining a common purpose, principles, and past—a necessity for monuments.

John Warren stressed the stabilizing functions of commemoration and the special fragility of republican states in his 1783 Fourth of July oration in Boston. He attributed the demise of Athens, Rome, and other ancient republics to "a forgetfulness of *fundamental principles.*" He warned, "So nearly is the most prosperous condition of a people allied to decay and ruin that even this flattering appearance conceals the seeds that finally must produce her destruction." To forestall the inevitable, Warren urged Americans to "go search the vaults, where lay enshrined the relicks of your martyred fellow citizens, and from their dust receive a lesson of the value of your freedom! . . . When virtue fails, when luxury and corruption shall undermine the pillars of the state, and threaten a total loss of liberty and patriotism, then solemnly repair to those *sacred repositories* of the dead."[5] But in the 1780s and for decades thereafter, Americans had no sacred repositories to which they could repair for philosophic or patriotic contemplation of the past personified in public or private ways.

Warren's remarks were premised on realization that the body of his brother Joseph, slain hero of the Battle of Bunker Hill, had been lost in a common grave on the battlefield "among the vulgar dead" for almost a year. When Bostonians located the hero's remains shortly after the British evacuation, they held a grand, patriotic funeral at King's Chapel on April 8, 1776. Perez Morton eulogized Warren, promising, "thy memory has been embalmed in the affections of thy grateful countrymen, who, in their breasts, have raised eternal monuments to thy bravery!"[6] Bostonians reinterred the patriot in another family's tomb in the Old Granary Burying Ground, but paid no attention to marking the new resting place.

Almost two decades later, the King Solomon Lodge of Freemasons, founded in Charlestown in 1783, erected a wooden, neoclassical monument, a hybrid form combining elements of an obelisk or squat pyramid, a monument type just beginning to win favor for funerary use in some old graveyards, replacing the traditional slab marker. They chose a site on the battlefield, however, rather than marking the hero's grave. A crowd of townspeople and officials gathered to consecrate the monument to Major General Warren and his associates in the spring of 1794. (Fig. 4.4.) They marched to the Charlestown site to the music of a dirge and listened to Master Mason John Soley declare that his generation would not be content "with having raised a monument of gratitude" in their hearts alone but desired to "present one to the eye of future generations" in tangible form. They renamed the hill containing "the graves of our departed countrymen" Mount Warren, calling upon fellow citizens to bring their children to the site to "teach them obedience to the voice of their country; inform them that their birth-right is Freedom." The monument would represent "the legacy left them by their countrymen to maintain its valor."[7] The General Court promptly passed an act to punish anyone defacing, injuring, or destroying the monument.

To remedy the newly perceived lack of historical monuments in Boston, Charles Bulfinch designed a sixty-foot Doric column on a pedestal, topped by a globe and an American eagle. Placed on Beacon Hill in memory of Independence in 1790, the monument was of wood and probably would not have lasted long, even if real estate speculators had not torn it down in 1811 to lower the hill for construction of homes of the city's new elite.[8] (Fig. 4.5.)

Shortly after the Revolution, foreign visitors began to remind Americans that their lack of common culture and sense of history could shorten the republic's longevity. Aware of their own need to create cultural alternatives to the Old Regime, the French were particularly concerned with ways to bolster society through material forms. Honoré-Gabriel Rigueti, the Comte de Mirabeau, a leader in the National Assembly during the early stages of the French Revolution and a rival of Lafayette, advised his American friends, "Multiply your monuments, rites, and commemorative ceremonies."[9] Some Americans, subsequently fearful of French spies, conspiracies, and extremist revolu-

Fig. 4.4. Masonic monument to General Joseph Warren, erected 1794 on Bunker Hill Battle site, engraving from Warren, *The History of the Bunker Hill Monument Association*, 1877.

Fig. 4.5. Monument to American independence designed by Charles Bulfinch, erected in 1790 on Beacon Hill, engraving, ca. 1830.

tionary fervor, questioned the motivations of such advice, but others harkened to his and more moderate French theories of the stabilizing utility of a "cult of heroes" or "cult of ancestors" in either material or literary form. For instance, James Wilson, in a 1790 law lecture at the University of Pennsylvania, proposed building a Temple of Fame in Philadelphia to honor Warren, Montgomery, and Mercer; Jeremy Belknap, who moved to Boston from New Hampshire after the Revolution, attempted to become "the American Plutarch" by publishing in 1794 the first volume of collected biographies of "Adventurers, Statesmen, Philosophers, Divines, and other remarkable characters."[10]

None of those heroes had the nationally unifying potential of George Washington, who died on December 14, 1799. His death spurred a new commemorative consciousness with patriotic dimensions such as that suggested by the Reverend Peter Whitney in an 1800 funeral sermon delivered in Brookfield, Massachusetts, "Weeping and Mourning at the Death of Eminent Persons a National Duty." The site of Washington's burial at Mount Vernon suggested the imagery of mourning pictures and funerary verse, a pastoral ideal coming into vogue that later inspired design of American "rural" cemetery landscapes. Washington's burial place—as it existed and as idealized—contrasted markedly in appearance with most burial grounds, especially those in cities. Just as the French drew inspiration from Rousseau's tomb in the romantic landscape at Ermenonville for designs of commemorative gardens, for proposals of picturesque cemeteries, and eventually for creation of Père Lachaise, Americans used Washington's grave at Mount Vernon as a secular shrine. Idealized images of the place proved compatible with new "rural" or pastoral aesthetics central to the cult of the melancholy and provided a model for proposals of "improved" burial places. Extensive literary description and visual interpretation in newspapers and books made the setting of Washington's tomb familiar to Americans in the first quarter of the century. Paintings, engravings, and mourning pictures depicted the place as romantic and picturesque—as people wished it to be rather than as it actually was. (Fig. 4.6.)

Travel narratives depicting Mount Vernon proved popular; they preceded by decades efforts to restore and preserve the estate itself. In a laudatory essay in the *New-England Galaxy* in 1823, one anonymous author described the simplicity and nobility of the rural setting and the extensive gardens, whose long gravel walks and alleys wound through a variety of fruit trees and shrubbery. Citing scriptural references to the garden as place of sepulcher to emphasize the sacredness of the place, the traveler made pilgrimage to the family vault "in which the dust of the hero reposes" on the bank of the river. The visitor could not imagine "a more romantic and picturesque site for a tomb." There, "a curtain of forest trees" on the steep hill separated it from the banks of the Potomac, "breaking the glare of the prospect and yet affording glimpses of the river when the foliage is the thickest." Large native oaks represented the virile president. "Venerable by their years," they surrounded the tomb and "annually strew the sepulcher with autumnal leaves, furnishing the most appropriate drapery for such a place." A copse of red cedar formed an evergreen backdrop for the scene and contrasted in winter "to the hoary and leafless branches of the oak." To the writer, the deciduous foliage indicated the decay of the body, while "the eternal verdure" of the cedar furnished "a beautiful emblem of the immortal spirit."[11] The account embroidered on reality, drawing more heavily on garden aesthetics than on a true description of the tattered formality of Mount Vernon after nearly a quarter-century's neglect. It presented a romanticized ideal yet to be achieved but certainly achievable, and more reasonable than other popular visual depictions of apotheosis of the first president, borne in triumph to heaven by angels.

Despite public interest in Washington's tomb, by the 1820s it had become a ruin of the sort that failed even to appeal to tastes conditioned by natural aesthetics of English gardens. Mount Vernon's landscape deteriorated as the heirs to Washington's fortune dwindled. British visitors were quick to criticize the shabby appearance of the place, to see there an indication of American's weak civilization that boded ill for the longevity of the republic. I. Finch thought that the tomb, which lacked an inscription, was "an insufficient memorial of the mighty dead."[12]

Neglect of the site suggested to E. T. Coke a general indictment of American taste: "The situation is a very pretty one, but scarcely any thing has been done by art to add to the natural beauty. The grounds are laid out in a tasteless style and kept in a slovenly manner, high coarse grass growing up to the very door. The Americans possess generally but little taste for ornamental gardening, or at least make no display of it." Coke wondered why the government did not purchase the property; he considered the nation's failure to erect a monument to the "man who was their idol while living and whose memory is still so revered amongst them" a "subject of surprise and reproach among foreigners."[13]

Other visitors called Washington's burial place characteristically American. J. S. Buckingham found a pleasing "air of simplicity" at Mount Vernon that would not appeal to those "accustomed to seeing the splendid mausolea erected to the memory of rulers, statesmen, and heroes in the old world."[14] Americans treated their first president's grave no differently from those of other heroes of the Revolution or of common citizens. By the end of the first quarter of the nineteenth century, however, as the debate over Washington's tomb demonstrates, many grew uneasy with the lack of material forms of postmortem remembrance. Some tried to rationalize their disregard for gravesites by perpetuating the names or virtues of notables in other places or patterns. According to Coke, Americans felt the city of Washington and its public buildings were a sufficient memorial to the first

Fig. 4.6. Washington's original grave at Mount Vernon, engraving from *Things as They Are, or Notes of a Traveller* (New York, 1834).

president. Other Americans remained reluctant to copy new English and French practices of creating monuments or shrines to leaders. Most visitors, however, expected to find formal monuments at the grave and in public places in the capital city, and they urged creation of the proper melancholy environment at the burial site patterned after English garden pastoralism.

Heeding Coke's advice, legislators proposed making a Congressional cemetery at Mount Vernon when the Washington family refused to exhume and reinter the first president's body in the national Capitol. Those with "romantic sensibilities," said Caroline Gilman, questioned whether "there is not something more touching in the lonely burial-place of our country's idol, even if its waving trees and natural flowers" did not stir "deep musings." The issue was one of aesthetics; the question, whether "improvements" on the rural estate to make a commemorative landscape reminiscent of the English garden, complete with a large funerary monument, would be preferable to leaving evidence of the process of natural decay and ruin indicative of time's passage and nature's resurgence. Americans had no taste for ruins, but they could not force removal of Washington's body to a more fitting site. Some asserted that Mount Vernon, even in disrepair, epitomized important American values—respect for private property, celebration of virtues grounded in the land, equation of nation with Nature, rejection of ostentation associated with Old World aristocracy. One visitor observed, "if feeling and taste be consulted, his dust will forever rest in the shades of his favourite retirement. I would prefer for myself or for a friend, the solitude and quiet of this rural spot where 'the birds sing over the grave' to the proudest columns of marble which a grateful country could rear." Mount Vernon became "the American Mecca" associated with "the agricultural pursuits and domestic concerns of the American Cincinnatus."[15]

The Reverend Hosea Ballou echoed the advice of many patriotic moralists to visit the site with his observation that "The American traveler, who visits the tomb of the hero and patriot whom we call the *father* of his country can never read the inscription of the beloved name of WASHINGTON without having a crowd of recollections, embracing the

Fig. 4.7. Washington's second grave in Gothic revival tomb, Mount Vernon, engraving by W. H. Bartlett, 1839.

events of that momentous conflict which led to the independence of our happy republic, press on his mind. Those recollections directly tend to awaken and strengthen sentiments and resolutions favorable to the defense and perpetuity of those political institutions which are the purchase of that valor which won our independence." Following such advice, parents took their children there as on pilgrimage. James Lowell visited Washington's grave at age eight in 1827 with his father, and fifty-nine years later took his own grandson to the site.[16]

Theodore Dwight found his visit to Washington's tomb a gratifying spiritual experience precisely because of the simplicity of the setting. Dwight wrote, "There is something much more congenial to my mind in the simple and indeed humble depository of the ashes of Washington than in the most splendid monuments of Italy or even of Egypt. Where there is no attempt made to captivate the eye, the mind is left at perfect freedom to form her own conceptions." Dwight had no objection to erection of monuments to Washington and hoped the day would come when every city, town, and village in the Union would have one "constructed in the purest taste"; however, he insisted "that any fabric of art" at Mount Vernon would only be "an impediment to the mind, which, if left to itself will create the noblest conceptions out of nothing."[17] Such rationalization of neglect proved less and less convincing to Americans intent on developing a national civilization. They looked at places of the past like Washington's tomb or New England graveyards and found no patriotic inspiration. Such landscapes did not remain naturally pristine and picturesque; they simply deteriorated. Even worse, because of the American abolition of primogeniture and the extreme economic vicissitudes of the new republic, many private burial grounds were lost by families along with other property within a generation of Independence.

Not until 1831 did Washington's executors follow the first president's will directing construction of a simple brick family vault and marble sarcophagus "of the ancient Roman shape . . . sculptured in relief, an eagle with the national escutcheon of America, the stars and stripes of her Union, and the word 'WASHINGTON,' only." The carving was done by John Struthers, an English marble mason living in Philadelphia. Work was not complete until 1837, when moving of the burials was done. Restoration of the entire estate did not begin until 1858, and then, not under auspices of the federal government but of the Mount Vernon Ladies' Association of the Union, chartered by the state of Virginia as one of its few nonprofit corporations.[18] (Figs. 4.7, 8.)

Fig. 4.8. Washington's second grave in Gothic revival tomb, Mount Vernon, engraving by W. H. Brooke, ca. 1840.

Such voluntarism rather than governmental action made the second quarter of the century an age of monument building, although American leaders turned their attention to stabilization of the nation in symbolic ways representative of patriotism and moralism, sacred yet secular and nondenominational. Public-spirited citizens debated the uses of art. Benjamin Henry Latrobe, an architect, landscape painter, new immigrant from England, and Republican, declared that "the history of Grecian art refutes the vulgar opinion that the arts are incompatible with liberty" for "Greece was free when the arts flourished."[19] Latrobe designed many of the public buildings in the national capital to double as monuments, and he encouraged neoclassical taste as an appropriate expression of republican ideals. Not until the 1820s would the likes of Nicholas Biddle, a leading Philadelphian and president of the Bank of the United States, take up the call for public works of art as proof of national and civic character. Mention of arts in this debate broadly referred to sculpture, architecture, monuments, and their place in the landscape.[20]

John Adams and Thomas Jefferson discussed uses of the arts in the correspondence of their declining years. Adams opposed a public policy for developing arts he considered traditionally "subservient to Priests and Kings, Nobles and . . . Monarchies," for "Sculpture, Painting, and Poetry have conspir'd against the Rights of Mankind."[21] Iconoclasm lingered from Adams's Puritan and revolutionary past, and art remained a symbolic enemy for Americans of Adams's mind.

For Americans of that generation, according to Neil Harris, art evidenced "dangerous age and decay"; and appearance of large numbers of artists portended "the beginnings of national declension." For many, "The actual conditions of many of the *objets d'art* themselves, the broken and mutilated torsos, suggested the shattered state of the societies which produced them."[22] Art and architecture explicitly symbolized society in form, durability, and preservation. Inevitable decay of monuments paralleled and represented decline of a civilization, and Americans at their semicentennial were loath to create material forms that might be harbingers of their own demise. Lacking a taste for ruins, they were reluctant to erect monuments of nondurable materials.

Jefferson, in contrast to Adams, was not concerned with the ultimate fate of the artifacts themselves. Art and architecture were agents of history, means by which his age would transmit its principles to the future, even if the duration of their usefulness might be limited. But the efficacy and durability of art depended on style. Neoclassical styles in particular represented ideals, "not what was to perish with ourselves, but would remain, be respected and preserved through other ages." To Jefferson, the neoclassical suggested a negation of luxury potentially destructive to the republic; its simplicity, visual purity, and lack of ornament were metaphoric of civic virtue. It was orderly and logical like the Constitution, an emblematic denial of baroque monarchy and aristocracy. It strengthened the conscious association of America with the heights achieved by classical cultures and political principles derived from ancient Greece and Rome. Jefferson wanted his generation's material culture to transmit a sense of national purpose just as the written documents of the federal government did. He wrote to James Madison that such monuments would present "to travellers a specimen of taste in our infancy, promising much for our mature age."[23] Popular taste signaled approval. Already in the decades following the revolution, Americans were erecting neoclassical funerary monuments—urns, obelisks, and steles—amid flat colonial stones in old graveyards.

Debate over the uses, value, and problems of art persisted through the first quarter of the new century. If, indeed, art represented the decay of an aging civilization, some argued, then lack of art indicated a society too young and immature and therefore weak and tenuous. This view fed fears that even after surviving the challenge of the War of 1812, the United States would remain merely a republican experiment resting on shallow foundations. The examples of restoration of monarchy in France in 1814 and revolution in 1830 renewed American insecurities. Jefferson, after all, had asserted each generation's right to revolt against the last. Conservative Americans in the age of Jackson feared democratic revolution; regional divisiveness also threatened the Union. In search of preventive mechanisms, even John Adams eventually wondered, "Is it possible to enlist the 'fine arts' on the side of truth, of virtue, of piety, or even of honor?"[24]

Through the decades following the War of 1812, leading Americans speculated that devising artificial props for the Founding Fathers' principles, through creation of a unifying material and literary culture, might convince all Americans of the republic's validity and permanence and muster patriotism for its preservation. Summarizing the philosophy well into the monument-building era, Hubbard Winslow, Boston's 1838 Fourth of July orator, predicted that art would "check the growing tendencies to insubordination and render all classes of citizens more humane, peaceful, and happy."[25] Commemorative landscapes and monuments, as in England and France, would embody political ideals and have powers of social control.

Winslow only repeated messages he and other Bostonians had been hearing for over two decades from their self-appointed cultural leaders. William Tudor, a merchant shipowner, was a great advocate of art for the sake of commemoration and creation of a past usable for city, region, and nation. Tudor insisted in 1816 that artists had a high duty to their country and "should feel something of a *missionary* spirit," their goal being "to excite the taste of the publick." Tudor considered it his personal mission to enrich national culture, to counteract foreign criticisms like those in the *Edinburgh Review* that great art and architecture would not suffice for creation of culture if they were borrowed and not developed indigenously. Tudor invoked other elite, Whiggish Bostonians to accept the calling to prove the critics wrong. Philanthropically minded merchants and professionals created institutions to foster cultural nationalism through the next decades, motivated by the belief that "correct taste" could strengthen "republican virtue" and hence ensure good and stable society.[26]

Tudor urged creation of a repository in Boston to enable American artists to improve their work and connoisseurs to refine their taste. Models and casts from Europe would suffice for aesthetic inspiration and education for a time, if no original art was immediately forthcoming. George Watson Brimmer assembled an art collection at Boston's Athenaeum. Tudor hoped to make it a "fashionable resort" and place of education, but that institution remained private and generally inaccessible to the public.

As with the rise of historical consciousness among mid-seventeenth-century Puritans when the founding generation of the Massachusetts Bay Colony was dying, a general sensibility to history blossomed in America as the nation celebrated its semicentennial, simultaneously marked by the deaths of Adams and Jefferson. In eulogizing the two founding fathers and presidents, whose deaths precisely coincided with the fiftieth anniversary of independence in 1826, Daniel Webster rationalized that "although no sculptured marble should rise to their memory, nor engraved stone bear record of their deeds, yet will their remembrance be as lasting as the land they honored." Webster asserted an overly bold and unprecedented confidence that "Marble columns may, indeed, moulder into dust, time may erase all impress from the crumbling stone, but their fame remains; for with AMERICAN LIBERTY it rose, and with AMERICAN LIBERTY ONLY can it perish." In similar terms, Edward Everett, presiding over the belated "funeral solemnities" for Adams and Jefferson at Charlestown, Massachusetts, on August 1, 1826, concluded, "The faithful marble may preserve their image; the engraven brass may proclaim their worth; but the humblest sod of Independent America, with nothing but the dewdrops of the morning to gild it, is a prouder mausoleum than kings or conquerors can boast. The country is their monument. Its independence is their epitaph." Yet Everett struck a fatalistic note, which resonated with the cataclysmic assumptions of the inexorable course of history shared by his Whiggish friends: "The contemporary and successive generations of men will disappear. In the long lapse of ages, the Tribes of America, like those of Greece and Rome, may pass away. The fabric of American Freedom, like all things human, however firm and fair, may crumble into dust. But the cause in which these our Fathers shone is immortal. . . . Their eulogy will be uttered in other languages, when those we speak, like us who speak them, shall be forgotten."[27]

The natural rights of man might be immutable and the righteousness of the American republic confirmed by Providence. Even so, the perception of a pressing necessity to give tangible manifestation to an American history based on commemoration of heroes and key events remained, challenging remembrance and interpretation in material terms by survivors and heirs, precisely as the nation celebrated having endured half a century intact. An awareness of the past and speculation of the uses of history were in the air, especially as counterpoint to escalating and unsettling social changes. Discontinuities of various sorts worried many. Emerson observed that with industrialization, "A cleavage is occurring in the hitherto firm granite of the past and a new era is nearly arrived."[28] Rapid, perceptible change premised a spirit of retrospection.

In Boston, in particular, despite successes in industrializing the hinterland, uncertainties arose about the city's future, as New York, Philadelphia, and Baltimore eclipsed it in prosperity. Some Bostonians wondered whether their city had not already, according to the anticipated pattern, had its heyday in the mid-eighteenth century and entered a period of irreversible decline. According to Tudor, it appeared that "Boston does and must decline," that other cities would inevitably run away with the "population and capital" of the "Metropolis of New England."[29] Such uncertainties fueled the spirit of retrospection as well as artistic innovation based on classical models, evidence of noble principles surviving and transcending the fall of civilization.

But Tudor, ever the avid urban booster, would not capitulate. He insisted that the example of Boston proved the value of a legacy of a principled past and provided ample evidence of its citizens' continuing worth. Tudor concurred with William Ellery Channing's exclamation, "What a monument is a city to the immortal energies of the human mind; and what a witness to man's spiritual destiny." Channing, Tudor, and their associates were confident that through voluntary associations meant to create high culture, they could make Boston into the "Athens of America," a latter-day "city on a hill."[30]

Despite this resolve to improve his city, Tudor's observation of the decline of Boston's place vis-à-vis other American cities was not based merely on the relatively greater growth and economic success of competitors. It revealed a latent pessimism premised in the cataclysmic view of history that still permeated much of western thought in the early nineteenth century. It reflected the notion that dramatic, violent beginnings and endings characterized the fate of cities, nations, and civilizations just as the human life was delimited by birth, maturation, decay, and death. Themes of cataclysm recurred in American art and literature: William Ware's *Zenobia; or, the Fall of Palmyra* (1827), Edgar Allen Poe's "The Fall of the House of Usher" (1839), and visionary paintings by Washington Allston and Thomas Cole in the 1820s and 1830s. James Fenimore Cooper summarized expectations of the inexorable in *The Crater*: "The earth revolves, men are born, live their time, and die; communities are formed and are dissolved; dynasties appear and disappear; good contends with evil; and evil still has its day; the whole, however, advancing slowly but unerringly towards that great consummation, which was designed from the beginning, and which is as certain to arrive in the end, as that the sun sets at night and rises in the morning."[31]

Dr. Jacob Bigelow shared this philosophy of history, first expressing it publicly in 1816 when he told a Harvard audience, "The power which men and nations exercise in regard to each other is temporary and transient. The greatest individuals have lived to see the decline of everything upon which their greatness reposed. Societies and political institutions, which have been distinguished in their ascent, have not been less remarkable in their fall. Those nations and governments which, in former times, have subdued their competitors and controlled, for a time, the destinies of the great portion of the world, are now erased from the list of empires, and perhaps, recognized only in name." Only knowledge was "permanent and progressive," immune to the vicissitudes and revolutions of Time. As an antidote, Bigelow urged Bostonians to expand all fields of learning and recognize the accomplishments of those who did so.[32]

Fatalism thus fed the commemorative impulse. Although the intellectual elite knew Sir Thomas Browne's warning that no one could become immortal in name alone through funerary inscriptions, leading Bostonians desired to leave to posterity material evidence of their social and cultural greatness, of republican political principles, and of citizens who distinguished themselves in areas of service to society. They took heart that their country was yet young, pristine, and bound to endure through a maturation of indefinite length. The United States still would go through the process depicted in Thomas Cole's five-painting series *The Course of Empire* (1833–36), graphically tracing a fictional, classical civilization from savage and Arcadian periods to a flourishing of ostentatious high culture and its inevitable destruction. (Figs. 4.9, 10.) This notion of history seemed correct to a generation that kept fresh memories of recent revolutions. Only nature was eternal, constantly renewing itself and resurgent after civilization's fall.

The cataclysmic concept of history paralleled the cult of the melancholy and its emphasis on individual mortality. The only difference was that one pertained to the public sphere and the other to the private; one to a city or nation, and the other to the individual. Some Americans argued for commemorative monuments as a means to preserve memories of a past worthy of emulation and a present soon to be past; others argued that the very act of monument building could forestall the inevitable decay of civilization.

Tudor, Brimmer, and their younger friend Bigelow were particularly sensitive to criticisms of Americans' lack of culture in the *Edinburgh Review*. The opinionated British essayist Sidney Smith particularly urged the commemorative impulse, reminding Americans that "great men hallow a whole people and lift up all who live in their time."[33] Tudor agreed but wished to redefine greatness in a particularly American way. He held to the doctrine of original equality, insisting that the criteria for recognition of greatness be based on talent, intellect, achievement, and service rather than on lineage. Because of his personal sense of mission to improve national and local culture, character, and intellect, Tudor naturally defined gentry status in terms of voluntary acceptance of stewardship of wealth and civic responsibility, traits that were prime criteria for elite status in Boston.

Perhaps in response to Sidney Smith and other critics of American culture, Dr. Bigelow proclaimed the uses and importance of recognizing and preserving the memories of great Americans in the address he delivered at Harvard upon being made Rumford Professor in 1816. Bigelow told his audience that commemoration of notable Americans would attract "the honorable notice of foreigners" and reflect "lustre upon the country of their birth." He proposed celebrating "men unambitious of fame, whose lives have passed in obscurity" yet who contributed to the development and improvement of the nation in various ways. He suggested that "if gathered from the ashes of obscurity, [their names] might serve to shed a gleam upon our literary reputation." Bigelow remained confident that many men had lived in America who were as learned as Franklin, "a native of New England," or as patriotic as any of the Founding Fathers. Only posthumous commemoration would resurrect such exemplary figures from oblivion. Bigelow found the past a source of inspiration and encouragement, especially for those "who would despond as to our future destinies."[34]

According to Bigelow, fame came naturally to those fortunate "to live in times of political importance" or those lucky enough "to find paths untrodden by predecessors," whereas patriots, philosophers, and scientists of his own era went unacclaimed and seemingly would have no place in history. Bigelow revealed a certain sadness that his generation did not have the advantages of that of the revolution, that the importance of an era intensified and immortalized individual reputations, a privilege that his generation might not have. Bigelow and his peers were anxious for fame. They strove to be renaissance men, to excel in many fields, to assert individualism, and to establish family names. Other forms of commemoration would have to compensate, even if artificially, thus creating a history composed of monuments, biographies, and other formal forms of recognition of individual merit.[35]

John Adams read the Rumford Address and congratulated Bigelow for refuting the criticisms in the *Edinburgh Review* predicting the imminent decadence of American culture. Adams added, "Our honors and glories and constant good fortune may make them giddy, as well as Napoleon."[36] Bigelow had articulated a new sense of mission for Bostonians to commemorate and celebrate their

Fig. 4.9. Thomas Cole, *The Arcadian Era,* painting from five-part series *The Course of Empire,* 1833–36, Metropolitan Museum of Art, New York.

past. In the next several decades, the new historical consciousness underlay publication of the monumental twenty-five-volume *Library of American Biography* (1833–49), edited by Jared Sparks, a Boston Unitarian minister and the first professor of secular history at Harvard; the building of the Bunker Hill Monument from 1825 to 1845; and the founding of Mount Auburn Cemetery in 1831, following Bigelow's 1825 proposal that Bostonians unite to create a multifunctional, extramural burial ground. Ralph Waldo Emerson correctly observed in 1836, "Our age is retrospective. It builds the sepulchers of the fathers. It writes biographies, history, criticism. The foregoing generation beheld God and nature face to face; we, through their eyes." More recently, David Van Tassel wrote that "reverence for ancestors" was so "unflagging" in that era that by mid-century, "filiopietistic regard for the dead was in danger of making hypocrites of historians" by a stretching of truth and objectivity about the past in the name of philosophic and patriotic idealism.[37]

Indeed, Americans of Emerson's generation worked assiduously to create a past, usable for their purposes, and Whiggish Bostonians led the crusade. In 1816, the leading Unitarian divine, William Ellery Channing, advised Bostonians, "Let the records of past ages be explored to rescue from oblivion, not the wasteful conqueror, but the benefactors to the human-race." Channing protested glorification of military heroes as symbols of superiority, triumph, and power. His ideal heroes were intellectuals and philanthropists working quietly and diligently to elevate all aspects of local and national culture. For Channing, altruism and cultural responsibility were prerequisites for gentry status. Channing encouraged the elite in active stewardship of their wealth and urged all citizens to have a sense of responsibility to community, believing that commemoration would instill such lessons.[38]

Many members of Boston's new commercial and industrial gentry heeded Channing's advice and sought ways to promote the ideals of character he stressed through historical biography. The entrepreneur William Appleton noted in his commonplace book his sense of his "duty to distribute [his] income, which is large, giving religious objects the first thought, and uniting with others in promoting the Arts and Sciences." Channing and other Unitarian ministers encouraged Bostonians to anticipate their ultimate mortality over the course of their lives, to give generously to community-spirited causes, and not to rely on a written will for the benevolence required of all good men in recognition of the wealth that God permitted them to accumulate. Following this pattern, the industrialist Amos Lawrence acted as "his own executor"; he kept only one-tenth of his income and gave away the rest, earning the reputation of "the greatest philanthropist of his age." Many prosperous Bostonians accepted the moral mandate to band together in voluntary associations to develop various projects for the common good.[39]

Cultivation of the arts and material commemoration were thus justified according to Bigelow, Channing, and other prominent Bostonians. Time and time again, in the 1820s and subsequent decades, leading Bostonians invoked their fellow citizens to use funerary commemoration for patriotic purposes. In 1813, Josiah Quincy described the first attachment of the citizen to the nation through filial affection that transcends death and fixes loyalties to a sense of place. "There is my fireside; there are the tombs of my ancestors," Quincy declared as proof of attachment to his hometown.[40]

Seven years later, on the bicentennial of the landing of the Pilgrims at Plymouth, Daniel Webster chose a similar message for his first major public address, acknowledging "a sort of *genius of*

Fig. 4.10. Thomas Cole, *Destruction of Civilization,* painting from five-part series *The Course of Empire,* 1833–36, Metropolitan Museum of Art, New York.

place" and elevating local associations to the level of national significance. Webster proclaimed that "by ascending to an association with our ancestors, by contemplating their example and studying their character, by partaking their sentiments, and imbibing their spirit, and rejoicing in their successes and triumphs, we seem to belong to their age and to mingle our own existence with theirs. We become their contemporaries." Monuments perpetuated the memories of the individuals who built them as well as the subject commemorated. Through a monument, the present generation could experience significant historical events, if only emotionally and vicariously. Webster declared that "a moral and philosophical respect for our ancestors elevates the character and improves the heart." He urged members of his generation to foster a sense of relationship both to the past and to posterity, to consider themselves as "interested and connected with our whole race, through all time, links in the great chain of being." Webster called upon his audience to leave "honorable memorials of themselves for the day when they would sleep with the fathers." He exhorted them to look to history, to be retrospective.[41] Webster echoed and reinterpreted the French debate on social uses of the "cult of ancestors"; and he domesticated and applied to public life the cult of the melancholy that had developed among political and religious liberals in eighteenth-century England. These were precisely the qualities, public and private, that seemed lacking in Boston in 1820.

The rapid growth of Boston and advances in technology accentuated the break between Webster's age and the past. Like many civic and cultural leaders of his era, Webster had to confront problems of the past and advise commemorative remedies to stabilize society for the future. These were, of course, national problems, but they seemed particularly acute in Boston in the 1820s. In 1822, Boston was incorporated as a city, thus leaving behind the traditional town form of government, the last vestiges, it seemed to many, of traditions dating back almost two hundred years, a past longer than that of any other major American urban area. Nathan Hale composed a lengthy meditation on and assessment of the state of community life in his *Chronicle of Boston and the Book of Retrospections and Anticipations,* bemoaning the lack of material evidence of the past:

> I looked for the monuments [the rich]
> had erected either to adorn the age
> in which they lived, or to humanize the age
> that was to come.
> For . . . "Without memorials of the past men
> would conceive
> that their own age was the original and father
> of all excellence,
> and thence would be vain and conceited."
> In contemplating antiquity . . . the mind itself
> becomes antique;
> it contracts from such venerable rust, far
> preferable
> to the point and polish of those wits
> who profane the memorials of former days
> with ridicule. . . .
> Yet how few among the great men of the world
> have founded their own monuments?
> Romulus, Alexander, Constantine, Peter,
> Washington,
> founded cities, those eternal monuments,
> which conquest cannot annihilate, nor time
> impair,
> but which all generations strengthen, extend,
> polish, and admire.
> But the monuments of the rich men of the city,
> where are they?[42]

Boston and America might be stronger for the absence of aristocracy, but Hale and others worried that city and nation would suffer from the lack of monuments traditionally erected by the rich. In fact, the Bowdoins, the Jays, and the Boudinots, leading families of the colonial period, had been eclipsed economically, culturally, and politically by a new elite; the duty of redefining the past through monuments fell upon those new leaders.

Bostonians called for private and public monuments precisely at a time when the few that existed seemed doomed to decay or oblivion. The old burial grounds of the city were crowded, chaotic, and threatened with displacement by legislation and urban development; only temporary memorials to the Revolution had been erected. By the 1820s, there were no permanent or durable commemorative structures or civic statuary in public places in the city, and open space that might be appropriate for them was rapidly disappearing.

Still, Josiah Quincy, Boston's second mayor, rationalized in 1830 that the legacy of the past was spiritual rather than material: "Right conceptions then of the glory of our ancestors are alone to be attained by analyzing their virtues . . . not seen characterized in breathing bronze, or in living marble. Our ancestors left no Corinthian temples on our hills, no Gothic cathedrals on our plains, no proud pyramid, no storied obelisk in our cities. But mind is there. Sagacious enterprises . . . these are the monuments of our ancestors . . . immutable and immortal in the social, moral, and intellectual condition of our descendants."[43] Although Quincy praised tradition and the New England mind, many Bostonians felt increasing discontent with the intangibility of history, especially when their spirit of urban competition was roused by the building of monuments in other cities. Monument building in Baltimore was of particular interest because of that city's strong mercantile and religious ties to Boston.

Baltimore, with its short history of prosperity, acquired the name "Monument City" based on commemorative structures erected in memory of Washington and local heroes of the War of 1812. As early as 1809, the Maryland legislature granted permission to a voluntary association to raise $100,000 by lottery for a monument to the first president, but war postponed the effort. On July 4, 1815, Baltimoreans laid the cornerstone on a hill north of the city in a dramatic public ceremony that attracted national attention. The young Bostonian Jacob Bigelow heard the news with envy from his brother Henry, boarding in Baltimore on business with "six full-blooded Yankees"; but he did not know of problems involving site choice.[44] Residents of townhouses rejected monument sites in the center of the city, fearing the stability of such a tall structure, and insisted that the column be placed at the urban periphery. Robert Mills, known as America's first native professional architect and later designer of the Washington Monument in the United States capital, furnished the plan. The marble column, of Doric style, which was considered symbolic of strength by Masons, topped by a sixteen-foot statue of Washington by the Italian sculptor Henrico Cancici, was completed in 1829. (Fig. 4.11.)

Fig. 4.11. Baltimore's Washington monument, designed by Robert Mills with portrait statue of Washington by Henrico Cancici, 1829, engraving by W. H. Bartlett, ca. 1835.

Similarly, in the summer of 1815, a public subscription campaign led by the Committee of Vigilance and Safety raised funds for a second monument in memory of citizens who died defending Baltimore against the British the previous fall in the Battle of Fort McHenry. The cornerstone for the Battle Monument was laid that September in a ceremony reminiscent of a pubic funeral with tolling bells and a processional of an estimated twenty thousand following a hearse bearing the plan of the proposed monument. Construction of Baltimore's second monument, a fifty-two-foot column de-

Fig. 4.12. Baltimore's Battle Monument, designed by Maximilien Godefroy, 1825, engraving by W. H. Bartlett, ca. 1835.

signed by French emigré architect Maximilien Godefroy, took a decade. It had a pyramidal, Egyptian Revival base, a pedestal adorned with eagles and bas-reliefs of two battles, and a column surmounted by a ten-foot-high female figure representative of the city, holding a laurel wreath and a ship's rudder. (Fig. 4.12.)

Perhaps it seemed ironic to leading Bostonians that such civic spirit and a sense of history were displayed in the very new commercial city of Baltimore before Boston. The example of civic monument building to the south was another impetus for Bostonians to plan their own commemorative structures and landscapes. They did not lag far behind. William Tudor, Boston's chief advocate for the creation of culture, urged erection of an equestrian statue to Washington in 1816, but he worried that the city had no suitable site. Although Massachusetts was full of major places of the Revolution, ideal locations for monuments to commemorate sacrifices of local heroes and to emphasize the importance of the region seemed scarce. Tudor favored hilltop locations for monuments to be visible from a distance and especially from the city. He considered a variety of nonsculptural monuments as well—pyramids, obelisks, triumphal arches, and columns. Yet he concluded, "The most ancient, the most durable monument of human labor on the surface of the globe is a tomb!" Tudor realized, however, that burial grounds in the city were totally inconducive to the accurate marking of the graves of notables, let alone to commemoration with grand monuments or mausoleums.[45]

Tudor also knew that Americans lacked the technological capabilities to quarry the enormous blocks of granite necessary for the building of obelisks or pyramids, despite rich deposits of the hard stone near the city. "No nation in modern times could have prepared the endless blocks of granite with the nice exactness of their fitting," he concluded. But that did not deter Tudor from urging construction of a suitable monument on "an advantageous situation . . . insulated as much as possible from others and not difficult of access."[46] Despite technological limitations and a shortage of cheap labor, Boston leaders decided to build a monument.

An even greater obstacle to commemoration was a historical controversy that raged through 1818, pitting a Federalist faction, which credited General Israel Putnam (1718–1790) for leading the Patriots at Bunker Hill, against Republicans who backed the leadership claims of Colonel William Prescott (1726–95). Partisans took the case to the public in the *Port-Folio,* the *Columbian Centinel,* and the *North American Review.* For a time, it seemed to Bostonians that history was more divisive than unifying.

For these reasons, Tudor's call for a patriotic monument in Boston, written with the example of Baltimore fresh in mind, was not answered for seven years until an appropriate site presented itself. In the spring of 1823, a notice appeared in a local newspaper that about three acres of land on Breed's Hill in Charlestown were to go to auction. The site, across the Charles River from the city, contained the remains of the patriots' earthen redoubt and breastwork as well as mass graves of an estimated five hundred soldiers from Massachusetts and Connecticut who fell in the Battle of Bunker Hill. General Henry Alexander Scammell Dearborn, nephew of the slain hero of the battle and a prominent Bostonian in his own right, protested to the *Boston Patriot:* "Here repose the ashes of the brave. Let not the glorious sepulchre of our Revolutionary warriors be profaned." Dearborn proposed "that some patriotic gentlemen of wealth" purchase the site and "have it enclosed with a stone or iron fence, to be held sacred."[47] (Fig. 4.13.)

Tudor immediately recognized the possibilities of preserving the place and using it as location for a major historical monument. The site of the "American battle of Marathon" was perfect, Tudor thought, atop heights commanding a view of the city, the harbor, and the countryside and towns for miles around.[48] Although connected to Boston by bridge, it was still essentially rural. Tudor easily mustered support from Dearborn and a number of the city's intellectual and financial elite—Edward Everett and George Ticknor of Harvard, Dr. John Collins Warren, Daniel Webster, Judge Joseph Story, and Thomas Handasyd Perkins, Boston's "merchant prince."[49]

Dearborn played a key role in planning and building the Bunker Hill monument. Born in 1783 in Essex, New Hampshire, he was far from provincial. While his father, General Henry Dearborn, served as Jefferson's Secretary of War, young Henry attended William and Mary College. On graduation, he asked the President for a diplomatic post abroad, but Jefferson genially refused, explaining that "no man ought to go to reside for any time abroad under the age of forty, for he would lose his American tastes and ideas . . . and grow incapable of becoming a loyal, useful, and contented citizen at home." Henry, determined to become the sort of citizen Jefferson proposed, took the President's advice and returned to New England to study law in Salem under Judge Joseph Story, then a Jeffersonian and close friend of John Marshall. During the War of 1812, Dearborn commanded defense of Boston's harbor as brigadier-general of the militia; he superintended construction of harbor fortifications in Portsmouth, New Hampshire, and was elected captain of the Ancient and Honorable Artillery Company in 1816. After the war, Dearborn tired of the law but developed wide-ranging expertise in civil engineering, architecture, politics, and horticulture. He became a central member of Boston's new elite and participated in a variety of voluntary associations meant to bolster local and national civilization—especially as vice president of the New England Society for Promotion of Manufactures and Mechanical Arts and as first president of the Massachusetts Horticultural Society. Dearborn was a force to be reckoned with, not only in terms of institutional influence but also for his high style, for he was immediately recognizable driving through the city streets in his stately carriage, drawn by a double span of horses with postilions.[50]

Under Dearborn's guidance, ambitious plans for the Bunker Hill Monument Association were developed. He urged friends to purchase not only the three acres of land advertised for sale but the entire battlefield. The group issued a circular letter in July of 1823 announcing intention to erect "a simple, majestic, lofty, and permanent monument, which shall carry down to remote ages a testimony . . . to the heroic virtue and courage of those men who began and achieved the independence of their country." The monument would display "the names and dates of all the distinguished characters and events which originated in New England." It would be a national monument but also one "dedicated to the Revolutionary glory which belongs to this portion of the Union." Edward Everett attempted to raise funds nationally, but focused his efforts on obtaining small donations from all classes in neighboring states. New Englanders were determined not to permit Southerners to usurp all of the credit for foundation and preservation of the nation.[51] A circular letter issued in the fall of 1824 soliciting donations argued, "Our fellow-citizens of Baltimore have set up a noble example of redeeming the arts to the cause of free institutions in the imposing monument they have erected. . . . If we cannot be the first to set up a structure of this character, let us not be other than the first to improve upon the example."[52] Local and regional pride proved a major impetus for the Monument Association.

The petition of twenty-six prominent Bostonians for a charter further stated: "As 'the first impulse to the ball of the Revolution' was given in the North; as the plains of Massachusetts were first stained with the blood of patriots,—THERE should be reared the FIRST PILLAR of the Republic." Without mentioning Baltimore, the petition noted that there were no northern monuments at Charlestown, Saratoga, Trenton, Monmouth, or Yorktown. "No statue, not even of Washington, adorns the Capitol, nor do his ashes repose under a national tomb." Petitioners concluded with a nationalistic argument for a charter from the state of Massachusetts: "If great actions, having for their object the public good; if individuals, renowned for their civil and military virtues, have in all ages, illumined the history and claimed the admiration of nations; — if they have been decreed worthy of the triumphal arch, the column, the temple, or the mausoleum, — what people ever had more cause thus to cherish the memory of their statesmen and heroes than those of the United States?"[53] Approving of these arguments, the Massachusetts General Court promptly incorporated the Bunker Hill Monument Association.

Through 1824, directors of the Association and others debated the merits of various monumental forms. Dearborn preferred a large but simple Ionic column as more economical and quicker to build, for he desired to see the monument completed in his lifetime. He opposed topping the column with a portrait statue, asserting that the monument "should be purely national" rather than commemorative of a hero like General Warren.[54] Although Washington assumed command of the Continental Army on Cambridge Common, his name was not mentioned, perhaps because he was not present at the Battle of Bunker Hill, which indeed the colonists lost.

Only William Ladd, president of the American Peace Society, proposed a mausoleum, so as not to produce "mortified pride" and increased "hatred and revenge" in the British that might lead to renewed hostilities. A mausoleum could serve as Boston's Westminster Abbey, a place of burial and commemoration for other patriots and notables. There, according to Ladd, "an American might meet with an Englishman as a reconciled brother, who might join him in admiration of English principles carried to perfection by descendants of Englishmen." Although the notion of creating a funerary depository for great individuals did not appeal to proponents of the Bunker Hill Monument Association, it lingered in Yankee minds, perhaps eventually giving Dr. Jacob Bigelow another reason for suggesting creation of Mount Auburn Cemetery.[55]

Most Bunker Hill Monument planners favored a simple obelisk. Joseph Story, vice president of the Association, Daniel Webster, and others particularly liked it and appointed a committee composed of Loammi Baldwin, George Ticknor, Samuel Swett, Washington Allston, and Bigelow to choose an appropriate, large-scale variation on the obelisk or pyramidal form. The Boston architect Solomon Willard presented a plan for a 221-foot structure, based on the cost estimates of Gridley Bryant, developer of the Quincy granite quarries.

Fig. 4.13. Portrait of General Henry A. S. Dearborn, painting, copied by Jane Stuart in 1850s from original by her father, Gilbert Stuart, ca. 1827, MHORT.

Still, the design committee awarded a premium to Horatio Greenough for his wooden model painted the color of granite and based on proportions from an obelisk at Thebes. Greenough called the obelisk "the most purely *monumental* form of structure," preferable to the column, which rightly belongs as part of a larger structure; many Americans seemed to agree with him, based on the number of obelisks used in lieu of slab gravestones in their burying grounds for several decades. In the end, however, the Association designated Willard "architect," charging him to superintend construction but precipitating a controversy over authorship of the design.[56]

The cornerstone of the Bunker Hill Monument was laid on June 17, 1825, the fiftieth anniversary of the battle, in what George Ticknor called "the most solemn ceremonies that have happened since Pericles made his funeral oration in the Ceramicus," the cemetery outside Athenian gates. Alexander Parris, who served as "official architect," was the presiding officer in the Masonic ceremony, which was followed by a brief speech by the visiting Marquis de Lafayette and an ode composed by the Reverend John Pierpont, a popular local Unitarian minister with a growing national

Fig. 4.14. Bunker Hill Monument with entire battlefield preserved, from membership certificate of the Bunker Hill Monument Association, engraving, ca. 1833.

reputation. Pierpont emphasized the funerary significance of the site:

> Here sleeps their dust; 't is holy ground;
> And we, the children of the brave,
> From the four winds are gathered round,
> To lay our offering on their grave.

Daniel Webster gave the chief oration, calling on Bostonians to "cherish every memorial of these worthy ancestors" to teach future generations "to venerate their piety." Webster proclaimed, "our object is, by this edifice to show our own deep sense of the value and importance of the achievements of our ancestors . . . to keep alive similar sentiments, and to foster a constant regard for the principles of the Revolution.[57] (Fig. 4.14.)

Webster revealed belief in the cataclysmic philosophy of history shared by many of his friends. "We wish," he said, "that in those days of disaster which as they come on all nations must be expected to come on us also, desponding patriotism may turn its eyes hitherward and be assured that the foundations of our national power still stand strong."[58] Bostonians anticipated that the Bunker Hill Monument would endure for millennia, standing to testify to the distant future and other nationalities of the republican principles upon which the United States had been founded and of the prominent role that the city had played in the revolution.

Alexander Everett similarly predicted in 1836 that the monument would be evidence of a golden age even "when our . . . metropolis and her sister cities shall have had their day of power, prosperity and glory, and passed away; when Boston, New York and Philadelphia shall have been what Rome, Athens, Memphis, and Babylon at their proudest period never were, and shall have sunk again, in conformity with the immutable law that regulates all human things, into the state of ruin in which those celebrated seats of empire are now; when of all the achievements of art and wealth that now surround us . . . the hand of Time shall have swept away everything except that simple granite obelisk, which will probably outlast all the structures it is destined to overlook." In that remote future, "the friends of liberty and virtue will come up from distant lands," perhaps from Australasia, in pilgrimage to that monument of the once-great American republic.[59]

Such lofty ideals impelled the undertaking of the ambitious construction project of a scale unprecedented in America to that time. Willard, later called "Father of the Granite Industry," and Bryant, an engineer, had to develop new technologies for quarrying and transporting stone before they could begin work in 1827. In the process, Bryant invented devices for the Granite Railway, the first railroad in America, which transported stone from the Quincy quarries to the shore, where they were loaded on sloops and schooners for the trip north along the coast to Charlestown.

Construction, therefore, proceeded slowly. Some viewed the incomplete structure as a negative sign, a message foreboding the future of the republic. In 1830, when the obelisk rose only forty feet, "surrounded by the massive stones prepared for the top half lying promiscuously at its base, like a sublime ruin," one pessimistic observer predicted it would remain "like a broken column, emblematic of a Republic of magnificent promise in its rise, but prematurely dismembered and inglorious in its fall."[60] Lack of funds further slowed work. The corporation, already virtually penniless by 1830, received meager contributions until Sarah Josepha Hale, editor of popular women's magazines, announced a national fund-raising campaign, complicated by the nation's plunge into hard economic times with the Panic of 1837. By 1838, it became evident that the Association's goal of preserving the entire battlefield as a national historic site would be impossible. The Association reluctantly sold ten acres, all except the land immediately around the monument, to developers of domestic real estate. (Figs. 4.15, 16.)

The capstone of the Bunker Hill Monument was not put in place until 1843; and the cost and difficulties of the project discouraged Bostonians from planning similarly ambitious public monuments for their city.[61] Rather, their thoughts turned to a more funerary and personal sort of commemoration that might be accomplished more quickly, on a less grandiose scale, and bit by bit as smaller voluntary efforts organized to celebrate individual merit and inspire historical consciousness. They remained avidly retrospective. Josiah Quincy, no longer mayor of Boston but president of Harvard College, observed on the 1830 bicentennial of Boston that the "natural and generous affections of man . . . connect him with ancestry . . . enlarge the sphere of his interests; multiply his motives to virtue; and give intensity to his sense of duty to generations to come, by the perception of obligations to those which are past." Appropriately, the topic of the 1832 Harvard commencement address of Joseph Stevens Buckminster Thacher was "Respect for Public Monuments, whether Triumphal or for the Dead." Thacher advocated a sort of commemoration serviceable to social stability through strengthened family cohesion, like the French "cult of ancestors." Many of the members of the Bunker Hill Monument Association readily responded to the appeal of Dr. Bigelow to found a cemetery under the auspices of the Massachusetts Horticultural Society, headed by Dearborn.[62]

Thaddeus W. Harris, a gentleman horticulturist, described a historic and commemorative rationale for creating a new cemetery. "Had such a cemetery with prophetic forethought of posterity, been laid out in the first settlement of the country, and

Fig. 4.15. Bunker Hill Monument, half-built, engraving from Caleb H. Snow, *A Geography of Boston,* 1830.

all our venerated dead—the eminent in church and state—been deposited side by side, with plain but enduring monuments, it would possess already an interest of the most elevated and affecting character." Harris anticipated that "in a Rural Cemetery the names and virtues of the departed would live in perpetual freshness and their souls seem to commune with those who come to do honor to their names." The place would attract local and foreign visitors, affording "the means of paying a tribute of respect by a monumental erection to the names and memory of great and good men, whenever or wherever they have died." It would become more than a simple, functional burial place. Harris hoped that the cemetery's "summit may be consecrated to Washington by a cenotaph inscribed with his name."[63] In that way, Boston, like Baltimore, would have two patriotic monuments: one commemorating local participation in a war for the nation and the other honoring the Father of the Country.

Once a dramatic, hilly site was chosen, William B. O. Peabody, another horticulturist, judged the summit "an admirable place for a monument intended to be seen at a distance," the best in the vicinity of the city. Cemetery founders anticipated that "Public sentiment will often delight in these tributes of respect, and the place will gradually become the honorary mausoleum for the distinguished men of Massachusetts."[64]

General Dearborn, Massachusetts Horticultural Society president, considered a cemetery, even more than patriotic monuments in public places, representative of the high culture of city and nation.[65] All agreed that the abysmal condition of

Fig. 4.16. Bunker Hill Monument, completed with small plot of property remaining, engraving, ca. 1845.

Fig. 4.17. Athenian Ceramicus, idealized view, engraving by H. W. Williams, 1839.

Boston's graveyards indicated only a disregard for the past and that pressures of urbanization on the limited space of the Shawmut peninsula made postmortem commemoration impossible in Boston, necessitating an extramural setting, a "rural" site outside city limits. Land close to the city, like that in Charlestown, was too valuable to reserve in large parcels for commemorative purposes. In founding a cemetery on rural land four miles west of Boston on the Cambridge-Watertown line, Dearborn, Bigelow, and their associates found a site that would not be threatened by high land values or urbanization for decades to come; and they created a commemorative landscape that would do far more than that initially proposed in the expanded setting for the Bunker Hill Monument. The institution and landscape would be full of complex commemorative symbolism—public and private—based on precedents from Egyptian and classical times as well as recent experiments in creating melancholy landscapes interpretive of a past in England and France.

Dearborn specifically referred to "the great Egyptian Cemetery . . . on the farther shore of the Lake Acherusia, near Memphis, ornamented with trees and water-courses, and answering to the Elysian fields of later times," a place produced by the golden age of Egypt, before the wealthy "sacrificed their true taste for nature to their ambition of splendor, their mummies gathered into catacombs."[66] This description had a particularly local reference, certainly not lost on those members of the Boston elite who had opposed recent plans for burials in church crypts. Dearborn, the idealist, hoped to make his era a new golden age; he emphasized the idea of the quest for new heights of civilization rather than that of stagnation preceding demise by founding urban institutions expressive of a new sense of past in a naturalistic context.

For that reason, Dearborn and his contemporaries looked to the best aspects of ancient civilizations for models to emulate or recycle in their new Arcadian age. He sought inspiration for a cemetery from the Elysian Fields, where Greeks "supposed the souls of the virtuous and illustrious retired after death and roamed through bowers, forever green, and over meadows spangled with flowers and refreshed by perennial streams." Another precedent was the Athenian Ceramicus (*Kerameikos*) outside the Dipylon gate; Dearborn's reference to it suggests that in planning Mount Auburn, Bostonians were compensating for the loss of the entire Bunker Hill battlefield, previously equated with the Ceramicus. Dearborn described the Ceramicus as "a pleasant resort for all who wished to borrow inspiration to noble deeds." (Fig. 4.17.) It was a place of commemoration, where "the illustrious men, who had either died in the service of their country or were thought deserving of the most distinguished honors" were buried. The Ceramicus was a pastoral "public promenade" for Athenians. There, Plato established his Academy and carried on philosophical discussions. To Bostonians, who named their private library the Athenaeum and called their city the "Athens of America," this analogy bore particular significance.[67]

Alexander Everett also cited classical public gardens as models for Bostonians in their attempt to fashion a pastoral landscape of burial and commemoration. According to Everett, the Ceramicus was an exemplary "public garden" outside the walls of the city and "near the spot appropriated to the sepulchers of distinguished men." It was a place of education. Aristotle's Lyceum was "another Athenian garden of the same description."[68] This analogy struck a particular chord with Bigelow and Everett's other Harvard classmates, who for decades had informally used Sweet Auburn, the estate destined to become Mount Auburn, as a similar scholarly retreat, albeit without the notable graves. Intent on modeling the new nation and its institutions on such classical examples, they naturally chose to preserve, refine, and extend the analogy of place at Sweet Auburn in such a manner.

As the French visitor Gustave de Beaumont observed after he and Alexis de Tocqueville dined with Alexander Everett and his friends on September 16, 1831, Boston's elite was preoccupied with shaping urban aesthetics; as heirs of the Puritans, however, they wanted their art and architecture to be useful and morally meaningful.[69] Everett hoped that the funeral ground of Mount Auburn, "consecrated to the memory of the patriots and heroes of the Revolution," would be the first of many such institutions and would inspire the reform of Mount Vernon with its "central situation in the Union, natural picturesque beauties, and noble position upon the banks of one of the finest rivers in the world." Everett proposed erecting an imposing monument to Washington at Mount Vernon similar to the one planned for Mount Auburn. "Towering majestically above the clumps of trees that adorn the grounds," it would be visible from a distance by "citizens as they ascended the river to visit the place." Mount Vernon, with commemoration of other founding fathers, would then become "a sort of sacred ground, like the plains of Elis in ancient Greece, where the Olympic games were celebrated.[70]

Planned from the start as prototype for other commemorative landscapes, Mount Auburn was to be exemplary. Like Boston itself when it was first founded by the Puritans, Mount Auburn would be "a city on a hill." It would be "one of the chief ornaments of the neighborhood . . . superior in its natural advantages of position to the famous sepulchral grounds of the ancient world." Everett predicted that "unless the sons of the Pilgrims should degenerate from their fathers, MOUNT AUBURN will hereafter record examples . . . of public and private virtue" that would offer lessons to the entire nation. Based on the model of ancient Greece, the place would become catalyst for "high national spirit," "public virtue," and fine arts worthy of a durable republic.[71] But Mount Auburn would, at the same time and in the short term, help to solve more practical problems of public health, cultural differences, and social factionalism evident in the burial controversy of 1823 in Boston.

5

An American Sensibility to Melancholy

So live, that when thy summons comes to join
The innumerable caravan, which moves
To that mysterious realm, where each shall
take
His chamber in the silent halls of death,
Thou go not like the quarry-slave at night,
Scourged to his dungeon, but, sustained and
soothed,
By an unfaltering trust, approach thy grave,
Like one who wraps the drapery of his couch
About him, and lies down to pleasant dreams.
—William Cullen Bryant, "Thanatopsis"
(1817)

As PURITANISM DECLINED in both New and Old England, melancholy gradually became the ideal emotional response recommended by ministers to their congregations and readers, replacing Calvinistic fears of man's postmortem fate. In 1714, Increase Mather told his congregation that the flight of the saved soul to heaven "should make the Believer long for death." Likewise, still recognizing the spiritual utility of certain fears, Leonard Hoar declared it "an error in the saints and people of God to be so much affrighted at death and to goe so mournfully out of this world." Excessive fear might be a sign of perdition, but cessation of doubt was no longer false assurance. Intense introspection on mortality served as a new sort of spiritual exercise, recommended by none other than Milton. According to David Stannard, "a tumultuous and exalted depression became their psychological ideal, the symbol and expression of their ultimate Salvation. This symbol suffered the fate so common to religious symbols, of being sought for and treasured as an end in itself . . . without regard for the . . . original inner meaning that it had possessed."[1] Hence, a predisposition to melancholy existed among descendants of Puritans even before appearing among other American colonists, especially the An-

Fig. 5.1. Jefferson's graveyard at Monticello, postcard view, ca. 1900.

glicans; it provided a major theme during the flowering of New England's material and literary culture in the first half of the nineteenth century.

Yet as with other cultural trends imported by New Englanders, melancholy did not become a major theme until decades after it flourished in the Old World. Unlike their English cousins, New Englanders only began shaping landscapes to commemorate a common past or to serve as catalysts for melancholy in the nineteenth century. They were fully aware of the powers of the built environment to epitomize larger ideals, however.

An early evidence of a new consciousness linking ideas of death and nature and emphasizing individual contemplation of those ideas appeared during the Revolutionary era, when Americans adopted the taste for melancholy of the Graveyard Poets and for the pastoral landscape gardening and commemorative monuments of Whiggish English estates. Despite nonimportation of commodities, American rebellion against British imperialism did not impede exposure to and acceptance of new cultural trends that ran counter to the Tory "establishment." Robert Blair's *The Grave* and Thomas Gray's *Elegy Written in a Country Churchyard* both appeared in popular editions from American publishers in 1771, 1773, and repeatedly thereafter. In fact, Whiggish sentimentalism and the English style of landscape gardening were considered on both sides of the Atlantic a counter-cultural response to Tory policy, like the Stamp Act, according to Arthur O. Lovejoy. The political significance of the aesthetics of melancholy thus helped spread the seeds of romanticism among American patriots. American leaders at the turn of the nineteenth century knew of the tastes of their Parliamentary allies for romantic gardens and monuments, which epitomized "a sort of party issue" displaying new political principles, faith in natural law, and an enlightened worldview.[2]

English garden design influenced Thomas Jefferson's 1771 plans for a romantic landscape at Monticello. Jefferson considered organizing his garden around a burial site and monuments in "some unfrequented vale in the park, where is 'no sound to break the stillness but a brook, that bubbling winds among the weeds; no mark of any human shape that had been there, unless the skeleton of some poor wretch, who sought the place out to despair and die in.' " Jefferson wrote, "Let it be among the ancient and venerable oaks; intersperse some gloomy evergreens" with "a small Gothic temple of antique appearance," illuminated at night by a dim lamp, a mausoleum to contain urns and inscriptions, and a pyramid of "rough rockstone" over the grave of "a favourite and faithful servant." Thinking of building into his landscape the symbolic contrasts between life and death, the present and the past represented by contrasts between secluded lawn, sheltering woods, vista, and panorama, Jefferson pondered whether "a view of the neighboring town would have a good effect." In 1773, he buried his best friend,

Dabney Carr, under a large elm where they had often read together; he inscribed the gravestone with a verse from the *Iliad* paraphrased by Alexander Pope:

> If in the melancholy shades below,
> The flames of friends and lovers cease to glow,
> Yet mine shall sacred last; mine undecayed
> Burn on through death and animate my shade.

In 1808, Jefferson planted a double line of weeping willows around the site of his own intended burial place. Although most of Jefferson's intentions to lay out his property in the English fashion were never realized, these plans still reveal the influence and resonance of British Whiggish sentimentality in revolutionary America.[3] (Fig. 5.1.)

Contemporaneously, themes of melancholy appeared in the writings of Philip Freneau and Charles Brockden Brown, labeled by Henry F. May "the leading radical intellectuals" of the revolutionary and Federal periods.[4] Freneau introduced the new nation to the imagery of sacred groves, the possibility of reattaining Eden through Nature, and the sublime significance of ruins; however, as in the case of Jefferson's romantic dreams for Monticello, the time was not entirely ripe for a wholehearted American espousal of such new aesthetics. Freneau's generation began to reject the old images of death, especially as represented in the dismal landscape of traditional graveyards. In "The House of Night" (1786), Freneau recounts the deathbed scene of Death personified, ending on a note of optimism with the light of dawn, a questioning of old pessimism, a new resolve:

> What is this Death, ye deep read sophists,
> say?—
> Death is no more than one unceasing change;
> New forms arise, while other forms decay,
> Yet all of Life throughout creation's range . . .
>
> When Nature bids thee from the world retire,
> With joy thy lodging leave, a fated guest;
> In Paradise, the land of thy desire,
> Existing always, always to be blest.[5]

Literary celebration of melancholy à la Freneau was rare during the Federal period; Fred Lewis Pattee calls "The House of Night" "the first distinctly romantic note heard in America."[6] It reflected new notions about both death and human history that would spread in the following decades.

Fig. 5.2. Willow-tree-and-urn motif on slate gravestone, ca. 1810, eastern Massachusetts, photograph by Alan Ward, 1982.

Fig. 5.3. Mourning picture inscribed "To the Memory of Susan K. White . . . 1833," with other names added in 1843 and 1848, engraving and watercolor.

At the end of the eighteenth century, material manifestations of naturalism and sentimentalism recurred in the form of the willow-tree-and-urn motif on gravestones and mourning pictures whose iconography was borrowed from the pastoral commemoration of the English garden. Willows and urns began to replace death's-heads and cherubs on gravestones in the last decades of the eighteenth century, just as white marble won favor over the more sober gray slate associated with Puritanism and the words "in memory of" replaced the blunter "here lies the body" or "*memento mori.*" The willow-and-urn motif symbolized secular, commemorative burial in a natural setting, as rare in colonial America as in England. (Fig. 5.2.) The combination of monument with melancholy tree was of modern origin but compatible with neoclassical taste.

The weeping willow (*Salix babylonica*) gained popularity after its introduction in the West from its native China in the 1730s. Alexander Pope planted one in his elegaic gardens at Twickenham; Masons carried willow branches and those of the acacia, a similar plant, at funerals. Folklore held that the willow dispelled evil, purified, and facilitated contact with the spiritual world. Its natural qualities predisposed it for symbolic usage. The *New England Farmer* reported in 1827 that in addition to the pensive drooping branches, "it weeps little drops of water . . . like fallen tears upon the leaves."[7] As one of the first trees to become green in spring and the last to shed its leaves even in the cold New England climate, it represented persistent life. Its easy regeneration from cuttings further intimated immortality.

English aesthetic theorists like Archibald Alison helped popularize the weeping willow because of its emotional associations. Alison considered it both melancholy and conducive to creation of a "beautiful" landscape. It formed a fine contrast with the oak in garden compositions as in mourning pictures. The oak bore even older funerary associations from Germanic lands, where folklore emphasized its powers against evil. The oak represented temporal human strength and the male family head. Depicted with trunk and branches severed, as on many nineteenth-century funerary monuments, it stood for the end of a family line. Many considered the willow more fitting for funerary planting than the oak, however, for functional reasons. William Prince, head of the Linnaean Botanical Gardens in Flushing, New York, reminded American horticulturists in 1828 that the extensive root system of *Salix babylonica* served to dry the soil in graveyards or to mark isolated tombs.[8]

This iconography recurred in mourning pictures popular through the early nineteenth century. These standardized compositions included weeping willows, "venerable" oaks, urns, and melancholy funerary landscape peopled by mourners or simply by a lone, grieving woman. (Figs. 5.3, 4.) Usually there were distant views of the landscape of the living left behind, as in the past, seen across symbolically reflective streams or ponds. The popularity of these images indicated a new, secularized, nondenominational spirituality tempered by liberal religion, the rise of affective individualism, and the beginnings of the domestication of death. Some even served more public purposes of patriotism. Mourning pictures appeared again and again, copied and interpreted in different media and in all parts of the nation—in German and Dutch Protestant households in Pennsylvania and New York, among French Huguenots, in Calvinist-Reformed homes in the Carolinas, and especially in both orthodox and liberal Presbyterian, Congregational, and Unitarian homes in New England. The willow-tree-and-urn motif was common in ordinary households for over half a century—on decorative panels over mirrors, as furniture ornamentation in silhouette or low relief, and in miniature on lockets, rings, and other jewelry pieces. Mourning scenes on cotton fabric and on wallpaper memorialized Washington, Franklin, Lafayette, Commodore Perry, and other national heroes. Snuffboxes, bellows, andirons, and, appropriately, handkerchiefs bore the conventional design. English Staffordshire and Liverpool dish-

Fig. 5.4. Mourning picture inscribed "Sacred to the Memory of Sarah, wife of James Merry . . . 1836," engraving and watercolor.

ware manufacturers turned out mourning patterns commemorating the patriots' deaths for the American market. Mourning pictures in various media introduced Americans of all classes to the visual, symbolic conventions of melancholy and pastoralism associated with eighteenth-century English art, literature, and garden design. Description of a similar scene appeared in the song "Sing All a Green Willow" from *Shakespeare's Dramatic Songs to all his Dramas,* a volume of music published in London in 1815 and imported in quantity by Americans, to be found even in Jefferson's Monticello library.

The landscape of mourning pictures was imaginary, stylized, symbolic, and strangely without precedent in existing American burial places. These pictures popularized the composition of Sir Joshua Reynold's last painting, *Et in Arcadia Ego* (1769), but replaced shepherds with female figures sadly musing over a funerary urn in a romantic setting; they introduced ordinary Americans, who did not read theories of landscape taste, to the melancholy and picturesque elements of English gardens. The focal point and constant element in the composition is the funerary monument of neoclassical form—either urn, squat obelisk or pyramid raised on a base, or sarcophagus—but rarely the traditional, flat, colonial style. When slab gravestones did appear in the pictures, they were secondary parts of the composition.

The urn was simply symbolic of death without specific reference to cremation, which would not become an issue of discussion for another half-century.[9] The central monument bore the name of a dead family member or friend, dates of birth and death, and often a bit of sentimental verse, further emphasizing the mourning picture's literary roots, similar to those of English gardens. The setting was usually a pastoral, rolling terrain. A panoramic or distant view of a town or at least of a church or country house could usually be seen to one side of the monument. Occasionally the burial place was set aside or isolated in the foreground by bodies of water—a stream, river, or pond—which defined landscape variety or heightened vistas just as water bodies did in English landscapes. Isolation of the monument in the foreground also symbolized the present and stressed the finality of death. Such mourning pictures suggested landscape elements later used at Mount Auburn and other American "rural" cemeteries.

According to Philippe Ariès, mourning pictures played the role of portable tomb or memorial adaptable to the mobility of the United States.[10] Even though such artifacts of melancholy did not substitute for the creation of secure, permanent burial places that would also be commemorative, they certainly helped to spread the demand for better funerary landscapes. The desire for material commemoration was growing, although most burials remained in settings quite unlike the romantic ideal. The vogue for mourning pictures preceded by decades of heyday of placing elaborate family monuments in pastoral cemeteries, and it conditioned public tastes to favor burial reform in order to make the ideal real.

The desire to ensure perpetuity of graves dates from the period immediately after the Revolution, when impermanency of property worried many Americans. James Hillhouse, a prominent New Haven citizen and sponsor of many public improvements, cited this as the reason for creation in 1796 of the New Burying Ground just north of the town and Yale College. Yellow fever had ravaged the city in 1794 and 1795, but Hillhouse did not refer to pubic health in documents he issued to launch the new burial institution. Although most New Englanders accepted burial in common burial grounds rather than in private graveyards, Hillhouse conceived of his plan for the New Burying Ground with permanent family lots defined in a larger landscape after he realized the insecurity of graves on private property when visiting a former family estate. Along with house and fields, "the family burying ground went with the rest into the hands of strangers, and the descendants had no control over the graves of their relatives and ancestors, which, though honorably protected in this instance, were liable, in other hands, to be neglected, injured, or entirely obliterated in the progress of time." To be sure, in the case of graveyards on private estates like Jefferson's Monticello, skillful legal arrangements might ensure the perpetuity of graves and the coherence of that portion of the property in perpetuity, but such instances were rare. Hillhouse desired to create "a sacred and inviolable burial place" for his own and other New Haven families.[11]

By 1796, New Haven's old common graveyard was nearly full and would either have to be extended onto valuable land in the center of the prospering commercial city, which was already "overbuilt," or replaced by a new site. Hillhouse wanted to make a new burial place "larger, better arranged for the accommodation of families, and by its retired situation, better calculated to impress the mind with a solemnity becoming the repository of the dead." The Yale divine Timothy Dwight thought that the old location "in the current of daily intercourse" made the graveyard "too familiar to the eye to have any beneficial effect on the heart." Public visibility degraded it "into a mere common object." Even the orthodox Congregationalist Dwight wanted a new burial place to be "a solemn object to man, a source of useful instruction and desirable impressions" rather than a reminder of grim, medieval notions of death.[12] Such a site would have plantings, unlike old New England graveyards, and sufficient space for families to erect commemorative monuments.

Removal of the burial place from the city's center conformed to principles articulated by the British aesthetic theorist Archibald Alison in 1790. Alison wrote that "The seasons of care, of grief, or of business, have other occupations, and destroy, for the time at least, our sensibility to the beautiful or the sublime, in the same proportion that they produce a state of mind unfavorable to the indulgence of imagination."[13] Whether or not they were familiar with Alison's views, Hillhouse and Dwight sensed the incongruity of the old burial site with the escalating activity at the center of their prosperous port city. They wanted to create a place conducive to melancholy in a more natural setting where their fellow citizens might plant weeping willows over neoclassical funerary monuments in imitation of the landscapes of mourning pictures. Such a place had no precedent in America; although the Dissenters' Bunhill Fields near London provided one modern example of an incorporated, extramural burial ground with freehold family plots, even it did not reflect the combination of neoclassical and melancholy aesthetics Hillhouse envisioned for the New Burying Ground.

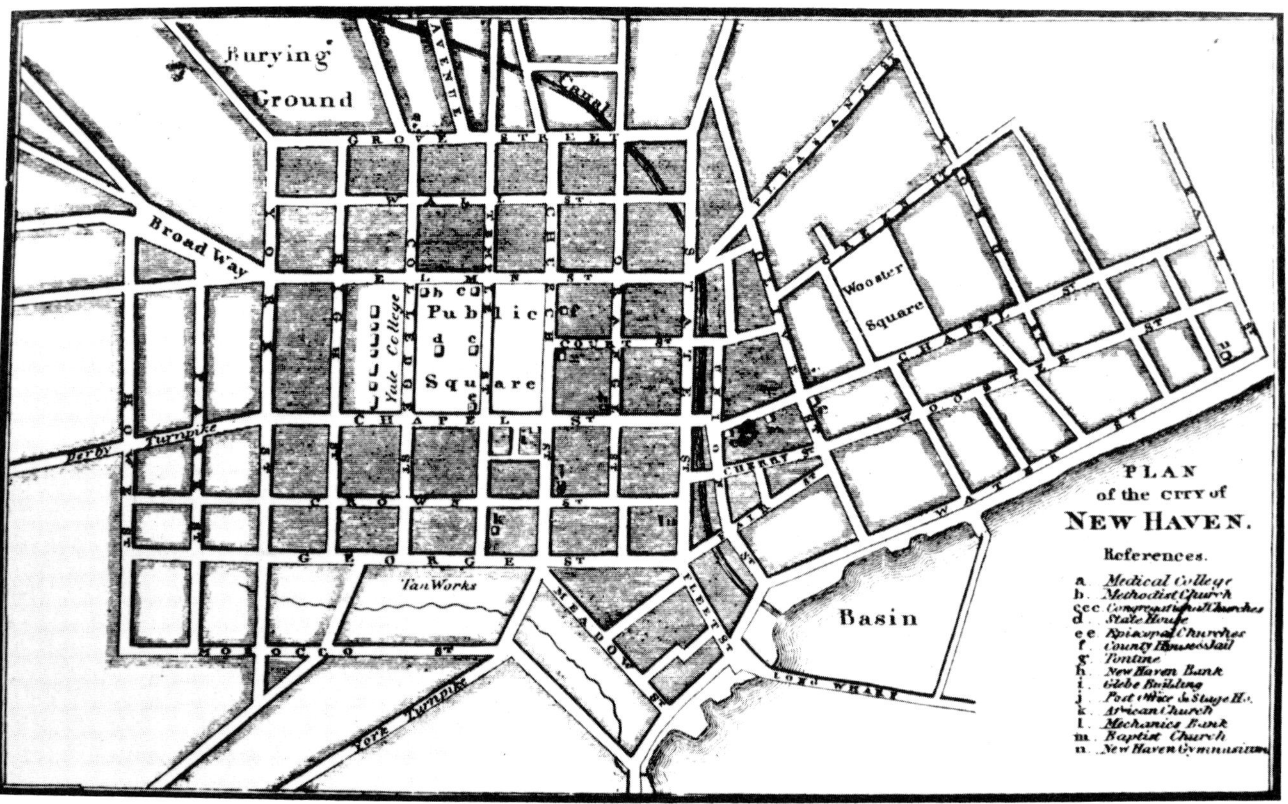

Fig. 5.5. New Haven, map of the town showing location of the New Burying Ground, 1837.

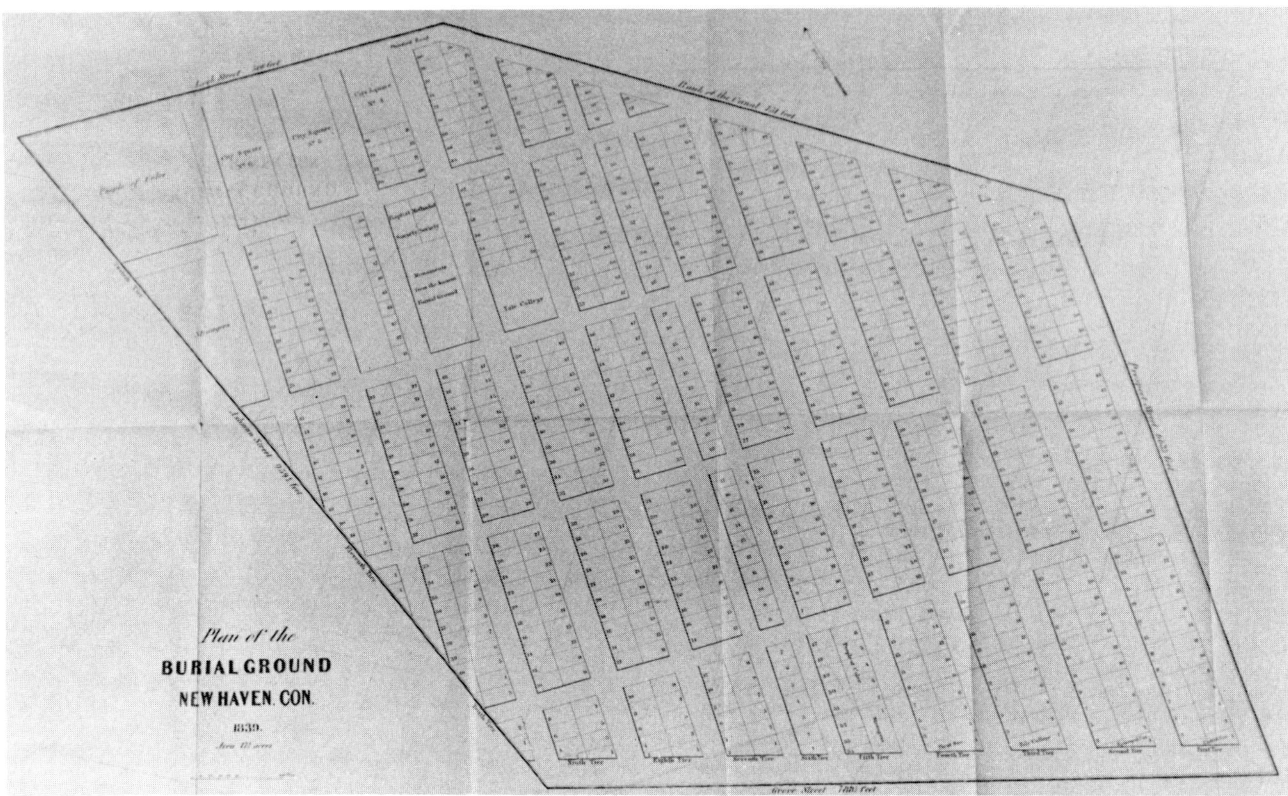

Fig. 5.6. New Haven's New Burying Ground, grid plan, engraving.

Hillhouse also wanted to secularize his city's burials in the spirit of his age, which called for separation of church and state. In contrast to those in most New England towns, the old graveyard in New Haven was not a purely civic place, because the original settlers, despite their Puritanism, "following the custom of their native country, buried their dead in a Church-yard," directly next to the first meetinghouse on the green or public square in the center of town. The Reverend Dwight later observed, "While the Romish apprehension concerning consecrated burial-places and concerning particular advantages supposed at the resurrection to attend those who are interred in them remained, this location of burial-grounds seems to have been not unnatural. But since, this apprehension has been perceived by common sense to be groundless and ridiculous, the impropriety of such a location forces itself upon every mind."[14] (Fig. 5.5.)

Hillhouse persuaded thirty-one leading New Haven citizens to subscribe $14 each for the privilege of choosing one of the first 284 family lots, each measuring 18′ by 32′ or 576 square feet in area, large enough for burial of several generations. The Connecticut legislature granted an act of incorporation to the Proprietors of the New Burying Ground in October of 1797, making an institution independent of the city. It was the first private corporation of its kind in the nation. The ten-acre graveyard contained essentially private space, governed by rules and regulations made by a board elected by proprietors of lots; it was not municipal like previous New England burying grounds. The Board possessed power to sell plots, at cost and not for profit, again in contrast to other corporations of the period, which were chartered for internal improvements but were profit-making ventures even if they provided amenities like bridges and turnpikes for public use. Proprietors of plots, with one vote each in the corporation, could tax themselves for maintenance and improvements on the entire burying ground; the body corporate and individual family lots of freeholds, however, remained exempt from payment of property taxes.

Professor Josiah Meigs of Yale surveyed and laid out the landscape of the New Burying Ground. Workers rolled and leveled the already flat terrain to permit imposition of a highly rational geometric symmetry with roads eighteen feet and twenty-four feet wide arranged in a grid of parallelograms, each thirty-five feet by sixty-four feet. (Fig. 5.6.) Hillhouse further rationalized the plan with a numbering system to permit keeping of accurate burial records and an accounting of property holdings. The landscape and institution were the products of the same rational mind-set revealed in the writing of the Constitution a decade before and in the laying of the gridded land survey in the Northwest Territory after 1785. One visitor was struck by the segmentation of the orderly design of the "square plot, of large extent, divided by smooth walks into small squares. These squares are again divided by railings into still smaller squares, and these again into squares so minute as to be reasonably occupied by two families; for the *square* not being lost sight of for a moment, and the smallest square being too large for the generality of families, no choice is left but to divide this smallest square into half squares."[15]

The landscape plan reflected the order and regularity of New Haven itself, unusual among New England towns for its square-grid arrangement. The New Burying Ground represented the town in miniature. Unlike previous graveyards, its road system permitted new hearses and carriages to enter the premises to deliver coffins and mourners in close proximity to graves. Fences, mostly made of wood, defined property lines as they did around house lots in town. Their horizontal railings were painted white, in contrast to black vertical posts. Hillhouse, whose street tree planting gave New Haven the reputation of a City of Elms, put fast-growing, columnar Lombardy poplars, expected "to grow with the least irregularity possible," in rows along roads in the burying ground. The Lombardy poplar had only recently been introduced into the United States and was much in vogue. These trees, along with the regularity of tidy roads and fences, made the place quite different visually from traditional, barren and chaotic graveyards in the region. Edward Kendall observed that Hillhouse undertook "the building of a new and entire city, in the immediate rear of the old one. He builds his houses of stone, in a very solid and costly manner; and has marked out the area of a spacious square, in which are to be ornamental plantations"; Hillhouse's plantings were formal, however, rather than naturalistic or picturesque.[16] The New Burying Ground was symbolically and aesthetically urban.

Dwight praised the plentiful space of family lots precisely because it precluded "use of vaults by taking away every inducement to build them." Dwight observed that "These melancholy and disgusting mansions seem not to have been dictated by nature and certainly not approved by good sense. Their salubrity is questionable; and the impression left by them on the mind transcends the bounds of mourning and sorrow, and borders, at least, upon loathing." Following the English example, association of earthen burial with lower-class status made entombment increasingly more popular with elite Americans than earthen burial. Construction of family tombs—whether subterranean chambers or shafts or above-ground rooms mounded over with turf—increased in New England at the end of the eighteenth century, perhaps indicating the desire for stronger family cohesion as communities became more complex, but more probably in response to crowding of burials into places not large enough to absorb the population growth. Proliferation of tombs in old New England graveyards resulted from the ever-diminishing space for individual graves. If family members wanted to remain together after death, tomb building was often the only way to ensure it. Dwight sanctioned the relatively new desire of families to be buried together as natural, and he approved of the way in which the New Burying Ground guaranteed it.[17]

Hillhouse considered the New Burying Ground semipublic; and the Board donated one lot to Yale College, one to each of the local "Ecclesiastical Societies" (Methodist, Baptist, and others), one for burial of strangers, three to the poor who could not afford family lots or were not members of local congregations, and one to "people of color." (Fig. 5.7.) Again, in 1800, the corporation deeded a large triangular lot to the town for common use, a second for strangers, and another for blacks. A

Fig. 5.7. Yale College lot, New Haven's New Burying Ground, photograph by Alan Ward, 1979.

public-spiritedness tempered exclusivity in the new burial institution, although a certain spatial distinction of status existed, unlike in the old graveyard.[18]

Perhaps the New Burying Ground was too innovative in the concepts it epitomized. New Haven families, faced with buying private burial space priced at $5 and $10 per lot, were slow to accept the system. By 1800, less than half of the lots were sold; and the corporation was $16,000 in debt. Hillhouse covered expenses by purchasing 155 unsold lots himself. For fifteen years, he personally retained control over the burying ground; few landscape improvements were made, due to lack of funds. Only in 1814, when all lots were sold, did the Board add eight more acres to the grounds. New Haven citizens continued to use the old graveyard on the central green, which was not officially closed until 1820, when it was finally judged "in a condition of total neglect and going to ruin in a manner deemed inconsistent with the religious and moral sense of this community and indicating a want of decent respect for the memory of the dead."[19]

By 1814, half of the fast-growing poplars originally planted by Hillhouse had reached maturity and were dying and unsightly. They were removed and not replaced. Only a few weeping willows planted by proprietors evidenced a nascent romanticism. There remained unfortunate similarities between the New Buying Ground and New England's traditional landscapes of death during this period, especially after many old colonial gravestones had been moved there in 1820 from the old graveyard on the common, causing crowding and increasing the number of two-dimensional vertical head and foot stones. Many proprietors continued to erect such stones, albeit favoring a new material—white marble, occasionally imported from Italy. The new vogue for the simple obelisk only added to the linearity and formality of the place. The monuments were "universally" aligned on lots, permitting the crowding of many stones together.[20]

Although certain characteristics of the New Burying Ground—perpetuity of family freehold plots, a state charter for an eleemosynary corporation, and plantings in a designed landscape—offered precedents for the creation of Mount Auburn Cemetery in 1831, the New Burying Ground was quite different aesthetically from the "rural" cemeteries that Americans would found in the decades to come. Still, Dwight rightly declared the New Burying Ground "altogether a singularity in the world." He took many American and foreign visitors there, "not one of whom had ever seen or heard of any thing of similar nature." He was confident that the example of the place would "extensively diffuse a new sense of propriety in disposing of the remains of the deceased."[21] Indeed, one wonders whether a Frenchman might have visited and returned home to insist that his countrymen stop theorizing about burial reform and make Père Lachaise, usually credited with being the first modern cemetery. The New Burying Ground actually created a "cult of ancestors" while the French were still debating how they could do just that as a means of stabilizing society, and it predated the Parisian cemetery by seven years.

Founders of the New Burying Ground meant it to be an institution of history, a repository for their past, a place for commemoration of lives lived rather than a traditional reminder of the final fact of death that displayed only the old message of *memento mori*. Dwight bragged that there, "an exquisite taste for propriety is discovered in every thing belonging to it, exhibiting a regard for the dead, reverential but not ostentatious, and happily fitted to influence the views and feelings of succeeding generations."[22] Hillhouse wanted to make memory visible, to perpetuate a sense of the past into the future, especially in terms of family; until the 1820s, however, only a few of his fellow citizens were ready to follow his lead. Although Hillhouse's generation, that of the Founding Fathers, realized the importance of fostering a sense of their all-too-short national past as a foundation of a strong republic, little was done in material terms. Only in the next generation did a taste for private as well as public commemoration really flourish.

New Haven residents did not fully accept their New Burying Ground until the third decade of the nineteenth century; likewise, the debate over the poor condition of Washington's tomb did not become earnest until the 1820s. By then, a commemorative consciousness dominated the national culture, stirred by the deaths of the last Founding Fathers, feeding the popularity of mourning pictures, and spreading the cult of the melancholy in literature, art, and landscape. In the process, Americans domesticated romanticism from abroad and reinterpreted it to meet personal as well as national needs.

Washington Irving's publication of *The Sketch Book of Geoffrey Crayon, Gent.* (1819–20) cultivated an American romanticism. Irving loved the picturesque and popularized the taste for it among Americans with accounts of travel in the English countryside. He united diverse strains of romanticism, drawing on British aesthetic theorists, Sir Walter Scott, and his friend Washington Allston, the Boston painter and poet. Irving found in "the fondness for rural life among the higher classes of the English . . . a great salutary effect upon the national character." A "moral feeling" pervaded English scenery, "associated in the mind with ideas of order, of quiet, of sober, well-established principles, of hoary usage and reverend custom"—in sum, the sense of a long and stable past, which America seemed to lack but Irving intended to tap and reinterpret, convincing his countrymen that they shared in it too. Irving believed that Americans could develop their own national character by drawing from the best of their British heritage—forms associated with the common life of Englishmen untainted by pomp and circumstance.[23]

For Irving, English country churchyards, without "haughty" memorials "which human pride had erected over its kindred dust," epitomized all that was good in English culture. There, rural funerals still evidenced beautiful and simple ancient customs, the "remains of some of the rites of the primitive church," if not of some "still higher antiquity, having been observed among the Greeks and Romans" in "the olden time." Such folkways were like ruins, "vestiges and reminders of a former age and a common past" that Americans should rightly share. They were purer and more prototypically democratic than medieval or more recent deathways. (Figs. 5.8, 9.) They were alternatives to the formalities of British high culture, rejected alike by Puritans and Revolutionaries and represented by the "mournful magnificence" of

Figs. 5.8., 5.9. Saint Giles churchyard, Stoke Poges, inspiration for Thomas Gray's "Elegy," postcard photographs, ca. 1900.

Westminster Abbey, "teaching no moral but the futility of that pride which hopes still to exact homage in its ashes and to live in an inscription." Irving declared Death the great democratizer, the ultimate revolutionary: "the equality of the grave . . . brings down the oppressor to the level of the oppressed." Westminster Abbey was a place of contradictions, Death's "great shadowy palace, where he sits in state, mocking at the relics of human glory and spreading dust and forgetfulness on the monuments of princes."[24]

In contrast, Irving aimed to popularize among Americans the simple graces of the English country churchyard. He praised "the rich vein of melancholy" running through the English character and giving it "some of its most touching and ennobling graces," traits epitomized in the burial traditions of common Englishmen. (Fig. 5.10.) He encouraged Americans to adopt those best features of their cultural heritage. Nostalgia and "sweet-souled melancholy" permeate Irving's prose in his celebration of rural scenes as catalysts for personal, sentimental memory. He repeated John Evelyn's belief that plants, "natural hieroglyphics of our fugitive, umbratile, anxious, and transitory life," were important additions to burial places; he urged Americans to start placing them in their burial grounds, to transform their graveyards from places "of disgust and dismay" to attractive sites of "sorrow and meditation."[25]

Conditions of most American burial grounds were much different from this romantic ideal, and Irving and his contemporaries recoiled from consideration of the decay of death. Calvinist ministers might still admonish their congregations to gaze into the grave to contemplate fate, to heed the lesson of *memento mori;* nevertheless, Irving admitted, "there is a dismal process going on in the grave, ere dust can return to its kindred dust, which the imagination shrinks from contemplating; and we seek still to think of the form we have loved

Fig. 5.10. Romantic English churchyard, engraving from *Gleason's Pictorial.*

with those refined associations which it awakened when blooming before us in youth and beauty." Irving rejected the "unlucky yew" and the "mournful cypress" along with the old grim iconography of death. He wondered why men sought "to clothe death with unnecessary terrors and to spread horrors round the tomb of those we love."[26]

Irving suggested burial reform in order to bolster a sense of national heritage in personal terms through perpetuation of memories. He counseled his readers to "go to the grave of buried love and meditate." He agreed with English and French romantics that "the natural effect of sorrow over the dead is to refine and elevate the mind." Melancholy as a source of a purified, natural culture was to be encouraged in every way possible. Creation of naturalistic burial places would permit Americans to engage in the "pleasures of melancholy, uplifting sentiments to improve the national character."[27]

Irving helped to spread English "rural" taste in the United States, and he fomented the desire for picturesque burial landscapes that would eventually result in creation of Mount Auburn and other pastoral cemeteries. Nature would "soften the horrors of the tomb," in Irving's words, "beguile the mind from brooding over the disgraces of perishing mortality," and "associate the memory of the deceased with the most delicate and beautiful objects . . . sweet-scented evergreens and flowers." Irving seemed to be paraphrasing the many recent French theories of burial reform by urging that "the grave should be surrounded by everything that might inspire tenderness and veneration for the dead; or that might win the living to virtue."[28]

Even more influential than Irving in bringing melancholy romanticism to New England was William Cullen Bryant, a poet whose youth paralleled the experience of many New Englanders of his generation. The orthodox Calvinist women in his family nurtured Bryant on the lessons of John Calvin and the hymns of Isaac Watts, teaching him actively to think of death. He watched his younger sister die at home, but reacted much differently from a good Calvinist. He sought solace in the pleasant rural landscape of the Berkshire Mountains around him, indulging there in the "pleasures of melancholy" while reading *The Remains of Henry Kirke White*, edited by Robert Southey, and other poems of the English Graveyard School. Bryant's father, a religious liberal, encouraged his adolescent son's sentimentalism with gifts of books like Blair's *The Grave* and the works of Addison, Pope, Gray, Wordsworth, and Coleridge.[29] The young Bryant took up the pen himself, setting the imagery of mourning pictures to verse in messages of consolation to similarly melancholy young friends. His work might have remained highly personal and private had not his father sent it to Boston, where literati had just begun a periodical to encourage indigenous American literature and criticism.

In founding the *North American Review* in 1815, William Tudor created a forum to foster American writing, hoping to disprove British criticisms that America was dangerously lacking in art and literature. Its first volume declared that the American environment could provide the stuff of culture: "These hills and forest hold romance; why may not majestic spirits have haunted them of old just as surely as they haunted the forests and mountains of Europe. Our country is alive with romantic possibilities if only one will grasp them before it is too late!"[30] Tudor and his friends feared the truth of British warnings that lack of a civilization, after discarding that of the mother country, would endanger the fragile American republic. Romanticism, based in cultivation of individual sentiment and a sense of the local past, might stave off the deterioration of a rootless new society. Edward T. Channing, editor of the *North American Review*, therefore, was seeking just what the elder Bryant submitted to him in 1817.

When Professor Channing and his cousin, Richard Henry Dana, Senior, read Bryant's poem "Thanatopsis," they could hardly believe it had been written in the small town of Great Barrington in western Massachusetts. Dana exclaimed, "That was never written on this side of the water!" "Thanatopsis," meaning "meditations on death," reminded him of the Graveyard Poets and Wordsworth, whom the *North American Review* avidly defended against "severe and unjust criticisms" of a common foe, the Edinburgh Reviewers. Bryant treated themes of death and nature in a manner particularly appealing to Boston's

Unitarian intellectuals. "Thanatopsis" described death in secular, pantheistic terms as a final reunion of the individual with the insensate universe. As in Shaftesbury's philosophy, Nature replaced God; death became universal, a force more powerful and invincible than man. Death and Nature were sublime, yet stoical acceptance of inevitable natural processes replaced traditional fears. Reason tempered emotion in a modern response to death quite unlike that urged by the old Puritan preachers.[31]

The popularity of "Thanatopsis" and other poems by Bryant spread the taste for melancholy to many Americans, reaching beyond the intellectual elite already familiar with English romantic sources and settings. In his poem "The Burial-Place," written in 1818 and published in 1821, Bryant contrasted the ideal of the English rural churchyard with American burial grounds, finding the latter aesthetically inferior. Echoing Irving and English Graveyard Poets, Bryant praises the willows, woodbine, and ivy that "hide / The gleaming marble" in contrast to the "naked rows of graves" surrounded by "coarse grass, between" that "shoots up its dull green spikes, and in the wind / Hisses." He delights in the power of resurgent Nature, which "rebuking the neglect of man, / Plants often, by the ancient mossy stone, / The brier rose."[32] Pantheism dominates Bryant's melancholy; and, in the same spirit as Irving, Bryant glorifies the English churchyard with the nostalgia of one who loves ideas symbolic of a common past absent in the present. Implicit in Bryant's celebration of rural burials in England is the suggestion of aesthetic reform of American burial grounds. Following the example of Wordsworth, Bryant encourages creation of naturalistic burial landscapes. He elaborates on this theme in later poems: "A Hymn to Death" (1820), "The Old Man's Funeral" (1824), and "The Two Graves" (1826).

Bryant's notions about death expressed poetically bridged a gap between the sterner outlook on the hereafter learned from a Calvinist parent, the liberal belief in the naturalness of death, and the expectation of universal salvation that was growing in his generation in New England and especially resonant in Unitarianism. His attitude toward death was shared by many of his contemporaries; Jacob Bigelow, for instance, expressed his feelings of personal resignation in a letter to his sister in 1820, shortly after the sudden death from "lung fever" of his six-month-old son and firstborn, William Scollay. Bigelow called it "the first domestic calamity which has befallen our house" and "our earliest discipline—how soon others are in reserve for us is only known to Providence." He concluded in a stoical manner, "Sufferings are the lot of humanity. Few years are all that remain for any of us."[33] Bigelow, John Quincy Adams, and Joseph Story wrote sentimental verse to assuage grief on the deaths of their children.

Melancholy had both public and private utility, according to both Irving and Bryant. Nature would help Americans create an indigenous culture and shape fitting places for private commemoration as the new nation strove to define a past in new terms. Through Irving and Bryant, the Wordsworthian notion of nature as moral force won American proponents. Bryant and the Boston literati domesticated Wordsworth, especially heeding his advance on burial reform. William Ellery Channing met Wordsworth in England. The poet read to the minister his passages on moral education to be gained from communion with Nature, and America's leading Unitarian returned home to Boston with messages on a naturalistic route to a new moral revival.[34] By the late 1820s, themes of death and nature in prose and poetry were juxtaposed in general circulation newspapers and magazines with local and national news and advertisements. Taste for the sentimental poets was far from limited to the readers of ladies' magazines and best-selling gift books.

One typical, romanticized account, "The Grave of a Mother," appeared in an 1823 issue of the *Boston Patriot and Daily Mercantile Advertiser*. An anonymous essayist wrote of "musing and wandering among the graves" one pleasant November evening as "the moon shone in her midnight meridian." Pausing over the grave of his mother, the visitor proudly noted that "no costly marble reared its head to tell that the slumberer beneath had once been great; it was marked by nought but the plain, simple stone . . . and the willow that had been planted by the hand of love." The natural setting only intensified the visitor's delight in melancholy: "Not a leaf stirred save some that were nipped by the pinching frosts of autumn from the trees, and as they slowly descended to earth, were silent monitors of the approach of winter and decay of man." The writer concluded, "There is something solemn and serious in the stillness of the graveyard; when the mind is made to feel its weakness, and to turn with reverence and admiration to that Being who governs the destinies of all."[35] The poem describes, however, an idealized landscape of mourning, certainly not the unpleasant conditions existing in the typical New England burying ground of that period, where few could plant the symbolic willow over the solitary graves of loved ones in a romantic, rural setting. Overuse of limited space would have prevented doing so even if the forces of religious conservatism had not protested pagan profanation of the common space of death.

For liberal and romantic Bostonians in the 1820s, discrepancies between this ideal and the unpleasant reality of urban graveyards were especially dramatic. One Bostonian observed, "Our burial places are in the cities crowded till they are full." Even in rural towns, it seemed that the only consideration in creating graveyards was "confining the remains of the departed to the smallest portion of earth that will hide them" in a place with few trees and inadequate enclosures. Graves in New England burial grounds were "indecently crowded together, and often, after a few years, disturbed."[36] Conditions were scarcely better, aesthetically, than in the churchyards of London and Paris.

Fig. 5.11. Pyramid monument designed by Solomon Willard for Franklin's parents' graves in Old Granary Burying Ground, Boston, photograph by Alan Ward, 1987.

Death had yet to be returned to the Garden, in spite of liberal religious denials of the universality of the wages of Adam's Fall. Still, idealism grew every year. The problem of the old burial grounds, therefore, was not entirely an urban phenomenon or the product of a crowded population. The landscapes and material culture of death inherited by the early nineteenth century generally reflected traditional, orthodox assumptions about death that did not include encouragement of optimism through an iconography or landscape representative of Eden, let alone Heaven. The exception was in the recent vogue for mourning pictures and the similar appearance of the willow-tree-and-urn motif on gravestones. But rapid urbanization and the advanced sensibilities of personal affection as well as sensitivities to unpleasant sights and smells, to say nothing of the latest trends in taste and liberal theology based on literary importation and cosmopolitanism, made the issue of burial reform for aesthetic and cultural reasons more pressing in Boston than in other major Atlantic seaboard cities or smaller New England towns.

William Tudor, Boston's chief cultural leader, described the new sensibility to the remains of the dead and attributed it largely to urbanization. During the colonial period, Tudor argued, burials were matters of community as well as personal concern because there was no separation between public and private life in the small, tight-knit, and traditional town. Family members remembered locations of burials of kin and neighbors in the common graveyard, even if there were no markers. Like oral lore, such knowledge often went unrecorded on stone or on paper, yet it was not forgotten. Indeed, gravestones appeared with increasing frequency precisely when New England towns became more complex, commercial, and diversified at the turn of the century, a time of community disintegration, social flux, and religious change.[37] But by Tudor's era, even the gravestones would not suffice for accurate marking, let alone the larger purpose of memory. Tudor wanted to promote public as well as private commemoration; he was representative of many members of the elite intent on the creation of culture in such terms.

Even more than New Haven's Hillhouse, leading Bostonians held "great objections to a place of sepulcher in a private field that in a few years" might pass into the hands of those who would "take no interest in preserving its sacred deposit from the plough." Articles in local newspapers bemoaned the lost, unidentified grave of Washington's mother in some Virginia field; but Bostonians realized that precise places of many of their own notable burials had been forgotten, even in the center of their city. For this reason, in 1827, a few citizens subscribed to erect a granite pyramid designed by Solomon Willard in the Old Granary Burying Ground over the graves of Benjamin

Fig. 5.12. Franklin's grave, Christ Church Burying Ground, a few blocks north of Independence Hall, Philadelphia, engraving, 1873.

Franklin's parents, Josiah and Abiah Folger. General Henry A. S. Dearborn delivered an address at a public ceremony on the laying of its cornerstone; and the governor and other state officials in attendance emphasized the importance of such a commemorative event.[38] (Fig. 5.11.)

The elder Franklins' funerary monument, then, was far grander than the plain, horizontal marble slab marking the grave of their illustrious son in a crowded Philadelphia burial ground. (Fig. 5.12.) Although throngs of visitors forged a path through surrounding graves to visit the Founding Father, many of them came away with negative judgments of the American character based on what they saw. One Frenchman observed, "They could have, after all, chosen for him a more honorable resting place than the obscure corner of an obscure graveyard, where his bones are thrown pele-mele with those of grossly ordinary men, under a stone that soon the weeds will hide from view." The unsightly grave proved "a cruel truth: no object in America is respected for the memories it engenders. The present generation is too occupied by business to have time to venerate historic images, or ancient services rendered, or great talents that are no more; there are enough other cares. Americans pick the fruits planted by their ancestors, or rather by their immediate predecessors," without giving them their commemoration due.[39]

Fig. 5.13. Dr. John Collins Warren, daguerrean portrait with skull, ca. 1850, courtesy of the Massachusetts General Hospital, Boston.

Certainly, the impulse to commemorate the dead was even less widespread in America than in France in the 1820s; and one of the first places it appeared was in Boston, impelling individual efforts to locate and mark the remains of long-deceased family members in the name of history. Boston burying grounds in the 1820s were places of greater chaos, disarray, and overuse than ever, but care to mark the precise locations of bodies in graves and tombs had never been great. Even the remains of the hero of the Battle of Bunker Hill, General Joseph Warren, were lost for a second time. His nephew, Dr. John Collins Warren, a leading citizen, had a difficult task in 1825 finding his illustrious ancestor's skeleton because its burial site in the Old Granary Burying Ground had been forgotten even within his family, and despite the elaborate, public obsequies accompanying the reinterment in 1776. (Fig. 5.13.) After a lengthy search, the younger Warren found his uncle's body in the family tomb of Judge George Richards Minot, a Federalist historian, only steps from his own new Beacon Hill residence. Dr. Warren identified it by the teeth and the fatal bullet hole behind the left ear. He moved the bones to crypts he recently had built in the basement of the new Saint Paul's Episcopal Church. Warren considered it a more permanent and appropriate resting place for the relics of such a hero, for his other, less distinguished family members, and for prominent Bostonians like himself—prosperous businessmen and civic leaders. Dr. Warren's solution to Boston's burial problems, however, was not for everybody; and the controversy that ensued revealed the complexity of conflicting interests and concerns preoccupying Bostonians as they tried to create new cultural forms expressive of their changing notions of death and community.

6

Grave Problems in Boston: The Burial Controversy of 1823

ಌ

The burying-place continues to be the most neglected spot in all the region, distinguished from other fields only by its leaning stones and the meanness of its enclosure, without a tree or shrub to take from it the air of utter desolation.

—William B. O. Peabody, "Mount Auburn Cemetery" (1831)

ಌ

The citizens of this metropolis buried their deceased friends in frequented parts of the city, crowding to the utmost capacity the spaces provided for them, and filling with sepulchres the cellars of their most central churches.

—Dr. Jacob Bigelow, *A History of the Cemetery of Mount Auburn* (1860)

PUBLIC HEALTH HAS TOO OFTEN been overemphasized as the major motivation for creation of Mount Auburn and other "rural" cemeteries. To be sure, burial reform preoccupied Bostonians and other urbanites in the 1820s and 1830s; however, the impulse to improve burial practices and places stemmed as much from changing sensibilities as from fears that retaining corpses in the midst of urban activities endangered health and precipitated epidemics. Throughout western civilizations at the turn of the century, the spread of gentility to larger portions of the population premised formulation of new criteria for urban cleanliness as well as new definitions of the proper and respectful ways to treat the dead. Many urbanites became sensitive to an unprecedented degree to the variety of foul smells that filled their environment; they began to consider repulsive the garbage and dirt that filled their streets. Burial reform was only one of many ways in which urbanites attempted to improve their surroundings.

The growing impulse to reform burial practices also reflected new attempts by municipalities to extend their powers over other corporate entities within their geographical limits. Attempts to regulate the practices of corporations as well as public services supplied by the municipality itself came

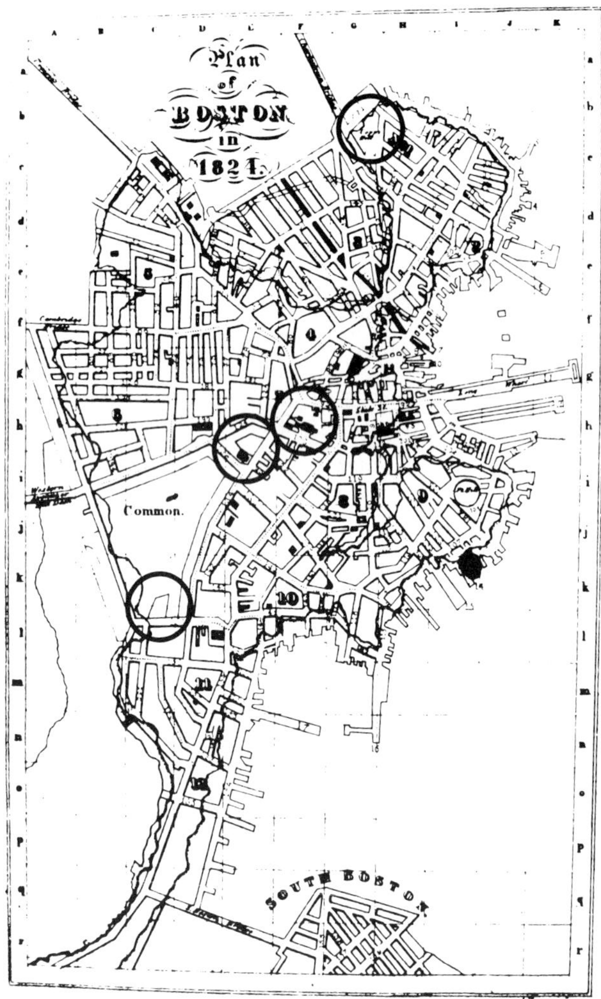

Fig. 6.1. Map of Boston on the Shawmut Peninsula with location of original burial grounds, engraving from Abel Bowen, 1824.

about of necessity at a time of crowding within old urban boundaries. Cities lacked adequate resources to create new solutions to the problem of too rapid growth and of strain placed on the traditional ways in which public services were supplied, and voluntary associations often filled the void. The 1823 burial controversy in Boston reveals the complexities underlying the reform impulse and illuminates many of the reasons for the founding of Mount Auburn, the nation's first "rural" cemetery, less than a decade later.

The tripling of Boston's population in the half-century following national independence created various environmental problems that confronted officials of the first city government installed in 1822. Portions of Boston were intensively overused. Little vacant land remained on the Shawmut Peninsula. (Fig. 6.1.) Sanitation and health were matters of growing concern, as were real estate values and the general appearance of the city. Reform-minded civic leaders, like James Hillhouse of New Haven two decades before, developed a dislike for narrow, treeless, dirty streets, so different from the winding rural roads near the country towns from which so many of them had only recently moved; they especially focused their attention on the old, chaotic burial grounds that formed pockets of wilderness amid escalating urban activity.

Filth and pollution of all sorts made cities in this era unpleasant if not actually unhealthy. The Boston Board of Health, created in 1799, had been slowly "correcting the atmosphere" for two decades with vague authorization to regulate the handling of fish and untanned hides, refuse sewers, privies, harbor dumping, and grave depth, in addition to establishing quarantines of ships suspected of carrying disease. The Board had power "to establish the police of burying grounds, appoint and locate the places where the dead may be buried, and cause the places for the deposit of the dead to be repaired and properly enclosed."[1] Yet the Board was subject to many political pressures and, characteristic of most municipal authorities in that era, generally took little regulatory action, especially in respect to quarantines, which slowed commerce and interfered with the economy of the city and the prosperity of the new elite. Burial regulation did not conflict with any powerful special interest group, however; the subject received general public support provided that no drastic changes in existing graveyards were proposed.

Bostonians had long recognized that their graveyards posed chronic problems. As early as the 1730s, Boston's three original burial grounds—King's Chapel, Copp's Hill, and the Old Granary—became so crowded that new burials were often made four-deep or in small, common trenches. (Figs. 6.2, 3.) A fourth graveyard was opened on the south end of the Common in 1756; tradition holds that it was first used by blacks.

Fig. 6.2. (*Above*) King's Chapel Burying Ground, Boston, engraving from F. W. P. Greenwood, *A History of King's Chapel,* 1833.

Fig. 6.3. (*Below*) Copp's Hill Burying Ground, Boston, engraving from Thomas Bridgman, *Epitaphs from Copp's Hill Burying Ground,* 1851.

There, during the Revolution, the British buried their common soldiers who died in Boston in combat or of disease. By the 1790s, physicians fearful of disease advised the town to ban the grazing of cattle in the burying grounds. Poor drainage led to further complaints. Water from the Granary Burying Ground flowed onto the Common and thence into the harbor. But, although Boston depended on individual wells for its water supply, few expressed worries publicly that urban burials would pollute the drinking water. Crowding of burials was the most serious problem, and creation of the fifth or South Burying Ground on the Shawmut Peninsula Neck in 1810 did not alleviate it. Even with this additional space, Boston's total burial land remained under five acres, much of that filled to capacity.

A flurry of public complaints about unsightly, overused burial grounds prompted the Massachusetts General Court in 1810 to honor the town's request for powers to regulate burials more closely. With new authority, in 1811 the town ordered disinterment of many old burials in order to gain space for future interments. The action was not unprecedented in light of the regular dissolution of graveyards in other cities whenever centrally located land was needed for construction of buildings. However, the idea of desecrating the graves of their forebears so offended some Bostonians that it was not easily forgotten. Ironically, Bostonians who showed little concern about identifying the precise locations of heroes of the Revolution reacted with strong emotions to the idea of displacing the community of the dead in their burial grounds. A decade later, a disgruntled citizen wrote to the editor of the *Boston Patriot and Mercantile Advertiser* of his lingering animosity over the plan to move the "mouldering bones of our ancestry respected by all nations, civilized and savage, from the long silence of the tomb for some pitiful object of economy."[2] Some Bostonians even used this issue as justification for opposition in 1822 to abandoning town government for a city charter because they felt they could not trust elected representatives.

Overcrowding of graveyards forced the town to ban burials in individual graves in 1816. Within two years, unmarked graves, four-deep, took up the remaining space in the Granary Burying Ground; parts of old coffins and bones regularly turned up when new burials were made in common or family tombs, many of which were in the form of vertical, brick-lined shafts. The Board of Health permitted construction of a few additional tombs as late as 1823. In an inventory a decade later, the King's Chapel yard had about 80 of these narrow, subterranean structures; Copp's Hill, 226, including one for infants, erected by the town; and the Neck Burying Ground, 172. (Fig. 6.4.) By 1823, Alderman Stephen Hooper found that even these tombs were nearly filled. He told Dr. John Collins Warren that "the question must soon be met by us or some other counsel which will not shrink from its responsibility, whether new and extensive places of deposit shall be opened *within* or *without* the city."[3]

Many members of Boston's elite remained reluctant to bury their dead far from their homes and the center of town; they did not support the creation of new burial places distant from around-the-clock public scrutiny. The new South Burying Ground contained primarily the graves of the poorer classes, including paupers from the Alms House and inmates of the House of Industry. It was further undesirable because it contained the gallows and was surrounded by dirty industries—candle manufacturers, slaughterhouses, and rope makers. It occupied damp, marshy ground; furthermore, its distant location made it subject to the periodic violations of grave robbers who removed individual bodies or vandals who ransacked groups of graves. Such incidents in 1822 and 1829 shocked the public; it was the regularity of body snatching that led health commissioners in 1823 to offer a $500 reward for information concerning "resurrection men," who provided Boston physicians with a constant supply of cadavers to further anatomical research and teaching.[4]

This concern for the security and permanency of burials was new. Formerly, Bostonians had tacitly accepted the fact that when a family became extinct, its tomb would probably be given or sold to another family. They regularly heard of unscrupulous grave diggers who "speculated in tombs" in the older burial grounds, erasing the family names on markers, emptying vaults of their

Fig. 6.4. Old family tombs in the Old Granary Burying Ground, Boston, photograph by Alan Ward, 1987.

contents at night, or compacting remains in order to resell the entire space to a new family or to bury dead strangers, charging between eight and twelve dollars for each.[5] Such corruption complicated the chaos that resulted from the graveyards' lack of general maintenance and persistent depredations.

Until the 1820s, most Bostonians took for granted that their burial grounds would be places of horror, but of horrors made by the living. For instance, urban lore held that despite elaborate obsequies for Governor John Hancock, following his lying in state for eight days in 1793, vandals severed the patriot's arm the night of his interment in the Old Granary. Vagrants occasionally took shelter in tombs and harassed passersby. Such seemed to be the status quo in Boston until changing sensibilities led to demands for assurances of permanency of burials and then for more pleasant places conducive to commemoration and even ornamentation of the center of the city.

From periodic reports in their newspapers, however, Bostonians knew that other cities had even greater problems with graveyards. Boston escaped many of the epidemic diseases that sporadically ravaged major mercantile cities along the Atlantic coast and were often attributed to miasmas or foul air in the vicinity of burial grounds. New Yorkers traced their recurrent epidemics to parts of the city near the overcrowded Trinity churchyard. A New York Board of Health study in 1806 determined the "malignant epidemic fever" was greatest in that neighborhood. It found that "a vast mass of decaying animal matter produced by the superstition of interring dead bodies near the churches, and which has been accumulating for a long lapse of time, is

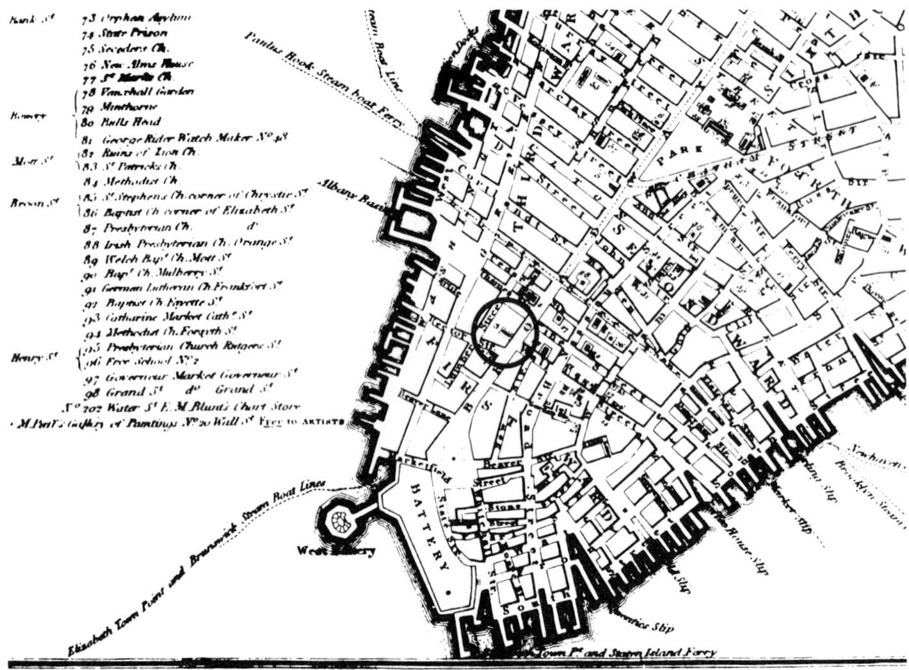

Fig. 6.5. New York City map, ca. 1820, showing location of Trinity churchyard on Broadway at the head of Wall Street.

now deposited in many of the most populous parts of the city." The Board concluded that it was "impossible that such a quantity of these animal remains should continue to be inoffensive and safe"; it recommended prohibition of future burials in the city. Rather than proposing complete dissolution of existing churchyards, however, Board members suggested that old burial places "might serve extremely well for plantations of grove and forest trees, useful and ornamental to the city." The planting would cleanse the soil, hasten natural decomposition of corpses, and purify the air.[6] With the exception of New Haven's New Burying Ground, there were few precedents for plantings in urban graveyards, and New York failed to implement these recommendations. City authorities ignored the report and continued to permit churches to extend burial crypts and tombs, even into areas under streets. (Fig. 6.5.)

Late in the summer of 1822, Bostonians read that yet another epidemic had made New York a "desolate city," resembling "a place afflicted with the panic, confusions and disorder of a siege." New York's "magnificent edifices" looked "like painted sepulchres; the spirit of life and gaiety had departed within." The rich fled north from the city center, which was then near the southern tip of Manhattan, to the "little village of Greenwich" to breathe fresh, rural air; the poor had no choice but to stay and take their chances with the fever in the polluted urban atmosphere.[7]

The New York publisher Francis D. Allen blamed the epidemic on urban burials in a pamphlet entitled *Documents and Facts, Showing the Fatal Effects of Interments in Populous Cities* that he compiled later that year. Allen presented a series of European examples to prove the deleterious effects of graveyards in the midst of cities. He urged removal of all burials to extramural sites, citing the example of burial reform in France. He acknowledged that the American public would be slow to accept suburban graveyards, despite growing fears and frequency of epidemic disease: "There are many whose feelings would revolt at the idea of taking their kindred and friends to a general cemetery three of four miles from the city." That, after all, was the usual fate of the poor consigned to potter's field. Proximity to the deceased's family and community after death seems to have taken on a similar, if secularized, importance in the American mind to the desirability of burial near the church altar in medieval times.[8]

Such old patterns and preferences were rapidly becoming anachronistic in rapidly growing cities like New York and Boston in the 1820s, as people began to separate home from work geographically and to make greater distinctions between the public and private spheres of life. No longer did tolling bells summon the entire community to accompany a bereaved family on foot to bury the dead in the graveyard; bells might still be tolled, at the expense of the estate, but unless the deceased was notable, funerals were no longer public events. Such a tradition conflicted with the new pace of urban life. Hence, Allen discounted the notion "that grave-yards within the city are absolutely necessary as mementos to the living."[9] Urbanites learned no valuable lessons of moral philosophy as they heedlessly hurried past burial grounds.

Allen published Dr. Samuel Akerly's opinion that Trinity Church Yard was "a great cause" of the yellow fever that ravaged the city in 1822. Akerly told the New York Board of Health that "an impure state of the atmosphere, caused by these and other masses of putrid matter greatly aggravates the malignity of the disease where it exists." In constant use since 1698, Trinity contained almost 120,000 bodies, some in graves less than two feet deep; the stench of decay was often obvious for blocks around. Many New Yorkers, if not all members of the medical profession, agreed with Akerly that there were real dangers associated with such "noxious effluvia."[10]

Uncertain notions about disease causation complicated and conditioned the response of physicians and the general public to problems of urban sanitation and burial reform. Most physicians in the early nineteenth century were aware that smallpox, measles, and other diseases with skin eruptions were contagious; yet anticontagionist theories regarded those diseases as exceptions to the rule. The general belief was that miasma engendered diseases, especially those with fevers. Dr. Benjamin Rush of Philadelphia had been a vocal miasmatist, and his influence on American medical opinion was substantial. Boston physicians attributed the "bilious remittent fever" that ravaged the southeastern portion of their city in 1796 to miasmata.

Self-interest impelled business leaders in mercantile cities to favor anticontagionist theories. Quarantines, the contagionist device for stemming the spread of disease, interfered with the free flow of trade; furthermore, cleaning up the urban environment, as advocated by the anticontagionists, was less costly and at the same time increased real estate values and appealed to new sensibilities offended by foul smells and visible filth. The medical historian Erwin Ackerknecht rightly observes that "powerful social and political factors" colored the scientific discussion of disease causation. The public debate over the sources of effluvia and the sort of disease engendered by miasma reflected religious, intellectual, and economic concerns as well during the 1820s.[11]

When Dr. Akerly urged burial reform in New York, therefore, his arguments were more economic than medical. He warned New Yorkers that property around churchyards would be "greatly injured and depreciated unless something effectual" was done to correct the overcrowding. The shift in the medical community was again evident after the New York City Council passed a law banning burials, under penalty of a $250 fine, south of Canal Street in March of 1823. Dr. David Hosack collected signatures from 130 local physicians petitioning that the law be rescinded in the name of property rights. Churches took the City to court in 1825 for infringing on their corporate property, but the State Supreme Court upheld the legality of the ordinance in 1827. Some New Yorkers boasted that their city was in the vanguard of a trend of burial reform soon to be followed in other major cities. Bostonians, however, handled the matter of burial reform quite differently.[12]

Since no major epidemics struck Boston in the early nineteenth century to raise questions of the association of disease, miasma, and burials, Bostonians' interest in burial reform centered on issues of space and aesthetics. Boston's burial controversy began in December of 1822, when directors of the new Saint Paul's Episcopal Church petitioned the first Boston City Council for "leave to erect tombs" and for its basement to be "recognized as a public cemetery." (Fig. 6.6.) A committee appointed by councilmen to study the matter readily approved the proposal, provided that City Council direct construction and retain perpetual control over crypt conditions. Alderman Ephraim Eliot declared that such burials would cause "no possible injury to the public health," that "no other mode, in common use, is more secure and less objectionable." Eliot quoted the authority of eight prominent local physicians that "decomposition of animal substances neither generates infection nor produces diseases." Furthermore, he noted that tomb burials had long existed in Boston at King's Chapel and at the Episcopalian Trinity and Christ churches with "no evil results."[13] The Board of Health and its president, Benjamin Whitman, remained silent on the issue, thus lending tacit support to approving the burials.

Religious factionalism, rather than public health, emerged as a major issue of public concern in the controversy following Saint Paul's receipt of approval for its crypts. Denominationalism had been growing in Boston for several decades and added a new element of discord to many civic concerns. Until the 1820s, most Bostonians harbored an antipathy to the Church of England inherited from the Puritans and heightened by the late-seventeenth-century imposition of Anglicanism on them along with revocation of their original charter. Since the days of Sir Edmund Andros's tyrannical Dominion of New England and, more recently, the revolutionary-period debates over American bishops in the episcopacy, many New Englanders despised that denomination as aristocratic, papist, corrupt, and, worst yet, an agency used for exerting control over them and their affairs. Many Bostonians, especially the Unitarians who rejected dogma and sectarianism, feared that establishment of Saint Paul's in 1819 signaled the beginning of a new British attempt to control America with Toryism and High Church forms. The local journalist Joseph T. Buckingham, outspoken editor of the weekly *New-England Galaxy,* articulated the region's traditional antipathy to Episcopalianism: "We have long looked upon the English form of worship as at variance with our republican institutions and repugnant to the views and feelings of our forefathers."[14]

Episcopalians declared the beginning of a new era in the 1820s as "men from the Orthodox, Unitarian, and Episcopal churches banded together to build a Church that would be of historic order but modern in spirit; of English inheritance, but American in character." Prominent Bostonians in the new congregation included Daniel Webster, George Sullivan, David Sears, and William Shimmin. Members of the congregation came almost exclusively from the town's new social, economic, cultural, and political elite. Some local critics called Saint Paul's a "movement on the part of men of wealth and prominence in the community to build a costly and impressive church building." Major subscribers to the fund for building the church were Dr. John Collins Warren, Harrison Gray Otis, William Tudor, Stephen and Henry Codman, William and Samuel Appleton, and Lucius M. Sargent—some of the city's wealthiest cultural leaders.[15]

The cornerstone of Saint Paul's was laid in September of 1819; the completed edifice was consecrated at the end of the following June. Its architect, Alexander Parris, assisted by sculptor Solomon Willard, designed the church in the form of a Greek temple, reminiscent of the Ionic structure at Illissue in Athens. Saint Paul's had a prime site, which alone cost $18,000, on Tremont Street by the corner of Boston Common, less than a block from the Granary Burying Ground, and close to the new homes of many of its members on Beacon Hill. The local historian Dr. Caleb H. Snow praised the project in 1825 as "the commencement of an era of art in Boston" and predicted the new church would have "a sensible influence on taste in architecture." The *Boston Intelligencer and Evening Gazette* boasted that "the whole design indicates the origin of a new taste among us by which high and uncouth steeples erected upon low buildings in bad proportions, will be abolished, —and a purer ideal of architectural beauty will be introduced."[16]

Saint Paul's builders spared no expense. The congregation budgeted a generous $50,000 for the project, but the church structure alone cost $83,000, and the total expenditure reached over $100,000. The congregation was in debt for over half that amount, an astronomical figure considering that the entire town budget in 1820 was only $150,000.[17]

Dr. John Collins Warren, a surgeon and specialist in anatomy, joined Saint Paul's in 1820; his subscription helped to build the new church. Dr. Warren was approaching the zenith of an active medical career and was a leader of local society. In 1811, he and Dr. James Jackson founded the Massachusetts General Hospital. Yet he found time to serve both as vestryman and senior warden for the new congregation and to tackle its high initial debt. Warren planned to alleviate financial difficulties by building and selling forty-seven family tombs in the church cellar. At the same time as crypt sales helped to defray the cost of the building, they also provided a secure and dignified place of burial for Boston's elite who might not own family tombs in the old burying grounds. Warren favored church burials, which were traditional in Anglicanism, although the form was one against which the founders of Massachusetts had deliberately reacted in creating common, secular graveyards situated away from the meetinghouse.[18] Although a few previous examples of crypt burials existed, they certainly were not central to the Boston tradition.

Even before the Council voted approval of Saint Paul's crypts, the *Columbian Centinel* observed that the issue "excited some interest" in the city.[19] A number of Boston newspaper editors publicized the controversy by invoking public health. The Republican *Boston Patriot and Daily Mercantile Advertiser* explicitly condemned church "cemeteries," meaning crypts, along with all urban burials, as conducive to disease: "A very fertile and reprehensible source of poisonous vapours contaminating the air is that of Church-yards in the middle of populous towns. The practice of depositing dead bodies in Churches is still more liable to censure, as this forms a constant source of putrid vapours, however imperceptible, which cannot fail to prove greatly destructive to health." Journalists sought to convince Bostonians that all urban burials posed health problems, yet no one seemed ready to ban them entirely. Indeed, the burial controversy became mainly an exercise in rhetoric, with issues defined primarily in religious and political rather than medical terms. Medical opinions were invoked only to strengthen other arguments against crypts.[20]

Joseph T. Buckingham, who oriented his *New-England Galaxy* to a readership of mechanics and the "middling sort," was most vehement in opposing crypt burials; he began a journalistic crusade against the City Council's action in favor of Saint Paul's petition. Emphasizing the traditional Yankee rejection of such "ignorance and bigotry," the

Fig. 6.6. Saint Paul's Church, Boston, photograph by Alan Ward, 1987.

belief in the sacredness of church burials, he challenged proponents of crypt burials to prove from the Bible "that there is anything sacred in stones and mortar, or that one piece of ground is more holy than another." He warned that such men would ultimately find that the cellars of their churches were, on the contrary, "the most dreadful of temporal curses." Buckingham invoked "the common sense of the community" to reject church burials, adding, "We have long looked upon the English form of worship as at varians [*sic*] with our republican institutions and repugnant to the views and feelings of our forefathers." Episcopalianism in general and the crypts in particular represented "undue attachment to a foreign nation and a haughty and aristocratic spirit." He concluded, "The quicker we get rid of them the better."[21]

Church burials posed the problem of privilege infringing on public welfare, especially given the "haughty and aristocratic spirit" associated with Episcopalianism. Buckingham invoked his era's nascent spirit of egalitarianism against creation of new marks of privilege, charging that "a more impudent and high-handed attempt to affect the selfish purposes of a purse-proud and obstinate aristocracy at the expense of the comfort, convenience, health, and even lives, of the whole city, is not on record." His sensationalistic effort to stir public opinion against church crypts relied most heavily on anti-elitist humor. Boston burial grounds were public places and common, whereas crypts would be reserved for a wealthy few members of exclusive congregations who could afford to purchase the private space. Buckingham printed one lengthy doggerel poem lampooning the wealthy churches. In part, it read:

Not many years ago, (as is well known,)
Some "meek and lowly" men wishing to hear
The *gospel* preached unto themselves, alone,
Far from the vulgar, (so it would appear,)
Did build a *costly* house to make each pew
Come high as possible — for seats so dear
Could not be purchased by the poor, they knew —
Beside, they had no *gallery,* for fear
That low and vulgar herd should creep in there.
And when the HOUSE was *dedicated,* they
Would let none in without a *ticket;* well,
Not satisfied with having their own way
In worshipping alone, in their stone *shell,*
They *now* do "want the liberty," they say,
"Of building TOMBS in it! — No — not to *sell,*
They wish to SLEEP alone, as well as pray:
Perhaps it *yet* may be our lot to tell
They have engaged a *private* room in ——.

Their petition might be granted, (as
'Twas doubtful) they did get eight learned men
To say, "that every *catching* fever" had
Been caused by "putrid *vegetables!*" Then
The common-council did decide it best
To grant them their request, "for," say they "when
They rot their *smell* no FEVER can molest;
For butchers, too have *ever* been
Snuffing such *scents,* and they are *healthy* men!

Now if our *rulers* think it best to build
Another place, where every man, that goes
To get fresh air, can have his nostrils fill'd
With fragrance sweeter than that of the rose,
Without expense or trouble — I can't say
Why they need tell what every body knows,
About those men: 'tis no *comfort* to me
To be informed, in poetry, or prose,
That BUTCHERS have such things beneath *their* nose.

But sure, in mercy, we've already got
Enough of *burying grounds* beside the MALL;
There's not a mortal walks there now, but what
He grasps his nose with all his might; nor shall
The greatest *snuff-taker* that ever had
A stuffed-up snout step on the common, and
Not grow quite sick — the stench is *now* so bad
None but a Council-man *unmoved* can stand
Upon that PUBLICK WALK — THE CITY'S LAND!

Therefore, I hope ST. PAUL'S will not be made
A Tomb, though, I must say, I always thought
It looked like one — but then I was afraid
To go and *see if 'twas,* — besides I sought
Not to creep in a place I should not go,
(Having no *ticket,* for none could be bought.)

Apropos: when the *tombs* are built d'ye know
If TICKETS will admit the *dead*? They ought —
For then each DEAD *intruder* will be caught.[22]

Democratic leanings played a stronger role in Buckingham's opposition to the crypts than did any other concerns, and he repeatedly stressed that issue in his own editorials as well as in the poems and articles he reprinted from other periodicals. He selected one item for a March 1823 issue of the *New-England Galaxy* addressing the question "What is death?" in a peculiarly Democratic way:

"Tis to be free! . . .
To join the great equality;
All alike are humbled there!
The mighty grave
Wraps Lord and slave;
Nor pride nor poverty dares come
Within that refuge-house, the tomb![23]

Buckingham went on to suggest that bribes bought the favorable vote of the aldermen authorizing "the location of charnel-houses and reservoirs of filth, corruption, rotten carcasses, plague and yellow fever, in the neighborhood of that spot consecrated to the goodness of health [the Common], — the only spot in the city where all classes may meet on terms of equality." The notion that miasmas from burials might cause epidemic disease was only one of many powerful arguments mustered against Saint Paul's crypts.[24]

Exaggerating, Buckingham credited "the industry, prudence and firmness" of the town's Board of Health with keeping Boston free for over twenty years from the epidemics that devastated other American cities, making Boston an asylum with "pure and healthful atmosphere." Boston literally lay under tons of filth removed by the wagonload from the streets during Mayor Josiah Quincy's administration; it was true, however, that yellow fever and cholera had not been the scourge in Boston that they were in New York and Philadelphia. Yet again, Buckingham's prime argument favored traditional ways of doing things and opposed rampant changes in procedures under the new City government.[25]

Buckingham predicted that permitting Saint Paul's to build tombs would precipitate many similar requests for church burials and make Bostonians "fugitives compelled to desert their homes and fly from a pestilence of their own creation" or compel them "to snuff up the effluvia of rotting carcasses when they take their morning promenades and inhale the pestiferous odour of animal putrefaction with every breeze." This precedent would turn the city into a "congregation of tombs and charnel-houses."[26] Buckingham appealed to growing urban pride to oppose such burials.

Indeed, Buckingham was right that Saint Paul's petition was not the last. Leaders of other churches quickly realized the economic benefits of crypt burials. The Prudential Committee of the Park Street Church proposed crypt burials to reduce its debt in 1822. Congregationalists built their Georgian church in 1809; as early as 1816, fundraisers considered erecting tombs beneath their structure to produce revenue. (Fig. 6.7.) Although many of the vaults in the Old Granary were virtually in the basement of the church, the Congregationalists did not petition to build additional crypts inside until Saint Paul's set the precedent. Park Street leaders argued that burial in church basements was "not an uncommon practice by religious societies of the day." Their church cellar was "large and deep"; thus, crypt burials would not differ greatly from

Fig. 6.7. Park Street Church adjacent to Old Granary Burying Ground, postcard photograph, ca. 1900.

those in family tombs in the graveyard a few feet away. Church spokesmen denied any potential danger to public health and echoed the argument that church cellars were standard repositories of the dead in almost all Christian nations.[27]

City Councilmen permitted the Park Street Church to erect one range of tombs on each side of its cellar, provided that the building's foundation not be injured; however, the Board of Aldermen rejected a proposed Strangers' Tomb in the church for burial of travelers who died while in Boston. Announcement of this second permission intensified public controversy over Boston burials. The Unitarian Buckingham's dislike for the orthodox Congregationalists, as much as his antipathy toward Episcopalians, tinged his rhetoric against the place nicknamed "Brimstone Corner." He even seemed to suggest that some civic-spirited Bostonian commit arson: "Fire, mingled with a suitable portion of refined flour of sulphur," he wrote, would be capable of settling the issue by disposing once and for all of the bodies of the dead in that church cellar.[28]

Attempting to keep the debate alive and to sell more newspapers, Buckingham reprinted English articles critical of church crypt burials with particular aesthetic appeal. One traveler's account of a Dublin church dwelt on how curiosity seekers regularly invaded the privacy of the dead on tours guided by a disrespectful sexton. "It is a poor privilege," the visitor concluded, "to hold together for a century or so until your coffin tumbles in about your ears, and then to re-appear, half skeleton, half mummy, exposed to the gazes of a generation that can know nothing of your name and character." Such "indignities" were scarcely less than "humiliating" than being "hung up in dissecting rooms," the fate of bodies snatched from their graves by the resurrection men who periodically pillaged Boston graveyards. The account had special meaning for those who worried about the theft of bodies for anatomical experimentation. Buckingham aimed to dissuade those interested in buying church crypts as a means of ensuring security for their dead.[29] It had a particular edge of religious criticism for those heirs of Puritans contemptuous of Catholic display and veneration of relics of saints—corpses and parts of corpses. An additional appeal of the article was to new sensibilities reacting against seeing the horrors of death in the form of the medieval depiction and display of the cadaver, mummy, skeleton, or skull.

Buckingham's various arguments mustered a certain amount of opposition to crypt burials, but Bostonians were becoming increasingly tolerant of religious diversity, exemplified by the proliferation of various ecclesiastical structures in the city. Boston's first mayor, John Phillips, the aldermen, and the common council were not prepared to rescind their permission for the Episcopalians or Congregationalists to build church crypts. When Josiah Quincy (1772–1864) became mayor in May of 1823, however, Buckingham found a new champion for his opposition to crypt burials. Mayor Quincy asserted his intention to improve the "health, security, and cleanliness" of Boston, to have an active administration, defining and extending the powers of the municipality. His inaugural address announced to Bostonians, especially those with "restricted fortunes," that he would use strong executive authority to improve their environment: "The rich can fly from the generated pestilence. The sons of fortune can seek refuge in purer atmosphere. But necessity condemns the poor to remain and inhale the noxious effluvia." The problem of urban burials was one of many urban issues Quincy tackled. He urged preventive measures, declaring it "not sufficient that the law, in its due process will ultimately remedy every injury and remove every nuisance." His motto was "Prevention should be the object of solicitude, not remedy." Quincy declared, "The criterion of an efficient government is that [nuisances] should be removed before complaint and without complaint."[30]

Quincy's political record favored Boston's mercantile interests. He became known as the "Great Mayor," responsible for an innovative program of city planning and municipal management. His concern with burial reform was part of a program including street cleaning, improving the antiquated sewerage system, initiating a city water supply, and creating new market facilities. Because of his own extensive speculations in Boston real estate, Quincy had a vested interest in improving the urban environment. The consummate politician enjoyed wholehearted support from a number of leading Bostonians of various classes—including Buckingham, advocate of mechanics and the "middling sort," as well as William Tudor, spokesman of the cultural elite. The mayor represented the forces of modernization in the new city government. He was instrumental in rationalizing the procedures and authority of the new municipal corporation and in imposing its authority over other corporations—schools, churches, and businesses. Quincy emphasized "efficiency" in all operations of the municipality. Those corporations or businesses that would not conform to new regulations could relocate beyond Boston's corporate boundaries. Otherwise, the major made sure that porches of churches did not infringe on new public sidewalks, that privies did not drain into streets, and that crypt burials did not emit foul smells noticeable on the Common.

Quincy spoke for sweeping burial reform, not limiting himself to criticism of church crypts. He echoed William Tudor's opinion that "cemeteries in cities must in time become so heaped up with the spoils of mortality as to require removal to prevent pestilence." Undoubtedly Quincy also knew of New York's burial problems, for his wife, Eliza Susan Morton, came from a prosperous mercantile family there. A clean city and issues of public health mattered more than tolerating diversity and permitting various religious institutions to determine their own separate burial places and practices. Tudor conceded, "It is solemn to place the remains of our friends within that sacred temple dedicated to God; it is affecting to offer our devotions, surrounded by the graves of those we have loved; but in great cities, it becomes as noxious to the living as it is useless to the dead, and a wise police has gradually prohibited it in most countries, or at least diminished the evil, by reserving such sepulture to those of high distinction."[31] Tudor's published opinions indicate that Quincy had the support of a substantial faction of Boston's elite in his crusade to reform the burial system.

One of Quincy's first orders of business was an attempt to undo the "dangerous precedent" set by the first city administration in permitting burials in church cellars. He feared that a growing number of Boston churches would try to take advantage of the precedent, "considering the pecuniary advantage." Indeed, on June 4, 1823, the mayor received a third petition for a crypt permit from the proprietors of the Methodist Episcopal Church on Bromfield Street. Quincy realized that to reverse permission already granted would be difficult if not legally impossible. Prominent members of Saint Paul's and the Park Street Church still held influential positions in city government and could argue that crypts were already built and in use. Nevertheless, on June 25, Quincy ordered a new, complete investigation of all urban burials and charged City Council to present a general report "on the expediency of prohibiting or limiting the erection of any New Cemeteries [*sic*] or tombs within the precincts of the city." To assure that the report would not reflect special interests, Quincy personally chaired the committee.[32]

One local physician supported Quincy's decision to scrutinize all urban burials. On July 4, 1823, Buckingham enthusiastically reported publication of a pamphlet dedicated to the mayor and condemning tomb burials. It would surely "have a tendency to counteract the pernicious effects of the atrocious act of our late city council." Dr. John Gorham Coffin, author of *Remarks on the Dangers and Duties of Sepulture; or, Security for the Living, with Respect and Repose for the Dead,* compiled an exposition of arguments against urban interments, presented with editorial remarks made in a moderate and rational tone. He signed the pamphlet simply "A Fellow of the Massachusetts Medical Society," to attest to his character, reputation, and knowledgeable authority, which he pitted against those of the eight other Boston physicians arguing against the dangers of miasma from crypt burials. Dr. Coffin distinguished himself from many other local physicians by his long crusade for preventive medicine of all sorts. Like so many other members of the city's new elite, he was a relative newcomer to Boston, from Essex County to the north. Still, he shared Quincy's interest in the welfare of the underprivileged and in making recommendations of constructive action to create an urban environment conducive to public health. Both Coffin and Quincy preferred this approach to the dramatic, heroic cure necessitated at a point of medical crisis—the standard bleedings, purgings, or quarantines of the day.[33]

The selection and synthesis of various writings against urban burials in Coffin's pamphlet emphasized anticontagionist or miasmatist views and drew primarily on the experience of France to condemn the role of animal putrefaction in fostering disease. Coffin reprinted portions of Francis D. Allen's pamphlet suggesting that "morbific exhalations" from New York's Trinity churchyard created a condition in which fevers repeatedly ravaged the city. Then, Dr. Coffin specifically addressed burials under Boston churches, cautioning that they might be "harmless while they remained without being moved" but wondering what would happen if a building centrally located "amidst the revolutions of a busy population" were disturbed by increasing urban activity or natural trauma. Like Buckingham, Coffin played heavily on new sensibilities and old hostilities to the idea of moving existing graves. "It is not long indeed," he reminded Bostonians, "since we have seen in this populous city, the mangled remains of the dead transported from one burying-ground into the other. We have also seen two church-yards opened, and deeply broken on extensive spaces, leaving exposed to our reluctant and pensive curiosity, shattered limbs of corpses and their decayed coffins, till they were closed again by a range of brick vaults."[34] Americans began to reject for themselves sights commonplace in London and Paris.

Dr. Coffin criticized all burials in the city, and he advocated creation of a burial place to permit speedy, natural decomposition of corpses. He wanted to ban all burials in family tombs, considering multiple burials a "pernicious custom," because such vaults had to be reopened for additions before "the time prescribed" for proper decomposition of previous burials. He wanted nothing less than a general prohibition of all burials in tombs, vaults, and even coffins—anything that would separate the body from surrounding earth and unnaturally inhibit decay. The physician stressed the salutary processes of nature rather than simply restating miasmatist medical opinion.[35]

Dr. Coffin intended to propose alternatives to urban burial and to urge Bostonians to create an extramural burial landscape similar to that in New Haven to "prevent the inducement to bury any longer in our city and churches, and prepare the way for a removal of the contents of these tombs, which are already sending forth no equivocal admonitions into some of our temples."[36] Bostonians might transfer existing remains and gravestones, following New Haven's example, from the center of the city to such a suburban location where grounds would be found extensive enough to permit only single burials in harmony with the natural processes of decay. The cemetery would function primarily for disposal of dead bodies; using coffins that virtually self-destructed on burial would hasten the process of decomposition. As was the practice in Europe, after a fixed interval of time, clean bones could then be disinterred and the spot reused.

Dr. Coffin anticipated opposition from those whose religious views held that the dead would rise intact on Judgment Day and who tried to preserve the corpse in the tomb or grave. He rationalized, "If the perished body is to be restored, it must be done by an act of creative power, and therefore to believe that human intervention is to have any influence in the case, is to suppose that human agency can interfere with the purposes of the Almighty." Evil alone arose when man arrogantly tampered with the system of Nature and hence with the will of God. Coffin's *Remarks* advocated naturalism and simplicity as essentially American, democratic, and anti-aristocratic; his ideal burial landscape would reflect all these principles. The grave, placed amid "the simplicity of nature," would be "eloquent" in teaching lessons to man. Death would be the great equalizer, the ultimate democrat, evident in the common grave rather than in the tomb, symbol of artificial status. The contrast between the two types of burial was great: the haughty tomb so different from the simplicity of the grave. As if echoing Buckingham, Dr. Coffin suggested that in choosing between the tomb and the grave Bostonians were choosing between aristocracy and democracy, superstition and natural law, human pretensions and the inexorable will of God.[37]

Coffin's ideal burial site reflected the growing romanticism of the era. The physician envisioned the repulsion and hasty retreat of the child from the grotesque sight in a parent's tomb. No persistent affection or quiet, commemorative melancholy would be possible in such a place. In contrast, the author observed, "I am differently affected when with the rising sun, or by the light of the melancholy moon, I go alone to my mother's grave. There I love to linger; and while there I hear the wind over one that sighed over me. I breathe an air refreshed by herbage, which draws its strength from the source whence I drew mine: and in the drops of dew that tremble on its leaves, I see the tears which so often bedewed her eyes as she breathed forth a prayer that her children might cherish her memory and escape from the pollutions of the world."[38] Dr. Coffin closely copied the work of several French theorists of burial reform. Pollution became figurative as well as literal. Putrefaction from urban burials symbolized social and cultural corruption. The ideal funerary landscape Dr. Coffin described, in contrast to the existing system, was that of William Cullen Bryant's and Wordsworth's poetry, or that imagery familiar to Bostonians from mourning pictures and the iconography of the willow tree and urn on their recent gravestones. Yet in America, with the exception of the isolated, rural family burying ground, few such landscapes existed. Again, the proposal of such a pastoral cemetery was in marked contrast to the reality of existing graveyards.

Dr. Coffin referred specifically to the classical literary ideal of burials outside of the city. He personally desired burial like that of Aristotle in a field, of Homer on the seashore, or of Lysander on a rural plain. Coffin's naturalistic burial site would reconcile changing notions about death and nature, harmonizing them with the taste for antiquity of Boston's elite. It would epitomize the liberal religious vision of the hereafter as Eden, rather than the vision of a fearsome place passed down from the European past and reinterpreted by the Puritans with emblems of their harsh expectations for postmortem fate, so vividly represented in the grisly forms of the New England graveyard at that time—disorder, chaos, noxious effluvia, and stern messages of *memento mori* etched on tumbling gray slate gravestones. Dr. Coffin's proposal suggested that the graveyard could be converted into a new sort of space, sanctified by nature, not by proximity to any church.[39]

Dr. Coffin's suggestions were not at all new. Such ideals of "rural" burial for urbanites had, in fact, been repeated frequently in Boston in the years before the burial controversy. Just months before the appearance of Coffin's pamphlet, the *Boston Patriot and Daily Mercantile Advertiser* reprinted a piece from a Charleston, South Carolina, newspaper praising the moral influence and simplicity of rural burial grounds. That anonymous essayist wrote in the spirit of Washington Irving: "What individual gazes upon the most obscure cemetery, without feeling the uncertain tenure of human existence?" Only the rural burial ground held such romantic attraction, making it a "melancholy pleasure" to visit such "habitations of the dead and meditate on the 'hoary text' that 'teaches the rustic moralist.' "[40] Such emotions were lost in graveyards crushed by urbanization or left behind in a distant hometown by rural New Englanders moving in increasing numbers to Boston to make fortunes and establish careers.

Even before the controversy over crypt burials, the idea of creating a new cemetery in a suburban location occurred to Bostonians interested in forming new urban institutions. William Tudor, Boston's chief cultural leader, suggested as early as 1820 that "a reform of our cemeteries would be honourable to public feeling." As an alternative to crowded graveyards with their "desolate look of abandonment," Tudor proposed that "an ample piece of ground selected in the vicinity of large towns" should be selected for all urban burials for Boston, New York, and other American cities. "It would be easy, without great expense," wrote Tudor, "to give the walls and entrance an appropriate appearance. The cypress, the willow, and other funeral trees, would form suitable ornaments within. A sufficient space might be allowed to different families to decorate as they choose, and where their remains would repose for ages untouched." Tudor suggested that "such a cemetery would be an interesting spot to visit," would be morally uplifting, and would represent the refinement of the city and its respect for the past. Tudor considered only a cultural rationale for the project, however, and made no mention of public health.[41]

Not surprisingly, therefore, when Mayor Quincy reported for his Joint Committee on Urban Interments, he recommended more than merely curbing additional crypt burials. He declared it "the duty of every successive city council to consult the health, safety, and prosperity of the city, independent of the opinions or decisions of any former city council." Within six months, Saint Paul's realized $13,000 in net proceeds from tomb sales, and the Park Street Church, $8,000, "a result which is offering to the proprietors of other churches a temptation perhaps too strong to be resisted." Quincy ensured denial of the request by the Methodist Episcopal Church on Bromfield Lane to build crypts because a third permit would definitely set a precedent; then, citing Dr. Coffin's contrasting view, he questioned the medical opinion of the physicians who considered crypt burials of no danger to public health. Quincy criticized the "vibration of opinion among learned men" and speculated that "it would not be surprising, if within the compass of the present generation, an entire revolution of opinion should take place and that of the effluvia arising from the decomposition of animal matter should *again* be held to be injurious to, or even destructive to health." Yet Quincy declared the medical debate irrelevant, only one manifestation of the "very great and honest diversity of opinions" of Bostonians concerned with more important issues of commonality versus privilege, the authority of the municipality versus interests of private property.[42]

Quincy concluded, "Grant that burying the dead within the city may be possibly innocent;—burying the dead out of it is certainly so." He deemed it "the duty of this and every other city council to limit as much as possible, consistent with existing property rights, all future burials within the precincts of this ancient peninsula; and also to adopt a prospective system, which shall terminate, ultimately, in some distant years the burying within it altogether." It would be impossible immediately to ban all burials within the city, but he urged creation of an alternative, extramural burial place as soon as possible.

Ideally, Quincy wanted the city to open a common place of burial with "wall and watch" and to "maintain the sanctity of the sepulchres," a place "where will finally repose all the inhabitants of the city." Not only would such a place solve the problem of crowding in Boston's old graveyards, it would "unite the interests and the natural prejudices and affections of the whole community," creating a civic spirit. There, democratically, "all classes [would] meet together." The elite, with their kin buried there, would not allow the lapses of security that had permitted graverobbing in the Neck or South Burying Ground and that premised the "powerful repugnance at present existing to being buried without the limits of the peninsula." Security was a prime concern, Quincy realized, that made Bostonians want to keep their burials under close surveillance at the center of urban life. Under Quincy's proposal, existing family tombs in the old graveyards and the two churches would remain in place because of respect for property rights, but additional burials would cease as soon as they became full.[43]

After filing the forty-page report, Quincy and the aldermen formed a second committee to select a site for creation of this new cemetery. The Common Council authorized the commission to erect tombs which the City might sell. Unlike Dr. Coffin, they had no general opposition to the idea of entombment. Yet, unfortunately, this second commission accomplished little else toward creation of new, extramural burial places.[44]

In July, the mayor wrote to Dr. John Collins Warren to elicit suggestions on how to end urban interments; but Warren replied that he would only favor finding additional land within the city, "such as can conveniently be devoted to the purpose without injury to more important interests." Cautious not to endanger the interests of Saint Paul's through his remarks, Warren noted that "it would be advantageous to the health and beauty of the city to open new cemeteries in different parts and especially in the vicinities of churches, in order to obtain the ventilation and comfort of such open spaces." Increased density of building along Boston's narrow streets impeded the circulation of fresh air. Warren, trained in medicine in Paris, probably knew French urban planning theories that simple open spaces and city squares, even without plantings, might function to circulate fresh air. The idea that burial grounds could provide open space beneficial to air quality was new and ran counter to miasmatists' arguments that all "domestic" interments fouled the urban atmosphere; but then, Warren's suggestion was compatible with his anti-miasmatic beliefs.[45]

The proposal was, however, unrealistic considering the paucity of space left on the Shawmut Peninsula for any sort of new building. Already proposals were made that parts of the Common be developed for residences and businesses. On behalf of the City, Mayor Quincy reappropriated a strip of property south of the Common in 1824 and held a referendum on its use, offering citizens five choices, including creation of a new burial ground. But since additional land would have to be *made* by filling in the salt marsh, nothing was done for over a decade, when the site became a public garden.[46]

Only as an afterthought at the end of his letter did Dr. Warren note that interments might not be restricted to the peninsular bounds of Boston. The physician speculated that a country site might be better than one in Boston "if a sufficient number of persons would be ready to defray the expense." He did not suggest that the municipality purchase land beyond its limits. Rather, the elite could continue to buy tombs in the city, associated with their churches, while everyone else would be sent outside the urban bounds to bury their dead.[47] Quincy did not consider this proposal, for he wanted to reestablish a common burial place for all Bostonians at the same time as he rid the city of interments.

Quincy's second committee never produced a report or established a site for Boston's burials beyond the municipal limits. In fact, no records remain of the committee's transactions. Under Quincy's administration, however, the Ordinance on the Burial of the Dead, passed in 1826, officially closed the Central (Common), King's Chapel, and Old Granary Burying Grounds, banning the opening or digging of new graves and the building of additional tombs on these sites. Under Quincy, the City also ended use of the old section of the North or Copp's Hill Burying Ground, but it permitted additional tomb construction in the new sections there as well as in the South Burying Ground on the Neck. The North and South graveyards alone retained sufficient room for continued use under increasingly careful regulation of a new Superintendent of Burying Grounds.

New restrictions permitted a family to reserve a spot for itself, for twenty years only, after a first burial if it placed a small stone slab engraved with name, age, and lot number on the spot. Burials would not be in perpetuity, although no mention was made of how the remains would be disposed of and the space recycled after the allotted time. Recycling of grave space in colonial times was sometimes practiced, if poorly documented. A large vault in the corner of King's Chapel Burying Ground functioned as a charnel house, indicating reuse of grave space and the necessity for a place to deposit bones after removal from the grave. Burial grounds would henceforth be "sufficiently secured by locks and bolts." From the 1820s on, Bostonians realized the need to regulate interments more closely by municipal codes.[48]

It would be wrong to judge that Quincy had not done enough for burial reform under his administration, which, after all, produced all sorts of new definitions of municipal action; but the mayor was dissatisfied because he had wanted to do more. At the beginning of his sixth term, Quincy noted that Bostonians remained "disgusted and sickened by that foulness which infects and contaminates the noble city of New York"; and he wanted to prevent such conditions from developing in his city. He lamented that "one law we lack yet, not only for the promotion of health, but for other cogent reasons" was that "no dead body in the future shall be buried or otherwise deposited within the city, or nearer half a mile from its limits." Quincy failed in an attempt to close the Middle Burial Ground on the Common in order to extend the tree-lined mall, because two or three families rejected the idea of moving the remains from their tombs. Bostonians were not as universally sickened by the idea of burials in their midst as he suggested. Quincy's crusades for public health and urban cleanliness in his first term gave way to more materially successful projects such as building Quincy market, widening streets, improving public schools, and creating a House of Industry.[49]

Quincy cannot be faulted for diverting attention from burial reform. He did succeed in curtailing the spread of crypt burials to other Boston churches, generally cleaning up the city, and creating an atmosphere of reform conducive to planning alternative institutions and landscapes through voluntary associations rather than under municipal auspices. Bostonians realized that their urban death rate was gradually but significantly falling to a point "less than in any other city of equal population on record."[50] Given that fact, burial reform in the name of public health was not a pressing matter in Boston; interments under city churches persisted until 1862, and tombs remained under Saint Paul's until 1878. Evidence that Boston's "rural" cemetery, Mount Auburn, was not founded *because of* public health issues that arose in the burial controversy of 1823 lies in the fact that one of the first acts of its founders was to acquire a crypt under the Park Street Church for regular use as a Receiving Tomb, to hold bodies under Mount Auburn auspices for up to three months when burial was not immediately possible at the cemetery or when decisions to transfer the dead elsewhere had yet to be made.

Quincy's spirit of urban improvement depended on voluntary action by all citizens. The new municipal corporation could more easily act negatively by banning, regulating, or removing environmental abuses, than positively by innovating with creative alternatives. The mayor reminded Bostonians that "a city would be noble if man would do but half as much for himself as nature has done for him." In retrospect, writing his *Municipal History of Boston* in 1852, Quincy wistfully noted that while the City Council failed to act on his proposal for a municipal, extramural burial ground, he remained proud that "the tone and policy of this report . . . have been since sanctioned by the establishment of the cemetery at Mount Auburn by an effective organization of private citizens."[51] In the end, Quincy was buried there atop a high hill facing east over Boston; Buckingham purchased an oversized family lot in a wooded area almost encircled by Willow Avenue in the heart of the grounds.[52]

7

The Cemetery Idea and Founding of Mount Auburn

The holiness of nature is ever a lofty contemplation; and it is well amidst the quiet wildwood and beneath the forest-shades, to be reminded sometimes of death.

—Cornelia Walter, *Mount Auburn Illustrated* (1847)

We see the futility of the old arts of preserving the body; we see the defects of the old theology; we learn that the race never dies, the individual is never spared. We give our earth to earth. We will not jealously guard a few atoms, selfishly and impossibly sequestering them from the vast circulations of nature; but at the same time we fully admit the divine hope and love which belong to our nature, and wish to make one spot tender to our children who shall come hither in the next century to read the dates of these lives.

—Ralph Waldo Emerson, "Address to the Inhabitants of Concord at the Consecration of Sleepy Hollow Cemetery" (September 29, 1855)

WHEN IT BECAME CLEAR that Mayor Josiah Quincy would not be able to create such a cemetery under municipal auspices, Joseph Buckingham advised his fellow citizens to take matters into their own hands. He addressed the growing spirit of benevolence, reform, and philanthropy, asking, "If we in life make sacrifices for the public good, shall we be selfish in death?" New Haven had already distanced its burial grounds from the civic center, and Bostonians might do likewise. Buckingham asked, "Who would wish to be buried in a close city and a crowded graveyard, to be deranged and knocked about, separated and disjointed, long before the last trumpet sounds? Would we not rather lie serenely where the pure breeze rustles the honeysuckles, and the field flowers, the long grass and the drooping willow, which cover and hang over our graves? Where, secure from unhallowed footsteps and boisterous mirth, the reeling tread of the drunkard, or the daily vapid gaze of the thoughtless, we lie quiet, undisturbed and happy?"[1] Buckingham publicized the ideal of rural burials to Bostonians not yet familiar with the literary recommendations of the likes of William Cullen Bryant, Washington Irving, and William Wordsworth.

Proposals for a pastoral cemetery appeared in

other Boston newspapers as well. One writer, identified merely as "A Traveller," suggested to the editor of the *Columbian Centinel* that an ideal site for a new cemetery would be on two lofty hills (possibly Fort Hill) available for purchase in South Boston, a site "superior to any thing in the vicinity" and "susceptible of great elegance at a trifling expense" because of the natural beauty of the place. A cemetery there would be far preferable to "a noisome appalling enclosure" in the city "from which we turn with disgust and dread." The City might purchase the property, enclose it, and convert it "into a delightful burying ground, which might be called the *Field of Repose,* as that of Père Lachaise of Paris." It would also be similar to New Haven's New Burying Ground. Thereby, "many objections to shutting up the old yards would be removed at once." The Traveller waxed poetic: "When we should behold from afar, a lofty column, or the more humble testimony of affectionate remembrance, a *white* stone, reared amidst waving willows, often would our feet thither turn, with mournful satisfaction." There Bostonians would pass some of their "most pleasant and improving hours in 'converse with the departed,' " visiting frequently to learn "the lesson of our own mortality; and, that, from those we love, even death itself cannot separate us." The site would be visible from the city. "When we saw the last rays of the setting sun illume the summits of these beautiful hills, the recollection that *there* was laid in peace the remains of a dear husband or wife or child would assuage our grief and chasten our sorrow; and many of those gloomy thoughts which come over the minds in the hours of sadness would thereby be dispelled."[2]

This writer did not simply react against urban graveyards and crypt burials but presented detailed, substantive recommendations for a new institution to teach lessons of moral philosophy, to inspire the beneficial emotion of melancholy rather than dread of death, and to foster a socially stabilizing cult of ancestors. The Traveller's proposed cemetery would provide democratized commemoration with posthumous remembrance based on accomplishments of the deceased in life and emotions engendered in survivors visiting the grave in a pastoral setting. The highly symbolic description was that of the mourning picture with neoclassical monuments under weeping willow and venerable oak, a romantic landscape with a view over the distant city. The white stone, not a stark gray stele, stood out framed in green in the light of the setting sun, another emblem of death. No further rationalizations based on public health arguments were necessary for the prescribed genius of place.

Proposals for alternatives to Boston's graveyards, after the burial controversy of 1823, focused cultural trends—a growing historical consciousness, a desire to create exemplary institutions through voluntary association to ameliorate city life, a sentimentalism shaped by affective individualism, and new notions of death conditioned by liberalized religion. Although several cemetery proposals and descriptions were tendered in the wake of the burial controversy, only one individual took action. Dr. Jacob Bigelow followed the public and private discussion of reform along with other Bostonians. (Fig. 7.1.) Later, he noted simply that in about 1825 he "had his attention called to certain gross abuses in the practice of Sepulture as it existed under churches and in other receptacles of the dead" in the city.[3] But Bigelow was not content simply to complain or debate; he took action and launched the project for creation of America's first "rural" cemetery.

In many ways, Bigelow was like other members of Boston's new elite, sons of small-town ministers who moved from the hinterland to the city in the 1820s and 1830s to establish careers and form the class that Oliver Wendell Holmes later labeled "Brahmin." Ambitious for a prosperous, professional future that could only be had in the region's "metropolis," Bigelow uprooted himself from his past in a New England town, leaving his parents' graves in the old Sudbury burying ground and his own rights to burial there. Like other newcomers to the city—Daniel Webster, Joseph Story—he had no family tomb in a Boston graveyard; furthermore, Mayor Quincy's regulations made certain that no new ones could be built on the Shawmut Peninsula. Some wealthy merchants with rural estates around the city's periphery installed tombs and burial grounds in their gardens in the English fashion, so many that Thomas G. Fessenden, edi-

Fig. 7.1. Dr. Jacob Bigelow, portrait photograph, ca. 1855.

tor of the *New England Farmer* and author of *The American Gardener* (1828), decried the practice as evidence of "gloomy" taste. Fessenden urged banishing "tombs and cemeteries" entirely from private gardens as "they always awaken melancholy reflections in old people, for they remind them of their approaching end." Mausoleums in estate gardens might have provided a temporary solution to crowding of urban graveyards as an alternative to church crypts, especially given the English precedent. But, whether because of a propensity for collective action and voluntary association or fears of the impermanence of property, New Englanders tended to reject private burial. Furthermore, Bigelow and others who owned only townhouses had no special provisions for their dead.[4]

Bigelow was a busy, ambitious thirty-eight-year-old physician in 1825. His intellectual qualifications and recently developed social connections predisposed his proposed cemetery venture to success. The son of a minister of modest means, he settled in Boston in 1811 after earning a degree from Harvard College and an M.D. from the University of Pennsylvania the previous year. His elder brother, Henry, an aspiring Boston merchant whose life would be cut short in 1815 by accident in Baltimore, helped him weather initial financial difficulties. Alexander H. Everett, his Harvard classmate, law student in the office of John Quincy Adams, and brother of Edward Everett, introduced him to a social circle with scholarly interests, including Nathan Hale and Edward Channing. They met on Saturday nights in George Ticknor's study for literary discussions emphasizing classical and English romantic works. Bigelow won election to the Anthology Club, the Athenaeum, the Massachusetts Historical Society, the American Association of Arts and Sciences (1812), the American Philosophical Society (1818), and several international medical and scientific societies. At Harvard College and its new medical school, he taught botany, materia medica (medicinal use of plants), and the application of the sciences to the useful arts—a field he termed "technology," introducing the word to American usage. By his early thirties, Bigelow had published four volumes on horticulture: *Florula Bostoniensis* (1814 and 1824) and *American Medical Botany* (1817–20), illustrated in color from copperplates by a method he invented.[5] These books won him an international reputation, including a certificate of "hommage" from the Société Linnéénne de Paris and commendation by the Royal Horticultural Society of London.[6]

Dr. James Jackson, one of the physicians who testified to the City Council that crypts under Saint Paul's would not endanger public health, took Bigelow into his prosperous medical practice. No records remain of Bigelow's specific position on the burial controversy, but his general medical philosophy opposed what he considered artificial interference in the processes of nature, especially the traditional bleedings and purgings that characterized disease treatment at that time, although he was one of the first Boston physicians to use chloroform to ease the pain of childbirth. Although Bigelow seemingly shared the antimiasmatist view of Boston medical leaders, the young physician's sympathies lay with more naturalistic solutions to burials of the city's dead than those proposed by Dr. Warren. Bigelow favored the tone and substance of Quincy's report on urban burials.

In November of 1825, Bigelow invited to his Spring Street home a dozen friends, all influential Bostonians—John Lowell, William Sturgis, George Bond, Judge Joseph Story, General Henry A. S. Dearborn, Edward Everett, Thomas W. Ward, John Tappen, Samuel P. Gardiner, and Nathan Hale—many of them active members of the Bunker Hill Monument Association and other Boston cultural institutions. Hale, son of a classmate of James Hillhouse at Yale, knew about New Haven's New Burying Ground. Bigelow proposed that his group form a voluntary association to create a similar extramural cemetery for Boston, "composed of family burial lots, separated and interspersed with trees, shrubs, and flowers, in a wood or a landscape garden."[7]

The suggestion was favorably received by all who knew the arguments for such an institution by Wordsworth, other English writers, French reformers, Washington Irving, and participants in the local burial controversy. Several prominent citizens not at the meeting had already promised Bigelow their support. They knew that Bigelow's proposed cemetery would put into practice a shared historical philosophy, summarized by Bigelow in his 1816 address when he was made first Rumford Professor at Harvard. Mount Auburn would preserve the memories of notable Americans to the credit of the region and the nation; it would perpetuate bonds of familial affection beyond death.[8]

But whereas Bigelow advocated institutionalizing the memories of lives lived, he criticized preservation of the corpse as unnatural. He spoke positively of the processes of decay, reminding Bostonians in a public lecture shortly after proposing the new cemetery that decayed physical material did not become "extinct or useless" but served as substance "from which other living frames are to be constructed." The dead body "contributes its remains to the nourishment of plants around it. . . . Were it not for this law of nature, the soil would soon be exhausted, the earth's surface would become a barren waste, and the whole race of organized beings, for want of sustenance, would become extinct." Existing urban burial places were unnatural and upset the equilibrium of a natural system that ensured fertility of the soil, crucial to development of experimental gardens and maintenance of rural agricultural production. In addition, they offended the sensibilities of people no longer willing to tolerate the smell of rotting human flesh and other "noxious effluvia."[9]

Bigelow condemned postmortem "preservative agents," or anything that would interrupt the process of decay, although embalming, cremation, and similar practices were virtually nonexistent in New England in the 1820s. Bigelow even disliked the "subterranean vaults and walls of brick" common in Boston graveyards as evidence of the pretension "to divide the clay of humanity from that of the rest of creation, and to preserve it separate for a time, as it were, for future inspection." According to Bigelow, "resistance to the laws of nature" could "at best only preserve a defaced and degraded image of what was once perfect and beautiful." His alternative was a burial system in which "nature is permitted to take its course, when the dead are committed to the earth under the open sky, to become early and peacefully blended with its original dust." Bigelow's proposals were based on changing sensibilities and a desire to restore the equilibrium of nature's processes rather than on explicit public health concerns. They were preventive rather than curative.[10]

As William B. O. Peabody, a minister, horticulturist, and early cemetery proponent, observed, "We cannot speak confidently with respect to the danger to health which arises" from burying in urban churches. Peabody believed that the danger to health from burials in cities had "probably been over-rated, if, indeed, it exists at all."[11] Bigelow, Peabody, and their friends had stronger motivations for proposing a naturalistic landscape than the desire for a site outside the city. Literary arguments for pastoralism and melancholy familiar from readings of the Anthology Club and from shelves of the Athenaeum—Wordsworth, Scott, Byron, Pope, Addison, and the Scottish rationalists—informed their taste. Bigelow especially liked the notions of the naturalness of death expressed in William Cullen Bryant's "Thanatopsis" (1817), in which nature assuages fear of death by inspiring acceptance of the inevitable surrender of individual existence. Like the poet, Bigelow accepted and even looked forward to the prospect "To mix forever with the elements, / To be a brother to the insensible rock / And to the sluggish clod." Nature became the great democratizer, "the great tomb of man." In proposing a pastoral cemetery in lieu of urban burials, Bigelow might have quoted Bryant:

> The groves were God's first temple . . .
> Ah, why
> Should we in the world's riper years, neglect
> God's ancient sanctuaries, and adore
> Only among the crowd, and under roofs
> That our frail hands have raised?[12]

The natural processes of decay as well as the worship of the divine belonged "in the retired valley or the sequestered wood, where the soil continues its primitive exuberance, and where the earth has not become too costly to afford to each occupant at least his length and breadth." There, the decay would "take place peacefully, silently, separately," and be "merged and lost in the surrounding harmonies of the creation."[13] There, each burial would have its own earthen grave, to remain untouched in perpetuity.

Bigelow and his associates began to consider the idea of natural decay of the dead "in the embrace of nature" beautiful. Bigelow cited the discovery of the remains of Major John André, executed for spying with Benedict Arnold against American revolutionaries. The workers disinterring André's body from the grave overlooking the Hudson River found roots of a massive tree wound through the Englishman's skull, "a natural and most beautiful coincidence" that "a faithful sentinel" had been posted "to watch till the obliterated ashes should no longer need a friend." Such sights occurred even on the streets of Boston, inspiring wonder rather than horror. The old Colonel Joseph May told of a similar discovery on his morning walk along Tremont Street. Gazing into the open tomb of the Cunningham family where James Otis lay in the Old Granary Burying Ground, May exclaimed, "Behold! the coffin was full of the fibrous roots of the elm, especially thick and matted about the skull." The sight reinforced May's equations of death and nature with a proto-Transcendental lesson. Glancing at an adjacent street tree, a "noble elm," May saw "in transfigured glory . . . all that was material of James Otis." Bigelow only wanted to create a more secluded place where such processes could take place in peace and privacy, for he considered them inappropriate and incongruent in the center of the bustling city. In a wooded cemetery, trees would hasten decomposition, stand as monuments to the deceased whose substance they consumed, and represent the divinely ordained system of nature.[14]

To permit and encourage decay of the dead "in the embrace of nature" also represented a pantheism shared by many Boston Unitarians. The Reverend Joseph Stevens Buckminster thought God could logically be seen in the design and organization of Nature; William Ellery Channing proclaimed, "God is in nature. God is in history." Channing considered nature a source of civilization, reminding Americans, "If we then are destitute of the antiquity of human institutions, we should never forget that we possess the antiquity of nature." The dead, history, and the role of God in Nature melded in Unitarian thought and premised Bigelow's proposal for a cemetery and a system in which "the forbidding and repulsive conditions which attend on decay" would be "merged and lost in the surrounding harmonies of creation."[15]

Stoicism and rationalism tempered old fears of death for Bigelow and fellow Unitarians. The Reverend William Ware declared in 1827, "Death, we regard not so much as even a temporary, momentary extinction of being, but simply as the appointed manner in which we shall pass from one stage of existence to another—from earth to heaven." The Reverend Hosea Ballou explained, "Our fleshly bodies, like the grass of the earth, are composed of the elements of nature; these elements support both the grass and our fleshly bodies; and as the grass finally withers and returns back from whence it came, is decomposed and joined with the elements of which it was composed, so do our bodies return to the earth from whence they came." Such religious liberals believed that "to the virtuous man death has no terror, it is the gate of life." They rationally accepted the message of *memento mori* of old colonial gravestones but without their Calvinistic suggestion of imminent damnation. Although they saw no horror in the skull or death's-head, they preferred to use more naturalistic and cheering symbols of death. Those of like minds only found sublime beauty and even intimations of immortality in the processes of nature that affected the human body after death.[16]

Until the nascent romanticism and the new taste of the elite for horticulture and picturesque landscapes of the 1820s, most New Englanders did not care about making a burial place beautiful or even about cleaning up existing burial grounds or placing plantings there. Bigelow observed, "Trees, whose inexpressible beauty has been provided by the hand of the Creator as the great ornament of earth, have rarely been planted about our graveyards; the enclosures are generally inadequate and neglected, the graves indecently crowded together and often, after a few years, disturbed; and the whole appearance as little calculated as possible to invite the visits of the seriously disposed, to tranquilize the feelings of surviving friends, and to gratify that disposition which would lead us to pay respect to their ashes."[17]

In addition to appeals to personal emotions and aesthetics, Bigelow called upon the pride and boosterism of civic leaders to win supporters for creation of a pastoral cemetery, an urban institution in a suburban location. He reminded his friends that leaders in Paris, London, Liverpool, and other European cities had either recently created such cemeteries outside their limits or were contemplating doing so. (Fig. 7.2.) These cemeteries served as showcases for local "ornamental taste" and attracted travelers. There, "the scenes which, under most other circumstances are repulsive and disgusting, are by the joint influence of nature and art rendered beautiful, attractive, and consoling." Art would complement Nature in "a landscape of the most picturesque character," where the "hand of taste" would scatter granite and marble memorials among the trees. Bigelow urged public-spirited Bostonians to create a silent city for their dead in a symbolic natural setting, for the cemetery would represent the city itself as repository of former residents and place of display of high culture.[18]

Bigelow's proposed cemetery would not be purely functional, for disposal of the city's dead, but would fill many other cultural needs—honoring the deceased, cultivating the civilizing emotion of melancholy, teaching moralistic lessons, and fostering a sense of the past as pertinent to the present and future. The cemetery would permit a sort of commemoration impossible in existing graveyards. Another early supporter of the cemetery, Thaddeus William Harris, observed, "In the public graveyard it is not always in the power of an individual to appropriate a single place of burial, space enough for the purposes of decent and respectful ornament." At the new cemetery it would be "in the power of every one, who may wish it, at an expense considerably less than that of a common tomb or a vault beneath a church to deposit the mortal remains of his friends and to provide a place of burial for himself, which, while living, he may contemplate without dread of disgust; one which is secure from the danger of being encroached upon,

Fig. 7.2. Liverpool Cemetery, engraving by T. M. Baynes, 1836.

as in the graveyards of the city; secluded from every species of uncongenial intrusion; surrounded with every thing that can fill the heart with tender and respectful emotions; beneath the shade of a venerable tree, on the slope of a verdant lawn, and with the seclusion of the forest, removed from all the discordant scenes of life."[19]

Harris, Bigelow, and others echoed Wordsworth in urging that burials be removed from "the tumultuous and harassing din of cities" and placed "amid the quiet verdure of the field," where "the harmonious and ever-changing face of nature reminds us, by its resuscitating influences, that to die is but to live again."[20] They had distinct ideas about the first qualities a cemetery site should possess—soil fit for burials without heavy boulders to make grave-digging difficult, with loose and sandy substance to hasten decomposition, and at enough distance from the city to isolate the site from rampant urbanization yet close enough to permit easy access given the transportation limitations of the day.

Immediately following Bigelow's first cemetery meeting, George Bond and John Tappan volunteered to search for a fitting site. They tried to acquire Augustus Aspinwall's estate in Brookline, just west of Boston, but the owner refused sale. They considered property on both sides of Western Avenue near the Punch Bowl on the road leading from the Shawmut Peninsula, but the land, so close to the city, proved too expensive. Real estate values soared in the 1820s, making it particularly difficult to procure land; Bigelow complained that some suburban landowners were reluctant to sell their property for a cemetery or to have one located in their vicinity. None of the sites Bigelow considered would have lent itself to creation of a pastoral landscape.[21] Fortunately, these initial efforts to procure land for a cemetery did not succeed; otherwise, Boston might have gotten simply an extramural burial ground with plantings but without a picturesque landscape design—a place similar to that created outside of New Haven three decades before and without further stylistic inspiration.

Bigelow's cemetery proposal languished for five years, and his friends did not put much work into the project. Bigelow had more pressing priorities, including publication in 1829 of his Harvard lectures "on the application of science to the useful arts," *Elements of Technology,* complete with his own mechanical and architectural illustrations. The national economic depression, which curtailed many projects requiring substantial expenditures, may also have delayed the cemetery's founding as it did construction of the Bunker Hill Monument. For five years, Bigelow succeeded only in attracting the attention of many of the city's cultural leaders, the same individuals with whom he discussed literature and creation of other voluntary associations for making Boston the "Athens of America."

Such an institution was the Massachusetts Horticultural Society, granted a charter in 1829 to develop the quality and diversity of plants grown in New England. Like the various societies for promotion of agriculture or of useful manufactures formed after the revolution, it was meant to strengthen American civilization through eco-

Fig. 7.3. Membership certificate, Massachusetts Horticultural Society.

nomic independence and to further regional prosperity through an increased and diversified variety of domestic plants. Its founders, Henry A. S. Dearborn and John Lowell, called horticulture "the most distinguished of the fine arts"; they described an intricate relationship between the "culture" of plants and the "culture" of the nation, glorying in the ambiguities of the term.[22] (Fig. 7.3.)

As first president of the society, Dearborn traced the history of horticulture to ancient Egypt, where "the stupendous temples, pyramids and obelisks" became wonders of the world along fertile Nile banks "adorned by a succession of luxuriant plantations." Dearborn saw the foundations of the arts and sciences in the horticultural achievements of ancient civilizations. Although Dearborn acknowledged advances in horticulture in ancient Greece and Rome, he found the greatest developments did not come until the "improved style of gardening" of eighteenth-century England described by Milton, Addison, Pope, and Kent. Dearborn suggested that if these precedents could be followed, and if only Americans would seriously develop their stock of plants and their skill in arranging garden landscapes, history pointed to America as the next great civilization. He proposed that Bostonians transform the Charles River into an artery of prosperity and culture similar to the Nile.[23] Such a call appealed to intellectual Bostonians, who ransacked ancient precedents for forms with which to fashion their new culture.

Bigelow lent his support to the horticulturists and became the society's corresponding secretary, expanding his already extensive international contacts to include the likes of Sir Walter Scott, an honorary member of the society from its inception. Zebedee Cook, Jr., vice president of the new society, stressed the importance of "reciprocal interchange of opinions and sentiments" between Boston and Paris, where a similar organization had been formed in 1826, following the model of the London Horticultural Society, which dated from 1805. Scientific naturalism spread internationally, conditioning the taste for pastoral landscapes as well as more practical attempts to develop diversified plants for ornamentation and cash crops. The Massachusetts Horticultural Society was not the first such organization in America but followed the New York Society, incorporated in 1822, and the Pennsylvania Horticultural Society, based in Philadelphia in 1827. As with monument building, Bostonians determined not to lag far behind.[24]

Despite the opening of a few commercial nurseries in the vicinity, Boston did not have the resources of other urban areas to furnish ornamental plantings for private gardens. John Lowell expressed the need in 1822, observing, "we are utterly destitute in New England of nurseries . . . on an extensive scale. We have no cultivators on whom we can call for a supply of the most common plants. . . . we have no place to which we can go for plants to ornament our grounds." Establishment of the Massachusetts Horticultural Society was one attempt to remedy the deficiency as Bostonians tried to compete with the amenities of "sister Cities"—New York, Philadelphia, Baltimore, and Charleston. Writing in the *New England Farmer,* Dearborn noted that the horticultural society would serve as a "branch of our domestic industry," an "association of men of taste, of influence, and industry," similar to those in other major cities. It would supplement individual efforts, which "generously and patriotically" were helping to develop and collect varieties of fruits, vegetables, and ornamentals.[25]

These gentleman horticulturists aimed to spread "rural taste" to their fellow Americans, permitting them to draw upon indigenous sources for the creation of culture rather than simply borrowing from abroad. The term "rural" implied far more than tilled fields. It reflected the perception that nature in the form of a tree-covered, green countryside—the "rural"—was rapidly disappearing along the Atlantic seaboard, like the deforestation that preceded the rise in the taste for the pastoral in England a century before. "Rural taste" involved both nostalgia for America's original, semi-forested landscape and desire for a way of life in harmony with nature associated in many minds with a vanishing or vanished primeval or Arcadian past.

Commemorative valuation of trees increased in New England as it had in Britain and France. Ancient and "venerable" trees, considered sublime, seemed especially threatened with destruction by

Fig. 7.4. Tree at Cambridge Common under which Washington assumed command of the Continental Army, engraving from *Gleason's Pictorial*, ca. 1845.

the hand of man. A number of particular old and notable trees served as landmarks or historical sites—oaks used by Indians as sites for councils or liberty trees with newer associations. In Cambridge alone, there was the "Whitefield tree" on the northwest side of the Common, where the Wesleyan evangelist preached in 1740 when denied use of the Puritan pulpit. The Rebellion Tree in Harvard Yard was the site where students traditionally gathered to protest against faculty. Even more important was the tree on the Common where Washington assumed command of the Continental Army on July 3, 1775. (Fig. 7.4.) The Massachusetts Historical Society, founded in 1791, solicited specimens of New England's natural history as well as written documents and other historical artifacts for its collection. Horticulturists in the 1820s considered other means of preserving ancient trees either individually or as entire pastoral properties threatened with displacement in the vicinities of cities.

By the end of the 1820s, old farms and estates ringing Boston often served as the only preserves of woodland and orchards—enclaves of the picturesque—from the hills of Milton and Roxbury to the south, to Cambridge and Watertown in the west, to Salem well into Essex County on the north. In this belt of rural culture, the first nurseries in New England sprang up. Horticulturists worried that because of America's lack of primogeniture, such estates would be sold and subdivided in subsequent generations or that their owners would hesitate to plant trees that would not mature in their lifetimes. They anticipated industries lining the shores of New England's rivers and streams; as urbanization spread, real estate values around the urban periphery would soar, and any remaining wooded land would be cleared for planting vegetables for the increasing demands of the city for food.

George Watson Brimmer, a merchant and member of the same circles as Bigelow, shared these concerns in 1825 when he purchased seventy-two acres of rolling, wooded land on the town line between Cambridge and Watertown. The property was four miles west of Boston, between two quiet towns undergoing rapid transition. Cambridge had a population of only 6,072 in 1830, yet the rural land on its western border seemed as destined to inevitable dissolution as its poetic namesake, Sweet Auburn. Harvard students had frequented the place, originally called "Stone's Woods," since the turn of the century. They renamed it "Sweet Auburn" in 1801 after Oliver Goldsmith's nostalgic poem "The Deserted Village" (1770), lamenting the erstwhile "loveliest village of the plain," one of the many small English and Irish towns destroyed during the eighteenth-century consolidation of estates. Jones Very, later a Transcendental poet, took his tutorial students to Sweet Auburn for discussions. Charles Francis Adams, Ralph Waldo Emerson, Bigelow, and Brimmer had fond recollections of time spent in Stone's Woods, the overgrown remnants of Simon Stone's farm, which dated from the early colonial period. (Fig. 7.5.) The poet Caroline Orne, who grew up in the neighborhood, described the farm's boundary as that river "whose waters flowed in many a graceful sweep," a place where "willows, bending downward, kissed the stream." It was one of the most picturesque places in the Boston metropolitan area.[26]

Orne and others with a romantic turn of mind considered it a "fairy place," magical because "the first dwelling, falling to decay, was left deserted, mouldering away," a ruin that touched a chord of nostalgia in those with a new taste for the picturesque. The place reminded them of New England's old colonial past, now just as completely obliterated as the cultures of Indians who once used the site for war councils before selling the land to Stone. Orne spent her youth in Sweet Auburn's grounds, its "cool retreats, the favorite walks, the hills covered with the fragrant wild strawberry or the various and beautiful tribes of

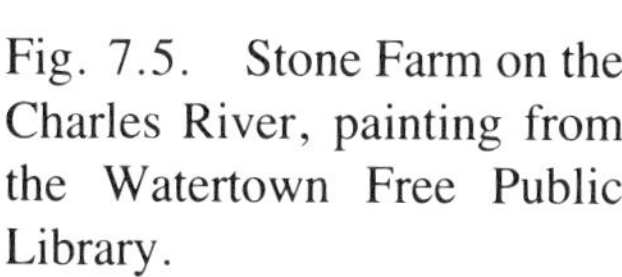

Fig. 7.5. Stone Farm on the Charles River, painting from the Watertown Free Public Library.

Fig. 7.6. (*Left*) Wooded view of Fresh Pond looking north from the summit of Sweet Auburn, engraving by Pendleton, ca. 1831, AAS.

Fig. 7.7. (*Opposite page, top*) Map of Boston and environs, engraved by Abel Bowen, ca. 1830. The hills of Sweet Auburn are four miles northwest of Boston and a mile from Harvard College. They lie on the Cambridge-Watertown line, north of the Charles River and south of Fresh Pond.

Fig. 7.8. (*Opposite page, bottom*) "Map of Boston and Its Vicinity from Actual Survey with Corrections in 1833," by John G. Hales.

mosses," describing as forming scenes of "pristine beauty." Similarly, James Russell Lowell remembered picking hazelnuts and watching chipmunks skirting the bogs there as a child, declaring in 1837, "Show me a place so sweet as that most delightful of spots, Sweet Auburn!"[27] (Fig. 7.6.)

Brimmer wanted to preserve Sweet Auburn's trees—some estimated to be over sixty years old, many old oak, beech, cedar, and pine. There was a walnut grove and a pear orchard. Brimmer determined to retain the natural, parklike landscape "for some public or appropriate use."[28] The property might otherwise have been a prime site for development. It was on a major public way, the River Road connected to the Boston Post Road, the major overland route through New England to New York. The navigable, tidal Charles River with salt marshes lining its banks stretched along the south side of the property. Mills, factories, warehouses, and wharves were rapidly being built along the river as far upstream as Waltham to the west, where the Boston Manufacturing Company started its first textile mill in 1815. Watertown had soap and candle manufactories, a paper mill, and a dye-house. In 1820 the federal government built the first part of its massive arsenal with a complex of storehouses, barracks, workshops, and wharves on forty acres across the river from the New England Lace Factory, half a mile upstream from Stone's Woods. (Figs. 7.7, 8.)

Initially Brimmer intended to create his own residence at Sweet Auburn just west of the prestigious old Tory Row, renamed Brattle Street, and near the new rural estates of some of Boston's elite. James Russell Lowell's country seat, "Elmwood," later home of Harvard's presidents, was just to the east. To the west and north lay Charles Davenport's "Fountain Hill," Harrison Gray Otis's "Oakley," and John P. Cushing's "Belmont." The natural qualities of the land resembled the ideal landscape achieved only through considerable artifice in an English landscape garden. Several acres of "wildwood," with large and varied forest trees, were separated from each other by lawns, ponds, old orchards, and rugged slopes and valleys. A glacial moraine crossed the property, creating a varied terrain of hills, grassy knolls, dells, bogs, rambling ponds, bosks, copses, and clearings. The landform was created in four successive periods of the Ice Age, part of the Boston Basin that stretched up the Charles River as far as Watertown; unlike land elsewhere in the region, however, there were few rock outcroppings. Rather, the soil varied between sand plains and clay beds over an underlying ledge of slate fifteen to two hundred feet

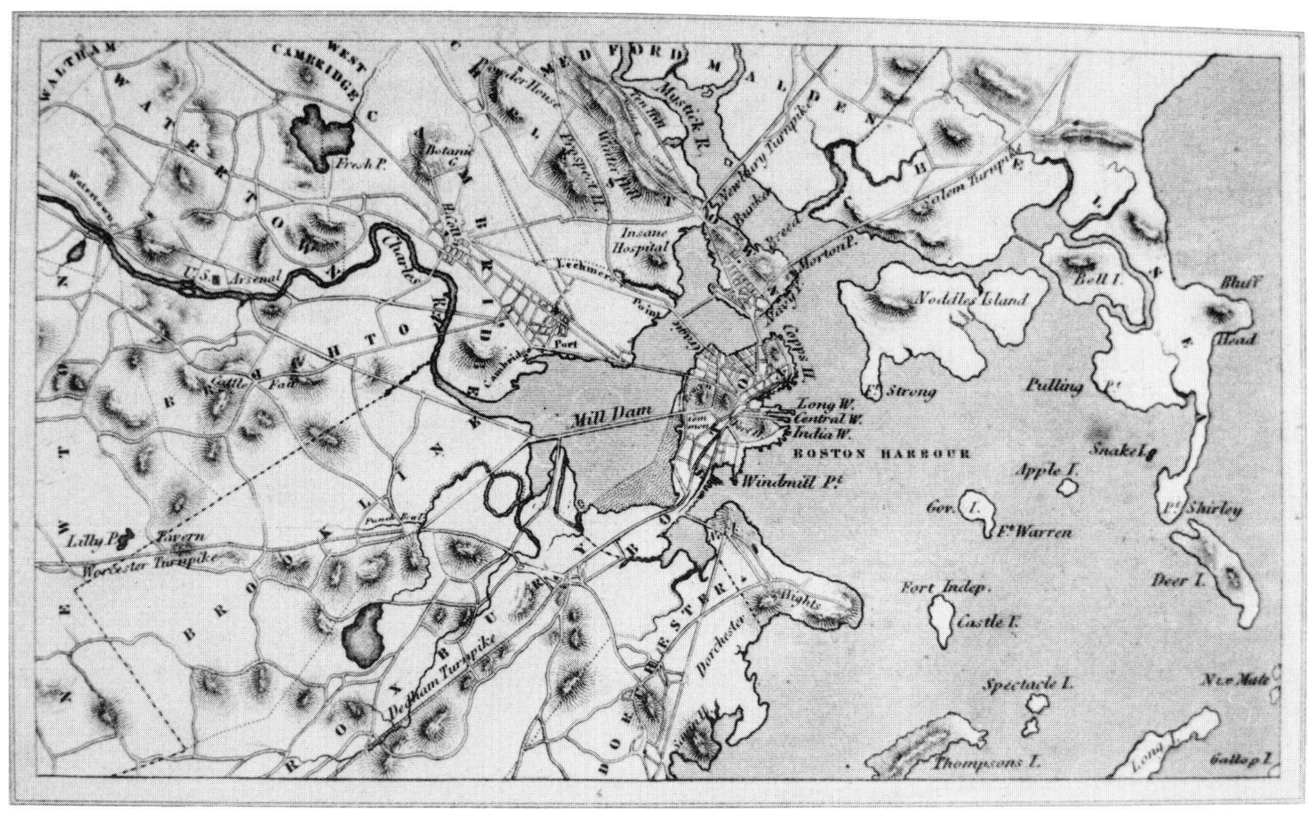

WALTHAM
WEST CAMBRIDGE
MEDFORD
MALDEN
WATERTOWN
CAMBRIDGE
Fresh P.
Botanic G.
Powder House
Mystick R.
Prospect H.
Winter Hill
Newbury Turnpike
Salem Turnpike
Bunker
Insane Hospital
Lechmere Point
U.S. Arsenal
Charles R.
Mill Dam
Noddles Island
Bell I.
Bluff Head
Pulling Pt.
Ft. Strong
Long W.
Central W.
India W.
BOSTON HARBOUR
Snake I.
Apple I.
Windmill Pt.
Gov. I.
Ft. Warren
Pt. Shirley
Deer I.
Fort Indep.
Castle I.
Spectacle I.
Thompsons I.
Dorchester Hights
Lilly P.
Tavern
Worcester Turnpike
Dedham Turnpike
Cattle Fair

WALTHAM PLAINS
Beaver Brook
WATERTOWN
CAMBRIDGE
Fresh Pond Hotel
Botanical Garden
Harvard University
U.S. Arsenal
Lechmere Point
CAMBRIDGE PORT
River
Mill Dam
BOSTON
BOSTON HARBOUR
Tremont Street
SOUTH BOSTON

below the surface.

Brimmer made a wise choice in buying Sweet Auburn, even if he was not to live there. He planted ornamental trees, created a few winding roads through the hills, and staked out sites for a new house and stables; by 1830, however, impeded by the nation's economic depression, construction had not yet begun on the estate. Perhaps increasing illness discouraged Brimmer's original plans, or he was simply motivated to preserve the pastoralism of the site rather than to develop it as a country seat. Brimmer may have visited Père Lachaise Cemetery in Paris and felt that Sweet Auburn would be perfect for creation of a similar burial landscape outside of Boston, but no documentary evidence remains to validate the supposition. It is even unclear whether Brimmer first approached Bigelow with the proposal that his property might be the proper site for a cemetery or whether Bigelow solicited it from his old college friend.[29]

Both agreed that many characteristics of Sweet Auburn predisposed it for the new cemetery. The site, peripheral to the developing city, was typical of those chosen for the sort of undesirable institutions then being removed from urban centers—prisons, insane asylums, hospitals, orphanages, and cemeteries. David Rothman characterizes places chosen for relocation of such "asylums" as having "tranquil, natural, and rural" grounds of ample proportions centered on "a low hillside with an unobstructed view of surrounding landscape." Nathan Hale, Bigelow's publisher friend, wrote that Sweet Auburn was as near the city "as is consistent with perfect security from the approach of these establishments [industries], usually found in the neighborhood of a large town, but not in harmony with the character of a place of burial." It was extensive enough that burials might be placed on the high ground toward the center of the property and the periphery reserved for decades as a buffer zone.[30]

Sweet Auburn was also newly accessible to Bostonians. Through the eighteenth century, the Charles River remained a barrier to easy travel from Boston to Cambridge and the nearby areas to the north and west; but in 1794, when the West Boston Bridge (on the site now occupied by the Longfellow Bridge) was constructed, it shortened the old eight-mile trip from Boston to Harvard College to two and a half miles. The next year, daily stage runs began along this route; by 1826, they became hourly. It was the first high-frequency route in America and preceded similar routes in the vicinity of Paris and London by two or three years. Bostonians, who from 1823 to 1826 considered only hilltops to the south of the city as possible locations for a rural cemetery, began to look to the north and west for appropriate sites. Hearses, introduced in 1796 in Boston for bearing coffins beyond the immediate vicinity of the deceased's house, and carriages, newly available for hire, could form funeral processions and carry mourners to burial places much farther from the city than had been possible in the old days when funeral processions proceeded on foot following the coffin borne by pallbearers to the nearby graveyard.

The outstanding feature of Sweet Auburn was its central hill rising 125 feet above the river, commanding what Bigelow called "one of the finest prospects which can be obtained in the environs of Boston." The Reverend William B. O. Peabody told his fellow horticulturists that the summit was "reached by a gentle ascent, which winds like a road round the hill, with valleys on each side, and is so exact in its bearing that it is difficult to persuade one's-self that man had no agency in forming it." From its top, one saw the serpentine course of the Charles River leading to the sea. The major part of the river's course, lined with tidal salt marshes, created a broad swath of open space between city and proposed cemetery. On all sides there stretched dramatic panoramas encompassing the metropolitan area. On a clear day, one could see as far as the Blue Hills of Milton to the south, Mount Monadnock in New Hampshire in the north, and the ocean to the east.[31]

The topography was ideal for creating a landscape in the English fashion, a standard feature of which was a "mount" or central high point reached by a spiraling path from which the estate owner could survey surrounding territory. Often a structure like a temple, pavilion, or tower topped the mount, providing places for contemplation or for experiencing the sublime inherent in the distant horizons. Those who read the first-century Greek philosopher Longinus, newly translated and popular among eighteenth- and early nineteenth-century literati, considered wide horizons and large rivers particularly sublime. Panoramic vistas were reminders of infinity and God, capable of flinging the imagination into "a pleasing astonishment." In *The General Scholium* of his *Mathematical Principles of Natural Philosophy,* Newton describes God's literal presence in space. Hence, distant vistas and panoramas suggestive of infinity were more than representative of the divine; they were actual attributes of God. Adding the political to the theological, Joseph Addison wrote that "a spacious horizon is an image of liberty." Following these theories, English landscape gardeners arranged plants and distant architectural elements called eye-catchers to maximize such prospects. Such examples and theories of landscape aesthetics were familiar to Boston literati and appealed to their liberal religious sensibilities.[32]

Panoramic views captured the imagination of Americans and Europeans alike in the early nineteenth century. Artists attempted to duplicate their sublime qualities in popular painted dioramas exhibited in many major cities. Landscape dioramas were often fashioned in a complete circle, with special effects created by lighting and multiple transparencies. Enthusiasm for these sweeping views was explained by the belief that dramatic perspectives and panoramas triggered powerful emotional associations, similar to those elicited by vistas in English landscaped gardens. One British writer described the sensations experienced on viewing a diorama exhibited in London in 1823: "The decided effect of the thing is that you look over an area of twenty miles. . . . You have, as far as the senses can be acted upon, all these things (realities) before you; and yet in the midst of all this crowd of animation, there is a stillness, which is the stillness of the grave. The idea produced is that of a region—of a world—desolated; of living nature at an end; of the last day past and over." Even Edgar Allen Poe described the sublime emotions elicited by distant, panoramic views, considered especially capable of being catalysts for melancholy and moralistic meditations.[33]

For these reasons, the site of Père Lachaise, with its panoramic view over the city of Paris, seemed particularly appropriate for an innovative cemetery inspired by English landscape taste. The example of the French cemetery, as well as the desire to preserve the highest point at Sweet Auburn for its unsurpassed view of the city and surrounding countryside, suggested to Brimmer and Bigelow that the ideal use for the property was for burials. The hilltop might also, they speculated, provide a fine site for a monument dedicated to George Washington to complement the Bunker Hill Monument, which was on a summit just to the east of the city—the sort of location recently advocated by William Tudor.

Other topographical features of Sweet Auburn were perfect for a romantic cemetery. The bodies of water and wetlands lent themselves to design of a picturesque landscape full of allegorical meaning. Folklore held that lakes and ponds as well as trees had powers to contain spirits. The presence of a deep, naturally circular dell in the middle of the property was symbolic, functioning like Walden Pond would as "mystic center" or *axis mundi* of Thoreau's cosmos, or, as Leo Marx points out, "like the 'naval of the earth' in the archaic myths studied by Mircea Eliade." It had the secluded feeling of a grotto, the womblike or tomblike enclosure of earth and rustic rock sheltering dark pools, brooks, or cascades—a basic fixture in English gardens. Yet Père Lachaise had no symbolic bodies of water. In their desire to form a landscape complete with reflective water, Mount Auburn's founders referred specifically to English precedents.[34]

Brimmer's willingness to provide Sweet Auburn gave new life to the proposal for an extramural cemetery. On November 27, 1830, Dearborn and John C. Gray joined Bigelow in calling a meeting of local gentlemen at the Exchange Coffee House to consider developing the cemetery there under the auspices of the new Massachusetts Horticultural Society rather than as an independent institution. Brimmer offered to sell his land for $6,000, taking a loss, and the horticulturists agreed to purchase it contingent on selling enough family lots to cover the cost.[35]

Dearborn, as president of the society, enthusiastically agreed with Bigelow and Brimmer that Sweet Auburn was ideal for a cemetery project.

The property was "consistent with perfect security" of burials, yet sufficiently distant from anticipated urban growth, which threatened to close existing Boston burial grounds. Dearborn assembled a committee including Bigelow, Brimmer, George Bond, John Lowell, Abbott Lawrence, and Thomas Handasyd Perkins to work out details. A week later, Dearborn publicly announced a plan for both a cemetery and an experimental horticultural garden, to be created separately on two sections of the grounds. Bigelow felt that the "young, active, and popular" horticultural society would ensure public acceptance of the innovative cemetery; in addition, the cemetery venture would enable the horticulturists to fulfill their own aspirations to establish an experimental garden. About forty acres were reserved for burials.[36]

Other horticulturists became active proponents of the cemetery project. Zebedee Cook, Jr., an insurance executive, lauded the idea of a multifunctional place "devoted to public uses" at the 1830 festival of Boston horticulturists. "Establishment of a public cemetery similar in its design to that of Père Lachaise in the environs of Paris, to be located in the suburbs of this metropolis," would further development of both horticultural and historical consciousness, Cook suggested. Being made "more alluring, more familiar, and imposing, by the aid of the rural embellishments," the place would connect "the present with the past" in a manner "peaceful and salutary to the physical and moral nature of man." Cook believed that "every generation of men is a link in the great chain that has been forming from the creation of the world, connecting the present with the past, and to be lengthened out through succeeding ages" with the assistance of the proposed cemetery. Cook advocated a landscape design following principles of the English style of gardening: "The skill and taste of the architect should be exerted in the construction of the requisite departments and avenues; and appropriate trees and plants should decorate its borders—the weeping-willow, waving its graceful drapery over the monumental marble and the somber foliage of the cypress should shade it; and the undying daisy should mingle its bright and glowing tints with the native laurel of our forests." Flowers "in their budding and bloom and decay" would be "silent and expressive teachers of morality," constant reminders of the fate of men and nations.[37]

Cook told his audience that the same salutary influences of the American System backed by John Quincy Adams and Henry Clay, a program that charged "the energies and hopes of our yeomanry," could be carried out on a local level by voluntary associations undertaking projects like the cemetery and garden to acculturate, educate, and produce better citizens. Thus, leaders could instill into the minds of ordinary Americans "a portion of their sentiments" and excite "in them a spirit of emulation, and the advantages that have accrued and still continue to follow their labors." Through institutional and material means, the elite could foster respect for authority and the work ethic at the same time as they elevated the taste of the "middling sort," stabilizing and improving the republic. The cemetery, according to Cook, would be a new sort of educational institution, affording "instruction and admonition" to all who visit it, not just to aspiring landscape designers. There, "the heart is chastened and the soul is subdued and the affections purified and exalted." There, "ambition surveys the boundaries of its powers, of its hopes, and its aspirations." These notions recalled those of French philosophers and advocates of the "cult of ancestors" preceding burial reform and establishment of Père Lachaise Cemetery.[38]

Emergence of a pattern of creation of culture in Boston similar to that of post-revolutionary France is not entirely surprising, despite conflicting trends toward anglophilia and francophobia among the New England elite. As Vernon Louis Parrington observes, "Changing its name and arraying itself in garments cut after the best Yankee fashion, the gospel of Jean Jacques presently walked the streets of Boston and spoke from its most respectable pulpits, under the guise of Unitarianism." Boston's cultural leaders shared Rousseau's belief in the excellence of human nature and the perfectibility of man. Whereas Mount Auburn's founders retained the sense of didactic mission of their Puritan ancestors, they abandoned Calvinist orthodoxy and notions of the universal consequences of Adam's sin. Their cemetery would be a silent "city on a hill," a corporate institution representative of communitarian ideals and providing a place of constructive spiritual and physical recreation for those still insistent on the useful and the moral but skeptical of empty, meaningless leisure.[39]

Mount Auburn would "teach those who have wealth and leisure, how they may make themselves happy not only without injuring others but with direct benefit to their fellow-men; to show them that in order to secure enjoyment for themselves, there is not need of inventing new pleasures . . . that Nature opens a never-failing paradise to those who are content to be innocent and well employed." Adding to Cook's moralistic ambitions for the cemetery, Dearborn asserted that it would "teach the community to pay more respect to the dead," an activity in which he judged America lagged far "behind other countries." There, visitors would engage in secularized meditation, an equivalent of religious activity in the sacred context of Nature in a manner most appealing to Unitarians. The cemetery would teach generalized, nondenominational lessons of moral philosophy and renew ambitions of self-improvement through work and self-denial.[40]

But most of all Dearborn emphasized the historical lessons of the cemetery: "There can be formed a public place of sepulture, where monuments can be erected to our illustrious men, whose remains, thus far, have unfortunately been consigned to obscure and isolated tombs instead of being collected within one common depository, where their great deeds might be perpetuated and their memories cherished by succeeding generations. Though dead, they would be eternal admonitors [*sic*] to the living—teaching them the way, which leads to national glory and individual renown." The great historical mandate Dearborn articulated would be, for many, the most compelling reason for creating such an innovative funerary institution.[41]

Because he anticipated that Boston's cemetery would be a multifunctional cultural institution mustering wide local support, Dearborn predicted that within three years it would "rival the most celebrated rural burial grounds in Europe and present a garden in such a state of forwardness" to serve as credit both to its sponsoring institution and to the city as well.[42] The argument of the necessity to compete with European cities in providing urban amenities, especially displaying a sense of their own history and high cultural achievement, convinced the Boston elite that the cemetery was necessary and justified, not just an idiosyncratic luxury.

As soon as the Massachusetts Horticultural Society undertook sponsorship of the cemetery, Dearborn sent to Paris and London for books and maps on similar landscapes and funerary monument design. He received the publications, including over two hundred engravings of art, architecture, and landscape, especially of Père Lachaise Cemetery. Dearborn personally translated portions of French historical and descriptive accounts of "that celebrated burial place, from a belief that it would be interesting to members of the Society," knowing that "establishment of rural cemeteries similar to Père Lachaise, has often been the subject of conversation in this country, and frequently adverted to by the writers in our scientific and literary publications." Before creation of Père Lachaise, "all was confusion, disorder, and irreverence towards the ashes of the dead in Paris. Causes, adverse to the indulgence of a recollection of our predecessors, seemed to have combined in the accumulation of everything which was capable of exciting terror and disgust." Certainly a similar situation existed in Boston graveyards. The model of the French cemetery offered many advantages to Bostonians. Père Lachaise was "the place of rendezvous for all the great and the opulent" of that city—before and after death—"for the illustrious in letters, the sciences and the arts; for those who were successful in commerce, and the numerous branches of national industry, for persons eminent for their public stations, and for men distinguished in political events." There, said Dearborn, "families are reunited, all opinions are confounded." The cemetery unified society, both on a private and a public, a personal, and a national level. Dearborn suggested that Bostonians and other Americans needed such an institution.[43]

Dearborn praised those aspects of Père Lachaise that reflected English landscape taste, and he determined to incorporate the best aspects of it in his new cemetery. Dearborn looked for design inspiration to English gardeners and aesthetic theorists as well as to the Parisian cemetery where many principles of picturesque landscape design had been put into practice. Dearborn lauded Bacon, Milton, Addison, Pope, Kent, Bridgeman, and other English landscape gardeners as "the champions of true taste." He quoted John Evelyn's condemnation of "the custom of burying in churches, and near about them, and especially in great cities," aware that that opinion would have particular resonance in Boston. He ordered all three of Sir Humphrey Repton's works on landscape gardening and consulted them in designing the new cemetery's landscape. Like the best English landscape gardeners, he permitted the terrain of Sweet Auburn to dictate a particular design that initially resembled Sir Uvedale Price's description of the "picturesque" rather than displaying the broad lawns, trimmed vistas, and specimen trees associated with the "beautiful" style of Capability Brown.[44]

Dearborn emphasized the compatibility of a cemetery and an experimental garden, speaking of the traditional sacredness of gardens in all cultures and advocating the practical development of plants to bolster the American agricultural economy. In this way, he mustered support for the project from Bostonians more interested in horticulture than in burial reform. When on June 23, 1831, the state legislature passed an amendment to the Massachusetts Horticultural Society charter, permitting the society to acquire real estate valued up to $10,000 to establish a "rural cemetery or burial ground" and "to plant and embellish the same with shrubbery, flowers, trees, walks, and other rural ornaments, and to enclose and divide the same with proper walls and enclosures" as a "perpetual dedication," Dearborn enlarged his committee membership, assembling twenty prominent Bostonians. They included Daniel Webster and Edward Everett, as well as ministers, merchants, lawyers, scholars, businessmen, and, of course, Bigelow, Brimmer, and Judge Joseph Story. Members of the select committee met repeatedly through the summer of 1831 and worked to publicize the cemetery venture among their friends.[45]

Bigelow consulted these and other individuals to help him name the cemetery, the first time an American burial ground was formally given a proper name. Edward Everett, editor of the *North American Review,* favored Bigelow's choice of Mount Auburn, a simple change of the existing nickname of the property, symbolic as well as descriptive of the site. Others suggested the classical name Necropolis; and Everett thought that Elysian Fields would be a "pretty" name, although just as objectionable as Sweet Auburn because of literary rather than religious associations. Everett rationalized that "use diminishes surprisingly all such associations, as is seen in the case of the new towns in New York—Troy, Utica."[46] The name Mount Auburn was of good Anglo-Saxon origin; like those of subsequent "rural" cemeteries, it resembled the names given to rural estates. By midsummer, 1831, Bigelow and the horticulturists were calling their cemetery Mount Auburn.

Dearborn, Bigelow, and the others publicized their cemetery project primarily by word of mouth, although they personally circulated subscription papers and placed many articles and progress reports in local periodicals. They encouraged site visits by their friends to appreciate "the scenery and natural advantages of the spot," emphasizing the importance of preserving the pastoralism of the place endangered by rising land values and industrialization. Dearborn stressed the potential historical and commemorative functions of a cemetery, and he reminded Bostonians that one of their major urban problems was about to be solved. Furthermore, an experimental garden at Mount Auburn would "develop the vast vegetable resources of the Union, give activity to enterprise, increase the enjoyment of all classes of citizens, advance the prosperity, and improve the general aspect of the whole country." Dearborn challenged Bostonians to support the venture as a matter of civic duty.[47]

Although horticulturists declared their proposed cemetery nondenominational, it was indeed the product of liberal religion, of Boston Unitarianism in its heyday. Toasts at the 1831 festival of the horticultural society revealed the new cosmology as well as mockery of the old. Malthus A. Ward drank to "*Eden*—the first abode of the living—Mount Auburn, the last resting place of the dead. If the Tree of Life sprung from the soil of the one, Immortality shall rise from the dust of the other."

Likewise, the Reverend John Pierpont's toast revealed the levity with which many of Mount Auburn's founders considered the old orthodoxy: "The tables turned since man first attended to Horticulture—then he had his worst *fall* in the Garden—now he has his best Garden in the *Fall.*" In 1829, Dearborn stressed the inherent sanctity of any garden based on the sanctioning by the Almighty of its "peerless beauties and refined pleasures" epitomized "by planting that of Eden, and consecrating it as a terrestrial paradise." Three years later, he described Mount Auburn as a sort of new Eden, reflecting "the beneficient precepts of our religion, the dictates of an exalted morality, a holy respect for the ashes of the dead, the kindest sympathies of the heart, and that active spirit of improvement which pervades every section of our country."[48]

Speaking to horticulturists in support of the cemetery venture, the Reverend William B. O. Peabody acknowledged, "there is something unpleasant to many in the idea of cultivating the place of death. This may be owing to the old prejudice, which regards nature and art as opposed to each other." Rather, he publicly praised the idea of creating a natural setting for burials that would be compatible with a new respect for the dead that "does not seem to partake of superstition." Peabody identified a new sensibility to death based on "enlightened, just, and manly sentiment, influencing not only the intelligent" but common Americans "who in general seem to be strangers to strong and delicate feeling." Peabody urged cultivation of sentiment among the general public or "giving a direction to public taste" as a way to strengthen the republic by creating more moralistic citizens. He equated the pastoral landscape of the "rural" cemetery with the "grandeur of the scene" of Niagara Falls. Both were places where the inexorable forces of nature instilled a sense of the sublime, where "the mind loses itself in earnest conjectures respecting destiny." Though Mount Auburn would be an educational institution, its lessons, he argued, would be primarily spiritual, but nondenominational, conveying a realization of morality in secularized aesthetic and intellectual terms.[49] Such arguments, along with supporting articles on international burial reform, appeared, almost as advertisements, in many Boston newspapers and periodicals in 1830 and 1831.

The Massachusetts Horticultural Society convened a public meeting of potential cemetery subscribers on June 8, 1831, to describe in detail plans, purposes, and functions of the cemetery. Purchase of the property would be complete as soon as one hundred subscribers of $60 were found. Then, subscriptions would be declared final, obligatory, and collectible; each subscriber would be entitled to a family burial lot of fifteen feet by twenty feet or three hundred square feet.[50] Lots were offered on relatively egalitarian terms, ability to pay being the sole criteria for becoming a proprietor. Members of the elite were accustomed to the purchase of burial space, although not in fee simple, for the building of tombs in common graveyards; they might consider an investment in a burial lot a sort of equivalent of buying a pew in the meeting house. Yet the only precedents for the idea of private burial plots were Père Lachaise and New Haven's New Burying Ground.

By the first of August of 1831, ninety-one families had purchased Mount Auburn's first hundred lots. Joseph P. Bradlee sold the last twenty-five subscriptions; Brimmer claimed ten lots in varied locations. Because of the initial favorable response and the need to raise additional funds to provide for extensive embellishment and security of the place, the subscription roll was enlarged to two and then four hundred. In the spring of 1832, the society charged Bigelow and Charles Curtis with obtaining new proprietors, authorizing them to employ an agent "to go round" to make sales; and George Bond, society treasurer, placed advertisements of cemetery lots in local newspapers. Subscribers received assurance that they would not be subjected to any charges beyond the burial plot price itself, the location of which was determined by lot similar to the land distribution pattern initially used in the formation of Puritan towns. Just having a plot at Mount Auburn was to be prestigious; thus, a circular pamphlet prepared in the fall of 1832 listed existing proprietors deliberately to encourage sales to Bostonians aspiring to associate themselves with members of the elite who already accepted the new cemetery.[51]

However, some subscribers paid for the privilege of choosing their own site. An auction was scheduled at the end of November at which subscribers who paid a premium selected the precise location of their lots. Samuel Appleton paid the highest, $100 for first choice; Bigelow and Dearborn each paid $72.50 extra; Brimmer paid from $60 to $71 for each of his ten lots. Other premiums ranged from $15 to $65. Yet even these proprietors chose lots in various parts of the grounds, some on fairly flat land near the Central Avenue and others on hills and in valleys. No one section seemed more desirable than another. The first four hundred lots sold were dispersed through the varied terrain in those areas first surveyed. Bigelow chose two contiguous lots on Beech Avenue, flat land near the Central Avenue leading southward from the entry to the major hill. Story preferred a more secluded spot on a low, wooded hillside overlooking Forest Pond and reached only by a small, earthen footpath. The heirs of industrialist Francis Cabot Lowell selected a similarly isolated location on a steep hillside reached by a path extending into the almost subterranean Consecration Dell. Josiah Quincy, former Boston mayor and Harvard president, placed his lot near the summit of the cemetery, with a commanding view of the city and the college he had governed. Samuel Appleton claimed the top of Cedar Hill on a path leading to the cemetery's highest point. Most early proprietors, however, preferred more visible lots located on avenues accessible to carriages rather than on narrow paths that wound through the more rugged valleys and over steeper hills.

Rapid acceptance of Mount Auburn by the elite ensured the success of the venture, which had attracted less than immediate support and patronage by the common people, not only because of the costs involved but because the location of the cemetery involved negation of New England superstitions inherited from medieval tradition. The cemetery location required Bostonians to transport their dead across the Charles River in violation of an old taboo against taking the dead over water. The necessity of fitting an excessive number of burials into crowded Boston graveyards had already led to elimination of the traditional alignment of graves on an east-west axis. At Mount Auburn, the placement of burial lots in the landscape indicated an official disregard of the old pattern once based on the belief that bodies of the elect had to be properly positioned to sit up in their graves on Judgment Day to face the Second Coming with the rising sun. Rationalism, sentimentalism, aesthetics, and necessity supplanted superstition and custom.

Bigelow was particularly concerned to counter Bostonians' reluctance to bury their dead far from their homes. He argued that the city's burial grounds were full and would have to be abandoned, perhaps after "the original tenants" had been "ejected," their bones removed to parts unknown. Because of increasing urban congestion, the public anticipated that Boston's graveyards might soon be closed. Bigelow concluded that "others must be formed in the country—the primitive and only proper location" for interring the dead. He overcame some hesitancy by "quiet interviews with selected friends of good judgment, of public spirit, and of high social influence," many of whom, in turn, became active advocates of lot sales. He recalled three decades later that "a change of place from the city to the country was not effected without difficulty"; and his biographer, the Reverend George Ellis, added that many people "were grieved and shocked at the proposal of carrying [their dead] far away across the river and burying them in wild, desolate woods, their graves exposed to violation."[52]

Although Bigelow's more enlightened friends, intellectual associates, civic leaders, and like-minded religious liberals championed his cemetery proposal, other practical and traditionalistic Yankees were not easily convinced of the advisability of paying for lots to locate their burials so far from their residences. The proposal of placing graves in "a distant wood" initially "met with lukewarmness, prejudice, and direct opposition." After all, burial outside the center of town had been the fate of social pariahs or of the poorer sort, whose graves were most often ravaged by resurrection men supplying corpses to physicians for anatomical study. Perhaps for this reason, some Bostonians even questioned the motivations of a doctor recommending creation of a rural cemetery. Undoubtedly, many fears of the vulnerability of distant graves were calmed by passage of 1831 of a law making human dissection legal in Massachusetts and hence eliminating much of the illegal traffic in cadavers.[53]

Some Bostonians resisted the idea of an extramural cemetery for more mundane reasons. They had yet to adopt the practice of visiting graves, which was just becoming popular in European countries, so they could not understand the desirability of creating a pleasant, pastoral setting for graves. Public hacks were scarce and expensive. Despite the regular stage and new bridges, there was little general transportation for those not prosperous enough to own carriages. With good Yankee frugality, many potential proprietors of Mount Auburn lots might have considered it an unusual expense to rent a hearse for funeral transportation to a place four miles away from the city.

Certainly, a large number of Bostonians could not even consider burying their dead at Mount Auburn because of the initial cost of a lot, an expense not always necessary in the old graveyards. Women working in the Lowell mills of the Merrimack Manufacturing Company at that time earned about $98.80 per year after paying for their board, a higher rate of pay than schoolteachers received. Male operatives at the same establishment and at the Waltham mills took home about $292 annually, before payment of rent. Common laborers in Boston in 1830 made about $230 a year; a master mason, $500. Estimated annual expenses for a family of four, living frugally, were $450. Purchase of a family lot at $60 would have been difficult to afford, especially as no provisions were made for spreading payment over time. Even a minister and academic of the caliber of Henry Ware, Hollis Professor of Divinity at Harvard, who had officiated at Mount Auburn's consecration, declared himself "ill able to spare the sum of money." Yet crypts under city churches sold for about $300, and a variety of Boston newspapers provided favorable publicity of the cemetery venture to convince mechanics and members of the growing middle class to join the elite in buying lots.[54]

Mount Auburn provided a "public" lot for permanent single graves, costing $10 each, for those who died without families or while visiting Boston. In that era, decades before the regular use of embalming, it was rare that the body of the deceased would be shipped back to a distant home. No special provisions were made at Mount Auburn for the burial of the poor, who would continue to be consigned to the anonymous graves of municipal burying grounds. Not surprisingly, cemetery founders assumed that most families would purchase property enough for their own burials. The indigent or solitary individual would be an exception. This was the old New England ideal, institutionalized first in the form of the Puritan town. Landlessness was only a relatively recent and limited urban phenomenon in 1830. The great tides of poor immigrants had yet to arrive in Boston. Certainly the small "public" lot named Saint James, twenty feet by ninety feet in size, divided into four sections, and surrounded by an iron fence and containing sixty single graves, was judged to be adequate to bury the widows, orphans, and travelers, exceptions to the social ideal; or so Mount Auburn's founders thought. (Fig. 7.9.) Perhaps the use of the saint's name was intended to win favor for the cemetery among local Episcopalians.

Proprietors of the Tremont House, Boston's new "modern" hotel, applied for a grant of land at Mount Auburn to erect a tomb for guests from out of town who died while in their establishment; however, the request was denied because the public lot was considered adequate for the purpose. Nevertheless, in 1833 the Tremont House, maintaining its reputation for innovation and for providing the most innovative amenities for guests, purchased its own lot on Hawthorne Path and erected a pentagonal tomb of Quincy granite surrounded by an iron railing. The six-foot-tall structure with sunken interior chamber contained three rows of horizontal cells (seven feet by two feet by eighteen inches) of mica slate, three across, along four sides, totaling thirty-six spaces, each of which was meant to be permanent, to be sealed with a marble tablet bearing the name and dates of the deceased. By 1839, the Tremont House tomb held two interments of guests, one from New York and one from Smyrna, the prosperous Ottoman port with an active trade with Boston. (Fig. 7.10.)

Mount Auburn particularly appealed to those with Harvard ties and memories of recreational

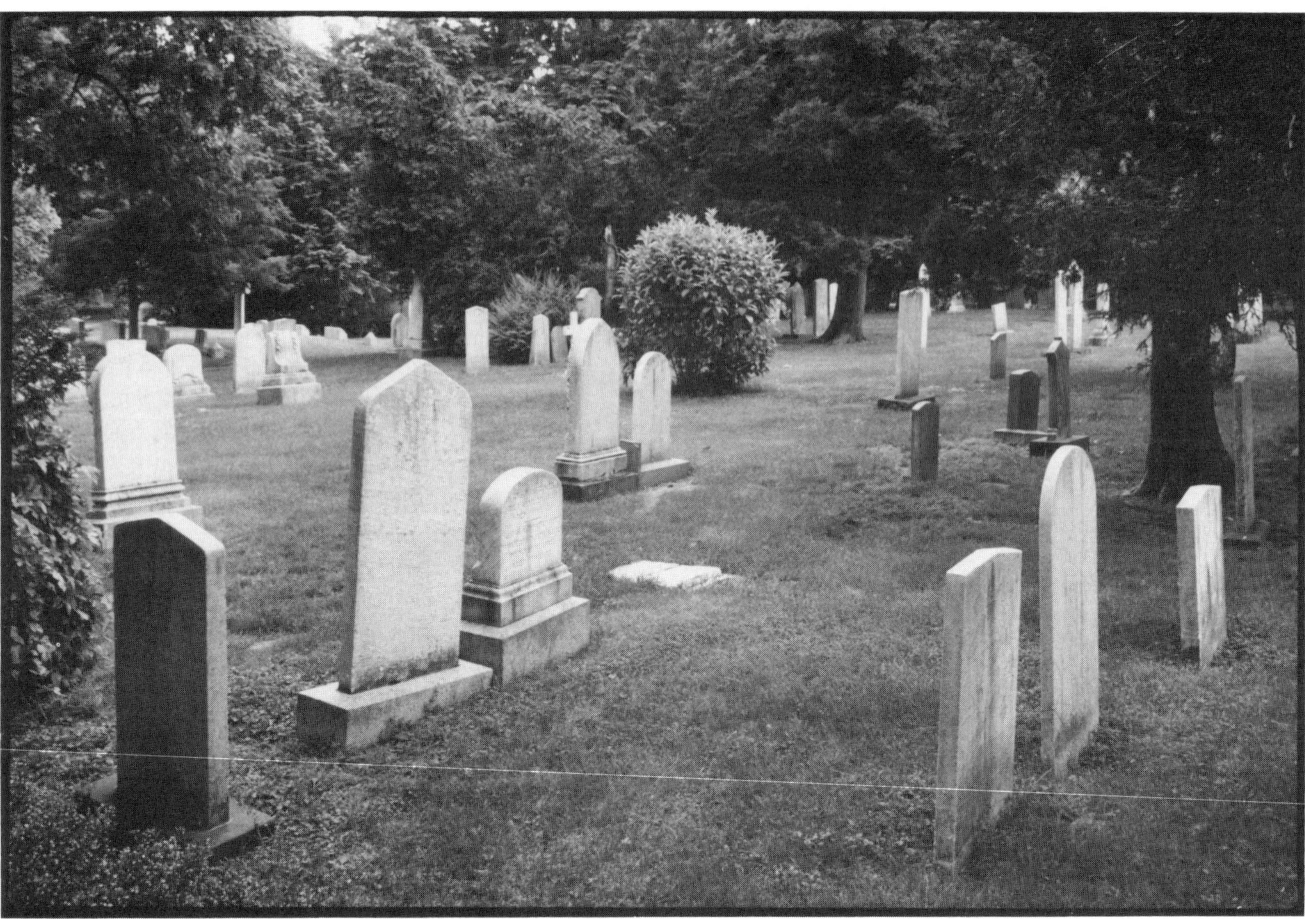

Fig. 7.9. Saint John's Public Lot, Mount Auburn's second public lot, photograph by Alan Ward, 1986.

time spent on the grounds during college days. The college corporation received a donation of a large lot for burial of students and professors who did not have burial rights in other family lots or who could not be shipped back to distant homes. The wooded site near the highest eminence in the cemetery was named Harvard Hill. Henry Blake McLellan wrote to his mother in 1833, shortly before his death at age twenty-two, that he wanted to be buried at the new cemetery because "with those pleasant places my college days are tenderly connected, *and I would love there to sleep my long, cold sleep.*" Despite the newness of the place, McLellan judged, "To such a place there is a permanence which is wanting to the common churchyard; the bodies there deposited rest quietly forever." Indeed, the notion of perpetuity of burial as institutionalized and guaranteed at Mount Auburn was innovative; and, although Mount Auburn provided a place for individualized, permanent burials, not all of the first proprietors took advantage of the guarantee.[55]

Fewer than half of the first four hundred lots sold were actually used as burial place of their original owners. Speculation in lots was not permitted; but many proprietors arranged with the Corporation to exchange their first, unoccupied lot for one on another site subsequently found preferable as new roads and paths were graded and improved. Sometimes they exchanged lots to be close to those of friends or relatives. Some lot owners took considerable time to decide. Other proprietors sold their lots back to the Corporation when they moved away from Boston.

Such was the case of the Reverend John Pierpont, Unitarian divine and orator at Mount Auburn's consecration. Pierpont was among the first proprietors, purchasing his lot when he left the Hollis Street Church. He chose a prominent spot on a hillside on Magnolia Avenue that curved around the Mount. Pierpont visited the place frequently to savor the "pleasures of melancholy," musing about his past and meditating on his inevitable fate. He waxed poetic, describing the site in the verse "To My Grave":

My grave! I've marked thee on this sunny slope,
The warm, dry slope of Auburn's wood-crowned
hill
That overlooks the Charles, and Roxbury's
fields,
That lies beyond it, as lay Canaan's green
And smiling landscape beyond Jordan's flood,
As seen by Moses.

The site had an intensely personal significance to the minister, looking back across the panorama of the city to recollections of his past career. He mused:

There stands the church, within whose lofty
walls
My voice for truth, and righteousness, and
God—
But all too feebly,—has been lifted up
For more than twenty years, but now shall soon
Be lifted up no more. I chose this spot,
And marked it for my grave, that, when my dust
Shall be united to its kindred dust,
They who have loved me—should there any
such
E'er stand beside it and let fall a tear,—
May see the temple where I toiled so long,
And toiled, I fear, in vain.

Pierpont's thoughts turned to death at a time of professional disappointment. He had lost his pulpit; indeed, he would even relinquish the cherished gravesite in 1845, returning the unused plot to the cemetery corporation when he was offered a position in Troy, New York.[56]

Because of acceptance of Mount Auburn by the likes of Pierpont and other respected public figures, Dearborn declared that the cemetery won immediate favor among "the affluent, the enlightened, the virtuous, the patriotic, the industrious and enterprising among all classes of society." Ready acceptance of Mount Auburn evidenced a strength of local and national character, a particular moral and patriotic sensibility in the Boston area beyond "that active spirit of improvement which pervades every section of our country," claimed Dearborn, not so much differing with Bigelow's assessment of the slowness of the public to favor burial at Mount Auburn as displaying an overly optimistic assessment of lot sales to the public. In Mount Auburn's first year, lot purchases and premiums produced $10,498.50. Of the first 250 proprietors, about half (122) were merchants, gentlemen, or physicians; 41 were mechanics or skilled workers; 3, widows; the rest were unidentified.

Still, in its first year Mount Auburn proved more popular than Père Lachaise was in its first two decades after its 1804 founding. Père Lachaise won acceptance slowly and only after a "revolution in customs and manners" shaped by the "universal gloom" following Napoleon's defeat at Waterloo, Dearborn explained in 1834. It had taken at least a decade for the Parisian cemetery to become "a resort of the admirers of the arts, the opulent and enlightened, as well as the common place of sepulcher for the most illustrious in letters, sci-

Fig. 7.10. Tremont House or "Strangers' " Tomb, Mount Auburn, engraving from *Picturesque Pocket Companion,* 1839.

ence, and arts, and of the humblest citizen of Paris." In contrast, prosperous Bostonians lost no time in purchasing burial space. The number of lots sold in the cemetery's first four years surpassed the number sold in the Parisian cemetery's first decade. Monument and tomb construction at Mount Auburn also exceeded that at Père Lachaise for the first year of both.[57]

Horticulturists tried to emphasize Mount Auburn's egalitarianism, declaring their intention "that every citizen should have an opportunity of participating in the advantages of the establishment." Although there were few provisions at Mount Auburn for the "humblest citizens" of the "Metropolis of New England," Dearborn spoke of lots "which every man in the community might acquire upon the same terms," simply financial, "at an expense considerably less than that of a common tomb [in a Boston graveyard] or a vault beneath a church [costing an average $300], to deposit the mortal remains of his friends or to provide a place a burial for himself, which, while living, he may contemplate without dread or disgust . . . removed from the discordant scenes of life." Dearborn encouraged applications for lots by farmers, mechanics, and dealers in building materials, proposing payment in labor or goods necessary for construction of the pastoral landscape. A good deal of bartered labor was used in laying out the grounds in Mount Auburn's first three years. In exchange for a cemetery lot, a neighboring farmer, Leonard Stone, constructed a two-story, clapboard cottage with shingled roof for the first superintendent, following Dearborn's specifications. (Fig. 7.11.) Dearborn concluded that "a very considerable portion of the expense in constructing roads, fences, gate-ways and various other edifices may be defrayed by compensation in cemetery lots." Mount Auburn's founders considered this practice both democratic and wise business. The bartering of lots for services and goods continued on a limited basis for several decades.[58]

* * * * *

Next, officers of the Massachusetts Horticultural Society prepared consecration ceremonies for Mount Auburn, scheduled for September 24, 1831. Brimmer headed a committee of nine that unanimously selected Associate U.S. Supreme Court Justice Joseph Story (1779–1845), one of its members, as orator of the day. Story had been active in the society and the planning of the ceme-

Fig. 7.11. Drawing for Superintendent's House by Henry A. S. Dearborn.

tery from the beginning. He was a national figure with regional roots, representative of the sort of notable individual Bigelow hoped would be recognized for the historical record by the cemetery.[59] (Fig. 7.12.)

Josiah Quincy had been instrumental in 1829 in persuading Story to move from Salem to Cambridge, where he became Harvard's first Dane Professor of Law, helping shift control of the college from clergy to attorneys. Story, then a Jeffersonian Republican, had served in the Tenth Congress with Quincy and received his appointment to the High Court by James Madison. Old friends knew him simply as "the poet of Marblehead," but his national reputation was immense. Arthur M. Schlesinger, Jr., called him second only to John Marshall as "main pillar" in the "fortress of conservatism." Story began his political career as a Jeffersonian but became a leading legal advocate of property rights and private corporations. He allied himself nationally with Henry Clay, Nicholas Biddle, and other Whigs against Jacksonian Democracy and sided with Daniel Webster in the Charles River Bridge case in 1831, insisting that common law protected sanctity of property. Along with John Quincy Adams, Massachusetts Governor Levi Lincoln, and Alexander Everett, according to Schlesinger, he "assisted in the transformation of right-wing Jeffersonianism into the National Republican party," a position Webster eventually joined in defense of the American System. Together with Nathan Appleton and Abbott Lawrence, these leaders attempted to manipulate culture for political purposes. Mount Auburn was a particularly appropriate project for Story to promote because of the ways in which its founders borrowed the ideologically loaded landscape aesthetics of the English garden, with their distinct Whiggish associations, and theories of Napoleonic cemetery reform meant to restore social order through a "cult of ancestors." Furthermore, the rights of property were ensured and enshrined at Mount Auburn as nowhere else in America through provisions that family burial lots were sacred in perpetuity and could not be lost because of debt.[60]

Story played a leading role in development of Mount Auburn despite his many academic and national commitments. Indeed, the cemetery venture was one of many local improvement causes he championed, like enclosing and planting trees on Cambridge Common. The Mount Auburn project seemed a particularly appropriate one for Story because of his well-known penchant for melancholy, shaped by the deaths of several of his children, his first wife, parents, and others close to him. His son, William Wetmore Story, realized this, especially after receiving a long, autobiographical letter from his father, aged fifty-two, in 1831, prefaced by the observation, "Perhaps, when I am in my grave you will take comfort in these little details." Story had an elegiac outlook on life, evident in his emphasis on the mystical significance of the simultaneous deaths of Jefferson and Adams on the fiftieth anniversary of independence in his 1826 Harvard Phi Beta Kappa lecture entitled *Characteristics of the Age*.[61]

Fig. 7.12. Joseph Story, engraved portrait from crayon drawing by William Wetmore Story, ca. 1845.

Story's son recalled that his father wrote Mount Auburn's consecration oration "to solace his wounded heart" following the death of his daughter, the fifth child lost in fifteen years: "In writing his address, he found a refuge from busy cares, and an outlet for crowding recollections, which found in utterance their best relief."[62] This instance illustrates still another reason why prominent Bostonians—leaders in the professions, business, politics, and intellectual pursuits—founded Mount Auburn. Mount Auburn provided a ritualized mechanism by which men, even more than women, might turn their grief—so frequent with the high infant and maternal mortality of the time—into a controlled mourning, permitting them to get on with life and work. They would temper their response to death by putting it aside, away from daily view so they could go about work in the public sphere. For middle-class and elite women of the period, there was the newly prescribed formalization through etiquette of mourning period and garb, but men could not retreat to a privatized sphere. Elimination of the visible presence of death of the old urban graveyards would help them carry on as usual in the most efficient manner.[63]

Creation of Mount Auburn reflected the modernization of American culture. Perhaps the twentieth-century American can best understand the functional significance with a fictional supposition. How would a Bostonian today, a leader of nationally important profession or even an ordinary citizen, feel about burying a close family member in ready public view on a major city street where graves frequently gaped open, revealing parts of contents not sealed in neat containers but emitting unpleasant odors? Would only the value of the land for development be considered? Would it be simply a matter of the intellectual and emotional "denial of death" to create a new sort of landscape, attractive in its naturalism, functional in preserving the beauty of the land and maintaining permanency of burials, and easily accessible to mourners although beyond the escalating crush of urban activity? Story, Dearborn, Bigelow, and many others were unabashed sentimentalists, knowing none of the negative connotations of that quality that would subsequently become part of mainstream male American culture. They mourned publicly, and they wrote as much melancholy verse—and just as bad from the point of view of modern literary criticism—as the better-published "scribbling women" of their day. However, they stoically got on with life and work, consigning emotions to leisure time and to places beyond the hustle of intensifying urbanization. They created Mount Auburn for those reasons.[64]

The control and ritualization of deathways represented by the "rural" cemetery did not simply represent a "beautification of death," to use Philippe Ariès's term, or the "denial of death" so often associated with twentieth-century America. Rather, it reflected new emotional sensibilities tempered by the exigencies of a modern way of life—the rise of affective individualism, intensified cohesion of the nuclear family, a growing cult of efficiency in service of business and industry, and separation of the public sphere of men from the private one of women. Matters of taste were also crucial—a repulsion with the odors of rotting bodies and refuse in urban areas, a renewed appreciation for the salutary influence of nature on the emotions through cultivation of reason, and a growing insistence on the canons of proper taste or gentility.

The contrast between the inappropriateness of the city as place of burial and the fitting naturalism of Mount Auburn proved a major theme in descriptions of the consecration and in Judge Story's address at the ceremonies. Story's son described the afternoon as ideal, "one of the serenest of those melancholy days which mark the early New England autumn." Dearborn remembered the day as cloudless: "the deep blue vault of heaven canopied the immense area with a dome of more resplendent grandeur than all that genius can conceive or art accomplish; whispering zephyrs rustled the many twinkling leaves . . . the glorious sun gilded, with his cheerful beams, the smiling landscape." Such was the poetic turn of mind of some Boston lawyers.[65]

Dearborn cleared one broad, shady avenue about halfway into the grounds from the entrance, then marked by only a common set of bars. Bostonians rode their carriages into Mount Auburn, leaving them in a grove of walnut trees to walk to their seats in a deep dell near the center of the property. The dell formed a natural amphitheater that easily accommodated between two and three thousand Bostonians on "rude benches." One newspaper account described the crowd as "the assembled Athenians in the venerable groves of Ceramicus," the cemetery and place of intellectual rendezvous of the ancient Greeks. The sixteen members of the Boston Band received $3 each to lead the procession of speakers, ministers, and dignitaries to a stage "fashioned of unshorn pine boughs and young trees, and decorated with festoons of flowers interwoven with the variegated leaves of the forest." To the right of the platform, an orchestra and choir performed in a grove on the hill overlooking the dell, resembling angels singing from on high. The younger Story described the scene as "novel and impressive beyond description, and the whole assembly seemed subdued to reverential feeling by this simple service in the great church of nature."[66] (Fig. 7.13.)

Dr. Henry Ware, Jr., Harvard's Hollis Professor of Divinity and a leading Unitarian, intoned the introductory prayer.[67] Judge Story then rose to speak, but, according to his son, "so overpowered was he by emotion that he could not begin." Regaining his composure, Story "faltered out" his

Fig. 7.13. Consecration Dell, photograph by Alan Ward, 1979.

first words, but "several times, during the delivery of his discourse, he was so much overcome as to be obliged to pause, and his own emotion communicated itself to the audience, who listened in reverential silence and with glistening eyes." The man, still actively mourning the sudden death by scarlet fever that spring of his ten-year-old daughter, wrote his oration "in his heart's blood" and it "could not fail to reach the hearts of all who had suffered like himself." This was the same Joseph Story whom Andrew Jackson called "the most dangerous man in America." Some historians have considered Unitarianism a stone-cold, rational religion devoid of emotion; however, the sentimentalism evident in Story's address, the response of his audience, and subsequent writings by Unitarians about Mount Auburn Cemetery contradict the generalization.[68]

Judge Story's address summarized the intention that the cemetery solace survivors by providing a personalized place for commemoration. He declared, "It is to the living mourner—to the parent, weeping over his dear dead child—to the husband, dwelling in his own solitary desolation—to the widow, whose heart is broken by untimely sorrow . . . that the repositories of the dead bring home thoughts full of admonition, of instruction, and slowly, but surely, of consolation also." Existing graveyards with their "sad spectacle of promiscuous ruins and intermingled graves" certainly offered little comfort to the grieving and often served to intensify bitter emotions. Even in rural New England towns, burial grounds were "left in a sad, neglected state, exposed to every sort of intrusion with scarcely a tree to shelter their barrenness or a shrub to spread a grateful shade over the new-made hillock."[69]

Story, who was familiar with the literary celebration of melancholy, praised the influence of contemplative visits to graves in a pastoral setting. Such a place admonishes, instructs, and instills "the reminiscences of the past, sources of pleasing melancholy reflection." Story explained,

> as time interposes its growing distances between us and them, we gather up, with more solicitude, the broken fragments of memory, and weave . . . into our very hearts the threads of their history. As we sit down by their graves, we seem to hear the tones of their affection whispering in our ears. We listen to the voice of their wisdom, speaking in the depths of our souls. We shed our tears; but they are no longer the burning tears of agony. They relieve our drooping spirits, and come no longer over us with a deathly faintness. We return to the world, and we feel ourselves purer, and better, and wiser, for this communion with the dead.

Story appreciated the "pleasures of melancholy" that would be cultivated in the "Garden of Graves." Mount Auburn would be a place "to gratify human feelings, or tranquilize human fears; to secure the best religious influences, and to cherish all those associations which cast a cheerful light over the darkness of the grave." The cemetery objectified new notions of death. Story viewed Mount Auburn "rather as means than as ends, rather as influences to govern human conduct, and to moderate human suffering." He observed, "Our cemeteries, rightly selected and properly arranged may be made subservient to some of the highest purposes of religion and human duty. They may preach lessons, to which none may refuse to listen, and which all that live must hear. Truths may be there felt and taught in the silence of our own meditation, more persuasive, and more enduring than ever flowed from human lips." The lessons of the rural cemetery would be moral philosophy as well as history. It would create a "cult of ancestors" as well as a "cult of heroes." It would take the place of the church or meetinghouse for spiritual activity.[70]

Story predicted that Mount Auburn would become a retreat, an asylum for the world-weary, especially for those overwhelmed by the new pace and demands of urban life, a place where one might "indulge in the dreams of hope and ambition, or solace their hearts by melancholy meditations." Nature provided forces for spiritual renewal absent in the city. Mount Auburn's site specifically objectified a growing contrast between urban and rural, creating a place of compromise

Fig. 7.14. Mount Auburn, view from central hill to Consecration Dell, photograph by Alan Ward, 1985.

and conciliation with its "variety of natural and artificial scenery." Story described the symbolic juxtaposition:

> All around us there breathes a solemn calm, as if we were in the bosom of a wilderness, broken only by the breeze as it murmurs through the tops of the forest. Ascend but a few steps, and what a change of scenery to surprise and delight us. We seem, as it were, in an instant, to pass from confines of death to the bright and balmy regions of life. Below us flows the winding Charles, with its rippling current, like the stream of time hastening to the ocean of eternity. In the distance, the city—at once the object of our admiration and our love—rears its proud eminences, its glittering spires, its

> lofty towers, its graceful mansions, its curling smoke, its crowded haunts of business and pleasure, which speak to the eye, and yet leave a noiseless loneliness on the ear.

Story added that in the cemetery, "We stand, as it were, upon the borders of two worlds," between those of the living and the dead as well as between the city and country. The place was a hierophany, a link between earth and heaven, a sacred space; topography and relationship of site to city further emphasized this. Mount Auburn lay to the west of the city, where the setting sun daily stressed that it was a place of death. Ancient associations attached to the garden, the mount, the valley, and the river as sacred and symbolic places of burial or worship and passageways to the afterlife were consciously revived and reinterpreted at Mount Auburn.[71]

As soon as Story declared the cemetery consecrated, the Boston Band played the music of the "reverend psalm of 'Old Hundred,' " to which the crowd sang "in one vast choral, that swelled into the sky and sounded down the aisles of the wood with a grandeur of effect beyond that of dome or cathedral" a hymn composed by the Reverend John Pierpont. Pierpont, nationally known for his popular, sentimental poetry, reinterpreted the message of Bryant's "Thanatopsis," emphasizing mortality as universal and natural:

> Decay! decay! 'tis stamped on all!
> All bloom in flower and flesh shall fade,
> Ye whispering trees, when we shall fall
> Be our long sleep beneath your shade.
>
> Here to thy bosom, Mother Earth,
> Take back, in peace, what thou hast given;
> And all that is of heavenly birth,
> O God, in peace, recall to heaven.

William Wetmore Story observed that "an electric thrill seemed to pervade the air when the last sound of voices died away, which touched every heart." One English visitor observed that the ceremony "seemed to touch the hearts of all who witnessed this impressive scene, with a spirit of humility, devotion, reverence, and awe."[72]

The Boston press stressed the spirit of boosterism or urban pride resounding after the consecration. Joseph T. Buckingham bragged that "there is not in all the untrodden valleys of the West, a more secluded, more natural or more appropriate spot for the religious exercises of the living." He predicted that in a few years, "when the hand of taste shall have passed over the luxuriance of nature, we may challenge the rivalry of the world to produce another such residence for the spirit of beauty." Buckingham was confident that Mount Auburn would "soon be a place of more general resort, both for [Bostonians] and for strangers, than any other spot in the vicinity." There was "no better spot for the rambles of curiosity, health or pleasure; none sweeter for the whispers of affection among the living; none lovelier for the rest of our kindred." Buckingham, who so vehemently and publicly opposed crypts under Boston churches during the burial controversy of 1823, became equally active in promoting and publicizing the new cemetery, of which he was one of the first hundred subscribers.[73] Despite the picturesque advantages of the site and the auspicious beginnings of the institution, Mount Auburn still required landscape design. The initial design, inspired by the funerary in English gardens and French cemeteries, allowed Mount Auburn to realize the potential foreseen by its founders, to make it more than simply a graveyard in a suburban setting. (Fig. 7.14.)

8

Cemetery and Garden: Landscape Design and Conflicting Institutional Purposes

Nature is a setting that fits equally well a comic or a mourning piece. . . . Within these plantations of God, a decorum and sanctity reign. . . . In the woods, we return to reason and faith. There I feel that nothing can befall me in life,—no disgrace, no calamity, (leaving me my eyes,) which nature cannot repair. . . . I become a transparent eye-ball; I am nothing; I see all; the currents of the Universal Being circulate through me; I am part or particle of God. . . . In the tranquil landscape, and especially in the distant line of the horizon, man beholds somewhat as beautiful as his own nature.

—Ralph Waldo Emerson, "Nature" (1836)

First follow Nature, and your judgment frame
By her just standard, which is still the same:
Unerring Nature, still divinely bright,
One clear, unchanged, and universal light.

—Alexander Pope, *Essay on Criticism* (lines 68–71) (1746)

Leaders of the Massachusetts Horticultural Society mistakenly anticipated that creation of a picturesque cemetery would require little work and very little expense for "the hand of art to fit it" for its purposes. According to General Henry A. S. Dearborn, "Nature has already done almost all that is required. Scarcely any thing is needed but a suitable enclosure, and such walks as will give access to the different parts of the enclosed space, and exhibit its features to the greatest advantage."[1] Dearborn also observed that the land was "so abundantly covered with forest trees," many over sixty years old, that it only required formation avenues, earthen planting of borders, clearing of underwood, and erection of fences, gateways, and appropriate edifices "to put the grounds in a sufficiently complete state for the uses designated and to render them at once beautiful and interesting." Dearborn proclaimed that "among the hills, glades, and dales . . . may be selected sites for isolated graves and tombs" to be focal points from the avenues winding through woods, hills, and dales and to approximate the landscape of the most admired English gardens."[2]

Dearborn took a leading role in the planning of Mount Auburn's landscape. In the garden area, he proposed conversion of "small ponds and mo-

Fig. 8.1. First Receiving Tomb, Green Briar Path, engraving from *Picturesque Pocket Companion,* 1839.

rasses into picturesque sheets of water, their margins diversified by clumps and belts of our most splendid native flowering trees and shrubs, requiring a soil thus constituted for their successful cultivation." Cleaning and deepening the ponds would benefit the experimental garden by producing valuable sludge for fertilizer. According to Dearborn and Harris, the area for burials would not require much cultivation, "improvement," or regular maintenance but would contrast with the orderly, functional experimental garden, a section reserved in the flat land north of the natural moraine called Indian Ridge. The garden would be a buffer zone, screening burials from public view from the Cambridge-Watertown road. Dearborn thought the cemetery could be completed in two years. The same task would have taken an estimated forty years had not large forest trees—"the venerable monarchs of the grove" and their "luxuriant progeny, which, in umbrageous contiguity, cover each hill and plain and sloping vale"—already cloaked most of the grounds.[3]

Although the horticultural society elected a nine-member Garden and Cemetery Committee, at least five of whom were owners of burial lots, most of the decisions and actual work in designing and laying out Mount Auburn's landscape were done by a subcommittee of Brimmer, Bigelow, and Dearborn.[4] Dearborn was away for months on end, serving in the Massachusetts legislature and United States Congress, but he attended almost half of all committee meetings from 1831 through 1834, when Joseph Story took over as committee head. By then, plans for the system of avenues and paths and other landscape features were fully drawn and well on the way to completion.

George Brimmer's major task was to procure a receiving tomb in the city. It would be used during the winter months when gravedigging with the simple tools of the time was difficult or for the temporary storage of bodies to be interred at Mount Auburn in tombs or graves that might not be ready or to be shipped elsewhere. Use of a receiving tomb for initial storage of the dead may also have been elected by some as a way to ensure against "suspended animation" and live burials, often repeated fears in that era.[5] The sexton charged $1.50 to place a body in the tomb. Brimmer paid $300 for a crypt in the basement of the Park Street Church, belying the belief by some historians that a prime motivation behind advocacy of the extramural cemetery was fear that burials under urban churches categorically endangered public health.

At the same time, J. C. Gray and Benjamin A. Gould oversaw construction by the superintendent and workmen of a receiving tomb at the cemetery, a simple structure in the form of a quadrangular tumulus of massive granite blocks covered with sod, meant to be functional rather than ornamental. (Fig. 8.1.) Bodies deposited in either location during the warm months from April through September could remain for only two months; those left at other times would have to be removed in less than four months. But analysis of deposits in the Receiving Tomb in the 1830s reveals that only about a third were recent (within one month) deaths. Another third died within a year of placement there; the rest were older deaths, perhaps the equivalent of the second burial frequent in many cultures. Despite requiring posting of a bond, often bodies were left unclaimed in the receiving tombs for much longer periods or simply abandoned to be buried anonymously by authorities at Mount Auburn.

For the first three and most important formative years, General Dearborn was leader and landscape designer at Mount Auburn. He was self-taught in the principles of classical design, having written and illustrated by hand a two-volume "Treatise on Grecian Architecture" (1828), dedicated to his children and urging self-improvement through study of historic design. Dearborn looked to ancient Greece as an ideal place where "ev'ry mechanic who excelled in his vocation was enabled to eternize his name, which was considered the greatest possible blessing, as the most important prayer which the Greeks addressed to their Gods was for the conservation of their memory." Dearborn anticipated that the new cemetery would offer such opportunities to enterprising Bostonians. Even before Mount Auburn's consecration and increasingly through the fall of 1831, he worked actively on the grounds, chalking and staking out a few eighteen- to twenty-foot-wide avenues and five- to six-foot-wide paths. Creation of a picturesque landscape "in conformity to the modern style of laying out grounds" first required formation of avenues curving to fit the site's remarkably varied topography and providing easy access to all portions of the grounds for horse-drawn hearses and carriages. He simply followed the natural features of the land in positioning avenues and paths "to run them as nearly level as possible by winding gradually and gracefully through the valleys and obliquely over hills, without any unnecessary or unavoidable bend, and especially to avoid all sinuosities." In order to create a picturesque landscape, he used elliptical or parabolical curves to replace "stiff circular lines which are incompatible with elegance of form and a pleasing effect." This graceful design method was, Dearborn argued, "a discovery of the Greeks, for all the mouldings in their architecture and the beautiful forms of their vases are profiles of the sections of a cone, and are either parabolical, elliptical, or hyperbolical." The cemetery was a walking garden with paths separated from carriageways, following the example of Père Lachaise. It permitted pedestrians to stroll through most of the grounds without distractions, except at intersections. And at both cemeteries, avenues made all of the grounds accessible, even to the aged and infirm not able to walk great distances through the hilly terrain. Those interested only in viewing the area of horticultural experimentation could visit Mount Auburn without venturing into the area reserved by burials.[6] (Fig. 8.2.)

Dearborn also formed "sheets of water," carved from bogs and shallow ponds between 1832 and 1833 to provide appropriate settings for aquatic plants, rhododendrons, azaleas, magnolias, and others requiring damp and rich soil. He planned to preserve Mount Auburn's "rural" nature, ensuring that the landscape not be built up in a congested fashion as was already the case at Père Lachaise. To achieve this, he created minimum setbacks or margins of six feet between lots and each avenue and path; spaces at least three feet wide were reserved between neighboring lots. The standard 300-square-foot lot, therefore, required a total area of about 550 square feet. Mount Auburn's seventy-two acres seemed so large in contrast to the area of old urban graveyards that the Garden and Cemetery Committee readily agreed to be generous with space, preserving decorative margins to ensure the naturalistic aesthetics into the foreseeable future. No lots would be permitted in focal areas like Central Square, the junction of the main avenue into the grounds near Consecration Dell; the committee also determined to preserve the wooded areas on hillsides unless special orders were issued for the building of tombs.

Determined that "the general appearance of the whole grounds should be that of a well-managed park" in the English fashion, Dearborn sketched planting plans of shrubs and flowers in generous ten-foot-wide border strips along major avenues. Flowers would include new bulbous varieties and perennials as well as those of the indigenous or "wild" sort. Ideally, any ornamental plantings added would be made to appear natural rather than creating the impression of a "dense and wild coppice or a neglected garden whose trees and plants have so multiplied and interlaced . . . as to completely destroy all that airiness, grace, and luxuriance of growth which good taste demands," even in areas where proprietors might substantially "improve" their lots with their own plants. Dearborn declared, "I established as a principle the method pursued in England in laying out extensive ornamental plantations of forest trees, shrubs, and flowers." Dearborn transplanted elms and other forest trees from his estate nurseries at Brinley Place in Roxbury to the open areas near the cemetery's front; he also recommended that moving and rearranging of trees be done in following years to "render their plantations a picture, varying and contrasting the masses by different tints," creating as an artist "factitious scenes," each "connected with the whole design." He thinned the woods in places to admit sunshine in "lawns" or clearings, especially along Central Avenue, "more open to the sun than most parts of the cemetery."[7] (Figs. 8.3, 4.)

Through the autumn of 1831, Dearborn labored "with hands as well as mind, without money and without price" at Mount Auburn. As soon as he returned from Washington in the spring of 1832, he was at the cemetery "hoe in hand, day after day, at the head of his laborers, levelling and grading the walks, taking his dinner with him, which he would step into the Wyeth House [an inn] across the road to eat." Oxen helped with heavy earth-moving; and Dearborn and workers carefully plowed, leveled, and rolled the ground to retain the character of the original terrain.[8] After the rains of April, the more arduous task began of laying road-beds of fine gravel on the avenues and smoothing the dirt surfaces of paths. Dearborn's private journal detailed his activity. In 1832 alone, he completed nearly six miles of avenues and paths, providing carriage access to the summit. He even made a road outside the grounds along the cemetery's eastern periphery (today's Coolidge Avenue) to the river and to existing highways on the south and northeast, "thus furnishing a new and most interesting approach to the establishment from Brighton, Brookline, Roxbury, and other towns south of the Charles River, as well as from the city." Dearborn's initial work in laying out earthen avenues and paths cost $3,000, one-third of the initial income from lot sales. By the middle of that year, Mount Auburn was acclaimed as "the pleasantest place of resort" in the area; visitors thronged the grounds through the fall, "numerous beyond all expectation."[9]

Alexander Wadsworth, a civil engineer adept at surveying and map-making, worked for Dearborn to produce "an accurate topographical survey and to locate the numerous avenues." Wadsworth simply drew a detailed map to show "general outlines of the projected improvements," as Dearborn staked them out himself. Wadsworth created a map or "plan," in the common parlance of the day; this did not mean that he was responsible for landscape design.[10]

After leveling ground along the Watertown road for erecting the fence, that first September, Dearborn set aside his tools for nine months to enter the legislature's winter session. Charging George Brimmer to oversee continuing landscape construction, Dearborn sent detailed, written instructions, stipulating the precise thickness of surfaces for avenues and paths, the way to sod gutters, and where to obtain good gravel. If Brimmer had to go south, Dearborn suggested, Bigelow could temporarily take over, since a more permanent resident manager had yet to be hired. In preparation, Brimmer oversaw the building of a gardener's cottage following Dearborn's designs.[11]

In the spring of 1833, Dearborn was back at work on the grounds, setting hitching posts outside the gate, finishing paths for the experimental garden, grading the public lot, laying a path around Forest Pond, and staking out fifty more lots. By 1834, however, his schedule in Washington kept him from spending time at the cemetery. The need for someone to oversee construction, lay out lots, direct Wadsworth's survey, and take on increasing routine demands for supervision of burials, record-keeping, and individual monument building forced the Garden and Cemetery Committee to hire a full-time superintendent, James E. Rupert.

Through this formative period, Bigelow was subordinate to Dearborn in landscape design. Bigelow's professional and academic careers, plus his activities in local literary societies, kept him consistently busier than Dearborn. Bigelow summered in New York City in 1832, hard at work investigating an Asiatic cholera epidemic ravaging the city; he returned to Boston surreptitiously to evade quarantine. In the spring and summer of 1833, Bigelow traveled to Europe for

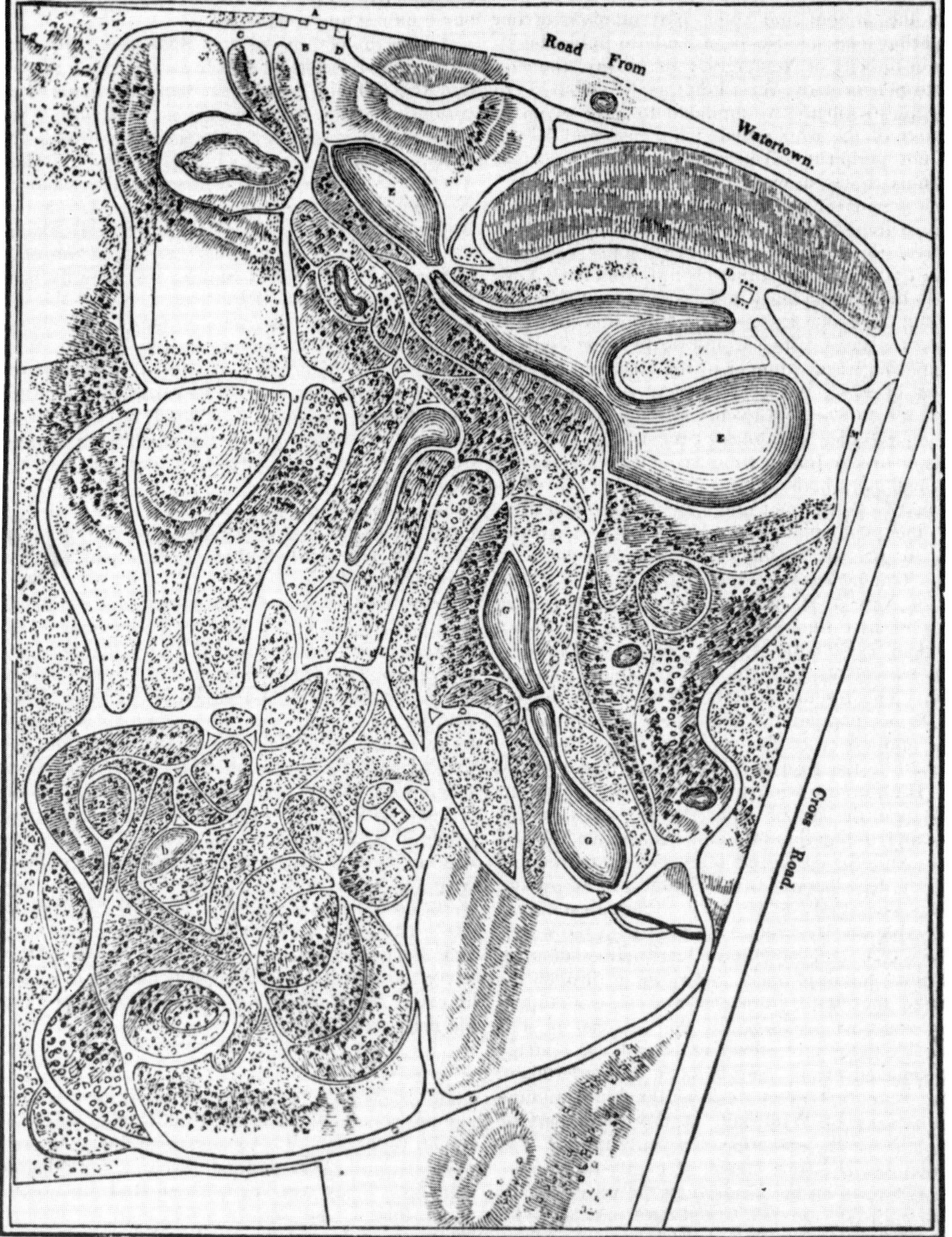

MOUNT AUBURN.

EXPLANATION OF THE VIEW OF MOUNT AUBURN.

A. Entrance from great road to Watertown.
B. Central Avenue.
C. Pine Avenue.
D. Garden Avenue.
E. Garden Pond.
F. Forest Pond.
G. Meadow Pond.
H. Cypress Avenue.
I. Cedar "
J. Central "
K. Beach "
L. Willow "
M. Maple "
N. Walnut "

O. Mountain Avenue.
P. Chestnut "
Q. Oak "
R. Larch "
S. Magnolia "
T. Mount Auburn.
U. Harvard Hill.
V. Juniper Hill.
W. Cedar Hill.
X. Temple Hill.
Y. Pine Hill.
Z. Laurel Hill.
a. Central Square.
b. Consecration Dell.

Fig. 8.2. First map of Mount Auburn, engraved after landscape design of General Henry A. S. Dearborn, 1831.

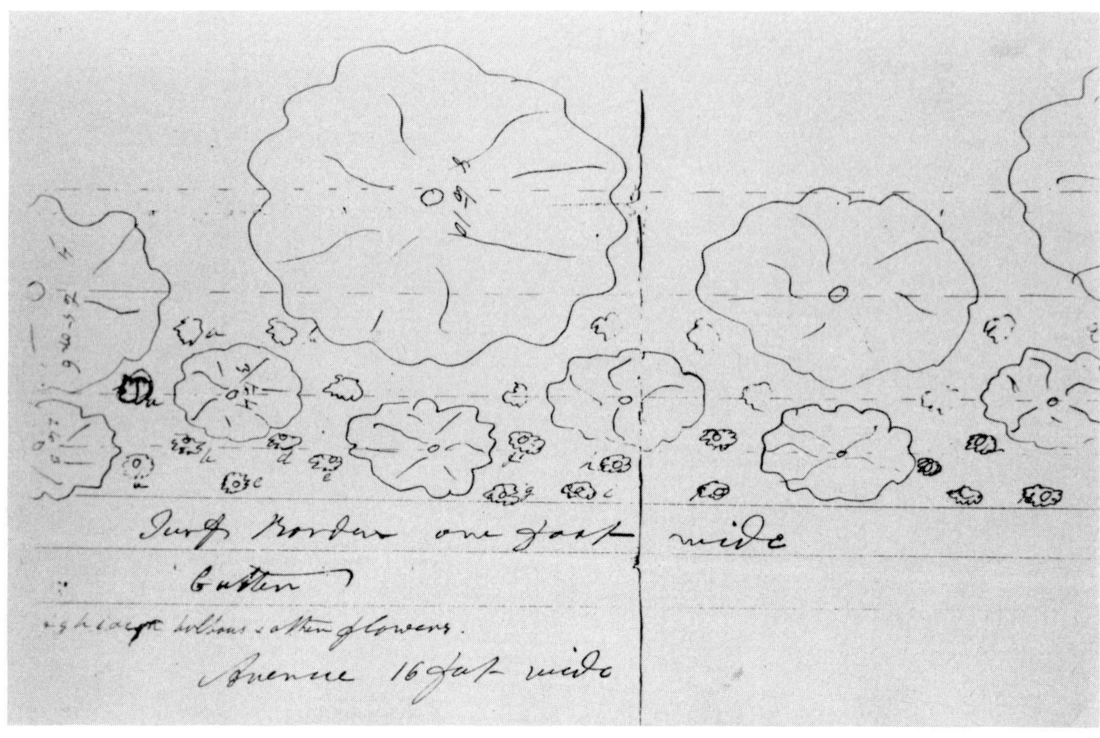

Figs. 8.3., 8.4. Henry A. S. Dearborn, drawings of planting plans, 1831.

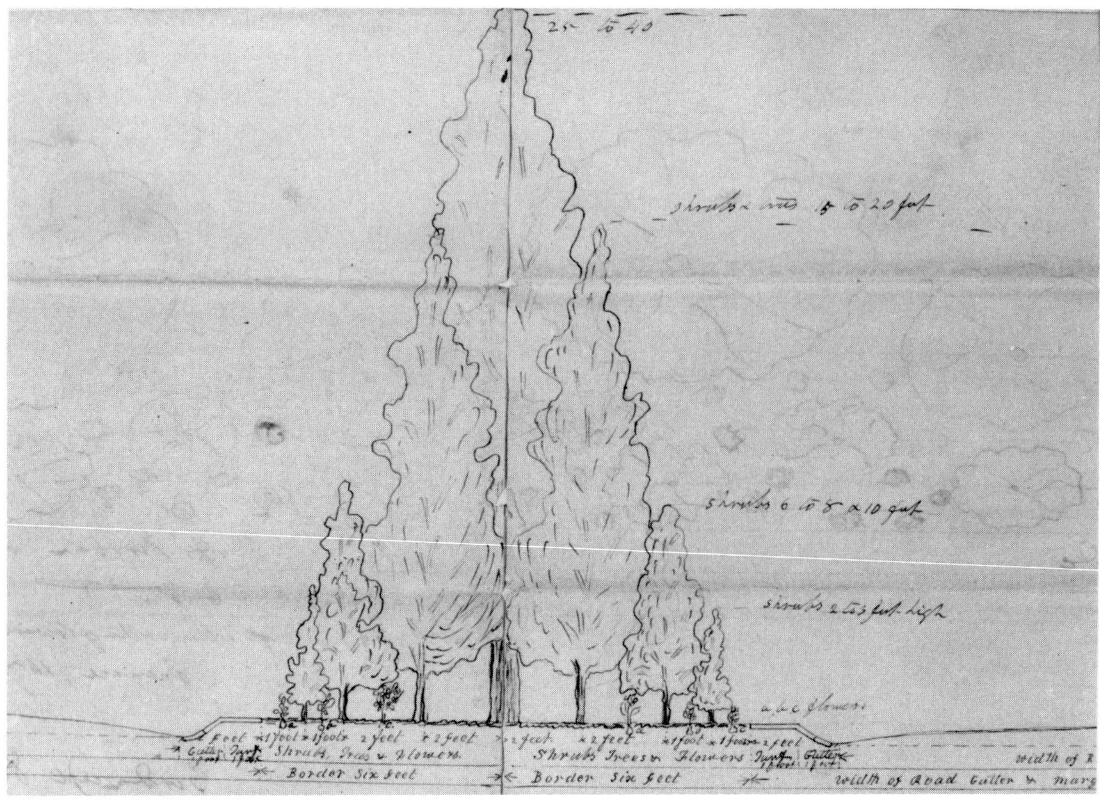

five months with over a dozen prominent Bostonians—the Whitwells, the Kembles, Dr. Oliver Wendell Holmes, Thomas Appleton, Mrs. Kirk Boott, and their families. One of the first things Bigelow and his friends did after arriving in Paris in early May before proceeding to other tourist sights—the Tuileries, the Opéra, the Panthéon, and Versailles—was to ride out to Père Lachaise Cemetery. The doctor wrote to his children, "It truly equals our expectations, especially in its superb view of the city." Although the landscape was more crowded than he anticipated, Bigelow considered some of the monuments "magnificent." Personal, sentimental inscriptions touched him "most deeply."[12]

Precisely when Dearborn was busy designing and laying out Mount Auburn, Bigelow was absent. Yet Bigelow attended all but four Garden and Cemetery Committee meetings in the cemetery's first four years, a record topped only by Treasurer George Bond. When Dearborn returned to Boston in the summers of 1832 and 1833, Bigelow happened to leave; and when most Garden and Cemetery Committee planning meetings were held, attended by Bigelow, Dearborn was out of town.

Still, Dearborn made most of the initial decisions about plantings and landscape. Bigelow performed many tasks in these years—buying $100 worth of shrubs, directing their placement by workmen, and giving plant names to avenues and paths identified by signs that were initially painted on small, white wooden boards. This naming, rather than actual landscape design, is what Bigelow's biographer referred to in crediting the doctor with "designating" the cemetery's ways. Although Bigelow called for creation of a rural cemetery in 1825, he did not specify what sort of landscape design it should have. All documentation gives that credit to Dearborn.[13]

Yet Cornelia Walter, editor of the *Boston Transcript,* gave almost sole credit for creating the cemetery to Bigelow in her book *Mount Auburn Illustrated,* published in 1847, a year before Dearborn founded and designed the landscape of Forest Hills, the second "rural" cemetery in metropolitan Boston. Echoing Bigelow's claims, Walter wrote, "By him the plan for the rural cemetery was first conceived. . . . By him the capacities of the ground were studied, and the avenues and paths chiefly laid out, whilst the belt of trees in front of the Cemetery were planted at his expense." Walter failed even to mention Dearborn. She was correct only in noting that after Mount Auburn's founding "much of its care has, by the Trustees, been vested in the direction of Dr. Bigelow," but that was the case after proprietors of burial lots separated their institution from the horticulturists.[14]

Others, however, credited Dearborn with Mount Auburn's founding. Five months after the general's death in 1851, Samuel Walker, Massachusetts Horticultural Society president, asserted in a national publication that "the history of Mount Auburn will be a record, in all coming time, that the members of this Society . . . were founders of that 'Garden of Graves,' . . . and that to its first President, General Henry A. S. Dearborn, are the public indebted for the beautiful and chaste arrangement." No mention was made of Bigelow, an officer of the society at that time.[15]

Controversy heated up even more after Dearborn's death. The Reverend George Putnam eulogized the general as "the head and the working member" of the subcommittee for laying out Mount Auburn. "With an eye so keen to detect the beautiful and a heart so warmly loving it, he knew how to make the most of every nook and dell, the tangled bog, the sandy level, the abrupt declivity, every tree and shrub and rock. In a word, he, after God, created Mount Auburn." Putnam conceded that "The first *conception* of a Forest Cemetery in America is not claimed for" Dearborn, but he minimized the importance and originality of Bigelow's 1825 proposal of an extramural cemetery: "Scores of men through scores of years had doubtless thought and talked of the subject; but it was when [Dearborn] as president of the horticultural society took up the project, and not before, that any thing was *done.*" Dearborn simply was not "the man to take a secondary and subordinate part in a matter in which official right and duty gave him a leading one . . . in which he felt perfectly at home, which was congenial to his life-long tastes and pursuits, and for which he had at the time entire leisure." Putnam insisted that "the *inception* and accomplishment of the *work*" were Dearborn's; Mount Auburn was "emphatically his creation," if "not his alone." Dearborn played "a leading and efficient part in changing a people's whole system of burial, in redeeming the waste places of death, in surrounding the very grave with nature's choicest adornments, and investing the dreary sepulchre with the scenes and objects that are fraught with the most soothing and elevating associations, and has directed the steps of the living multitudes of cities and villages to the abodes of the dead, as the quietest shades and the loveliest resorts." When the eulogy appeared in Boston newspapers, Bigelow found himself simply listed among many others "associated with [Dearborn] in maturing and executing the plan." Despite their essential truth, these were strong words for Bigelow, then cemetery president, to read.[16]

Bigelow personally and immediately determined to correct the record and disprove contentions of Dearborn's instrumentality in the cemetery's founding. In 1860, at age seventy-three, Bigelow published his own *History of the Cemetery,* characterizing himself as "a witness and an agent in most of the movements" producing Mount Auburn. He called the ill-fated experimental garden merely a concession "to accommodate the wishes of the horticulturists." He insisted that the avenues and paths were laid out by a subcommittee including himself, Dearborn, and Brimmer. Although Bigelow used the passive voice skillfully to avoid the question of agency in much of his account of early landscape development and although he referred to himself in the third person, he made a persuasive claim for himself as prime mover and decision maker. Bigelow concluded, undoubtedly with Dearborn's Forest Hills in mind, "Mount Auburn, in most respects, takes precedence over other cemeteries which have been founded in imitation of it."[17]

Again in 1866, Bigelow complained directly to the horticultural society that "in all the late publications, discourses, and records of the Society, all notice of my name has been avoided, and the credit given to other parties, whom I now gratefully recall as friendly and efficient collaborators." He protested, "For 36 years, I have officially devoted to the care and improvement of Mount Auburn most of the leisure time which I had to spare . . . and have gratuitously watched its interests as of those of my own child." He correctly claimed responsibility for the design of major cemetery structures; however, although he brought the idea of a rural cemetery to Bostonians' attention, it certainly was not his innovation. Indeed, others like William Tudor and Josiah Quincy were earlier to propose such a place to Bostonians. Nevertheless, on December 29, 1866, the society tried to lay the controversy to rest by issuing a general resolution acknowledging Bigelow's "aid and counsel" in the initial cemetery venture.[18]

Soon after publication of Bigelow's history, the *Mount Auburn Memorial,* a small weekly paper produced for a while by the cemetery gatekeeper and his son, featured a biographical sketch of General Dearborn, asserting "it was he who performed the chief part of the work of laying out the grounds. . . . The skill and taste with which he performed his task is fully acknowledged in the admiration of those who have seen the beauties of that sacred ground . . . a magnificent and beautiful monument to him—to his industry and taste."[19] Not surprisingly, publication of that newspaper ceased abruptly less than six months later; it is unclear whether Bigelow's adverse reaction to the article, lack of sales, or the onset of the Civil War shortened the life of the weekly.

Two decades later, Bigelow's eulogist, the Reverend George E. Ellis, took up the cudgels, claiming that the doctor "was called upon to lay out and adorn Mount Auburn, to designate its avenues and paths, to draft its lodges, gateway, and fences, and to plan its tower and chapel" because of his "taste and skill, and knowledge of materials, and eye for proportions, and judgment of construction." After attributing the design of the entire cemetery and its structures to Bigelow, Ellis boldly declared that Bigelow deserved greatest praise as "the first—we may say, in Christendom—to conceive, propose, and earnestly and patiently to guide on to a most complete triumph, the plan of an extensive forest-garden cemetery, combining the wildness of nature with the finish of culture, with all appropriate arrangements and adornments." Ellis claimed originality for Bigelow's idea, conceived "without aid or guidance from any similar device in this country, nor on the scale which it was organized and carried out, had he any previous example in Europe to follow." Ellis chose the seldom-used term "forest-garden," indicating a response aimed at discrediting Putnam's eulogy of Dearborn and undermining Putnam's praise of Forest Hills Cemetery in Roxbury. Ellis's assertion that Bigelow did not look to European precedents also contradicted not only Dearborn's published accounts of use of printed materials from France and England but his repeated reference to the example of Père Lachaise Cemetery in his design for Mount Auburn's landscape.[20]

The debate over assigning credit for the founding of Mount Auburn only obscures the fact that it was a very important and influential *designed* landscape, not simply the work of "amateurs." Although trends in professionalization proceeded at an irregular pace in the flux of nineteenth-century American society, it is wrong to call the likes of Bigelow, Story, and Dearborn amateurs. They excelled in many different fields, although not on a full-time, income-earning basis. As in England of the previous century, members of the gentry easily became physicians, clergymen, barristers, architects, and landscape gardeners, occasionally combining fields of expertise. In Boston in 1830, members of the local elite—Bigelow, the physician, horticulturist, and architect; Story, the jurist; and Dearborn, the nonpracticing lawyer, but active politician, engineer, and landscape gardener—still found it easy to be renaissance men. Together in the Massachusetts Horticultural Society and similar new institutions, they fostered their eclectic expertise and developed a variety of projects to improve their society and culture.[21]

The controversy over agency of individuals in historical accounts of Mount Auburn was only a distant echo of a more substantive controversy that plagued the cemetery's first years. Bigelow's faction of cemetery proponents resented that permanent structures could not be built immediately. Horticulturists, on the other hand, begrudged extensive development of the cemetery at a time of limited income and at the expense of the experimental garden. Ambitious plans to make Mount Auburn an "Institution for the Education of Scientific and Practical Gardeners" were quickly thwarted, although Dearborn urged support of an educational garden: "In this age of general improvement, when institutions and associations have been formed for inculcating intelligence in every branch of knowledge and among all walks of society . . . it is not only desirable, but highly important, that measures should be taken for extending similar advantages" as in instruction in the mechanic arts "to those persons who may wish to become accomplished Gardeners." Dearborn proposed nothing less than a practical school of horticulture, staffed by instructors teaching "a science and an art . . . requiring an extensive acquaintance with Natural History and Physics, Botany, Mineralogy, Hydraulics, Mechanics, Architecture, Chemistry, and Entomology." There would be lessons in topographical analysis, drawing, projection of maps, laying out of grounds, and design of "rural" buildings to complement the "modern" or English style of landscape gardening. Dearborn hoped that at Mount Auburn practical gardeners might teach both theory and practice "that science and skill may be contemporaneously acquired . . . in a well-managed establishment." Dearborn wished Mount Auburn to become a school of design, complete with library, models, maps, and plans and elevations of buildings, as well as studio space, to teach students to create a "rural architecture," that would include gravel walks, artificial caverns, fish ponds, and observatories extending over at least half of the grounds.[22]

Dearborn's ideas were not unprecedented. The London Horticultural Society gardens proved an important training ground for Joseph Paxton, the landscape gardener who achieved international fame second only to John Claudius Loudon; they attracted aspiring professionals like Adolph Strauch from Prussia, who later became a major American cemetery and park designer based in Cincinnati. Dearborn hoped that his experimental garden and school combining design and horticultural curricula would become a similar place of professional training for American landscape gardeners. Its interdisciplinary focus would resemble that of Bigelow's Harvard course on technology; however, such an ambitious, formalized course of landscape study would not be available in America until seventy years later.

One wonders whether Dearborn's school, if created, might not have eventually become formally affiliated with Harvard, precisely at a time when the college was busily adding new professional curricula. It might have become the first professional design school in the nation, perhaps as influential as the systematic course of study of the law established in 1845 by Story, which within a decade became the model for proliferating professional law schools across the country and eventually made obsolete the older, informal practice of the aspiring attorney simply reading the law in the office of an established practitioner, as Dearborn had done in Story's Salem office. Instead, for the next seventy years, America lacked professional academic training of landscape architects.

The need for an experimental garden for development of better and more diversified plants to be grown in America preoccupied other founders. Zebedee Cook, vice president of the horticulturists, reminded his friends, "We have been too long accustomed to rely upon foreign nurseries for fruit trees and other plants. . . . We should depend more upon our own resources." Cook recalled a time when "everything that bore the impress of a foreign original was sought after, admired and eulogized without much regard to its intrinsic merits"; now, he observed, "these antinational prejudices and predilections are fast receding before the beaming and unquenchable light of intellect and patriotism." Cook wanted a place to domesticate foreign plants and develop new hybrids, with sections devoted to fruit trees, timber trees, ornamentals and shrubs, vegetables, flowers, orangeries, hotbeds, vineries, and greenhouses. Nurseries, melon grounds, strawberry fields, and a "culinarium" would fill the large northeastern portion of the ground and the southeast corner as well. Dearborn agreed about the necessity of an experimental garden to "develop the vast vegetable resources of the Union, give activity to enterprise, increase the enjoyment of all classes of citizens, advance the prosperity, and improve the general aspect of the whole country."[23] Thus, Mount Auburn would become an institution of the American System.

Horticulturists wanted to see what seeds received from various parts of the country and other nations could be naturalized to New England's soil and climate. As early as the spring of 1832, anxious over delays in planting potatoes, corn, peas, and carrots, Dearborn charged Brimmer to hire a gardener to prepare the soil in the large, flat land in the front of the grounds, north of the section reserved for burials, on and beyond the glacial moraine called Indian Ridge. Although the garden was to remain separate from the burial grounds, Dearborn had staked out walks and chosen locations for bridges interconnecting the two areas at several points. There was to be "a line of demarcation rather than of disconnection," with the garden shielding the cemetery from view from the public road but blending into it on the interior. As in the English garden, borders and barriers were to be inconspicuous if not invisible if at all possible.[24]

News of the joint garden and cemetery venture quickly spread internationally through a network of horticulturists who sent contributions: seeds of the *magnolia acuminata* from Ohio forests, trees from an upstate New York nursery, scions of plums and apples from Montreal, vegetable seeds from the London Horticultural Society, and over a hundred different seed varieties from the Calcutta Botanical Garden. The Naples Botanic Garden sent a large box of mixed seeds. By the end of 1833, Dearborn inventoried over 1,300 forest, ornamental, and fruit trees, a wide selection of vegetables, and 450 varieties of other seeds, including strawberries, wild rice, skinless oats, Normandy garden cress, tree of heaven, willows, nuts, and a newly discovered vegetable from Chile, the *Oxalis crenata,* then hoped to rival the potato as a staple crop. He had to keep many of the plants in his own nurseries on his Brinley Place estate in Roxbury, just south of Boston. The *New England Farmer* regularly listed plants received by the horticultural society for Mount Auburn.[25]

David Porter, American chargé d'affaires to the Ottoman empire, sent seeds of the oriental cypress, allegedly responsible for the beauty of Turkish cemeteries. Porter had read discussions in American newspapers of trees "most proper to decorate or to conceal the gloomy aspect of our neglected Grave Yards"; he earmarked his gift specifically for the cemetery rather than the garden. In Turkey, wrote Porter, "death is divested of half his terrors, by the cheerful aspect which their cemeteries present. They are places of resort during festivals and are visited by Christians as the most pleasant place for recreation." Many other writers had recently contrasted Turkish cemeteries with New England burial grounds, and Porter felt justified in predicting that when the cypress "decorated" American graveyards, "death will be deprived of his sting, the grave of its victory."[26]

Dearborn welcomed gifts of plants for both the cemetery and the garden, and he attempted to develop both sections of Mount Auburn simultaneously. In 1833, he persuaded the horticultural society to go $5,000 into debt and thirty-five Bostonians to loan $100 apiece to buy twenty-five acres of hilly, wooded land immediately to the west because the topography would permit better development of the picturesque funerary landscape by providing "beautiful sites for monuments." Most of the new land was quickly surveyed and sold for burial lots. It was so desirable that many of the first proprietors exchanged their lots for ones in this area. Mount Auburn had 110 acres in comparison to Père Lachaise, which began with only fifty-two acres and expanded to seventy-two by the 1830s.[27]

By enlarging the cemetery, Dearborn never accomplished his task of dividing the garden into "compartments" or "departments" to permit gardeners to conduct the "comparative experiments on the modes of culture . . . to attain a knowledge of the most useful, rare, and beautiful species, the best processes of rearing and propagating them, [and] the most successful methods of insuring perfect and abundant crops, as well as useful and ornamental planting."[28] Joseph Bradley, George Pratt, and Elijah Vose attempted to raise additional funds by a subscription campaign specifically for the experimental garden, since proceeds from cemetery lot sales were absorbed by general improvements in the burial area, but they met with no success. By the summer of 1833, a disheartened Dearborn realized he would have to abandon his hope of creating a school for landscape gardeners.

Nevertheless, Dearborn started an experimental garden on a limited basis. He hired David Haggerston, a commercial gardener from Charlestown and member of the horticultural society, who with the help of two laborers and the porter at the main gate, reputed to be a "practical" gardener, planted seeds in hotbeds for culinary vegetables and decorative plants. In the spring of 1833, Haggerston set out three hundred different forest, ornamental, and fruit trees throughout the grounds. Dearborn still hoped to develop a mutually beneficial, symbiotic relationship between the garden and the cemetery, but he grew increasingly pessimistic. Tensions escalated between horticulturists and proprietors of burial lots over public access to the grounds. Brimmer reminded Dearborn that there was indifference if not outright opposition to an experimental garden among cemetery supporters. Bigelow may well have been an opponent, despite his personal knowledge of plants and position of leadership in the horticultural society; he suggested several decades later that the garden was merely a matter of expediency, a concession to horticulturists necessary in order to have institutional auspices under which to begin the cemetery venture.[29]

Burial lot owners like Bigelow and Story may have feared for the security of their graves because of free public access to the grounds, or perhaps they were offended by visitors' behavior. Those Bostonians who became the first cemetery proprietors insisted on making Mount Auburn a new sort of private place—or rather a congregation of private family burial grounds in a single landscape. After all, many objections to the old urban burial grounds were that they were so very public, exposed to the view of, if not physically accessible to, common passersby on Boston's streets.

To provide security if not total privacy, Zebedee Cook and George Bond oversaw enclosure of the grounds in the spring of 1833, after Dearborn tended to major details. He ordered seven-foot cedar and spruce posts from Maine to be held together by iron rails and painted a dark color. Some described it as made of "neat and substantial" pickets; others, as "rough sawed pales." Such an open fence was "not so liable to be shaken and injured by the wind," but would remain "secure against cattle," until horticulturists could afford to make the more expensive but preferable "stone or brick wall all round." A sturdy fence was crucial in winning confidence of Bostonians that their dead would remain buried, safe from grave robbers. One Newton resident queried Dearborn in 1833, "How will the bodies be protected at Mount Auburn? by some ponderous concave rock placed over the grave for a time and lifted and moved from place to place by powerful machinery?" In lieu of a cemetery system to ensure against grave robbing, many individual proprietors used mortsafes, temporary iron grilles rooted in the ground over graves, to prevent disturbance of their dead.[30]

Countering these concerns, avid horticulturists charged that cemetery proprietors had no interest in their activities but made up an increasingly large portion of their society's membership, automatically receiving life tenure with purchase of a burial lot. Through 1833 and 1834, Massachusetts Horticultural Society meetings became increasingly stormy; by 1834, many burial lot holders professed "a positive aversion" to the idea of an experimental garden. Dearborn sided with the horticulturists; Bigelow, with cemetery advocates.[31]

Others also took sides. Zebedee Cook wrote that Dearborn always felt Mount Auburn "was purchased with the intention of establishing a garden of Experimentation, that the *cemetery* was secondary, the proceeds thereof to be devoted to the *garden and* the cemetery." Despite Cook's urging, Dearborn hesitated to state these views in writing. He remained on friendly terms with Bigelow, but his increasing commitments in Congress and elsewhere eased him away from the growing unpleasantness at an opportune time. By 1834, Dearborn was the only conciliator of the two factions. Brimmer resigned in 1832 because of ill health to travel abroad; he died in Florence, Italy, in 1838 and was buried far from the cemetery he was instrumental in creating.[32]

The public ignored the internal conflict, continuing to use Mount Auburn as a new amenity, constantly improved for their use, with free access granted to all on foot, on horseback, or in carriages. In April of 1833, the famous actress Fanny Kemble judged Mount Auburn "a pleasure garden instead of a place of graves." Extensive publicity of the new institution in regional and national newspapers as well as in a variety of guides and travel narratives attracted more visitors than proprietors. Almost immediately, Mount Auburn earned an international reputation.[33]

Ralph Waldo Emerson continued to go there as he had during his college days to enjoy the natural landscape. He wrote in his journal of a visit in the spring of 1834, a whole day spent in the woods except for a brief lunch taken at the Fresh Pond Hotel, another "pleasure ground" in the vicinity. Emerson "forsook the tombs and found a sunny hollow where the east wind would not blow." There, he sat against a tree for the day, communing with nature, "and let what would pass through [his eyes] into the soul." He found a variety of plants, four gilding snakes, a chick-a-dee, and a black-capped titmouse. Emerson observed, "I saw no more my relation, how near and petty, to Cambridge or Boston; I heeded no more what minute or hour our Massachusetts clocks might indicate—I saw only the noble earth on which I was born, with the great Star which warms and enlightens it. . . . It was Day—that was all Heaven said. The pines glittered . . . and seemed to challenge me to read their riddle. . . . This gay and grand architecture, from the vault to the moss and lichen on which I lay,—who shall explain to me the laws of its proportions and adornments?" Such was the good behavior expected of visitors to Mount Auburn; such were the lessons of pantheistic philosophy that they were supposed to "read" in the picturesque, wooded landscape sheltering Bostonians' burials.[34]

Many other visitors to Mount Auburn sought only present pleasures and not the "pleasures of melancholy," lessons of moral philosophy or of transcendentalism, or even simple appreciation of nature. Founders observed that the cemetery was used "in a manner very different from what they had expected, destroying the solemnity and quiet" intended for their new burial place. Proprietors complained that conditions were becoming worse than those in the city's old graveyards. Visitors mutilated trees, broke fences, and trampled lots. Dearborn's hand-lettered signs were not effective: "Visitors are desired to confine their walks to the avenues and paths and to avoid treading on the borders." "Pause—this is hallowed ground, Sacred to the dead and the living. Pluck not a shrub—touch not a flower. Leave every thing in its beauty." "Walk Your Horse." Those on horseback proved the most disruptive and damaging, riding on narrow paths intended for contemplative strollers, and tethering their mounts to trees and shrubs. First, the society employed officers to police the grounds on holidays like the Fourth of July. The problem of visitors' behavior was chronic, however, becoming intolerable for those interested primarily in Mount Auburn's burial functions just at the time when Dearborn resigned the chairmanship of the Garden and Cemetery Committee to pursue other activities.[35]

Dearborn resigned as president of the horticultural society on September 10, 1834, explaining his intention to move west, although he never did. He attended his last Garden and Cemetery Committee meeting in July. Cook, who briefly succeeded him, left a month later to head a major insurance institution in New York. Perhaps Dearborn or Cook eventually could have conciliated Mount Auburn's two factions had they stayed on.

Judge Joseph Story, rather than Bigelow, took over from Dearborn despite pressing personal and professional concerns. Story had only a passing interest in horticulture, and he lent a sympathetic ear to complaints of burial lot owners that visitors with free access to Mount Auburn "destroyed the solemnity and quiet" of the place and even perpetrated real damage. The great judicial defender of property rights supported proprietors' claims that the cemetery should be a collection of private holdings ensured in perpetuity under institutional auspices rather than a public place open and accessible to anyone. He heeded suggestions that "such indiscriminate admissions" impeded growth of the cemetery, after some potential proprietors told him they would not take lots while Mount Auburn was so open.[36]

After eighteen months of diminishing lot sales and increasing complaints from proprietors that the grounds were "used in a manner very different from what they had expected," Story persuaded Garden and Cemetery Committee members to deny permission to enter the grounds to all persons on horseback or in carriages, with exception of those attending funerals. Proprietors protested, however; Story quickly modified the regulation to admit lot owners, family members, and guests in carriages if they presented to the gatekeeper a nontransferable ticket, to be issued annually. No mention was made of horticulturists without lots. The general public could still enter freely on foot from sunrise to sunset, but absence of inexpensive public transportation to the site, which was four miles from Boston and a mile from Cambridge, limited access to the grounds for a time. Furthermore, only proprietors could enter the grounds on Sundays, the day that had brought "unusual concourses of people" to Mount Auburn, the one day of rest for the working classes. Story observed "that the injuries done to the grounds and shrubbery were far greater on that day than on any other day." Only committee members could make exceptions to these restrictions by issuing temporary tickets to out-of-town visitors. Sabbath meditations in the sacred groves of the cemetery would no longer be interrupted by mere pleasure seekers who lacked a proprietary stake in the place, possession of which was the equivalent of having purchased a pew in one of Boston's fine churches.

Six days a week, nonproprietors who came by horse or carriage without tickets could secure their animals at hitching posts provided outside the gate and proceed on foot through the grounds. Story ordered the south gate permanently locked so the porter could scrutinize everyone entering or leaving from the north. Many new people bought lots just to have the privilege of entering in a carriage, and those who already had lots liked the increased exclusivity of the place. Still the committee insisted on acquiring supplementary legislation on March 21, 1834, making it a misdemeanor to "destroy, mutilate, deface, or remove any tomb, monument, gravestone or other structure . . . tree, shrub, or plant" or to discharge firearms in the cemetery under penalty of a $5 to $50 fine and prosecution for trespass. Story deemed regulations "indispensable to the quiet and good order of the grounds." He posted new signs detailing them and again warning proprietors in carriages to go no faster than a walk.[37]

Despite the rules, regulations, and restricted admissions, Mount Auburn's popularity continued to grow, justifying Dearborn's 1831 prediction that it would be "a holy and pleasant resort for the living . . . one of the most instructive, magnificent and pleasant promenades in our country. From its immediate proximity to the Capitol of the State, it will attract universal interest, and become a place of healthful, refreshing and agreeable resort." Story's Garden and Cemetery Committee did not wish to ban visitors altogether; it merely wanted them to be fewer and more well-behaved. Indeed, the committee placed benches at various locations in Mount Auburn for the convenience of those walking miles through the grounds on foot. Mount Auburn was to be a walking garden precisely at a time when Boston, rapidly expanding, was ceasing to be a compact walking city.[38]

Story was gratified in the fall of 1834 that Mount Auburn was "a place of general resort and interest, as well to strangers as to citizens; and its shades and paths, ornamented with monumental structures, of various beauty and elegance, have already given solace and tranquilizing reflections to many an afflicted heart, and awakened a deep moral sensibility in many a pious bosom." Once rowdy visitors were excluded, Alexander Everett could muse, "How salutary the effect which a visit to its calm and sacred shades will produce on souls too much agitated by the storms of the world! It was surely fitting that Art and Nature should combine their beauties to grace a scene devoted to purposes so high and holy." Ironically, however, visiting Mount Auburn had not calmed the souls of those whose behavior brought the "storms of the world" into the cemetery. The place was meant for those already confirmed to gentility.[39]

The new regulations prompted public criticism of Mount Auburn reminiscent of the charges of elitism leveled against the congregations of Saint Paul's and the Park Street Church in the 1823 burial controversy. Only this time, Joseph Buckingham's *New-England Galaxy* did not lead a journalistic crusade against privilege, because the editor was a cemetery proprietor and ardent advocate. Story attempted to dispel the "erroneous" public opinion that Mount Auburn was a "private speculation for the private benefit of members of the [Massachusetts Horticultural] Society, or of the individuals, who originally advanced the money to purchase the grounds . . . and that considerable profits [had] been already realized from it." He asserted that the cemetery was "in the truest and noblest sense a public institution . . . of which the whole community [might] obtain the benefit upon easy and equal terms . . . the usual sum fixed for the purchase of a lot." Story strongly denied that anyone had "any private interest" in the venture. In fact, by the end of 1834, cemetery development produced a $2,000 deficit.[40]

By that time, differences between horticulturists and cemetery proprietors proved irreconcilable. A major cause of friction between the two factions leading to official separation of the institutions was the failure of lot sales to produce enough revenue for development of the experimental garden. Limited admissions and stricter regulations gave greater grounds for contention. Those with burial lots generally had no interest in activities and aspirations of the horticultural society and demanded that land allotted for the experimental garden be given over to burials, although there was no pressing need for additional space. Development of the cemetery as a pleasant, pastoral place was simply more important than experimental gardening; it was a personal priority for Bigelow, Story, and others who, unlike Dearborn, Cook, and other horticulturists, owned no country estates on which to create family burial grounds in the fashion of English gardens. Dearborn and Cook, however, unlike many of their friends with rural estates, sympathized with those who wanted the cemetery, not only because they realized that it would provide for interments outside of old urban graveyards but also because such an institution would have other functions as well. Indeed, both men subsequently helped found other rural cemeteries—Forest Hills in Roxbury south of Boston and Green-Wood across the East River from New York, respectively.

Elijah Vose, third president of the society, did not own burial space at Mount Auburn, lacked Dearborn's enthusiasm for the venture, and realized that a fully developed garden would not be forthcoming for years, if ever. The Garden and Cemetery Committee belatedly and halfheartedly ordered specific improvements to make the garden "productive and profitable" late in 1834. Then, however, cemetery proponents Bigelow and Story insisted that major structures mentioned in the original plan—a chapel, observatory tower, granite gate, and permanent enclosure—be built before energy and funds would be allocated to the intri-

Fig. 8.5. Corporate seal of the Massachusetts Horticultural Society, 1829.

cacies of cultivating better cabbages and cauliflower. Neither horticulturists nor cemetery proprietors remained satisfied with development of Mount Auburn under Massachusetts Horticultural Society auspices.

By the end of 1834, both horticulturists and cemetery proprietors realized that their differences were irreconcilable in a single institution, and Joseph Story headed a committee to negotiate an institutional separation. The Massachusetts General Court issued a new act of incorporation, an inviolable contract in the name of the Proprietors of the Cemetery of Mount Auburn, on March 31, 1835. The horticultural society relinquished ownership of the experimental garden; proprietors of burial lots ceased to be members of the society by signing the charter on April 21, 1835. On June 19, the society deeded all land to the new cemetery corporation. The state exempted the cemetery from paying taxes; and the new charter empowered the board to add fifty more acres of land and to receive money for maintenance of buildings, tombs, monuments, and grounds yet to be developed. Most of the original rules, regulations, and procedures established by the horticultural society continued in effect under the new corporation, whose charter formalized bans on shooting firearms, playing music, or harming monuments, structures, and plants in the cemetery under penalty of misdemeanor. No longer able to use the society emblem, Bigelow and Story devised a seal for Mount Auburn bearing the Latin motto *Sic panditur immortalis* or "Thus extends the path of immortality." (Figs. 8.5, 6.)

The agreement separating the two institutions included stipulation that the cemetery pay the horticultural society a retroactive and henceforth annual sum of one-fourth the proceeds from lot sales after deduction of $1,400 per year for operating expenses, provided that the society apply the money to an experimental garden or "the promotion of the Art and Science of Horticulture" only. With minor modifications in 1858 and 1910, which excluded applicability of the agreement to subsequent purchase of land, this financial arrangement remained in operation until 1975, although the society unsuccessfully tried to claim a quarter of all burial fees in addition in 1845. For over a century, horticulturists reserved the right to inspect the cemetery's financial records. Although the society never attempted to establish another

Fig. 8.6. Corporate seal of the Proprietors and Trustees of Mount Auburn Cemetery, 1835.

experimental garden, funds from Mount Auburn eventually made possible the building of two Horticultural Halls, the first designed by Gridley J. Fox Bryant for a central Tremont Street location in 1865; the second, a large, three-story English Baroque structure in Boston's South End across from Symphony Hall in 1901. Horticultural Society President Leverett Saltonstall called establishment of Mount Auburn "one of the most fortunate events" in the financial history of his organization, despite the institutional schism.[41]

Mount Auburn's charter vested ownership of the entire cemetery in lot owners and provided for preservation of perpetual control of each burial lot within the family that originally purchased it in fee simple. Cemetery trustees publicly announced that they made provisions to keep proprietors from using lots for profit; only relatives would be permitted burial in a single lot. The new corporation kept meticulous records of proprietors and burials, facilitated by an innovative system established from the start of numbering of lots consecutively as surveyed, rather than in sequence along avenues and paths. Books registering names and dates of interments contained other vital information as well—city of residence, date of death, original place of interment in cases of bodies moved from previous graves and receiving tombs. Records show no discontinuity with rechartering of the cemetery. Lots remained indivisible, once occupied by burials, and passed intact to heirs of the deceased proprietor with preference given to males over females, with "proximity of blood and priority of age having due regard" in addition to "proximity of residence" to the cemetery.[42] Cemetery trustees reserved the right to act as jury, determining a new lot representative to assume the sole vote in the corporation after the death of the original owner. This arrangement provided for continuous family control of each cemetery lot through a sort of primogeniture. It also meant that there were few if any voting women in the corporation, unless they were proprietors in their own right or sole surviving descendants. Cemetery organization recapitulated the order of Victorian society at large.

Proprietors met annually at a time and place advertised publicly in local newspapers. They then had the opportunity to make suggestions about the cemetery, although usually they simply cast their votes and proxies to elect a board of from seven to twelve trustees, a number that fluctuated between nine and ten in the first decade. The annual proprietors' meeting resembled the old New England town meeting in procedure and function, and trustees were like selectmen. Many of the first nine trustees had also been active on the horticultural society's Garden and Cemetery Committee. They met monthly, first at Treasurer George Bond's Boston home, then at Charles Curtis's office, and by 1844 at Dr. Jacob Bigelow's Summer Street house, but rarely at the cemetery itself. Through the 1830s, trustee attendance was so erratic that the board often lacked a quorum for months on end, delaying the few decisions to be made. Development and maintenance of the cemetery during that period were shared by four small standing committees—Grounds, Lots, Finance, and Regulations and Interment Records—with prime responsibility usually resting on Jacob Bigelow.

Officers of the new corporation were distinguished and, therefore, could devote only limited time to the cemetery. President Joseph Story enjoyed national renown as a justice of the United States Supreme Court. Benjamin R. Curtis (1809–74), first secretary of Mount Auburn, was a young lawyer who would follow in Story's footsteps, winning appointment to the Supreme Court in 1850 and resigning seven years later after writing the minority opinion in the Dred Scott case. Curtis then served as chief defense counsel in President Andrew Johnson's impeachment trial. Curtis received $100 per year for his services to the cemetery. Although Dr. Bigelow held no office other than trustee until 1845 and continued his Harvard teaching and medical practice, he played a leading role in directing decisions on a day-to-day basis.

Mount Auburn is an early example of corporations founded in the early nineteenth century to answer varied individual and community needs. New Englanders pioneered in the art of founding eleemosynary corporations, legal instruments of private collective action to accomplish projects with public benefits. By 1820, Massachusetts had granted both profit and nonprofit charters so readily that the state had more corporations than all of

Europe. New corporations assumed functions formerly filled by the state, the community, or the family, privatizing and systematizing services previously performed informally or publicly.

The newness of the eleemosynary corporation and the distinguished status of officers and trustees led to public skepticism of the cemetery as elitist and antidemocratic. Despite relatively high lot prices that they set, trustees disclaimed any "design to confine the sale of lots to any class of citizens." Burial space was "advertised for sale without discrimination."[43] Many of Boston's "middling sort" managed to accumulate enough money to purchase lots at Mount Auburn, and the cemetery drew proprietors from the ranks of prosperous mechanics and farmers in the metropolitan area.

Mount Auburn's first interment in July of 1832 was a stillborn infant of Mr. and Mrs. James Boyd of Boston. Of seventeen burials that year, only two were recent deaths; others had died from four months to twenty-one years previously and were reinterred from older graveyards. Joseph Story moved the remains of five of his children to Mount Auburn, bringing four from Salem and one from Cambridge's common burial ground. When Mary Hastings, a young woman aged twenty-six, died, her widower decided to rebury the bodies of two infants, perhaps her sisters, dead since 1815 and 1819, at the same time as he laid his wife to rest. Sometimes more than two burials were placed in the same grave in lots without family tombs. Reinterments made up a major portion of all burials through Mount Auburn's first decade, most coming from Boston and occurring during the cool spring months of April and May. Many proprietors were anxious to move bodies of loved ones from crowded urban graveyards, fearing that old burial places would be forcibly discontinued and the bones carted away to unknown sites. But there were no attempts to remove the remains of colonial ancestors to Mount Auburn, because precise locations of burial even of grandparents, let alone of the founders of the colony, had been forgotten. Burial records reveal that the earliest death dates of the reinterments at the cemetery were 1792 for Mary Sargent, 1796 for Simon Elliot and Captain John Stanton, and 1797 for a Mrs. Green and John S. Ellery. Bostonians took renewed consolation, as Bigelow observed, in the pleasant, pastoral place for postmortem reconstitution of immediate families.[44]

By 1825, Mount Auburn's basic corporate and landscape structure was in place in forms that would endure, relatively unchanged, for decades and even through the twentieth century, providing precedents to be emulated in the founding of many other "rural" cemeteries. The urban institution was called "rural" because of the "picturesque" landscape laid out on a suburban site over the irregular terrain, further sculpted with earthen avenues and paths. Trees formed a major element of landscape structure. It was the sort of forest garden advocated by English designers like William Kent, Sir Uvedale Price, and Sir William Chambers. It reflected its founders' knowledge of and ability to apply a formula derived from these and other eighteenth-century English theorists, from many of the first literary proponents of romanticism, and from French cemetery reformers. Such was a fitting site for development of an American cult of commemoration.

9

Art and Nature Balanced: A Marble History in the Forest Cemetery

Nature and Art here harmonize with each other, and mingle their powers "to lend enchantment to the scene."
—Enoch Cobb Wines, *A Trip to Boston* (1838)

The care with which the rural aspect of the enclosure is preserved affords the best illustration of the harmony which exists between Nature and Man, even in his decay.
—"Burial," *North American Review* (July 1861)

MOUNT AUBURN'S "ARCADIAN LOVELINESS" distracted thoughts from the horrors of death, according to one visitor from Philadelphia. Enoch Cobb Wines concluded that "though corruption is not less foul here than elsewhere, and the worms are as sure to banquet upon the poor remains of humanity, yet death would seem disrobed of half its terrors, if one could be assured of a final resting place beneath the deep shadows of its trees and amid its profusion of flowers." Wines echoed Keats in praise of personal consolation found in a romantic burial place amid Nature. The same sentiments were repeated by many other visitors and paraphrased by Thoreau, who wrote in *Walden* in 1845, "There can be no very black melancholy to him who lives in the midst of Nature."[1] (Fig. 9.1.)

Mount Auburn's founders equally valued nature's powers to soothe grief and serve as balm for the world-weary; indeed, nature dominated the spirit of place through the first decades of Mount Auburn's existence. Development of the cemetery proceeded slowly, impeded by the hard economic times following the Panic of 1837 and by separation of Mount Auburn from the Massachusetts Horticultural Society. For a time, Jacob Bigelow, Joseph Story, and their associates were more intent on re-forming the cemetery as an independent in-

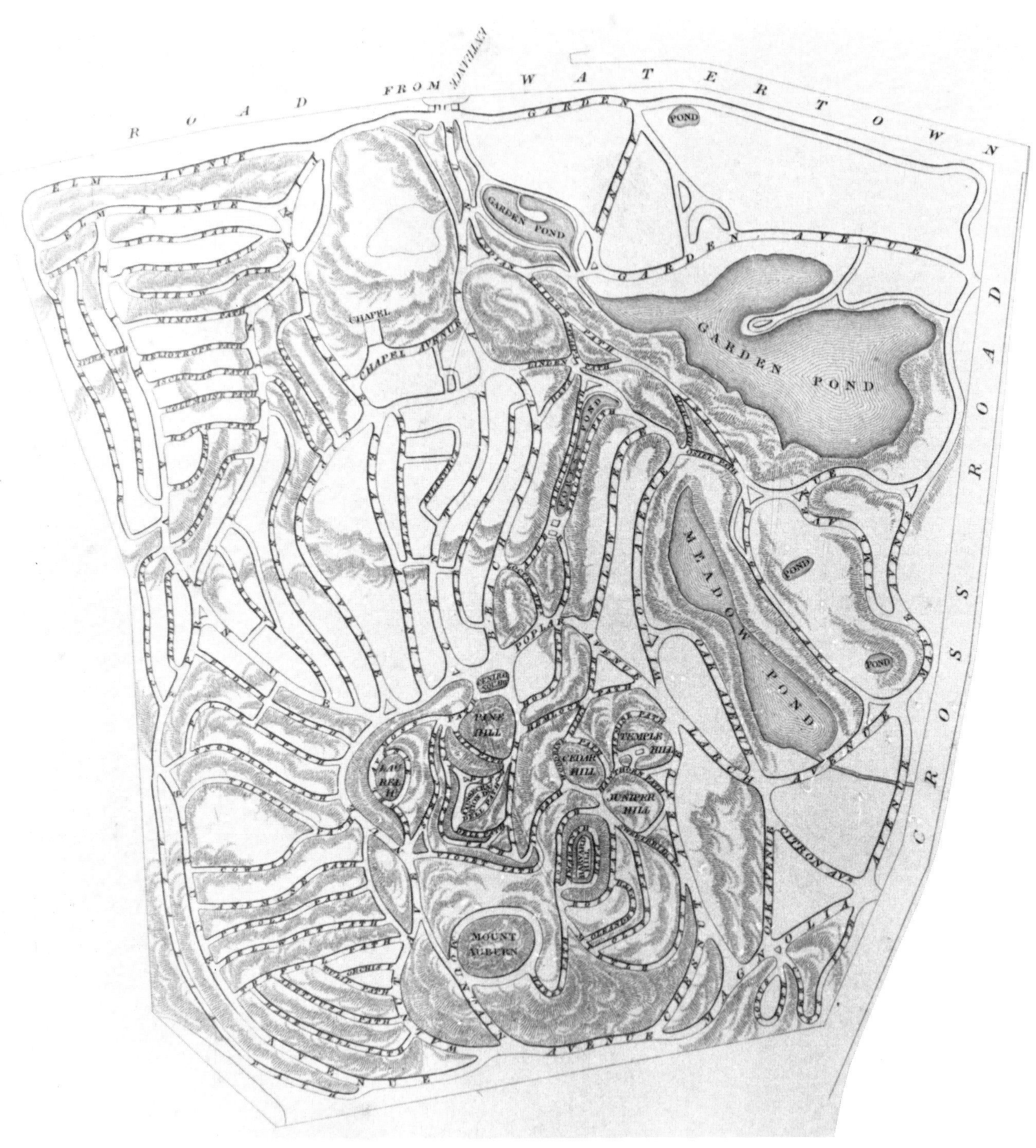

Fig. 9.1. Map of Mount Auburn, engraving by James Smillie, 1847.

stitution than on "embellishing the picturesque." Early "improvements" to the landscape by individual proprietors or by the cemetery corporation did not mar the woodsy rusticity of the original site as General Henry A. S. Dearborn left it, and Mount Auburn remained the same size until purchases of land in 1842 and 1844 expanded the property to 116 acres. Art and Nature were well balanced in the landscape.

The cemetery provided the sort of site that romantic writers fantasized had once been commonplace in the rural towns of Old England; but Mount Auburn's founders revealed no grandiose genealogical ambitions to reassemble the bones of their forebears, despite what a number of family monuments suggest. Mount Auburn served more immediate commemorative functions for the nuclear family. One writer observed in 1835, "A wise man, indeed, would not complain if his child were buried in the bed of the ocean or entombed in a far distant region; but it would be his choice that some neighboring grove or valley afford it a grave, which he may visit and there dwell upon the virtues of the beloved one." Mount Auburn was a place that mourners "could visit without publicity and without interruption." It ensured privacy for both mourners and the dead, in dramatic contrast to the old burial grounds immediately in eye- and earshot of the increasing hustle of urban life. Creation of Mount Auburn came at a time of the formalization of mourning customs intended to privatize grief, especially for women; by removal of burials from the public sphere of urban life, to a secluded domain, it permitted men to do likewise despite a less rigid code of male mourning behavior.[2]

Most additions to Mount Auburn's landscape in its first decade were products of private initiative, such as Hannah Adams's monument, which erroneously proclaims the deceased writer Mount Auburn's "first tenant." It was the first monument, however, erected by voluntary subscription of her female friends, who recognized the "Historian of the Jews and Reviewer of Christian Sects," the only woman who had been granted access to the Athenaeum Library and a member of one of Massachusetts's most distinguished families. She was a person deemed worthy of public commemoration; the horticultural society donated a free lot and even appropriated $35 for an iron fence to protect her neoclassical marble stone. Miss Adams was in fact Mount Auburn's ninth burial, moved there in November of 1832, a year after her death. (Figs. 9.2, 3.)

New Englanders began to take unprecedented interest in erecting monuments and protecting them with ornate cast-iron fences. During the cemetery's first decade alone, they built 190 tombs and 164 monuments, many on the same lots. Through the 1840s, most Mount Auburn proprietors chose simple, neoclassical marble monuments that stood out well in the wooded landscape, appearing as if placed in niches where trees were cleared away to form a series of tableaux. Occasionally Connecticut freestone was chosen, its reddish hue harmonizing well with the surrounding earth that characterized the surface of some family lots and paths before the mid-century spread of the taste for well-mown turf. Inscriptions on the freestone, not readily legible, were usually gilded to make the engraved letters clearer. Those carved in marble were frequently accentuated with black paint. A few early monuments at Mount Auburn were of bluestone or brownstone.

Despite increasing availability of granite in the Bay State, marble remained the stone of choice until after the Civil War, when technological ad-

Fig. 9.2. Hannah Adams monument, Central Square, engraving from *Picturesque Pocket Companion,* 1839.

Fig. 9.3. Hannah Adams monument on Walnut Avenue near Central Square, engraving by James Smillie, 1847.

vances made the harder stone cheaper, easier to carve, and hence more common. Marble gained popularity after it was first quarried in Vermont in the 1780s and began to replace slate as the preferred stuff of gravestones even in New England's old burial grounds. It was even shipped out of the region. Residents of New Orleans imported it from the 1820s for their highly architectural cemeteries, finding it better for above-ground tombs than structures of stucco-faced brick. Marble could be cheaply, easily, and ornately sculpted, an important advantage at that time of diversifying iconographic taste. Although it was generally known that the stone was not very durable, especially in northern winters, its whiteness was considered highly desirable; it added an optimistic symbolic value to monuments and represented a new attitude toward death and the hereafter, more appropriate in the mind of the times than the old gray slate. Not only did it stand out, fashioned in three dimensions in the landscape and glowing against the greenery of trees and shrubs or the gray walls of mausoleums, it also suggested the purity of heaven-bound souls and the assurance of salvation provided by liberal religion. It served visually as an affirmative religious statement in contrast to the two-dimensional, austere slate stones linked in many minds with the old Puritan view of death, rejected by religious liberals and evangelicals alike.

New Englanders associated marble with neoclassicism, a style chosen increasingly over forms from the colonial past. Insistent that their new burial place not resemble the old graveyards, Mount Auburn's founders issued a circular letter in 1833 prohibiting perpendicular slab gravestones and the use of slate in particular, although relatively flat marble steles were permitted. Dearborn and his associates thought the "stiff and ungainly" slate headstones "would not harmonize with the natural and artificial beauties of a rural cemetery but give a gloomy aspect to the scenery which is intended to banish the cheerless associations connected with the burial-places of our cities and country towns." Any old stones moved to Mount Auburn during reinterments, which were common at that time, had to be set horizontally in the earth; few of them are visible in the cemetery today. Only monuments "of a form approved by the committee" of trustees were permitted. These regulations conformed to tastes shared by the likes of the architect and critic Henry Russell Cleveland, who as early as 1836 cited Mount Auburn as the first place in the United States to display fine "sepulchral architecture." Cleveland pointedly discounted "the rude gravestones of our burying-grounds" from consideration as art at the same time as he warned that monuments at the new cemetery "should be in good taste" rather than displaying the ostentation of Europe.[3]

Fig. 9.4. Joseph Story monument in wooded setting, engraving by William Hunt, 1834, AAS.

While Mount Auburn's founders rejected New England's traditional material culture of death, they reinforced the characteristic Yankee aversion to ostentation, discouraging excesses of baroque, ornamental taste. Joseph Story told proprietors that funerary monuments should not be "for the poor purpose of gratifying our vanity or pride" but should serve as texts from which man might "read" his "destiny and duty."* Similarly, Mount Auburn's first guidebook advised in 1839, "Let us employ some of the superfluous wealth now often expended in luxury worse than useless in rendering the place where our beloved friends repose decent, attractive, and grateful at once to the eye and the heart."[4] The monuments, tombs, and even landscape of the cemetery reflect the new expendable wealth in the region from industrialism and international commerce, but Mount Auburn's moral lessons negated nascent conspicuous consumption. President Story advised lot owners to maintain a fine balance between display of wealth and investment of sufficient funds in funerary monuments to represent virtues and to display family prosperity, the fruit of the work ethic and evidence of righteousness—old lessons taught in a new style.

For themselves and their families, Story and Bigelow chose simple, neoclassical monuments, two of the first nine scattered through the wooded landscape by the spring of 1833. Story's is a marble obelisk atop a pedestal, decorated with Egyptian iconography similar to that on the gate. Story hastened to erect this single, family monument, as he was among the first to reinter five previously deceased children at Mount Auburn and anxious to make an attractive setting for their graves. (Figs. 9.4, 5, 6.) The obelisk became a favored funerary monument, especially for heroes, in the last decades of the eighteenth century. The form had been

*It is difficult to determine the architect, sculptor, or monument dealer responsible for many of the monuments at Mount Auburn since the cemetery has not kept correspondence from the nineteenth century in the individual files kept for each family lot; a meticulous inventory of the funerary art and architecture of the cemetery remains to be done.

Fig. 9.5. Joseph Story monument on Narcissus Path, engraving, from *Picturesque Pocket Companion,* 1839.

used extensively for commemoration in English landscaped gardens, borrowed in turn from Italian villa gardens. It was, therefore, considered more Roman than Egyptian.[5] (Fig. 9.7.)

Bigelow placed a family monument on his lot before any burials, although he anticipated the 1834 reinterment of his six-month-old son, William, dead since 1820. Bigelow, like the other proprietors who erected monuments in the first years, did much of the contracting himself. He purchased precut marble in November of 1832 from the Massachusetts State Prison; he commissioned the architect Solomon Willard to carve a low relief festoon of olive leaves around the severed column (now disappeared), symbolic of life cut short, atop the neoclassical plinth and pedestal. The monument cost $168.13, including $22.63 for labor of three men and a derrick for setting stones. Bigelow's simple iron fence, erected by Safford and Low in 1833, cost an additional $13.70, and sodding of the lot, $10. By 1834, the total cost of Bigelow's lot, central monument, plantings, and fence came to over $300, more than the annual income of a Boston laborer. Yet the taste displayed by Bigelow was in no way ostentatious. This example serves as an index of the money expended by the "average" proprietor in the 1830s. (Fig. 9.8.)

In his writings and by personal example, Bigelow urged the building of monuments before they were actually needed to mark burials. Erecting one's own monument was a way to come to terms with mortality, to learn important lessons of moral philosophy, and to commemorate one's self and family. Mount Auburn's founders urged each family head "to provide a place of burial for himself, which while living he may contemplate without dread or disgust . . . surrounded with every thing that can fill the heart with tender and respectful emotions . . . removed from all the discordant scenes of life." Cemetery publicists also stressed the civic function of "improving" Mount Auburn's landscape with tasteful structures like the cenotaphs and commemorative architectural features that decorated English gardens.[6] Mount Auburn provided a place in which New Englanders could create the private, rural burial places celebrated in the melancholy, nostalgic poetry of the

Fig. 9.6. Joseph Story family monument engraved with genealogy, photograph by Alan Ward, 1987.

Graveyard Poets, Wordsworth, and William Cullen Bryant but rarely found in reality. There, patriarchs could fulfill their old responsibility as teachers of spiritual values, a role long proclaimed by New England ministers but increasingly relegated to matriarchs. There, they could express in material terms New Englanders' strong valuation of family, an institution weakened by geographic mobility and other sorts of social change.

Bigelow encouraged patriarchal monument building as self-commemorative and to strengthen longevity of family names. He urged his peers to be conscious of their own role in creating personal reputation and establishing lineage, of contemporary if not historical origin, especially since in America "prescriptive and hereditary positions [were] declining in social influence." In his essay "On the Limits of Education," Bigelow declared it "better to be the founder of a great name than its disreputable survivor." Rephrasing the French aphorism "I am my own ancestor" with reference

Fig. 9.7. George Bond monument in wooded setting, engraving by William Hunt, 1834, AAS.

Fig. 9.8. Jacob Bigelow monument on Beech Avenue (original column is now missing), engraving from *Picturesque Pocket Companion,* 1839.

to a new individualism, Bigelow observed, "In this great and original country, which is now treading in the vanguard of a new reformation, we have thousands yet untaught who are to become ancestors in fame, ancestors in fortune, ancestors in science, ancestors in virtue. May their descendants be worthy of them."[7] Mount Auburn provided a place for teaching subsequent generations about the accomplishments of Bigelow's era in shaping a new American society and civilization in hopes of contributing to a linear history that would endure despite the natural cataclysmic forces feared by pessimists. Bigelow was intensely conscious of the significant accomplishments of his era—development of industries, institutions, art, and literature in a thriving, expanding republic. He intended that his generation's monuments and epitaphs at Mount Auburn challenge posterity to strive to surpass contemporary accomplishments in order to merit its own status as distinguished ancestors of yet future generations. Monuments could instill ambition by perpetuating the examples and spreading the fame of a new sort of American hero and heroine—role models rather than relics.

Material manifestations of a symbolic consciousness appeared throughout Mount Auburn's landscape and early structures. Many Bostonians reacted against forms inherited from their Puritan and colonial past just as surely as the Puritans had rejected earlier forms associated with papism. Although there would be none of the grim, medieval symbolism of death's-heads and skeletons, there were certainly few marks of traditional Christianity present in the first monuments at the cemetery, deliberately declared nondenominational. Indeed, Philippe Ariès labeled the trend as one of "de-Christianization," although that assessment is relative and applies more to France than to New England. Many of Mount Auburn's first proprietors were Unitarians, who continued to reject traditional Christian symbolism, even the simple cross. Many of them shared their ancestors' antipathy to display of the cross as "an object of veneration" because it was "the ignominious engine used for the destruction" of Christ. Some considered its use "the first step towards our subjection to the Pope of Rome." Rather, in their effort to expand the expressive range of their iconography, they turned to the examples set by political and

Fig. 9.9. Monument of André-Ernest-Modeste Grétry at Père Lachaise, engraving from Arnaud, 1817, a book used by Mount Auburn founders as a source of monument patterns, MHORT.

Fig. 9.10. Monument of Q. M. A. Verhuell at Père Lachaise, engraving from Arnaud, 1817.

philosophical liberals in Britain and France and to use of diverse symbols and architectural styles, especially those drawn from ancient Egypt, Greece, Rome, or other pagan precedents, which lacked the dangers of papism seen in traditional Christian motifs.[8]

Symbolic meaning quickly gained public currency through literary and mass-circulation newspapers and journals, sentimental poetry, pattern books, and guidebooks. Masons particularly developed what Neil Harris termed an "extensive vocabulary of formal symbols," used in commemorative places like Mount Auburn and other cemeteries copied after its example. For antebellum Americans, taste became consciously symbolic, a matter of "aesthetic ideology."[9] Ideology, or at least symbolic representations of notions about life, death, nature, and the sacred, was self-consciously evident in trends in taste displayed on monuments at Mount Auburn and elsewhere. Through the first decades of the nineteenth century, many Americans who could afford to do so chose simple, marble, neoclassical structures in lieu of traditional gravestones, even though the new structures were placed amid slabs and simple tombs in old burial grounds. The shift from standard two-dimensional stones to three-dimensional monuments indicates an intellectual shift from the dualism of orthodox Protestantism to a more modern perspective on history, a move away from the force of a fixed and formal community culture to dimensional individualism. The shift in historical consciousness occurred gradually, however. Yet, except in the case of monuments to notables, most of the new structures were not exclusively commemorative of individuals but honored several individuals associated in a family, broadly defined and privatized. These monuments, often erected over chamber tombs, evidence anticipation of inevitable mortality and assertion of family cohesion in the face of increasingly disruptive forces of mobility, modernization, and death.

By providing a setting in which to place new three-dimensional commemorative structures, the founding of Mount Auburn intensified the desire for such monuments, although there were few local craftsmen or architects prepared to meet the demand. A diversity of designs was available in the books on Père Lachaise by Arnaud and Joli-

Fig. 9.11. Monument of Nansouti at Père Lachaise, engraving from Jolimont, 1821, a book used by Mount Auburn founders as a source of monument patterns, MHORT.

Fig. 9.12. Monument of Méhul, Père Lachaise, engraving from Jolimont, 1821.

Fig. 9.13. Monument of Dugazon, Père Lachaise, engraving from Jolimont, 1821.

mont, and Bigelow ordered additional sketches for two standard neoclassical monuments from Solomon Willard in 1832. (Figs. 9.9–13.) He recommended the architect's design services to proprietors. William Kenrick of Newton expressed his hope that "ingenious artists" might construct such monuments for sale, especially once the opening of railroads made larger blocks of marble available in the Boston area. Robert Gould Shaw anticipated the growing demand for marble monuments in 1833 by sending to Italy for an assortment of neoclassical structures "as an adventure, thinking they would be wanted" the following summer. (Figs. 9.14, 15, 16.) Again in 1837, the board allocated $100 to commission various designs to be available to proprietors wishing to order custom-made monuments from local quarries. In 1838, Bigelow offered a prize of $50 for the best monument design, but no record remains of competition results. Many early monuments at Mount Auburn were designed or produced to order by Alpheus Carey, a local stonecutter and engraver.[10] The Reverend William B. O. Peabody raised a lone voice in favor of eliminating monuments of stone. "Let the monuments be found in the noble forests of our land," he advised, "let them not be such as the elements waste, but such as time only strengthens and repairs."[11] While Bostonians rapidly acquired the taste for placing plantings on their graves, they also determined to set memories of their dead in marble and demanded new and varied designs for their funerary stones.

When J. S. Buckingham visited Mount Auburn in 1838, therefore, he praised the monuments, "some of beautiful design and many executed from the finest Italian marble, having indeed been made in Italy." Many similar monuments were being produced in Boston "with great taste and

Fig. 9.14. Oliver Carter family monument, Roman Revival style, ca. 1840, photograph by Alan Ward, 1987.

Fig. 9.15. Ward family monument, ca. 1837, photograph by Alan Ward, 1987.

skill; though this is a branch of art but recently cultivated in the city." At about the same time, a writer in the *American Magazine* described Mount Auburn's monuments as evidence of "a pure and classical taste." Some were "elaborate and highly ornamented," but the critic favored the "elegant but plain," which made up the majority at that time. Most were products of local artists, architects, and craftsmen like Carey.[12] (Figs. 9.17, 18, 19, 20.)

The taste for the neoclassical harmonized with an American valuation of nature as the primitive, sacred source of law and culture. Bostonians, perhaps even more than other Americans of the era, associated naturalistic aesthetics with moralism. (Fig. 9.21.) Those who looked to ancient civilizations for purer political forms than those inherited from the old regimes of Europe considered neoclassical architectural styles representative of natural forms drawn from Arcadian eras, when man was closer to nature and natural law. Tree trunks of the forest inspired the form of columns; the burial mound or mount suggested pyramids. Obelisks were hierophanies, symbolic and ceremonial points of linkage between the sacred and the profane, heaven and earth. Many of Mount Auburn's early monuments were inspired by Athenian grave markers of the ninth and eighth centuries B.C., an era that art historian Vincent Scully describes as embodying attitudes attempting to reconcile newly perceived oppositions between Man and Nature. Americans in the antebellum decades shared many of these notions with the ancient Greeks, whose funerary stones and urns, like their latter-day equivalents at Mount Auburn, "celebrated the family cult and contrasted in all major ways with nature's forms around them."[13] Such Greek Revival forms particularly appealed to elite Bostonians, who thought of themselves as citizens of the Athens of America and commissioned sculpted busts of themselves in classical togas for the Athenaeum Library.

Fig. 9.16. Robert Gould Shaw monument, Pine Avenue, engraving from Nathaniel Dearborn's *Guide,* 1852.

Fig. 9.17. Stone and Stevens neoclassical monuments on Beech Avenue, engraving from N. Dearborn, 1852.

Fig. 9.18. (*Above*) John W. Webster neoclassical monument, Narcissus Path, engraving from N. Dearborn, 1852.

Visitors to Mount Auburn usually interpreted the style of monuments placed in the innovative funerary landscape as evidence of new, more optimistic notions of death; they realized that a major cultural change was under way based on beliefs in universal salvation and family reunion in heaven. Writers in the popular press and periodicals repeated the desire of cemetery founders to create a place that was "beautiful, attractive, consoling—not gloomy and repulsive." According to one contemporary commentator, Americans had formerly neglected their dead because "we are inclined, *generally,* I know, to disparage external appearance. We have a contempt for ceremonies. We are a hard, practical people, intensely absorbed in business, surrounded by circumstances which accustom us to the livelier kinds of excitement, educated and impelled in every way to undervalue and lose sight of what may be called the graces of civilization." Such was increasing less so in Boston in the 1830s and 1840s, especially among the most successful in international commerce and industrial capitalism. Criticism of the "want of feeling" toward the dead as a national "fault" was rapidly disproven at Mount Auburn and the many cemeteries American urbanites fashioned after its example. Indeed, the writer admitted in 1839, "We are not, in our mortuary observances, quite so heathenish as we have been."[14]

Mount Auburn provided for a private cult of ancestors enshrined in carefully defined family burial lots even more than for a cult of heroes meriting public fame. Some Bostonians used the cemetery for genealogical purposes, determining to honor founders of families even though their bones lay elsewhere. Such was the case of Dr. George Shattuck, Jr., who in 1836 chose a large, 1,600-square-foot lot on a yet-unsurveyed eleva-

Fig. 9.19. Alexander Wadsworth monument, Indian Ridge Path (moved to a more conspicuous location on Spruce Avenue in the 1860s), engraving from *Picturesque Pocket Companion,* 1839.

Fig. 9.20. John Tappan monument (erected over a chamber tomb) on Linden and Narcissus Paths, engraving from N. Dearborn, 1852.

tion covered with oak, cedar, and walnut trees in the western portion of the grounds. His father had in 1833 disposed of one family lot on flat ground near Central Square, and he donated another on a prime, hilltop site to Harvard College. Shattuck persuaded Bigelow to name the walkway to his lot Pilgrim Path in lieu of the usual plant name. (Fig. 9.22.) Shattuck wrote his friend, cemetery Treasurer George Bond, of his intention to commemorate a forefather who came to Massachusetts in 1638. He constructed an underground tomb ample enough to hold several future generations of his family; and he commissioned a simple, rectangular, four-sided monument designed by Washington Allston, built by Alpheus Carey, and inscribed with a detailed family genealogy, including the name of a seventeenth-century ancestor who left no male descendants to carry on his name. Each side of the simple sarcophagus lists members of branches of Shattuck's family tree. (Fig. 9.23.) The physician declared, "I wish to associate in the minds of my children the names of their maternal ancestors at the family burial place." He included names of paternal ancestors buried elsewhere, especially one "Pilgrim Father, one of a handful God hath multiplied into a nation"; but he did not attempt to retrieve and reinter their remains at Mount Auburn. A simple iron fence topped by small but symbolic acorn finials surrounds the Shattuck lot.[15]

Fig. 9.21. (*Above*) Martha Coffin Derby sarcophagus on Iris Path near Consecration Dell, engraving by James Smillie, 1847.

Others shared Shattuck's genealogical sensibility and used Mount Auburn lots as sites for its material expression. Another marble sarcophagus placed on a Locust Avenue lot in the late 1830s traced a family lineage to Bartholomew Cheever, born in Canterbury, Kent, England, in 1607. The Cheever family patriarch, according to the stone, came to America in 1637 and died in 1693, aged eighty-six. He was a "Pilgrim Father, one of a handful God hath multiplied into a nation!" The

Fig. 9.22. Dr. George Shattuck, Jr., family lot on Pilgrim Path, engraving by James Smillie, 1847.

Fig. 9.23. Shattuck family monument with detail of genealogical inscriptions, photograph by Alan Ward, 1987.

monument also recognized Caleb Davis, "born in Woodstock, Connecticut in 1739 . . . educated a merchant, resided in Boston; died July 6, 1797, aged 58. Caleb was Speaker to the first House of Representatives under the Commonwealth's new constitution, distinguished alike for piety and patriotism. Eleanor Cheever, daughter of William Downs Cheever, was born February 1, 1749–50—married to Caleb Davis, September 9, 1787—died January 2, 1825, aged 75 years." According to the inscription, "the records of the Boston Female Orphan Asylum tell of her associated labors in the cause of suffering humanity." The stone also proclaimed to God that Richard Bartholomew, Daniel, William Downs, Eleanor, and Elizabeth, "who now likewise rest from their labors, were of the generations who have risen up to bless thy name." Such was the testimony and gratitude of subsequent generations for the accomplishments of predecessors. Lengthy proclamation of achievement and narratives of family history appeared on many monuments erected at Mount Auburn through mid-century. (Fig. 9.24.)

At the new cemetery, the distinction between civic monument and private funerary stone blurred. Story described the function of monuments to teach "our destiny and duty," to elucidate exemplary and notable lives in the same manner as Jared Sparks's collected biographies. Bigelow encouraged development of a cult of ancestors within each family as well as celebration of heroes for the community, region, and nation. A major purpose of Mount Auburn, he insisted, was to "afford the means of paying tribute of respect by monumental erections to the name and memory of great and good men, whenever or wherever they have died." Through the first decades, many cenotaphs, monuments unrelated to actual burials but meant for commemoration of notables buried elsewhere, were erected for this purpose. The author of the first guidebook to Mount Auburn expressed the hope that one day that cemetery would display as many great names as seen in the chief cemetery of Paris: "See how the dust of Père Lachaise teems with them! What monuments—what historical and classical accumulations—what scholars, conquerors, and bards—what hints and helps to patriotism and perseverance and high ambition!" With Mount Auburn, the time had been "hastened when even the pilgrim who comes from other climes to visit . . . may read wherever he wanders on the face of the soil, the character and praise of the living generation in the works which shall indicate their remembrance of those that have passed away."[16]

Commemoration was twofold. It proclaimed the values of the present as well as of the past. Many monuments, especially those erected by subscription campaigns and voluntary associations, note the virtues of the monument builders as well as of

Fig. 9.24. Ellery-Sargent stone on Greenbriar Path with genealogical inscription, photograph by Alan Ward, 1986.

Fig. 9.25. Clement Durgin monument on Narcissus Path, engraving from *Picturesque Pocket Companion,* 1839.

the deceased. A subscription by "friends" in the late 1830s provided funds for a monument to Clement Durgin, associate principal of the Chauncey Hall School. The stone reads, "A student and lover of nature, in her wonders he saw and acknowledged and through them adored her beneficent Author. His life was a beautiful illustration of his philosophy; his death of the triumph of Faith." It added, "His pupils have reared this monument as an imperfect memorial of their grateful affections and respect." (Fig. 9.25.) Students at the Charlestown Female Seminary erected a stone to their teacher Martha Whiting, who died in 1850. (Fig. 9.26.) Other subscription campaigns for monuments honored relatives rather than the deceased; for instance, Boston mechanics raised funds for a cenotaph to Edwin Buckingham, son of the prominent newspaper editor, who died at sea in 1833 at age twenty-three. (Figs. 9.27, 28.)

Story instigated a campaign among former classmates to build an Egyptian sarcophagus on the grave of his friend and colleague John Hooker Ashmun, Royal Professor of Law, who died in 1833 at age thirty-three. The monument was placed on the grave on Harvard Hill, the 5,226-square-foot burial area near the highest point in the cemetery that had been donated to the College in large part by George Shattuck, Sr. Charles Chauncey Emerson, Ashmun's student, who eventually died of the same disease, composed his teacher's epitaph, which reads, "He went behind precedents to principles; and books were his helpers, never his masters. There was the beauty of accuracy in his understanding, and the beauty of uprightness in his character. Through the slow progress of the disease which consumed his life, he kept unimpaired his kindness of temper and superiority of intellect. He did more sick than others in health. He was fit to teach at an age when common men are beginning to learn, and his few years bore the fruit of long life. A lover of truth, an obeyer of duty, a sincere friend, and a wise instructor. His pupils

Fig. 9.26. Martha Whiting monument, engraving from N. Dearborn, 1857.

Fig. 9.27. Edwin Buckingham monument on Willow Avenue, engraving from *Picturesque Pocket Companion,* 1839.

Fig. 9.28. Buckingham family lot, including monument erected by subscription to son Edwin, lost at sea, and the more simple marble slab stones of the publisher-journalist Joseph T. Buckingham, his wife, Melinda, and her sister, Lucinda, photograph by Alan Ward, 1987.

raise this stone to his memory." Ashmun's monument was meant to serve as a spiritual tract, a sermon to visitors that they should leave with new resolve to live similarly in hopes of being equally righteous, accomplished, and remembered. (Figs. 9.29, 30.)

In an attempt to assemble Harvard's recent notables in the college lot, Bigelow and Story joined an appeal to the widow of John Thornton Kirkland, president of Harvard at the height of the Unitarian controversy, that she permit reinterment of her husband at Mount Auburn; but she refused "to disturb the repose of his present resting place" in the Cambridge burying ground across from the college yard. Mrs. Kirkland replied to a Committee of Harvard Alumni that despite "the peculiar beauties of Mount Auburn," she had "no pleasing associations with the new and great city of the dead." She suggested that honoring and perpetuating Dr. Kirkland's memory could be accomplished "without the removal of what at best must soon be dust." Undeterred, the commemorative committee of Bigelow, Charles P. Curtis, F. W. P. Greenwood, Charles Francis Adams, and Jared Sparks raised funds for a cenotaph at Mount Auburn. As Mrs. Kirkland predicted, few visitors "pause to think if he sleep beneath the marble."[17] The monument was meant to impart the lesson of a life rather than simply to mark mortal remains.

Bostonians, following the advice of William Ellery Channing, rejected the notion that heroism was founded only on military bravery and dramatic deeds. Rather, they wanted to celebrate exemplary

Fig. 9.29. Harvard Hill with monuments to President John Kirkland (foreground) and John Hooker Ashmun (center), engraving by James Smillie, 1847.

Fig. 9.30. Harvard Hill with monuments of Ashmun (center) and Kirkland (behind to right), photograph by Alan Ward, 1985.

lives, especially those reflecting character and personal virtue in the service of the community. Channing preached self-culture and self-improvement to workingmen. Character and learned accomplishments mattered more than power and prestige; the melancholy tale of a promising life cut short in youth appealed more to proponents of "conspicuous commemoration" at Mount Auburn than great and daring deeds or accumulated wealth.[18]

Such was the case of the Reverend Samuel H. Stearns, born in 1802, graduated from Harvard in 1832, and ordained at Boston's Old South Church in 1834. Stearns resigned his ministry in 1836 because of illness and, like many other ailing Bostonians with the means to do so, was traveling through Europe to regain his health when he died in Paris. Stearns was buried at Père Lachaise, but by 1839, his family, friends, and former congregation arranged for the return of his body to Boston, interment at Mount Auburn, and erection of an obelisk proclaiming a man who was "Discriminating, tasteful, magnanimous, devoted, uniting uncommon eloquence with fervent and confiding piety . . . a full believer in the doctrines of grace." (Fig. 9.31.)

Even if it required the ritual of reburial, risking reinstitutionalization of veneration of relics, Bostonians were especially intent on commemorating their ministers, in particular the liberal leaders of Universalism and Unitarianism, who championed an optimistic belief in universal salvation against the old orthodoxy of Predestination. In 1837, the Reverend John Murray was reentombed at Mount Auburn under a simple marble monument "Erected at the recommendation of the United States General Convention of Universalists," and intended, according to the Reverend Hosea Ballou, "to accommodate future generations with a knowledge of the spot" so that they might learn "to cherish and preserve the memory of those whom the wisdom of God has distinguished as benefactors of mankind." (Fig. 9.32.) Since his death in 1815, Murray's body "had mouldered [anonymously] in the Sargent [family] tomb in the Granary Burying-Ground, without a stone or inscription of any kind to denote the ashes of the man who had stirred the country with the tidings of universal love." Ballou urged such funerary commemoration while warning "against the pageantry of pride, displayed in costly garnishings [at the grave], and also against monkish superstition, which attributes efficacy and merit to that which is but dust." A visit to Murray's new burial place, properly marked and surrounded by nature, would supplement the reading of the biography of the great man but not lead the visitor astray in the superstitious way associated with High Church ritual, Ballou protested. Similarly, in 1839, George Bond and George W. Coffin, on behalf of a number of other Bostonians, petitioned Theodore Lyman of the Brattle Street Church or "Society" to have the remains of the Reverend Joseph Stevens Buckminster moved from a common graveyard to a lot at Mount Auburn donated by Amos Lawrence, where a proper monument could be erected to his memory.[19]

Many voluntary associations adopted the cause of monument building in the cemetery's first decade. In 1834, the Garden and Cemetery Committee granted a lot to the "Committee of the Young Men of Boston," headed by Charles Francis Adams, H. F. Baker, and L. M. Walter, for their intended construction of a cenotaph in memory of General Lafayette; the association must have failed to raise

Fig. 9.31. Reverend Samuel Stearns monument on Moss Path, engraving from *Picturesque Pocket Companion,* 1839.

Fig. 9.32. Reverend John Murray's monument on Vine Path near Consecration Dell, photograph by Alan Ward, 1980.

sufficient funds, however, because a monument was never erected and the lot was forfeited without record.

When the internationally famous Prussian phrenologist Gaspar Spurzheim died while lecturing in Boston in the fall of 1832, several local leaders determined to honor him at the new cemetery. His theories so captured the imagination of the scientifically minded that the mayor, aldermen, Harvard faculty, and the city's entire medical profession marched *en masse* through Boston's streets to his funeral service, which featured an ode composed for the occasion by the Reverend John Pierpont. Perhaps fervent espousal of Spurzheim's theories and the desire to commemorate his life were part of their general reaction to the charge by the *Edinburgh Review* that he was a charlatan, for literary Bostonians made themselves steadfast champions of all those attacked and criticized by the British journal. Or perhaps Bostonians were aware that in 1828 the British Phrenological Society had erected a monument with portrait bust over the tomb in Père Lachaise of Franz Joseph Gall, acclaimed for locating the position of the "hump of crime" on the skull, and they wanted to honor a similar luminary of phrenology at Mount Auburn. Nevertheless, William Sturgis, a Harvard professor and local politician, personally contributed the bulk of funds to a subscription campaign to buy Spurzheim a lot at Mount Auburn and place a pol-

Fig. 9.33. Gaspar Spurzheim's monument (cenotaph), engraving from *Cyclopoedia of Useful Knowledge,* 1836.

ished Italian marble sarcophagus on it. (Figs. 9.33, 34.) The monument, in imitation of the Roman tomb of Scipio Africanus, was surrounded by a simple oval iron fence on a prominent lot atop the first hillock on the left of Central Avenue just inside the cemetery, a site meant "to excite in the minds of some a classical recollection" corresponding to a description of a place of sepulcher in Virgil's Ninth Eclogue. The English visitor Harriet Martineau, however, complained that she and others did not understand how the form of the sarcophagus was appropriate for Spurzheim. Use of the monument was a matter of expediency, she thought, saving the committee the trouble of com-

Fig. 9.34. (*Below*) Spurzheim's monument on Central Avenue, engraving by James Smillie, 1847.

Fig. 9.35. Frederick P. Leverett monument on Vine Path near Consecration Dell, erected ca. 1833, photograph by Alan Ward, 1987.

Fig. 9.36. (*Below, center*) Frederick P. Leverett monument, engraving from *Picturesque Pocket Companion*, 1839.

Fig. 9.37. (*Below, bottom*) Warren Colburn monument, Locust Avenue, engraving from Nathaniel Dearborn, 1852.

missioning a custom-made structure. Fortuitously, it arrived in Boston just at the time of the phrenologist's sudden death, one of the first imports intended by Robert G. Shaw, Sr., for purchase by anyone favoring neoclassical commemoration. Spurzheim epitomized the sort of popular scholar that elite Bostonians hoped to honor at Mount Auburn.[20]

Bostonians particularly commemorated those whose teaching or scholarship furthered the recent cultural, industrial, and commercial success of their region. One early monument at the cemetery praised Frederic P. Leverett, superintending teacher of the Boston Latin School and author of the nationally known Latin Lexicon, which went to press the day he died. The monument proclaims Leverett's work, which "reflects honor not only on the person engaged in its preparation, but on our country . . . the result of American ability and industry and American enterprise." (Figs. 9.35, 36.) Another monument honored the example, "cherished for imitation," of Warren Colburn, a forty-year-old mathematician, who died in 1833. Colburn authored standard texts on arithmetic and algebra used in New England schools, providing a practical education for a new generation of industrialists and engineers who might later take Bigelow's courses on technology at Harvard; he also contributed mathematical research to development of Lowell manufactories. (Fig. 9.37.)

Fig. 9.38. (*Above*) Nathaniel Bowditch monument at Central and Cypress avenues, engraving by James Smillie, 1847.

Fig. 9.39. (*Below*) Bowditch monument by Robert Ball Hughes, 1847, photograph by Alan Ward, 1987.

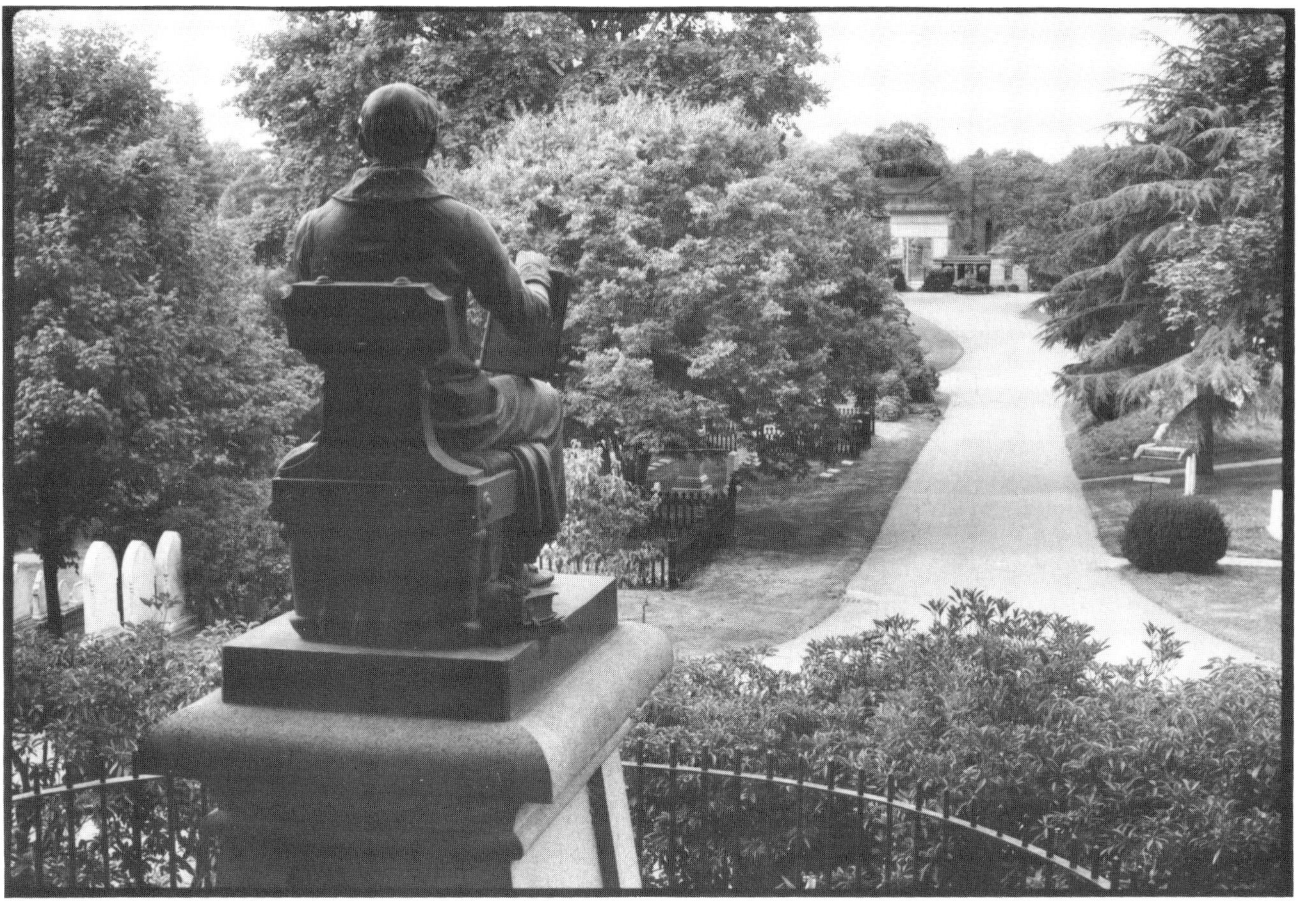

Fig. 9.40. Bowditch monument sited near cemetery entrance as focal point greeting the visitor entering on Central Avenue, photograph by Alan Ward, 1987.

For similar reasons, the death of the astronomer and mathematician Nathaniel Bowditch in 1838 inspired the voluntary commemorative impulse of many mercantile leaders who owed their prosperity in international trade to his perfection of practical navigation techniques and instruments. Although Bowditch already owned a family lot and monument nestled far inside the cemetery, an association of urban leaders was formed in 1843 to build a second monument, a cenotaph, in a very visible location; it was by far the most elaborate form attempted to date for an individual in any American funerary setting. At first, the committee contemplated an obelisk but then agreed on a life-sized, seated portrait statue of the scientist with globe and navigational instruments. The iron sculpture, the work of Robert Ball Hughes, an English immigrant recently settled in Boston, was the first large bronze figure cast in the United States, a product of the Boston foundry of Gooding and Gavette. In 1847, Hughes exhibited the original sculpture in the vestibule of the Athenaeum; the Mount Auburn trustees declared that the monument was in its own right representative of the latest advances in American art and industry. The corporation reserved a prime piece of land across Central Avenue from Spurzheim's sarcophagus, at the first rising hill as one enters the cemetery, and allotted funds to protect the monument with an iron fence and to reserve a band of space around it in perpetuity for ornamental purposes.[21] (Figs. 9.38, 39, 40.)

Requests from commemorative committees for free land at Mount Auburn became so numerous, however, that by the end of 1838 the trustees declared it henceforth "inexpedient to make gratuitous appropriations for erection of monuments to distinguished individuals."[22] Perhaps they worried that those already honored were not as inherently "distinguished" as they might have hoped, or else they simply realized that the number of those deserving honors in New England at a time of industrialization, technological invention, and cultural renaissance would soon lead to a landslide in requests for free commemorative space. Their final "gratuitous appropriation" of seventy square feet of land was made in 1839 for the Reverend Noah Worcester of Brighton, the Unitarian abolitionist called the "Friend of Peace." Trustees did not want to act as jurors, deciding which individuals merited commemoration. Neither did they want to give away large quantities of land only to have to raise lot prices inordinately or to lose incoming funds for maintenance of the entire institution. Already, because of the Panic of 1837, they found they could not afford to build several structures that they had originally planned to ornament the grounds following the fashion of English gardens.

This decision did not entirely impede the commemorative impulse of groups intent on building cenotaphs and other monuments at Mount Auburn; it simply meant that subscription campaigns had to raise additional money for purchase of lots if the individual in question did not already have right to burial at the cemetery. Irregularities in the rolling terrain and the winding system of avenues and paths resulted in many odd pieces of ground that could not be sectioned into regular three-hundred-square-foot parcels; in 1840 the Committee on Lots proposed that these be reserved for "public monuments," to be sold for 26⅔ cents per square foot plus a premium of $20 for site choice, provided that funds be donated for perpetual care.

The Massachusetts Horticultural Society bought a lot on Yarrow Path in 1838 for interment of Thomas Green Fessenden, deceased the previous year. The Massachusetts Society for Promoting Agriculture joined the horticulturists to help finance the monument to the editor of the *New England Farmer,* a neoclassical marble structure set in place in 1839.

Mount Auburn's board stuck to this new policy and did not make special provisions of land or fences when William Ellery Channing, "the Unitarian Pope," died in 1842. Channing's family exchanged lots originally purchased on Chestnut Avenue, which had become a busy road winding up to the cemetery's summit, for a pair of more secluded plots on the newly surveyed Greenbriar Path on the low hill west of the entrance; 112 members of the Federal Street Church congregation contributed $1,780 for a monument to the subscription campaign run by Thomas Handasyd Perkins. The prominent landscape painter Washington Allston, Channing's classmate and brother-in-law, designed the monument, which defies precise description as neoclassical; it was constructed of Italian marble by Alpheus Carey, the new local monument dealer who provided many of Mount Auburn's early monuments. (Fig. 9.41.)

Fig. 9.41. William Ellery Channing monument on Greenbriar Path, engraving by Nathaniel Dearborn, 1852.

The cenotaph of Margaret Fuller Ossoli (1810–50) was placed on her family's lot between Pyrola and Belwort paths. Her father, Timothy, who died in 1838, was a U.S. congressman, but his monument did not draw the constant procession of visitors who through the 1850s and 1860s beat a path to the stone erected in memory of Margaret, feminist, Transcendentalist, and the first woman admitted to Harvard Library. Margaret Fuller edited the *Dial,* wrote for Horace Greeley's New York *Tribune,* and established an international literary reputation before she visited Italy, met Giovanni Angelo Marquis Ossoli, a captain of the Italian Civic Guard and ten years her junior, and bore a son, Angelo. After working together in the ill-fated Roman Revolution of 1848, Margaret and

Giovanni sailed for New York, only to meet with tragic death by shipwreck off Long Island's Fire Island on July 19, 1850. The bodies of wife and husband were never found, despite Thoreau's exhaustive search of miles of beaches; but sailors retrieved Angelino Nino and temporarily buried his small body in a sea chest in the sand until family could remove it to Mount Auburn.

Thomas Carew, Carey's competitor in the new funerary monument business, custom-made Fuller's arched marble stone inset with a bronze plaque that read: "By birth a child of New England, by adoption a citizen of Rome, by Genius belonging to the World. In youth an insatiate student, seeking the highest culture. In riper years Teacher, Writer, Critic of Literature and Art. In maturer age, companion and helper of many earnest reformers in America and Europe." The stone also remembers Ossoli, who "gave up rank, station, and home for the Roman Republic, and for his wife and child." It concludes, "United in life by mutual love, labors, and trials, the Merciful Father took them together, and in death they are not divided." The star above Fuller's low-relief portrait medallion was her signature on her writings. The book represents her literary career; the sword, the Italian struggle she and her husband shared. The decorative elements of oak and laurel suggest strength and accomplishment. (Fig. 9.42.)

Some of the founders, like Bigelow, retained their desire to make Mount Auburn a repository of notables of national as well as regional repute. A case in point is Hugh Swinton Legare, who was President John Tyler's attorney general and secretary of state after being defeated for Congress in 1838 by John C. Calhoun because of the Nullification Controversy. When Legare died unexpectedly in Boston while attending ceremonies on completion of the Bunker Hill Monument in 1843, he was given a public funeral. Dr. Bigelow attended him as "chief physician" on his deathbed in George Ticknor's house, and Legare was temporarily placed in Ticknor's family tomb. Bostonians eulogized Legare's personality, surpassing those "of all our Northern statesmen." He was compared to Edward Everett (who was, however, quite alive) and found to have "the same exquisite classical taste, the same love and veneration for antiquity"; both were "eminently conservative in politics and eminent as literary writers." In 1851, Legare's sister, Mrs. Mary Bullen of South Carolina, purchased through Henry D. Cruger a small, triangular, forty-foot lot near the entrance of Gentian and Mimosa paths and planted four of the "most luxuriant weeping willows in the cemetery . . . bowed down in grief and suffering." She declared her intention to erect a monument over his new grave there but did not do so because she lived far from Boston and could not make arrangements through Ticknor, who was out of town. By 1856, however, Richard Yeadon, the editor of the Charleston *Courier,* persuaded Mrs. Bullen to transfer the body to Charleston; and he raised funds for a public monument there.[23]

Fig. 9.42. Cenotaph to Margaret Fuller Ossoli, engraving by Nathaniel Dearborn, 1857.

An association called the Friends of the American Slave also took advantage of the new cemetery policy of selling irregular parcels of land for "public monuments" after the 1846 death of the abolitionist minister Charles T. Torrey. A native of Scituate, Massachusetts, Torrey earned the title "martyr of liberty" when he died of tuberculosis after serving five years in a Baltimore prison, sentenced for his antislavery activism. His monument, a capped obelisk with bronze medallion portrait, bears some of Torrey's last words, "It is better to die in prison with the peace of God in our breast than to live in freedom with polluted conscience." (Fig. 9.43.)

Fig. 9.43. Charles T. Torrey monument, erected ca. 1846, daguerreotype by Albert Sands Southworth and Josiah Johnson Hawes, ca. 1850, George Eastman House.

The trustees' only deviation from their new rule against granting whole lots for commemoration of individuals occurred in the early 1840s when they donated land on Central Avenue for a stocky, twenty-foot white marble obelisk, decorated with swags of roses in low relief. The cenotaph proclaimed the memory of officers and other members of the U.S. Exploring Expedition—Lieutenant Joseph A. Underwood and Midshipmen Wilkes Henry, James W. Reid, and Frederick A. Bacon—"pioneers in civilization," who died in the Fiji Islands in the South Seas in 1839 and 1840. It was designed and erected by their associate officers and

Groups of abolitionists visiting the Torrey cenotaph made sure to stop at the grave of the fugitive slave Peter Byus on the corner of Citron Path and Magnolia Avenue to see the monument with low relief of a slave breaking his chains. It was copied from Josiah Wedgwood's famous black and white jasper cameo, "Am I Not a Man and a Brother" (1787), made for the Society for the Abolition of the Slave Trade and widely circulated via Franklin among American antislavery advocates. Byus's stone proclaims the life of a man "born in Hampshire County, Virginia, a slave. At the age of about thirty-six he fled to Boston for freedom, where he resided for the last thirty years of his life." Byus died in 1867, aged sixty-six, proclaimed by those who contributed to his stone to be "a Sincere Christian, a True Friend, and an Honest Man." (Fig. 9.44.)

Fig. 9.44. Peter Byus monument, 1867, low relief of freed slave copied after low-relief engraving by Josiah Wedgwood, photograph by Alan Ward, 1987.

Fig. 9.45. U.S. Exploring Expedition monument on Central Avenue, engraving by James Smillie, 1847.

Fig. 9.46. (*Below*) U.S. Exploring Expedition monument, detail, photograph by Alan Ward, 1987.

the scientific corps at a cost of $200. (Figs. 9.45, 46.) The expedition, Thoreau complained, had been the object of considerable "parade and expense"; the monument proclaimed the men heroes of a venture of international importance.[24]

Religious societies, like other voluntary organizations, had to raise their own funds for purchase of burial ground as well as erection of commemorative monuments. In 1859, for instance, three men—Charles Tufts, Silvanus Packard, and Maturin M. Ballou—petitioned the board for permission to unite their contiguous lots into one enclosure, eliminating intervening spaces in order to create an appropriate site for erection of a life-sized marble portrait statue of the Reverend Hosea Ballou, the famed Universalist minister. In order to extend the privilege of contributing to the monument to Universalists nationally, the Boston Society ruled that no single subscription be over one dollar. Ballou died in 1852 at age eighty-one, after a long and active theological career. From his teens, Ballou believed in universal salvation as an outgrowth of the Calvinist doctrine of election, which he held to apply to all mankind; he "assaulted the Calvinism of his day" and denied the inevitability of any postmortem punishment. In the

Fig. 9.47. Reverend Hosea Ballou monument by Edward Augustus Brackett, 1860, photograph by Alan Ward, 1979.

Fig. 9.48. Thomas Handasyd Perkins family lot on Central Avenue with marble Newfoundland watchdog sculpted by Horatio Greenough, ca. 1840s, half of a stereographic photograph, ca. 1860.

thirty-four years Ballou served as pastor of the Second Universalist Society in Boston he contributed to the atmosphere of religious liberalism that premised the founding of Mount Auburn as a second Eden, regardless of Adam's Fall; it was entirely appropriate that he be commemorated there. The sculptor Edward Augustus Brackett (1818–1908) completed the life-sized, standing portrait statue of Ballou "in the full vigor of adulthood" in 1860.[25] (Fig. 9.47.)

Boston's Baptists similarly raised funds for a monument at Mount Auburn to the Reverend Daniel Sharp, who died in 1853 at age seventy near Baltimore. The structure, designed by the architect George Snell and erected in 1856, was "in the early English style of pointed architecture," described in one contemporary guidebook as displaying "refined taste which distinguishes this monument from most of the miscalled Gothic structures in the grounds." Although many Yankees shared a taste for Gothic Revival architecture, they reflected their Puritan forebears' rejection of things considered papist in their descriptions of the style, which had begun to replace the neoclassical in favor. Styles as well as trends in commemoration were changing rapidly by the mid-1850s.[26]

Most monuments erected at Mount Auburn in its first decades celebrated the importance of ministers, mothers, merchants, and mechanics in the life of the metropolitan region; in particular, the cemetery attracted commemoration of merchants and industrialists active in the economic development of New England, for such was usually the product of self-commemoration. Still, many of these monuments are quite unpretentious, reflecting the frugality and moderation of taste characteristic of even the most prosperous of Yankees. For instance, the business associates of Francis Stanton financed a simple monument to "An upright merchant, a useful citizen, a valued friend." The family of Jesse Putnam, who died in 1837 at age eighty-three, erected a discreet monument of Italian marble with simple Egyptian emblems under a "noble" oak tree on Beech Avenue. Putnam's stone marks the grave of the "Father of the merchants of Boston, a distinction not claimed by himself, but accorded by others in consideration of the intelligence, energy, and integrity with which for

Fig. 9.49. Samuel Appleton family lot between Woodbine and Hawthorne paths, engraving by James Smillie, 1847.

more than half a century at home and abroad, he followed and adorned his profession." The same monument remembers Putnam's wife, Susannah: "Having discharged with unwearied fidelity and devotion the duties of this relation as well as those of a daughter and mother, she sank into the sleep of death with hope full of immortality." Epitaphs such as this reflected the notion that exemplary women had important social functions, albeit in separate spheres from husbands active in the business world.

Thomas Handasyd Perkins, Jr., known as the "Merchant Prince," avoided proclamation of his family's central position in the economic life of the city and region when he commissioned the single monument to be placed in the center of his lot on Central Avenue and over the full-chamber, masonry tomb completely and discreetly hidden beneath the turf. No epitaphs adorn the marble monument, which was less than two feet high and in the form of a reclining, faithful Newfoundland watchdog, sculpted by Horatio Greenough. (Fig. 9.48.)

The prosperous merchant Samuel Appleton, on the other hand, erected a more elaborate structure, a miniature Grecian temple fashioned of marble in Italy and measuring twelve by six feet. At $10,000, it was unquestionably the most costly funerary monument at Mount Auburn and perhaps in the nation in the 1830s, and visitors were alerted to that fact by many articles and publications. The small structure is encircled by a flight of three steps and topped by nonfunctional sepulchral lamps. Low-relief Corinthian columns appear to support the entablature. Symbolic elements—a serpent coiled in a circle with spread wings over it representing eternity and evergreen wreaths indicating perpetual remembrance—decorate its sides. The whiteness of the marble stands out against the backdrop of a dense grove of evergreens, creating an almost theatrical composition in the lot of one of New England's most prosperous merchants, which occupies a dramatic site near the summit of the cemetery. Seen from a distance, the monument seems to take on far grander proportions than its diminutive size would indicate. (Figs. 9.49, 50.)

In 1866, members of the express companies of the United States contributed to have T. A. Carew design an elaborate monument to William Frederick Harnden, "Founder of the Express Business in America," replacing a modest marble stone adorned with a conventional dove clasping a broken flower in its beak. Harnden, who died in 1845 at age thirty-one, established one of the most successful private postal companies in Boston in 1839, with door-to-door pickup and delivery between Boston and New York. By 1844, over forty such firms existed in Boston alone. The monument, with canopy supported by columns, shelters a draped marble urn guarded by a faithful dog. Two low-relief sculptured panels on sides of the base depict domestic scenes of mail being sent and delivered. The front panel bears the verse from 1 Samuel 21, "Because the King's Business Required Haste." The grand monument is not unlike an advertisement for the new and growing communication industry. (Figs. 9.51, 52, 53.)

The Harnden monument was one of many placed in the cemetery by professional and business colleagues of innovative individuals—entrepreneurs, educators, inventors, and bureaucrats. A simple obelisk proclaims Barnabas Bates, who died in 1854, the "Father of Cheap Postage." It represents an attempt by Whigs to claim credit for the postal reform that was being attributed to Jacksonian Democrats. The remains of a once more elaborate monument on Spruce Avenue proclaims Thomas Blanchard, who died in 1864 at age seventy-six, "An eminent American Inventor, whose great mind conceived ideas and brought into operation works of art that will live for ages." Two sides of the stone bear low reliefs of his "works of art," the industrial machines he created; the back takes note of other family members. (Fig. 9.54.) By the 1860s, Bostonians were less willing to contribute to subscription campaigns to build commemorative monuments at the cemetery to such individuals, despite merit and accomplishments; the task was left to families to mention noteworthy careers on stones that doubled to mark burials of other, less notable family members.

Fig. 9.50. Appleton monument, made in Italy ca. 1838, photograph by Alan Ward, 1985.

Whereas Mount Auburn's founders encouraged the building of lot enclosures and monuments, they actively discouraged construction of crypts, tombs, and mausoleums. Bigelow was particularly vocal in urging the resolution "that the resources of art shall not be wasted in vain efforts to delay or modify the inevitable course of nature," that is, decay of the corpse that could be hastened by earthen burial. He described the process of decomposition in a natural setting as something good and beautiful, citing Biblical authority to bolster his argument: "Then shall the dust return to earth as it was, and the spirit shall return to God who gave it." He reasoned with Bostonians that "the common grave affords the most simple, natural, and secure method by which the body may return to the bosom of the earth, to be peacefully blended with its original dust." He recommended expenditures for improvements only "above the surface of the earth—not under it," because "a beautiful monument is interesting to every one . . . a far more soothing object than the most costly charnel house." Besides, the cemetery provided abundant space to ensure each individual his own grave, guaranteed by the charter in perpetuity;

Fig. 9.51. William Frederick Harnden monument on Central Avenue, 1866, photograph by Alan Ward, 1987.

Fig. 9.52. (*Below, left*) Harnden Monument, detail of low relief, "The Express Business," photograph by Alan Ward, 1987.

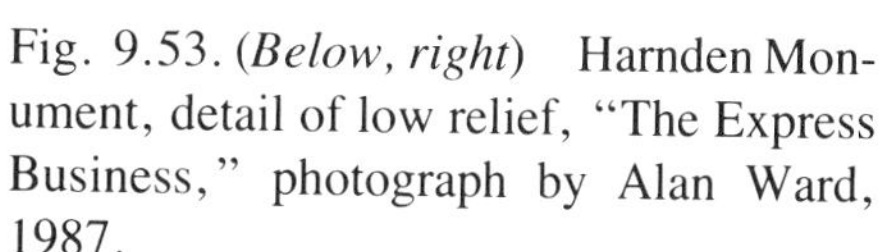

Fig. 9.53. (*Below, right*) Harnden Monument, detail of low relief, "The Express Business," photograph by Alan Ward, 1987.

Fig. 9.54. Thomas Blanchard, inventor, monument erected ca. 1865 with low reliefs of machines he invented, photograph by Alan Ward, 1987.

there was no longer need to cram the remains of one family together in a crypt in order to guarantee their postmortem proximity or simply to provide identifiable burial space.[27]

Although Bigelow eloquently advocated earthen burials, many proprietors constructed single-chamber tombs at Mount Auburn in its first decades; and the board did not attempt to ban them as it had slate gravestones. In the first year alone, proprietors built eighteen tombs but only sixteen monuments, many on the same lots. By 1841, almost half of all lots sold were used for construction of tombs; 164 monuments punctuated the picturesque landscape, some erected on lots with tombs hidden underground. Through the first decade, an average of twenty tombs was completed annually. Many proprietors like Thomas Handasyd Perkins built subterranean tombs, eight-foot-high rooms with floors ten feet below the ground surface and roof covered by two feet of earth, roughly following designs of tombs at Père Lachaise illustrated by Arnaud. (Fig. 9.55.) These structures were more elaborate than the shaft or chamber tombs in the region's old burial grounds. Such a tomb cost about $190 if constructed of brick or cement block, and $270 if of stone covered with mica slate and flat granite. Entrance was by a locked iron door at the bottom of a flight of stone steps covered by a removable stone that itself could be turfed over so that no evidence of the structure was visible to the casual visitor. A single monument in the center of such a lot usually contained just the family name or vital dates of those buried in the chamber, although presence of a single monument is not an automatic indication of a subterranean tomb. Such was the case of the Perkins lot.

Similar tombs were built partially above ground, nestled in hillsides or mounded with dirt to conceal masonry, revealing only stone façades with locked doors. (Figs. 9.56, 57.) They might cost between $300 and $1,500. The first extensive use of granite at Mount Auburn appeared on the façades of these tombs—either simply consisting of slabs forming a front wall and protective wings or more carefully crafted in the Egyptian style. Many of these had marble doors or inserts to receive inscriptions. An exception to this rule is the Winchester brownstone mausoleum of simple Gothic Revival style, almost a free-standing building erected on Narcissus Path on the shore of Forest Pond in the 1840s. Others are the twin classical tombs of W. Read and S. O. Mead on Ailanthus Path at Central Avenue, structures only partially settled into a small hill and surrounded on all sides by an ornate cast-iron fence. (Figs. 9.58, 59.)

Locations of many Mount Auburn tombs, if not site choice and landscape design as well, seemingly correspond to "geomancy," the systematic theory of topographical siting of domestic and burial structures developed by the Chinese. Descriptions of proper Chinese tomb burials emphasize death as "an inherent aspect of the cosmos," part of natural processes in terms close to those used by

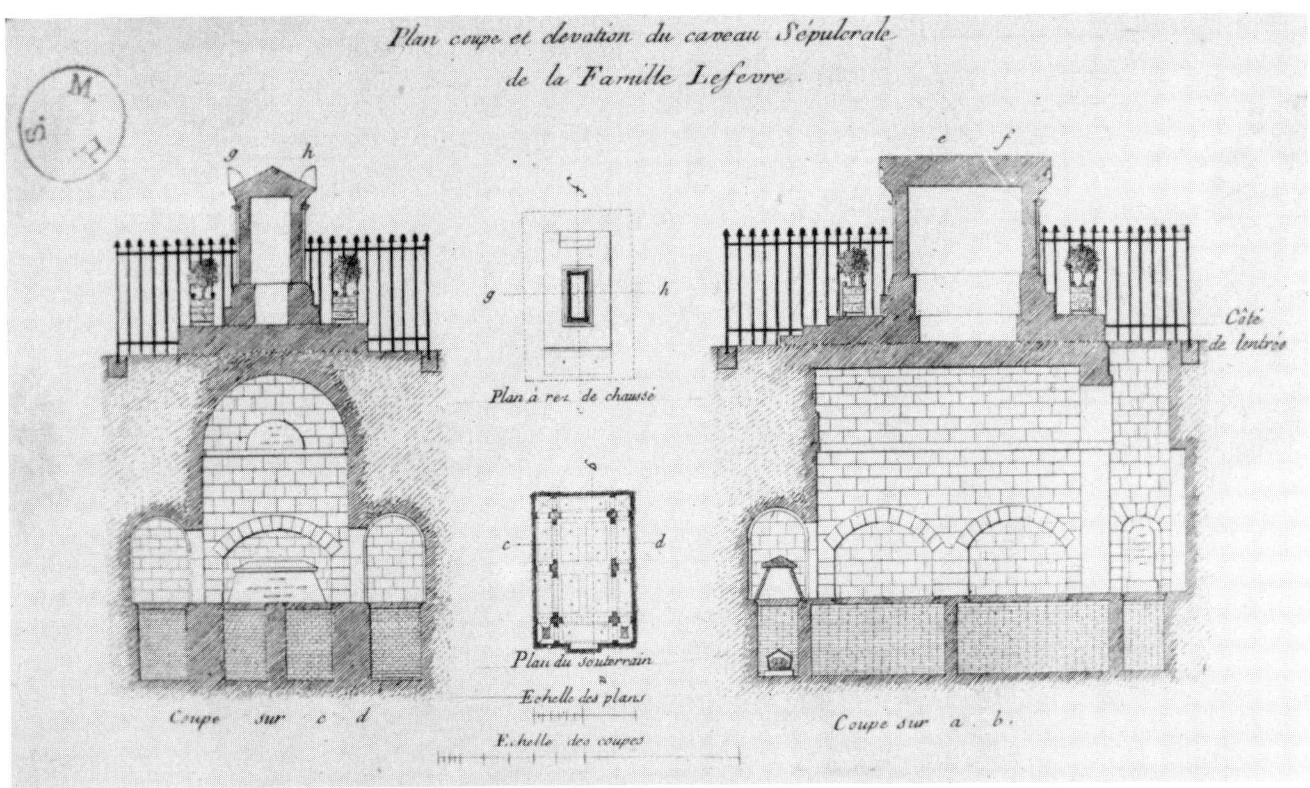

Fig. 9.55. (*Above*) Structure of subterranean chamber tomb at Père Lachaise, engraving by Arnaud, 1817, book used as reference for the building of Mount Auburn, MHORT.

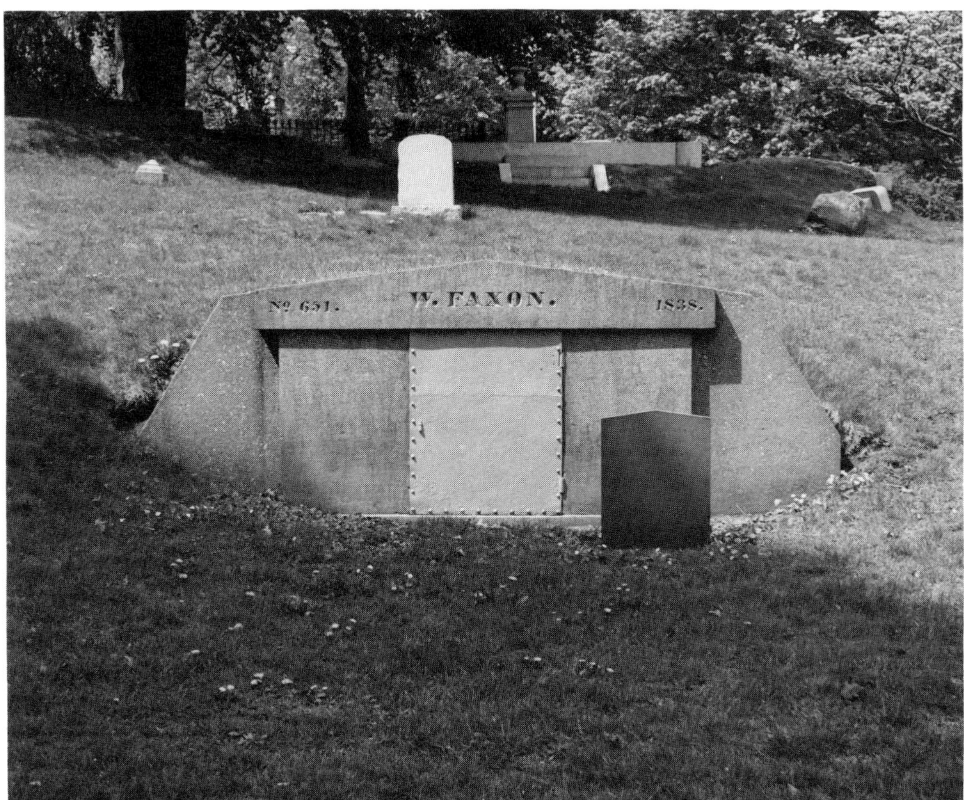

Fig. 9.56. (*Right*) William Faxon family chamber tomb on Yarrow Path, 1838, photograph by Alan Ward, 1983.

Fig. 9.57. Family chamber tomb between Deutzia and Lily paths, photograph by Alan Ward, 1983.

Fig. 9.58. Read and Mead tombs, daguerreotype by Southworth and Hawes, ca. 1850, George Eastman House.

Bigelow. *The Burial Book* (*Tsang Shu*), written by Kuo P'u in the fourth century B.C., and subsequent *feng shui* literature by siting theorists also describe how proper burial extends the fortunes of the dead to the living. The ideal burial site has a view of a water body, either a distant ocean, a river, or a pond, for water symbolizes, among other things, money. The Chinese located tombs in parabolic land formations with adjacent sheltering hills affording protection from the elements; more important, these were places of vital *ch'i*. *Ch'i* is the force thought to circulate between heaven and earth and along ridges and valleys in the land. Topography influences the flow of *ch'i* to "energize" the dead, thereby preserving links with living and future progeny and ensuring their prosperity. In addition, the Chinese favored white stone as particularly lucky. Even more than the post-revolutionary French, the Chinese cultivated a cult of ancestors through burial landscapes. Some Bostonians might well have been familiar with geomancy through cultural contacts of the China trade, and they may have borrowed inspiration from it in locating their tombs in Mount Auburn's terrain, especially rich in ancient geological formations like the moraine forming Indian Ridge.[28]

Unlike Boston's old graveyards, Mount Auburn provided plenty of space for the construction of tombs large enough to hold several generations of a family. Its topography permitted a wide variety of site choices that may or may not have had deeper meanings. Certainly, from the first, forms of burial and commemoration at Mount Auburn engendered controversy. Dearborn cautioned that entrances to hillside tombs could easily seem "offensive to good taste"; but, unlike Bigelow, he did not discourage attempts to isolate the bodies of the dead from contact with the soil. Indeed, he suggested that proprietors who could afford to do so consider the combination of a tomb and monument in a single, large structure. In offering this advice, Dearborn might have had in mind the grandiose funerary buildings that characterized Père Lachaise Cemetery, after which he modeled Mount Auburn.[29]

Dearborn, like many of Mount Auburn's proprietors, differed with Bigelow over ideals of proper burial. In 1832, the general counseled lot owners that even those families without chamber tombs could have their graves "so constructed as to possess most of the advantages of tombs." He explained that the cemetery's grave digger could make a brick platform to hold the coffin a foot above the bottom of the grave and then construct a brick arch over it before filling the rest of the hole with dirt. In this manner, the grave would be "more secure" and would remain undisturbed when other graves were dug nearby. Initially, the impulse to place a body in a tomb and to avoid true earthen burial probably stemmed more from the desire to deter grave robbers and to keep the remains away from the ground than from the desire to prevent decay and preserve the corpse intact. Certainly there were no recorded attempts at Mount Auburn in the 1830s and 1840s to seal

Fig. 9.59. William P. Winchester mausoleum on Narcissus Path by Forest Pond, daguerreotype by Southworth and Hawes, ca. 1850, GEH.

tombs hermetically to prevent decay; frequently, published accounts of visits to tombs included graphic descriptions of the process of decomposition. Indeed, opponents of tomb burial described in grisly detail the condition of bodies in tombs periodically reopened for addition of the newly dead, and they complained of the invasion of the privacy of the dead that that represented.[30]

Prevalence of chamber tombs at Mount Auburn in its first decades indicates little concern with theories that miasmas from decaying bodies could endanger health. Indeed, the family of Dr. John Gorham Coffin, outspoken crusader against the dangers of crypt burials in cities, erected one of Mount Auburn's first chamber tombs. (Fig. 9.60.) The issue came up only once during this formative period, when trustees deemed it the duty of their Committee on Lots to prevent construction of "any tomb without its being so secured as to prevent the escape of effluvia from within." Those already built were to be secured if necessary. Trustees ruled in 1841 that no proprietor could rent or sell space in tombs to unrelated individuals, but this regulation was related to a similar ban on burials of unrelated individuals in family lots. The ruling against rental or sale of space in private tombs resulted from the chronic need for places of temporary deposit of bodies, especially during winter months.[31]

Fig. 9.60. George W. Coffin chamber tomb and monument on Chestnut Avenue from *Picturesque Pocket Companion,* 1839.

Once the landscape was laid out and the institution established as a nonprofit corporation, and until the mid-1840s, most of Mount Auburn's trustees showed little concern for additional cemetery development and maintenance. Trustees regularly delegated authority to Bigelow and a few others who, as the Committee on Lots or Committee on Grounds, actually visited Mount Auburn and made minor decisions. They assumed that the naturalistic landscape required little general maintenance. From 1833 to 1834, a local gardener, David Haggerston, periodically aided the horticulturists with additions and changes to plantings, while the surveyor Alexander Wadsworth continued to stake out newly numbered lots and to locate the direction of new avenues and paths according to the board's instructions.

In 1834, John W. Russell became Mount Auburn's first superintendent, serving primarily as a caretaker for the grounds in exchange for the handsome annual salary of $600 plus use of a house where he had to board cemetery laborers with his family for $2.50 per person per week. As an additional benefit, the superintendent had use of a piece of the grounds for his own vegetable garden to satisfy the needs of family and boarders. Russell functioned as sexton, employing workers for digging and filling graves; he also supervised funerals inside the grounds, making sure that bans on music and the firing of volleys were observed.[32] Russell helped the surveyor lay out lots so as to permit digging of graves without damaging existing trees—an indication that preservation of the original plantings of the site continued to be a priority and that the design and layout of the grounds were shaped to a certain extent by trees already in place. The superintendent maintained cemetery records based on numbered lots and kept certain small accounts. He kept track of lots sold and improved, structures built on lots, and the vital statistics of individuals buried at Mount Auburn. Trustees generally left Russell unsupervised until 1838, when they began to suspect that he "permitted many trees to be removed improperly," probably to ease the task of surveying lots and digging graves. They dismissed him in 1841 under suspicion that he had been selling firewood from Mount Auburn for profit.

Rufus Howe replaced Russell in the spring of 1841; he was the first and last person elected superintendent by proprietors' ballots. The board insisted on formally stipulating Howe's duties, holding him "personally responsible for the preservation of the trees," allowing none to be removed unless the Committee on Lots approved. Howe had to account to the treasurer for all brush or wood produced from tree trimming because, in those hard economic times, the cemetery, as well as the superintendent, needed additional revenue. Bigelow, in particular, insisted on controlling each tree planted in or removed from Mount Auburn. Sale of hay from grass-cutting twice a season produced additional income, and the board required a meticulous accounting from the superintendent of all such transactions.[33] Howe served for fourteen years, until 1855.

Through its first decade, Mount Auburn remained "almost a wilderness," with simply graveled avenues and paths barely staked out, forming a labyrinth "perplexing to the stranger" through the wooded grounds. Descending from the mount with its panoramic view, the visitor found himself "within the shadows of the deep forest and secluded glade, where he may be as much shut off from the visible world, as if he were a thousand miles from any habitation." Yet the journalist Joseph T. Buckingham observed as early as 1838: "What a change has a period of seven years produced! The native wildness of the place is softened and subdued, but not destroyed, by the hand of labor and art." Buckingham wrote, "The visitor now sees in all directions the marble urn, the sarcophagus, and the granite obelisk. . . . Seven years ago, Mount Auburn was the habitation only of the field-mouse and the squirrel, or of wild animals and reptiles more unfit for the companionship of man; it is now a City of the Dead, populous with all degrees and qualities of our race, rich with the treasures of memory, of love, or friendship, and affection."[34] For a time, Art and Nature remained balanced at Mount Auburn. But with each passing year and the accumulation of more and more artifacts, the rural aspects of the landscape faded. (Figs. 9.61, 62, 63.)

Increasingly, despite separation of the cemetery from the Massachusetts Horticultural Society, tastes for ornamental plantings grew among proprietors and trustees like Bigelow who were charged with making aesthetic decisions about the landscape. Buckingham praised the melding of cultivated plants with those indigenous to the site: "The native oak now waves its foliage over an exotic shrubbery; the anemone, the violet, and the aster, long the lonely and the unobtrusive spontaneous product of the soil, now gracefully mingle with the daisy, the narcissus, and the lily; the wild rose and sweetbriar unveil their blushing beauties and exhale their incomparable fragrance in presence of more gaudy varieties of foreign origin. Most of the trees and shrubs that are indigenous to our New England forests are to be found within the limits of Mount Auburn, and the nurseries of exotic plants have made bountiful contribution to add to the native establishment."[35] (Figs. 9.64, 65, 66.)

In 1838, Enoch Cobb Wines from Philadelphia found "an accumulation and variety of classical beauties" and "scenes of Arcadian loveliness" at "the most romantic of burial-places," Mount Auburn, "which certainly no spot in America can match and which probably few places can equal in any part of the world." Wines concluded, "death would seem disrobed of half its terrors" in such a place. Similarly, John Ross Dix praised the simplicity and dominance of Nature at the cemetery: "There is a life, joyous life beneath, around, and above us—insects chirp in the grass—bright-eyed, variegated squirrels run gracefully up the boles of trees, or peer curiously out from amongst turfed grass—bright-winged birds glance athwart the leafy gloom . . . yea, every thing tells of life." Dix, like so many early visitors, echoed Keats that such a natural setting "would almost make one in love with death to be buried in so sweet a place."[36]

Buckingham complained as early as 1838, however, that in certain portions of the grounds, near Central Square and Consecration Dell, "the monuments thicken upon the view." A number of tombs, "embosomed in the deep shade of a grove of pines," ranged to the south of the grounds.[37] Even as monuments filled the grounds through the 1840s, Mount Auburn retained its picturesque appearance, as the Grounds Committee made sure to plant a number of forest trees in close proximity to each other even in the areas that did not originally have them. In 1842, for instance, trustees approved adoption of a more efficient plan submitted by Waldo Higginson for laying out lots in the southeast part of the cemetery before the planting of native forest trees in that area.[38]

Even through the cemetery's second decade, visitors described Mount Auburn as "a large extent of wild, unreclaimed, hilly ground, covered with oak and pine . . . enclosed for a public burial place."[39] As late as 1853, another observer saw the woods "hewn away in various spots for the purpose of sepulture and to open the many avenues . . . and afford to those who love such a holy and secluded spot, the most interesting retreats and delightful walks." This was a forested, truly "rural" cemetery, a series of secluded lawns, open spots "thickly overshadowed" by a canopy of trees, captured by the pen of James Smillie in the mid-1840s.[40] Although a delicate balance between Art and Nature remained—the monuments added to the forested landscape, and the ornamental plants interspersed among those common to the region—the initial, Arcadian phase of Mount Auburn's landscape was beginning to draw to a close as the cemetery neared its third decade.

Fig. 9.61. Henry Dexter's sculpture of Emily on the family lot of C. J. F. Binney on Yarrow Path, engraving by James Smillie, 1847.

Fig. 9.62. Visitors in the "forest" cemetery, engraving by James Smillie, 1847.

Still, Art did not obliterate the dominance of picturesque Nature at Mount Auburn for at least two decades. Cornelia Walter, who grew up in the neighborhood, celebrated the cemetery's "forest umbrageousness" in verse. In 1847, she lauded the lakes "so cleansed, deepened, and banked as to present a pleasant feature in this widespread extent of forest loveliness." Through the 1840s, Mount Auburn still sheltered "thickly wooded vales, yet fresh with the growth of centuries." In places, new plantings, the acacia and the willow chosen for symbolic significance, added a note of cultivated melancholy; "the sombre shade of its groves, the solemn calm of all things around, appeal to the religious sense." Unlike her Puritan ancestors, Walter considered this "deep, dark wood . . . holy."[41]

Fig. 9.63. The "picturesque" cemetery landscape, engraving by James Smillie, 1847.

Bigelow took great personal pride in the ceme-

Fig. 9.64. Forested area on Vine and Aster paths near Consecration Dell, photograph by Alan Ward, 1986.

tery, to which he devoted increasing amounts of time and effort after the separation of the institution from the Massachusetts Horticultural Society. Through the 1830s and 1840s, Bigelow retained his taste for the picturesque, enjoying Mount Auburn's rough, naturalistic landscape, further sanctified by the pantheistic spirit expressed by Wordsworth, Delille, Bryant, and Bigelow's fellow Unitarians. The physician even attempted to capture the poetics of place in verse, privately penning his thoughts about the cemetery before burying the poem amid the correspondence of his wife and children:

Mount Auburn! thou divine enchanting spot
Whom Nature has embellished and adorned
With all the pride of her luxuriance,
Thee I salute: and Muses invoke thine aid
 To guide me through the maze of poesy
 Which I have entered heedless and alone. . . .
Auburn! it is not language can express
The majesty and beauty of thy groves;
Description's efforts are inadequate
To paint the charms of the thrice favoured spot
Whose gifted soil supports thy forests wide.
Let him who wills to know thy beauties fair
Come to thy depths and pay his homage there.

As the Bostonian who took credit for proposing creation of the "forest cemetery" and as a founding trustee conscientious of his continuing stewardship of the place, Bigelow uttered both invocation and invitation. At Mount Auburn, the businessman could find moral recreation and self renewal:

> Let him forget,
> Reposing on thy soil, the toilsome cares,
> Vicissitudes, and labours of the little world
> Which he inhabits. Let his weary soul
> Find rest amid the silence of thy groves
> And let the waving of thy foliage breathe
> A pleasing calm throughout his harassed soul
> And lull him into visions of repose.

The privacy found in Nature would also sooth the mourner, wrote Bigelow:

> Let him come sit amid thy solitudes,
> And meditate on his departed friends:
> Let him recline upon the turf, and list
> To the sweet song of heav'n inspired birds,
> Till all his faculties are deep absorbed
> In Nature's charms. Then let his stricken *soul*
> Spurn the stern shackles of despondency,
> Shake off the cares that clung around his *soul*
> And turn towards home, a new created man.[42]

Bostonians and visitors from beyond the metropolitan area heeded Bigelow's advice in increasing numbers. But for many, the emotionally salutary influence of Nature was not enough. Proprietors and voluntary associations intent on commemorating notables strove to create a "marble history" of "the good and great" at Mount Auburn. Mnemonic monuments could "improve" upon Nature, serve as catalysts for specific associations or memories, and even ornament the grounds in the style of English gardens.

A more personal, sentimental sort of commemoration also began to appear at Mount Auburn with the return of economic prosperity in the mid-1840s, urged on by a growing number of advocates of sentimentalism like Buckingham, who wrote, "The monuments in our cemeteries are not simply valuable as specimens of the sculptor's skill or as artistic embodiments of beauty." An increasing number of stones were "erected to preserve the decaying memory of one whom the world never missed when he passed away." Owners of family lots desired to reshape Mount Auburn into a "sculptured garden." They enclosed lots with cast-iron fences, creating a place objectifying trends in the "domestication of death." With the accumulation of private as well as public monuments and a new taste for the "gardenesque" to supercede the "picturesque," the balance between Nature and Art at Mount Auburn tipped in favor of the latter by mid-century.[43]

Fig. 9.65. Monuments from the 1830s on Ivy Path overlooking Consecration Dell, photograph by Alan Ward, 1979.

Fig. 9.66. Kendall family monument near Consecration Dell, photograph by Alan Ward, 1979.

Map of Mount Auburn from Nathaniel Dearborn's 1839 catalogue.

10

Embellishing the Picturesque: Structures in the Landscape and Elements of Style

The Rhine has its castled crags, its vine-clad hills, and ancient villages; the Hudson has its wooded mountains, its rugged precipices, its green undulating shores—a natural majesty, and an unbounded capacity for improvement by art. . . . Without any great stretch of the imagination we may anticipate the time when the ample waters shall reflect temple, and tower, and dome in every variety of picturesqueness and magnificence.

—Thomas Cole, "Essay on American Scenery" (1835)

There sits the Sphinx at the road-side, and from age to age, as each prophet comes by, he tries his fortune at reading her riddle. There seems to be a necessity in spirit to manifest itself in material forms.

—Ralph Waldo Emerson, "Nature" (1836)

MOUNT AUBURN'S FOUNDERS REALIZED that creation of a picturesque funerary landscape would entail more than simply choosing an appropriately varied terrain with rambling, reflective ponds, laying out gracefully curving drives and paths, and planting ornamental trees and shrubs among the natural forest growth. They planned from the start to "embellish" the grounds with "public" structures that would be both functional and ornamental. Art would "improve" upon Nature. After all, chief features in English gardens were the ruins, arches, grottoes, temples, towers, chapels, monuments, and gates that served as eye-catchers as well as reminders of a real or mythical past; the Scottish aesthetic theorist Archibald Alison deemed such an assembly of structures intensely sublime.[1]

The French architect Brongniart had similar intentions for Père Lachaise in designing a central pyramidal chapel (never built) and other funerary structures of diverse architectural styles. From his intensive readings, Henry A. S. Dearborn was well aware of the importance given to architectural elements in the planning of Père Lachaise, although he did not concern himself with the way in which the rage for architecture completely changed landscape aesthetics of the French cemetery after only three decades. He also knew that Londoners, formulating plans for their own cemetery, intended to display "exact models of the superb temples, triumphal arches, columns and public monuments of Greece and Rome, as receptacles or memorials of departed worthies of the empire," in a central part of the grounds.[2]

In aspiring to create such a picturesque landscape blending the pastoral with structures with rich associations to a long and venerable past, Mount Auburn's founders reflected both the trends in taste and the historicism of their age. They would have agreed with the painter Thomas Cole, whose "Essay on American Scenery" (1835) proclaimed that "Poetry and Painting . . . purify thought by grasping the past, the present and the future—they give the mind a foretaste of its immortality." Cole complained, however, that American scenes had minimal historical and legendary associations. Rather, they were "not so much of the past as of the present and the future. . . . You see no ruined tower to tell of outrage—no gorgeous temple to speak of ostentation . . . . We are still in Eden; the wall that shuts us out of the garden is our own ignorance and folly." Like Boston's Unitarians, Cole considered Eden achievable or at least recreatable. Art could aid in the process. Cole applied Burkean theories of sensory creation of emotion to his painting, knowing that Burke originally referred primarily to landscape gardening. It is no coincidence, then, that many of the scenes depicted by Cole contain many of the same mnemonic elements as both eighteenth-century landscaped English gardens and Mount Auburn—aerial perspectives heightening a sense of distance and stirring thoughts of the past, the future, or the infinite; mirror lakes and dark pools encouraging melancholy introspection; a varied terrain of hills and valleys framing perspectives, inspired by the taste for the picturesque; luxurious and "venerable" trees testifying to the inexorable processes of Nature and Time; and, most important, neoclassical and medieval structures or their ruins covered by clinging ivy, representing a long and distant past. Cole's paintings *The Departure* and *The Return* (1837), as well as *Thanatopsis* (1850) by Cole's close friend Asher B. Durand, bear striking resemblance to Mount Auburn's landscape, with the addition of more structures to embellish the picturesque.[3] (Figs. 10.1, 2, 3.)

Cemetery founders were anxious to place ornamental structures at Mount Auburn as soon as lot sales had produced a sufficient surplus or a subscription campaign had been mounted by local philanthropists desirous of improving cultural institutions. Although design competitions were to be held eventually for the structures, Bigelow submitted models and drawings of a Gothic Tower, a Grecian tower, and a Doric temple even before consecration of the cemetery. He urged that at a later date a "stupendous monument" to Washington might also be erected at Mount Auburn.[4]

In the preprofessional era, both Dearborn and Bigelow were well qualified to design Mount Auburn's landscape and buildings. Walter Muir Whitehill observes that "at the beginning of the nineteenth century the practice of architecture was considered to be within the grasp of any literate gentleman who had a mind to try his hand at it."[5] Neither Dearborn nor Bigelow can be considered a dilettante, dabbler, or amateur at design. Both were multitalented renaissance men and shared a sense of mission to create a usable past in material terms for their nation, region, and city. Their ideologies and taste for the revival and reapplication of architectural styles, as well as for Nature, were the same. Both should be given credit as founders and designers of America's first "rural" cemetery because of various tasks and responsibilities each assumed in Mount Auburn's development in its first four years.

Whereas Dearborn provided initial landscape design, Bigelow's major contribution, beyond proposing the cemetery in the first place, was architectural. Bigelow was as qualified as any of America's architects of his generation to prepare a design. At Harvard, as first Rumford Professor of the Application of Science to the Useful Arts, he lectured on architecture and building technology using a set of models and drawings he made himself. He drew his own comparative scale illustration of major classical and modern buildings for his 1829 book *Elements of Technology,* and Charles Bulfinch declared it accurate. Bigelow's architectural expertise reflected itself in his ambitions for

Fig. 10.1. Thomas Cole, *The Departure,* 1837, painting. Courtesy of New York Historical Society.

Fig. 10.2. Thomas Cole, *The Return,* 1837, painting. Courtesy of New York Historical Society.

Fig. 10.3. Ashur B. Durand, *Thanatopsis,* 1850, painting. Courtesy of Metropolitan Museum of Art, New York.

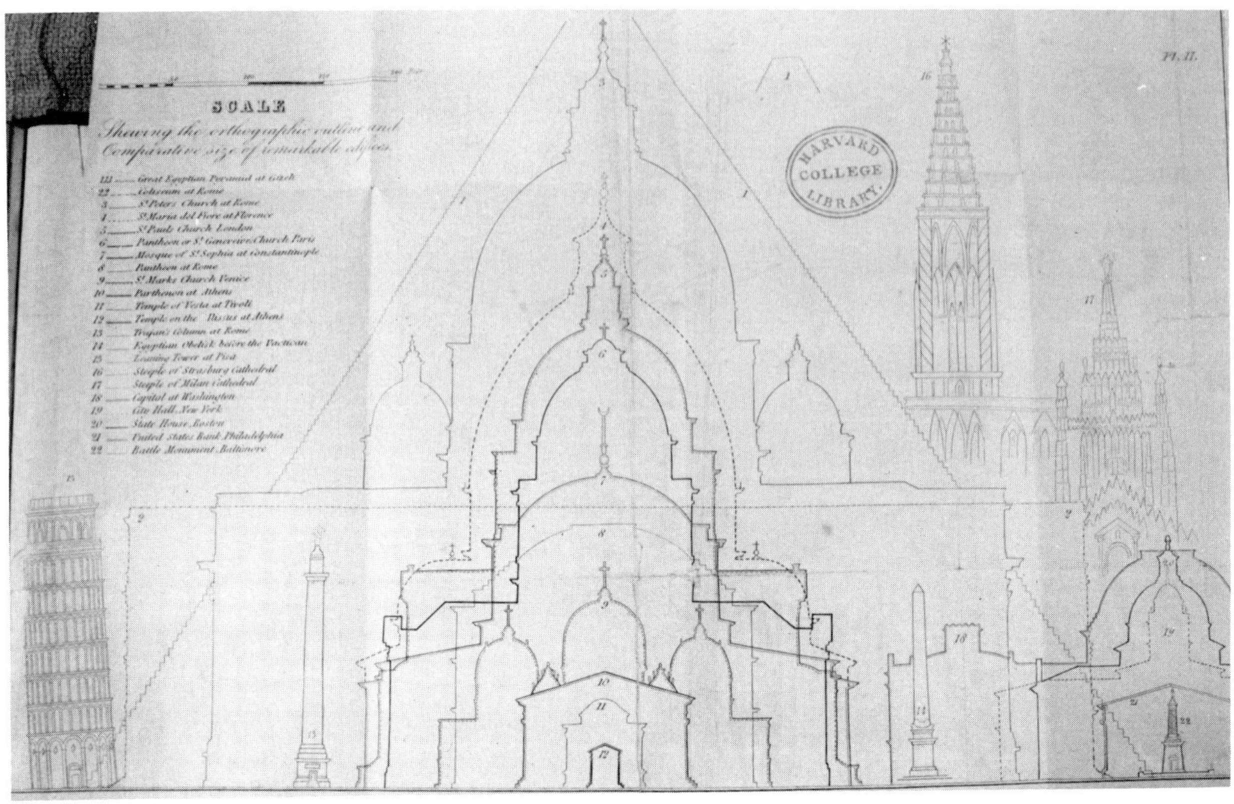

Fig. 10.4. (*Above*) Jacob Bigelow, "orthographic outline and comparative sizes of remarkable edifices," frontispiece in *Elements of Technology,* 1829.

Fig. 10.5. (*Below*) Jacob Bigelow, Egyptian architecture, engraving from *The Useful Arts,* 1840.

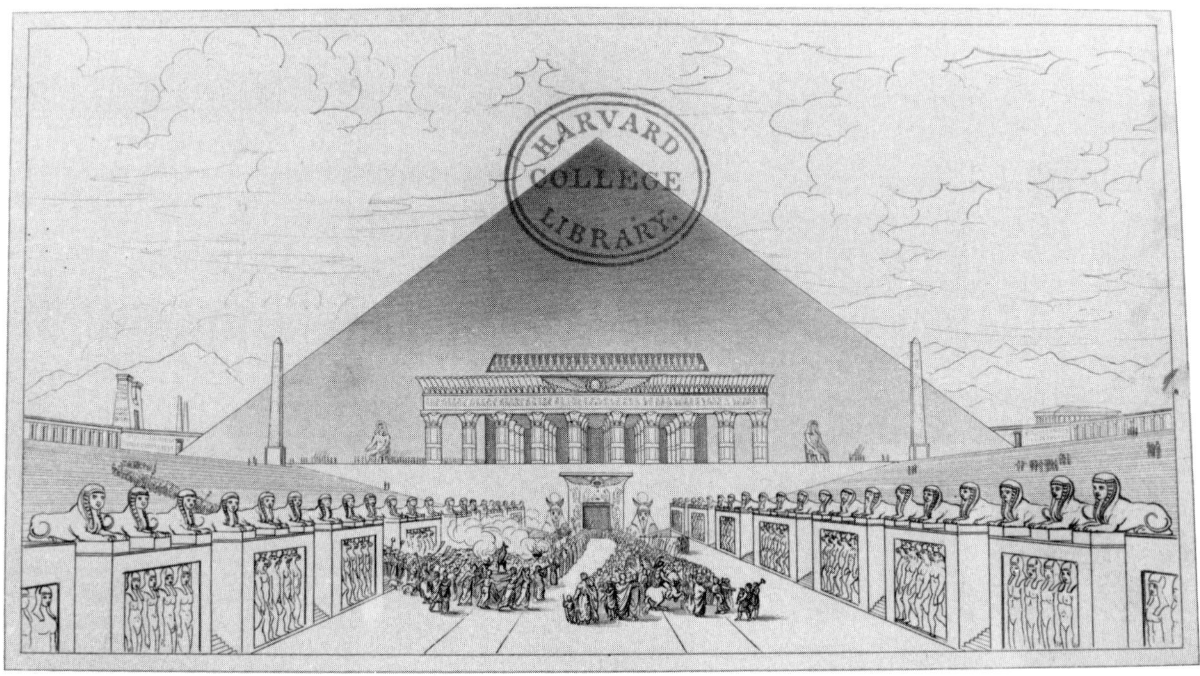

Mount Auburn.[6] (Figs. 10.4, 5.)

Bigelow provided designs for the gate, claiming them as his own; he also closely supervised gate construction by local farmers who traded labor for burial plots. Work began in 1832 on the twenty-five-foot structure of wood, which was painted gray and dusted with sand while it was wet to simulate stone. The gate was to be a temporary facsimile until sufficient funds from lot sales permitted its reconstruction in stone. Bigelow paid special attention to iconographic detail. He wrote Dearborn in Washington in January of 1833 that "the winged globe is a splendid ornament, worthy of being oftener copied in modern times. . . . In most of the Egyptian cornices there is on each side of the globe, a fabulous sort of animal with an inflated body and a head like a serpent or crocodile." Yet some of his friends suggested "that an uncouth Egyptian Idol might give offense to some persons." Bigelow directed the carving of the decorative detail, modifying it without substantially changing it by positioning a drooping Egyptian lotus, symbolic of eternal life, "so as to conceal the head of the monster, leaving the spectator to imagine what he pleases behind it."[7] Perhaps Bigelow, intent on recreating Eden at Mount Auburn, was loath to place a snake at the entrance. (Figs. 10.6, 7.)

Because of economic restraints associated with the cemetery's founding and subsequent hard times in the aftermath of the Panic of 1837, the first corporate structure, and the one major addition to the cemetery during its first decade, was the Egyptian Revival Gateway. The gate, symbolic in many ways, was more often used and recognized as a logo for the cemetery than the seal devised by Bigelow and Story. It appeared on a number of engraved views in guidebooks, on stationery, and even on memorabilia like china cups. (Fig. 10.8.) It was an unprecedented architectural element for an American burial landscape. Most graveyards had only simple openings in enclosing walls or pale fences, with an unobtrusive gate, if any. The architect Goddé's 1835 design for the gates of Père

Fig. 10.6. Mount Auburn's Egyptian gate, engraving by James Smillie, 1847.

Fig. 10.7. Detail of Egyptian iconography modified by Jacob Bigelow for Mount Auburn's gate, photograph by Alan Ward, 1980.

Fig. 10.8. China teacup with Mount Auburn gateway, ca. 1850. Courtesy of Mount Auburn Cemetery.

Lachaise Cemetery was not as grandiose as Bigelow's. The addition of such a ceremonious entrance, more elaborate than those of Boston's new churches, indicates the complexity of new notions about the cemetery and expectations that it would be a place of great civic and cultural importance.

Bigelow's choice of the Egyptian style responded to intellectual and cultural trends of the era. From the Renaissance on, western Europeans used obelisks and pyramids in funerary monuments, but more elaborate and explicit use of Egyptian architecture and symbols was radically new. Interest in the Egyptian grew through the first decades of the century, following publications of archaeological findings of Napoleon's Near Eastern campaigns. A major catalyst for the Egyptian vogue came in 1822 with a discovery that challenged the basis of western thought. News of Jean-François Champollion's deciphering of hieroglyphics precipitated an international debate on the origins of knowledge; and that accomplishment perfectly coincided with the spirit of the times, the quest for taxonomies of reality in varied forms—linguistics, mastery of modern languages, codification of the law, increasing use of numbers in all aspects of everyday life, technology, and history.

In 1823, Edward Everett wrote two articles in the *North American Review* on the importance of Champollion's work in the intellectual history of the times. In 1831, he ranked the discovery with those of Leibniz and Newton, "destined to throw a flood light on a chapter of the history of mankind." Indeed, as John T. Irwin observes, "the decipherment of the hieroglyphics and Darwin's theory of evolution were probably the two severest blows delivered by nineteenth-century science to the credibility of Genesis and accepted Biblical chronology." In England, according to Everett, it excited "violent party spirit." Such a discovery particularly appealed to religious liberals who challenged old orthodoxies, rejected traditional superstitions, and refused to believe in the universal wages of sin from Adam's Fall.[8] The Fall was reinterpreted as man's discontinuity with the natural world rather than with Adam's literal expulsion from Eden; therefore, the Egyptian style represented restoration of naturalism and was particularly appropriate for the entrance to a gardenlike cemetery established by liberal Protestants.

Fig. 10.9. Archaeological view of gate at Thebes from Denon.

Champollion's discovery struck a particular chord in scientific minds intent on developing hieroglyphical methods of interpreting physical shapes through signature analysis, physiognomy, and phrenology. Bigelow, who attempted to found a Linnaean Society in Boston, in order to catalogue New England plant materials and teach the principles of technology to Harvard students, was an enthusiast of things Egyptian because of the implications of Champollion's work. His taste for the Egyptian was further whetted by arrival of the first Middle Eastern artifacts in Boston in 1823—a Theban mummy of Padihershef, an ancient stonecutter in his sarcophagus—strengthening associations of the style with death. A Dutch merchant donated it to the Massachusetts General Hospital.

The Egyptian style also captured the imagination of arbiters of American culture intent on finding new symbols representative of their nation. Many Americans in the 1830s equated their country with Egypt, another "first civilization" capable of providing an alternative cultural idiom to that inherited from England. They nicknamed the Mississippi the "American Nile" and gave the names of Memphis, Cairo, Karnac, and Thebes to new towns along its banks. One amateur archaeologist even theorized in 1839 that Egyptians migrated to America via Asia; and Joseph Smith claimed to have translated his *Book of Mormon* (1830) from hieroglyphics he personally deciphered. Furthermore, Freemasonry fostered the taste with its symbolism and publications like Jeremy Cross's *The True Masonic Chart; or Hieroglyphic Monitor* (1819).

The Egyptian interested architects searching new archaeological texts for styles to meet the growing demand for public buildings of increasingly grand scale. The aspiring young architect Alexander Jackson Davis spent considerable time with Bigelow in Boston, as if in an apprenticeship, copying illustrations from the doctor's personal architectural library, from that of Dr. George Parkman, and from works in the Athenaeum. Ithiel Town had sent Davis to Bigelow in 1827 with a letter of introduction for that purpose, to prepare for a professional career in architecture with the doctor in the same manner as aspiring lawyers read in the law libraries of their elders.

Fig. 10.10. Alexander Jackson Davis design for Egyptian cemetery gate, 1828, courtesy of Metropolitan Museum of Art, New York.

Fig. 10.11. Egyptian tomb of C. Monce, Père Lachaise, engraving from Jolimont, the book Dearborn ordered as an aid in design of Mount Auburn.

Davis stayed in Boston for two years and together with Bigelow pored over French reports from Napoleon's 1798–99 expedition. They avidly read Dominique Vivant Denon's three-volume *Voyage dans la Basse et la Haute Egypte pendant les Campagnes du général Bonaparte,* first published in New York in 1803. They used its illustrations as models for their own fanciful drawings of Egyptian cemetery gates and other buildings, predating Mount Auburn's founding by three years. (Fig. 10.9.) Bigelow's design for Mount Auburn's gate closely resembles gates drawn by Davis, vertical structures with flaring cavetto cornices and flanking pylons, inspired by gates of Thebes, Karnac, and Denderah that were entrances to burial grounds along the Nile. (Fig. 10.10.) It is also strikingly like the tomb of C. Monce in Père Lachaise, a design Bigelow knew from the Jolimont book ordered by Dearborn.[9] (Fig. 10.11.)

Davis favored cemetery gates "constructed so that even in ruins" they would "testify to posterity

Fig. 10.12. Kirk Boott family tomb in the Egyptian style, ca. 1840, on 453-square-foot lot on Amaranth and Rose paths, photograph by Alan Ward, 1985.

the sense which the age had of the event commemorated." Mount Auburn's gate did not commemorate an event as did the Bunker Hill Monument; Bigelow created a design to be just as durable, however, anticipating that the structure, once it was rebuilt in granite, would stand even after the parent civilization was in ruin. His was a fatalistic, cataclysmic view of history. Yet at the same time, Bigelow and other Americans interpreted the Egyptian style as promise and symbol of permanency. It was an architecture that had endured longer than other monuments of ancient mankind—even the wonders of the world. The Egyptian was intrinsically historic as well as sublime, stirring awe by reminding of a nonrecurring past. Bigelow noted, "No man can look upon the splendid ruins of Karnac without feeling humbled by the greatness of a people who have passed away forever."[10] The style indicated the pastness of the past and the mortality of all. It bore subtle hortatory messages updating and reinterpreting the medieval *memento mori*. For that reason, its association with ancient funerary structures aside, it seemed particularly appropriate for a cemetery.

A British visitor agreed, praising that gateway "which looms up in all its gloomy grandeur and exhibits on its front the awful emblems of Time and Eternity! It stands like a solemn milestone on life's broad highway, intimating to every traveller that he is another stage nearer the end of his journey, and that when the weary race shall terminate, 'THEN SHALL THE DUST RETURN TO THE EARTH AS IT WAS, AND THE SPIRIT SHALL RETURN TO GOD WHO GAVE IT.' " The latter was the quote from Ecclesiastes 12:7 added by Bigelow to the face of the plinth to be read by all entering the grounds.[11]

Indeed, Egyptian style and symbols baffled some critics, who considered them reminiscent of tyrant kings and heathenism. John Frazee of New Jersey, founder of the National Academy and a specialist on funerary sculpture, wrote in 1835 that the Egyptian would "never harmonize with the glorious principles of republican achievement nor with Christianity." Henry Russell Cleveland presented a similar opinion on "American architecture" in 1836, calling the Egyptian "anterior to civilization," reminiscent of the "most degraded and revolting paganism which ever existed." Cleveland considered it "the architecture of embalmed cats and deified crocodiles." Cleveland had nothing but praise for the rest of Mount Auburn's landscape as a model for sepulchral architecture, but he doubted whether the Egyptian style so prevalent in "uncouth structures" at the cemetery was "appropriate to a Christian burial-place." Although the Egyptian was "solid, stupendous, and time-defying," the critic thought it out of place where "religion should be present to the mind."[12]

Cleveland acknowledged that few Bostonians had the same disagreeable associations with the Egyptian as he did. The style had the "great merit of combining cheapness and durability," considered preferable by many to the more expensive and fussy Gothic, furthermore associated with papism. Many of the first proprietors at Mount Auburn followed the lead of Joseph Story and chose the Egyptian style for monuments. Sometimes, as on the Samuel Appleton monument, only a symbol or two appeared eclectically on a neoclassical monument. Others, like Kirk Boott, superintendent of the first textile mills in Lowell, or the family of Francis Cabot Lowell, the mills' chief entrepreneur, favored it for their tombs. (Figs. 10.12, 13.)

Dearborn defended the Egyptian as "the architecture of the grave, particularly adapted to the abode of the dead," with an "enduring character" emblematic of immortality.[13] The Boston minister William B. O. Peabody interpreted the Egyptian, like the entire landscape of Mount Auburn, as symbolic of death. Addressing members of the Massachusetts Horticultural Society, Peabody traced to Egypt the practice of "placing the tomb in the midst of the beauty and luxuriance of nature." He equated Mount Auburn with "the great Egyptian cemetery . . . on the farther shore of the Lake Acherusia, near Memphis, ornamented with trees and water-courses."[14]

The local writer Cornelia Walter presented one

Fig. 10.13. Francis Cabot Lowell II family tomb in Egyptian style on 1,620-square-foot lot on Ivy Path, photograph by Alan Ward, 1979.

of the best explanations for the extensive use of the Egyptian at Mount Auburn. Probably based on the rationale she heard from her friend Dr. Bigelow, Walter argued that "the now mythologized doctrines of Egypt seem to have been the original source of others more ennobling; and hieroglyphical discoveries have traced and are tracing them far beyond the era of the pyramids to an unknown limit, but to a pure, sacred, and divine source. When the art of writing was unknown, the primeval Egyptians resorted to symbols and emblems to express their faith; and these, as correctly interpreted, certainly present many sublime ideas in connection with those great truths which in an after age constituted the doctrines of *Christianity.*" Walter explained that some Egyptian sculptures and paintings were "undoubtedly symbolical of the resurrection of the soul, a dread of the final judgment, and a belief in Omnipotent Justice."[15]

Walter expanded on Bigelow's reasoning, suggesting that the symbolism of Mount Auburn's landscape had Egyptian origins. The pyramid was representative of "*the mountain,* the holy hill, the divine sanctuary cut in the mountain, i.e., *the tomb,*" she explained. "The *mountain* was sacred among the Egyptians as the abode of the dead, and was identical with the sepulchre . . . the future state." Walter observed that for Mount Auburn's founders, as for the ancient Egyptians, "the image or figure of a hill became an emblem of *death,* and the pyramidal form, which imitated it, was a funereal symbol—an object consecrated to the abode of the departed." She omitted consideration of more immediate precedents in English gardens or at Père Lachaise.[16]

Walter specifically defended the symbol of the winged globe that appeared so frequently at Mount Auburn in its early years. She considered it "a most beautiful emblem of benign protection." The image of the sun with outstretched wings was "the primitive type of the divine wisdom—the universal Protector." There could be no "more fitting emblem than this for the abode of the dead," for the symbol represented "the protecting wings of Him who is the great author of our being—the 'giver of life and death.'"[17] Mount Auburn's founders favored the Egyptian because it was considered sacred and sublime; equally, it appealed to cosmopolitan and nondenominational tastes.

Some critics of Mount Auburn's gate disliked material more than style. One visitor from Philadelphia in 1838 called the gate a "paltry deception" and belittled "the taste that could paint wood in imitation of granite at the entrance of a City of the Dead." The visitor attempted to shame his hosts: "In a city like Boston, rich beyond most others and proverbial for its liberality," cost "never ought to be an obstacle it *cannot* be now, when vast sums must have been realized from the sale of lots."[18] He ignored the frequency with which ornamental structures in English gardens were fashioned of wood and then painted to resemble stone, with full intention of permanency without replacement. Sir William Chambers, for instance, placed a number of ornamental buildings of wood at the Kew gardens outside London; they were strong enough to withstand the nearby blast of German bombs in World War II.

Following the example of Mount Auburn's gate, the Boston architect Isaiah Rogers designed a small Egyptian gate, constructed in 1840, for the Old Granary Burying Ground. Three years later he used an almost identical structure for the old Touro Jewish Cemetery in Newport, Rhode Island. But Rogers built in granite, for the technology of cutting and carving that hard stone had newly been perfected. (Fig. 10.14.) Until the 1840s, use of granite remained expensive and difficult, slowing completion of even the Bunker Hill Monument, a simple and austere obelisk, until 1843. That year Mount Auburn's gate was finally redone in Quincy granite.[19]

Return of financial prosperity by the spring of 1841, investment of proceeds from lot sales in fifteen different securities—primarily federal bonds, banks, and railroad stock—and accumulation of savings of over $26,000 by 1843 and $82,000 in 1844 permitted Mount Auburn's board to undertake a series of major construction projects intended to complete the picturesque landscape as originally intended. Trustees also planned on obtaining subscriptions "from munificent individuals in aid of such funds," since they were reluctant to sell stock to finance projects. They chose Octavius T. Rogers of Quincy as contractor for the $9,500 project of reconstructing Bigelow's

Fig. 10.14. Egyptian gate by Isaiah Rogers, 1840, at Boston's Old Granary Burying Ground, engraving from Moses King, *Hand-Book of Boston,* 1878.

temporary wooden gate in fine hammered granite "of substantially the same form, mode, and dimension." Rogers was reputedly the only one capable of making and raising the twenty-two-foot-long, monolithic cap or cornice stone in a single piece, the largest piece of sculpted granite placed in an American structure to that date. Rogers shipped the stone by barge from Quincy, south of Boston, and up the Charles River. Teams of oxen dragged it to Mount Auburn's entrance, where it was raised into place by means of screws on a wooden frame. Yet despite his expertise, Rogers left an "unseemly" joint, and the monolith had to be reset. Work was complete in October of 1843.[20]

The new gate could be locked at night by the superintendent, and it had a signal bell for summoning the gatekeeper after hours. In 1852, a larger bell was installed, "which could be heard throughout the grounds for giving concerted signals to workmen, ringing out visitors at sundown and the like." The central carriage entry was flanked symmetrically by two pedestrian doors and two rooms used as porter's and superintendent's offices. Obelisks, separated by a short expanse of fence, punctuated the entrance on either side.[21]

Next, the trustees determined to complete the front and eastern side of the grounds by removing the fence of wooden pales and replacing it with a permanent one; they abandoned the original idea of erecting "a wall of stone of a substantial and elegant design." By the 1840s, the taste for ornate cast-iron fences reigned supreme. In England, John Claudius Loudon advocated use of iron railings rather than high walls around public gardens. Mount Auburn's trustees were confident that metal could provide "due protection and security" for their grounds. In the spring of 1844, Bigelow submitted a design for a ten-foot-high fence with the

Fig. 10.15. Mount Auburn's cast-iron fence designed by Bigelow, ca. 1844, section restored 1982, photograph by Alan Ward, 1987.

Egyptian motif carried out with lotus flower finials. Octavius Rogers laid a firm foundation, a low granite curb set four feet deep to prevent dislocation by frost heaves; the firm of Adams, Whitredge and Cummings of Boston prepared and assembled the cast iron. (Fig. 10.15.) The corporation expended $15,000 for the granite base alone, three times more than trustees committed to he initial construction of the chapel. Although the board originally allocated only $15,000 to $17,000, expenses soared because of the need to regrade the Old Cambridge Road along the entire front of the cemetery. Installation of the iron cost $12,400. Eventually, trustees reluctantly sold $10,000 in stock to complete the work—the portion along the front by 1848 and the Coolidge Avenue side in 1851, a total length of 4,364 feet.[22]

The south and west borders of the cemetery were enclosed in 1851 by a "substantial timber fence," replacing the original flimsy palisade; to increase protection, trustees voted to plant a live hedge of buckthorn or a similar shrub, "believing that in a few years in this way a very handsome and permanent hedge may be obtained at a comparatively trifling expense," under $1,000. There was no need to provide an ornamental enclosure for peripheral parts of the grounds that would not be seen by large numbers of passersby from outside and that might be screened by plantings from within.[23]

The new iron fence made the interior of the cemetery visible from exterior streets. Approaching visitors saw monuments in "the surrounding verdure, like bright remembrances from the heart of earth."[24] Some visitors, however, still found fault. J. S. Buckingham, an Englishman otherwise quite praiseful of the landscape, found only "one defect" in Mount Auburn—the combination of a cast-iron railing with the Egyptian style. He found the relatively small scale of the fence "diminutive" compared to the "colossal size. . . . massiveness and durability of material" of authentic Egyptian structures. He concluded that "the effect of the whole is to produce a strange combination of heaviness and littleness, quite unworthy of the place, and to leave a most unfavourable impression on the visitors." Buckingham especially opposed "the cumbrous and inappropriate gates and railings along the entrance." He even hoped that the Egyptian structure would eventually be replaced by a Greek or Roman entrance, a truly "triumphal gateway," perhaps "with a fine open colonnade of the Ionic order."[25]

Although Mount Auburn was nondenominational, founders planned from the start to construct a chapel for funeral services. Original plans called for a Doric temple on one of the minor hills in the eastern portion of the grounds. The site was even labeled "Temple Hill" on the 1839 map in anticipation of the building. Bigelow prepared a design "of simple and classical character" and obtained an estimate for its construction in the fall of 1834, but the legal separation of cemetery from horticultural society followed by the Panic of 1837 delayed construction until the mid-1840s. By then, tastes had changed.

Whereas Bostonians generally favored Egyptian or neoclassical styles for monuments placed in Mount Auburn in the 1830s, by the 1840s they turned increasingly to the Gothic, perhaps heeding Henry Russell Cleveland's advice that that style should be "chosen for the prevailing architecture" of the cemetery. American interest in the Gothic was fueled by discussion of the writings of Augustus Welby Pugin in various periodicals. At the same time, criticism of the Egyptian and the Greek as pagan lessened the vogue of those revival styles. By 1845, Andrew Jackson Downing happily proclaimed that "the Greek temple disease has passed its crisis. The people have survived it." Similarly, the New Yorker George Templeton Strong decried both the Egyptian and the Greek as the "revived Pagan style." He felt that "this recurrence of heathen taste and anti-Christian usage in architecture or art of any sort is, or should be, unreal and unnatural everywhere." The Boston architect and sculptor Hammatt Billings remained skeptical in 1857 that "the symbols, utterly unmeaning to our unsymbolical minds are supposed to convey some suggestion of immortality." Billings represented the next generation of professionalized architects, who favored the Gothic. There were many theories and rationalizations mustered to justify the new vogue for the Gothic.[26]

The Gothic weathered controversy through the eighteenth century. Bigelow told his students that "Gothic" was a term of derision traced to Sir

Christopher Wren. Many of the Whiggish proprietors of English gardens contemptuously rejected the "Gothick" as "barbarous and tasteless." Quatremère de Quincy wrote that the style was "born not in the infancy but in the decrepitude of the social state," thus signaling impending ruin. Addison considered it symptomatic of a "meanness of manner" to be expected of an outmoded, decaying order rather than of a youthful, simple civilization. Many associated the style with Tory politics and High Church ideology. Most often when it appeared in landscaped gardens, it was in the form of ruins, symbolic of the demise of the Old Order.[27]

Batty Langley was an early and influential advocate of the style, however; he preferred to call it "Saxon" and to associate it with an era of simple Christianity and an English tradition of freedom. Other advocates, following the explanations of German critics Friedrich and August Wilhelm Schlegel, said the Gothic also represented "a spiritual striving for the infinite" as well as for a mythical past. Influenced by the Schlegels, Coleridge wrote, "Grecian architecture is a thing, but the Gothic is an idea" or "symbolical expression of the infinite." Beginning in the 1770s, romantics on both sides of the Atlantic favored reinterpretations of the Gothic for that reason.[28]

Proponents of the revival associated the Gothic with nature, referring to the arboreal theory of the origin of the style made current in England in Bishop William Warburton's 1751 edition of Pope. In *Elements of Technology* (1829), Bigelow provided one of the first American descriptions of Gothic architecture and also traced the principles of the style to "the imitation of groves and bowers under which the Druids performed their sacred rites." John Henry Hopkins, the Episcopal bishop of Vermont, repeated this theory in 1836 in the first American book on Gothic architecture, researched at the Boston Athenaeum (where his path must have regularly crossed Bigelow's). Even Emerson echoed such notions of the origins of the style in the *Dial* in 1841. Bigelow, Hopkins, Emerson, and others therefore associated the Gothic with pantheism rather than Christianity, with Nature rather than the Roman Church; thus they found it acceptable for modern applications. A renewed taste for the Gothic had common origins and proponents with the taste for romantic landscape gardening. Bigelow and other proponents preferred to use the simply descriptive terms "pointed" or "perpendicular" and to trace the style to an arcadian past more distant than the Dark Ages.[29]

Bigelow, a firm believer in derivative culture, also identified the "Greco-Gothic" or "Romanesque" as early manifestations of the style. A similar account appeared in an anonymous essay in the *American Journal of Sciences and Arts* that drew comparisons between the Gothic and older Greek forms while speculating that the style originated in Rome. These arguments aimed to disassociate the Gothic from the popish, making it usable by Low Church Protestants. Although Bigelow got most of his information from the archaeological writings of John Britton and Augustus Welby Pugin, he favored the Gothic for essentially the same symbolic reasons as did his friend Alexander Jackson Davis. Neither Bigelow nor Davis used the Gothic in an archaeological spirit. Rather, they saw it as a symbolic and poetic form suggestive of the passing of time. That, after all, was a major function of the picturesque landscape of the cemetery itself; that was also the aspect of the Gothic captured by Thomas Cole in his 1837 set of paintings, *The Departure* and *The Return,* which are so suggestive of sections of Mount Auburn. Like other revival styles, the Gothic reminded Americans of a past much longer than that which they had as a nation but which they could still make their own.[30]

Certainly Sir Walter Scott's role as an early corresponding member of the Massachusetts Horticultural Society and the popularity of his historical novels whetted the interest of Bigelow and his friends even further. Even Hawthorne, the latter-day Puritan, exclaimed in his *English Note-Books,* "Oh, that we had cathedrals in America were it only for the sensuous luxury." In an age of religious declension, intellectual Americans realized art's power to revive faith through the senses.[31] Such were the powers attributed to the picturesque landscapes of eighteenth-century English gardens; Bigelow knew too that the Gothic as well as structures of other diverse styles were favored by Richard Payne Knight and Sir Uvedale Price as architectural ornamentation for such gardens because of

Fig. 10.16. Gore Hall (library), Harvard College, designed by Richard Bond, 1838, engraving by Warren, ca. 1855.

their rich romantic associations.

Bigelow's decision to use the Gothic in the cemetery was bolstered by the growing popularity of the style in America as well. Once disassociated from papism, the style appealed even to Unitarians. In 1803, William Ellery Channing requested that his friend, the architect Charles Bulfinch, design the new Federal Street Church in the Gothic style. The architectural firm of Town and Davis began using the Gothic in 1832; the detailing of the estate house at Lyndhurst in Tarrytown, New York, designed in 1838 by Alexander Jackson Davis a decade after he and Bigelow read architecture together, is very similar to that of Bigelow's chapel. Washington's second tomb, designed by William Yeaton of Alexandria in 1835, was in the form of a plain brick wall with Gothic entry, reflective of the many literary and artistic attempts to depict the first president's grave in a romantic setting. The architect Solomon Willard, Bigelow's friend, who occasionally provided working drawings if not the original designs for Mount Auburn, used the Gothic for granite structures: the Bowdoin Street Church (1830), Temple Street First Methodist Church (1833), Saint Peter's (1833) in Boston, and the First Unitarian Church of Salem (1836). Harvard's library, Gore Hall, designed of Quincy granite by Richard Bond in 1838, was a Latin cross 104′ by 81′ vaguely reminiscent of King's College Chapel in Cambridge, England. (Fig. 10.16.) Boston was a fertile field for the growing American taste for the Gothic in the 1830s.[32]

By the 1840s, the style reached its heyday, urged on by the aesthetic preaching of Ecclesiologism, an Anglican and Episcopalian movement devoted to propagation of a taste for the Gothic with renewed religious associations. The Cambridge Camden Society, organized in England, began publication of the *Ecclesiologist* in 1841 to counteract the effects of Puritanism on church architecture. Americans were already familiar with the simple or Norman architecture of the rural English parish church through illustrations in the *Gentleman's Magazine and Historical Chronicle,* imported regularly from England from the 1780s on; the missionary work of Ecclesiologists along with the simultaneous rise of Episcopalianism, especially new and noteworthy in New England, hastened acceptance of the "Christian" style.[33]

Development of mortuary chapels in cemeteries produced a new building type akin to architectural follies in English gardens and provided opportunities for use of the Gothic. Henry Edward Kendall won the competition over forty-five other entries with his Gothic design for a chapel for London's new Kensal Green Cemetery in 1832, and Bigelow may have read the favorable review of the controversial design in the *Gentleman's Magazine* that year. Similarly, John Notman, a Scotsman recently settled in Philadelphia, designed a chapel in miniature (50′ by $24\frac{1}{2}$′) collegiate Gothic in 1837 for Laurel Hill, the joint stock cemetery founded in partial emulation of Mount Auburn in 1836. (Fig. 10.17.) Henry Russell Cleveland praised the Gothic in an 1836 article in the *North American Review,* finding its peculiarly Christian ornaments reminiscent "of the joys of life beyond the grave." Cleveland's only reserva-

Fig. 10.17. Gothic chapel designed by John Notman, 1837, for Philadelphia's Laurel Hill Cemetery.

tion was that the style would prove too expensive for American projects, a point Bigelow had made in 1829.[34] Trends in taste and rising prosperity made it virtually inevitable that a number of Gothic monuments and structures would become part of Mount Auburn's eclectic landscape.

Bigelow cited these examples to Mount Auburn's trustees, and the spirit of cultural competition as well as accumulation of surplus funds by 1843 encouraged the board to allocate $5,000 for a chapel, provided a like sum could be raised by subscription within one year. Trustees did not want to sell stocks as they did to pay for the granite gateway and fence, and philanthropic Bostonians contributed to the project. Dr. George Parkman, despite a reputation for miserliness, donated $100; Samuel Appleton and Dr. George C. Shattuck, $1,000 each. Although $7,000 in contributions was raised, the board learned that the chapel would cost at least $25,000.

Some proprietors, however, saw no need for a chapel at the cemetery. To many heirs of Puritans, addition of a chapel amounted to making Mount Auburn into a churchyard. Most Bostonians held funeral services in their own homes, an old custom established when Puritans made burials a civil rather than a religious matter. It was only in the late eighteenth century that Boston's religious liberals began to conduct obsequies in the church itself; even then, such services were more often held for prominent citizens rather than common members of the congregation. Given the pleasant landscape of the new cemetery, however, many proprietors held services in the open at the grave rather than in their homes. Bigelow urged construction of a chapel before any other "public" structures to provide shelter for these services in inclement weather. Still, Cornelia Walter speculated that the chapel would probably primarily serve Episcopalians, because they required a place for the priest to read a more formal burial service.[35]

In the spring of 1844, Mount Auburn's trustees invited half a dozen prominent local architects, including Richard Bond, Gridley J. Fox Bryant, and Ammi B. Young, to submit plans for the chapel. They stipulated that it be "in a chaste style and taste and of the most durable materials, and upon a plan which will admit of great additions and enlargements at a future period without injury to the symmetry and proportions" of the original building "when the religious services and the erection of monuments" inside would necessitate expansion. The chapel would eventually "constitute the Nave or part of the Nave of a future Church which shall become with its future transept a Latin or Greek cross." The lack of built-in pews and pulpit would permit varying uses of the interior. Movable furnishings would be of either iron or wood. Although the concept of movable seating differed greatly from colonial meetinghouses and New England churches, where pews were permanent structural divisions of interior space sold to members of the congregation, it was characteristic of most older European churches.

Trustees intended that the chapel, like English churches, "become the repository of Marble Busts and Statues and other sepulchral monuments which may from time to time be placed there by liberal Benefactors and Friends in memory of the Dead, and which would not bear the exposure of the open air" in the harsh New England climate. Trustees also suggested that the chapel be lit by a dome, lanterns, or skylight to leave the walls free for other uses such as display of commemorative monuments. Additionally, such lighting would have a dim quality appropriate to the deliberately funereal nature of the place. Coming from above, it would be symbolic of the light of heaven and life after death.[36]

Bigelow anonymously placed his own entry in the competition for the chapel; when trustees met at Bigelow's house to select a design, they unanimously chose his. Bigelow proposed a structure of the style sometimes termed "Protestant Gothic," although his plan called for simple decoration suggestive of the Egyptian, including exterior octagonal columns rather than buttresses. Its simple nave, sixty feet by forty and eighty feet high, is lit only by small, circular clerestory windows and high rose windows at either end, leaving plenty of interior wall space. Bigelow undoubtedly knew that aestheticians like Archibald Alison and Pugin thought that detailed ornamentation kept the Gothic from being sublime, but he was also aware that a structure built in granite could not include elaborate detail. His design resembles Harvard's

Fig. 10.18. Mount Auburn's first chapel, view from south, engraving by Bufford of Boston, ca. 1846.

Gore Hall in its simplicity. As Douglass Shand Tucci observed, this chapel, like so many other Boston buildings of its era, possesses "fundamental characteristics that proceed, if not from the Greek Revival, not from the Gothic either. Rather, these characteristics proceed from one thing all these buildings, Greek, Egyptian, and Gothic, have in common: granite." Tucci labeled this and other local structures from the 1840s examples of the "Boston Granite Style."[37] (Figs. 10.18, 19.)

Fig. 10.19. Mount Auburn's first chapel, view from north from Lawn Avenue, carte de visite photograph by G. K. or W. S. Warren, ca. 1865.

Bigelow's claim to complete authorship of the chapel, however, is open to question. In November of 1845, the board received a letter from Ammi B. Young "in relation to a design and plans furnished by him for a Chapel" and voted to respond with thanks for "donation of his bill for a valuable design." Yet Young, known for his Boston Custom House (1837), excelled in a neoclassical rather than a Gothic idiom.[38]

When Bigelow persuaded the board to choose his design for the chapel, he also won acceptance of a new location. The low Temple Hill on the carriage drive winding to the summit of the cemetery already had several family lots and a receiving tomb; moreover, it did not have the appropriate flat topography or central location for proper siting of a Gothic structure. Bigelow favored use of the plateau just west of Central Avenue near the front of the cemetery. The corporation had only to repurchase four lots to lay out a new avenue, providing access to the chapel and making it one of several major focal points in the landscape.[39]

Bigelow served as contractor for the chapel's construction. Based on the recommendation of D. R. Hay of Edinburgh, author of a philosophic treatise on harmony of colors, Bigelow hired the firm of Ballantine and Allan of Glasgow, noted for its "glass painting" and appointment by the Royal Commission in the Fine Arts to execute the painted windows for the House of Lords, rebuilt in 1836. He rejected their suggestion of distinctly Biblical scenes with major windows depicting the Resurrection and the Ascension and smaller semicircular panes picturing the twelve Apostles in the style of the thirteenth century. He also asked them not to use the symbolic letters $^{\mathrm{P}}_{\mathrm{X}}$, Greek for Christ, or the letters Alpha and Omega, signifying the beginning and ending of life. Rather, Bigelow sent them templates for the north rose window inspired by the famous low-relief carving "Night," by the internationally acclaimed sculptor Bertel Thorwaldsen, with a winged female figure asleep in the clouds, cradling two sleeping infants. (Fig. 10.20.) Wilson Flagg said it was meant "to symbolize the tranquility of death"; Cornelia Walter remarked that it reminded her of Mrs. Hemans's sentimental verse:

> Free, free from earth-born fear,
> I would range the blessed skies
> Through the blue divinely clear,
> Where the low mists cannot rise.

Bigelow requested that the rose window on the front or south of the chapel depict two cherubs from Raphael's painting of the Madonna di San Sisto gazing upward to a source of heavenly light, representing belief in immortality. He suggested that the representation of Death in the north window be in cold or somber tints, while that of Immortality facing the sun be in bright and dazzling colors.[40] (Fig. 10.21.)

Bigelow commissioned Gridley Bryant, architect of City Hall and proprietor of the Quincy quarries, to draw up working plans for the chapel. Octavius T. Rogers constructed the building quickly,

Fig. 10.20. Thorwaldsen's *Night*, stereographic photograph, ca. 1860, of often-copied low-relief medallion.

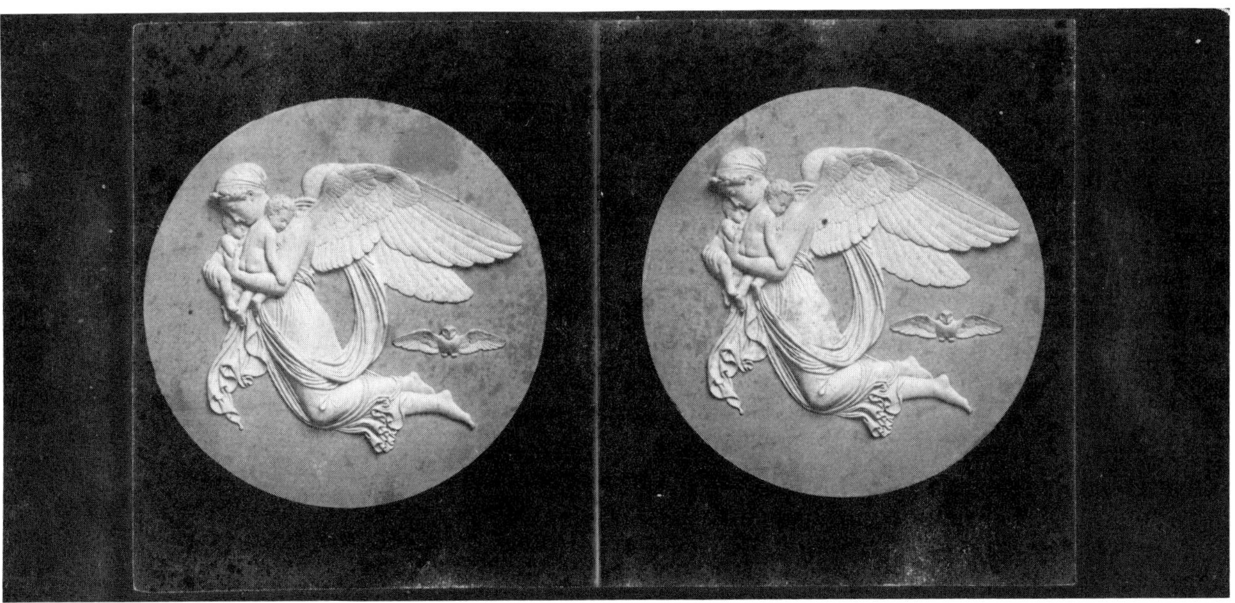

Fig. 10.21. Nave windows, chapel, photograph, ca. 1900. Courtesy of Mount Auburn Cemetery.

completing work in 1846. The effects of the haste became evident, however, in less than a year. The ashlar granite pieces were flawed by veins of iron, which discolored the entire structure. In the spring of 1848, Superintendent Rufus Howe spent $100 on experiments to remove exterior stains, but the defective stone had already begun to disintegrate, creating chronic leaks in the roof that grew worse each year. Inspectors from the firm of Washburn, Treadwell, and Standish complained that in addition to structural problems, "the walls of the clerestory cracked as if shaken by the wind," making a very disquieting noise. Engineers convinced the board in 1851 that the defects were great enough to raise doubts of the safety of the entire chapel. The pinnacles were particularly unstable, and walls admitted wind and rain. No restitution could be obtained from Rogers, despite conclusive evidence of "gross violation of the building contract," a result of subcontracting work.[41] Piecemeal reconstruction was impossible. The *coup de grace* came in February of 1852 when a storm destroyed the precariously mounted north rose window. Trustees reluctantly concluded that there was no alternative to tearing down and rebuilding the entire chapel. Work began late in 1853 and proceeded slowly and cautiously; it was completed in 1858 at a total expense of $50,000.

The second chapel was essentially the same as the first, with only minor differences in ornament. The building was six feet longer; the new stained glass rose window had only geometrical designs rather than the allegorical depiction of Immortality. It had parlor-like rooms off the right side of the nave where a grieving family might have privacy, screened from public view by heavy velvet curtains. The finishing touch of interior paving with multicolored English burnt tiles was installed in 1861. The structure needed only one minor cleaning of lime marks and proved entirely strong and satisfactory except for a new, unsettling flaw. An echo, annoying if not actually eerie, made proprietors reluctant to schedule funeral services in the rebuilt chapel; they also complained that the structure still seemed particularly damp and cold. Although trustees provided suitable books and a reading desk, hoping that it would serve as a place for quiet, melancholy contemplation like the hermitages in English gardens, the chapel never received much use.[42]

Most proprietors complained that trustees should not have expended proceeds from lot sales on such a building in the first place; they vocally opposed plans to make the chapel a historical museum, housing "a collection of mere curiosities or relics of ancient times," no more appropriate to the general purposes of the cemetery than "establishment of an historical library, though that [would be] in some sense the best monument to the worthy dead." Others countered that it was entirely fitting to make the chapel and, indeed, the entire cemetery a historical repository.[43]

In her 1847 book on Mount Auburn, Cornelia Walter repeated Bigelow's hope that the chapel would become a museum. The English visitor Sir

Charles Lyell wrote in 1849 that the building was "to serve as a Westminster Abbey, Pantheon, or Valhalla," commemorating "distinguished men." Some speculated that the cemetery charter might even be interpreted to "allow the heir of any . . . military heroes to hang the trophies of . . . victories above a mural tablet in the Chapel." These artifacts and "relics" would constitute a collection entrusted to the corporation's care. No one wondered who would define the "worthy dead" or evaluate credentials of historical note, but many of the newer trustees were vehemently unwilling to assume that task. They felt the cemetery should be simply functional for burials and opposed attempts to make something more of the cemetery, especially if it involved creation of high culture.[44]

Advocates of commemoration seized upon the death of Joseph Story in September of 1845, and Bigelow mounted a subscription campaign to fund a statue of the Supreme Court justice and Mount Auburn's first president for placement in the chapel. Bigelow, Charles Curtis, and Martin Brimmer formed a Statuary Committee to find an artist; in January, they reported that the son of the deceased, the young lawyer William Wetmore Story, despite a lack of formal art training, had designed a bust of his father and a small model of a life-length statue, "both of which bid fair to convey a more just impression of the character, expression, and likeness of the deceased." They made a contract with the twenty-nine-year-old Story, who promptly left his Boston law practice for Rome to set up a sculpture studio.[45]

By 1847, trustees had collected $2,630, more than enough to complete the commission; they invested the surplus in a special account that eventually was used for further embellishment of the grounds. Work of the statue took longer than anticipated, however; in 1851, the sculptor asked for an extension in the contract, which some newer trustees favored canceling. Bigelow urged Story to return to Boston to complete the work, believing that use of American marble would produce a satisfactory product and that work could progress more quickly under the trustees' watchful eyes; but Story refused, resigning his commission. The board reconsidered, persuaded Story to continue the work in Rome, and negotiated a new contract. Story promised delivery in October of 1854, three years after first promised, but the statue did not arrive in Boston until the following spring. Edward H. Eldredge exhibited it in the Athenaeum vestibule and kept it insured until cemetery trustees procured a suitable pedestal, designed by Richard Saltonstall Greenough. In ceremonies at the Athenaeum the board formally accepted the statue, deeming it "an exact and living likeness of its distinguished original, a just conception and appropriate expression of character," and "a truthful and life-like embodiment of what marble can give successfully to commemorate the dead."[46] (Fig. 10.22.)

William Wetmore Story returned briefly to Boston for the ceremonies and halfheartedly resumed his law practice, but in 1856 he went back to Italy to devote his life to sculpture. Hawthorne visited Story's studio and modeled the story *The Marble Faun* (1860) on the life of the expatriate Bostonian. Mount Auburn's commission of the Story statue not only launched the career of a major American sculptor; William's two sons, Julian Russell and Thomas Waldo, also found careers in art, and his daughter married a Medici. It was relatively easy for a cultured young man or woman to take up sculpture in Italy without worrying about lack of craftsmanship, for artists routinely hired teams of skilled stonecutters, some of whom specialized in the intricate carving of drapery or working the texture of skin and hair, to execute their designs in marble.

William Wetmore Story was only one of many aspiring American artists who went to Italy from the 1830s through the 1850s to produce sculpture for American patrons, who, inspired by neoclassical taste and the desire to commemorate notable individuals, provided a steady stream of commissions. Bigelow proposed additional historic statues for Mount Auburn in his 1853 annual report, quoting Joseph Story's report a decade earlier on possible uses of the chapel and the expectation that "marble busts and statues and other sepulchral monuments . . . *may from time to time be placed there by liberal benefactors and presented in memory of the dead.*" For a year, Bigelow argued with fellow trustees that the original plan of Mount Auburn included addition of statuary at corporate expense to the buildings and grounds. He quoted Samuel Johnson's definition of "embellishment" as "adventitious beauty" and "adscititious grace," or "that which is taken in to complete something else." Webster's dictionary described "embellishment" as "any thing that adds beauty or elegance, that which renders anything pleasing to the eye."[47]

Trustees Charles Curtis and Secretary Henry M. Parker rendered their legal opinion that "*commemorative statues* are an embellishment of a Cemetery" and therefore within the lawful power of the board to commission art. They added that the articles of incorporation, furthermore, could be construed "properly [to] allow the heir of any of our military heroes to hang the trophies of his father's victories above a mural tablet in the chapel," entrusting the artifacts to corporate care. Since a "good estate" usually reserved about $360 for funeral expenses, the bulk of which paid for a gravestone, some trustees speculated that a similar sum might be expended on a portrait of the deceased—a painting or low relief—for display in the chapel rather than as a separate monument to the family lot. Curtis and Parker joined with Bigelow in hopes that "memorials of the worthy dead might thus gradually accumulate under [trustee] care and eventually the number of these relics of various kinds may make up such a collection that [the Corporation] would not be authorized, in the first instance, to establish as an independent thing, as an embellishment of the Cemetery." Mount Auburn would then have a collection of historical artifacts and art "appropriate to and in harmony with the place," not unlike that in the Parisian Museum of the Invalides, attached to the funerary chapel including Napoleon's tomb.[48] No one questioned, however, the process for defining the "worthy dead" or for evaluating credentials of historical note.

In a split decision, the board allocated $15,000, to be divided to provide three full-length statues "to be prepared under contracts to be made with proper artists, the said statues to be those of persons distinguished in American History." Bigelow and his Statuary Committee encountered "great difficulty" in choosing the subjects because of "the equality of conflicting claims, especially of those which crowd about the revolution." Bigelow felt that "difficulty would be somewhat diminished by selecting a representative man," using Emerson's term, "for each four distinct epochs or periods of our history"—the colonial settlement of America and foundation of Boston, the first resistance to "aggression of British power," independence and establishment of republican government, and the triumph of constitutional law or "realization growing out of the others of the period of supremacy of law and of intellectual, moral, and social progress." Story's statue already represented the last stage, according to Bigelow.[49]

Extensive discussion focused on the choice of notables to symbolize the other three periods. Bigelow solicited advice from the likes of John Gorham Palfrey, who was then writing a history of Massachusetts. Former mayor and Harvard president Josiah Quincy suggested John Jay, John Marshall, and John Pickering as representative Americans on criteria of "morals, motives, and intellect." Others proposed John Cotton and John Eliot. The decision finally rested on sons of Massachusetts: John Winthrop, James Otis, and John Adams, presenting the characteristically regional interpretation of national history.[50]

Opposition to the statuary remained, however, generally among new proprietors and trustees who argued that the cemetery was founded for purely functional reasons to remove burials from the city and not to become a museum or "an historical library." George Crockett and Isaac Parker were most vocal in opposition to corporate expenditures for art that was not part of the chapel as originally designed; they encouraged public debate that filled local papers and carried over to the 1856 annual proprietors' meeting.[51]

The editor of the Boston *Advertiser* supported erection of statues; W. F. Brown, writing for the Boston *Daily Courier,* praised the sculptors' ability to show "a just appreciation of the historic enterprise to which they have given their talents." Brown believed that "the appropriate ornaments of cemeteries are memorials of the dead, and of these memorials, works of statuary are, by common consent of the enlightened world, the most beautiful, expressive, and desirable. Their historic truth enhances their value, and their costliness restricts their multiplication." Brown defended the rights of trustees to embellish the cemetery, and expressed confidence that the effort would be respected by "a cultivated and discerning community."[52]

J. M. Wightman countered to the editor of the *Atlas* that defenders of the statues were not acquainted with the opinions of the majority of Mount Auburn's proprietors. He complained that the $15,000 allocated for the statues was especially objectionable after the $50,000 already spent on the chapel, "for which there has not been and probably will not be any use." Wightman did not categorically oppose commemorative statues; he merely thought they would be better if financed by voluntary subscription and placed in Faneuil Hall, the State House, or the library, public sites in the city where a larger portion of the population would come in contact with them. Furthermore, he objected, "The statues of Winthrop, of Otis, and Adams ought not to be immured within this monument [Mount Auburn's chapel]; their dust rests in other places; they have no connection with this cemetery. . . . their statues should stand out boldly in the light of day—in places which when living, they had graced and honored by their presence, their virtues and their patriotism, and where they may be often present to the eye, as bright exemplars for the present and future generations."[53]

A writer to the *Christian Examiner* favored the statues, anticipating, "How rich we shall be in works of art when these have arrived to reconsecrate, by their almost speaking presence, the hallowed regions of our unforgotten dead!" The writer cautioned proprietors not to be swept along

Fig. 10.22. Joseph Story portrait statue by William Wetmore Story, 1854, half of a stereographic photograph, ca. 1865. SPNEA.

by materialism, for they were capable of evil as well as good in their attempt to commemorate the great and the ordinary: "The chief charm of Mount Auburn is the peaceful shade which its deep groves fold around the sorrowing heart—and marble shafts are no compensation for destroyed trees—least of all, is one of these gloomy tombs a grateful substitute for the blended beauty and fragrance of pine and elm."[54]

The debate continued. A letter to the *Daily Courier* alleged that the corporation had perverted money "from its legitimate purposes without even consulting proprietors." The writer, identified only as a lot owner himself, judged it a "decided improprietory [*sic*] to place statues of statesmen in such a place"; he questioned the authority of trustees to do so based on his "experience in corporations." He, too, favored the idea of the statues but proposed moving them to "suitable public places or buildings."[55]

Two days later, another letter to the *Courier* from one of Mount Auburn's first proprietors defended the decision to commission statues and complained that the controversy served only "to keep off persons who are disposed to purchase lots." This writer warned that "agitation and party excitement would doom Mount Auburn to "the fate of too many modern corporations"—dissolution and bankruptcy. The controversy created bad public relations.[56]

Wightman strengthened his criticism of the financial impropriety of corporate commissioning of statues a week later in the *Atlas*. He would not object to display of costly works of art at the cemetery, he argued, if proprietors were "not taxed for them without their consent." He mustered a summary of Mount Auburn's budget to prove his point. In the previous year, corporate expenditures were $37,342, but receipts amounted to only $26,439, depleting investments by $10,650 at a time when there was no permanent fund to ensure future maintenance and preservation of the grounds. To make matters worse, limited corporate investments of $30,000 had only a $25,000 market value. Wightman reminded Bostonians that Bigelow himself had announced at the 1856 annual meeting, "If, for the next thirty years, the Trustees should sell all the available lots, and spend as they

Fig. 10.23. John Winthrop portrait statue by Richard Saltonstall Greenough, 1857, half of a stereographic photograph, ca. 1865, SPNEA.

Fig. 10.24. James Otis portrait statue begun by Thomas Crawford and completed by Randolph Rogers, 1857–58, half of a stereographic photograph, ca. 1865, SPNEA.

have been doing since the first establishment of the cemetery, at the end of that time the Corporation would be without any income with which to keep the grounds in order." Furthermore, the annual interest on each statue would pay for one grounds worker for a year. By mid-1856, alterations and additions under way on the gate and superintendent's house had to be stopped because of the statuary expenses.[57]

Wightman echoed the views of insurgent trustees who had proposed only six weeks before that the contracts for the statues be canceled, that monies saved be placed in a permanent fund, "and the income derived from it be spent upon the grounds,—in keeping them in more perfect order than has hitherto been the case, that it would be far more for the reputation of the place and the pleasure and comfort of the visitors and proprietors than would be the exhibition of the statuary, however beautiful." In order to curb future spending, this minority faction of trustees amended Article 25 of the By-Laws to stipulate that no new expenditure over $1,000 could be made unless voted on by the board at a meeting held at least seven days after the proposal had been presented. This measure would prevent a few influential board members, like Bigelow, from rushing through projects that other trustees might oppose if given time for due deliberation.[58]

Fig. 10.25. John Adams portrait statue by Randolph Rogers, 1857, half of a stereographic photograph, ca. 1865, SPNEA.

The insurgent trustees were not averse to spending money for amenities to the grounds if the additions provided new facilities or conveniences for proprietors and visitors. In 1855, new board members Mace Tisdale and Isaiah Bangs joined Bigelow on the Committee on Grounds. They urged installation of benches, improvement of lighting in the lodge, and placement of privies in the grounds, the last item strongly opposed by Bigelow. Tisdale, who had narrowly won reelection in 1855, in turn threatened to resign over the statues controversy, following the example of George W. Crockett, a trustee of twelve years. Isaac Parker dissented so vocally on the issue that he lost his sixteen-year board seat; and like-minded proprietors elected three new trustees who joined Tisdale in opposition to the statues, forcing the board to issue majority and minority reports for and against rescinding the contracts, although two pedestals and one statue were already in place in the chapel.[59]

Bigelow pointed out that the corporation had entered into binding contracts with three sculptors and had given a $1,000 down payment to two after approving four daguerreotype views of maquettes. Richard Saltonstall Greenough (1819–1904), designer of the Story statue pedestal, was chosen to execute the statue of Winthrop. Thomas Crawford (1814–57), one of the first American sculptors to settle in Rome to study with Thorwaldsen, after working with John Frazee and Robert Launitz in New Jersey carving funerary monuments, won the commission for the Otis portrait. Randolph Rogers (1852–92) was to do the John Adams, his first major commission. Work, however, did not progress smoothly.[60] (Figs. 10.23, 24, 25.)

Crawford began the Otis statue and completed a seven-foot-tall plaster model, but he died suddenly in 1857 before it could be executed in marble. Crawford's widow, the sister of Julia Ward Howe, arranged for Rogers to complete the work. Rogers had just finished his Adams "of the heroic size, in the costume of the period when he lived and all in admirable taste" and shipped it off to Boston; but it was lost at sea and the sculptor had to make a duplicate. In 1859, the ship bearing the second Adams statue put into Savannah in distress, and the statue was not forwarded to Boston until the following year. John Adams, who had always been skeptical about art, even when used in the name of history, would have found the difficulties ironic, especially on the eve of the Civil War. Throughout the difficulties and delays, however, Bigelow remained confident that the wait for such "a valuable and most appropriate embellishment" was well worthwhile and would ultimately give Mount Auburn "precedence over all other cemeteries in this country" at a relatively minor expense.[61]

The editor of the short-lived *Mount Auburn Memorial* echoed Bigelow's confidence in the commemorative value of the statues, wondering, "What parent as he conducts his son to Mount Auburn will not, as he pauses before their monumental statues, seek to heighten his reverence for virtue, for patriotism, for science, for learning, for devotion to the public good." Luxuriating in the twilight of a Whiggish historicism, he exclaimed, "Winthrop, Otis, Adams, Bowditch, Story—these are our jewels, these our abiding treasures." He only bemoaned the lack of a memorial to John Hancock, either in Boston or at the cemetery, and proposed that trustees select a choice location for reinterment and suitable honors: "Let there be placed upon his mausoleum a colossal figure of the Genius of America, supporting upon her left arm an emblematic shield of the American Union, and in her right hand grasping the staff surmounted by the 'Cap of Liberty.' "[62] A poem by "Justitia" published the following week in the *Memorial* stressed the same argument for commemoration of Hancock:

First of the band who rent Britannia's chain,
And her proud mandate sent back o'er the main,
Is there no shrine or urn to speak thy fame?
No spot where youth may learn thy deeds to name?

Shame to thy natal place, shame to the land,
Neglecting thee to grace, itself doth brand,
And to the stranger's eye seemeth imbrued [*sic*]
With crime of deepest dye—Ingratitude.

"Give honor," saith our God, "Where honor's due."
Who broke the tyrant's rod, claims it of you.
Raise where his ashes sleep, a marble bust;
Place it where willows weep o'er his dust.

But write no eulogy upon the stone;
Under his bust let be his name alone.
No epitaph or song his fame shall swell;
For in proud history his deeds shall dwell.[63]

The same honors would be due Sam Adams, the editor suggested; but "no one present could say positively" where his ashes "reposed" in Boston's Old Granary Burying Ground.[64]

The 1856 controversy over historical statues signaled a growing unwillingness, however, to use Mount Auburn as a place of public commemoration. Indeed, with the exception of Bigelow, most trustees discouraged it. In 1858, the board defined "public monuments" erected by subscription campaigns as "memorials" and stipulated that endowment of a perpetual care fund be mandatory before their erection. Since the corporation stopped granting land for such memorials, subscription campaigns would have to raise funds to buy lots and to assure their care as well as to erect monuments. Bigelow knew from experience the necessity of such a regulation to ensure repair as well as routine maintenance. Since 1845, the corporation had held a $72 endowment fund for the memorial to Dr. Kirkland, Harvard president; after less than a decade, it was needed for repairs. The cemetery did not hold such funds for the statue of Nathaniel Bowditch. Since 1853, Bigelow had been trying unsuccessfully to repair damage done to the cast bronze by New England weather. Piecemeal efforts of workers trying to stop the many holes that developed and to cover the patching with bronze-colored paint proved insufficient and unsightly. Eventually, the statue of the mathematician and astronomer had to be taken down and shipped to Munich for recasting in Europe's best foundry.

Bostonians willing to contribute to construct

commemorative monuments began to look to public sites rather than to Mount Auburn. In 1867, when a subscription campaign raised funds so that William Wetmore Story could design a life-sized portrait statue of Edward Everett (1794–1865) in a dramatic histrionic pose, cast in bronze in Munich, they chose a site on the Beacon Street side of the Public Garden. There, passersby could easily read that Everett was "Orator, Minister, Classics Professor, Magazine Editor, Statesman, Congressman, Governor, Ambassador, President of Harvard, Secretary of State, Senator." (Fig. 10.26.) Everett has a fine neoclassical monument of red and white granite proclaiming his accomplishments even more extensively at the cemetery; but it is difficult to find, blending in with a host of similar monuments on a steep hillside near Mount Auburn's summit. (Fig. 10.27.)

The demise of public commemoration in the "rural" cemetery was not solely a matter of the waning of romantic nationalism or Whiggish historicism. With the rise of sentimentalism and the growing accumulation of small stones representative of trends in affective individualism and the domestication of death, there were no longer proper places there for conspicuous display of monuments of great public significance. Also, Adolph Strauch, superintendent and landscape gardener of Cincinnati's Spring Grove Cemetery, observed in 1857, "Memorials of love adorn our rural Cemeteries; those which we dedicate to the memory of the great—of public benefactors—must be too grand and imposing to accord well with those gentler feelings symbolized in our more modest monuments; they may suitably adorn public buildings as to be useful for public purposes."[65] At Mount Auburn by mid-century, the distinction between public and private monuments blurred, especially amid the proliferation of stones and other structures in the landscape. The failure of the commemorative purpose, one of the chief reasons for Mount Auburn's founding, was not simply a matter of insurgent trustees with alternative visions for the cemetery and more businesslike methods.

Although after Joseph Story's death differences emerged on the board over what additional amenities should be funded by the corporation, trustees unanimously agreed to build the observatory or tower that had been anticipated by cemetery founders as soon as the chapel was built. Bigelow had provided Greek and Gothic designs for a tower in Mount Auburn's first year, arguing that when the hill 125 feet above the Charles River was so "crowned," it would become "a most interesting place of resort, as commanding an extensive panoramic view of that richly variegated region of magnificent scenery, embraced within the far distant heights which encircle the metropolis." Dearborn rightly predicted that a tower would "present a prominent and imposing feature in the landscape, of which it becomes the center."[66] Bigelow intended it to "serve the double purpose of a landmark to identify the spot from a distance and of an observatory commanding an uninterrupted view of the country around it."[67]

Dearborn had also speculated that "a stupendous monument to the most illustrious benefactor of his country," George Washington, might be built in lieu of a tower "when the munificence of the citizens shall be commensurate with their debt of patriotic gratitude." Yankees like Joseph Story and Josiah Quincy had organized to erect a monument to the first president in the "Capital of New England" as early as 1811; but, although the Massachusetts legislature appointed commissioners and allocated funds for the project in 1816, no monument was built. William Tudor encouraged the venture to "do honour to the good taste and judgment of those who erect it . . . to the state and town" as well as to Washington; he worried, however, about lack of appropriate sites in the city even for a small equestrian statue. Tudor had favored an architectural rather than a sculptural monument, and he considered steep hills that were "not difficult of access" and near Boston ideal. Mount Auburn provided such a location.[68] Its tower could be dedicated to the first president, adding a third function of commemoration and giving the city historical monuments atop hills to the east and to the west.

The tower would also "embellish the picturesque" in a way characteristic of many English gardens. Mount Auburn's founders knew that towers imbued with mythical or historical associations were common elements in such landscapes. Claremont in Surry had a Belvedere Tower, designed in

Fig. 10.26. Edward Everett portrait statue by William Wetmore Story, cast in bronze in Munich, 1867, half of a stereographic photograph, ca. 1870.

1715 by Sir John Vanbrugh for the summit of the principal knoll, called the Mount. Studley Royal in North Yorkshire contained a short, octagonal tower atop the estate's highest hill. Henry Hoare, proprietor of Stourhead in Wiltshire, commissioned Henry Flitcroft to erect an imposing 160-foot "gothick" tower in 1762 on Kingsettle Hill, where King Alfred reputedly planted his flag against Danish invaders in 879. Whigs, like Voltaire in his *Histoire Générale,* venerated Alfred,

Fig. 10.27. (*Below*) Edward Everett funerary monument at Mount Auburn, photograph by Alan Ward, 1986.

Fig. 10.28. Castellated tower at Whitton, England, engraving, ca. 1780.

Fig. 10.29. (*Below*) Octagon tower on Constitution Hill at Studley Royal, added by the proprietor, William Aislabie, in 1738 to replace a classical pavilion, photograph by Alan Ward, 1985.

"The Father of His People" and "Founder of the English Monarchy and Liberty," as quintessential guardian of their liberties and the founder of trial by jury, a militia, and a naval force. He was the monarch who confirmed the old Saxon institution of Parliament. Many towers bore Alfred's name. (Figs. 10.28, 29, 30, 31.)

Frequent placement of "gothick" towers in English gardens was also a matter of taste. Sanderson Miller, an English "gentleman architect," played a seminal role in England's Gothic revival in the 1750s and 1760s as it was linked to the taste for the picturesque. The octagonal, battlemented tower he built at his own estate at Radway Grange in Warwickshire was on the spot where legend held that King Charles I raised his standard in the Battle of Edgehill in 1642; many of Miller's other towers were follies or garden ornaments without specific historical significance, however, serving simply to embellish the landscape. Miller specialized in sham castellated ruins, especially in the form of round towers providing panoramic views suggestive of infinity. Sir Horace Walpole and Richard Payne Knight, apostles of the picturesque, particularly favored the castellated "gothick" style over the Greek or Roman. Archibald Alison, the Scottish aesthetic philosopher read by many of Mount Auburn's founders, remarked that "an old tower in the middle of a deep wood," like ruins, stirred emotional responses similar to the sublime,

Fig. 10.30. Tower (160 feet) commemorating King Alfred's victory over the Danes in A.D. 879 on Kingsettle Hill in the gardens at Stourhead, Wiltshire, designed by Henry Flitcroft, 1762, photograph by Alan Ward, 1985.

Fig. 10.31. Belvedere tower, probably designed by John Rocque, ca. 1740, Claremont gardens, Surrey, photograph by Alan Ward, 1985.

triggering a realization of the passage of time and the pastness of the past.[69] Towers continued to be favored for commemoration in Britain into the nineteenth century. In 1811, the wealthy banker Sir William Paxton built a castellated tower at Dyfed in memory of Lord Nelson.

Impelled by his aesthetic historicism, Bigelow did not forget that a tower was part of the original plan when in 1843 trustees considered allocation of their surplus for a permanent gate, fence, and chapel, but those construction projects took precedence. It was not until the summer of 1852 that work on the tower began. No architectural competition was held for its design. Bigelow took credit for the concept of the circular, castellated Norman structure, although Gridley J. Fox Bryant was hired to produce plans, models, and working drawings. Indeed, one local newspaper reported that the structure was "designed by the indefatigable G. J. F. Bryant under direction of Bigelow, President of the Corporation."[70] Bryant was Boston's leading commercial architect at mid-century specializing in granite construction. His major projects include the Mercantile Wharf Building, the State Street Block, the City Hospital, the City Hall, and the first Horticultural Hall. The firm of Whitcher and Sheldon, which rebuilt the chapel, served as contractors, using Quincy granite to build the sixty-two-foot tower. Whereas many observers referred to the tower, like the chapel, as being of "Dissenters' or Perpendicular" Gothic style, Bigelow called it Norman. Perhaps he, like Henry Adams a generation later, attached particular historical associations to the Norman as source of Yankee heritage.[71] (Figs. 10.32, 33.)

Although the new structure was called Washington Tower, no dedicatory ceremonies were ever held. The commemorative functions of the structure were overshadowed by its immediate popularity as a tourist attraction. Guidebooks had long bragged of the spectacular panoramic view from the summit of the cemetery; the tower only served to dramatize the view further for those willing to climb the dark, circular staircase to the platformed deck and the top. One visitor judged the view "equal perhaps to what is obtained from the monument of Bunker Hill or the cupola of the Capitol" atop Beacon Hill. The "observatory" was acclaimed "a work of art and public enterprise."[72] On a clear day, one could survey the entire metropolitan area, seeing as far as the ocean, the Blue Hills of Milton, and the mountains of New Hampshire.

Fig. 10.32. George Washington Tower, Mount Auburn, engraving from Nathaniel Dearborn, 1856.

With construction of the tower, Mount Auburn's trustees completed all the major projects initially intended to "embellish" their picturesque landscape. Further "improvements" would be left up to proprietors of lots. Bigelow increasingly turned his attention to diversifying the ornamental plantings at Mount Auburn, especially as American tastes shifted from the picturesque to the gardenesque. Although the landscape of the cemetery would go through successive periods of change, losing its original woodsy charm, the eclectic "public" structures dating from its first quarter-century remain today, as durable and timeless as the granite from which they are made.

Bigelow's last major contribution to Mount Auburn was donation "to the proprietors" in 1870 of "a monumental statue imitated from the Sphinx of antiquity and designed to commemorate the Great War of American Conservation." He pro-

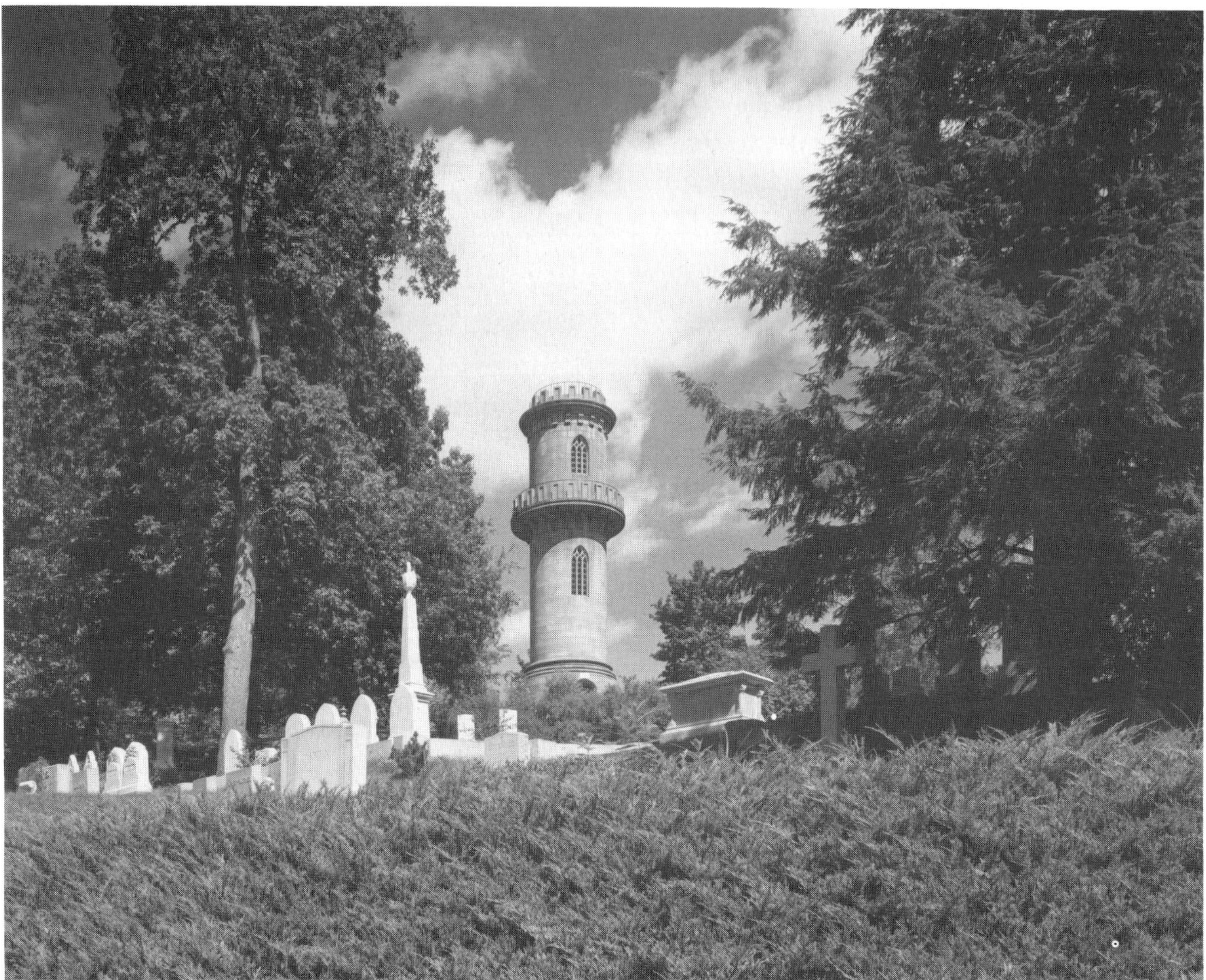

Fig. 10.33. Washington Tower, 62 feet, designed by Jacob Bigelow and built by Gridley J. Fox Bryant, 1843, photograph by Alan Ward, 1979.

posed use of surplus corporate funds to augment a subscription campaign for erection of a "public monument" to the Union dead as early as 1865, although there was no single lot reserved for the war dead at Mount Auburn. The previous year, a campaign in Cincinnati raised $25,000 to finance a statue of a Union "Soldier of the Line" sculpted by Randolph Rogers and cast in bronze in Munich for placement near the soldiers' burial section in Spring Grove Cemetery. Despite the controversy over corporate funding of historical statuary a decade before, patriotism in the immediate wake of the war led Mount Auburn's board tentatively to agree to allocate part of the funds, not exceeding $15,000; the subscription campaign was never undertaken in earnest, however. Trustees could not agree on an artist or a design in their informal discussions. Perhaps they considered sufficient the monument erected by the Company of Independent Cadets in 1867 in memory of eight members who died "in Defense of the Union During the Rebellion" in the South, but that monument also remembered previous wars fought by association members. (Fig. 10.34.) Besides, so many other campaigns were being mounted to build elaborate Civil War monuments in public places across New

England; and many proprietors erected monuments to their own war dead on Mount Auburn lots. (Fig. 10.35.) Nevertheless, Bigelow determined to proceed with the project at his own expense and following his own sense of mission to embellish Mount Auburn's landscape with commemorative structures compatible with the picturesque aesthetics that inspired the cemetery's original design.[73]

Bigelow insisted on the importance of erecting "a general and comprehensive" structure at Mount Auburn "To apply either to the magnitude of these events or to the greatness of their consequences"; however, he felt that "the wide range

Fig. 10.34. (*Below*) Soldiers' and Sailors' (Civil War) monument in Winthrop Square, Charlestown, Massachusetts, sculpted of Hallowell granite by Martin Milmore and dedicated 1872, photograph by Alan Ward, 1988.

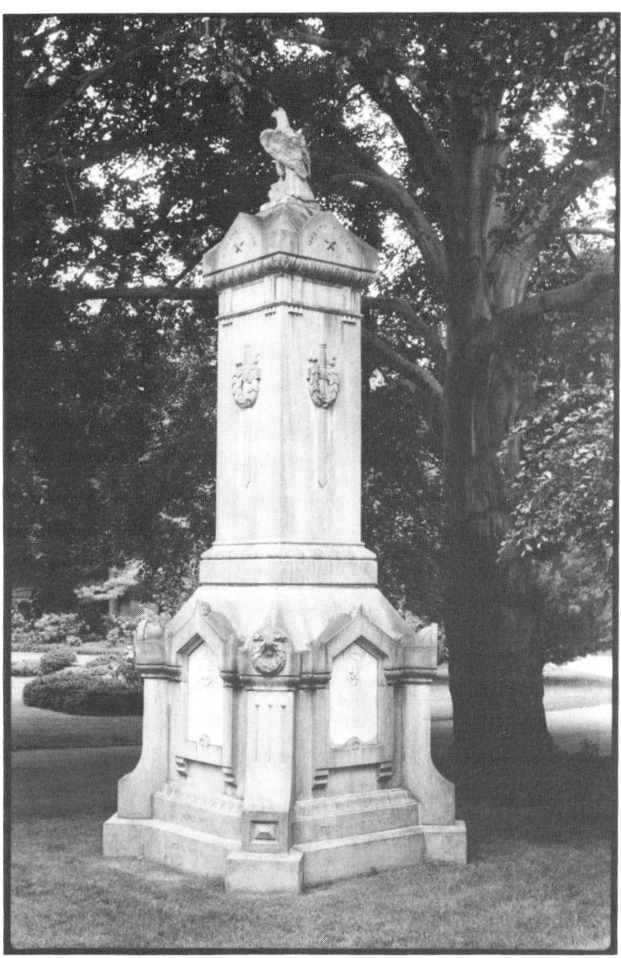

Fig. 10.35. (*Above*) Monument of the Company of Independent Cadets, Mount Auburn, 1867, photograph by Alan Ward, 1987.

of architectural ideas and combinations exhibited in pillars, pyramids, obelisks, altars, sarcophagi, and mausoleums, have been produced and reproduced in inexhaustible variety," while "the more significant creations of expressive sculpture have hitherto been less frequently attempted" in America "because they are more difficult of satisfactory execution."[74] He resolved that his cemetery should have a monument of heroic size and form, like the lion erected by Belgians on the battlefield of Waterloo[75] or the dying lion carved in a natural sandstone cliff at Lucerne in memory of the Swiss Guards massacred by the mob at the Tuileries Palace in Paris in 1792 in defense of the royal family of Louis XVI, considered the first

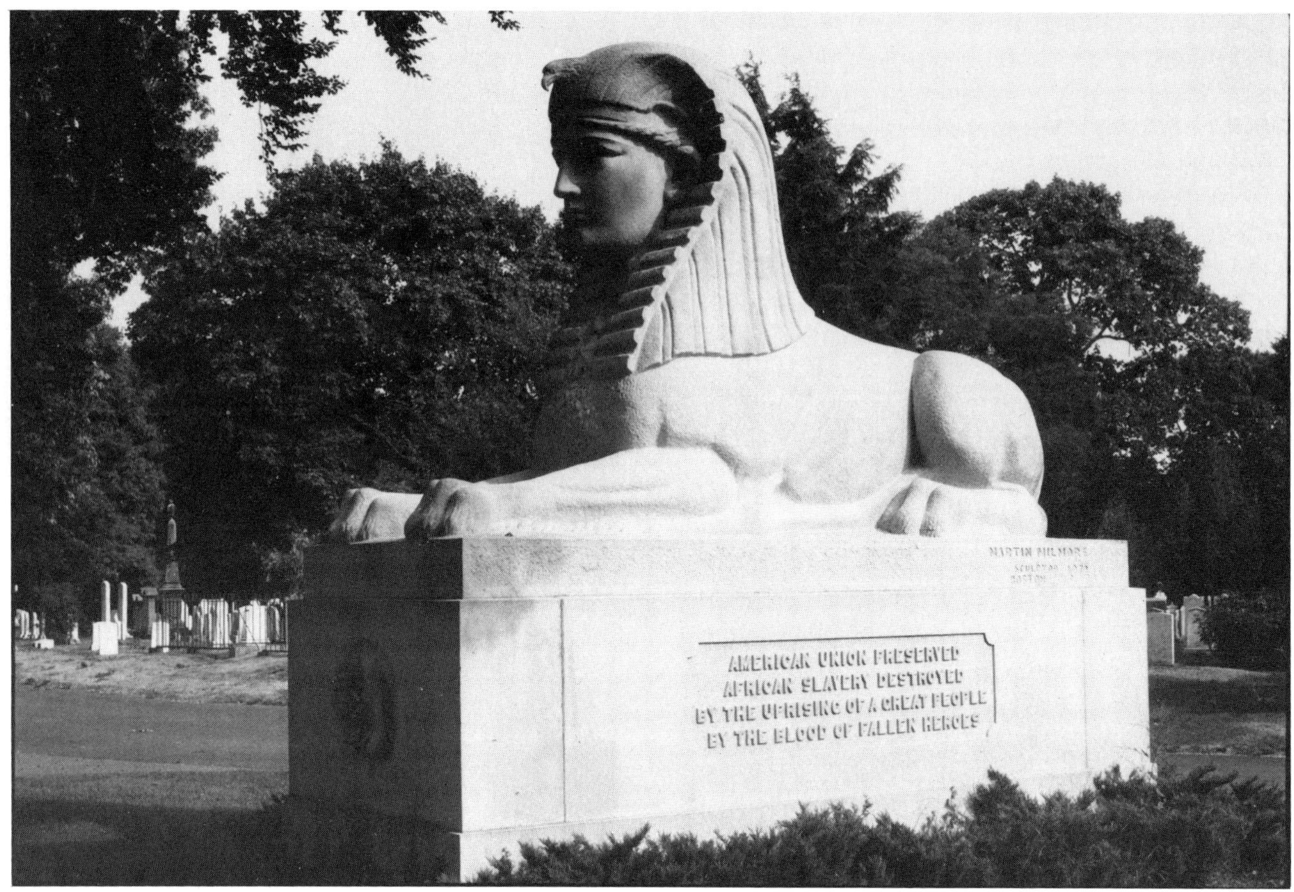

Fig. 10.36. Sphinx to the Union Dead sculpted by Martin Milmore, 1871, donated by Jacob Bigelow, photograph by Alan Ward, 1987.

monument erected in modern times to dead soldiers.

Bigelow took matters into his own hands, personally commissioning the sculptor Martin Milmore to execute a monumental sphinx out of a single block of Hallowell granite, fifteen feet long and eight high with a face three feet long. (Fig. 10.36.) Bigelow undoubtedly drew inspiration from the painting *The Questioner of the Sphinx* (1863) by Elihu Vedder in the collection of Mrs. Martin Brimmer, but Bigelow explained that he chose the mythical figure with obtuse, inscrutable symbolism "to restore for modern application the ancient form" with its "associations of repose, strength, beauty, and duration." (Fig. 10.37.) He considered it "an ideal personification of intellect and physical force"—an embodiment of the Yankee culture that emerged triumphant from the war.[76]

Use of the form of the sphinx in the cemetery made sense to Bigelow, who knew of its international popularity as a garden ornament and its use as a ceremonial device on important public buildings. A female sphinx, supposedly intended to evoke a spirit of melancholy musing on the past, occupies a central position in the garden grotto on Goethe's summer estate on the banks of the Ilum in Weimar. Edmund Burke praised the tendency of that landscape "to fill the mind with that sort of delightful horror, which is the most genuine effect and truest test of the sublime." Whether intended to be sublime or merely decorative, the form of the sphinx recurred in the gardens of Chenonceau and Versailles in France, at Blenheim in England, and in Edinburgh, to mention only a few examples of revivalistic uses of the sphinx in modern Europe.[77] (Fig. 10.38.)

The female sphinx was the sort described by early Greek poets, rather than the male sphinx, symbolic of monarchy and Egyptian in origin. Bigelow referred Milmore to views of restored sphinxes in Casas's *Voyage Pittoresque en Egypte et Syrie*. There was, Bigelow wrote, great historical variety in the appearance of the sphinx "from the almost Nubian and sometimes brute profile to the most perfect Caucasian face." Most Egyptian sphinxes, he judged, "though African . . . exhibit many examples of the most perfect intellectual human head" and even "some of the finest examples of the Indo-European faces."[78] Ironically, although Bigelow's notions of style betray a latent racism that even the most enlightened Yankee seldom escaped, his monument proclaims in Latin and English: "American Union Preserved, African Slavery Destroyed, By the Uprising of a Great People, By the Blood of Fallen Heroes."

Bigelow chose the sphinx "to typify in the present age of social transition a result of greater

Fig. 10.37. Elihu Vedder, *The Questioner of the Sphinx*, 1863, painting. Courtesy of the Boston Museum of Fine Arts.

magnitude in the history of the world than were all the revolutions and conquests of the primeval East." He wanted it "to express the present attitude and character of a nation perhaps as far remote in time from the building of the pyramids as was that event from the earliest constructions attempted by man. The same ideal from which . . . on the dividing ridge of time has looked backward on unmeasured antiquity, now looks forward to illuminate progress. It stands as a landmark of a state of things which the world has not before seen—a great, warlike and successful nation, in the plentitude and full consciousness of its power, suddenly reversing its energies . . . to resume the still familiar arts of peace and good will." Bigelow wondered, "What symbol can better express the attributes of a just, calm, and dignified self-reliance than one which combines power with attractiveness, strength of the lion with the beauty and benignity of woman."[79]

Mount Auburn's sphinx is of Greek rather than Egyptian origin, and indeed the word "sphinx" is Greek. This derivation suggests additional symbolic significance Bigelow had in mind in commissioning such a monument to the Union dead. The Greek sphinx was a ghostlike monster with a female head and body of a lion, believed arbitrarily to carry off youths and to be present at fatal battles. The most famous of the Greek sphinxes is the one encountered by Oedipus on the road from Corinth to Thebes, unknowingly to fulfill his destiny. Oedipus overcomes the ordeal, answers the riddle of the omniscient questioner, and proceeds on his way to the predetermined future. Likewise, Americans emerging from the Civil War with the Union intact could turn away from the divisive past to future progress.

Fig. 10.38. Sphinx in the English gardens of the Petit Trianon, Versailles, photograph by Alan Ward, 1985.

According to Bigelow's meticulous instructions, Milmore carved an Egyptian lotus, symbolic of human life, on the south side of the pedestal and an American water lily on the north. Another inscription on the monument is the words "Jacob Bigelow Statuit et Dedicavit." The doctor vehemently protested to John T. Bradlee, his successor as Mount Auburn's president, that his name not be displayed conspicuously as "ostentation rather than the gratitude to the donor." Some trustees wanted to place Bigelow's name prominently on the front of the pedestal, in essence turning the sphinx into a monument to the man who had originally proposed creation of the "rural" cemetery in 1825, who had served as a trustee for forty-eight years and as president for twenty-six, but Bigelow threatened not to transfer ownership of the statue to the corporation unless such personal recognition was relegated to a less conspicuous place on the side.[80]

In accepting the statue in August of 1871, trustees described it as "illustrated and inscribed" by Bigelow's own "classic pen." It was "an evidence alike of his private virtues and of his patriotism . . . a most fitting crown to all the valuable services rendered to the Cemetery, as chief among those who originated and planned it." The board funded its installation in a central location in front of the chapel, symbolically facing North. It engendered only minor controversy when one proprietor cautioned that in such a place, encircled by a carriageway, it would "occasion fright to horses."[81]

Jacob Bigelow never *saw* the completed sphinx in place. Cataracts deprived him of sight in his last years. By early 1871, he complained that he could no longer read or write. The architectural historian Wayne Andrews exaggerated the story of Bigelow's demise, however, claiming that the doctor "lost his mind—though only after translating *Mother Goose* into Latin." Bigelow did the translation, finding intellectual recreation in his declining years as he undoubtedly rationalized that the work would provide an early introduction to classical studies for very young Americans of the future. Work on such a project does not indicate dementia but continuation of intellectual acuity and didactic intentions that underlay most of the projects Bigelow undertook over his long and productive life. Andrews colored his description of Bigelow's inspection of the completed sphinx in a most unsympathetic way: "The day was to come when he would totter through the gates of Mount Auburn on the arms of his friends; reaching the Strange Sphinx Monument he set up in memory of the Civil War dead, he would finger it fondly."[82] Indeed, friends led Bigelow to the statue and watched sympathetically as the blind physician feebly fingered its contours as the only way he could discern them. Over the next six years, Bigelow progressively succumbed to deafness and paralysis as well, spending his last years bedridden but rationally complaining to loved ones of his diminishing physical capabilities. His papers give no evidence of senility.

On Bigelow's resignation in 1871, the eleven-member board immediately sent "the originator and founder of Mount Auburn" an "unanimous and urgent solicitation" that he delay his retirement. Bigelow complied, attending his last board meeting on September 25, 1872. Trustees issued the resolution that "every object [at Mount Auburn], its entrance gateway, its chapel, its beautiful avenues, paths, and fountains, all bear witness to his science, skill, and taste, and signally identify him with Mount Auburn." Bigelow was not, as we have seen, solely responsible for creation of Mount Auburn's landscape; its initial design was the product of Henry A. S. Dearborn and the efforts of other trustees, workers, and superintendents. But Bigelow must be credited with having made many substantial contributions to its subsequent development. Trustees commissioned a marble bust of Bigelow from the "celebrated" sculptor Henry Dexter, who had done many of Mount Auburn's monuments. This "suitable testimonial and token of appreciation of the long and continued and faithful services" of the aged physician was placed on a bracket over the main entrance of the chapel in November of 1872.[83] (Fig. 10.39.)

Bigelow drew consolation in his last days from letters of thanks sent to him by the likes of a Brookline, Massachusetts, mother who wrote that by his gift of the sphinx she was assured "that the blood of her sons had not been shed in vain."

Along with his wife, Mary, who frequently hosted meetings of the Widows' Society in her home in those years, he spent even more time than other Americans in mourning Civil War losses. Bigelow's eulogist, the Reverend George E. Ellis, portrayed him as "placid and tranquil, occasionally speculating as to what he was or what he was waiting for." In the end, Bigelow even rationalized his blindness, reminding "a friend that it was our human wont, as we lay down at night, to close our eyes before we actually fell asleep." Bigelow died on January 10, 1879. After services at the Unitarian King's Chapel in Boston, he was buried under the modest neoclassical marble sarcophagus he had erected more than four decades before.[84]

The death of Jacob Bigelow marked the passing of the formative era of Mount Auburn Cemetery, characterized by development of a picturesque landscape and a Whiggish historical sensibility. Younger generations of Bostonians, who began to assume control of the corporation in 1850s, had less complex ambitions for the institution as an agency of culture than did its founders. They did realize, however, that Mount Auburn was an important place to preserve, although not in static form. Even after their cemetery had ceased to attract throngs of visitors and to be emulated for its landscape design, it would remain through the next century very usable for burials, personal commemoration, and display of horticultural taste—if not for a usable past.

Fig. 10.39. Portrait bust of Dr. Jacob Bigelow by Henry Dexter, 1872.

11

The Rage for Mount Auburn: Sacred Site or Pleasure Ground

Where else shall we go with the musings of Sadness, or for the indulgence of Grief; where to cool the burning brow of Ambition, or relieve the swelling heart of disappointment? We can find no better spot for the rambles of curiosity, health, or pleasure; none sweeter for the whispers of affection among the living.

—"Cemetery at Mount Auburn," *New England Farmer* 10:11 (Sept. 1831)

Then let this haunt be sacred. For the feet
Of strangers, here in future days shall turn,
As to some Mecca of philosophy;
And here the admiring youth shall come to seek
Some relic of the great and good—whose fame
Shall gather greenness from the hand of Time.

—Mrs. Lydia H. Sigourney, quoted by Cornelia Walter in *Mount Auburn Illustrated* (1847)

IMMEDIATELY AFTER ITS FOUNDING, Mount Auburn captured the public imagination, and its popularity extended far beyond the local genteel class of its founders. It became a favorite "resort" for both New Englanders and visitors, who read the monuments or simply communed with nature. Couples frequented the cemetery for courtship walks, cultivating melancholy emotions by reading sentimental verses engraved on the stones of those who died young. Teachers urged youth to visit the cemetery to learn from the exemplary lives of notables interred there, to acquire proper ambitions and aspirations for their own lives. Ministers and moralists further argued that the place served as a catalyst for virtue. It displayed family values and enduring social cohesion in the face of the ultimate disruptive force—death. Visitors would profit spiritually from its many lessons. (Fig. 11.1.)

The popularity of Mount Auburn can only fully be understood in the context of the growing sentimentalized romanticism in the second quarter of the century, which elaborated upon the semi-secularization of devotional values that had begun in the wake of the revolutionary era. The cemetery duplicated the melancholy, allegorical landscapes found in mourning pictures, the stylized painted

Fig. 11.1 Mount Auburn panorama looking toward the Chapel and Fresh Pond to the north, engraving by James Smillie, 1847.

and embroidered compositions regularly executed by schoolgirls and young ladies for display in family parlors after the turn of the nineteenth century. Neoclassicism fostered a taste for pastoral landscapes as a new Arcadia, symbol of the new nation. English landscape aesthetics further loaded taste for such landscapes with associations that permeated romantic literature and material culture in America into the 1840s.

Many people went to Mount Auburn, however, simply to find an "asylum" from the increasingly hectic life of the burgeoning city, a pleasant pastoral place to promenade. Mount Auburn was one of the few parklike settings in the metropolitan area at a time when the mall on the Common was the only green, open space in Boston. Although Horace Gray, Charles P. Curtis, and other horticulturists had won a charter as Proprietors of Botanic Gardens to be located next to the Common in 1837, this venture was short-lived; and the Public Garden was not completed as parkland until 1860. The "Emerald Necklace" park system designed by Frederick Law Olmsted did not provide extensive recreational space until the 1880s and 1890s. For these and other reasons, Mount Auburn was Boston's chief attraction during its first half-century.

Mount Auburn's founders created the sort of place proper Yankees considered acceptable for recreation. Just as their Puritan forefathers rejected frivolity of leisure at the Maypole of Merrymount, many mid-century Boston Brahmins disapproved of new forms of recreation appearing in the metropolitan area. For instance, the vicinity of Mount Auburn gained favor for leisure even before the making of the cemetery. In 1792, Jacob Wyeth began development of a "rural resort" on eight acres of his father's farmland on Fresh Pond just north of Sweet Auburn. Wyeth built a tavern, which was called a hotel in the 1830s; until the Civil War, it won a thriving business, with diversions like lawn bowling and boating. But genteel New Englanders frowned on such amusements, preferring contemplative strolls through Sweet Auburn or the rural countryside still close to the city.

Mount Auburn provided for passive, edifying recreation for the humble and the great, the young and the old, especially if one's family owned a burial lot to ensure free access to the grounds by carriage. George Ticknor Curtis, Joseph Story's son-in-law, observed in 1834 that the cemetery permitted people "to rid themselves of Time among the final homes of those who have exchanged it for eternity." (Fig. 11.2.) Impressionable schoolgirls like Mary Tyler Peabody gloried in the romantic melancholy of the place. Mary wrote to her friend Miss Rawlins Pickman of Salem in the fall of 1835 about the wonderful emotions stirred by a visit to the new cemetery one Friday evening: "How can I describe the feeling with which I looked again upon our gorgeous woods and heard the song of the wind in the pine groves. I should like to sleep there, with that beautiful soul sighing my requiem. Nothing that the hand of man has done was so interesting to me as the grave of a young wife, whose simple monument is surrounded by a railing and decked with beautiful flowers." Mary concluded, "I always feel as if I wanted to stay when I get there."[1]

The textile industrialist Amos Lawrence, who had renounced drink, smoke, and theater in his youth, told his diary of many days spent at Mount Auburn, where he and his three brothers had enclosed the largest family lot in the cemetery. Lawrence mused, "A better taste is growing among us. . . . It is decidedly better than the old fashion of making these tenements look as dreary as anything in the world can look." He hoped that proprietors would avoid ostentation in monuments, so as to "speak to their living owners and induce them to labor to merit . . . a good word from the future lookers on."[2] (Fig. 11.3.) Charles Sumner, a peace activist and abolitionist, used the cemetery as retreat from the heat of national politics on the eve of the Civil War. Lore also holds that a messenger found Franklin Pierce sitting under a tree at Mount Auburn when he came to notify the future president that the 1852 Democratic convention in Baltimore had nominated him compromise candidate.

Many New Englanders purchased lots at Mount Auburn primarily to have full access to the place for themselves and their guests. Cleveland Amory called "the love of funerals and funeral going" the favorite custom of Proper Bostonians and the basis of First Family social history; Mount Auburn was the focal point of such activity. James Russell Lowell described a trip through Mount Auburn as a necessary part of the ritual of Boston hospitality, *de rigueur* after a Beacon Hill dinner "with people you never saw before nor ever wish to see again." Lowell mused, "Your memory of the dinner is expected to reconcile you to the prospect of the

Fig. 11.2. Solitary contemplation at the Judge Story monument on Narcissus Path, engraving by James Smillie, 1847.

graveyard." Lowell aimed his criticism at social convention and not at the cemetery, where he personally loved to stroll, consulting the Muse. Lowell admitted his view of the cemetery was jaundiced to the point of "getting treasonable," especially in contrast to the many others who waxed poetic after visits to the cemetery. For instance, it was called the "Gateway to Heaven" by one Boston lady and her seamstress in a three-part verse about Mount Auburn "as it was on the day of creation, as it is, and as it shall be on the day of resurrection."[3]

Such was the intended response. In consecrating Mount Auburn in 1831, Story promised that the cemetery would "preach lessons to which none may refuse to listen, and which all that live must hear." Three decades later, Wilson Flagg called the place "a school of both religion and philosophy." He urged, "To these consecrated grounds we would resort as we attend service in the house of God, to indulge in serious meditation and to ponder on those themes which are neglected by the multitude during the hurry of business or in the idle whirl of pleasure." In the interim, many individuals followed and echoed advice received from clergy and sentimental writers promoting the idea that Mount Auburn was a new sort of sacred place, an Eden minus Adam's Fall with Nature resanctified and each visitor apt to be saved. The cemetery's naturalism harmonized well with lessons of

Fig. 11.3. Family lot of the four Lawrence brothers, 1,300 square feet, the largest at Mount Auburn, between Cypress and Chapel avenues, photograph by Alan Ward, 1979.

Fig. 11.4. Mount Auburn's chapel, engraving by James Smillie, 1847.

liberal religion and proper Christian optimism. John Greenleaf Adams urged acceptance of the idea of death represented by the cemetery: "Old and crude notions of the ghastly and the awful should be exchanged for sentiments more befitting believers in Him who is the Resurrection and the Life. . . . If earth must be a sepulchre, let it also be a garden." Unitarian ministers like William Ellery Channing, Henry Ware, George Putnam, and John Pierpont proved particularly instrumental in promoting the cemetery locally and nationally in print and from pulpits as an educational institution imparting lessons of moral philosophy; most emphasized the nondenominational appeal of the place. Flagg observed, "We need not be the disciples of a theological faith to feel the truth," to hear "a new gospel of consolation," albeit secularized, and to learn lessons of "moral philosophy."[4] (Fig. 11.4.)

Secular writers proved even more active than the clergy in stressing the moral influences of Mount Auburn. They urged visits there to rouse "religious sentiments" even in unbelievers caught up in contemporary "uncertainty of religious truths." The Boston newspaperman Joseph Buckingham offered the cemetery as spiritual medicine: "Reader! if you would have the sympathies of your nature awakened, your earthly affections purified, your anxieties chastened and subdued, go to Mount Auburn. Go not for the gratification of idle curiosity, to comment with the eye of a critic upon the forms of the monuments or the taste of those who placed them there. . . . Go not there with cold indifference to shock the sensibility of the bereaved with your antic and unseemly behavior. . . . But go to read and to learn the lesson

Fig. 11.5. (*Above*) Monument of John H. Gossler of Hamburg on Yarrow Path, engraving by James Smillie, 1847.

Fig. 11.6. (*Below*) John Lowell monument on Willow Avenue, engraving by Smillie, 1847.

which you must transmit to those who come after you."[5] (Fig. 11.5.)

Similarly, Cornelia Walter, the author of *Mount Auburn Illustrated* (1847), advocated "meditative wanderings" on which one might "gain a lesson from nature." At the cemetery, visitors would "learn to conform our lives to the order of her [nature's] works in view of both the present and future." Walter echoed Bigelow's thoughts about the cemetery and recommended Mount Auburn because of the lessons of moral philosophy built into the landscape. "Those periods of meditation," Walter promised, "derived from the enticements of Mount Auburn will remain constantly fixed in the recollection as bright oases in the pilgrimage of life." Mount Auburn was a place for "intellectual indulgence" to the liking of those preferring the "pleasures of melancholy" to more frivolous leisure.[6] (Fig. 11.6.)

Walter repeated a philosophy of place familiar to literary Bostonians who read Shaftesbury, Pope, Burke, and other British advocates of the philosophic values of landscaped gardens: "Thus it is seen that *taste*, whether exhibited in flower-crowned mounds, or in the chaste and classic monument, may exist in a rural cemetery in close connection with *morals;* and it is no less true that every pure ideal of religion and virtue grows in beauty by the food upon which it feeds."[7] Proper Bostonians hoped that their cemetery would provide spiritual nourishment and be an agent of progress toward cultural as well as moral excellence, the means to a great and ambitious end; it would thus exert social control through acculturation.

Intellectual Bostonians agreed with Walter and Buckingham, the latter of whom declared, "it is wise and beneficial for men to familiarize themselves . . . with the certainty of that death from which none can hope to be exempt, to contemplate more frequently the tomb to which they must all descend." What better place to do so than in a natural setting, where the processes of birth, maturation, decline, and renewal with the seasons reminded one that death was part of an inexorable system? Nature provided metaphoric forms replacing the grim imagery of death inherited from the Puritan past. Buckingham concluded, "There can be no good reason why death should be associated with sorrow and gloom, as it is the common practice of mankind to do." The cemetery itself represented more optimistic notions of death, "the still higher and more ennobling light of a passage from mortality to immortality—from the darkness, doubt, and ignorance of mere humanity, to the light, the confidence, and the full meridian of intelligence and happiness to which this immortality will lead the spirit." Mount Auburn promised to condition acceptance of death "with resignation and joy."[8]

In her *Advice to Mothers* (1831), Lydia Maria Child urged women to take their children on Sunday walks through the cemetery. "So important do I consider cheerful association with death, that I wish to see our graveyards laid out with walks and trees and beautiful shrubs as places of promenade," she wrote, and certainly Mount Auburn fulfilled her desire.[9] Indeed, James Smillie's illustrations of Mount Auburn in the mid-1840s show parents introducing toddlers to the cemetery. (Fig. 11.7.)

Mount Auburn was to be more than a pleasant place in which to pass leisure time in a manner acceptable to liberal Protestant moralists, however. One writer in the *Christian Examiner* in 1836 believed the cemetery would stir "the sentiment of retrospection and reverence" for a common American past grounded in moralistic principles and also provide antidotes for the disagreeable effects of the modern age, "the busy competition . . . the hurried, ambitious spirit" rampant in prosperous cities. The English moralist Henry Tuckerman thought such cemeteries fostered "that association with the past essential to intellectual dignity." which was fast disappearing. Lessons learned in the cemetery would counteract a growing materialism that seemed to be leading Americans to live only in the present, forgetting their personal and public past. According to Tuckerman, "Sentiment is the great conservative principle of society; those instincts of patriotism, local attachment, family affection, human sympathy, reverence for truth, age, valor, and wisdom . . . constitute the latent force of civil society." Mount Auburn objectified these qualities. Emotional and moral "primal instincts" rediscovered by a visit to the cemetery, according to this view, would bolster and renew

Fig. 11.7. Mother bringing children to William Ellery Channing monument, engraving by James Smillie, 1847.

republican virtue.[10]

Nostalgia as well as the taste for pantheism and historicism current in American romanticism colored the opinions of many authors who considered Mount Auburn a moralistically didactic place. For instance, one Lowell mill girl wrote in 1840: "Mount Auburn! how soothing and tranquilizing is the remembrance of thy deep and quiet beauty! . . . As we stray through thy pleasant woods . . . we go back in imagination to our own homes and stand by the graves of our loved ones; and we remember the crushing weight of utter loneliness which pressed upon us as the green turf hid them from our view." This young woman found Mount Auburn an asylum from the industrialized work-place into which she had been thrust, which was a severe contrast to life in the rural New England hometowns of herself and her co-workers.[11] Those yearning for a sense of community lost or for the timeless rhythms of pre-industrial life found gratification at Mount Auburn, which, after all, drew its name from Oliver Goldsmith's Sweet Auburn.

The moralistic sentimentalism focused on Mount Auburn recurred in local newspapers, ladies' magazines, and gift books from the 1830s through the 1850s. One writer in the *Ladies' Repository* observed that "a poet looking for a time" upon Consecration Dell "will have his heart stirred and may indite words of holy import or be reminded of the soul-language of a brother bard, 'Thou, God, art here; thou fill'st the solitude. Thou art in the soft winds that run along the summit of those trees.' " The writer suggested that the visitor, so moved, should "kneel down and consecrate his soul to God." The essay urged the visitor to select his own burial spot to be "occasionally visited and cultivated" as a reminder of mortality and "of the great work we have to do prior to our departure to the other world, and of the value of that faith which makes it safe to die." The designed pastoral landscape seemed far more appropriate to liberal religious convictions than did the traditional burying grounds that epitomized the old Calvinism, and a host of writers found poetic inspiration at Mount Auburn.[12]

Mrs. Sarah Josepha Hale, one of the most prolific of the sentimentalists, attempted through verse to convince the public to accept the naturalistic earthen burial system proposed by Jacob Bigelow: "Away with human pageantries, the Temple's solemn gloom! / No need of Mausoleum, if ye give the Dead but room."[13] The theme of cemetery hallowed by Nature rather than by Church appealed equally to the Cambridge poetess Caroline F. Orne. In her long verse *Sweet Auburn and Mount Auburn* (1844), Orne nostalgically described how a pristine natural landscape, the Arcadia of her childhood, had been transformed into a "City of the Silent . . . sacred to the deepest affections."

Two hundred years! and, lo! the forest deep
Becomes the silent land of dreamless sleep.
Ye spirits of my sires! while earth shall stand,
Be guardian genii of this hallowed land.
Methinks your spirit voices oft I hear.

Orne sensed her relationship to the past during visits to Mount Auburn; she recognized as well the spiritual functions of the place for others. She invited her readers:

Unto their Cities of the Silent come,
And look with faith's clear eye beyond the tomb.

But, like Dearborn and Story, Orne reminded visitors to be on their best behavior:

'Tis holy ground—this City of the Dead
Let no rude accents of untimely mirth
Break the calm stillness of this sacred earth.

Although mistaken in many of her other judgments about the cultural origins of Mount Auburn, Ann Douglas rightly observes that "the cemetery functioned not like experience but like literature." Literary descriptions of melancholy landscapes inspired its design, and it was intended that the landscape function like literature in instilling certain sentiments in visitors. But Mount Auburn also inspired numerous poems, religious tracts, short stories, moralistic essays, and travel narratives, which augmented its fame nationally and even internationally.[14]

Yet some of the sentimentalists displayed a mournfulness too negative for many of the cemetery's Unitarian proponents. William Ellery Channing found Mrs. Felicia Dorothea Hemans's poetry too gloomy, "her sense of the evils of life . . . too keen." Channing declared his "love to be touched, moved, but not depressed." Mount Auburn aided cultivation of a proper optimism, Channing thought; he resented attempts to exploit the sentimentalism inherent in the cemetery. Still, tragic personal loss, nostalgia, and durable resolve of family cohesion became formulaic themes in mid-century popular culture, purveyed by the likes of Mrs. Hemans, Mrs. Lydia Huntley Sigourney, and Mrs. Sara Payson Willis (1812–72). Mrs. Willis, better known as Fanny Fern, sold almost a hundred thousand copies of *Fern Leaves from Fanny's Portfolio* in 1853, the first year of its publication.[15]

It was not only the sentimentalists who consulted the Muse at Mount Auburn. Nathaniel Hawthorne found the stuff of romance in the allegorical landscape. His tale "The Lily's Quest," published in 1839 in Mount Auburn's first guidebook, described lovers' futile search for an appropriate place on which to build a temple of love. Adam Forrester and Lilias Fay are followed through various seemingly ideal, picturesque landscapes by a melancholy, black-caped old man who repeatedly quashes their plans with tales of tragedies associated with each site. In the end, after they select a spot on an old rural estate and when construction of the building is nearly complete, Lilias dies. The lovers have built a temple with white marble columns and dome "planned after an ancient mausoleum" and "intended for a tomb."

Hawthorne concludes, "the pilgrim lovers were seeking not a temple of earthly joy but a tomb for themselves and their posterity." Each place they liked was reminiscent of parts of Mount Auburn; and the story seems almost like an advertisement offering desirable, romantic plots on which real-life couples could erect their own elegaic structures after the fashion of the fictitious lovers.[16]

Sylvester Judd's *Margaret: A Tale of the Real and Ideal: Blight and Bloom,* published in Boston in 1845, is similar to Hawthorne's romance. A young man and woman, Evelyn and Margaret, establish a utopian community called Mons Christi; the parallels between it and Mount Auburn are many. Mons Christi was intended to embody liberal religious principles, albeit with a huge, central cross rather than a tower, and, like the cemetery, it fostered high culture in many ways. It had a tasteful display of marble statuary and sites named after plants. There were also fountains and gardens, music rooms, observatories, halls of art, crops of rye and corn on adjacent land, statues of Peace and Truth, and marble muses—all the amenities Dearborn originally proposed for Mount Auburn. Judd described it as an earthly paradise where men of all nations met. Undoubtedly, he drew inspiration from Mount Auburn, which he frequented in the 1830s while a Harvard Divinity student.[17]

Edgar Allen Poe provided a more critical description of a similar landscape in his "Domain of Arnheim" (1847). Ellison, Poe's fictional landscape gardener, chose "a spot not far from a populous city" for his estate on "land of wonderful fertility and beauty, affording a panoramic prospect very little less in extent than that of Aetna, and . . . surpassing the far-famed view from that mountain in all true elements of the picturesque." There, "The thought of nature still remained, but her character seemed to have undergone modification . . . Not a dead branch—not a withered leaf—not a stray pebble—not a patch of brown earth was anywhere visible . . . it bewildered the eye." When Poe visited Boston, maintenance at Mount Auburn undoubtedly had yet to reach this level of perfection, although increasingly as the century progressed, professionalizing superintendents aspired to achieve this ideal. Poe, however, considered it unnatural.[18]

Poe described Arnheim as an attempt to re-create an Eden built on a foundation of inheritance. He warned that as in Eden, "In the most enchanting of natural landscapes, there will always be found a defect or an excess—many excesses and defects. While the component parts may defy, individually, the highest skill of the artist, the arrangement of these parts will always be susceptible to improvement." Poe considered "geological disturbances . . . of form and color grouping," at Arnheim as in New England, "prognostic of *death.*" Accumulations of detail made Arnheim's landscape mature and change gradually. These messages had currency through the romantic era, but they struck a particular chord of recognition with those familiar with Mount Auburn. The highly controlled garden at Arnheim marked an effort to transcend natural change and death, but continual attempts at "improvement" bore the seeds of destruction of Nature in Poe's fictional world and indeed, eventually, for a time in the late nineteenth century, in the real landscape of the cemetery.[19]

Few accounts of the cemetery contained negative opinions. The orthodox Congregational minister Nehemiah Adams of the Essex Street Church, later author of the sentimental "Agnes and the Key of Her Little Coffin," worried in 1834 that public enjoyment of Mount Auburn would foster pantheism and obliterate the fear of death that theological conservatives still attempted to foster. The Reverend Adams wrote, "if it is possible by natural means to lose the dreadful associations of dissolution in the grave, a burial in some of the lovely places of Mount Auburn seems sure to assist it. All that meets the eye there above and around the grave is pure and beautiful." He decried the calm submission to death represented in the new cemetery, preferring the sterner Calvinistic warnings of postmortem fate. He exhorted the orthodox to consider the scene when the graves give up their dead on Judgment Day. Adams did not foresee the purely recreational enjoyment many people would find there independent of spiritual lessons.[20] Love of nature developed in a straightforward, secular way, despite the best efforts of ministers and cemetery guidebook writers.

Many writers recognized the importance of

imagination in stirring visitors' retrospection and melancholy, and literature preconditioned the proper state of mind for appreciation of Mount Auburn. Early guidebooks contained as much prose and poetry as they did detailed descriptions of the cemetery landscape. *The Picturesque Pocket Companion and Visitor's Guide Through Mount Auburn* (1839), the first publication on the cemetery for the general public, included an essay by John Pierpont, "The Grave and the Tomb," advocating earthen burials; Hawthorne's "Lily's Quest"; and sentimental poems by William Cullen Bryant, Mrs. Felicia Dorothea Hemans, Charles Sprague, and others. The editor interspersed more verse with the engraved illustrations of over fifty monuments and tombs. This and subsequent books and pamphlets functioned as spiritual guides in addition to pointing out major sights. The anonymous author of the *Picturesque Pocket Companion* pondered, "Will [the musing moralist of future generations] not think how once, with the first flush of spring's verdure, and how again in the summer's sultry hours, the denizens of the city's populous streets *here* at least could wrap themselves so in solitude and gloom? How *here*, even those to whom trial and toil had made the world a weariness for the time, might learn from the depths of nature in intervals of solemn but refreshing meditation to look forth with complacency and renew themselves as they looked through the tree-tops of the mountain-summit on many a glorious vision."[21] *The Picturesque Pocket Companion* aided use of the cemetery as a spiritual retreat and place of philosophical recreation.

Nathaniel Dearborn, a Boston publisher, had much the same intent in issuing *Dearborn's Guide through Mount Auburn . . . for the Benefit of Strangers*, a slim, portable, fifty-page booklet published annually through the 1850s and 1860s and sold for twenty cents. (Fig. 11.8.) It contained a map, over sixty engravings, and a good deal of the secular moral philosophy so popular with Unitarians and Evangelicals alike. It led visitors through the cemetery along a prescribed route, pointing out noteworthy interments and monuments and providing short pieces of sentimental verse to set the proper melancholy frame of mind. Many of the moralistic poems had practical, hor-

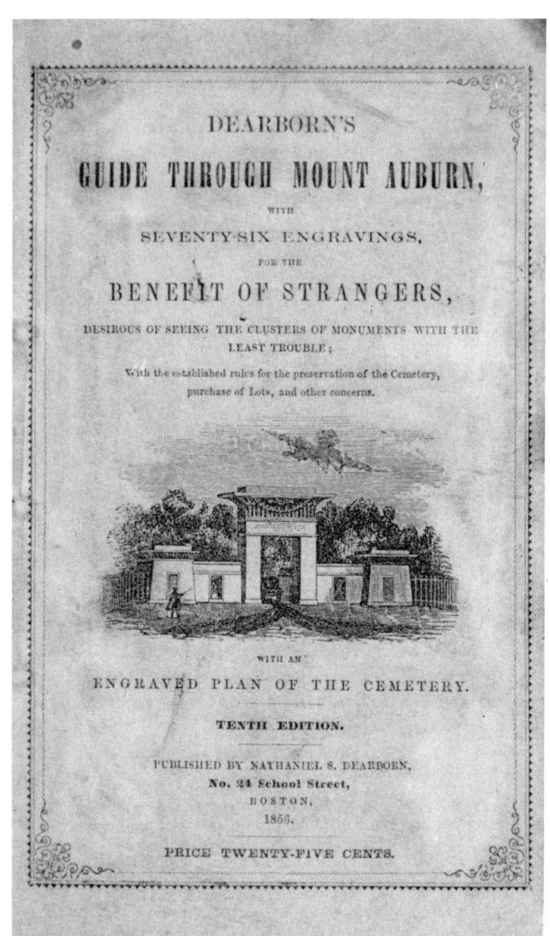
DEARBORN'S

GUIDE THROUGH MOUNT AUBURN,

WITH

SEVENTY-SIX ENGRAVINGS,

FOR THE

BENEFIT OF STRANGERS,

DESIROUS OF SEEING THE CLUSTERS OF MONUMENTS WITH THE LEAST TROUBLE;

With the established rules for the preservation of the Cemetery, purchase of Lots, and other concerns.

WITH AN

ENGRAVED PLAN OF THE CEMETERY.

TENTH EDITION.

PUBLISHED BY NATHANIEL S. DEARBORN,
No. 24 School Street,
BOSTON,
1856.

PRICE TWENTY-FIVE CENTS.

Fig. 11.8. Cover from *Dearborn's Guide*, 1856.

Fig. 11.9. Illustrations and verse in *Dearborn's Guide*, 1856.

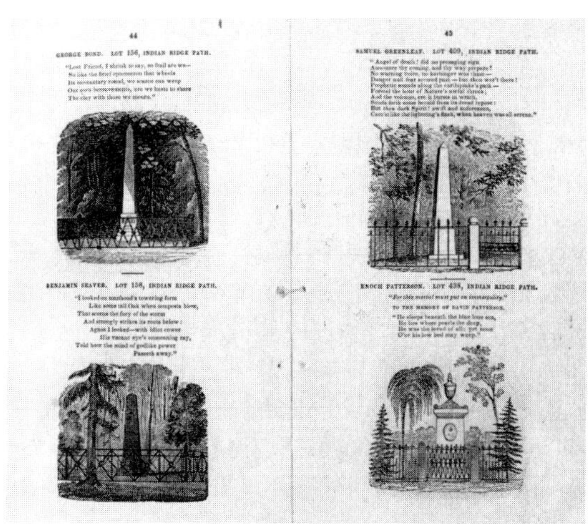

tatory messages reminiscent of *Poor Richard's* aphorisms. (Fig. 11.9.) For instance, when the visitor reached the monument to Robert Gould Shaw, Sr., he read:

Be wise to-day; 'tis madness to defer:
Next day the fatal precedent will plead;
Thus on, till wisdom is push'd out of life
Procrastination is the thief of time;
Year after year it steals, till all are fled,
And to the mercies of a moment leaves
The vast concerns of an eternal scene.

The verse placed next to the view of Richard Haughton's monument offered advice for the visitor harried by the pace of urbanized life:

We censure Nature for a span too short;
That span too short, we tax as tedious too;
Torture invention, all expedients tire,
To lash the lingering moments into speed,
And whirl us (happy riddance) from ourself.

A similar truism accompanied the illustration of S. P. Allen's lot:

At thirty man suspects himself a fool;
Knows it at forty, and reforms his plan;
At fifty chides his infamous delay,
Pushes his prudent purpose to resolve;
In all the magnanimity of thought
Resolves and re-solves; then dies the same.

Poems in *Dearborn's Guide* urged wisdom, diligence, work, moderation, humility, stewardship of wealth, and other civic virtues. Verse expressing more personal, melancholy sentiments was taken directly from monuments. Although Nathaniel Dearborn published his guide independent of aid from the corporation, trustees made sure that a supply of these, their own maps, and catalogues of proprietors was kept on hand by Mount Auburn's gatekeeper.[22]

Levi Merriam Stevens claimed that his competing *Guide,* subtitled *A Handbook for Passengers over the Cambridge Railroad,* aimed "not to describe Mount Auburn as any one thinks it should be, but to lead the visitor through the most interesting portions of the Cemetery, to call attention to

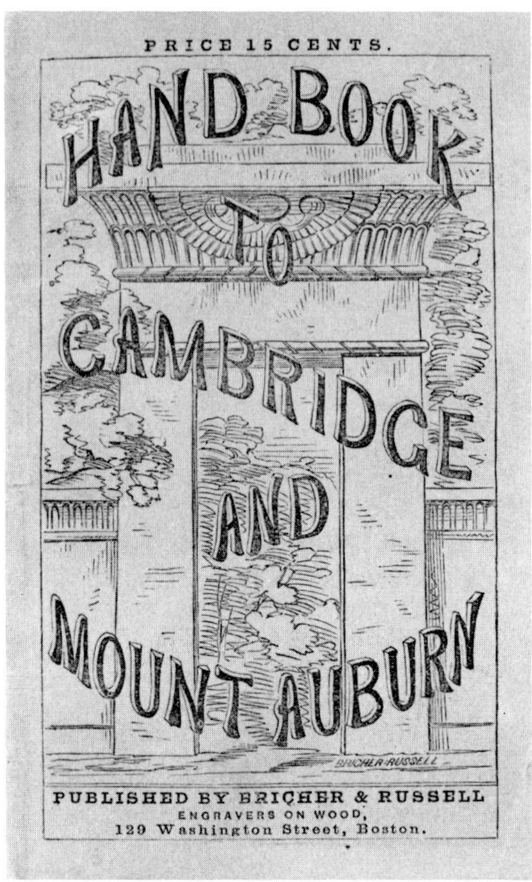

Fig. 11.10. Cover from fourth edition of the *Handbook for Passengers over the Cambridge Railroad,* 1860.

everything on the route worthy of observation, and thus enable him to view Mount Auburn as it is—as Nature, Art and Affection have made it." The seventy-five-page Stevens *Guide,* first published in 1856 and updated annually into the 1860s, provided illustrations and detailed descriptions of major monuments as well as selected epitaphs and funerary verse. (Fig. 11.10.) It emphasized Mount Auburn's moralistic functions: "To what better place can we go . . . to cool the burning brow of ambition, or to relieve the swelling heart of disappointment? We can find no better spot for the rambles of curiosity, health, or pleasure; none sweeter for the whispers of affection among the loving." He urged people to visit the cemetery to "renew our failing resolutions for the dark and boundless future."[23]

Wilson Flagg, author of *Mount Auburn: Its Scenes, Its Beauties, and Its Lessons* (1861), was particularly active in proclaiming "the moral influence of graves" in a picturesque setting. Flagg believed visitors derived great benefit "from scenes that tend to conquer an excess of frivolity, or to moderate that entire devotion to mammon which, like intemperance and vice, has ruined many a noble heart." The visitor was "not to be saddened, but to be sombered; to think more earnestly of the higher purposes of life, of its transient duration, and of the importance of neglecting no duty of religion, charity, or benevolence." There one would "read lessons which heaven, through nature, conveys to us in many a pleasing emblem of light and beauty. The winds represent the vicissitudes of life; but they inculcate the lesson that there is no adversity that is not followed by the tranquility of a better day. The flowers bud and bloom, and, in their vernal loveliness, represent the morning of our days and the spring-time of our life; but they perish like our own corporeal frames, to indicate by their revival that new life, of which death is but the celestial dawning. The trees that spread their branches and extend their benevolent shade over the graves . . . are a manifestation of that unseen power that has assembled the departed spirits under his providential care."[24] Flagg's emphasis on the moral functions of Mount Auburn reflect his particular pantheistic liberalism, which was shared by many prominent Bostonians of his day.

Flagg and Mount Auburn's founders knew that sensibility to the spiritual messages of the cemetery did not permeate all levels of society. Flagg judged, however, that "those who possess an ordinary amount of cultivation" would benefit from the "melancholy pleasure" of meditation among the tombs. Restating views of eighteenth-century romantics from England and the Continent, Flagg deemed "agreeable" the emotion of melancholy "when gently excited" by an elegaic landscape. For Flagg and like-minded Bostonians, "the contemplation of the graves of our fellow beings produces a pensive state of mind that overcomes our natural horror of death, especially when associated with certain fanciful images emblematical of peace and immortality." Mount Auburn served as a place of spiritual exercise for the genteel. There, "the mind is enabled to extend its thoughts further into infinity."[25] The cemetery, by implication, would not stir such intellectualized emotions in the common man.

Flagg recognized the particular appeal of Mount Auburn to an educated elite interested in literature and philosophy. He, therefore, presented a selection of readings interspersed with his own essays revealing opinions on such matters as the moral influence of cemeteries, epitaphs, and symbols, humility in architecture, proper funerary sculpture, and uses of varied plants at the cemetery. He included accounts of ancient funeral practices and descriptions of Old World burial places. He reprinted Bernardin de Saint-Pierre's essay "The Pleasure of Tombs," inspired by Rousseau's burial at the picturesque country seat at Ermenonville, which in turn inspired Père Lachaise and eventually Mount Auburn. Flagg published parts of *Solitude Considered* by Johann Georg von Zimmerman, an eighteenth-century Swiss physician, who praised the pleasures of mourning in "the salutary shades of the country," and he seasoned the ensemble with plenty of sentimental verse. Flagg left detailed descriptions of the cemetery to Nathaniel Dearborn's guidebooks and to Thomas Safford's weekly newspaper, the *Mount Auburn Memorial*.[26]

Safford, the cemetery gatekeeper, enjoyed the support of the corporation in his venture to edit with his son the eight-page newspaper, which was published weekly in Cambridgeport. In the first issue in June of 1859, they stated their purpose: "to open a medium of communication for [elegaic] subjects and embody the history of the place." They would present "matters of historical interest capable of awakening all the finer sensibilities of our nature and of quickening the ties of love and affection." Others harbored lofty ambitions for the publication. One letter to the editor proclaimed, "There is more literary ability among the proprietors of Mount Auburn than was ever engaged in any literary enterprise in the world." If only they would submit prose and poetry, the new journal would prosper. Another writer predicted that the paper would "call attention to the condition of old neglected places of interment and aid in the good work Mount Auburn has already done . . . that of renovating the burying-places of the whole country."[27]

The paper was on sale at the cemetery gate, the Bowdoin Square Railway Station in Boston, the Cambridge Post Office, and the publisher's office. However, it appealed primarily to the genteel and to proprietors of cemetery lots. Safford quoted "a gentleman of taste and culture" as calling the paper "*unique,* the only one in the world so far as we know, which is devoted to these chronicles of the departed, in the spirit which Scott's 'Old Mortality' would have deemed congenial in its reverent carefulness." Members of the general public were less receptive. Safford acknowledged a skepticism overheard on the streetcar when a man wondered, "Isn't it rather a gloomy sort of sheet?" The editor feared that "many are at first disinclined to the reading of our paper; they say it treads mostly upon a subject the most gloomy . . . Death." But he countered, "Surely no person can complain . . . if his mind is rightly directed to those things which improve and elevate."[28]

As Safford wrote, the era of popularity of sentimental and melancholy subjects was rapidly drawing to a close, but more as a result of trends in mass culture than as a reaction to the carnage of the Civil War. Safford complained, "in this jostling, whirling age of change and novelty, the greatest favor is bestowed upon any thing which present a garish, over-showy exterior." His newspaper lasted barely a year and a half, probably prolonged in its longevity by support of the corporation. Still, the rise of materialism and a more entertaining sort of popular culture cannot be exclusively faulted for the failure of the public to respond to the *Mount Auburn Memorial.* The onset of the war gave the public a more pressing basis for melancholy of the sort that could not long sustain the sentimentality of the preceding decades. Yet for the three antebellum decades, Mount Auburn and a literature related directly or indirectly to it remained in vogue.[29]

Despite the popular sentimentality, however, not all visitors appreciated the genteel purposes of the cemetery; many came with less than pious intentions, seeking recreation rather than reverence. The young heard of the "magic wilderness of its beautiful and almost endless variety." One writer told them, "You are not only lost in astonishment at what you see, but are in danger of losing yourself among its mazes, through which you might wander for hours without finding a clue to an escape."[30] Mount Auburn appealed to a sense of mystical excitement and even adventure, so much a part of romanticism. It was a fantasy landscape.

Many came primarily as tourists, having heard that a walk through the cemetery was "one of the indispensables to a stranger sojourning in or near Boston, and few places present, within an equal space, either to citizens or strangers, a more varied combination of elements to attract attention and awaken thought." They knew that "neither care nor expense has been spared in the efforts to enhance its great natural advantages." According to the *American Cyclopoedia of Useful Knowledge* (1835), it was "justly celebrated as the most interesting object of the kind in our country"—not unlike twentieth-century museums or amusement parks in its appeal. Andrew Jackson Downing observed that "people seem to go there to enjoy themselves, and not to indulge in any serious recollections or regrets." Certainly those Bostonians who had captured the spirit of urban boosterism were proud to read that the cemetery was "a becoming appendage, an interesting ornament of the town."[31]

Such had been the case from the start, and the issue of tourist access and behavior was a major bone of contention leading to the split between cemetery proprietors and horticulturists. Three years after Mount Auburn's founding, one English visitor commented that "parties of pleasure come hither from the city in great numbers . . . sometimes at the rate of six hundred a day." Caroline Gilman noted in 1838, "The city does indeed throng to the spot so sacred . . . leaving the dusty world behind. Daily, hourly, a line of carriages stands at its lofty gate, and countless guests pause at the solemn inscription . . . and then enter to meditate among the unrivalled varieties of Mount Auburn." Gilman, touring with her minister husband, chose to ignore the purely secular uses of the grounds. The young Englishman Henry Arthur Bright, a close friend of Hawthorne, visited Mount Auburn with Longfellow in 1852 and observed, "Cemeteries here are all the 'rage'; people lounge in them, and use them (as their tastes are inclined) for walking, making love, weeping, sentimentalizing, and every thing in short." One local writer admitted that "quiet, home-keeping citizens, even in Cambridge, may not be aware of the great number of persons who daily visit Mount Auburn."[32]

Bostonians were anxious to present Mount Auburn as their city's major showplace, for the cemetery had been designed as a place to display Yankee accomplishments and taste. Samuel Swett took the Cuban horticulturist Ramon de la Sagra there, pointing with pride to his family lot and monument "as if he were showing off a vacation house." The author of Mount Auburn's first guidebook wondered in 1839, "What object in or near Boston will be equally attractive?" As early as the summer of 1833, participants in a national conference of physicians meeting in Boston visited the cemetery.[33]

Most visitors were ordinary Americans who made certain, when in Boston, to see the cemetery about which they had read so much and wrote about the experience only to their diaries. Arozina Perkins, a twenty-two-year-old New Haven schoolteacher, visited Boston in 1849 for a day en route from seeing her widowed mother in Marshfield, south of the city. After a morning's stroll on the Common and climb up the State House dome and before seeing Faneuil Hall and the Museum, she and her brothers drove to Mount Auburn "and rambled about there for hours." Arozina declared, "I could have spent days there, and still have found something new—something to admire." The cemetery particularly appealed to her melancholy temperament shaped by the death of her father, the scattering of eleven siblings across the country, never to be seen again in life, and her separation from her beloved rural childhood home in Johnson, Vermont.[34] The personal upheavals of mid-century mobility as well as mortality conditioned the taste for melancholy places like Mount Auburn, which promised reunion with loved ones in the hereafter, if not physically in the family plot.

Visitors proved the best publicists. Sir Charles Lyell, Joseph Story's British friend, visited the cemetery on trips to Boston in 1842 and 1849; he praised it highly in his travel account. The sixteen-year-old Emily Dickinson made sure to see Mount Auburn as well as the Bunker Hill Monument, the Chinese Museum, two concerts, and a horticultural exhibition when in Boston in 1846; she wrote her friends that literary descriptions did not do justice to the place. Harvard President Edward Everett took Lady Emmeline Wortley on a carriage ride through Mount Auburn when she visited in 1849, and she described the experience favorably in her travel narrative.[35] That year, the New Yorker Andrew Jackson Downing, who visited the cemetery many times, wrote in the *Horticulturist* that the cemetery "idea took the public mind by storm. Travelers made pilgrimages to the Athens of New England solely to see the realization of their long cherished dream of a resting place for the dead."[36] It was precisely the resonance of complex tastes and ideas made manifest at Mount Auburn that led to the cemetery's great popularity.

Over the years, a host of notables made Mount Auburn as major a stop as the Erie Canal or Niagara Falls on their grand tours of the United States. Charles Dickens and Emperor Dom Pedro of Brazil praised the cemetery. In October of 1860, trustees Uriel Crocker and Charles Nazro escorted Lord Renfew, the Prince of Wales and future King Edward VI, followed by a throng of celebrity-seeking Bostonians who watched him plant a yellowwood and a purple beech in front of the chapel. Newspapers across the country reported that Napoléon III "gave the palm to Mount Auburn for its natural beauty of position" and for its designed landscape.[37] One Boston newspaper bragged, "Every visitor goes to Mount Auburn as a matter of course."[38]

Mount Auburn received nearly unanimous accolades in many travel accounts, a major literary genre in the mid-nineteenth century. The Swedish visitor Carl David Arfwedson, like so many others, paraphrased Keats, exclaiming that "a glance at this beautiful cemetery almost excites a wish to die."[39] Enoch Cobb Wines of Philadelphia commended the picturesque drive to Mount Auburn past "the country seats of opulent citizens, which . . . gave indubitable tokens of the wealth and taste and comfort of their occupants." He praised the cemetery landscape, "which certainly no spot in America can match, and which probably few places can equal in any part of the world."

Fig. 11.11. Fictional view of Mount Auburn's landscape from an unidentified German illustrated book of views of the United States, engraving, 1859, collection of the author.

Wines concluded after inspecting the monuments, "nowhere else can the evidence be met with of such invariably pure taste in so large a number of persons." Having toured the cemetery's "primeval forests" and ascended to the top of the "quite lofty mountain," Wines came away with the impression "that it was expressly designed by the Creator for its present use."[40]

Views of Mount Auburn appeared in various European compendia of the pictorial sights of America, attracting still more visitors from abroad. In one instance, a German illustrator even composed a fanciful view of the landscape, a pastiche of real and nonexistent monuments.[41] (Fig. 11.11.)

The Englishwoman Isabella Lucy Bird delighted in the picturesque aspects of the cemetery "far removed from the din of cities," where "the neglectfulness and dreariness of the outer aspect of the graves are completely done away with and the dead lie peacefuly under ground carpeted with flowers and shaded by trees." Similarly, John Ross Dix exclaimed, "There is life, joyous life beneath, around, and above us . . . every thing tells of life."[42] The phrenologist George Combe, close friend of Boston's educational reformer Horace Mann, found edification at the tombs of notables, where "lessons of wisdom and benevolence may for ages be learned." He predicted that "many a pilgrim from distant lands will preserve as a precious memorial, a flower from the sod which covers what was mortal of these saints in the calendar of a coming age."[43] Combe did not realize that picking flowers as souvenirs was an offense subject to fine. Nevertheless, Bostonians savored the positive publicity their city received from visitors because of Mount Auburn, especially because, as with Tocqueville's observations on *Democracy in America,* the visitors' opinions echoed the diverse rationales and ideas expressed by the cemetery's founders.

Great praise of Mount Auburn came from the Englishwoman Harriet Martineau, who received a personally guided tour by Joseph Story in August of 1847. She judged the cemetery a particularly American phenomenon indicative of New England's dominance in the national culture. "As might have been predicted," wrote Martineau, "one of the first directions in which the Americans have indulged their taste and indicated their refinement is in the preparation and care of their burial places." She attributed this tendency to "the pilgrim origin of the New-England population, whose fathers seemed to think that they lived only in order to die." Hence, in America, thoughts of death filled "a large space in the people's mind," Martineau explained.[44]

Yet despite the centrality of death in antebellum American culture, Martineau saw evidence at Mount Auburn of a nascent trend in the national mentality—a trend later to be labeled the "denial of death." She wrote, "A visitor from a strange planet, ignorant of mortality, would take this place to be the sanctum of creation. Every step teems with the promise of life. Beauty is about to spring out of the ashes, and life out of dust; Humanity seems to be waiting, with acclamations ready on its lips, for the new birth. That there has been any past is little more than a matter of inference." Ironically, despite their attempt to create a usable past, cemetery founders seemed to Martineau to have denied it.[45]

Martineau moderated her criticisms of American culture precisely because she considered Mount Auburn representative of it and also "the most beautiful cemetery in the world," with an "air of finish and taste, especially in contrast to Père Lachaise." Mount Auburn epitomized hope; the French cemetery, mourning. At Père Lachaise, Martineau observed, "there is no light from the future shining over the place. In Mount Auburn, on the contrary, there is nothing else." Martineau thought Boston's cemetery appealed particularly "to us, in whom education, reason, the prophecies of natural religion, and the promises of the gospel unite their influence to generate a perfect belief in a life beyond the grave." She admitted that the place must appear much different to the doubtful. Still it was "a mazy paradise, where every forest tree of the western continent grows and every bird to which the climate is congenial builds its nest." Martineau looked at the cemetery as metaphor for travel and life, presenting lessons of transience with which she, appropriately, ended her two-volume travel narrative of the United States.[46]

The immense popularity of Mount Auburn and the numbers of nonproprietors seeking admission in carriages led to the breakdown of the ticket system established by Joseph Story to limit access to the grounds. (Fig. 11.12.) By the early 1850s, several new trustees of a younger generation relaxed the restrictions for anyone appearing to be

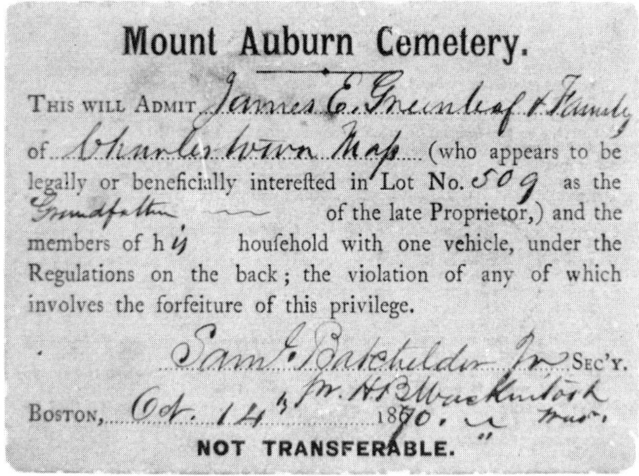

Mount Auburn Cemetery.

THIS WILL ADMIT James E. Greenleaf & Family of Charlestown Mass (who appears to be legally or beneficially interested in Lot No. 509 as the Grandfather of the late Proprietor,) and the members of his household with one vehicle, under the Regulations on the back; the violation of any of which involves the forfeiture of this privilege.

Saml. Batchelder Jr. SEC'Y.

BOSTON, Oct. 14, 1870.

NOT TRANSFERABLE.

Fig. 11.12. Proprietor's ticket for entrance by carriage to Mount Auburn, with regulations, ca. 1860–70.

REGULATIONS.

1. The gates are opened at sunrise, and closed at sunset.
2. No money is to be paid to the Gate-keeper.
3. No vehicle is admitted unless accompanied by a Proprietor or a member of his or her *household, with his or her ticket.*
4. No refreshments, and no party carrying refreshments, will be admitted.
5. All persons who shall be found within the Cemetery conducting themselves unsuitably to the purposes to which the grounds are devoted, will be required instantly to leave the grounds, and, upon refusal, will be compelled to do so. Such persons will also be prosecuted.
6. No vehicle is to be driven in the Cemetery at a rate faster than a walk.
7. No horse is to be fastened except at the posts provided for this purpose. No horse is to be left unfastened without a keeper.
8. No person is admitted on horseback.
9. All persons are prohibited from gathering any flowers, EITHER WILD OR CULTIVATED, or breaking any tree, shrub, or plant.
10. All persons are prohibited from writing upon, defacing, or injuring any monument, fence, or other structure in or belonging to the Cemetery.
11. All persons are prohibited from discharging fire-arms in the Cemetery.
12. *This ticket is not to be loaned or transferred.*

The Superintendent has the care of the Cemetery, and is authorized to remove all those who violate these regulations or commit any trespass. Trespassers are also liable to be fined FIFTY DOLLARS respectable. They liberalized the granting of tickets for Sunday admission to those with relatives in public lots; they gave three tickets to the Scots Charitable Society, the institutional owner of a large burial plot. They permitted the gatekeeper to admit anyone claiming to be a proprietor or family member even without a ticket, although the superintendent, gatekeeper, and other employees were authorized to ask for identification from anyone entering the cemetery and were granted discretionary powers to exclude anyone giving a false name.

Some proprietors criticized the authoritarian attitude of the gatekeeper; a visitor denied entry complained that B. F. Wyeth shut the gate in his face with "offensive alacrity." Trustees concluded the exclusion was not "in a manner rude, cruel, or uncalled for," although they made the excuse that Wyeth was "an excitable person and too apt perhaps to take offense unnecessarily." The board dismissed him in 1856 for accepting money thrown by persons leaving the grounds to supplement his $450 annual income. He was asked to return to the corporation the estimated additional $10 he had thus collected annually. Wyeth may indeed have been surreptitiously charging and pocketing admission to the cemetery for several years.[47]

Perhaps the gatekeeper's temper was shortened in 1853 when Henry M. Parker began issuing more than one ticket per lot, readily reissuing "lost" tickets without written applications, giving tickets to holders of small lots who had no vote in the corporation, and even granting tickets to nonproprietors living in the Boston area. The liberalized admission policy certainly would have cut into Wyeth's source of illicit revenue. Trustees determined to maintain only "a mild and reasonable enforcement of the rules" so as not to turn Mount Auburn into "a pleasure drive for all pleasure seekers who may chance to pass that way," perhaps en route to Fresh Pond. They gave the gatekeeper discretion to "prevent abuses which might otherwise necessarily creep in." Still, the gatekeeper reported the unpreventable "surreptitious use of tickets by many residents of the area who were not proprietors." Trustees responded not by issuing a new sort of ticket in more limited numbers but by agreeing to issue a ticket good for one carriage entrance to anyone who requested it. They deemed the new policy "quite sufficient to make the grounds as public as can reasonably be required." Still complaints were heard, and the board voted that the gatekeeper was "to admit persons of respectable appearance and demeanor to ride into the Cemetery without tickets or permits until further orders."[48]

The question of admission to the cemetery was "a delicate one." Trustees concluded that "Mount Auburn, although strictly a private institution, may in some senses be considered a public one." Conscious that Mount Auburn was "the pioneer of ornamental cemeteries—the delight and pride of our citizens and the admiration of strangers," they felt a sense of responsibility to make the place more accessible to visitors since "its fame extends wherever Boston is known" and it was repeatedly copied in other cities. Trustees considered it "natural, therefore, that all strangers visiting this part of the country should be desirous of seeing it" and determined "to grant every facility for the gratification of this desire and also for the accommodation of resident non-proprietors."[49]

Prior to 1853, the secretary and nine trustees were more anxious to issue tickets to "strangers" than to residents of the Boston area who did not own burial lots. Story had discovered, after all, that the fringe benefit of buying a burial lot was receipt of an unrestricted admissions ticket for a carriage-load of family and guests; hence, restricted admissions for nonproprietors increased lot sales. By the 1850s, however, Mount Auburn's lot prices had increased substantially, and it now faced competition from other "rural" cemeteries in the metropolitan region. Indeed, some families sold their Mount Auburn lots and purchased others that were less expensive and closer to home at Forest Hills, Sleepy Hollow, or elsewhere. Competition from these institutions may have helped to liberalize Mount Auburn's admission policy as trustees attempted to keep the place the focus of public attention. Furthermore, the board wanted to counter the negative criticisms of exclusivity that led democratically minded Bostonians away from Mount Auburn. In 1861, therefore, they changed the term "tickets" to "cards of admission."[50]

The gatekeeper was discreet in regulating admissions. The young Englishwoman Isabella Lucy Bird was impressed on her 1854 visit that being an obvious stranger "produced a magic effect." The gatekeeper readily admitted her carriage and refused a gratuity.[51] The cemetery continued to issue tickets to Boston's principal hotels and to individual visitors from out of town, each ticket bearing the name of the party to be admitted. Cards were for one-time use and were supposed to be surrendered at the gate, although few were collected in this way. But although trustees welcomed visitors from out of town, they were not ready to permit mass tourism. They banned charabancs, omnibuses, and excursion wagons from the cemetery. Although James Cheever suggested that the cemetery make carriages available at the gate for use by strangers who needed them to see the grounds, such an amenity was never provided. The board also rejected several requests from enterprising individuals seeking permits to operate a carriage-for-hire inside the cemetery.

Issuance of tickets to limit admission of carriages was not sufficient to prevent problems. With over three thousand proprietors holding tickets and with a constant stream of tourists from out of town, traffic in the cemetery on weekends was heavy. Complaints were heard of fast driving and injuries caused to the grounds by it. Many drivers leaving funerals were habitually guilty of speeding. Drivers of public hackney coaches, bringing ticketed passengers from downtown hotels, were perhaps the greatest offenders; so, for a time, trustees banned hired hacks until they heard complaints that the measure limited access for out-of-town visitors. Drivers caught speeding were barred from future entry, and hotels giving tickets to banned drivers also lost visiting privileges for their guests.

Periodic improvements in public transportation helped to bring greater numbers of visitors to Mount Auburn. Many visitors to the cemetery in its first years used hired hacks if they did not own carriages; this made the trip an expensive proposition and kept many people away. Hourly runs by the Cambridge Stage Company from Boston to Harvard made Mount Auburn, a mile and a half to the west, accessible to many Bostonians. In 1834, the first large-capacity, horse-drawn omnibuses went into service in Cambridge; by 1838, several regular lines provided hourly runs between Harvard and the cemetery gate. The route ending at the cemetery was so important that in 1838 the City of Cambridge renamed the old road Mount Auburn Street.

In 1856, the Cambridge Horse Railroad, the first in New England, extended its line from Boston's Bowdoin Square through Cambridge to the Mount Auburn gate, forming a central line in the new metropolitan network and increasing public access to the grounds. (Figs. 11.13, 14.) Cars made 175 trips each way per day, at fifteen-minute intervals until 11:30 at night, although the cemetery was open only to carriages from sunrise to sunset. Use of wrought-iron rails assured a smooth ride to the cemetery along the tree-lined Brattle Street past the Longfellow House. In 1863, an additional line brought visitors past Fresh Pond to the cemetery via Garden and Craigie streets.

Jacob Bigelow, his family, and other proprietors who did not own carriages used the horse railroad to travel to Mount Auburn; the corporation supplied trustees with free tickets for the new mass transit. Although Martin Brimmer, a trustee, wanted to limit admittance at the gate to exclude many members of the general public who came to Mount Auburn on the horse railway, a good deal of cooperation existed between the transit company and cemetery officials. In fact, the three founders of the company owned burial lots at Mount Auburn, and two subsequently became cemetery trustees. Perhaps that accounted for the higher fare charged for trips to Mount Auburn than to any other stop along the line, a fare about which proprietors complained. Major stables were located near Mount Auburn with room for 35 cars and 220 horses; and the adjacent station provided for connections to the Waltham and Watertown Railways. The horse railroad, initially located to improve access to the cemetery, eventually helped make Cambridge into a suburb from which businessmen could commute in half an hour to Boston offices. Electrification of the system dated from the 1890s, and the last horsecar ran in 1900. By the 1880s, the Union Railway Company had more lines ending at the Mount Auburn terminus than at any other site. Passengers would catch cars in either Bowdoin or Scollay Square in Boston.[52]

Fig. 11.13. (*Above*) Horse-drawn railway car for Mount Auburn terminus, engraving by Kilburn, ca. 1860.

Fig. 11.14. (*Below*) Horse-drawn railway car, Boston to Mount Auburn, engraving by John Andrew for *Ballou's Pictorial*, 1856.

Cemetery trustees worried more when the Fitchburg Railroad and the Cambridge Branch Railroad Company began to provide passenger service to the Watertown side of the cemetery in 1847 and built a station near the northwest corner of Mount Auburn. (Fig. 11.15.) They feared that "the grounds [would] be overrun by crowds of persons who [would] make it a resort for pleasure and amusement and thus disturb the sacred quiet of the place." However, they were powerless to stop trains from making the cemetery a major stop, attracting just as many passengers as the Fresh Pond Hotel, a popular local day resort just to the north and the next stop on the line. The board immediately rejected the 1853 request by the railroad superintendent that the cemetery open a gate nearer the station "for the accommodation of the great concourse of visitors which it is anticipated will thus be brought to Mount Auburn," although the idea proved very popular with proprietors. In 1856, Philip Hickborn and twenty-five other lot holders delivered a similar petition to the corporation, arguing that trustees should entrust a key to the station agent so that only proprietors and not the general public would be able to use the entrance. But trustees persistently rejected the idea, which was raised every few years until the end of the century.[53]

Meanwhile, the board confronted the persistent problem of policing the grounds. Because after 1841 Superintendent Rufus Howe had more extensive record-keeping responsibilities than his predecessor, the board hired a watchman to supplement the work of gatekeeper and superintendent in overseeing visitors' conduct and in suppressing nuisances and "improper practices." Specifically, trustees ordered the watchman to prevent the "various depredations of late committed upon the flowers and shrubs" and to regulate behavior of "large parties assembled within the ground with refreshments and for purposes utterly incompatible with those to which the grounds are devoted."[54]

Offenses involved deliberate damage to plants, and trustees repeated their ban on gathering flowers. Anyone found possessing them would be automatically judged to have taken them from the grounds and prosecuted. Flowers brought into the

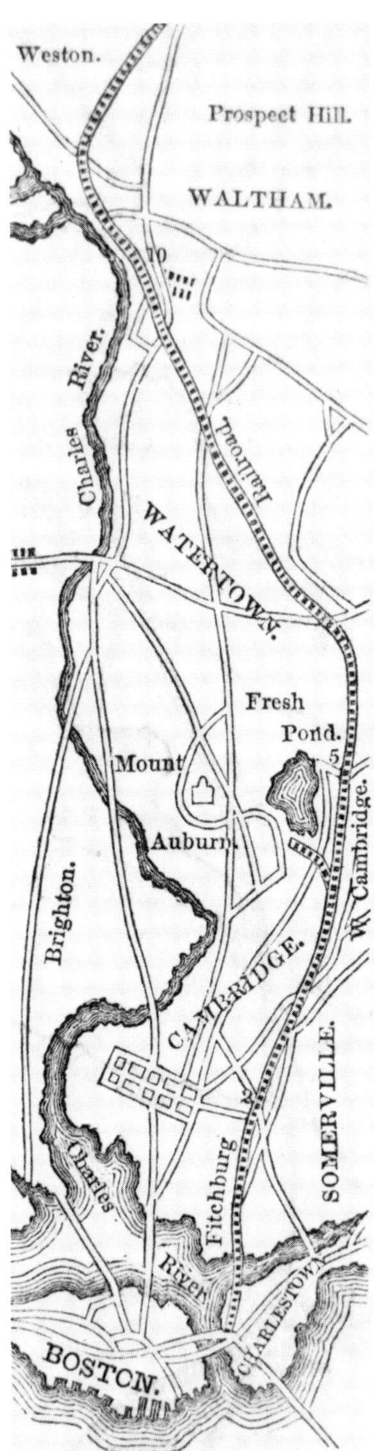

Fig. 11.15. Map of Fitchburg railway line with stop at Mount Auburn, from the Boston *Almanac,* 1847.

cemetery had to be registered with the gatekeeper. Other damage was more serious. In 1846, one proprietor complained of injury to furniture on his lot; trustees offered a $100 reward for detection of the offender, who was never apprehended. As soon as the tower was built, trustees had to approve repair of injury done to its woodwork by cutting and defacing—graffiti. The superintendent even had to place a fence around the large oak tree in front of the chapel to deter whittling and carving, a predilection of the times that endangered street trees in cities as well. The board offered a $20 reward for information to convict anyone found damaging plants or monuments or committing any other act of "trespass"; it gained authorization from the legislature to deem damage to plants or structures and improper firing of guns in the cemetery a misdemeanor subject to a fine from $5 to $50.

Property damage to the cemetery was not the only problem. Visitors complained of "unseemly noises" made by those "conducting themselves unsuitably to the purposes to which the grounds are devoted." Rowdiness just outside the cemetery proved as bothersome as that within the grounds, and the gatekeeper, B. F. Wyeth, could not control it. Repeated publication and posting of rules and regulations proved ineffective in curtailing obnoxious and damaging behavior of visitors. A watchman hired in 1841 to prevent and suppress nuisances was equally powerless. The gatekeeper and watchman were supposed to be the ultimate judges of behavior and to have the authority to require offenders of the rules of propriety to leave the grounds immediately. Superintendent Daniel Winsor thought that posting notices in various parts of the grounds warning visitors against walking across lots would "remedy the evil complained of" by proprietors, but other proprietors criticized signs as "not suitable to the character of the place." Visitors were not to bring picnic goods into the grounds. Trustees Benjamin Gould and Charles P. Curtis looked into deputizing a local man as police officer exclusively for the cemetery, but no such appointment was made until the 1850s.[55]

Fig. 11.16. Victorian pump house, carte de visite photograph by G. K. or W. S. Warren, ca. 1865.

After the hiring of a new gatekeeper, Truman H. Safford of Watertown, the board determined to gain more formal authority for him to preserve the peace in the vicinity of the gate as well as within the cemetery. Isaiah Bangs persuaded the City of Cambridge to make Safford a "special policeman," albeit on the cemetery payroll. In 1857, Cambridge and Watertown deputized Superintendent Jonathan Mann and two other cemetery workers as well. By 1861, deputized employees wore badges on "suitable occasions" like the Fourth of July to assert their authority. Since the cemetery's founding and until establishment of Decoration Day in 1868, great crowds flocked to Mount Auburn on Independence Day, necessitating employment of extra "officers or servants" to care for the grounds. Entire conventions visited Mount Auburn. In 1864 a hundred members of the Grand Lodge of Odd Fellows of the United States meeting in Boston received permission to come to Mount Auburn in a group. By 1866, the corporation employed a "police force" during the summer months.[56]

Through the 1850s and 1860s, trustees considered adding various amenities for visitors to the cemetery. Mace Tisdale, new to the board in 1850, urged the building of a well or pump house just inside the gate to provide pure, fresh drinking water for visitors. Older trustees spoke publicly in opposition to such a structure "for the benefit of outsiders." One wrote the editor of the *Evening Transcript,* "The quiet of Mount Auburn is already too much disturbed by the avalanche of foot and railroad passengers which is daily discharged upon it." He feared the pump house would become

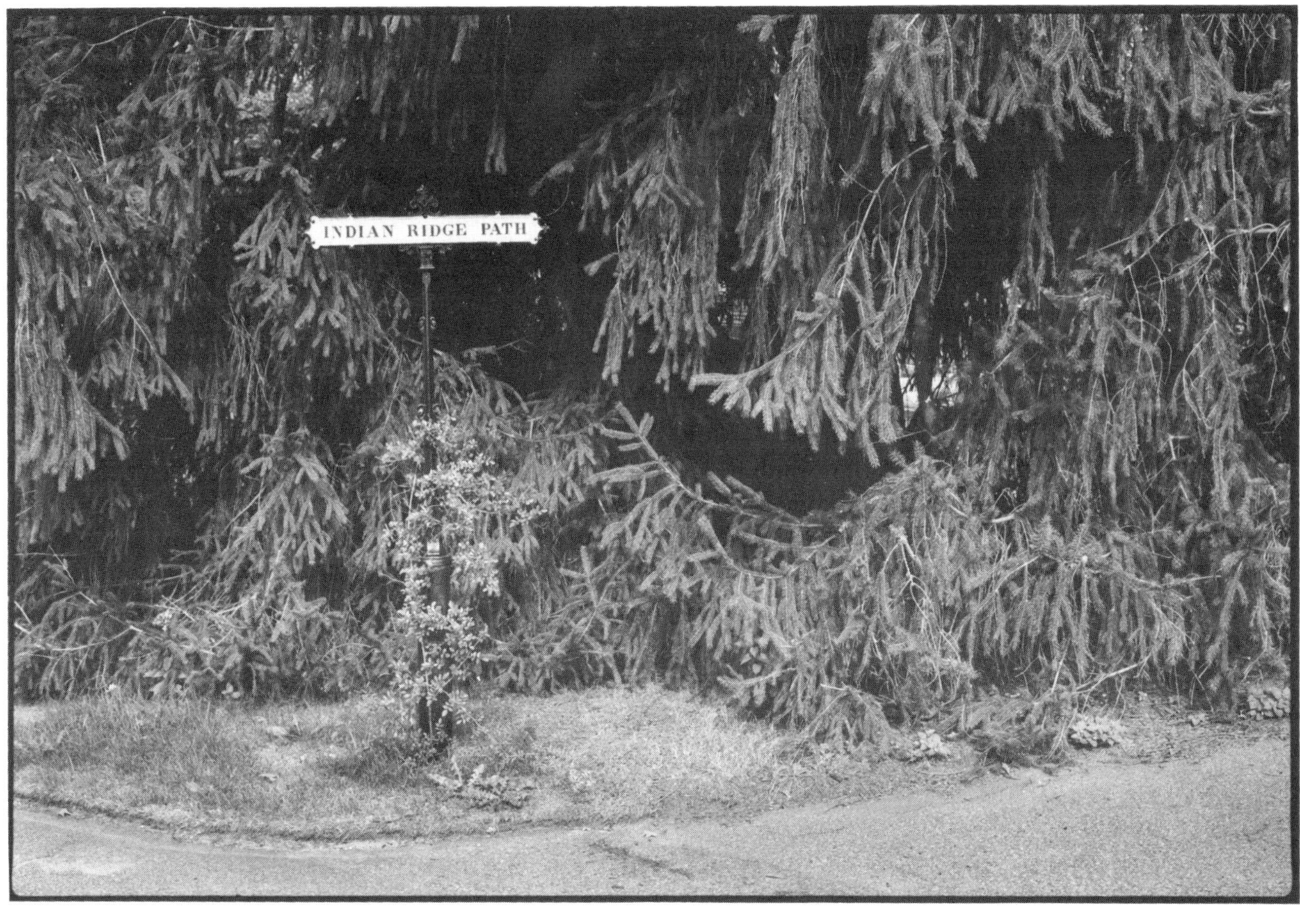

Fig. 11.17. Cast-iron sign at intersection of Central Avenue and Indian Ridge Path, photograph by Alan Ward, 1987.

a "lounging place and a nuisance." But even if that did not happen, his objection remained to the structure of carved Victorian gingerbread woodwork, judged "so gross a violation of good taste" especially as located near the Egyptian gate.[57] Tisdale presented the design of the elaborate, Victorian wooden pavilion or gazebo and supervised its construction in 1853 just to the left of the Central Avenue as the visitor entered the cemetery. (Fig. 11.16.) Some welcomed the amenity "embowered amidst a mass of green foliage," while others, like the architect Hammatt Billings, criticized it as having "rather too much the appearance of a garden summer house to be strictly in keeping with its position in a cemetery." Still, it remained in place until 1896, when, perhaps because of the diminishing number of visitors, it was moved to the rear of the grounds.[58]

Visitors appreciated this and other new conveniences—new cast-iron signs at the corners of all avenues and paths and $195 worth of iron settees placed around the grounds. Trustees also authorized construction of a well and pump on Spruce Avenue near Yarrow Path so proprietors could water their ornamental plants. (Fig. 11.17.)

In 1860, they decided to make major changes in the interior of the Egyptian gate to shelter visitors from sun and rain. A temporary awning placed over two recesses on either side of the entrance had proved insufficient. They allocated $1,600 to enclose two recesses or rooms next to the lodges with granite walls, a roof, and Egyptian columns facing into the cemetery, following Bigelow's design modifications. They were constructed by J. B. Whitcher for $1,600. (Fig.

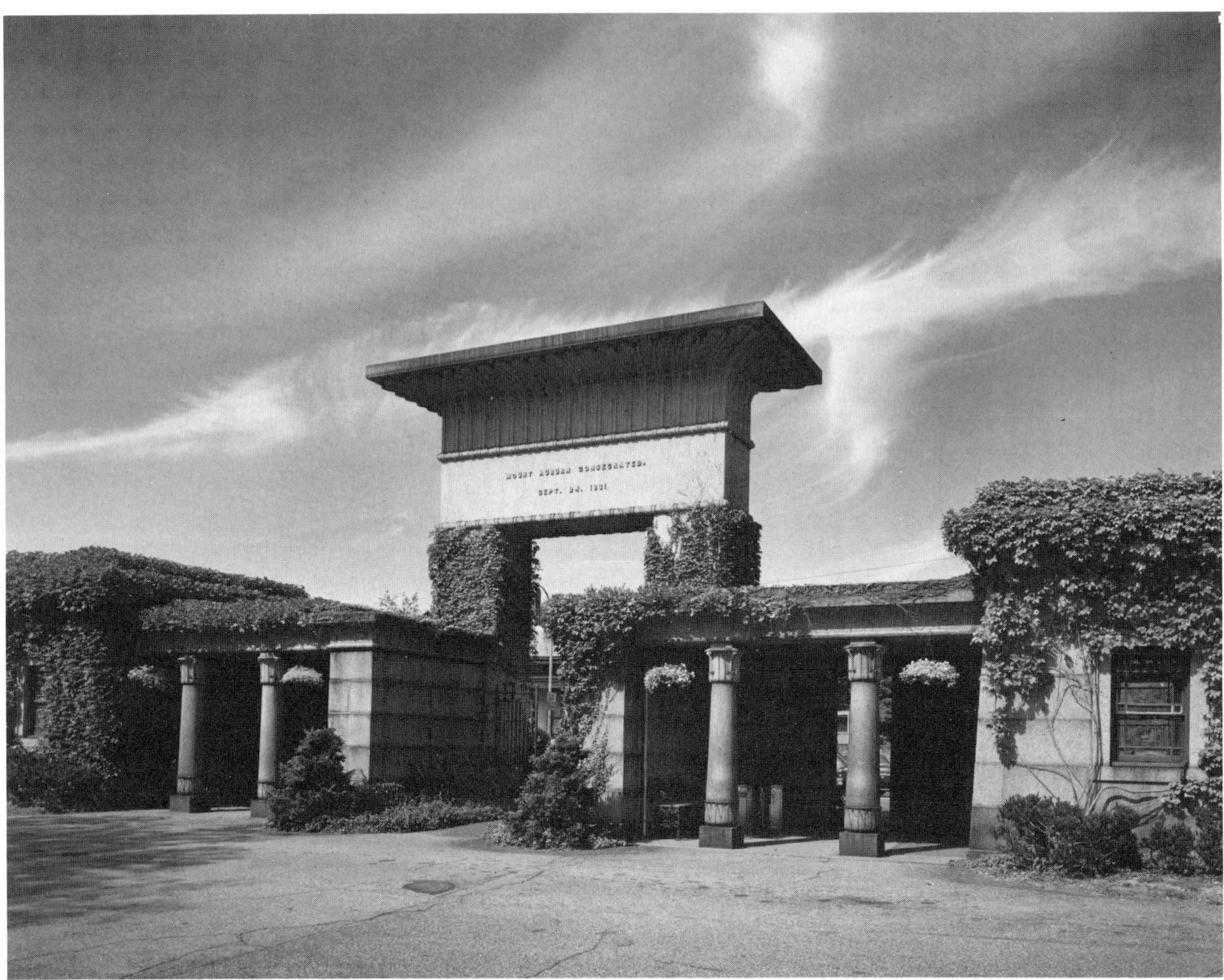

Fig. 11.18. Sheltered recesses added to south side of Egyptian gate in 1860, photograph by Alan Ward, 1979.

11.18.)

The board responded favorably to the needs of visitors. In 1861, despite Bigelow's opposition, privies or water closets were constructed near the front of the cemetery between the gate and office, for the use of ladies and children. Superintendent Jonathan Mann urged the board to lease land across the road from the cemetery entrance for a reception house where Charles F. Belcher could sell refreshments and provide "respectable quarters" in which ladies could wait for escorts or trolleys. In 1869, the architects William Washburn and Son presented drawings for a rest house completed in 1871 on Wyeth Estate land immediately across Mount Auburn Street; and the following year, the City of Cambridge agreed to pave the street up to fifty feet on each side of the gate with granite blocks, with the cemetery and the Cambridge Horse Railroad paying half the cost.[59] (Fig. 11.19.)

By mid-century, trustees permitted new sorts of active but genteel recreation at Mount Auburn. As winter approached in 1859, the editor of the *Memorial* observed, "If the coming season is as favorable to the lovers of skating as past years have been, soon the quiet little lake will be covered with a graceful, gliding multitude of merry ladies and gentlemen. . . . It is a fortunate circumstance that Fashion has lately countenanced this amusement as one in which the feminine part of the community can take a part." Use of ponds by local residents pursuing the new sport of ice skating did not seem inharmonious with the dignity and funereal purposes of Mount Auburn, and no attempt was made by the board to regulate it.[60] (Fig. 11.20.)

The board even considered admitting certain individuals on horseback in 1861, although trustees realized that "a person riding in the saddle can very easily cross through the narrow paths or even over the lots," doing great injury to monuments and plants. Opponents of the measure noted that "there is a class of persons . . . by no means a small one, who can be made to respect the rights of their fellow citizens only the enactment of a strict code of laws and the rigid enforcement of them." They regretted that they could not grant "the privilege to one without to all"; but they determined to use their own precedent, monetary controls. Already they curtailed "indiscriminate" building of tombs by charging a fee for the right. They applied the same principle by charging a "bonus" of ten dollars for a ticket to ride horseback in Mount Auburn, provided that the rider remain on regular avenues and proceed no faster than a walk.[61]

By the mid-1860s, however, the public thought of Mount Auburn less as a "pleasure ground" or museumlike institution and more as simply a repository for the dead. The tragic consequences of the Civil War impressed images of a grim and ugly death on the national consciousness, bringing an abrupt halt to the romanticization of death. The pump house and reception house were amenities for mourners and those visiting graves rather than attractions for the general public, which might still throng to the cemetery but came primarily on occasions for patriotic memorial such as the newly established Decoration Day or the funerals of notables. (Fig. 11.21.)

At the same time as the cemetery's popular appeal diminished, Americans began a public park movement. Cities across the nation created landscapes similar to Mount Auburn but without graves—places in which to picnic and to ride horses. They were truly public places open to

Fig. 11.19. Reception house across Mount Auburn Street from Mount Auburn's gate, half of a stereographic photograph, SPNEA.

Fig. 11.20. The skating "rage," genteel recreation in Regent's Park, London, half of a stereographic photograph, ca. 1860.

Fig. 11.21. Crowds of visitors at Mount Auburn on Decoration Day, half of a stereographic photograph, ca. 1875.

anyone who had a carriage or wanted to rent one, appropriate places for voluntary associations to erect monuments commemorative of notables and important events. The management of Mount Auburn and similar cemeteries must have breathed a collective sigh of relief that the "rage" had run its course, and they could get down to the business of running an efficient funerary institution.

Epilogue: Putting the Past under Grass

This generation reclines a little to congratulate itself on being the last of an illustrious line. . . . There are the Records of the Philosophical Societies and the public Eulogies of *Great Men!* . . . 'Yes, we have done great deeds, and sung divine songs, which shall never die,'—that is, as long as *we* can remember them.

—Henry David Thoreau, *Walden* (1854)

After the Civil War, the cultural climate was much different from that which had premised creation and development of Mount Auburn. Gone were the genteel tastes, the romantic idealism, the intentions to fashion a usable republican past through forms borrowed from the heights of civilizations, ancient and modern, and the shared belief that national stability could be assured by building material and literary monuments. Belief in philanthropy, which in earlier years had resulted in community action to finance funerary monuments to exemplary individuals in hopes of cultivating shared civic values and producing a virtuous citizenry through moral philosophy, was redirected into sponsorship of new forms and institutions of high culture reflecting more cosmopolitan tastes and the love of art for art's sake.

For the generation of Yankees born in the first third of the century, Edward Waldo Emerson observed, "life was still serious, amusement occasional and secondary; they still lived in the preserve of the unseen; they worshipped and went apart for solitary thought."[1] Mount Auburn was an institution compatible with their mentality, and cemetery founders resented the frivolous use of it as a "pleasure ground" by those who did not share their aversion to misspent leisure. The next generation, however, set aside the old values and adopted new concepts of culture and leisure that diminished the importance of the cemetery as an agent of moral philosophy and consensus history.

As Van Wyck Brooks remarked of the new era, "Other ways were coming; and other seasons, not without heights and depths of thought and feeling; but the spring days of the young republic, with all their aspirations and resolves, the Virgilian days, the Homeric days, were passing with the poets who pressed them. . . . Last things were in order . . . and all the Boston men could do,—or all they thought they could do,—was to bury the dead. Mount Auburn was becoming over-crowded."[2] No longer valued as a historical repository, the cemetery became more simply a place for burial of the dead and for display of familial sentiment in material terms. Bostonians created other new and specialized institutions—museums, parks, tourist attractions, and showplaces of urban worth—that took over many of Mount Auburn's former functions.

A new generation of urban leaders redefined culture and their roles as cultural arbiters. Through the last decades of the century, a striving, self-interested, scientifically minded elite arose and adopted the hard-nosed doctrine of social survival of the fittest. Darwinism left no room for the virtuous or the anachronistic. Heroes of yesteryear lost their pertinence and their appeal. The past was past; the dead, buried. Americans abandoned the pleasures of melancholy for progress, the past for the future. By emerging from the Civil War intact, the nation stayed the ultimate cataclysm, the death of the Union, which had so often been predicted in preceding decades as a phenomenon of the natural processes of time, if not of a quicker rise of divisive factionalism. The cataclysmic notion of historical processes itself became passé. Yankees successfully fought the demise of the nation, and their victory served as harbinger for similar successes in everyday life—advances in medical sciences, promulgation of the germ theory, conquest of pain through anesthesia, triumph over post-mortem decay with embalming, unification of the nation through material goods, and development of a mass culture based on optimism and insistence on the pristine newness of the present.

Preservation of the Union, in particular, despite the war's immense toll in mortality, seemed to contradict antebellum historical pessimists, who equated history with commemoration of the dead past and planned for the day when a few monuments—like that at Bunker Hill or those to notables at Mount Auburn—would provide lone testimony of the heyday of American civilization to visitors from some distant nation where enlightened ideals and republican government were again vibrant and new. Even more than the War of 1812, the Civil War provided assurance to the heirs of Calvinism that their nation was divinely sanctioned, tested, regenerate, and chastened for self-doubt. Because of Providence, so the train of thought went, the nation was redeemed from the fate of Adam, the consequences of the Fall, expulsion from the Garden, and subsequent, inevitable aging, death, and decay. The successful passing of the great test, the crucible of domestic war, confirmed Yankees' self-assurance. They turned with relief from contemplation of the troubled past and got down to business. Thus, by 1889, Moorfield Storey (whose son and grandson would serve as Mount Auburn trustees) complained that "the conditions of society have changed."[3] Many members of the gentry abandoned politics as public service, content to become administrators. Too many gentlemen set aside their sense of social and cultural mission to devote their energies to enterprise and self-interest.

The time had passed when Whiggish creators of culture believed that memory of a past shaped by individual virtue would forestall lawlessness and the demise of the republic. Once, commemoration of the exemplary person, the Puritan "Saint" or later the secular "Great Man," functioned in the same didactic way as Winthrop's proposed "city on a hill." After the war, only the notion of exemplary community—the Nation—remained, but it was seen as a new Eden, forever exempt from sin, change, aging, dissension, destructive divisiveness, and finally death. Americans abandoned romanticism and the cult of the melancholy for the cult of the new. The new mentality was characterized by denial of death, rejection of ruins or evidence of aging and decay, and a dogged optimism. This optimism arose from a revivalistic sense of national self-assurance accompanied by a militant moralism, which eventually took on international dimensions only hinted at by Winthrop in his coining of the phrase "city on a hill." Gone was the muted, resigned optimism in the face of catastrophe cultivated by Voltaire and the "pleasures of melancholy" of the romantics.

There had been, of course, high-minded individuals of the earlier generation who could not accept the Whiggish mission of Mount Auburn's founders to teach lessons of history and moral philosophy through the landscape and artifacts of the place. Emerson signaled the beginning of the transition in mentality in his essay "Nature" (1836). He criticized the retrospection of his era at the same time as he identified it as a major theme of the age. He asked Americans intent on looking to their past, "Why should not we also enjoy an original relation to the universe?" Henry David Thoreau became even more explicit. Much of his *Walden* (1854) can be read as a diatribe against the materialism of memory epitomized by the cemetery. Thoreau ranted, "It should not be by their architecture, but why not even by their power of abstract thought that nations should seek to commemorate themselves? . . . In Arcadia, . . . I did not see any hammering stone. Nations are possessed with an insane ambition to perpetuate the memory of themselves by the amount of hammered stone they leave. . . . One piece of good sense would be more memorable than a monument as high as the moon. I love to see stones in place. The grandeur of Thebes was a vulgar grandeur. . . . Most of the stone a nation hammers goes toward its tomb only. It buries itself alive." He complained that "we have built for this world a family mansion, and for the next a family tomb. The best works of art are the expression of man's struggle to free himself from this condition, but the effect of our art is merely to make this low state comfortable and that higher state to be forgotten."[4]

Horace Bushnell also criticized the institutionalization of memory when he questioned the uses in his day of lessons of the past in *The Moral Use of Dark Things* (1868). Bushnell decried the "history of oblivion" or "dead history," asking, "Do the vegetable growth repine or sicken because they cannot remember the growth of previous centuries? Is it not enough that the very soil that feeds them is fertilized by the waste of so many generations moldering in it?" Although the liberal minister continued to use organic imagery suggestive of an earlier romantic era, he rejected the old historicism and the Hegelian dialectics that tempered the writing of American romantic historians, who believed in the natural changes of time, the inevitable cycles leading to decline and fall of civilizations. Bushnell, however, like his contemporaries, believed in progress and preferred to live in the present.[5] Theirs was a linear view of history pointing away from the past and toward the future.

Some of Bushnell's generation who could accept neither the new business-oriented, scientific mentality nor the older Whiggish values epitomized by Mount Auburn became disillusioned and retreated abroad rather than simply to the New England woods. They quested for new ideals to compensate for the failure of the old and their disenchantment with the new. Richard Henry Dana II, for instance, was scorned by the "establishment" for his idealistic, active resistance to the Fugitive Slave Law. His career arbitrarily curtailed by unprincipled enemies, he became an expatriate, dying in Rome in 1882. There he was buried near Shelley and Keats in the pastoral Protestant Cemetery, a fact that gave his remaining Boston readers greater pride than if he had been returned for burial at Mount Auburn. For the young adults of 1870, wrote Van Wyck Brooks, "The old culture had broken down, the old causes were dead and forgotten, and no new ideal had arisen to rally the minds of the younger men." Those of the new generation who still harbored shreds of the old idealism "felt as if the labours of their fathers had been mocked, as if their country had been wrested from them; and they looked across the sea again, despairing of a nation that had passed beyond their powers of comprehension . . . as if three generations of history had gone for nothing." Even Jacob Bigelow's grandson, William Sturgis Bigelow, turned away from his Brahmin heritage to Buddhism, willing that after his death in 1926 half his ashes be placed in the Hōmōyōin Temple on the shores of Lake Biwa in Japan rather than all in the family plot at Mount Auburn.[6]

Even among those who stayed at home, the

Fig. E.1. Colonel William Prescott statue by William Wetmore Story, 1881, in front of the Bunker Hill Monument, photograph by Alan Ward, 1988.

change in mentality had spiritual dimensions. Lessons of moral philosophy drawn from examples of the secular past were no longer seen as the key to good citizenship. Unitarianism waned in Boston, and High Church Episcopalianism finally won over the elite. Liberal religion under a new generation of leaders like Doctors James Freeman Clarke and Edward Everett Hale (neither of whom chose burial at Mount Auburn) became simply ethical culture; Mount Auburn, the quintessential product of Unitarianism, seemed passé to many, despite its policy of nondenominationalism. It was an era, according to Brooks, when "people who loved goodness had ceased to 'adore' it, with the burning heart of the saint who lay in Mount Auburn; and, ceasing to adore, they ceased to struggle."[7] By the turn of the century, as Henry Adams also realized, history could no longer be taught as morality. The reality of the past provided little that was usable to the extent that idealistic, Whiggish leaders had once hoped—even in New England. The older historical consciousness passed; the past was buried. Death was either beautified or objectified or denied. Mount Auburn became more purely functional, for disposal of the dead, when a new generation discounted many of the prime historical and cultural reasons for which it had been founded.

The new generation was far more objective about the past, if they thought of it at all. Bostonians heeded the controversial, critical history of Richard Frothingham, who marshaled evidence to disprove local claims that General Israel Putnam or General Joseph Warren rather than Colonel William Prescott led the patriots in the Battle of Bunker Hill. Thereafter, schoolchildren were taught to associate the battle with Prescott's words, "Don't fire until you see the whites of their eyes." Public recognition of Prescott impelled a subscription campaign to erect a nine-foot-tall, bronze statue of Prescott by William Wetmore Story. Placed immediately in front of the Bunker Hill Monument, it staked in material form a commemorative claim that had originally been Warren's. Story's Prescott strides forward in a flaring greatcoat, seeming to be the common man impelled to the greatness of leadership, quite in contrast to the reserved and even aristocratic demeanor of Warren in the marble portrait statue sculpted for the interior of the monument by Henry Dexter in 1857. Robert C. Warren lauded Prescott as prime hero of the battle in ceremonies at the unveiling of the Prescott statue on June 17, 1881.[8] (Figs. E.1, 2.)

The problem of redefining a commonly acceptable past was greatest in New England at the end of the century precisely because of the region's previous lofty ambitions to set the moral and historical keynote for a national culture conceived in romantic terms. By the 1880s, Yankees became receptive to the debunking approach of Richard Hildreth, whose work dispelled old notions of "a colonial golden age of fabulous purity and virtue" that had been promulgated by antebellum filiopietists in search of local roots for a nation thought of as an Arcadia in the past. With this shift in ideas about history, the original goal of creating for Boston, New England, and even the nation a Ceramicus, Valhalla, or Westminster Abbey at Mount Auburn did not succeed because a second generation of trustees either would not or could not promote the place as the chief historical, let alone funerary, repository of the area. But even more important was the failure of Yankees by mid-century to reach consensus about their own public heroes, or about where and how they should be commemorated.[9]

The story of William Thomas Green Morton illustrates the point. When Morton, a Boston dentist, died in 1868 at age forty-nine, a dispute lived on over whether or not he should receive credit for the "discovery" of anesthesia. Morton's friends, "Citizens of Boston," erected an appropriate monument over his grave on Spruce Avenue at Mount Auburn. Morton died without funds to will for self-commemoration, having expended much of his estate and vitality over the previous two decades attempting to claim credit for discovery of sulphuric ether, the use of which he first successfully demonstrated to the medical profession at the Massachusetts General Hospital in 1846. The monument, a fluted column topped by a conventional draped urn, proclaims the "Inventor and Revealer of Anaesthetic Inhalation / Before Whom in All Time Surgery was Agony / By Whom Pain in Surgery was Averted and Annulled / Since Whom Science Has Control of Pain." (Fig. E.3.)

A Boston "chemist" (pharmacist), Charles T. Jackson, who initially had been skeptical of Morton's experiment but nevertheless supplied the dentist with the ether required for the demonstration, belatedly attempted to claim the discovery for himself. When Jackson died in 1880, he was also buried at Mount Auburn. He, too, received a commemorative stone, albeit more modest in scale, proclaiming at his grave his discovery of anesthesia: "Eminent as a Chemist, Mineralogist, Geologist and Investigator in All Departments of Natu-

Fig. E.2. General Joseph Warren statue by Henry Dexter, 1857, photograph by Alan Ward, 1988.

ral Science. Through His Observations of the Peculiar Effects of Sulphuric Ether on the Nerves of Sensation, and His Bold Deduction Therefrom, the Benign Discovery of Painless Surgery Was Made." Jackson's family added a verse to the stone: "Thy Godlike Crime Was to be Kind / To Render with Thy Precepts Less / The Sum of Human Wretchedness / And Strengthen Man with His Own Mind." (Fig. E.4.)

The controversy became more than a personal or local matter, however, in the wake of the Civil War. Although Morton received public acclaim for having gained international acceptance of the use of ether in surgery, the medical profession generally credited Crawford Williamson Long of Georgia with first using the substance in 1842 to remove a neck tumor, despite the southerner's failure to publicize the accomplishment until 1849.

Thomas Lee, "a citizen of Boston" and philanthropist of the Public Garden, attempted to solve the dilemma by donating in 1867 an entire monument in generalized gratitude for his own receipt of ether during an operation. But, at the same time, he skirted the Morton-Jackson controversy and ignored recognition of Long, simply proclaiming the discovery of anesthesia as a matter of local pride. The monument was placed in Boston's new Public Garden "To Commend the Discovery that the Inhaling of Ether Causes Insensibility to Pain—First Proved in the World at the Massachusetts General Hospital, Boston, October, A.D. MDCCCXLVI." The monument bypassed the controversy by quoting from Isaiah, "This also cometh forth from the Lord of Hosts which is wonderful in counsel and excellent in working." The elaborate Victorian monument, topped by a figure of the Good Samaritan kneeling over a wounded man, includes low-relief sculptures of scenes showing use of anesthesia during the Civil War as well as in the operating room. The simple inscription reads, "In gratitude for the relief of human suffering by the inhaling of ether." (Fig. E.5.)

The dilemma of public commemoration of heroes, however, had deep roots in cultural change and cannot be simply attributed to rival claims of individuals or localities. William Dean Howells identified a basic shift in "the American ideal of greatness" from older ideals in *A Traveller from Altruria* (1894). Asked to describe the concept of greatness in his own era, Howell's fictional banker replies, "I should say that within a generation our ideal has changed twice. Before the war, and during all the time from the Revolution onward, it was undoubtedly the great politician, the publicist, the statesman. As we grew older and began to have an intellectual life of our own, I think the literary fellows had a pretty good share of the honors that were going; that is, such a man as Longfellow was popularly considered a type of greatness. When the war came, it brought the soldier to the front, and there was a period of ten or fifteen years when he

Fig. E.3. William Thomas Green Morton monument, 1868, on Spruce Avenue, Mount Auburn, photograph by Alan Ward, 1987.

dominated the American imagination. That period passed, and the great era of material prosperity set in. The big fortunes began to tower up, and heroes of another sort began to appeal to our imagination." Howells's banker concluded that at the turn of the century, "the millionaire is now the American ideal."[10] Such a Gilded Age hero simply did not fit in at Mount Auburn, where avoidance of ostentation and conspicuous display of wealth had been institutionalized by trustees, mirroring the tastes and psyches of many Yankees, although other garden cemeteries in more prosperous cities readily welcomed the grandiose self-commemoration of the captains of new industry and enterprise. Mount Auburn, therefore, could not and would not provide a site for the sort of conspicuous self-commemoration required by many of those who rose to fame and prominence in the new era.

Widening gaps between classes in the last decades of the century further fragmented cultural cohesion in New England, with consequent ramifications on Mount Auburn, its functions, common commemorative purpose, and local prominence. Ronald Story describes the "crisis years" in mid-century Boston, "when the entire hard-wrought infrastructure of the elite seemed in danger of dilution, seizure, and collapse," paralleling political fragmentation, social pluralism, and escalating egalitarianism.[11] By the 1850s, Brahmins felt under siege from newcomers. They experienced challenges to their authority in the Athenaeum in 1853, at Harvard from 1850 to 1865, and at the Lowell Institute through the 1850s. Mount Auburn's trustees, led by President Jacob Bigelow, staved off attempts by insurgent proprietors and younger trustees to democratize cemetery administration and to lower prohibitively high lot prices in 1856. Controversy over corporate funding of historical statuary, demands by new trustees for investment of corporate monies in a permanent maintenance fund, and provisions for more amenities for public use evidence the trend at Mount Auburn as well as a negation of the agenda set at the founding to make the cemetery an agent of history. The insurgents finally found solutions to the stalwart exclusivity of Brahmins and their narrow agendas by founding alternative institutions—a public library as alternative to the Athenaeum, new colleges to challenge Harvard's intellectual hegemony, competitive banks and textile mills, and, finally, additional garden cemeteries. Certainly, in the process, the primacy of Mount Auburn as one of Boston's major historical and cultural institutions was weakened if not permanently sabotaged.

Fig. E.4. Charles T. Jackson monument, ca. 1880, on Mountain Avenue, Mount Auburn, photograph by Alan Ward, 1987.

In his declining years, Bigelow worried that subsequent generations of trustees would be worse than the insurgents of the 1850s and 1860s, willing to change the landscape and institution of Mount Auburn entirely, reshaping in radical new ways the forms and policies he had labored to develop over

Fig. E.5. Ether monument, dedicated 1868, donated by Thomas Lee, Boston Public Garden, photograph by Alan Ward, 1987.

four decades. In 1869, Bigelow persuaded the board to petition the state legislature to amend the cemetery's charter to provide for rotating terms for trustees, hence lessening the threat of future insurgency. From Mount Auburn's inception, board membership varied from seven to twelve trustees, although after 1857 the number ten was fixed in the charter. Bigelow described several unsuccessful attempts by proprietors "to supercede the existing Board by a new and less experienced body." He worried "that the funds designed for the preservation and improvement of the cemetery [had] become so large as to tempt the cupidity of improper and irresponsible persons. At the same time, the largely increased number of proprietors affords a greater opportunity than heretofore for clandestine and revolutionary movements." Proprietors of lots were becoming more demanding by 1870, but their complaints were generally related more to the care of the landscape than to any attempt to undermine the management of the institution and the Brahmin control of the corporation.[12] Once Bigelow won the major organizational change to forestall insurgency, he stepped down from the presidency in 1871, an old and ailing man but finally assured that his institutional legacy would endure.

Bigelow retired with confidence that Mount Auburn had been and would remain an exemplary institution. It reflected a more refined taste and new sensibilities toward death and nature that hastened the reform in the 1830s and 1840s of many of the traditional, unsightly burial grounds of the area. Thomas Bridgman decried New England's "neglected, unfenced, and uncared for graves exposed to horses, cattle, and dogs," and the intrusion of busy city life, with not "a tree nor a flower suffering to shade or bloom there, and neither walk nor path laid out among the falling straggling stones, for the pensive mourner." He credited Mount Auburn with instituting a new ideal. A local antiquarian, Nathaniel Shurtleff, agreed that "until the purchase of 'Sweet Auburn' for a rural burialplace, very little had been done towards ornamenting and beautifying the graveyards in Boston and neighboring towns." Since then, however, "much has been done to expel from the old graveyards their forbidding appearances."[13]

Actually, planting of the first trees in Boston's Old Granary Burying Ground predated Mount Auburn's founding by a year. A group of prominent citizens, reflecting the same impulse that underlay Mount Auburn's founding, proposed renaming the site Franklin Cemetery in honor of the Founding Father's parents, who were buried there, and ornamenting the grounds with plants. The superintendent of burials, Samuel H. Hewes, dedicated his last years before his 1845 death at age eighty-five to the "improvement" of this and other Boston graveyards. Using both public and private subscription funds, Hewes added trees to all the old sites. He reset the ancient, toppled stones in "geometrical rows on the borders" of newly laid paths, regardless of the locations of burials the stones were meant to mark. The fencing of Boston's burial grounds with iron proceeded from 1839 through the 1840s. By 1841, thanks to a crusade led by Samuel Downer, Dorchester's graveyards, south of Boston, had walks, shrubbery, flowers, silver maples, and green, sodded ground. Similar improvements to other colonial burial grounds in the metropolitan region transformed them into the pleasant places they have remained through the twentieth century.[14]

Mount Auburn's founders hoped that their institution would "ultimately offer an example of landscape or picturesque gardening in conformity to the modern style of laying out grounds." Indeed, Mount Auburn's most enduring significance is as catalyst for the burial reform and the elevation of landscape taste of the "rural" cemetery movement. Through the antebellum decades, cultural elites from many cities admired Mount Auburn so much that, time and time again, they determined to copy it. Funerary landscapes created with explicit reference and comparison to Boston's prototype appeared in Philadelphia's Laurel Hill Cemetery in 1836, Baltimore's Green Mount and New York's Green-Wood in 1838, Pittsburgh's Allegheny and Cincinnati's Spring Grove in 1845, Richmond's Holly-Wood and Louisville's Cave Hill in 1848, and Charleston's Magnolia in 1850—to name only a few of the major pastoral cemeteries founded during the heyday of Mount Auburn's national renown. (Figs. E.6, 7, 8.) The number of American "rural" cemeteries founded by 1860 was far greater than any of Mount Auburn's most optimistic founders might have predicted in 1831.

Bigelow, however, certainly did not foresee that other Yankees in his own backyard would not accept Mount Auburn as the "Westminster Abbey" of New England—and, in fact, that his policies would be responsible for the alienation. He and other longtime trustees insisted on increasing lot prices to a prohibitively high level. By 1845, Mount Auburn lots cost \$80 to \$100, and an additional premium was charged for choice of a site. By 1854, the minimum cost rose to \$150, before premium. The increasing size and pluralism of the population in the metropolitan Boston area, in fact in all of eastern New England, could not and would not be accommodated by Mount Auburn alone, given the changing expectations popularized by the expanding mass media and their promotion of the aesthetics of burial in a romantic, rural place. The area within a hundred-mile radius of Boston was dotted with towns and cities with leaders zealous to have their *own* rural cemeteries.[15]

Urged on by the displacement of the town's first four graveyards by urban construction and the railroad, Worcester's civic fathers were early to found their twenty-four-acre Rural Cemetery in 1838. James Barnes, engineer of the Western Railroad, and a committee of cemetery trustees laid out the funerary grounds according to the landscape design formula established at Mount Auburn. It has walks and carriageways "sweeping in gentle curves," despite the flatness and small size of that property. Trustees of Worcester's generically named Rural Cemetery set prices of standard 300-square-foot family lots, the same size as those at Mount Auburn, at \$30, half of the rate charged when Mount Auburn opened and a third of the

Fig. E.6. (*Left*) View of Laurel Hill Cemetery, near Philadelphia, designed by John Notman, 1836, engraving ca. 1840.

Fig. E.7. (*Below, left*) Plan of Green-Wood Cemetery, Brooklyn, New York, designed by Major David Bates Douglass, 1838, engraving by James Smillie, 1847.

Fig. E.8. (*Below*) Plan of the Cemetery of Spring Grove, Cincinnati, designed by Howard Daniels, 1845, engraved map by surveyor John Earnshaw, ca. 1850.

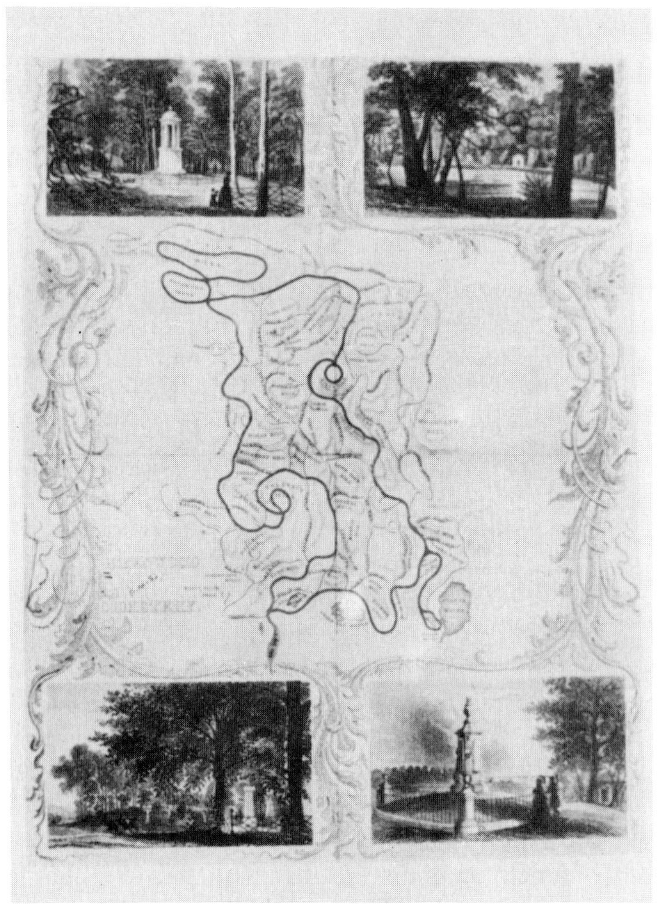

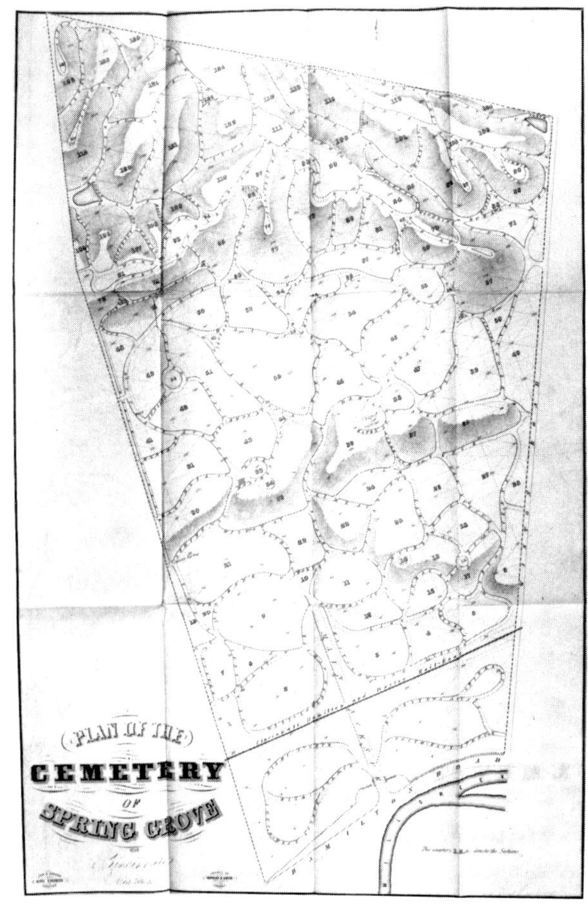

going rate in 1838. Unlike the Boston cemetery, half-lots were available in Worcester and sold at prices "very properly put so low as to come within the means of the great mass of the community."[16] Worcester's cemetery was intended to be more democratic than Mount Auburn.

Less-than-affluent New Englanders and those without easy access to Mount Auburn desired affordable burial lots in pastoral landscapes, albeit closer to their own residences. The Rural Cemetery of New Bedford was chartered in 1837 and opened in 1842; Harmony Grove was dedicated in Salem in 1840; Blue Hill in Braintree, in 1839; the Springfield Cemetery, in 1841; Oak Hill in Newburyport, in 1842; Woodlawn or the Garden Cemetery in Chelsea-Everett, in 1851; and Green Lawn in Nahant, in 1858. Sleepy Hollow in Concord had consecration services in 1855 that included an address by Ralph Waldo Emerson and the reading of a poem by the late William Ellery Channing.

Mount Auburn was no longer unique by mid-century, even in the Boston metropolitan area. Nor did it focus the historical consciousness of Yankees, especially after the founding of Boston's second "rural" cemetery. Urged on by local resident General Henry A. S. Dearborn, the first mayor of Roxbury, John J. Clarke convinced his City Council in 1846 of the necessity to establish a cemetery to replace the old town graveyards, which were filled up and in "repulsive condition." Mount Auburn was "too distant, and but comparatively few feel able to procure lots there," Clarke argued. Although most Roxbury residents lived on estates and in fine suburban homes, many complained that Mount Auburn did not supply the demand of all classes, the high and the low, the rich and the poor, let alone the "middling," for "laying the remains of their friends in grounds made beautiful as well as sacred." Clarke surmised that "taste and refined feelings are not measured by wealth, nor are they confined to the opulent."[17] Roxbury residents wanted their own cemetery to give larger portions of the population the opportunity of burying their dead in a pleasing, picturesque setting.

Despite minor opposition by the frugal few who felt Roxbury should only provide a simple potter's field for those who could not afford private burial

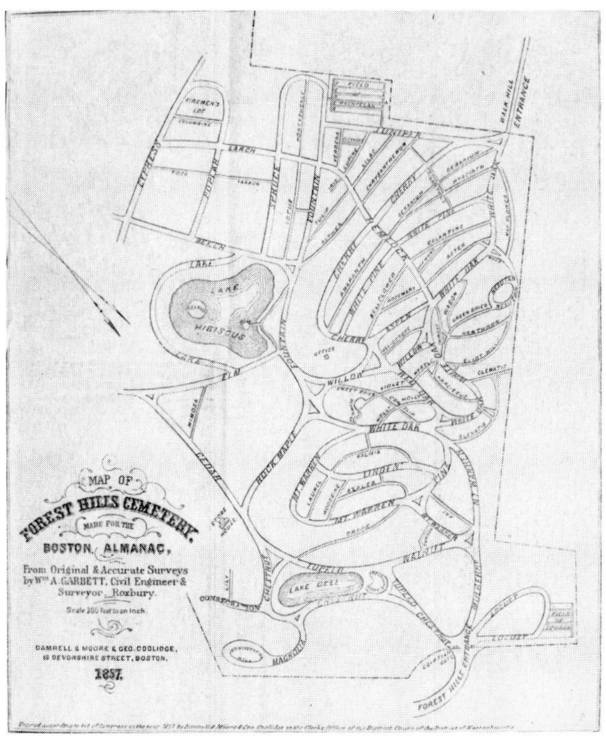

Fig. E.9. Forest Hills Cemetery, Roxbury (Boston), designed by General Henry A. S. Dearborn, 1845, map by William A. Garbett, 1857.

arrangements elsewhere, the municipality allocated $27,895 to purchase a farm with high ground, little lakes, and adjacent land totaling seventy-one acres. In 1847, assisted by the surveyor Daniel Brims, Dearborn designed and laid out the Rural Cemetery of Roxbury, later named Forest Hills, following the same manner he used at Mount Auburn sixteen years before. (Fig. E.9.) By 1858, Forest Hills expanded to 104 acres. Although initially the cemetery provided space for public burials free of charge, Forest Hills sold private family burial lots. Many members of the Massachusetts Horticultural Society, earlier disenchanted by Mount Auburn, and prominent Bostonians like Dr. John Collins Warren purchased lots there rather than at Mount Auburn. At $50 apiece, Forest Hills lots were about half the price of those at Mount Auburn. The economical price provided incentive to a substantial number of Mount Auburn proprietors to sell their lots and move bodies of kin across town to Roxbury. Despite this competition, Mount Auburn's older trustees insisted on raising their lot prices further, although in 1855 they yielded to pressure from their younger colleagues and, for the first time, permitted sale of quarter-lots of seventy-five square feet, provided that owners not become members of the corporation. In its first seven years, Forest Hills sold over nine hundred lots; by comparison, two-thirds that number were sold in Mount Auburn's first seven years (when there was no competition). By 1854 after twenty-three years, Mount Auburn had sold only 2,425 lots. Forest Hills matched Mount Auburn's appeal both in landscape taste and in intention to serve the entire metropolitan area. The second intention was made particularly explicit after 1868, when the City of Boston annexed Roxbury, necessitating rechartering of Forest Hills as a nonprofit, private corporation. Still, the City of Boston claimed the place as its own cemetery, purchasing in 1857 several thousand square feet of land for the Boston Fire Department. Forest Hills proved more economical than Mount Auburn and provided an equally fitting site for the fine monument bearing the statue of a noble but unnamed fireman.[18]

Fig. E.10. Egyptian revival gate, wood painted to resemble stone, designed by General Dearborn for Forest Hills Cemetery, 1845–65, engraving by John Andrew.

Proceeds from lot sales rather than public monies paid for all landscape improvements at Forest Hills. Dearborn designed an Egyptian gate. As had been initially the case at Mount Auburn, it was built of wood, but painted and sanded to resemble brownstone. (Fig. E.10.) There was, however, "a difference of opinion as to the propriety of using, as is much the custom, the Egyptian architecture about our burying places," wrote the author of the 1855 Forest Hills guidebook. Many considered the Egyptian gates a "relic of paganism," although the apologist for the style described it as "essentially the architecture of the grave" and "reminiscent of remote ages, of buried cities, and of peoples. Imposing and somber in form and mysterious in its remote origin . . . peculiarly adapted to the abode of the dead, and its enduring character contrasts strongly and strangely with the brief life of mortals." By the time funds accumulated to rebuild the gate in stone, tastes had changed and advocates of the Egyptian had lost their enthusiasm. In 1865, a "modern Gothic" structure of Roxbury stone and Caledonia freestone took its place. By 1876, the financial prosperity of Forest Hills also permitted construction of a twenty-five-foot-high rustic observatory on Consecration Hill. Parallels to the picturesque landscape at Mount Auburn were many.[19] (Fig. E.11.)

When Dearborn died in 1851, his eulogist praised the man who gave "his time and skill" freely in "designing and preparing" not only Forest Hills but cemeteries in many towns.[20] These may have been in the metropolitan area, although few specific records remain. The trend in voluntary burial reform, begun at Mount Auburn to compensate for Boston's failure to create new municipal burial grounds in pleasant landscapes beyond city limits, escalated through the 1850s. Voluntary associations in New England manufacturing towns developed their own rural cemeteries as their populations skyrocketed, although many of the industrial capitalists and their agents owned prominent lots at Mount Auburn. Lowell dedicated its Rural

Fig. E.11. Views of Forest Hills Cemetery, from Moses King's *Hand-Book of Boston,* 1878.

Cemetery in 1841; Providence, Swan Point in 1846; Waltham, Mount Feake in 1848; Lynn, Pine Grove in 1850; and Fall River, Oak Grove in 1853. Manchester, New Hampshire, further upstream on the industrialized Merrimac River, boasted the "improvement" of a public cemetery in the picturesque style, "deserving the attention of travelers." Pine Grove, opened in 1850, was in "a beautiful grove with a deep ravine traversed by a rivulet and tastefully intersected by winding paths" and "arranged somewhat like Mount Auburn."[21] All of these cemeteries, however, were more conveniently located to the populations of these burgeoning industrial cities and far less expensive (let alone prestigious) than Mount Auburn.

Although the movement to create pastoral cemeteries escalated in New England in particular in the antebellum decades, it was not without opponents. At the 1850 consecration of Brighton's small, fourteen-acre Evergreen Cemetery, the orator acknowledged a lingering controversy among the orthodox over the landscape inspired by liberal theology and taste: "Still to some it may yet appear a superfluous work, a work not quite in keeping with the essential elements of the New England character." The speaker argued that old burial landscapes proved "uninstructive" and were "unfrequented by our people." Graveyards, particularly in urban areas, had rarely been "places of habitual resort, where encouraging moral and religious reflections might be awakened." By mid-century, however, the pastoral ideal for a burial place had gained acceptance, albeit sometimes reluctant, among orthodox Calvinists and even those whose religious rites and symbols they had been most intent on rejecting.[22]

Finally, even Boston-area Catholics followed suit by founding "rural" cemeteries, despite traditional Church opposition to creating cemeteries apart from established churches or permitting plantings around graves. In 1857, the Catholic Cemetery Association of Dorchester (after 1877, the Boston Catholic Cemetery Association) incorporated an organization in reaction to a Boston Board of Health order to close Saint Augustine's Cemetery, the first Catholic burial ground in the metropolitan area since 1818. Bishop John Bernard Fitzpatrick protested vehemently, but he recognized that municipal restrictions of burial grounds in places like Charlestown would have dire consequences for the recently expanded Catholic community. Cambridge and Roxbury had recently sought legislation to close old graveyards, to require special permits for all burials, and to prohibit establishment of new cemeteries not under direct municipal control, measures aimed specifically at Catholics. Doctrinal reasons remained, however, for the archdiocese to provide its own burial places. Nondenominational cemeteries like Mount Auburn hung out no signs equivalent to the "No Irish Need Apply" in Yankee shop windows. Rather, the Church's insistence that communicants be buried in consecrated ground limited the choice of cemeteries for practicing Catholics, who were not even supposed to accept the inexpensive option of municipal burying grounds.[23]

Plans made in 1857 by the Catholic Cemetery Association for Holyhood in Brookline, just west of Boston, called for ponds and sinuous roads around the periphery of the grounds, vaguely reminiscent of "rural" cemetery design, but these were never installed. A steepled chapel was designed by the influential Catholic ecclesiastical architect Patrick Heeley, making the grounds a sort of churchyard. Still, despite traditional Church opposition to burial landscapes suggestive of pantheism, the entire cemetery reflects the intention to create a moderately romantic landscape.

Such was not the case in other Catholic cemeteries. In 1870, the bishop of Boston purchased for \$65,000 a 6½-acre wedge of land to establish a cemetery in Watertown, immediately to the west of Mount Auburn's wall; its landscape, however, remains purely functional for burial, with graves arranged in a formal, linear manner on either side of one straight, central road. Curiously, there is no chapel. Although this cemetery eventually accumulated several fine Victorian funerary monuments over graves covered only by dried grass and weeds, they are crowded together among plain stones in rows unadorned by trees or shrubs, in dramatic contrast to the backdrop of Mount Auburn's naturalistic landscape on the other side of the wall. (Fig. E.12.)

The municipality of Boston did not acquire an extramural cemetery to replace its old town grounds until 1857, when it annexed the five-year-old Mount Hope Cemetery with 106 acres of ponds and trees located in the valley just south of Forest Hills between Dorchester and West Roxbury. That year marked the first time a city document used the word "cemetery" in lieu of the simple, traditional reference to "burial grounds." Finally, in 1862, after establishing its own alternatives, the City banned further burials in church crypts; their contents were eventually moved to suburban cemeteries, including Mount Auburn.

Through the 1870s, despite facilities provided by Mount Auburn, Forest Hills, and other private rural cemeteries, in addition to Catholic cemeteries, many municipalities in the Boston metropolitan area founded public funerary landscapes designed more or less following the pastoral ideal. In 1870, the town of Watertown, site of over 90 percent of Mount Auburn itself, expended \$10,000 to purchase and lay out a garden cemetery to be given the local Indian name Weetomac. Although many town officials hoped the cemetery would become "a second Mount Auburn," selectmen could not agree whether to permit Catholics to consecrate part of the grounds for themselves; the property was sold when no decision could be reached. A similar dispute prevented the neighboring town of Arlington from establishing its own "rural" cemetery.

The City of Cambridge was more successful. In 1854, it purchased twenty-four acres of land on the Charles River from Mount Auburn. The property was separated only by a peripheral road; and City Engineer J. G. Chase followed the landscape design of the original in laying out the municipal cemetery with picturesque, winding roads given plant names. The landscape seemed to be an extension of Mount Auburn, although on slightly flatter terrain. Only in the twentieth century did the contrast become pronounced, due to poor maintenance, lack of restorative planting, and crowding of individual graves in the public cemetery. Despite formal disestablishment, political separation of church and state, city authorities stipulated that only those who resided in Cambridge and assisted in supporting some religious denomination there could purchase family lots in the cemetery.[24]

The illustrious, intellectual James and Howells families, relative newcomers to New England, chose family plots at the Cambridge Cemetery, a fact that many visitors, expecting to find such notables at Mount Auburn, find curious. Van Wyck Brooks offers one possible explanation of why the elder James favored the new public cemetery. The patriarch "was convinced that property was not a final fact of history, since men were ashamed of the deference they paid it." He was skeptical of institutions like churches and colleges; he especially decried "a feeble Unitarian sentimentality" as far less desirable than the "old virile religion," represented by the old, common burial grounds of New England. But then, no more burials were permitted in the first Cambridge graveyard once the new public cemetery was opened. Still, James, Senior, rejected Mount Auburn, the quintessential product of a Unitarianism that he considered "not itself a religion, but rather a kind of cultural substitute for religion." Brooks wrote, "his pet aversion was 'flagrant morality' or any sort of conscious virtue." James, Senior, was "a mystical democrat" and "an absolute libertarian,"

Fig. E.12. Catholic Cemetery in Watertown, just west of Mount Auburn, a study in contrasting landscape taste, photograph by Alan Ward, 1987.

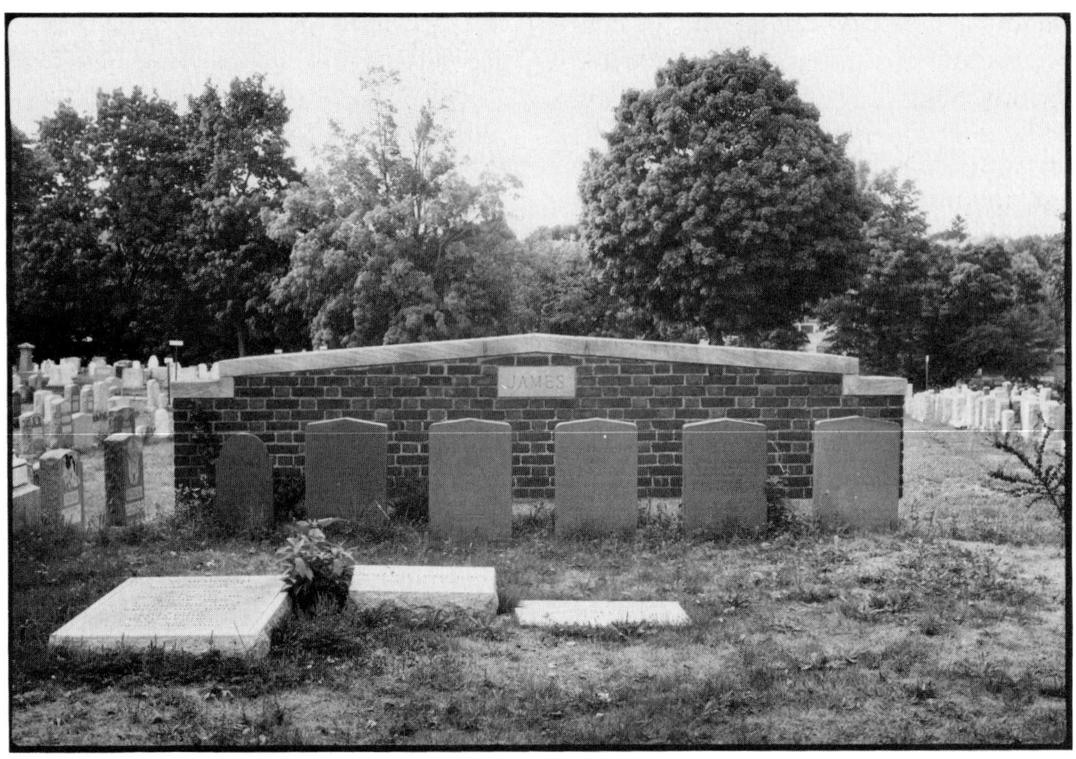

Fig. E.13. (*Above*) Henry James family lot, Cambridge Cemetery, photograph by Alan Ward, 1987.

Fig. E.14. (*Below*) William Dean Howells family lot, Cambridge Cemetery, photograph by Alan Ward, 1987.

who, like Whitman, "preferred the company of stage-drivers to that of 'our' literary men." According to George Santayana, the elder James "escaped the limitations" of the "genteel tradition." The man who described "a crowded horse-car" as the "nearest approach on earth to the joys of heaven" chose burial with common Cambridge citizens; there, in the new municipal cemetery, he was laid to rest in 1882, followed a decade later by the ashes of his daughter Alice and then by his sons William and Henry.[25] (Fig. E.13).

Influenced by Tolstoy and horrified by America's growing class divisions, the Ohio-born democratic realist and socialist writer William Dean Howells followed the example of the James family and purchased a lot near theirs. (Fig. E.14.) Thomas Wentworth Higginson, an abolitionist and minister of a gospel too liberal even for Unitarians, also chose burial in the Cambridge cemetery rather than at Mount Auburn. As if to challenge the claim made for Colonel Robert Gould Shaw, Jr., whose family lies at Mount Auburn, Higginson's stone rightfully proclaims his command of the first black regiment in the Civil War, the 1st South Carolina Volunteers, later the 33rd U.S. Colored Troops, the first Negro unit in the U.S. Army and the first in the South. (Fig. E.15.)

As picturesque cemeteries in the Boston metropolitan area proliferated, Mount Auburn had considerable competition to be the resting place of New England notables. Daniel Webster, who had added his voice to those calling for the first "rural" cemetery in 1830, ultimately chose burial in his native New Hampshire, perhaps as much excluded by those alienated by his stance on the Fugitive Slave Law as choosing to return to rest at home. Emerson, Hawthorne, Thoreau, and the Alcotts lay along Authors' Ridge at Concord's Sleepy Hollow Cemetery. The abolitionist William Lloyd Garrison, the sculptor Martin Milmore (whose funerary monument commemorates his work on Mount Auburn's sphinx), the writer and orator Edward Everett Hale, the playwright Eugene O'Neill, the poet e. e. cummings, and others eventually came to rest across town at Forest Hills.

Mount Auburn accumulated a long list of the graves of notables through its first century and after—many with the potential of becoming the sort of role models if not heroes that cemetery founders hoped would shape the lives of successive generations by their examples and lessons of individual commitment to virtue, work, and excellence. But, reflecting the general failure of commemoration in the nation at large, such graves drew little public notice except from a few antiquarians. Perhaps now and then some devotee of American poetry or legal scholar made pilgrimage to the grave of Longfellow or Story. In the last decades of the century, associations of "colored" citizens of Boston came *en masse* to the grave of abolitionist Senator Charles Sumner, who in 1878 received a commemorative monument in the Public Garden in contrast to his simple family monument at the cemetery. (Figs. E.16, 17.) But from

Fig. E.15. Thomas Wentworth Higginson stone, slate, 1911, Cambridge Cemetery, photograph by Alan Ward, 1987.

Fig. E.16. Charles Sumner portrait statue, $9\frac{1}{2}$-foot bronze by Thomas Ball, 1878, on granite pedestal in Boston Public Garden, half of a stereographic photograph, ca. 1880.

the end of the Civil War on, Mount Auburn was no longer recognized as the general, public place for creation of regional, let alone national, heroes and history as its founders had hoped.

Some individuals who had intentions to erect elaborate commemorative monuments abandoned them. For instance, visiting her childhood home in Watertown from her studio in Florence, Italy, the sculptor Harriet Hosmer looked for a site in Mount Auburn where she could place a sculptural monument to her noted physician father, Hiram. She purchased a family lot but did nothing more. Their

Fig. E.17. Charles Sumner funerary monument, Arethusa Path near Walnut Avenue, photograph by Alan Ward, 1988.

Fig. E.18. Hosmer and Homer (left rear) family monuments, Lily and Hemlock paths, photograph by Alan Ward, 1988.

simple, modern memorial, of the new, mass-produced sort purchased from a company rather than custom-made and shaped by the sculptor's hand with evocative intent, offers no evidence of the distinction achieved by either father or daughter in their lifetimes; it simply records their lives and deaths. Like the plain stone of Winslow Homer just across Lily Path, it is purely funerary.[26] (Fig. E.18.)

To imply that Mount Auburn failed to achieve the idealistic commemorative ambitions of its founders would be to repeat the mythic theme of declension characteristic of much of the perception of New England's past. Like the Puritan town, the cemetery changed considerably over time; that change was adaptive to new notions about the relationship of the individual to community, God, and Nature as well as to growth of a diversified population, development of technology, and spread of mass culture. Like the models of landscape and social organization provided by early Puritan towns, Mount Auburn was deliberately designed to be a prototype of design and a definition of community. The "rural" cemetery movement, like the "hiving off" of New England townspeople and town form to the west, only indicates a persistent strength of form capable of adaptation to meet changing social and cultural circumstances.

Mount Auburn did not *fail* in its mission to become exemplary, to teach lessons of moral philosophy, to be a "silent city on a hill." As Americans gradually shifted their tastes and assumptions about death, Mount Auburn's appearance and functions were altered, as were those of other "rural" cemeteries patterned after it that eventually became "garden" cemeteries. The place

Fig. E.19. Urban streets at Père Lachaise Cemetery, Paris, photographs by Alan Ward, 1985.

Fig. E.20.

and the institution never went into a state of decline, disuse, or rejection; they simply changed. Idealism gave way to pragmatism and a more simple functionalism. And as pluralism in the Boston metropolitan area increased, no single exemplary institution would suffice; there was a diversity of material definitions of individual identity, family cohesion, status, and community consciousness transcending death.

The fact that Mount Auburn and *its* prototype, Père Lachaise, developed so very differently after beginning with essentially the same landscape aesthetics and design intentions is an indication of the differences between American and French culture over the course of two centuries. As early as 1838, Harriet Martineau "read" the two landscapes as documents of national cultures. That year, Charles Sumner wrote to Judge Joseph Story from Paris that he could not see why Mount Auburn was so often compared to "that immense city of the dead." There, at least 50,000 monuments were already crowded together "as thick and close as corn that grows in the field; tomb touches tomb and monument adjoins upon monument. The eye is wearied by the constant succession; it solicits in vain the relief of a little green grass." Sumner hoped that "many years will pass away" before Mount Auburn's pastoralism would be similarly obliterated. Happily, it never has been. Sumner concluded, "Give me our Mount Auburn, clad in the russet dress of nature, with its simple memorials scattered here and there, its beautiful paths and its overshadowing grove. Nature has done as much for Mount Auburn as man has for Père Lachaise, and I need not tell you how superior is the workmanship of Nature."[27]

Through the second half of the nineteenth century, other visitors took note of the widening differences between "manners and customs" revealed in the artifacts and landscapes of the two cemeteries. One reviewer wrote, "The parent cemetery of Père Lachaise . . . has been surpassed by its descendants. . . . The French graveyard shows too plainly the pruning hand of man.

Fig. E.21.

Artificial landscape, prim parterres and mathematically clipped bowers, give it too much that stiff and constrained aspect which is the failure of Versailles. Ostentatious monuments and sculptured tombs . . . are laid out in streets, instead of being scattered about the grounds." (Figs. E.19, 20, 21.) Another writer found Père Lachaise "only remarkable for its historical interest. There is nothing bright nor beautiful. The tombs, with few exceptions are hustled together like houses in a large city. It is grand, sad, and silent."[28] (Fig. E.22.)

Bigelow and subsequent trustees were indeed responsible for setting policies that led to prohibitively high lot prices and rules that limited proprietors' freedom to erect ostentatious monuments and tombs, thereby limiting the popularity of Mount Auburn and its development as a "Westminster Abbey" for the region. But those very policies also contributed to preservation of some of the original pastoralism of the place. (Fig. E.23.) Meanwhile, creation of parks and museums provided other institutions to relieve the cemetery of its role as chief pleasure ground and place for display of fine art and architecture in the urban area.

By the 1860s, most of Mount Auburn's trustees and proprietors agreed with Wilson Flagg that cemetery grounds should not "be made a place for general recreation. The idea of connecting them with a public garden was unwise." Flagg proposed, "If our citizens feel the want of a place for rural recreation, where they can employ themselves in cheerful festivities and enjoy the beauties of nature, they should purchase a pleasant and extensive tract of pasture and woodland and devote it to these purposes."[29] Over the next decades, Bostonians heeded Flagg's advice by participating in the public park movement.

Organizers of subscription campaigns for commemorative monuments selected places like Boston's Public Garden, the Commons, the State House grounds, and other park areas for public remembrance of the likes of Josiah Quincy, William Ellery Channing, and Charles Sumner, notables who were buried in Mount Auburn. A distinction was made between the civic and the funerary monument. The monument would thus be regularly seen and enjoyed by a wider portion of the general public than it would at the cemetery, and it would become an ornament in the urban fabric at the time when civic leaders became more concerned with beautifying Boston. Furthermore, contributions to the monument would not have to include funds to pay for cemetery land or to maintain it.

By the last quarter of the century, few Bostonians still referred to Mount Auburn as a museum or hoped to develop it as a repository of art. The Boston Museum of Fine Arts, chartered in 1870 and opened in 1876, provided the public with a place to see fine art and architecture that previously could only be found at Mount Auburn, unless one was a member of the Athenaeum. The public preferred to see authentic Egyptian artifacts rather than American renditions of the style, although both were equally out of context. At the museum, one could find impeccable marble sculptures by the likes of William Wetmore Story and Randolph Rogers protected from the wear and tear of the harsh New England environment, unlike those exposed to winter snows and acid rain at the cemetery.

The cultural centrality of Mount Auburn was lessened further by the rapid fading of the American taste for sentimentality. Mark Twain, in *The Adventures of Huckleberry Finn* (1884), finds the old melancholy anachronistic. Twain's satire of old deathways signaled the transition to what some critics of culture have labeled the modern "denial of death."[30] Trends in privatization made mourning and sentimentality increasingly a family matter to be kept under the wraps of strictly prescribed women's mourning dress, hidden behind an emotionless façade for men, and consigned to domestic places even more private than the Victorian parlor. Following the trend, even the display of familial emotions in words and symbols at the burial place faded from fashion. Only the most standardized, simple, mass-produced "memorial" stone remained, and these accumulated in newer sections around the periphery of Mount Auburn into the twentieth century.

Ironically, when Americans put the past under grass, explicitly equating history and death in funerary institutions like Mount Auburn, they made the past no longer usable. Mount Auburn and other landscapes of memory lost their purpose as histor-

Fig. E.22. Bird's-eye view of Père Lachaise, built up as a City of the Dead, engraving by Ledot, ca. 1880.

ical agents well before the last quarter of the century. Significantly, in Edward Bellamy's utopian novel *Looking Backward* (1888), Julian West passes his last day in the nineteenth century visiting Mount Auburn on Decoration Day with his betrothed, Edith Bartlett, before waking from an extended mesmerized sleep in Boston in the year 2000.[31] Once the past was past and the dead of the New England Renaissance buried, even Yankees became so intent on getting on to the future that they had no time for cemeteries. Musing on the past, like excessive mourning, was counterproductive and an inefficient use of time. Funerary directors and cemeterians professionalized, making death a matter of business and bringing an end to the "domestication of death" that characterized the early nineteenth century.

An appropriate parable for the cultural change appeared in Lucretia Hale's "Peterkin Papers." An American family, presumably elite Bostonians, is lost in Europe along with their luggage. Similarly, turn-of-the-century Bostonians had lost their old cultural baggage. According to Brooks, the Bostonians "had no Lady from Philadelphia to tell them to meet at the Sphinx." They had abandoned all of their old guides. Indeed, back in Boston was their real sphinx, commemorative of the Union dead but financed solely by Dr. Jacob Bigelow as his last personal gesture of Whiggish idealism. It sat silently facing north at Mount Auburn, by then well off the tourist's beaten path. Brooks adds, metaphorically, "Whether they could have found the Sphinx and what the Sphinx might have had to say were questions which they scarcely dared to ask."[32]

Yet, in the end, after a hundred and fifty years, Mount Auburn's private, sentimental significance remains, along with vestiges of its original naturalistic landscape. There are even hints that it is being rediscovered as a place of history. Tastes change, as does the tenor of the times. The author of the cemetery's first guidebook in 1839 may have been prescient: "Future generations may be prouder of it than we are, but can they be as fond? Will not the musing moralist of those days, sometimes weary of sensations and splendor, turn or seek to turn back in imagination to this uncrowded quietude and primitive simplicity—this glistening turf—these cool, sweet-winding avenues and paths—this green, fresh beauty of the woods?"[33]

Fig. E.23. Bigelow Chapel from Cypress Avenue, photograph by Alan Ward, 1977.

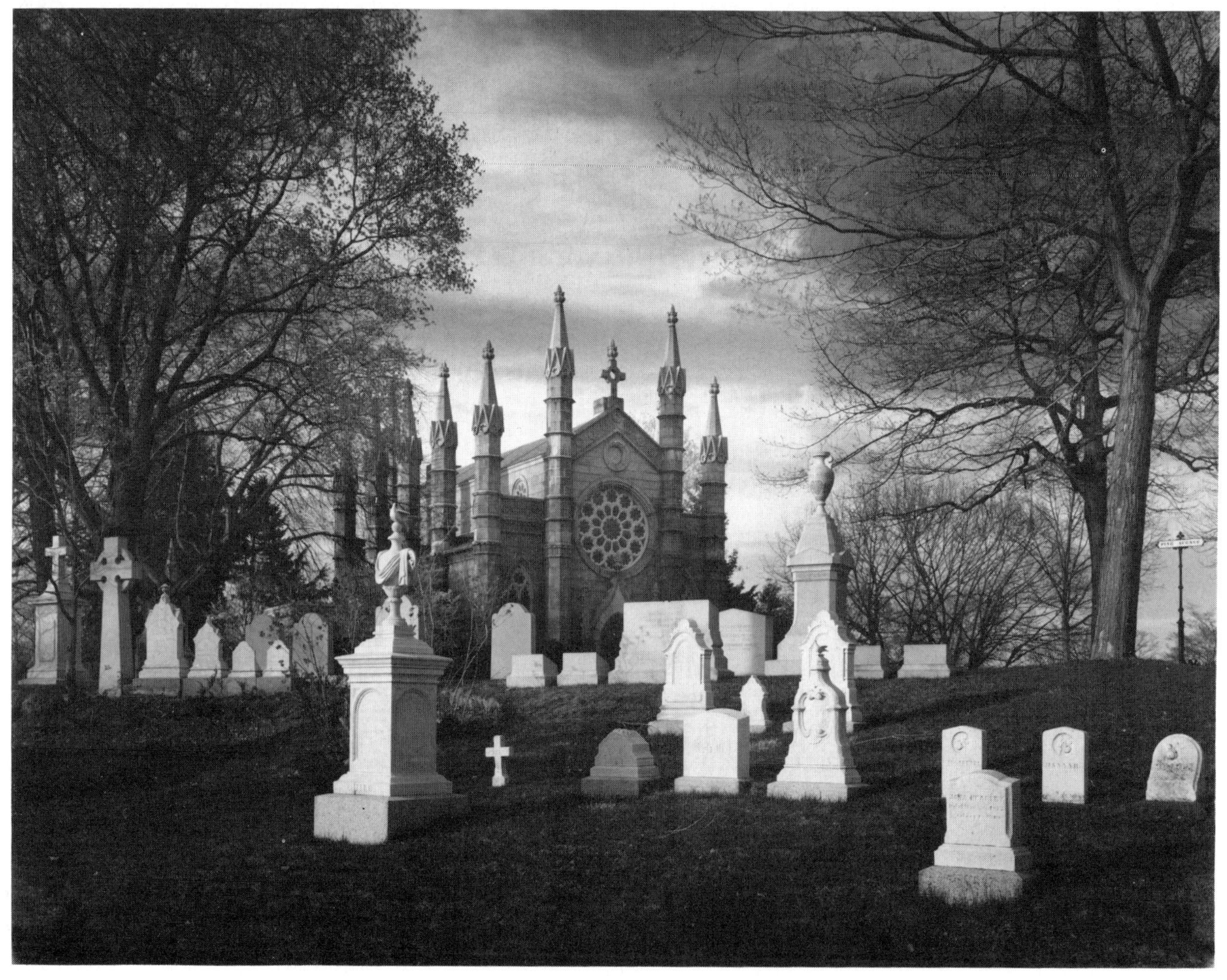

Appendix:

Trustees and Officers of the Corporation in the Nineteenth Century

PRESIDENTS:	Joseph Story	1835–1845
	Jacob Bigelow	1845–1871
	John T. Bradlee	1871–1874
	Israel M. Spelman	1874–1905
SECRETARIES:	George W. Pratt	1831–1832
	Charles P. Curtis	1832–1835
	Benjamin R. Curtis	1835–1844
	Henry M. Parker	1844–1855
	Austin J. Coolidge	1855–1870
	Samuel Batchelder, Jr.	1870–1876
	J. Harris Reed	1876–1882
	Lewis G. Farmer	1883–1907
TREASURERS:	George Bond	1831–1842
	George William Bond	1842–1867
	Austin J. Coolidge	1868–1870
	Henry B. Mackintosh	1870–1900
SUPERINTENDENTS:	David Haggerston	1833–1834
	John W. Russell	1834–1840
	Rufus Howe	1841–1855
	Jonathan Mann	1855–1861
	Daniel L. Winsor	1861–1870
	Charles W. Folsom	1870–1873
	James W. Lovering	1873–1896
GARDENERS:	Anthony Apple	1858–1860
	William H. Spooner	1860–1862
FOUNDERS AND TRUSTEES:	Joseph Story	1831–1845
	Jacob Bigelow	1831–1879
	George Bond	1831–1842
	Benjamin A. Gould	1831–1859
	Henry A. S. Dearborn	1831–1833
	George W. Brimmer	1831–1832
	Charles Wells	1831–1832
	Edward Everett	1831–1832
	George W. Pratt	1831–1832
	Zebedee Cook, Jr.	1832–1833
	Joseph P. Bradlee	1833–1837

Charles Brown	1833–1837
Charles P. Curtis	1833–1864
Samuel Appleton	1834–1837
Elijah Vose	1834–1837
James Read	1835–1870
Benjamin R. Curtis	1837–1851
Martin Brimmer	1838–1847
Isaac Parker	1838–1854
Samuel T. Armstrong	1839–1840
George W. Crockett	1843–1855
John C. Gray	1845–1849
John J. Dixwell	1847–1851
Mace Tisdale	1850–1853, 1855–1858
George H. Kuhn	1852–1855
Charles C. Little	1852–1869
Isaiah Bangs	1854–1859
James Cheever	1856–1870
Uriel Crocker	1856–1865
William R. Lawrence	1856–1860
Henry S. McKean	1856–1857
Charles C. Nazro	1856–1865
William T. Andrews	1859–1863
Jacob Sleeper	1859–1870
Edward S. Tobey	1859–1863
Edward Austin	1860–1870
Edward S. Rand	1860–1871
George Livermore	1864–1865
Otis Norcross	1864–1870
J. Ingersoll Bowditch	1865–1870
Paul Adams	1865–1870
Loyal Lovejoy	1865–1870
Isaac Livermore	1866–1874
John T. Bradlee	1870–1877
Nathaniel J. Bradlee	1870–1880
Alfred T. Turner	1870–1874
Thomas M. Brewer	1870–1880
Edward Lawrence	1871–1881
Charles F. Choate	1871–1911
William Perkins	1871–1880
Samuel T. Snow	1871–1880
James L. Little	1871–1877
Henry W. Pickering	1872–1877
T. Quincy Browne	1874–1899
Israel M. Spelman	1874–1905
Charles U. Cotting	1877–1885
Alanson Bigelow	1877–1884
Henry A. Rice	1877–1895

Notes

INTRODUCTION

1. Alexis de Tocqueville met members of the Boston elite, many of whom were founders of Mount Auburn, at a dinner hosted by Alexander Everett.

2. The term "culture" is used in its nineteenth-century sense, often closely associated with art and hence akin to meanings of "high culture" or civilization. The word was also frequently closely associated with "the idea of care . . . or superintendence of the landscape." Both uses implied spiritual purpose. See Edgar Allan Poe, "The Domain of Arnheim" (1847), in *Edgar Allan Poe: Selected Prose, Poetry, and Eureka,* ed. by W. H. Auden (New York: Holt, Rinehart, & Winston, 1950), 401–2.

3. William Wordsworth, quoted in F. R. Cowell, *The Garden as Fine Art* (Boston: Houghton Mifflin, 1978), 185. Mortuary themes used in English gardens were drawn from Virgil, Seneca, Lucretius, and Ovid.

4. William B. O. Peabody, "Mount Auburn Cemetery: Report of the Massachusetts Horticultural Society upon the Establishment of an Experimental Garden and Rural Cemetery," *North American Review* 33 (Oct. 1831), 397–98; and "Mount Auburn," *New England Magazine* (Sept. 1831), 236–39. Wilson Flagg, *Mount Auburn: Its Scenes, Its Beauties, and Its Lessons* (Boston: James Munroe, 1861), 272. See Gordon S. Wood, *The Creation of the American Republic, 1776–1787* (Chapel Hill: Univ. of North Carolina Press, 1969), 33; also reprinted as "The Whig Science of Politics," in James Kirby Martin, *Interpreting Colonial America: Selected Readings* (New York: Harper & Row, 1978), 340.

5. See the history of usage of the term "revolution" in the *Oxford English Dictionary.*

6. Malcolm MacColl, *Lawlessness, Sacerdotalism, and Ritualism discussed in Six Letters Addressed . . . to the Right Hon. Lord Selborne* (London: J. T. Hayes, 1875), 418–19.

7. [John Calvin], *The Forme of Prayers and Ministrations of the Sacraments, etc., Used in the English Congregation at Geneva; and Approved by the Famous and Godly Learned Man, Iohn Caluyn* (1556), reprinted in *The Liturgical Portions of the Genevan Service Book* (Edinburgh and London, 1931), 161. Also see Horton Davies, *The Worship of the English Puritans* (Westminster: Dacre Press, 1948), 121–22. In England, secularization of churches included substituting images of Queen Elizabeth for those of Christ, Mary, and the saints.

8. See Allan Ludwig, *Graven Images: New England Stonecarving and Its Symbols, 1650–1815* (Middletown, Conn.: Wesleyan Univ. Press, 1966); Edward Young, *Night Thoughts on Life, Death, and Immortality* (Philadelphia: Benjamin Johnson, 1805), I:143.

9. John Bunyan, *Pilgrim's Progress,* ed. by J. B. Wharey (1678; Oxford: Oxford Univ. Press, 1928). This is considered the standard edition.

10. Jacques Delille, "Preface by the Translator," in René Louis Marquis de Girardin, *An Essay on Landscape; or, on the Means of Improving and Embellishing the Country Around our Habitations* (London: J. Dodsley, 1793), xxxvi. The term "tourism" developed at the end of the eighteenth century in reference to making the principal stops on the Grand Tour. By that time, however, the itinerary had become far more extensive, bringing international travelers into contact with one another to escalate the rate of cross-cultural borrowing. The painter Washington Allston from Boston met Coleridge in Rome in 1806. In 1826, Harvard's President Kirkland and his wife visited the pyramids in Egypt. Mary Bigelow to [her mother], (June 20, 1826), Bigelow Papers, MHIS.

11. Allegory and historicism were intricately related, as French architectural critic Antoine-Chrysostome Quatremère de Quincy recognized: "By means of allegory, the art of architecture is made *historian* and *narrator:* It explores to us the general and particular subject of which it treats, and it informs us of the moral aim as well as the physical use of the building. Allegorical decoration takes the place of inscriptions; and it speaks better." "Décoration," in *Encyclopédie Méthodique,* 2, pt. 1, 179, quoted in Anthony Vidler, *The Writing of the Walls* (Princeton: Princeton Architectural Press, 1987), 161–62. Vidler also argues for major Masonic influence on and use of English gardens, factors which may carry over in aesthetic influences of the landscape style on "rural" cemeteries but which I have been unable to document for this study.

12. Rev. William Mason, quoted in Edward Malins, *English Landscaping and Literature, 1660–1840* (London: Oxford Univ. Press, 1966), 87.

13. Arthur O. Lovejoy, *Essays in the History of Ideas* (Baltimore: Johns Hopkins Univ. Press, 1948), 134. A. A. Tait, *The Landscape Garden in Scotland, 1735–1835* (Edinburgh: Edinburgh Univ. Press, 1980), 7. Christopher Hussey, *English Gardens and Landscapes, 1700–1750* (New York: Funk & Wagnalls, 1967), 112, 89, 100–101. My study deliberately avoids the landscape reform of the "beautiful" by Lancelot "Capability" Brown because it had few of the allegorical or historicist references of other landscape gardeners of the "picturesque" style and because it had little influence on other landscapes of memory or "rural" cemeteries during the period under consideration in this book.

14. Lawrence Stone, *The Family, Sex and Marriage in England, 1500–1800* (New York: Harper & Row, 1977), 3–4. Stone, "Death and Its History," *New York Review of Books* 25:15 (Oct. 12, 1978), 22. David Hume used the word "sentiment" to mean both feeling and thought, thus giving a different interpretation to "sentimentality" than it would acquire in the nineteenth century. David Daiches, Peter Jones, and Jean Jones, eds., *A Hotbed of Genius: The Scottish En-*

lightenment, 1730–1790 (Edinburgh: Edinburgh Univ. Press, 1986), 18.

15. Delille, "Preface," iv.

16. Wood, 340. William Wordsworth, *The Prelude,* Book 11 (composed ca. Feb. 1804) (New York: Appleton. 1850); Edward Everett, *An Oration Pronounced at Cambridge before the Phi Beta Kappa Society, Aug. 27, 1824* (Boston, 1824).

17. Alain Corbin, *The Foul and the Fragrant: Odor and the French Social Imagination* (Cambridge: Harvard Univ. Press, 1986).

18. Justin Winsor, ed., *The Memorial History of Boston, 1630–1880* (Boston: James R. Osgood, 1881), IV:86.

19. Harrison Gray Otis to George Harrison (Mar. 2, 1823), in Samuel Eliot Morison, ed., *The Life and Letters of Harrison Gray Otis* (Boston: Houghton Mifflin, 1946), I:449. [Thomas Green Fessenden,] *New England Farmer* 9:7 (Sept. 3, 1830), 53.

20. Odell Shepard, ed., *The Journals of Bronson Alcott* (Boston: Little, Brown, & Co., 1938), 15.

21. [Henry A. S. Dearborn,] "Mount Auburn Cemetery: Report of the Massachusetts Horticultural Society upon the Establishment of an Experimental Garden and Rural Cemetery, Boston, 1831," *North American Review* 33 (1831): 403.

22. Ronald Story, *The Forging of an Aristocracy: Harvard and the Boston Upper Class, 1800–1870* (Middletown, Conn.: Wesleyan Univ Press, 1980).

23. Alexander H. Everett, *An Address Delivered before the Massachusetts Horticultural Society at their 5th Annual Festival, Sept. 18, 1833* (Boston: J. T. Buckingham, 1833), 19.

24. Ann Douglas, *The Feminization of American Culture* (New York: Knopf, 1977).

25. Andrew Jackson Downing, "Improving the Public Ground of the City of Washington," letter to President Millard Fillmore, Winterthur Document (n.d., 1851?) no. 4838, 6–7, quoted in Walter L. Creese, *The Crowning of the American Landscape* (Princeton: Princeton Univ. Press, 1985), 207.

26. Clarence Cook, *A Description of the New York Central Park* (1869; New York: Benjamin Blom, 1972), 15. So significant is Mount Auburn's landscape design that the misconception is often repeated that Frederick Law Olmsted laid it out. Yet Olmsted was only three when Dr. Bigelow proposed the cemetery in 1825, and only nine in 1831, when General Dearborn worked out the initial design from English and French books. By the time Olmsted began his design career in 1858, shifting from writing to supervising construction of Central Park, Mount Auburn was a mature landscape over a quarter-century old.

CHAPTER 1

1. Institutionalization of burials appeared at different times in different areas following the conversion to Christianity of native peoples. The Saxons were not converted until the eighth century, nor the Danes until the tenth.

2. *Monumenta germaniae historica* (Hanover, 1875–89), Leges 5, Capitula de partibus Saxoniae, year 777, p. 43, quoted in Philippe Ariès, *The Hour of our Death,* trans. by Helen Weaver (New York: Knopf, 1981), 38, 50–51. Ariès, *Images de l'homme devant la mort* (Paris: Seuil, 1983), 20–21.

3. Ariès, *The Hour,* 39–41.

4. Ariès, *Images,* 24–29.

5. Henry Martyn Dexter, *The Congregationalism of the Last Three Hundred Years* (New York: Harper & Brothers, 1880), 11 and 26.

6. Léon Vafflard, *Notice sur les champs de sépultures anciens et modernes de la ville de Paris.* (Paris: Charles de Mougues Frères, 1867), 22–23, 34. Robert Hertz observes the prevalence in many societies of a second burial of remains after decomposition. He attributes the practice to social and psychological as well as practical motivations. In French and Italian cemeteries of the seventeenth and eighteenth centuries, it was a functional necessity to free grave space for reuse; the practice persisted even into the mid-nineteenth century in Boston, however, as records of reinterments at Mount Auburn Cemetery reveal. Robert Hertz, *Death and the Right Hand,* trans. by R. and C. Needham (Glencoe, Ill.: Free Press, 1960), chap. 6.

7. Michel Ragon, *The Space of Death: A Study in Funerary Architecture, Decoration, and Urbanism,* trans. by Alan Sheridan (Charlottesville: Univ. of Virginia Press, 1983), 51. In 1783, the French considered introducing wolves surreptitiously into England as a means of weakening British power. Fernand Braudel, *Capitalism and Material Life, 1400–1800,* trans. by Miriam Kochan (New York: Harper & Row, 1973), 34. For a depiction of wolves lurking outside cemetery walls, see the mid-nineteenth-century painting *Les Lupens* by Maurice Sand (1828–89) in the Musée Goya, Castres, France.

8. See Maud de Leigh Hodges, *Crossroads on the Charles: A History of Watertown, Massachusetts* (Canaan, N.H.: Phoenix, for the Watertown Free Public Library, 1980), 31. Howard S. Russell, *A Long, Deep Furrow: Three Centuries of Farming in New England* (Hanover, N.H.: Univ. Press of New England, 1976), 23, 83. Edward Doubleday Harris, "Introduction," in Thaddeus William Harris, *Epitaphs from the Old Burying Ground in Watertown* (Boston: n.p., 1869), ii. By 1855, Henry David Thoreau noted that the "rav'nous howling Wolf" observed in 1633 by William Wood had long been exterminated. Surely it is not merely a change in cultural tastes that permitted Yankees to plan on founding new burial grounds on the periphery of urban development only a decade after the passing of the threat of wolves.

9. Betty Willsher and Doreen Hunter, *Stones: A Guide to Some Remarkable Eighteenth-Century Scottish Gravestones* (New York: Taplinger, 1979), 60. Henry A. S. Dearborn, "Report," in "Proceedings of the Massachusetts Horticultural Society . . . 1831," *New England Farmer* 9:49 (June 22, 1831), 385. On the French cypress, see C. P. Arnaud, *Recueil de tombeaux des quatres cimetières de Paris* (Paris: Arnaud & Germain Mathiot, 1824), I:42.

10. The yew, *Taxus baccata Linnaei,* was called *Iw* in Saxon and *Yw* in Welsh. F. E. Warren, *The Liturgy and Ritual of the Celtic Church* (Oxford: Clarendon Press, 1883), 94. James Stevens Curl, *The Victorian Celebration of Death* (London: Trowbridge, 1972), 45. John Potenger, "Pastoral Reflections on Death" (1691), quoted in John Draper, *The Funeral Elegy and the Rise of English Romanticism* (New York: New York Univ. Press, 1929), 66–69. T. H. W., "Botanical History of the Yew Tree," *Gentleman's Magazine* 56, pt. 2, no. 5 (Nov. 1786), 941. The frequent appearance of yews in Scottish graveyards has been attributed to the order by Edward IV that every man must have a bow; the strong but flexible yew branches were perfect for bow making. Yew wood was so precious for long bows that Venetians shipped it to England from Turkey until the sixteenth century, when the supply ran out and the Turks had to import it for themselves from Germany. Fernand Braudel, *The Mediterranean and the Mediterranean World in the Age of Philip II,* trans. by Sian Reynolds (New York: Harper & Row, 1973), II:800–801. T. J. Pettigrew, *The Chronicles of Tombs* (Edinburgh: H. G. Bohn, 1859), cited in Willsher and Hunter, 60. Indeed, the blooming yew produces a hallucinogenic chemical. Also see Vaughan Cornish, *The Churchyard Yew and Immortality* (London: F. Muller, 1946).

11. The name "Druid," for instance, means "knowing the oak tree" and applies to an elite Celtic class charged with guarding sacred oak groves and other sites holy to Celtic peoples (*loci consecrati,* according to Caesar). Carlo Borromeo, *Instructiones Fabricae et Suppelectilis Ecclesiasticae* (Milan, 1577), cited in Richard A. Etlin, *The Architecture of Death: The Transformation of the Cemetery in Eighteenth-Century Paris* (Cambridge: MIT Press, 1984), 90 and 380. Borromeo, *Arte Sacra: De Fabrica Ecclesiae* (Milan, 1952), capo 27, "Sepolcreti e Cimiteri," 88: "Non vi si devono piantare viti, alberi, arbusti, sterpi di alcun genere, no solo di quelli da frutta, ma nemmanco di quelli che producano bacche d'alcun genere. Anzi non vi si lasci neppure crescere erba o fieno che serva per pascolo angli animali." M. [Henri] Bourde de la Rougerie, *Le Parlement de Bretagne, l'évêque de Rennes et les ifs dans les cimetières, 1636–7* (Rennes, 1931), quoted in Ragon, 115; and in John McManners, *Death and the Enlightenment: Changing Attitudes to Death among Christians and Unbelievers in Eighteenth-Century France* (Oxford: Clarendon Press of Oxford Univ. Press, 1981), 305.

12. (Bishop) Henri de Sponde, *Les Cimetières sacrez* (Bordeaux, 1598), quoted in Ariès, *The Hour,* 315–7.

13. Dexter, 46 and 73.

14. Jean Calvin, *Institutes,* trans. by T. Norton (London: n.p., 1611), IV:x:29. City Lands Committee of the Corporation of London, *History of the Bunhill Fields Burying Ground with Some of the Principal Inscriptions* (London: Charles Skipper & East, 1902). *Bunhill Fields Burial Ground: Proceedings in Reference to its Preservation with Inscriptions on the Tombs* (London: Hamilton, Adams, 1867).

15. "The Cemeteries and Catacombs of Paris," *Quarterly Review* 21:42 (Apr. 1819), 381.

16. In 1777, John Wesley presided at ceremonies laying the cornerstone of the Methodist chapel just across the City Road from Bunhill Fields. The small graveyard behind the structure contains the tombs of Wesley, Clarke, Benson, and Watson, leading Methodist ministers. By the late eighteenth century, many of the newer Protestant sects were more accepting of burial near their own churches than their Dissenting ancestors had been in the previous two centuries. T. D. Woolsey, "Cemeteries and Monuments," *New Englander* 28 (Nov. 1849), 493.

A gardener was employed at Bunhill Fields in the 1880s. Paths and plantings were added after new burials ceased; and removal of soil, monuments, or remains from the grounds was prohibited by law.

17. The Lady Marie Andros died Jan. 22, 1687/8 and was buried Feb. 10. Henry Wilder Foote, *Annals of King's Chapel from the Puritan Age of New England to the Present Day* (Boston: Little, Brown, 1882), I:74–76.

18. Increase Mather, *Meditations on Death* (Boston: Timothy Green, 1707). William Cooper, *A Sermon Concerning the Laying of Deaths of Others to Heart . . .* (Boston, B. Green for B. Eliot, 1720), 27.

19. *Historical Sketch and Matters Appertaining to the Granary Burial-Ground* (Boston: Municipal Printing Office, 1902), 8. *Historical Sketch of King's Chapel Burying-Ground* (Boston: Municipal Printing Office, 1903), 41 and 52. *Historical Sketch of the First Burying Place in Roxbury* (Boston: Municipal Printing Office, 1904), 41–45. The practice of erecting fences around burials in these graveyards arose from the desire to protect graves and stones from browsing cattle more than from the desire to stake out posthumous property. When the grazing of cattle in burial grounds ceased in the Boston area, following complaints about the practice by physicians in the 1790s, no attempt was made to introduce ornamental plantings or to provide maintenance to keep down weeds. As late as 1841, for instance, during the first campaign to add plantings to the first burial ground in Dorchester, Massachusetts, Samuel Downer found he had to clear the stubborn growth of "Suckery, Brambles and Full grass" before the ground could be sodded. *Historical Sketch of the First Burying Ground in Dorchester* (Boston: Municipal Printing Office, 1903), 56.

20. Peter Benes notes that in the case of Plymouth County, Massachusetts, only about half of the population received a stone although the town had a native stone-

carver. Benes, *The Masks of Orthodoxy: Folk Gravestone Carving in Plymouth County, Massachusetts, 1689–1805* (Amherst: Univ. of Mass. Press, 1977), 12 and 41.

21. A Looker-On, [John Ross Dix,] *Local Loiterings and Visits in the Vicinity of Boston* (Boston: Redding and Co., 1845), 18, reprinted as "An Englishman's Opinion of Mount Auburn," *Mount Auburn Memorial* 2:3 (July 18, 1860), 19.

22. "The Cemeteries and Catacombs," 380. Parliament considered banning iron coffins from London burial grounds in the 1810s in land granted for a limited term of years but not in space purchased in fee simple. Parliament did not close the old, church-controlled cemeteries in London until 1814. Joseph Stevens Buckminster Thacher, "Address at the Commencement . . . 1832," manuscript in "Exhibition and Commencement Performances" (1831–32), HUA.

23. P. Lorrain, quoted in David E. Stannard, *The Puritan Way of Death: A Study in Religion, Culture, and Social Change* (New York: Oxford Univ. Press, 1977), 106. Philippe Habert, *The Temple of Death: A Poem,* trans. by John Sheffield Buckingham (London: Daniel Brown, 1701). Louis-Sébastien Mercier, *Le Tableau de Paris, nouvelle édition, corrigée et augmentée* (Amsterdam, 12 vol., 1782–88), III:178, quoted in French in McManners, 63.

24. Stone, 3–4.

25. Pierre Patte, quoted in Etlin, "Landscapes of Eternity: Funerary Architecture and the Cemetery, 1793–1881," *Oppositions* 8 (Spring 1977), 18. Nicher-Cerisy, *Des Tombeaux* (Paris: n.p., n.d. [ca 1796]), 20–21. François-Marie Marchant de Beaumont, *Manuel et itinéraire du curieux dans le cimetière du Père la Chaise* 3rd ed. (Paris: Emler Frères, 1828), v–vi, 244 (1st ed., Paris: Plassan, 1820).

26. Leon Bernard, *The Emerging City: Paris in the Age of Louis XIV* (Durham, N.C.: Duke Univ. Press, 1970), 188–89. Felix Vicq-d'Azyr, *Essai sur les lieux et les dangers de sépultures* (Paris, 1778). For a discussion of the new sensibility to smells see Alain Corbin, *The Foul and the Fragrant.*

27. Wordsworth, "Essay upon Epitaphs," in Wordsworth, *The Excursion: A Poem* (New York: C. S. Francis, 1850), 329–40.

CHAPTER 2

1. Ariès, *The Hour,* 298 passim. Stone, "Death and Its History," 22.

2. Draper, 21.

3. Louis Cazamian, *Modern Times (1600–1914),* in Emile Légouis and Louis Cazamian, *A History of English Literature,* trans. by W. D. MacInnes and Louis Cazamian (New York: Macmillan, 1929), 853. For this reason, the best-known poems of the eighteenth century were Young's *Night Thoughts,* Pope's *Essay on Man,* and Thomson's *The Seasons.* These works were published and republished in full and in excerpts into the middle of the nineteenth century in America as well as England. Bostonian Nathan Appleton owned copies of Thomson and Gessner that are now in Harvard's Widener Library.

4. John Milton, *Il Penseroso* (Oxford: Clarendon Press, 1883).

5. Samuel Clarke and George Cokayne, in Draper, 190.

6. Isaac Watts, "The Church-Yard," in *Reliquiae Iuveniles: Miscellaneous Thoughts in Prose and Verse, on Natural, Moral, and Divine Subjects* (London: James Brackstone, 1742), 107.

7. Ludwig, *Graven Images,* 283–87.

8. Sir Thomas Browne, *Hydriotaphia: Urne-Buriall, or A Discourse of the Sepulchrall Urnes Lately Found in Norfolk* (London: Henry Browne, 1658).

9. John Evelyn, *Silva; or, A Discourse of Forest-Trees, and the Propagation of Timber in His Majesty's Dominions . . . together with an Historical Account of the Sacredness and Use of Standing Groves, with Notes by A. Hunter, M. D.* (1664. York, England: Longman, Hurst, Rees, Orme, & Brown, 1812), I:319, 322.

10. Ibid., 341–42.

11. Evelyn, quoted in "Cemeteries and Catacombs," 381.

12. James Stevens Curl, *A Celebration of Death: An Introduction to Some of the Buildings, Monuments, and Settings of Funerary Architecture in the Western European Tradition* (New York: Charles Scribner's Sons, 1980), 102.

13. E. S. DeBeer, ed., *The Diary of John Evelyn* (London: Oxford Univ. Press, 1959). Robert Burton, *The Anatomy of Melancholy* (1621), pt. 2, sec. 2, mem. 4, quoted in John Dixon Hunt, *The Figure in the Landscape: Poetry, Painting, and Gardening during the Eighteenth Century* (Baltimore: Johns Hopkins Univ. Press, 1976), 65.

14. Erwin Panofsky, "*Et in Arcadia Ego:* Poussin and the Elegiac Tradition," in *Meaning in the Visual Arts* (Garden City, N.Y.: Doubleday, 1955), 312.

15. Edmund Arwaker, J. H. Esq., and Sir F. F., Knight of Bath, quoted in Draper, 148–49. These verses also contrasted dramatically with the fate of the remains of Oliver Cromwell after the restoration. Charles II ordered that the Lord Protector's embalmed remains be removed from a Westminster Abbey tomb and publicly hung at Tyburn, site of criminal executions. When Cromwell's body was finally buried beneath the gallows, it was without the head, which remained impaled atop Westminster Hall through the remainder of Charles II's reign.

16. Anthony Ashley Cooper, Third Earl of Shaftesbury, *Characteristics of Men, Manners, Opinions, Times* (London, 2d edition, 1714), II:388–95.

17. Shaftesbury, quoted in Basil Willey, *The Eighteenth-Century Background: Studies on the Idea of Nature in*

the *Thought of the Period* (London: Chatto & Windus, 1949), 63.

18. Alexander Pope, "Epistle IV to Richard Boyle, Earl of Burlington: Argument of the Use of Riches," in James E. Willington, ed., *Alexander Pope's Epistles to Several Persons (Moral Essays)* (Coral Gables, Fla.: Univ. of Miami Press, 1976), 130–31, lines 51–58. Pope has often been misquoted by zealous landscape gardeners intent on accentuating the prescriptive message for those who would impose Art on Nature by the imperative voice (eliminating the "s" from "calls . . . catches . . . joins . . . varies . . . breaks . . . paints . . . and . . . designs"), taking away control from the Genius of Place and assigning it to the Hand of Man.

19. [Anon.,] *The Rise and Progress of the Present Taste in Planting Parks, Pleasure Grounds, Gardens, etc. . . . in a Poetic Epistle to the Right Honourable Charles Lord Viscount Irwin* (London: for C. Moran, 1767), 17.

20. Ibid., 17, 20, 23, passim.

21. Kent, quoted in Malins, 31. John Dixon Hunt, "Pope's Twickenham Revisited," *Eighteenth-Century Life* 8 n.s., 2 (Jan. 1983): 29–30.

22. James Thomson, "Autumn," lines 964 and 1031 in *The Seasons* (Newburyport, Mass.: John Mycall for the Boston Book-Store, 1790), first American edition.

23. For definitions of "elysium," see Joseph Addison, *Tatler* no. 123 (Jan. 21, 1710) and *Spectator* no. 417 (June 28, 1712).

24. Stephen Switzer, *Ichnographia Rustica; or, the Nobleman, Gentleman, and Gardener's Recreation* (London: D. Brown et al., 1718), iii, xi.

25. Batty Langley, *New Principles of Gardening* (London: Bettesworth, Batley, 1728). Speculation on the location of the site that inspired Sweet Auburn has varied. Many literary scholars consider it Goldsmith's native Lissoy in Ireland. Others identify English sites like the village of Nuneham, moved in 1760 a mile away from the place where Horace Walpole, first Lord Harcourt, intended to develop as his pleasure gardens, Nuneham Courtenay. Or it might refer to the village of Stowe, displaced two miles from its original site in 1730 for the same reason by Lord Cobham. David Jarrett, *The English Landscape Garden* (New York: Rizzoli, 1978), 8 and 130.

26. Peter Gay, *The Enlightenment: The Rise of Modern Paganism* (New York: W. W. Norton, 1966), 59.

27. Bridgeman, who designed the gardens of Claremont, was the first professional gardener to reject the rigid formality of landscape taste previously imported from France. Pope, "Epistle IV," lines 69–70.

28. Peter Willis, *Charles Bridgeman and the English Landscape Garden* (London: A. Zwemmer, 1977), 121–22. Willis notes that the design of the Elysian Fields recreates a dream allegory of Virtue, Honour, and (Modern) Vanity published by Addison in *Tatler* no. 123 (Jan. 21, 1710) and expanded upon in other writings. Cobham opposed Robert Walpole after the Excise Bill of 1733. The statue of Cobham was destroyed by lightning in 1957.

29. Madame du Boccage, *Lettres sur l'Angleterre* (published in English in 1770), quoted in Dora Wiebenson, *The Picturesque Garden in France* (Princeton: Princeton Univ. Press, 1978), 26–27. The Duchess of Portland, quoted in B. Sprague Allen, *Tides in English Taste (1619–1800): A Background for the Study of Literature* (Cambridge: Harvard Univ. Press, 1937), II:175. Laurence Whistler, Michael Gibbon, and George Clarke, *Stowe: A Guide to the Gardens* (London: n.p., 1974), 22–3.

30. Major contemporaneous guides to Stowe and other gardens included Samuel Boyse, "The Triumphs of Nature; A Poem," *Gentleman's Magazine* 12 (Aug. 1742); Daniel Defoe, "Appendix," *Tour Thro' the Whole Island of Great Britain, Divided into Circuits or Journies* [sic] (London: J. Osborn, 1742, 4th ed.); B. Seeley, *Description of the Gardens of Lord Viscount Cobham at Stowe in Buckinghamshire* (Northampton: W. Dicey, 1746); William Gilpin, *Dialogue upon the Gardens of the Right Honourable the Lord Viscount Cobham at Stowe in Buckinghamshire* (London: B. Seeley, 1748, 1749, and 1751); George Bickham, the Younger, *The Beauties of Stowe* (London, 1750, 1753, and 1756); Thomas Whately, *Observations on Modern Gardening* (London, 1770).

31. Kenneth Woodbridge, *Landscape and Antiquity: Aspects of English Culture at Stourhead, 1718–1838* (Oxford: Clarendon Press, 1970); and Woodbridge, *The Stourhead Landscape* (London: National Trust, 1982), 25.

32. Mrs. Elizabeth Singer Rowe, quoted in Draper, 254.

33. Thomas Gray, *An Elegy Written in a Country Churchyard* (London: R. Dodsley, 1751).

34. Michael Symes, "Nature as the Bride of Art: The Design and Structure of Painshill," in Robert P. Maccubbin and Peter Martin, eds., *Eighteenth-Century Life* 8, n.s., 2 (Jan. 1983), 63–73.

35. Switzer, *Ichnographia Rustica.*

36. Batty Langley, advertisement in *Daily Advertiser* no. 138 (1731), quoted in Bernard Denvir, *The Eighteenth Century: Art, Design, and Society, 1689–1789* (London: Longman, 1983).

37. Lady Irwin, quoted in Hussey, 115; and in Etlin, *Architecture,* 172.

38. [Anon.,] *The Rise and Progress,* 15.

39. Nicholas Penny, *Church Monuments in Romantic England* (New Haven: Yale Univ. Press, 1977), 44.

40. John Adams (ambassador to the Court of St. James) and Thomas Jefferson (ambassador to France) visited several English gardens together in the spring of 1786 using Whately's *Observations,* Seeley's *Description . . . of Stowe,* Heely's *Guide to Hagley and the Leasowes,* and a volume by Shenstone.

41. *Connoisseur* (Mar. 1756), quoted in Gay, 41; and/or *Connoisseur* (1755), quoted in Denvir, 152–53.

42. Edmund Burke, *A Philosophical Inquiry into the Origin of our Ideas of the Sublime and the Beautiful* (Philadelphia: D. Johnson, 1806), 35, 40, 103.

43. James T. Boulton, ed., *Edmund Burke's Philosophical Enquiry into the Origin of Our Ideas of the Sublime and the Beautiful* (South Bend: Univ. of Notre Dame Press, 1968), part I, sec. xiii, 44; part II, iii.

44. Sir Uvedale Price, *Essays on the Picturesque, as Compared with the Sublime and the Beautiful* (London: J. Mawman, 1810), 68–70. "The Chinese Origin of a Romanticism," in Lovejoy, 129. Sir William Chambers, *A Dissertation on Oriental Gardening* (London: W. Griffin, printer to the Royal Academy, 1772), 37–38; also quoted in Lovejoy, 130–31.

45. Chambers, 37–38.

46. Archibald Alison, *Essays on the Nature and the Principles of Taste* (1790; reprint, Boston: Cummings & Hilliard, 1812), 179–80.

47. Sir Horace Walpole to Rev. William Mason (Nov. 27, 1775), in Horace Walpole, *Letters,* ed. by Mrs. P. Toynbee (Oxford: Oxford Univ. Press, 1925).

48. Tait, 203 and 207. See Sir H[erbert] J[ohn] C[lifford] Grierson, ed., *The Letters of Sir Walter Scott* (London: Constable & Co., 1932–37), 12 vols.

49. Wordsworth, "Essay," 408.

50. Hans Huth, *Nature and the American: Three Centuries of Changing Attitudes* (Lincoln: Univ. of Nebraska Press, 1957), 57.

51. Daniel Webster, "An Address Delivered at the Laying of the Cornerstone of the Bunker Hill Monument" (1825), in *The Writings and Speeches of Daniel Webster in 18 Volumes, Vol. I: Memoir and Speeches on Various Occasions* (Boston: Little, Brown, & Co., 1903), 180.

CHAPTER 3

1. McManners, 170–71. Claude-Adrien Helvétius, *De l'esprit; or, Essays on the Mind and Its Several Faculties* (London: J. Dodsley, 1759). Abbé Rémi, *Les Jours, pour servir de correctif et de supplement aux Nuits de Young* (Paris, n.p., 1770).

2. François-Marie Arouet de Voltaire, "La Considération due aux gens de lettres," *Lettres Philosophiques* 12, in André Lagarde and Laurent Michard, eds., *XVIIIe Siècle: Les grands auteurs français du programme* (Paris: Bordas, 1965), IV:124.

3. Lucretius and Voltaire quoted in Gay, 102–04.

4. Voltaire, "Enterrement," *Oeuvres complètes: Dictionnaire philosophique portatif, ou la raison par alphabet,* (Paris: Garnier Frères, 1878), II:550–51.

5. Jean Le Rond d'Alembert, *Preliminary Discourse to the Encyclopedia of Diderot,* trans. by Richard N. Schwab (Indianapolis: Bobbs-Merrill, 1963), 53–54, 100. George Armstrong Kelly, *Mortal Politics in Eighteenth-Century France,* in *Historical Reflections* 13:1 (Spring 1986): 49–50.

6. Salomon Gessner, *Idyllen* (1756), trans. into French by Michel Huber, *Idylles et poèmes champêtres* (Lyon: J. M. Buryset, 1762). Delille, "Preface by the Translator," in René-Louis Marquis de Girardin, *An Essay on Landscape; or, on the Means of Improving and Embellishing the Country Around our Habitations,* trans. by R.-L. Girardin Vicomte d'Ermenonville (London: J. Dodsley, 1793), vi.

7. Georges-Louis LeRouge, *Cahiers des jardins anglo-chinois à la mode* (Paris: LeRouge, 1776–85).

8. Claude-Henri Watelet, *Essai sur les jardins* (Paris: Chez Perault, 1764). Delille, *Les Jardins; ou, l'art d'embellir les paysages* (1782), quoted in Ariès, *The Hour,* 520–51. Delille, "Preface," iv.

9. Jean-Jacques Rousseau, *Les Rêveries du promeneur solitaire* (Paris: Garnier, 1960).

10. René-Louis Marquis de Girardin, *De la composition des paysages sur le terrain, ou, des moyens d'embellir la nature* (Geneva: Chez F. M. Delaguette, 1777).

11. René Mathieu, *Ermenonville* (Paris: Nouvelles Editions Latines, 1985).

12. Girardin, *Promenade ou itinéraire des jardins d'Ermenonville* (Paris: Chez Mérigot, 1788). Louis-Stanislas-Cécile-Xavier, Comte de Girardin, brother of the Marquis, affixed his name as author to a book by the same title published with the Marquis' *Promenade ou itinéraire des jardins de Chantilly* (Paris, Desenne, Gattey, Guyot, et Hédouin, 1791).

13. Four of the most useful works on the English garden style in France are Alexandre L.-J. de Laborde, *Déscription des nouveaux jardins de la France et de ses anciens châteaux* (Paris: Delance, 1808[–15?]); J[ean] C[harles] Krafft, *Plans des plus beaux jardins pittoresques de France, d'Angleterre, et d'Allemagne* (Paris: Levrault 1809 and 1810), 2 vols.; Wiebenson, *The Picturesque Garden in France;* and Vidler, *The Writing of the Walls.*

14. Laborde, 109.

15. Jan Ingenhousz, *Experiments on Vegetables, Discovering their Great Power of Purifying the Common Air in Sunshine, and of Injuring It in the Shade and at Night, to which is Joined a New Method of Examining the Accurate Degree of the Salubrity of the Atmosphere* (London: P. Elmsley & H. Payne, 1779). Girardin, *An Essay,* 121–22.

16. Jacques-Henri Bernardin de Saint-Pierre, *Etudes de la nature,* vol. 5 (Paris: Didot jeune, 1792), also quoted in Amaury Pineu Duval, *Des Sépultures chez les anciens et les modernes* (Paris: Panckoucke, an IX [1801]), 76–81.

17. Ibid. See Leo Marx, *The Machine in the Garden: Technology and the Pastoral Ideal in America* (New York: Oxford Univ. Press, 1964); Mircea Eliade, *The Sacred and the Profane: The Nature of Religion* (New York: Harcourt, Brace, & World, 1957).

18. Bernardin de Saint-Pierre, *Etudes*, vol. 5, 405. Bernardin's essay "On the Pleasure of Tombs" was first made available to Americans in the translation by Henry Hunter (Worcester, Mass.: J. Nancrede, 1797).

19. Christian Cayus Lorenz Hirschfeld, *Theorie der Gartenkunst* (Leipzig: Weidmanns Erben & Reich, 1779–85), five volumes, simultaneously published in French as *Theorie de l'art des jardins*.

20. P. A. Vieillard, "Fouché," in Ferdinand Hoefer, ed., *Nouvelle Biographie Générale*, vol. 18 (Paris: Firmin Didot Frères, 1870), 262. Norman Hampson, *The Life and Opinions of Maximilien Robespierre* (London, 1974), 181.

21. Pierre-Gaspard Chaumette, *Arrêtés du Conseil-Général de la Commune de Paris rélatif aux différents cultes et aux prêtres* (Paris: le 17 vendémiaire, an II [8 Oct. 1793]), 106–07. Vieillard, 262. Four days later Chaumette decreed destruction of all "barbarian monuments" from the Old Regime and publicly staged the mock funeral of an aristocrat.

22. Chaumette, 106–07. [Avril,] *Rapport de l'Administration des travaux publics, sur les cimetières, lu au Conseil-Général par le citoyen Avril* (Paris: n.p., n.d. [1793?]), 7.

23. [Abbé] F[rançois]-V[alentin] M[ulot,] *Vues d'un citoyen, ancien Deputé de Paris à l'Assemblé Législative sur les sépultures* (Paris: n.p., n.d. [1796?]), 5. Delille, "L'Imagination," song 7 (1794), in *Oeuvres* (Paris: Michaud 1824), 9:146.

24. M[ulot,] *Vues*, 15–19.

25. Doliver, *Essai sur les funérailles* (Versailles, Jacob, an IX [1801]), I:4–7.

26. Nicher-Cérisy, 23–24, 26.

27. [Pierre-Louis] Roederer, *Des Institutions funéraires convenables à une république qui permet tous les cultes et n'en adopte aucun* (Paris: Mathey & Desenne, an II [1793]), cover. C. Guillon, *Sur le respect du aux tombeaux; et l'indécence des inhumations actuelles* (Paris: n.p., an VIII [1800]), 1. Doliver, i. Général F.-R.-J. Pommereul, *Mémoire sur les funérailles et les sépultures, Question . . . jugée par l'Institut* (Paris: Onfroy; and Tours: Billault, an IX [1801]), cover and v.

28. Amaury Duval, *Des Sépultures chez les anciens et les modernes* (Paris: Panckoucke, an IX [1801]), 37, 82–88.

29. Duval, 20.

30. Ibid., 45–46, 71–73, 85–86.

31. Mulot, *Discours sur les funérailles et le respect du aux morts, lu le 15 thermidor, an IV au Lycée des Arts* (Paris: n.p., 1796), 15–19. Also see Mulot, *Discours . . . sur cette question: Quelles sont les cérémonies à faire pour les funérailles et le reglement à adopter pour le lieu de la sépulture?* (Paris: n.p., an IX [1801]). For an extended appeal for support for the prize-winning proposals by Duval and Mulot, as well as for the runner-up Girard, see A. Gauthier-Lachapelle, *Des Sépultures* (Paris: DuPont, an IX [1801).

32. Mulot, *Discours sur les funérailles*, 13, 16, and 23. M[ulot,] *Vues*, 6.

33. Pommereul, 4–5, 7, 32, and 37.

34. Athanase-Charles Détournelle, *Mémoire sur les funérailles et les sépultures* (Paris: n.p., an IX [1801]), 3–4, 7, 25.

35. J.-M. Coupé, *De la mortalité des sépultures, et de leur police* (Paris: Chez Calixte Vollant, an IX [1801]), 22, 25, and 27.

36. J[oseph] de Girard, *Des Tombeaux, ou de l'influence des institutions funèbres sur les moeurs* (Paris, an IX [1801]), quoted in Ariès, *The Hour*, 506–11.

37. [J.-B. Leclerc,] Corps Législatif, Conseil des Cinq-Cents, *Motion d'Ordre par J.-B. Leclerc sur l'existence et l'utilité d'une religion civile en France* (Paris: n.p., 9 fructidor, an V [1797]). J.-B. Leclerc, *Rapport . . . sur les institutions rélatives à l'état civil des citoyens, Corps Législatif, le 16 brumaire, an VI* (Paris: n.p., 1798), 2–4, 21, 41.

38. J[acques] C[ambry,] *Rapport sur les sépultures, presenté à l'Administration Centrale du Départment de la Seine* (Paris: n.p., an VII [1799]), 13.

39. Abbé Henri Grégoire, *Second rapport sur le vandalisme* (Paris: n.p., 1794), 6. Also see Vidler, 168–69.

40. Département de la Seine, *Rapport fait au Conseil-Général sur l'instruction publique, le rétablissement des Bourses, le scandale des inhumations actuelles, l'érection de cimetières, la restitution des tombeaux, mausolées, etc.* (Paris: Imprimerie nationale, n.d. [ca 1800]), 25–32. Also see Quatremère de Quincy, *Rapport fait au Conseil-Général le 15 thermidor, an VIII, sur l'instruction publique, le rétablissement des Bourses, le scandale des inhumations actuelles, l'érection de cimetiéres, la restitution des tombeaux, mausolées, etc.* (Paris: n.p., an VIII [1800]).

41. Jules Michelet, *Ma Jeunesse* (Paris: C. Lévy, 6th ed., 1884), 45. See discussion of Lenoir's Museum and its historiographic significance in Vidler, 168–87. Mme. Roye de la Rochefoucault sponsored construction of the tomb of Abélard and Heloïse to provide "a richer monument to models of love and constance." See F.-G.-T. Jolimont, *Les Mausolées français, receuil des tombeaux les plus rémarquables par leur structure, leurs épitaphes, ou les cendres qu'ils renferment, ériges dans les nouveaux cimetières de Paris* (Paris: Firmin Didot, 1821), n.p.

42. On 22 floréal, an XII (May 1, 1804), Napoleon banned all burials in churches, temples, and synagogues and inside the boundaries of cities and towns.

43. Two other cemeteries were established at the same time north and south of the city at Montmartre and Montparnasse, although they could not compare with Père Lachaise in terms of either landscape design or social prestige. No cemetery was placed west of the city, as had once been suggested, probably because prevailing winds would blow any noxious effluvia from burials there into and over Paris.

44. Jolimont, 5–6. Jolimont bore the title of Ingenieur employé au cadastre.

45. Molière had been buried at night, as befitted one active in theater, in a common grave in the cemetery of Saint-Eustache in 1673. La Fontaine was placed in a common pit in Saint-Josephe's Cemetery in 1792. Alexandre Lenoir's antiquarian repository was officially closed in 1817 and many of its holding moved to Père Lachaise. Lenoir kept with the cenotaph to Abélard and Héloïse only a few of the bones that he did not distribute to friends and patrons as souvenirs. Vidler, 223, n. 55. From exile on the island of Saint-Hélène, Napoleon wrote of his wish to be buried at Père Lachaise, his grave marked by a plain, classical stele. Frederick Brown, *Père Lachaise: Elysium and Real Estate* (New York: Viking, 1973), 18.

46. Marchant de Beaumont, *Manuel et itinéraire,* 3rd ed., 42–44. Another major guidebook published in numerous editions was Richard [and Jean Marie Vincent Dudin,] *Le Véritable conducteur aux cimetières du Père La Chaise, Montmartre, Montparnasse et Vaugirard; ou, Guide le plus complet, le plus nouveau et le plus exact, de l'étranger, du curieux, et du promeneur dans ces cimetières* (Paris: Chez Roy-Terry, 1830). Also see Marchant de Beaumont, *Le Nouveau conducteur de l'étranger à Paris en 1826,* 13th ed. (Paris: Moroval, 1826). (The 6th edition appeared in 1818.)

During the siege of Paris on March 30, 1814, students of several military schools unsuccessfully tried to defend Paris from the strategic vantage point of the cemetery; but the Russians overtook the site, setting up camp among the graves and cutting down many of the trees for firewood and to clear lines of fire for cannon batteries. Still, only two decades later the English visitor Mrs. Frances Trollope observed, "the thickly-planted trees and shrubs have grown so rapidly, as in many places to make it difficult to pass through them." *Paris and the Parisians in 1835* (New York: Harper & Brothers, 1836), 116.

47. "Cemeteries and Catacombs," 391. Delille, "Preface," v.

48. Delille, "Preface," v. Augustus Charles Pugin and C. Heath, *Paris and Its Environs Displayed in a Series of Picturesque Views* (London: Robert Jennings, 1829), II:129.

49. Marchant de Beaumont, *Manuel et itinéraire,* 34 and 270.

50. *Atlantic Souvenir,* quoted in Huth, 66–67.

51. Marchant de Beaumont, *Manuel et itinéraire,* 35, 173, and 182.

52. Ibid., v–vi, 244.

53. One British critic was certainly mistaken in his judgment of Père Lachaise: "Such exhibits cannot have a salutary tendency; they foster that disease of mind in which melancholy madness has its foundation. . . . Public feeling would not tolerate them in Protestant countries." *Quarterly Review,* 394. Indeed, the cemetery represented a basic rebellion against High Church forms; slightly a decade after the opinion was expressed, Americans and their British cousins set to work in various cities to found a host of similar cemeteries.

CHAPTER 4

1. A number of Puritan histories were reprinted in the early nineteenth century, such as Cotton Mather, *Magnalia Christi Americana; or, The Ecclesiastical History of New England from its First Planting in the Year 1620 unto the Year of Our Lord 1698* (New Haven: S. Converse, 1820). A prime example of New England's commemorative celebration of the founding decades was Thomas Bridgman, *The Pilgrims of Boston and their Descendants, with Introduction by Edward Everett, also Inscriptions from the Monuments in the Granary Burial Ground* (New York: D. Appleton, 1856). Also see Bradford Smith, *Bradford of Plymouth* (Philadelphia: J. B. Lippincott, 1951), 300; William Hubbard, *General History of New England from the Discovery to MDCLXXX* (Cambridge: Massachusetts Historical Society, 1815); Edward Johnson, *A History of New England from the English Planting in the Yeare 1628 untill the Yeare 1652* (London: Brooke, 1654).

2. Only late in the nineteenth century, after the cleaning and planting of King's Chapel Burial Ground, did Bostonians erect a funerary monument to Winthrop at a spot that may not be the precise resting place of the Puritan leader and with a table stone of traditional form but with distinctly Victorian iconography. For an overview dispelling some misconceptions and assessing dimensions of the iconophobia of American Puritans, see Dickran Tashjian, "Puritan Attitudes toward Iconoclasm," in *Puritan Gravestone Art II: Annual Proceedings of the Dublin Seminar for New England Folklife* (June 24–25, 1978), 4–5.

3. Samuel Willard, "The High Esteem Which God Hath of the Death of His Saints" (Boston, 1685), in Perry Miller and Thomas E. Johnson, eds., *The Puritans: A Sourcebook of Their Writings* (New York: Harper & Row, 1963), 371–74.

4. Willard, quoted in Stannard, *The Puritan Way,* 130.

5. Warren quoted extensively from Montesquieu and Voltaire. John Warren, *An Oration, Delivered July 4th, 1783, at the Request of the Inhabitants of Boston in Celebration of the Anniversary of American Independence* (Boston: John Gill, 1783), 55–67.

6. Perez Morton quoted in George Washington Warren, *The History of the Bunker Hill Monument Association*

(Boston: James R. Osgood, 1877), 13,

7. John Soley quoted in George Warren, 10–12.

8. The Massachusetts General Court authorized reconstruction of the Bulfinch monument in 1865, but it was not rebuilt until 1898, when the Bunker Hill Monument Association hired the architectural firm of Little and Browne to complete the task.

9. Honoré-Gabriel Riqueti, the Comte de Mirabeau, quoted in Neil Harris, *The Artist in American Society: The Formative Years, 1790–1860* (New York: Simon & Schuster, 1966), 18.

10. Jeremy Belknap, *American Biography: or, An Historical Account of Those Persons who Have Been Distinguished in America, as Adventurers, Statesmen, Philosophers, Divines, Warriors, Authors, and Other Remarkable Characters, Comprehending a Recital of the Events Connected with their Lives and Actions* (Boston: Isaiah Thomas & Ebenezer T. Andrews, 1794–98). Robert McCloskey, ed., *The Works of James Wilson* (Cambridge: Harvard Univ. Press, 1967), I:72. The Reverend Peter Whitney also encouraged patriotic commemoration in his funeral sermon, *Weeping and Mourning at the Death of Eminent Persons a National Duty* (Brookfield, Mass.: E. Merriam, 1800).

11. "Mount Vernon," *New-England Galaxy* 6:276 (Jan. 24, 1823): 1.

12. I. Finch, *Travels in the United States of America and Canada Containing Some Account of their Scientific Institutions, and . . . An Essay on the Natural Boundaries of Empires* (London: Longman, Rees, Orme, Brown, Green, & Longman, 1833), 218.

13. E. T. Coke, *A Subaltern's Furlough: Descriptive of Scenes in Various Parts of the United States . . . during the Summer and Autumn of 1832* (New York: J. & J. Harper, 1833), I:99.

14. Ibid., 99. J. S. Buckingham, *America: Historical, Statistic, and Descriptive* (London: Fisher, Son, & Co., n.d., [ca. 1840]), III:569.

15. Caroline Gilman and Rev. S. Gilman, *The Poetry of Traveling in the United States* (New York: S. Colman, 1838), 7 and 19.

16. Rev. Hosea Ballou, "Address on the Re-Burial of Rev. John Murray," (June 8, 1837) in Thomas Whittemore, ed., *The Life of Rev. Hosea Ballou: With Accounts of His Writings* (Boston: James M. Usher, 1855), III:245.

17. Theodore Dwight, *Summer Tours; or, Notes of a Traveler through Some of the Middle and Northern States* (New York: Harper & Brothers, 1847), 14.

18. Henry Tudor, *Narrative of a Tour in North America* (London: James Duncan, 1834), 68–69. J. S. Buckingham, *The Slave States of America* (London: Fisher, Son, & Co., 1842), I:568–69. Washington's remains were removed from the original wooden coffin, shards of which were distributed around the country like relics. The Philadelphia architect William Strickland assembled a pamphlet on the new sarcophagus in order to spur public demand for such funerary monuments and increase his own commissions. *Tomb of Washington at Mount Vernon* (Philadelphia: Carey & Hart, 1840).

19. B[enjamin] Henry Latrobe, "Anniversary Oration Pronounced before the Society of Artists of the United States, by Appointment of the Society, on the eighth of May, 1811," *First Annual Exhibition of the Society of Artists of the United States* (Philadelphia, 1811), bound with *The Port-folio* n.s. 5:6 (June 1811).

20. Nicholas Biddle, quoted in Neil Harris, 43. For one comprehensive definition of the arts of this period, see Jacob Bigelow, *Elements of Technology, Taken Chiefly from a Course of Lectures Delivered at Cambridge, on the Application of the Sciences to the Useful Arts* (Boston: Hilliard, Gray, Little, & Wilkins, 1829).

21. Neil Harris, 28. John Adams to Thomas Jefferson (Dec. 16, 1816), in Leslie J. Cappon, ed., *Adams-Jefferson Letters* (Chapel Hill: Univ. Of North Carolina Press, 1959), II:507. Adams to Jefferson (Jan. 1, 1817), quoted in Theodore Sizer, ed., *The Autobiography of Colonel John Trumbull, Patriot-Artist, 1756–1843* (New Haven: Yale Univ. Press, 1953), 311.

22. Neil Harris, 35.

23. Jefferson, quoted in ibid., 42. I have found no correspondence in which Jefferson reminds Adams of the symbolic, commemorative use of the architecture and landscape they discovered together on their visit to Stowe in 1786. Jefferson to Madison (Fall 1785), quoted in Wayne Andrews, *Architecture, Ambition, and Americans: A Social History of American Architecture* (New York: Free Press, 1964), 64.

24. John Adams to Benjamin Waterhouse. (Feb. 26, 1817), quoted in Adrienne Koch and William Peder, eds., *Selected Writings of John and John Quincy Adams* (New York: Knopf, 1964), 199–200. The nuances of their debate on the uses of art aside, Henry A. S. Dearborn wanted to publish the Jefferson-Adams correspondence to give "to all future generations an important lesson amidst periods of civil discord." Dearborn called the correspondence an "everlasting monument to the holyness [*sic*] of friendship and the sacredness of confidential intercourse." Dearborn to Jefferson (Nov. 24, 1823), HLH.

25. Hubbard Winslow quoted in Neil Harris, 195.

26. [William Tudor,] "Instruction for the Fine Arts," *North American Review* 2 (Jan. 1816): 161. *Monthly Anthology* 4 (May 1807): 230.

27. Daniel Webster, "Adams and Jefferson" (1826), in *The Writings and Speeches of Daniel Webster: Vol. I: Memoir and Speeches on Various Occasions* (Boston: Little, Brown, 1903), 322. Edward Everett, *An Address Delivered at Charlestown, Aug. 1, 1826, in Commemoration of John Adams and Thomas Jefferson* (Boston: William L. Lewis, 1826), 35–36.

28. Emerson, quoted in John Burchard and Albert Bush-Brown, *The Architecture of America: A Social and Cultural History* (Boston: Little, Brown, & Co.,

1961), 24.

29. William Tudor to Harrison Gray Otis (Sept. 2, 1815), in Samuel Eliot Morison, *Harrison Gray Otis, 1765–1848: The Urbane Federalist* (Boston: Houghton Mifflin, 1969), 235.

30. William Ellery Channing, "The True End of Life," quoted in Albert Fein, "The American City: The Ideal and the Real," in Edgard Kaufman, Jr., ed., *The Rise of American Architecture* (New York: Praeger, 1970), 54.

31. James Fenimore Cooper, *The Crater* (Cambridge: Belknap Press of Harvard Univ. Press, 1962), 444.

32. Bigelow, *Inaugural Address, Delivered in the Chapel at Cambridge, Dec. 11, 1816* (Boston: Wells & Lilly, 1817), 11–13; reprinted in *North American Review* 4 (Jan. 1817), 271–72.

33. Sidney Smith in the *Edinburgh Review* (Jan. 1820), quoted in Daniel J. Boorstin, *The Image; or, What Happened to the American Dream* (New York: Atheneum, 1962), 47. Edward Everett particularly attacked "our transatlantic critics" in his Harvard Phi Beta Kappa presentation, "An Oration Pronounced at Cambridge . . . Aug. 27, 1824," *North American Review* 20:11 (1825): 422–23.

34. Bigelow, *Inaugural Address,* 17–18, 23–26.

35. Ibid.

36. John Adams, quoted in George E. Ellis, *Memoir of Dr. Jacob Bigelow* (Cambridge: John Wilson & Son, 1880), 46.

37. Ralph Waldo Emerson, *Nature* (1836), in *Ralph Waldo Emerson: Essays and Lectures* (New York: Library of America, 1983), 7. David D. Van Tassel, *Recording America's Past: An Interpretation of the Development of Historical Studies in America, 1607–1884* (Chicago: Univ. of Chicago Press, 1960), 72.

38. William Ellery Channing, "War: Discourses before the Congregational Ministers of Massachusetts," (1816), in *The Works of William E. Channing, D.D.* (Boston and New York: American Unitarian Association, 1848), 3:40–41. A similar opinion was expressed that year by Francis C. Gray, in "An Address Before the Society of Phi Beta Kappa on Thurs., the 29th of Aug., 1816," *North American Review* 3 (Sept. 1816): 289.

39. Frederic Cople Jaher, *The Urban Establishment: Upper Strata in Boston, New York, Charleston, Chicago, and Los Angeles* (Urbana: Univ. of Illinois Press, 1982), 64. William Lawrence, *The Life of Amos A. Lawrence* (Boston: Houghton Mifflin, 1888). George Warren, 256.

40. Josiah Quincy, "Speech on the Invasion of Canada" (Jan. 5, 1813), in *Speeches Delivered in the Congress of the United States, 1805–1813* (Boston: Little, Brown, 1874), 396.

41. Webster, "First Settlement of New England" (Dec. 22, 1820), in *Writings and Speeches,* I:182–199.

42. [Nathan Hale,] *Selections from the Chronicle of Boston and the Book of Retrospections and Anticipations, Compiled in the Last Month of the Last Year of the Town, and the First Month of the First Year of the City* (Boston: [Nathan Hale], 1822), 64–65.

43. Josiah Quincy, *An Address to the Citizens of Boston on the XVIIth of Sept., MDCCCXXX. The Close of the Second Century from the First Settlement of the City* (Boston: J. H. Eastburn, 1830), 9–10.

44. Henry Bigelow (Baltimore) to Jacob Bigelow (July 2, 1815), in the Bigelow Papers, CLMH.

45. [William Tudor,] "Monument to Washington," *North American Review* 2:6 (1816): 329–40.

46. Ibid., 334.

47. Henry A. S. Dearborn, "Bunker Hill," *Boston Patriot* (Apr. 1823).

48. George Warren, 31–35.

49. Ibid., 38.

50. George Putnam, *An Address Delivered before the City Government and Citizens of Roxbury on the Life and Character of the Late Henry A. S. Dearborn, Mayor of the City, Sept. 3rd, 1851* (Roxbury: Norfolk County Journal Press, 1851), 6. He was elected fellow of the American Academy of Arts and Sciences in 1823 and two years later led a state survey of western Massachusetts in a quixotic search for a canal route to link Boston to the new Erie Canal. Dearborn's historical consciousness was evident two years before the laying of the Bunker Hill Monument cornerstone when, two days after visiting John Adams, Dearborn wrote Jefferson urging publication of the correspondence of the two former presidents. Dearborn to Thomas Jefferson (Nov. 24, 1823), HLH.

51. George Warren, 47.

52. Ibid., 115–16.

53. Ibid., 41-43.

54. Ibid., 171–72. Dearborn knew that history could be more divisive than unifying if focused on controversial issues, as proven by the public argument in 1818 between his father, Henry Dearborn, and General Israel Putnam over Joseph Warren's role in the Battle of Bunker Hill.

55. Ibid., 176–77.

56. The popularity of the obelisk may have been inspired by the Wellington monument, a 175-foot obelisk with an interior winding staircase to the top, erected in 1817 in Somerset, England, and financed by the local gentry to perpetuate the memory of the Iron Duke. Ibid., 157–59. Gridley Bryant purchased the Quincy quarries in 1825 and sold them to the Bunker Hill Monument Association for $350. Loammi Baldwin was also at times credited with the design.

57. John Pierpont, "Ode Written for the Laying of the Corner Stone of the Bunker Hill Monument, June 17, 1825," in *Airs of Palestine and Other Poems* (Boston: James Munroe, 1840). Daniel Webster, *An Address Delivered at the Laying of the Corner Stone of the*

Bunker Hill Monument (Boston: Cummings and Hilliard, 1825), 8.

58. Webster, *Address, 9.*

59. Alexander H. Everett, "June 7, 1836 Celebration," in *A Memorial of the American Patriots who Fell at the Battle of Bunker Hill, with an Account of the Dedication of the Memorial Tablets* (Boston: By Order of the City Council, 1889), 274.

60. George Warren, 253–54.

61. As at the inception of the monument project, Daniel Webster delivered the address at ceremonies for its completion. President John Tyler and his cabinet attended. Many Bostonians contributed to the subscription campaign begun in 1836 to build a monument to Washington in the nation's capital. Robert Mills designed a 555-foot obelisk surrounded by a circular, colonnaded temple, a structure far more ambitious than the Bunker Hill Monument. Work did not begin until 1843, but stopped in 1854 when funds ran out. The monument was not finished, albeit in much simplified form without the temple base, until 1885 and after the federal government assumed control, assigning the project to the Army Corps of Engineers.

62. Josiah Quincy, quoted in Frederic Cople Jaher, "The Boston Brahmins in the Age of Industrial Capitalism," in Jaher, ed., *The Age of Industrialism in America: Essays in Social Structure and Cultural Values* (New York: Free Press, 1968), 82. The retrospective spirit was also evident in the renaming of Cambridge streets with historical names like Dunster and Holyoke, replacing the generic Wood, Crooked, Creek, Water, and Marsh.

63. T. W. Harris, *A Discourse Delivered before the Massachusetts Horticultural Society in Celebration of its Fourth Anniversary, Oct. 3, 1832* (Cambridge: E. W. Metcalf, 1832), 71–73.

64. Peabody, "Mount Auburn Cemetery," 397–98, 406.

65. [Dearborn,] "Mount Auburn Cemetery," 399.

66. Ibid., 401–05.

67. Ibid.

68. Alexander Everett, *Address,* 18.

69. Gustave de Beaumont, *Lettres d'Amérique, 1831–2,* ed. by André Jardin and George W. Pierson (Paris: Presses Univérsitaires de France, 1973), 146.

70. Alexander Everett, *Address,* 22–23.

71. Ibid.

CHAPTER 5

1. Increase Mather and Leonard Hoar, quoted in Stannard, *The Puritan Way,* 80.

2. Lovejoy, 134.

3. Henry S. Randall, *The Life of Thomas Jefferson* (New York: Derby and Jackson, 1858), I:60–61. Edwin M. Betts, *Thomas Jefferson's Garden Book* (Philadelphia: American Philosophical Society, 1944), 25–27. Robert H. Kean, *History of the Graveyard at Monticello* (Charlottesville, Va.: Thomas Jefferson Memorial Foundation, 1972), 4. Jefferson's plans predated by fifteen years his visit to English gardens in the company of John Adams. Also see Edith Philips, *Louis Hué Girardin and Nicholas Gouin Dufief and Their Relations with Thomas Jefferson* (Baltimore: Johns Hopkins Univ. Press, 1926).

4. Henry F. May, *The Enlightenment in America* (New York: Oxford Univ. Press, 1976). 243.

5. Philip Freneau, "The House of Night" (1786), quoted in Edwin H. Cady, *Literature of the Early Republic* (New York: Holt, Rinehart, & Winston, 1967), 349.

6. Fred Lewis Pattee, *The First Century of American Literature, 1770–1870* (New York: D. Appleton-Century, 1935), 33–34.

7. "The Weeping Willow," *New England Farmer* 5:43 (May 18, 1827): 338.

8. William Prince, *A Short Treatise on Horticulture* (New York: T. & J. Swords, 1828), 216. This was the first original horticulture book published in America; it was written by the head of the Linnaean Botanical Gardens in Flushing, New York.

9. More recently in Europe, urns were used for burial of the heart separate from the body or for second burial of bones removed from a temporary grave.

10. Philippe Ariès, *Western Attitudes toward Death from the Middle Ages to the Present,* trans. by Patricia M. Ranum (Baltimore: Johns Hopkins Univ. Press, 1974), 80.

11. *Report of the Committee Appointed to Inquire into the Condition of the New-Haven Burying Ground and to Propose a Plan for its Improvement* (New Haven: B. L. Hamlen, 1839), 4.

12. Timothy Dwight, *Travels in New-England and New York* (New Haven: T. Dwight, 1821), II:191.

13. Alison, 144.

14. Timothy Dwight, 191.

15. Edward Augustus Kendall, *Travels through the Northern Parts of the United States in the Years of 1807 and 1808* (New York: I. Riley, 1809), I:253.

16. Ibid., 254–56.

17. Timothy Dwight, 192–93.

18. *Report,* 9.

19. Timothy Dwight, 192–93.

20. Ibid.

21. Ibid.

22. Ibid.

23. Washington Irving, *The Sketch Book of Geoffrey Crayon, Gent.* (1819–20, reprint, New York: Dutton, 1963), 55 and 60.

24. Irving, 134–35, 161–68, and 171–72. The parallels between Irving's criticism of Westminster Abbey and that of Voltaire a century before are remarkable. See discussion of Voltaire's critique in chapter 3.

25. Ibid., 90, 96, and 130–36.

26. Ibid., 137.

27. Ibid., 166.

28. Ibid.

29. Pattee, 301–02.

30. Ibid., 269 and 273.

31. F. W. P. Greenwood, "The Miscellaneous Poems of William Wordsworth," *North American Review* 9 n.s. (Apr. 1824): 356–70. Van Wyck Brooks, *The Flowering of New England, 1815–1865* (New York: E. P. Dutton, 1940), 112.

32. William Cullen Bryant, *Poems* (Philadelphia: A. Hart, 1851), 53–55.

33. Jacob Bigelow to Elizabeth B[igelow] Wheeler (June 16, 1820), in Bigelow Papers, CLMH. John Quincy Adams, "Death of Children," *Mount Auburn Memorial* 1:39 (Mar. 7, 1860): 310. Joseph Story, "Lines Written on the Death of a Daughter in May 1831," in *The Miscellaneous Writings, Literary, Critical, Juridical, and Political* (Boston: James Munroe, 1835), 167–69.

34. [William Ellery Channing,] "Remarks on National Literature," *Christian Examiner* 7 (1830): 269.

35. "The Grave of a Mother," *Boston Patriot and Daily Mercantile Advertiser* 1720 (Jan. 9, 1823): 2.

36. [William Tudor,] "On Certain Funeral Ceremonies," in *Letters on the Eastern States* (New York: Kirk & Mercein, 1820), 17.

37. Ibid.

38. *Report,* 4. Dearborn and Dr. John Collins Warren were major contributors to the Franklin monument.

39. Le Capitaine Basil-Hall, *Voyage dans les Etats-Unis de l'Amérique du Nord* (Paris: Arthus Bertrand, 1834), II:9–11.

CHAPTER 6

1. Boston Board of Health, 1799, quoted in John Ballard Blake, *Public Health in the Town of Boston, 1630–1822* (Cambridge: Harvard Univ. Press, 1952), 167–70.

2. See *Boston Patriot and Daily Mercantile Advertiser* (Dec. 17, 1821), quoted in Blake, 213.

3. Blake, 51, 167–70, 192, and 200.

4. Edward H. Savage, comp., *A Brief Mention of the Dates of More than 5000 Events that Transpired in Boston from 1630 to 1880* (Boston: Tolman & White, 1884), 21. *Boston Intelligencer and Evening Gazette* 11 (March 8, 1823). *Columbian Centinel* 4049 (Jan. 29, 1825), 2. *Boston Patriot and Daily Mercantile Advertiser* 1843 (June 3, 1823). Thomas Bridgman, *Epitaphs from Copp's Hill Burying Ground, Boston, with Notes* (Boston: James Munroe, 1851), xx–xxi.

5. Bridgman, *Epitaphs,* xx–xxi. Samuel Adams Drake, *Old Landmarks and Historic Personages of Boston* (Boston: Little, Brown, 1872), 296. When the last of the Bellingham family died, the family tomb in the Old Granary was given to the family of Governor James Sullivan.

6. [Francis D. Allen, comp.,] *Documents and Facts, Showing the Fatal Effects of Interments in Populous Cities* (New York: F. D. Allen, 1822), 14–15. This report included a letter from Dr. Samuel Akerly to F. D. Allen dated Oct. 12, 1822. John Duffy, *A History of Public Health in New York City, 1625–1866* (New York: Russell Sage Foundation, 1968), I:98.

7. "The Desolate City," *Columbian Centinel* 4011 (Sept. 18, 1822), 2.

8. [Allen,] *Documents,* iii. Nicholas Penny notes that in England, "It is only in the middle of the nineteenth century that burial in the earth was at all favoured by the upper classes . . . only then that the soil was likely to remain undisturbed." N[icholas] B. Penny, "The Commercial Garden Necropolis of the Early Nineteenth Century and Its Critics," *Garden History* 2 (Summer 1974): 61.

9. [Allen,] *Documents,* iv.

10. Ibid., 7. Dr. Samuel Akerly considered vault burials preferable to earthen graves. Bodies decomposed there three to four times faster or in about a year's time. Still, he noted the incidence of offensive effluvia in New York City vaults.

11. Anonymous letters to the editor, *Columbian Centinel* (Sept. 10, 17, 24, 28, and Nov. 16, 1796), quoted in Blake, 159–60. Erwin H. Ackerknecht, "Anticontagionism between 1821 and 1867," *Bulletin of the History of Medicine* 22 (1948): 567. In 1824, Boston merchants persuaded the Board of Health to shorten the summer quarantine season by two months. Caleb H. Snow, *A History of Boston: The Metropolis of Massachusetts* (Boston: Abel Bowen, 1825), 406.

12. [Allen,] *Documents,* iv.

13. "City Council," *Columbian Centinel* 4037 (Dec. 18, 1822), 2. [Joseph T. Buckingham,] "Tombs Under St. Paul's," *New-England Galaxy* 6:273 (Jan. 3, 1823): 2. *Boston Patriot and Daily Mercantile Advertiser* 12:1714 (Jan. 2, 1823). The physicians were John Collins Warren; James Jackson, Warren's close friend and senior partner in practice with Jacob Bigelow; Aaron Dexter, Warren's brother-in-law; John Dixwell; William Ingalls; John Randall; John Gorham; and Enoch Hale, Jr. The term applied to the place of burial in a church crypt or cellar was "cemetery," meaning dormitory or sleeping room, in contrast to the words "graveyard" or "burial ground," generally applied to existing outdoor places of interment in Boston. An additional definition of "cemetery" developed in early nineteenth-century Boston, following the example of the French, to distinguish the old burial places from the "cemeteries. . . . all situated in the outskirts of the city." The change in terminology signaled not only a new usage and form but also, as in France, a shift in notions about death itself. Bostonians did not overlook the fact that both Doctors Warren and Hale were wardens of Saint Paul's. *Columbian Centinel* 4037. *New-England Galaxy* 273.

14. *New-England Galaxy* (March 12, 1824).

15. William Lawrence, *A Sermon on the 75th Anniversary of Saint Paul's Church, Boston* (Boston: By the Parish, 1895), 12–13. Some Bostonians criticized certain elite factions as forming the "Aristocratical Party," a group said to show their attachment to England of a political, social, and religious nature. See "The Boston Aristocracy," *Boston Patriot and Daily Mercantile Advertiser* 12:1814 (Apr. 30, 1823). Rejection of Episcopalianism in Boston runs counter to the pattern observed in Philadelphia, according to E. Digby Baltzell, *Puritan Boston and Quaker Philadelphia: Two Protestant Ethics and the Spirit of Class Authority and Leadership* (New York: Macmillan, 1979). Douglas, 25. Phillips Brooks, "The Episcopal Church," in Winsor, ed., *Memorial History of Boston,* 3:455. Snow, 356. Lawrence, *Sermon,* 13–15. *Bacon's Dictionary of Boston* (Boston: Houghton Mifflin, 1886), 355. Samuel Appleton also provided the largest initial contribution for creation of Mount Auburn.

16. Snow, 356. Savage, 32. "St. Paul's Church," *Boston Intelligencer and Evening Gazette* 6 (Oct. 23, 1819): 1. Snow, 347. See subscription papers in vol. 12, The Papers of Dr. John Collins Warren, MHIS.

17. Robert A. McCaughey, *Josiah Quincy, 1772–1865: The Last Federalist* (Cambridge: Harvard Univ. Press, 1974), 99. Lawrence, *Sermon,* 15–16. James M. Bugbee, "Boston Under the Mayors, 1822–1880," in Winsor, 225.

18. Dr. John Collins Warren's diary, quoted in Lawrence, *Sermon,* 18. Samuel Farrar Jarvas, *A Narrative of Events Connected with the Acceptance and Resignation of the Rectorship of St. Paul's Church, Boston* (Boston: n.p., Nov. 1825), n.p. John and Abigail Adams were laid to rest beneath Quincy's First Church Unitarian. One medical historian notes that in 1793 in Philadelphia, "local Republican civic leaders like editor Andrew Brown and merchants John Swanick and Stephen Girard supported Dr. Deveze's explanation that burying the dead inside the city had produced the disease." Martin S. Pernick, "Politics, Parties, and Pestilence: Epidemic Yellow Fever in Philadelphia and the Rise of the First Party System," *William and Mary Quarterly* 29 (1972): 559–86.

19. "City Council," *Columbian Centinel* 4041 (Jan. 1, 1823), 2. Also see *New-England Galaxy* (Jan. 3, 1823). "The Church-Yard," *Boston Patriot and Daily Mercantile Advertiser* 11:1703 (Dec. 20, 1822).

20. "Church Cemeteries," *Boston Patriot and Daily Mercantile Advertiser* 11:1708 (Dec. 26, 1822).

21. *New-England Galaxy* (Jan. 3, 1823). Buckingham, born in rural Connecticut in 1779, was an outspoken proponent of freedom of the press who garnered many foes and even libel suits for his journalistic vehemence. But as editor of the Boston *Courier* and the *New England Magazine* as well as the *Gazette,* he established public confidence to elect him to several terms in both houses of the Massachusetts legislature and to positions of influence in many civic associations. *New-England Galaxy* (Mar. 12, 1824).

22. "Squam Poet," "Inscribed to S.C.," *New-England Galaxy* 6:275 (Jan. 17, 1823), 3.

23. "'Death' from Mr. Croly's *Illustrations of Gems,*" *New-England Galaxy* 6:282 (March 7, 1823).

24. Oliver Smith, a philanthropist who helped found the Boston Dispensary, had just planted trees on the Mall to replace those destroyed in the war. Gravel walks crisscrossed the area, making it suitable for strolling ladies in long dresses. John Gorham Coffin, *An Address Delivered before the Contributors of the Boston Dispensary at the Seventeenth Anniversary, October 21, 1813* (Boston: John Eliot, 1813), 9. "City Council," *Columbian Centinel* 4049 (Jan. 29, 1823), 2. Perhaps the charge of bribery was valid. A month after the City Council ruling, David Sears, wealthy warden of Saint Paul's, donated an estate called City Market to Boston.

25. [Joseph T. Buckingham,] "Sacred Ground" *New-England Galaxy* 6:277 (Jan. 31, 1823):2.

26. Ibid.

27. H. Crosby Englizian, *Brimstone Corner: Park Street Church, Boston* (Chicago: Moody Press, 1968), 76–77. The site of the church was called "brimstone corner" in reference to the hellfire-and-brimstone style of preaching there by the Rev. Edward Beecher from 1826 to 1830. Some folklorists, however, attribute it to gunpowder stored in the church cellar during the War of 1812.

28. The Park Street Church was a relatively new congregation formed in 1809 with a core of twenty-six members, twenty-one from other Congregational churches recently divided by the Unitarian Controversy. Until the building of the Somerset Street Church, it boasted the highest steeple in town, the capitals of which were designed by Solomon Willard. The Park Street Church, like Saint Paul's, revealed the pride and status that accompanied membership in a congregation housed in an architecturally prominent edifice at the foot of Beacon Hill, Boston's new elite residential area. *Bacon's Dictionary,* 162. "City Council," *Boston Evening Gazette* 9 (Jan. 18, 1822), 2. "City Council," *Columbian Centinel* 4049 (Jan. 29, 1823), 2. Englizian, 77. The Park Street Church built thirty crypt tombs. [Buckingham,] "Another Cemetery," *New-England Galaxy* 6:275 (Jan. 17, 1823). Similarly, Buckingham suggested that the tombs of Saint Paul's would remain a curse on the city and "nothing but their final conflagration" would be able to remove them. *New-England Galaxy* 6:293 (March 16, 1823).

Such was the caustic journalist style that earned Buckingham a landmark libel suit from Methodist minister J. Maffitt, a case challenging freedom of the press before the bench of then-judge Josiah Quincy in 1822. Because of Quincy's decision in favor of Buckingham, the editor became a vocal proponent of Quincy as mayor.

29. "The Vaults of St. Michan's," *New-England Galaxy* 6:275 (Jan. 17, 1823).

30. Josiah Quincy was a religious liberal who sat in the congregation of Rev. William Ellery Channing in the Federal Street Church; he refused to call himself a Unitarian, however, or to participate in denominational discussions. He greatly disliked sectarianism and was thus representative of many religious liberals in Boston. Edmund Quincy, *The Life of Josiah Quincy of Massachusetts* (Boston: Ticknor & Fields, 1868), 532–33. Quincy was also antiaristocratic by disposition. He made many political coalitions and considered himself a champion of the common man as well as a member of the city's cultural and intellectual elite. McCaughey, 92. Josiah Quincy, *A Municipal History of the Town and City of Boston during Two Centuries* (Boston: Little, Brown, 1852), 62, 65–66. *New-England Galaxy* 8:290 (May 2, 1825), 2. Few enforcement mechanisms existed to aid Quincy in implementing his resolution. The mayor made himself chairman of all committees of the Board of Alderman. Otherwise, his emphasis on "internal police"—maintenance of cleanliness and order, abatement of nuisances, suppression of vice and crime, and protection of public health—was well intentioned but fairly ineffectual.

31. Blake, 202–04. Tudor, quoted in ibid., 210. See William Tudor, "On Certain Funeral Ceremonies," in *Letters,* 5–17.

32. *Columbian Centinel* 4094. Boston City Records, *City Council Proceedings* (June 25, 1823), 271, microfilm reel 18, BPL.

33. *New-England Galaxy* 6:299 (July 4, 1823). *New-England Galaxy* 6:300 (July 11, 1823). [John Gorham Coffin,] A Fellow of the Massachusetts Medical Society, *Remarks on the Dangers and Duties of Sepulture; or, Security for the Living, with Respect and Repose for the Dead* (Boston: Phelps & Farnham, 1823). This pamphlet has been erroneously and repeatedly attributed to Dr. Jacob Bigelow in the Countway Library and Harvard Union catalogues and in other references. A close reading of the work, however, put the authorship in question. Whereas Bigelow did propose a "rural" cemetery to Bostonians two years after publication of the pamphlet and was a Fellow of the Massachusetts Medical Society in 1823, he was a youth and had not left Sudbury, Massachusetts, for Harvard College in early 1801. The pamphlet's author, on the other hand, recounted a visit to Nice, France: "In 1801, I visited this place as a commissioner of public health, during the prevalence of a bad fever," 2. Documentation of the authorship of the pamphlet by Dr. Coffin appears in Buckingham's reviews in the *New-England Galaxy*. Furthermore, Bigelow's papers and his biographer make no reference to the younger physician's authorship of such a pamphlet. See Ellis. [Coffin,] 3–4. Coffin championed preventive medicine as editor of the *Medical Intelligencer* in 1826. From 1818 to 1820, Coffin lectured and wrote on the dangers to health of bathing "longer than two or three minutes at a time or more often than once every other day." Blake, 240. Perhaps confusion over authorship of the pamphlet stemmed from Bigelow's subsequent theories on "self-limiting" diseases and approaches to preventive medicine similar to Coffin's.

34. [Coffin,] 45 and 5.

35. Ibid., 33–34 and 57.

36. Ibid., 61 and 64–65.

37. Ibid., 64–65.

38. Ibid., 71.

39. Ibid.

40. "City Council," *Columbian Centinel* 4041 (Jan. 1, 1823), 2. Also see *New-England Galaxy* 6 (Jan. 3, 1823). "The Church-Yard," *Boston Patriot and Daily Mercantile Advertiser* 11:1703 (Dec. 20, 1822).

41. [Tudor,] "On Certain Funeral Ceremonies," 17.

42. Boston City Records, "Quincy Commission Report," *City Council Proceedings* (Aug. 4, 1823), 311–20.

43. Ibid., 330–36. Quincy's egalitarianism was also evident in his complaint about crypt burials that "the great mass of citizens cannot afford the right, nor could it be extended to all, if they could afford it." He asserted, "Why a minority of the population of any city should be permitted to have the exclusive privilege of poisoning the atmosphere of the majority of all the citizens, is a question not easily answered." Ibid., 326.

44. The ban of 1823 was rescinded to permit construction of a double line of tombs in the Common Burying Ground in 1836.

45. John Collins Warren to Josiah Quincy, draft of "Letter on Interments, July 1823 Answer," The Warren Papers 10:82, MHIS.

46. Nathaniel B. Shurtleff, *A Topographical and Historical Description of Boston* (Boston: Rockwell & Churchill, 1891), 359.

47. Ibid.

48. The last recorded burial at King's Chapel occurred in 1796. *Bacon's Dictionary,* 278. *The Charter of the City of Boston and Ordinances Made and Established by the Mayor, Aldermen, and Common Council, with Such Acts of the Legislature of Massachusetts as Relate to the Government of Said City* (Boston: True & Greene, 1827), 183–85. Savage, 21 and 44. Also see "An Ordinance to Regulate the Interment of the Dead" (passed Sept. 26, 1822), in Thomas Wetmore and Edward G. Prescott, eds., *The Charter and Ordinances of the City of Boston together with the Acts of the Legislature Relating to the City* (Boston: J. H. Eastburn, 1834), 186–92. *Columbian Centinel* 4103.

49. Josiah Quincy, *An Address to the Board of Aldermen, Members of the Common Council of Boston, on the Organization of the City Government at Faneuil Hall, January 1, 1828* (Boston: Commercial Gazette Office, 1828). Also quoted by Dr. John Gorham Coffin, editor of the new journal dedicated to preventive medicine, *Boston Medical Intelligencer* 5:36 (Jan. 22, 1828), 578. Mayor Samuel Armstrong's administration finally cut a swath off the corner of the Common Burial Ground, eliminating a row of tombs, to extend Boylston Street to connect with Tremont Street in 1836. One member of the Massachusetts Society for Promoting Good Citizenship later credited Quincy as catalyst for creation of Mount Auburn. Mellen Chamberlain, *Josiah Quincy: The Great Mayor* (Boston: By the Society, 1889), 18.

50. Savage, 44. McCaughey, 90–100. "Burials in Cities," *Boston News-Letter and City Record* (March 4, 1826), 126. "Extract of an Address of the Mayor of Boston to the City Council," *Boston Medical Intelligencer* 5:36 (Jan. 22, 1828), 577–78 (at that time Dr. Coffin was editor). From 1813 to 1823, there was one death for every 42 Bostonians annually. The average for 1824 to 1827 was one in 48, and annual figures continually improved to one in 55 for 1826–27 or one in 63 for 1827 alone.

51. Quincy, *Municipal History,* 100. In fact, an 1849 ordinance authorized the City of Boston "to purchase and hold land, for a public cemetery, in any town in this commonwealth" and to establish rules and regulations similar to those existing for intramural burials. Peleg W. Chandler, *The Charter and Ordinances of the City of Boston together with the Acts of the Legislature relating to the City* (Boston: John H. Eastburn, 1850), 201.

52. Despite subsequent purchase of a family lot at Forest Hills, Boston's second "rural" cemetery, which opened in 1848, Dr. John Collins Warren ordered that after his death his skeleton should be properly prepared and presented to the Massachusetts General Hospital.

CHAPTER 7

1. [Joseph T. Buckingham,] *New-England Galaxy* 290 (May 2, 1825), 2.

2. Abel Bowen, "Burial in Cities," *Boston News-Letter and City Record* (March 4, 1826), 126–29.

3. Jacob Bigelow, *A History of the Cemetery of Mount Auburn* (Boston and Cambridge: James Munroe, 1860), 2–3.

4. Ellis, 33. Fessenden, 187. This was not such a concern for Dearborn and Zebedee Cook, who had estates in Roxbury and Dorchester, respectively, although no evidence remains of their plans to place burials there.
   Bigelow considered himself a self-made man, recalling in old age, "It is enough for me that I have led a long and happy life, beginning at the bottom of the ladder and ending with the esteem and good opinion of many." Bigelow to an unidentified friend (Jan. 17, 1871), Bigelow Papers, CLMH.

5. Both of Bigelow's parents died in 1816, a year after his brother. Bigelow's *Florula Bostoniensis* (Boston: Cummings & Hilliard, 1814) preceded Sir Joseph Dalton Hooker's *Flora Scotica* (1821) and John Claudius Loudon's *Et Fruticetum Britannicum* (1821).

6. See Dirk Struik, *Yankee Science in the Making* (Boston: Little, Brown, 1948), for an assessment of the importance of Bigelow.

7. Bigelow, *History,* 137.

8. Bigelow, *Inaugural Address.*

9. Bigelow quoted in Cornelia W. Walter, *The Rural Cemeteries of America: Mount Auburn Illustrated in a Series of Views from Drawings Taken on the Spot . . . with Descriptive Notices* (New York: R. Martin, 1847), 29–30.

10. Ibid., 33–34. Bigelow, "On the Burial of the Dead, and Mount Auburn Cemetery," in *Nature in Disease, Illustrated in Various Discourses and Essays to which are Added Miscellaneous Writings, Chiefly on Medical Subjects* (Boston: Ticknor & Fields, 1854), 16; and in *Modern Inquiries: Classical, Professional, and Miscellaneous* (Boston: Little, Brown, 1867), 119–36. Bigelow, "Extract from 'Nature in Disease,' " *Mount Auburn Memorial* 1:2 (Aug. 31, 1859), 90.

11. Peabody, "Mount Auburn Cemetery," 397–406.

12. Bryant, "A Forest Hymn" (1829), in *Poems* 130–34. [Bryant,] "Thanatopsis," *North American Review* (Sept, 1817).

13. Bigelow, quoted in Walter, 30.

14. Bigelow, "On Burial," 133. Colonel Joseph May quoted in Walter, 33–34. *Historical Sketch and Matters Appertaining to the Granary Burial Ground,* 19.

15. Channing, "Self-Culture" (1828), 456. Channing, "Botany" (1818), 345.

16. William Ware, "Unitarian Belief," *Unitarian* 1 (Nov. 1827), 19. Universalists claimed to have taken the lead in avowing Unitarianism. Maturin M. Ballou, *Biography of Rev. Hosea Ballou* (Boston: Abel Thompkins, 1852), 331.

17. [Robert Manning, ed.,] *History of the Massachusetts Horticultural Society, 1829–1878* (Boston: Rand, Avery, for the Society, 1880), 74. Walter, 33–35. Also Bigelow, "Extract," quoted in "Mount Auburn," *Gleason's Pictorial Drawing Room Companion* (Aug. 13, 1853), 104–5.

18. Walter, 35.

19. T. W. Harris, *Discourse,* 76–78. The term "friends" often referred to relatives rather than close acquaintances.

20. Wordsworth, "Essay upon Epitaphs," 239–40.

21. Several decades later, William Aspinwall's heirs sold his Brighton estate for creation of Evergreen Ceme-

tery. The Brookline Hospital Church occupies part of the nearby Aspinwall property. Bigelow, *History,* 137.

22. Henry A. S. Dearborn, *Address Delivered before the Massachusetts Horticultural Society on the Celebration of their First Anniversary, Sept. 19, 1829* (2d ed., Boston: J. T. Buckingham, 1833), in *Transactions of the Massachusetts Horticultural Society, 1829–1838* (Boston: William D. Ticknor, 1847), I:5 (published orations and other proceedings bound together, hereafter referred to as *Transactions*), MHOR. Zebedee Cook, Jr., *An Address Pronounced before the Massachusetts Horticultural Society in Commemoration of its Second Annual Festival, the 10th of Sept. 1830,* (Boston: Isaac R. Baits, 1830), 10; also in *Transactions.*

23. H. Dearborn, "General Dearborn's Address: Delivered before the Massachusetts Horticultural Society on the Celebration of their First Anniversary, Sept. 19, 1829," *New England Farmer* 8:26 (Jan. 15, 1830), 203.

24. Z. Cook, 17. The Horticultural Society of Paris elected Dearborn, Cook, John C. Gray, Enoch Bartlett (breeder of the pear), and Bigelow honorary members in February of 1830. *New England Farmer* 8:31 (Feb. 1830), 243. The Caledonian Horticultural Society was founded in Edinburgh in 1809.

25. In 1824 Captain Jonathan Winship and his brother Francis established a nursery in Brighton specializing in ornamental trees and shrubs. It was one of the first such ventures in the Boston metropolitan area. [Manning,] 52, 57, 60.

26. Simon Stone held an Indian deed for the property. Colonel George Sullivan and Charles W. Green named the old estate "Sweet Auburn." Debate remains among literary scholars over whether Goldsmith referred to his hometown of Lissoy, County Westmeath, or to Nuneham Courtenay, the Oxfordshire town destroyed in 1761 by Lord Harcourt for construction of his landscaped garden. "George W. Brimmer" [from *Boston Daily Advertiser,* Sept. 1838], *Mount Auburn Memorial* 1:44 (Apr. 11, 1860), 345. Caroline F. Orne, *Sweet Auburn and Mount Auburn with Other Poems* (Cambridge: John Owen, 1844), 19.

27. Orne, 1–16. James Russell Lowell, "Cambridge Thirty Years Ago" (Introduction to the *Biglow Papers*) and Lowell to George B. Loring (1837), in Charles Eliot Norton, ed., *Letters of James Russell Lowell* (New York: Harper & Brothers, 1894), I:19.

28. *Mount Auburn Memorial* 1:1, 2. T. W. Harris, *Discourse,* 76–78.

29. Benjamin A. Gould, mutual friend of Bigelow and Brimmer, visited Père Lachaise. Gould to Bigelow (Jan. 11, 1829), in Bigelow Papers, MHIS. David B. Chase, "The Beginnings of the Landscape Tradition in America," *Historic Preservation* 25 (Jan.–Mar. 1973): 41.

30. David J. Rothman, *The Discovery of the Asylum: Social Order and Disorder in the New Republic* (Boston: Little, Brown, 1971), 137–38. Nathan Hale, "Mount Auburn," *Boston Daily Advertiser* (1831), clipping in the files of the Corporation. It is only coincidental that an eighteenth-century ferry across the Charles River was located between Brighton and the current site of Mount Auburn on the Cambridge-Watertown Road, close to the old center of Watertown. No cemetery founder referred to the latent symbolism of a ferry site as suggestive of the mythical route to the nether world across the River Styx.

31. Bigelow, *History,* 16. Peabody, "Mount Auburn Cemetery," 406.

32. [Dionysius Cassius] Longinus, *An Essay on the Sublime,* trans. by Nicholas Boileau-Despreaux (1674) (Oxford: Leon Lichfield, 1698). Isaac Newton, *Mathematical Principles of Natural Philosophy,* ed. by Florian Cajori (Berkeley: Univ. of California Press, 1934), 544–45. Joseph Addison, "Panoramas," *Spectator,* no. 412, quoted in Walter Jackson Bate, *From Classic to Romantic: Premises of Taste in Eighteenth-Century England* (Cambridge: Harvard Univ. Press, 1946), 99.

33. Many dioramas also presented romantic landscapes. A major example was Louis-Jacques-Mandé Daguerre's Holyrood Chapel, exhibited in Paris and London between 1823 and 1825, depicting a gothic ruin by moonlight and a white-robed woman praying in front of a funerary monument; it was an elaborate mourning picture. Daguerre's *View of Paris from Montmartre* (1831), presenting a panorama similar to that seen by visitors to Père Lachaise Cemetery. Daguerre also produced dioramas of *The Tomb of Napoleon at St. Helena* and the *Campo Santo at Pisa* (1830), a famous Italian cemetery. A diorama, *Transparent Panoramic View of West Point and Adjacent Scenery,* attracted almost as much attention in Washington in 1829 as President Jackson's inauguration. Also see Poe, 403.

34. Ronald Rees, "The Scenery Cult: Changing Landscape Taste over Three Centuries," *Landscape* 19:3 (May 1975): 42. Marx, 246.

35. Brimmer took a $1,000 loss on the property. Martin Brimmer to Bigelow (n.d. [1856?]), in Bigelow Papers, box 3 (1854–69), MHIS.

36. T. W. Harris, *Discourse,* 70.

37. Z. Cook, 27–28. Another reference to the precedent set by Père Lachaise was Alexander Everett, *Address,* 18, 37–46.

38. Z. Cook, 27–28.

39. Vernon Louis Parrington, *Main Currents in American Thought. Vol. 2: 1800: The Romantic Revolution in America* (New York: Harcourt, Brace, & World, 1927), 314.

40. Z. Cook, 10–28. H. Dearborn, "Historical Sketch," *Transactions* I:68–70.

41. H. Dearborn, "Report," in "Proceedings of the Massachusetts Horticultural Society . . . the 18th of June 1831," *New England Farmer* 9:49 (June 22, 1831), 385.

42. H. Dearborn, "The Cemetery of Père Lachaise," *New England Farmer* 11 (Sept. 12, 1832), 66–67.

43. Ibid. H. Dearborn, "Proceedings of the Massachusetts Horticultural Society . . . Sept. 8, 1832," *Transactions.* Albert Emerson Benson, *History of the Massachusetts Horticultural Society* (Norwood, Mass.: Plimpton Press, for the Society, 1929), 41. The books Dearborn ordered and relied on included: Jolimont, *Les mausolées français,* folio vol.; Arnaud, *Recueil de tombeaux des quatre cimetières de Paris;* Marchant de Beaumont, *Manuel et itinéraire;* Evelyn, *Silva;* George Maliphant, *Designs for Sepulchral Monuments* (London, n.d.); and various works by Sir Humphrey Repton. Dearborn and his associates may also have been familiar with Augustus Pugin's *Paris and its Environs,* containing ten engravings of Père Lachaise, including detailed descriptions of landscape and monuments. Bigelow also regularly ordered books to be imported by the Boston firm of Cummings & Hilliard.

44. H. Dearborn, *Address . . . 1829,* 7. Dearborn recognized and reinterpreted Sir Humphrey Repton, a major English garden theorist, a decade before John Claudius Loudon did, although Loudon is often credited with assembling Repton's writings and propounding the importance of his taste in garden design.

45. H. Dearborn, "Address," *New England Farmer* 8:27 (Jan. 22, 1831): 211. The Act of the General Court, chap. 69, sec. 1 (June 23, 1831), did not mention the experimental garden. The Committee of Twenty formed in June of 1831 to determine how to proceed included Story, Webster, Dearborn, Bigelow, Charles Lowell, Samuel Appleton, Edward Everett, George Brimmer, George Bond, Alexander H. Everett, Abbott Lawrence, James T. Austin, Franklin Dexter, Joseph P. Bradlee, Charles Tappan, Charles P. Curtis, Zebedee Cook, John Pierpont, L. M. Sargent, and George W. Pratt.

46. Edward Everett to Bigelow (June 20, 1831), quoted in Ellis, 73. Reference may also have been made to Lake Avernus, the Italian place famous to travelers on the Grand Tour as site of the grotto of the Cumaean sibyl where Aeneas began his descent into the underworld. Designers of English gardens and landscape painters like Richard Wilson often tried to reinterpret views of the site.

47. H. Dearborn, "Historical Sketch," 68–70. Peabody, "Mount Auburn Cemetery," 405.

48. H. Dearborn, "Second Annual Report," 105.

49. Peabody, "Mount Auburn Cemetery," 406. Peabody's assertion that Mount Auburn was product of "manly sentiment" belies the more recent interpretation of the cemetery as evidence of the "feminization of American culture" by Ann Douglas in a book by that name (New York: Knopf, 1977).

50. H. Dearborn, "Proceedings . . . Sept. 8, 1832," *Transactions* I:35–36.

51. Bigelow, *History,* 138. Although Mount Auburn did not initially levy additional charges, the City of Boston did: "for the use of one horse and car and leader, $1.50; for each additional horse, 75¢. For carrying the corpse from the house to the car and from the car to the grave, tomb, or vault, and placing the same therein and closing the same, including the assistance of the funeral porters, $3." The bereaved were charged "$1 per mile for any distance that a funeral car may be sent out of the City." Charges did not include extra services like special permission for the tolling of bells, notification of friends, services in the home, placing the corpse in a coffin, taking it down stairs, etc. A single funeral done in "proper" style with burial at Mount Auburn could cost as much as the family lot itself. See [84,] Sec. 11, "An Ordinance to Regulate the Interment of the Dead [Passed Sept. 26, 1833], in Wetmore and Prescott, 191.

52. Bigelow, *History,* 138. Ellis, 74.

53. Ibid.

54. Rev. Henry Ware to George Bond (July 4, 1832), Rare Books Room, BPL. Dearborn proposed scattering single graves through the grounds among the family lots, but other founders vetoed the idea. Malthus A. Ward, *An Address Pronounced before the Massachusetts Horticultural Society in Commemoration of its Third Annual Festival, Sept. 21, 1831* (Boston: J. T. & E. Buckingham, 1831), 47, also in *Transactions.*

55. Henry Blake McLellan, quoted in "Sweet Auburn," *Mount Auburn Memorial* 1:2 (June 22, 1859): 12. McLellan is buried in his family's tomb, not on Harvard Hill.

56. John Pierpont, "To My Grave," in *Airs of Palestine and Other Poems* (Boston: James Munroe, 1840), 65–72.

57. Bigelow, *History,* 138. "Proceedings . . . Oct. 1st, 1831," *New England Farmer* 10:12 (Oct. 5, 1831), 90–91. Advertisements appeared in the *Boston Evening Gazette* in the late summer of 1832.

58. H. Dearborn, " Proceedings . . . 1832," *Transactions* I:36.

59. The committee planning the consecration included Story, Dearborn, Cook, J. T. Buckingham, Brimmer, George W. Pratt, Z. B. Adams, Charles P. Curtis, and the Reverend Charles Lowell.

60. Arthur Schlesinger, Jr., *The Age of Jackson* (Boston: Little, Brown, 1945), 144–45 and 322–26.

61. William Wetmore Story, ed., *Life and Letters of Joseph Story* (Boston: Little, Brown, 1851), I:2 and II:60–61. Also see "Sketch of the Life of Judge Story," *Mount Auburn Memorial* 1:1 (Aug. 24, 1859): 81. Story suffered what might be considered a nervous breakdown when his first wife's death was almost immediately followed by that of his father in 1815.

62. W. Story, II:60–61.

63. See the chapter "The Domestication of Death," in Douglas.

64. W. Story, II:62–65.

65. Bigelow wrote sentimental verse on the deaths of his children. Also see J. Q. Adams, 310.

66. H. Dearborn, "Historical Sketch," *Transactions* I:71 and 76. [Manning,] 82. Bigelow, *History,* 11. The Horticultural Society expended $50.82 for putting up seats for the crowd.

67. W. Story, II:63. David Brion Davis, *Antebellum American Culture* (Lexington, Mass.: D. C. Heath, 1979), 146. It was Ware who invited Josiah Quincy to the Harvard presidency.

68. Ware's election to the Harvard chair of theology in 1805 was a major event in the Unitarian controversy. Ware was colleague of Ralph Waldo Emerson at the Second Church in Boston until 1832.

69. W. Story, II:64–65. "Judge Story's Address," in *The Picturesque Pocket Companion and Visitor's Guide through Mount Auburn* (Boston: Otis, Broaders, 1839), 74–75.

70. W. Story, II:64–65.

71. Ibid., 65–67. *Picturesque,* 79.

72. W. Story, II:67. J. S. Buckingham, *America,* III:146.

73. "Cemetery at Mount Auburn" [reprint of article from *Boston Courier*], *New England Farmer* 10:11 (Sept. 28, 1831): 82.

CHAPTER 8

1. Bigelow, *History,* 134. Henry A. S. Dearborn, "The Proposed Cemetery," in T. W. Harris, *Discourse,* 70.

2. H. Dearborn, "Proceedings . . . 1831," 1.

3. H. Dearborn, "An Account of the Proceedings in Relation to the Experimental Garden and the Cemetery of Mount Auburn," *Transactions,* I:68. [H. Dearborn,] "Proceedings . . . Oct. 1st, 1832," *New England Farmer* 10:12 (Oct. 5, 1831): 90–91.

4. Members of the Garden and Cemetery Committee were Story, Dearborn, Bigelow, Brimmer, Edward Everett, Benjamin A. Gould, Charles Wells, George W. Pratt, and George Bond. Zebedee Cook, Jr., vice president of the horticultural society, also participated.

5. *New England Farmer* 3 (1824): 77 and 22.

6. H. Dearborn, "A Treatise on Grecian Architecture," (1828) 2 vol. manuscript folio, Rare Books Room, BPL. Manuscript letter from Dearborn (Jan. 18, 1842), included in "Constitution, Reports, Addresses and Other Publications in Relation to the Massachusetts Horticultural Society and the Cemetery at Mount Auburn from 1829 to 1837," MHOR. Dearborn, "Plan of the Avenues of Mount Auburn and Plan of the Cottage for the Gardener of Mount Auburn and Report of the Garden and Cemetery Committee of the Massachusetts Horticultural Society" (Sept. 17, 1834), signed Joseph Story, Chairman, manuscript in NYPL. Also see Robin Carver, *History of Boston* (Boston: Lilly, Wait, Colman, & Holden, 1832), 148. Provision of carriage as well as foot access to all parts of the grounds responded to a criticism of English gardens Dearborn had gleaned from his readings of Humphrey Repton in "The 'Red Book' for Blaise Castle" (1795–96), excerpt reprinted in John Dixon Hunt and Peter Willis, eds., *The Genius of Place: The English Landscape Garden, 1620–1820* (New York: Harper & Row, 1975), 363–64.

7. H. Dearborn, "The Proposed Rural Cemetery," in "An Account," 84. Dearborn to G[eorge] W. Brimmer, "On the Work to be Done at Mount Auburn," from Roxbury (Nov. 30, 1831), NYPL. By 1833, Dearborn counted over 1,300 forest, ornamental, and fruit trees at Mount Auburn. [Henry M. Parker,] *Notes on Mount Auburn, Edited by an Officer of the Corporation; Intended to Serve as a Stranger's Guide Book* (Boston: James Munroe, 1849), 16. Dearborn, "English Gardens," in "Writings on Horticulture and Other Branches of Rural Industry," manuscript vol. 2, 117–19, Rare Books Room, NYPL. [Manning,] 94–95.

8. John B. Russell, quoted in [Manning,] 86–91.

9. The exterior road near Pomroy's mill cost $200 for a right of way, $700 for land, and $250 for materials to surface it. [Mount Auburn Cemetery,] "Records of Committees " (Nov. 3, 1831–Jan. 23, 1835), manuscript book (hereafter referred to as "Records"), 15, MTA. The roads were "smoothly gravelled" from the start, according to Carver, 148. H. Dearborn, "Historical Sketch," 77–79.

10. A major example of this misunderstanding read, "Wadsworth's imaginative solution—no doubt supervised by Bigelow who is traditionally credited with the design—was to wind the roadways around the hills and ponds, their routes dictated by the terrain in order to achieve picturesque vistas and make efficient use of the ground." Bainbridge Bunting and Robert H. Nylander, *Survey of Architectural History in Cambridge: Report Four: Old Cambridge* (Cambridge: Cambridge Historical Commission & MIT Press, 1969), 70. An example of Wadsworth's map-making, "Plan of the Village of Old Cambridge," 1833, appears as figure 6 in that same volume. Use of the word "plan" in that example certainly did not imply that Wadsworth provided the landscape design for Cambridge, which was established in 1630!

11. Additional evidence appears in Dearborn to George W. Brimmer, "On the Work to be Done at Mount Auburn during the Winter of 1831–2 and the Spring of 1832" (Nov. 20, 1831) from Brinley Place, Roxbury, NYPL. Also see Dearborn, "Plan of the Avenues of Mount Auburn and Plan of the Cottage for the Gardener of Mount Auburn and Report of the Garden and Cemetery Committee of the Massachusetts Horticultural Society" (Sept. 17, 1834), signed Joseph Story, Chairman, manuscript, NYPL.

12. Bigelow to his family in Boston from the Hotel des Princes, rue Richelieu, Paris (May 2–4, 1833), in the Bigelow Papers, NYPL.

13. Bigelow's biographer, George Ellis, credits him with "designating" avenues, but that only meant that the physician chose names for the routes for carriages and pedestrians laid out by Dearborn. Still, considerable confusion exists in historical accounts of who deserves credit for creating Mount Auburn—confusion largely produced by competitive claims originating with Dearborn and Bigelow, reinterpreted and perpetuated by their eulogists, and then misunderstood by historians relying only on secondary sources. Attribution of credit is further complicated because the cemetery began as a voluntary association, developed under auspices of another Boston institution, and finally was incorporated independently. Through these phases, committees made many organizational and design decisions, misinterpreted even by contemporaries. One observer from Baltimore listed Joseph Story, Daniel Webster, Governer Levi Lincoln, Abbott Lawrence, Samuel Appleton, the Everett brothers, Brimmer, and Dearborn as instrumental in creating Mount Auburn, omitting mention of Bigelow entirely. Although Bigelow did not design the landscape, he remained a constant proponent of the cemetery through all initial phases and for decades to come. [Stephen Duncan Walker,] *Rural Cemetery and Public Walk* (Baltimore: Sands & Neilson, 1835), 4. By 1833, Mount Auburn had 110 acres. And if the debate over authorship of the cemetery was not confused enough by partisans of Dearborn and Bigelow, many more recent writers have further confused the historical record. One article even attributed the design to Nathaniel Dearborn, the prominent Boston printer and author of a series of guidebooks to the cemetery. Jules Zanger's "Mount Auburn Cemetery: The Silent Suburb," *Landscape* 24:2 (1980): 23–28, is perhaps more erroneous and full of misinterpretations than any other source.

14. Walter, 10.

15. Samuel Walker, "Horticultural Societies," *Horticulturist* 6:2 (Feb. 1851): 92.

16. Putnam, 12–14. Versions of the eulogy were printed in local newspapers: "Putnam's Address," *Boston Courier* (Sept. 4, 1851); Putnam, "Address," *Boston Daily Advertiser* (Sept. 9, 1851). Subsequently Robert Manning became a partisan in the debate when he edited his *History of the Massachusetts Horticultural Society* (1880).

17. Bigelow, *History*, 6, 19, and 96.

18. Bigelow to Massachusetts Horticultural Society (Sept. 1866), quoted in [Manning,] 115–17.

19. "Gen. H. A. S. Dearborn," *Mount Auburn Memorial* 2:14 (Oct. 3, 1860): 105.

20. Ellis, 34, 61–62. Ellis, a minister graduated in the Harvard class of 1834, was a close friend of Francis Parkman, Bigelow's son-in-law. Ellis omitted to mention in the eulogy that subsequently in the 1850s and 1860s Bigelow was responsible for altering the original "rural" aesthetics of Mount Auburn's landscape, making the place "gardenesque" rather than "picturesque" by eliminating half of the original tree canopy in order to plant ornamentals. I will discuss that process of landscape change in another book.

21. Burton J. Bledstein, *The Culture of Professionalism: The Middle Class and the Development of Higher Education in America* (New York: Norton, 1976), 20. The term "landscape architect" had yet to be coined by Andrew Jackson Downing.

22. H. Dearborn, "Historical Sketch," 68–70. "Mount Auburn Cemetery: Report of the Massachusetts Horticultural Society upon the Establishment of an Experimental Garden and Rural Cemetery," *North American Review* 33 (1831): 405. John Claudius Loudon closely paraphrased Dearborn in speculating that cemeteries might double as educational institutions of architecture and landscape gardening in his essay "On the Laying Out and Uses of Cemeteries" (1843).

23. Z. Cook, in *Transactions* I:75. Cook also called for protection and preservation of useful birds at Mount Auburn, a secondary function that would have made the place America's first bird sanctuary. H. Dearborn, "Historical Sketch," 68.

24. H. Dearborn, *Transactions* I:75. Dearborn, "Historical Sketch," 68.

25. H. Dearborn, "Historical Sketch," 69–70, 73, 78. Dearborn, "Garden and Cemetery Committee Report," *Transactions* (1831), I:48. Dearborn to Brimmer (Nov. 20, 1831). Letter from S. P. Hildreth to the Massachusetts Horticultural Society (Feb. 25, 1833), quoted in "Plants Grown," *New England Farmer* 11 (Apr. 3, 1833), 299.

26. David Porter letter, quoted in *New England Farmer* 11 (May 22, 1833), 354–55. Other periodic reports of plants and seeds received by the horticultural society for Mount Auburn appeared through the *New England Farmer* 10–13 (1832–34). Eastern Orthodox Christians in the Ottoman empire did not have the same ban on cemetery plantings as Roman Catholics after the Counter-Reformation.

27. Dearborn to George Bond (Sept. 10, 1832), BPL. Samuel Appleton loaned $1,000, the largest single amount.

28. Bigelow, *History*, 6.

29. Brimmer to Dearborn (Dec. 9, 1830), *New England Farmer* 11 (May 22, 1833), 354–55. David Haggerston, the gardener, exhibited produce grown at Mount Auburn at the horticultural society in June of 1834.

30. J. Story, "Report" (Sept. 1932), *Transactions* I:47. William Kenrick to Dearborn (June 11, 1833) in the Dearborn Papers, Rare Books Room, BPL.

31. George Bond to Dearborn (Sept. 10, 1832), Dearborn Papers. Benson, 40–41. Oakes I. Ames, "Mount Auburn's Sixscore Years," *Publications of the Cambridge Historical Society* 34 (1951–52): 80. By September of 1833, 259 of 400 lots laid out had been sold, producing revenue of $17,229.72.

32. Z. Cook to Dearborn (Dec. 30, 1834), in Josiah Little

Papers, MHIS. Dearborn had hoped to establish "Seminaries of trees and shrubs" as late as that fall. Dearborn to Z. Cook (Sept. 10, 1834), in John C. Gray, *An Address Delivered before the Massachusetts Horticultural Society at the 6th Anniversary, Sept. 17, 1834* (Boston: J. T. Buckingham, 1834), 29.

33. H. Dearborn, "Historical Sketch," 77–79. "Records," 15. [Fanny Kemble,] *The Journal of Frances Anne Butler, Better Known as Fanny Kemble* (1835; New York: B. Blom, 1970), 175–76.

34. Ralph Waldo Emerson (April 11, 1834), in Edward Waldo Emerson and Waldo Forbes Emerson, eds., *Journals of Ralph Waldo Emerson with Annotations* (Boston: Houghton Mifflin, 1910), III:270–71. Bliss Perry, ed., *The Heart of Emerson's Journals* (Boston: Houghton Mifflin, 1926), 82–83.

35. "Proceedings of the Massachusetts Horticultural Society," *Transactions* I:106–07. J. Story, "Report" (Sept. 1832), *Transactions* I:47.

36. "Records" (April 29, 1833), 14. H. Dearborn, "Report," *Transactions* I:104.

37. H. Dearborn, "Report," *Transactions* I:104.

38. "Records," 15. H. Dearborn, "Historical Sketch," 73–74.

39. "Report of the Garden and Cemetery Committee" (Sept. 17, 1837), in "Records," 27. "Records" (July 19, 1834), 22, and (Oct. 17, 1834), 24. Alexander Everett, *Address*. Everett gave a large dinner for Alexis de Tocqueville when the Frenchman and his traveling companion de Beaumont visited America in 1831 in order to introduce Tocqueville to many of the Bostonians active in the Bunker Hill Monument Association, the Massachusetts Horticultural Society, and the founding of Mount Auburn.

40. "Report of the Garden and Cemetery Committee" (Sept. 17, 1837), in "Records," 27.

41. Leverett Saltonstall [President of the Massachusetts Horticultural Society], quoted in Flagg, 33.

42. Commonwealth of Massachusetts, "An Act to Incorporate the Proprietors of the Cemetery of Mount Auburn" (1835), in *A Catalogue of Proprietors of the Cemetery of Mount Auburn* (Boston: James Munroe, 1846), xvii–xviii.

43. "Report of the Garden and Cemetery Committee" (Sept. 17, 1837).

44. Attempts to move older remains, if located, may have been impeded by the new Boston code "That no person shall remove any bodies, or the remains of any bodies from any of the graves or tombs in this city, or shall disturb, break up, or remove any body in any tomb or grave without the special permission of the Superintendent of Burials." "An Ordinance to Regulate Interment of the Dead," [86,] Sec. 13 in chap. 24, "Health," in [City of Boston,] *The Charter and Ordinances of the City of Boston* (Boston: J. H. Eastburn, 1834), 192.

CHAPTER 9

1. [Enoch Cobb Wines,] *A Trip to Boston in a Series of Letters to the Editor of the United States Gazette* (Boston: Little, Brown, 1838), 45. Henry David Thoreau, *Walden* (1854; New York: Thomas Y. Crowell, 1961), 173.

2. "Mount Auburn," *Cyclopoedia of Useful Knowledge* (1835), 9, an anonymous clipping in the files of the Cemetery, Cambridge.

3. Peabody, "Mount Auburn Cemetery," 406. Henry A. S. Dearborn, "An Account of the Work Done at Mount Auburn during the Year 1832," in *Transactions*. "Records" (Oct. 1833), 17, and (Nov. 3, 1831), 2. Slate stones were later permitted at Mount Auburn during the vogue for the neocolonial style at the turn of the twentieth century. Henry Russell Cleveland, "American Architecture," *North American Review* 43:93 (Oct. 1836): 378.

4. *Picturesque,* 75.

5. Hunt, "Pope's Twickenham Revisited," 32.

6. Ibid., 12–13.

7. Jacob Bigelow, "On the Limits of Education," in *Modern Inquiries: Classical, Professional, and Miscellaneous* (Boston: Little, Brown, 1867), 32.

8. Ariès, *The Hour*. "A Conservative Unitarian" to the Senior Warden of King's Chapel (Nov. 1841), in Foote, II:470–71.

9. Jeremy Cross, *True Masonic Chart or Hieroglyphic Monitor* (New Haven: J. C. Gray, 1819). See also Neil Harris.

10. Much valuable historical documentation on monuments and family lots was lost in the 1960s when "efficiency" experts serving as consultants to the corporation "cleaned" the files. Willard initially received $14 for his designs. William Kenrick (Newton) to Henry A. S. Dearborn, in the Dearborn Papers, BPL. On Robert Gould Shaw's order of monuments, see Bigelow to Dearborn (Jan. 13, 1833), BPL. In 1837, the cemetery expended $100 for monument plans. "Records," 1 (March 22, 1837), 39.

11. Peabody, "Mount Auburn Cemetery," 406.

12. J. S. Buckingham, *America,* 3. [Anon.,] "Mount Auburn," *American Magazine* 10, clipping in the files of the cemetery.

13. Vincent Scully, *The Earth, the Temple, and the Gods: Greek Sacred Architecture* (New York: Praeger, 1969), 42–43. Also see Eliade, especially chap. 1, "Sacred Space and Making the World Sacred."

14. *Picturesque,* 193–94. The precedent for Mount Auburn's trustees to vote for exclusion of any offensive monument or effigy had been set at Père Lachaise, where all inscriptions had to be approved by the superintendent. The provision was included as the seventh "condition" or "limitation" on the "Form for Conveyance of Lots" issued to each proprietor, reprinted in *Catalogue of the Lots in Mount Auburn Cemetery* (Boston: Rand & Avery, 1857), 29, and elsewhere.

15. Josiah Quincy, then president of Harvard, acknowledged the elder Shattuck's donation of lots in April of 1833. George Shattuck, Jr., to George Bond, n.d., the Shattuck Papers 33:4, MHIS.

16. Bigelow, *History,* 142. *Picturesque,* 206 and 195.

17. Mrs. E. C. Kirkland to the Committee of the Alumni of Harvard University Who Propose Erecting a Monument to the Memory of Dr. Kirkland (n.d.), Bigelow Family Papers, MHIS.

18. *Picturesque,* 189.

19. Thomas Whittemore, ed. *The Life of Rev. Hosea Ballou,* IV:242–47.

20. *Picturesque,* 89. Harriet Martineau, *Retrospect of Western Travel* (London: Saunders & Otley, 1838), II:232–33. George Combe, *Notes on the United States of North America during a Phrenological Visit in 1838–9–40* (Philadelphia: Carey & Hart, 1841), I:135. According to the usually meticulous interment records of the cemetery, Spurzheim's embalmed body (embalming was unusual for that era) was never buried at Mount Auburn, although it was temporarily deposited in the cemetery's receiving tomb under Boston's Park Street Church. Present whereabouts of the remains are unknown, although the Boston Phrenological Society followed Spurzheim's wishes and preserved the scientist's brain, "floating in alcohol and hermetically sealed," as well as the skull in their iron safe for further study as "a very interesting addition to their collection of casts and skulls"; but they, too, have been lost. In 1987, Dr. Richard Tyler, professor of Neurology at Brigham and Women's Hospital in Boston, claimed to have located documentation that Spurzheim's body actually was interred at Mount Auburn; I have not seen that reference, however.

21. Although his minister, the Rev. Alexander Young, felt that Bowditch had "built his own monument, more enduring than marble," he urged erection of "a material and visible monument" at Mount Auburn: "Let the shipmasters and mates throughout the United States and all seamen who have actually used the *Practical Navigator* give one dollar each (those who please may give more) towards the erection of a monument of white marble in a style of severe and simple grandeur, befitting his character; and let the amount be collected in every seaport by the Chamber of Commerce, the Marine Society, and if neither of these exist, by some Insurance Company, or by the Collector of the port. Let the monument be a four-sided figure." Young detailed a proposed design: On one face, "a few geometrical figures, a circle, a triangle, &c around a ship in the center full sail with the American flag flying at the mizzen-peak" and the motto "DIRIGO—I guide." On another face, a relief of two books inscribed THE PRACTICAL NAVIGATOR and MECANIQUE CELESTE along with a sextant and compass, the ringed planet Saturn, and the constellation Ursa Minor with polestar. Inscriptions on the two remaining sides would proclaim Bowditch "The American Pilot and Mathematician . . . The Expounder of the Mechanism of the Heavens" and acknowledge the contributions for the monument to "their Guide and Benefactor" from the Seamen of the United States.

Indeed, as news of Bowditch's death spread nationally, flags flew at half-mast on vessels out of Baltimore and midshipmen at the Naval Academy donned black crepe armbands for thirty days. No evidence remains of how many of them contributed to the monument, which was far more elaborate and innovative than that proposed by the Rev. Young. Young, *A Discourse on the Life and Character of the Hon. Nathaniel Bowditch, LL.D., F. R. S., Delivered in the Church on Church Green, Mar. 25, 1838* (Boston: Little, Brown, 1838), 98–99.

As if competing on behalf of local notable Thomas Godfrey, inventor of the marine quadrant, who died in 1749, the Mercantile Library Company of Philadelphia and citizens of Germantown, Pennsylvania, erected an obelisk in Laurel Hill Cemetery over the remains of Godfrey and his parents, recently moved from the old colonial family burial ground.

22. "Records," 1 (Dec. 13, 1838), 48–49.

23. For a description of Legare's Mugwump career, see William R. Taylor, *Cavalier and Yankee: The Old South and American National Character* (Cambridge: Harvard Univ. Press, 1979), 53–57. Mrs. C. H. Putnam, "Letters from Home: Mount Auburn Cemetery," *Young Lady's and Gentleman's Parlor Album* (New York, ca. 1843), 309–12, clipping in the files of the Cemetery.

24. Charles Wilkes, *Narrative of the U.S. Exploring Expedition during the Years 1838, 1839, 1840, 1841, 1842* (Philadelphia: Lea & Blanchard, 1848), II:310–11. Wilkes retaliated for the deaths by killing eighty-seven "Fejee" villagers. Less than three months after the tragedy, a committee aboard ship, still in the South Seas, decided to place the monument at Mount Auburn. Final design was done by Drayton and the monument erected by John Struthers and Son, Philadelphia. Perhaps erection of the monument stimulated Thoreau's rancor against the "parade and expense" of the expedition. Thoreau, 424.

25. Ballou's body was first placed in a tomb in the Boston Common Burying Ground; but "it was the intention to regard this merely as a temporary burial" and to move the body to a more fitting, permanent site.

26. Damrell V. Moore and George Coolidge, eds., *The Boston Almanac for the Year 1857,* no. 22 (Boston: John P. Jewett, 1857), 59. The lot was donated by Amos Lawrence. A decade before, the industrialist also gave lots near his own at Mount Auburn to the Reverends J. S. Buckminster and Lothrop to ensure their nearness to him in death. Although he accepted the secularized cemetery, Lawrence seemed to want to

have his burial near those saintly men of God, as if it were the best alternative to a churchyard he could find in the Boston area. After all, Amos had his son Amos Adams Lawrence confirmed as an Episcopalian at Saint Paul's in 1842. The event signaled the shift of many leading Unitarian families in Boston to acceptance of High Church forms. Perhaps this accounts for the industrialist's desire to surround his family lots with the graves of ministers, albeit of many denominations; it may even suggest his influence in determining the form and location of the cemetery's first chapel near the Lawrence family lot. William R. Lawrence, ed., *Extracts from the Diary and Correspondence of the Late Amos Lawrence* (Boston: Gould & Lawrence, 1855), 176. Whittemore, IV:304–05, 317, 341.

27. Bigelow, *History,* 531. Bigelow, *Boston Daily Advertiser,* quoted in ibid., 95. "Mount Auburn Cemetery," *New England Farmer* 10:5 (Aug. 17, 1831), 38.

28. Steven J. Bennett, "Chinese Topographical Thinking," *Boston University Journal* (Jan. 1978): 14–27. The term and concept of "geomancy" (*feng shui* in Chinese) was known to Bigelow and appeared in his correspondence, manuscript page (1854), Bigelow Family Papers, box 3 (1854–69), MHIS. Also see Sarah Rossback, *Feng Shui: The Chinese Art of Placement* (New York: E. P. Dutton, 1983), 51–55.

29. *Transactions,* 81–82. There is also a striking, if only superficial and visual, similarity between Mount Auburn's hillside tombs and Hindu temples in the form of simple chambers or caves, the *garbhagrhas* or "womb-houses," built into rock under moundlike hillsides and often having only plain stone façades. The same elite Bostonians whom Oliver Wendell Holmes later dubbed "Brahmins," self-conscious of parallels based on learning and lineage between themselves and the Indian ruling caste, may well have drawn stylistic inspiration from these temple structures, seen during trade with India. Bostonians may have adapted the structural form to an entirely new cultural use—burial—unprecedented in the parent culture, which used cremation. Thanks are due to Dr. Barbara Ramusak for showing me the engraved view of "The Temple of Mandeswara near Chaynpore, Bahar" by Thomas Daniell, 1808.

The seven-foot by nine-foot roughstone tomb with thirty-body capacity on lot 493 with a slate top (hidden under mounded earth) and door cost $200.

30. Dearborn, "An Account of the Work Done at Mount Auburn during the year 1832," in T. W. Harris, *Discourse,* 81–82.

31. "Records," 1 (June 5, 1841), 72.

32. Ibid., 1 (June 7, 1838), 46.

33. Ibid., 1 (March 9, 1841), 71.

34. Joseph T. Buckingham, "Mount Auburn," *Boston Courier* (Sept. 28, 1838), reprinted in *Mount Auburn Memorial* 2:1 (July 4, 1860), 10. J. S. Buckingham, *America,* 391–92.

35. J. S. Buckingham, *America,* 391–92.

36. [Wines,] 44–45. [John Ross Dix,] A Looker-On, *Local Loiterings, and Visits in the Vicinity of Boston* (Boston: Redding, 1845), 17–9.

37. J. T. Buckingham, 10.

38. "Records," 1 (July 14, 1842), 83.

39. Charles Lyell, *A Second Visit to the United States of North America* (London: John Murray, 1849), I:171.

40. "The Tomb of Spurzheim at Mount Auburn," *Family Magazine* (1853): 404.

41. Walter, 5, 8–9, and 15.

42. Bigelow, "Mount Auburn!" manuscript poem in the Bigelow Family Papers, MHIS.

43. *Mount Auburn Memorial* 1:38 (Feb. 29, 1860), 301. Douglas, chap. 6, "The Domestication of Death."

CHAPTER 10

1. Alison, 180.

2. Henry A. S. Dearborn, "Report," in *Picturesque,* 46.

3. Thomas Cole, quoted in John Lunsford, *The Romantic Vision in America* (Dallas: Dallas Museum of Fine Arts, 1971), n.p.

4. H. Dearborn, "Report," in "Proceedings . . . 1831," 90.

5. Walter Muir Whitehill, Foreword, in Douglass Shand Tucci, *Built in Boston: City and Suburb, 1800–1950* (Boston: New York Graphic Society, 1978), viii.

6. Bigelow's parlor had a "beautiful array of classical and artistic adornments—the arch of Constantine, models of ancient columns, temples, and amphitheatres, *bas reliefs* and bronzes, Apollo and the Muses, the busts of the Caesars, the models of York Minster made by his own hand." Charles Bulfinch to Bigelow (Nov. 20, 1828), in the Bigelow Papers, MHIS. Ellis, 88. Charles Bulfinch to Bigelow (Nov. 20, 1828), Bigelow Family Papers, MHIS. Dearborn, "Report: The Annual Meeting of the Horticultural Society, October 1, 1831, The Committee on Laying Out the Grounds and Forming the Plan of the Experimental Garden and Cemetery at Mount Auburn," *Transactions* 1:77.

7. Bigelow to Dearborn in Congress, Washington, D.C. (January 13, 1833), BPL.

8. Edward Everett, "The Zodiac of Denderah," *North American Review* 17:41 (1823): 233–42. Everett, "Hieroglyphics," *North American Review* 32:70 (Jan. 1831): 95–126. John T. Irwin, *American Hieroglyphics: The Symbol of the Egyptian Hieroglyphics in the American Renaissance* (Baltimore: Johns Hopkins Univ. Press, 1980), 8. Everett's 1831 piece reviewed J. G. H. Greppo, *Essay on the Hieroglyphic System of*

M. Champollion, Jr., on the Advantages which It Offers to Sacred Criticism, trans. by Isaac Stuart (Boston: Perkins & Marvin, 1830). Also see Henry Wheaton, "Egyptian Antiquities," *North American Review* 30:65 (Oct. 1829): 361–88, on books concerning Champollion from England, France, and Denmark.

9. See Richard G. Carrott, *The Egyptian Revival: Its Sources, Monuments, and Meaning, 1808–1858* (Berkeley: Univ. of California Press, 1978), 87–88. An even more encyclopedia study was *Déscription de l'Egypte; ou, Recueil des observations et des recherches qui ont été faites en Egypte pendant l'expédition de l'armée française, publié par les ordres de Sa Majesté, l'empereur Napoléon le Grand,* from Denon's Commission on Egyptian Monuments, issued in twenty-one volumes between 1809 and 1823. Harvard received copies in 1822, the gift of W. H. Eliot. William Dunlap called the Athenaeum the "only respectable library of the Fine Arts" in the nation in his *History of the Rise and Progress of the Arts of Design in the United States* (New York: Scott, 1834), II:409. Jolimont, 5–6.

10. Alexander Jackson Davis, quoted in Carrott, 53. Bigelow, *Elements of Technology,* 131.

11. [Dix,] 18.

12. John Frazee, "The Statue and Monument to Washington," *North American Review* 5 (Mar. 1835): 350–52. Cleveland, 379.

13. Henry A. S. Dearborn, *An Address Delivered before the Massachusetts Society for Promoting Agriculture in Brighton, Oct. 14, 1835* (Boston: George C. Barrett, 1835), 7. Dearborn, "General Dearborn's Address: Delivered before the Massachusetts Horticultural Society on the Celebration of their First Anniversary, Sept. 19, 1829," *New England Farmer* 8:26 (Jan. 15, 1830): 203.

14. Peabody, "Mount Auburn Cemetery," 397–406.

15. Walter, 17–20. The intellectual defense of the style might have drawn on "sacred" historians like the seventeenth-century Jesuit Athanasius Kircher and Bishop Jacques-Bénigne Bossuet, who praised Egyptian civilization as origin of orderly government, law, and philosophy. Peter Gay, *The Enlightenment,* 77–78.

16. Ibid.

17. Ibid.

18. [Wines,] 44.

19. S. Geary built an Egyptian entrance of stone at London's Highgate Cemetery in 1838. Through the 1840s, Egyptian gates appeared at Rochester's Forest Hills and Philadelphia's Odd Fellows Cemetery; others were proposed but rejected for Philadelphia's Laurel Hill and Baltimore's Green Mount. The architect Henry Austin designed an Egyptian Revival gateway for New Haven's Grove Street Cemetery in 1845. Solomon Willard sometimes receives credit for design of the Old Granary gates.

20. "Trustees' Minutes," in "Proprietors' and Trustees Records," I (July 14, 1842), 82–83; (Sept. 29, 1843), 99–100; (Apr. 13, 1844); (May 21, 1844), 114. The board failed to take Cleveland's advice that a permanent gate take the form of a Gothic "wall pierced by three pointed arches, the middle one very lofty and broad for the admission of carriages." After all, as Cleveland acknowledged, the Gothic was more expensive than the Egyptian. The suggestion of such an entry, "surmounted by a battlement of open-work, or machicolated . . . supported by buttresses or by octagon towers terminating in light pinnacles," may have inspired Upjohn's designs for gates at Green-Wood Cemetery in Brooklyn. Cleveland, 381.

21. "Trustees' Minutes," I (June 1, 1852), 231.

22. *Picturesque,* 35. "Trustees' Minutes," I (July 14, 1842), 83; (Sept. 29, 1843), 93–101; (May 21, 1844), 114.

23. "Trustees' Minutes," I (July 14, 1842), 83.

24. Isaac Smith Homans, *Sketches of Boston, Past and Present and of Some Few Places in its Vicinity* (Boston: Phillips, Sampson, & Co., 1851), 106.

25. J. S. Buckingham, *America,* III:392.

26. Cleveland, 380. Andrew Jackson Downing, quoted in Andrews, 108. George Templeton Strong, *Diary,* ed. by Allan Nevins and Milton Halsey Thomas (New York: Macmillan, 1952), I:229. Hammatt Billings, "Mount Auburn," in Moore and Coolidge, 52.

27. Lovejoy, "The First Gothic Revolution and the Return to Nature," in *Essays,* 136, 142, 150–55.

28. Batty Langley, *Ancient Architecture Restored and Improved by a Great Variety of Usefull Designs, Entirely New, in the Gothic Mode for the Ornamenting of Buildings and Gardens* (London, 1742). Augustus Welby Pugin and Augustus Charles Pugin, *Examples of Gothic Architecture* and *The True Principles of Pointed or Christian Architecture* (London: Bohn, 1853).

29. S. Williams, "Notes on Bigelow's Rumford Lectures," manuscript, 13th lecture, HVA. Bigelow, *Elements of Technology,* I:293–94.

30. "Architecture in the United States," *The American Journal of Sciences and Arts* 18:2 (July 1830): 220–29. Andrews, 120. See John Britton's various works on the architectural antiquities of Great Britain (1807–26) and the history and antiquities of cathedrals (1814–35). Bigelow had read Britton.

31. Nathaniel Hawthorne, *English Note-Books,* quoted in Neil Harris, 148.

32. Appropriately, America's greatest Gothic architect, Richard Upjohn, was in training in Boston from 1834 to 1835, working for Alexander Parris. Alexander Jackson Davis had recently designed a Gothic hall for New York University.

33. American Ecclesiologists favored architects like John Notman and Richard Upjohn, noted for work on cemeteries (particularly Philadelphia's Laurel Hill, New York's Green-Wood, and Richmond's Holly-Wood).

34. Cleveland, 356–84.

35. Walter, 36.

36. "Trustees' Minutes," I (Sept. 29, 1843), 99–100 and 102.

37. Many of the chapel competition drawings are now at the Society for the Preservation of New England Antiquities, Boston. Bigelow, Charles P. Curtis, and James Read formed the Building Committee, with power to sign contracts for the chapel; Martin Brimmer and Joseph Story joined Bigelow as a committee to solicit subscription funds. See Tucci, 18.

38. "Trustees' Minutes," I (Nov. 15, 1845), 130.

39. Homans, 108.

40. Hay initially recommended use of his own work, "scrolls for the walls with illuminated mottos . . . in oil painting and gilding upon a cloth or paper medium . . . easily permanently fixed to the wall . . . by any common painter." D. R. Hay to Bigelow (Feb. 28, 1845), manuscript in the files of the Corporation, Cambridge. "Trustees' Minutes," I (June 13, 1845), 127. Bigelow to Ballantine and Allen (Apr. 21, 1845, and June 14, 1845), manuscript drafts in the files of the Corporation. Flagg, 16. Walter, Ballantine and Allen charged £150 for the nave and £20 each for four aisle windows.

41. [Parker,] 21.

42. "Trustees' Minutes," I (Apr. 18, 1848), 170.

43. "Trustees' Minutes," II (Sept. 4, 1854), 4.

44. Walter, 37. Lyell, I:171. "Trustees' Minutes," II (Sept. 4, 1854), 1–4. At the beginning of 1850, Mount Auburn was worth $121,529; the figure had soared to $190,040 four years later.

45. Subscribers for the Story statue included Bigelow, Samuel A. Eliot, Nathan and William Appleton, William Sturgis, C. G. and F. C. Loring, Ignatius Sargent, Charles P. Curtis, Richard Fletcher, N. J. Bowditch, J. C. Gray, C. T. Bigelow, William Gray, and J. A. Lowell. "Trustees' Minutes," I (Jan. 16, 1846).

46. Ibid., II (June 1, 1855), 37; II (Sept. 4, 1854), 7.

47. [Mount Auburn Cemetery,] *Annual Report of the Trustees of the Cemetery of Mount Auburn* (Boston: By the Corporation, 1853). *Annual Report of the Trustees of the Cemetery of Mount Auburn . . . January 1843* (Boston, 1843) (hereafter referred to as *Annual Report*). "Trustees' Minutes," I (Jan. 3, 1854), 253; II (Apr. 21, 1856), 85; II (Sept. 4, 1854), 5. Ellis, 74.

48. "Trustees' Minutes," II (Sept. 4, 1854), 4–7; I (Oct. 2, 1854), 282; II (Apr. 14, 1856), 78; II (Apr. 21, 1856), 81–84, 87–88.

49. Ibid., I (Aug. 7, 1854), 276.

50. Bigelow to John Gorham Palfrey (Oct. 20, 1854), HLH. Ellis, 74.

51. "Trustees' Minutes," II (Apr. 14, 1856), 78; II (Apr. 21, 1856), 81–84, 87.

52. [W. F.] B[rown,] "Crawford's Statue of James Otis," *Boston Daily Courier* (June 17, 1856).

53. [J. M.] W[ightman,] "For the *Atlas:* Mount Auburn Cemetery, letter to the Editor," *Atlas* (June 20, 1856), also reprinted in the *Evening Transcript.*

54. H., "Mount Auburn," *Christian Examiner* (June 21, 1856).

55. H., A Proprietor, "Mount Auburn Cemetery," *Boston Daily Courier* (June 22, 1856).

56. "A Proprietor since 1831," "Letter to the Editor: Mount Auburn Cemetery," *Boston Daily Courier* (June 24, 1856).

57. W[ightman,] "To the Editor: Mount Auburn Cemetery," *Atlas* (June 30, 1856).

58. "Trustees' Minutes," II (Apr. 21, 1856), 86–87.

59. "Trustees' Minutes," II (Aug. 4, 1856), 97.

60. Millard F. Rogers, Jr., *Randolph Rogers: American Sculptor in Rome* (Amherst: Univ. of Massachusetts Press, 1971), 25–32.

61. Ibid., 25–32. Because of additional work, Rogers received $8,000 instead of the original $5,000. Thomas Crawford wrote to his wife that the commission "pays very well."

62. "Hiram Powers the Sculptor—Inauguration of Powers' Statue of Webster," *Mount Auburn Memorial* 1:15 (Sept. 21, 1859): 117. A Bostonian, "To the Editors" (Sept. 16, 1859), *Mount Auburn Memorial* 1:15 (Sept. 21, 1859): 116.

63. Justitia, "John Hancock," *Mount Auburn Memorial* 1:17 (Oct. 6, 1859): 134.

64. "Hiram Powers."

65. [Adolph Strauch,] "Monuments" (from *The Report of Spring Grove Cemetery for 1857*), *Mount Auburn Memorial* 1:28 (Dec. 21, 1859): 218.

66. "Records," (June 23, 1832), 9. [Henry A. S. Dearborn,] "Garden and Cemetery Committee Report" (1831) and "Report: The Annual Meeting of the Horticultural Society, Oct. 1, 1831," in *Transactions,* 46 and 77.

67. Bigelow, *History,* 16. Funerary associations of towers dated from the Middle Ages, when many were used as "limbos," places for entombment of unbaptized infants, who were not permitted burial by the Church in hallowed ground. Ragon, 77. An even more ancient funerary analogy may be between the tower and the tree. Lore holds that King Alfred was buried in a hollow oak trunk. Dedication of many towers to Alfred, making them cenotaphs, may have drawn inspiration from that story.

68. [H. Dearborn,] "Proceedings . . . 1831," 90. *Proceedings of the Association of Citizens to Erect a Monument in Honour of Gen. George Washington* (Boston: Greenough & Stebbins, 1811). [William Tudor,] "Monument to Washington," 329–34.

69. Alison, 37–38.

70. "Mount Auburn Cemetery," *Cambridge Chronicle* 7:37 (Sept. 11, 1852): 2.

71. Henry Adams, *Mont-Saint-Michel and Chartres* (New York: American Institute of Architects, 1913), chap. 1.

72. "A Stranger's View of Mount Auburn," *Mount Auburn Memorial* 1:46 (Apr. 25, 1860), 362.

73. Only about thirty bodies of Civil War dead were shipped home for burial at Mount Auburn by private initiative. *Annual Report* (1872).

74. *Evening Transcript* (Oct. 23, 1872).

75. Ragon, 111.

76. Bigelow, *An Account of the Sphinx of Mount Auburn* (Boston: By the Corporation, 1872). Bigelow's sphinx is also similar to that illustrated in Johann Bernhard Fischer von Erlach, *Entwurff einer Historischen Architectur* (Vienna, 1721) or in Van Laar.

77. A view of the sphinx in the English garden of the Prince Beneventi at Valence appeared in Jean Charles Krafft, *Plan des plus beaux jardins pittoresques,* Vol. I, plate 10. Burke, 64.

78. Bigelow, *Account.*

79. Ellis, 71–73.

80. "Trustees' Records," V (July 10, 1872), 162.

81. Ibid., V (Dec. 15, 1872), 193.

82. Andrews, 112. Bigelow to Otis Norcross (Apr. 17, 1871), HLH.

83. "Trustees' Records," V (Feb. 23, 1871), 65; (Mar. 13, 1872), 143.

84. Mrs. E. A. Dwight, Brookline, to Bigelow (Dec. 19, 1872), box 4, Bigelow Papers, MHIS. Ellis, 99.

CHAPTER 11

1. G[eorge] T[icknor] Curtis, "Mount Auburn," *New England Magazine* 7 (Oct. 1834), 316. Mary Tyler Peabody to Miss Rawlins Pickman, Salem (Oct. 8, 1835), Horace Mann II Papers, MHIS.

2. Lawrence, *Extracts,* 129, 175–76. The story about Franklin Pierce is repeated in John Francis Marion, *Famous and Curious Cemeteries* (New York: Crown, 1977), 57.

3. Cleveland Amory, *The Proper Bostonians* (New York: E. P. Putnam, 1947), 253 and 257. James Russell Lowell to Mrs. [. . .] (Apr. 19, 1876), in Norton, I:19.

4. Joseph Story, "Consecration Address," in *Picturesque,* 74. Flagg, "The Moral Influence of Graves," in Flagg, 36–38. John Greenleaf Adams, *Christian Victor; or, Morality and Immorality, Including Happy Death Scenes* (Boston: A. Tomplins, 1851). Putnam, 14. Also, see Rev. John A. Clark, ed., *Christian Keepsake and Missionary Annual* (Philadelphia: William Marshall, 1839). John Pierpont, "The Garden of Graves," in S. G. Goodrich, ed., *The Token: A Christmas and New Year's Present* (Boston: S. G. Goodrich, 1832), 374–87.

5. J. T. Buckingham, 3, originally from the *Boston Courier* (Sept. 28, 1838).

6. Walter, 5–7, 67, 95, and 113.

7. Ibid., 39.

8. Ibid., 5–7, 394–95. See also J. T. Buckingham.

9. Lydia Maria Child, *Advice to Mothers* (Boston: Carter & Hendee, 1831), 81.

10. Henry Tuckerman, "The Law of Burial and the Sentiment of Death," *Christian Examiner* 26 (1836), 338. Also see J. Brayer, "The Burial of the Dead," *Christian Examiner* 31 (1842): 137–64, 281–307.

11. Zillah, "Mount Auburn," *Lowell Offering* 1:1 (1840): 13–14. Also see E. E. T., "Burial and Burial Places," *Lowell Offering* ser. 2, vol. 1 (1840): 154–57.

12. "Consecration Dell," *Ladies' Repository,* reprinted in *Mount Auburn Memorial* 1:27 (Dec. 14, 1859): 213. Also see Mary S. B. Dana, "Mount Auburn," in *The Parted Family and Other Poems* (New York: Dayton & Saxton, 1842), 214–16. Caroline H. Gilman, "Sweet Auburn: Now Mount Auburn Cemetery," in *Verses of a Life Time,* (Boston: James Munroe, 1849), 154–56. Sarah Payson Willis, "Incident at Mount Auburn," in *Fern Leaves from Fanny's Port Folio* (Auburn, N.Y.: Derby & Miller, 1853), 260–62. Mrs. F. E. Browne, "Mount Auburn," in *Ruth: A Sacred Drama* (New York, Wynkoop & Hallenbeck, 1871), 34–35. For a longer discussion and extensive excerpts of sentimental verse about Mount Auburn, see Michael McEachern McDowell, *American Attitudes toward Death, 1825–1865,* diss., (Ann Arbor: Univ. Microfilms, 1978), 363–408.

13. Mrs. S[arah] J[osepha] Hale, "Mount Auburn Cemetery," *Godey's Magazine* (1844).

14. Orne, iii–v, 33 and 43. Douglas, 253.

15. Channing quoted in William Charvat, *The Origins of American Critical Thought, 1810–35* (Philadelphia: Univ. of Pennsylvania Press), 78–79.

16. Nathaniel Hawthorne, "The Lily's Quest," in *Picturesque,* 235–38.

17. Sylvester Judd, *Margaret: A Tale of the Real and the Ideal: Blight and Bloom; Including Sketches of a Place Not Before Described, Called Mons Christi* (Boston: Jordan & Wiley, 1845). See William B. O. Peabody, "Margaret," *North American Review* 62:130 (Jan. 1846), 102–40.

18. Poe, 397, 401–04.

19. Ibid.

20. Nehemiah Adams, "Mount Auburn," *American Quarterly Observer* 3 (July 1834): 156–61.

21. *Picturesque,* 208.

22. Nathaniel S. Dearborn, *Dearborn's Guide through Mount Auburn Cemetery* (Boston: N. Dearborn, 6th

rev. ed., 1852), 15–16. Mrs. F. E. Browne, 34–35. One English visitor attempted to intensify the experience of melancholy on his visit to Mount Auburn by reading "Thanatopsis" and other poems by William Cullen Bryant. See "An Englishman's Opinion of Mount Auburn," (1845) *Mount Auburn Memorial* 2:3 (July 18, 1860): 19.

23. [Levi Merriam Stevens,] *Guide through Mount Auburn: A Handbook for Passengers over the Cambridge Railroad* (Boston: Bricher & Russell, 1860), 26 and 29.

24. Flagg, 34–37 and 9.

25. Ibid., 11.

26. Ibid., 37–38. Bernardin de Saint-Pierre, quoted in ibid., 28–32.

27. "Introductory," *Mount Auburn Memorial* 1:1 (June 15, 1859): 6. Letters to the Editor, ibid., 1:4 (July 6, 1859): 29. "Notices to the Press," ibid., 1:21 (Nov. 2, 1859): 66. "Our Sheet," ibid., 1:24 (Nov. 23, 1859): 188.

28. "Our Sheet," 188.

29. A content analysis of poetry in the mass-circulation *Godey's Ladies' Book,* which reached an estimated readership of 150,000, reveals that in the period from 1830 through 1834, about one-third of fiction and poetry concerned themes of death, dying, and the hereafter. From 1850 to 1854, the proportion rose to 81 percent; but between 1875 and 1879, it fell to 30 percent. See Richard Meckel, "Consolation in American Periodical Literature, 1830–1880," unpublished paper delivered at the conference "A Time to Mourn" at the State University of New York at Stony Brook, Oct. 25, 1980.

30. Mrs. C. H. Putnam, 309–12.

31. Hammatt Billings, "Sketches at Mount Auburn," in Moore and Coolidge, eds., 51. "Cemetery of Mount Auburn," *American Cyclopoedia of Useful Knowledge* (1835), 9, clippings in the files of the Corporation. Andrew Jackson Downing, quoted in Huth, 69.

32. Edward S. Abby, quoted in Huth, 67. Gilman and Gilman, 158. Anne Henry Ehrenpreis, ed., *Happy Country This America: The Travel Diary of Henry Arthur Bright* (Columbus: Ohio State Univ. Press, 1978), 118. "Mount Auburn," from the *Cambridge Chronicle,* reprinted in the *Mount Auburn Memorial* 1:45 (Apr. 18, 1860): 357.

33. *Picturesque,* 14. D. Ramon de la Sagra, *Cinco Meses en los Estados-Unidos de la America del Norte desde el 20 de Abril al 23 de Setiembre de 1835* (Paris: Pablo Renouard, 1836), 333.

34. "The Diary of Arozina Perkins," in Polly Welts Kaufman, *Women Teachers on the Frontier* (New Haven: Yale Univ. Press, 1984), 69.

35. Lyell, I:14–16, 171–72. Emily Dickinson to Abiah Root, letter 13 (Sept. 1846), *Letters,* ed. by Thomas H. Johnson and Theodora Ward (Cambridge: Harvard Univ. Press), I:36. Lady Emmeline Wortley, *Travels in the United States . . . during 1849–50* (New York: Harper Brothers, 1851), 47–48. Also see Mrs. C. H. Putnam.

36. [Andrew Jackson Downing,] *Horticulturist* 4:1 (July 1849): 9–10.

37. [Marie T. Courcelles,] "Silent Cities," *Cincinnati Daily Enquirer* (Feb. 25, 1877).

38. *Boston Transcript* (1840), clipping in the files of the Corporation.

39. Carl David Arfwedson, *The United States and Canada in 1832* (1834; New York: Johnson Reprint, 1961), I:211–3.

40. [Wines,] 45–46.

41. I have not been able to locate the complete citation for the 1859 German illustrated guide to the United States, the source of the engraving by Verlager which I purchased separately from a dealer in antiquarian paper at a trade show of the Ephemera Society of America, a valuable source for historic visuals.

42. Isabella Lucy Bird, *The Englishwoman in America* (1856; Madison: Univ. of Wisconsin Press, 1966), 396–97. [Dix,] 17–19.

43. Combe, I:135. Also see C. A. Goodrich, *The Family Tourist: A Visit to the Principal Cities of the Western Continent* (Hartford: Case, Tiffany, 1848), 60–61.

44. Martineau, II:227–33.

45. Ibid., 231–33.

46. Ibid.

47. "Trustees' Records," I (July 14, 1842), 85; II (Apr. 7, 1856), 74.

48. Ibid., III (May 4, 1859), 57; (July 11, 1859), 69.

49. Ibid., III (July 11, 1859), 68–69.

50. Ibid., III (Aug. 5, 1861), 212.

51. Bird, 396. "Trustees' Records," II (July 5, 1853), 250; III (June 6, 1859), 63; (July 11, 1859), 64.

52. Founders of the Cambridge Horse Railroad were Gardner G. Hubbard, Isaac Livermore, and Charles C. Little. Little became a cemetery trustee in 1852; Livermore, in 1866.

53. "Trustees' Records," I (Dec. 26, 1846), 149; (May 3, 1853), 247; II (July 7, 1856), 96; V (Sept. 13, 1871), 97.

54. Ibid., I (July 14, 1842), 84–86.

55. Ibid., II (June 18, 1855), 44; (Sept. 4, 1855), 46.

56. Ibid., II (Aug. 3, 1857), 209–10; (Apr. 5, 1858), 244; III (Nov. 4, 1861), 247; "Records of Committees" (1832), 8; "Trustees' Records," IV (June 20, 1866), 77.

57. A Trustee to the Editor, "Mount Auburn Cemetery," *Evening Transcript* (Nov. 4, 1856).

58. "Introductory," *Mount Auburn Memorial* 1:1 (June 15, 1859): 6. Billings, 52.

59. "Trustees' Records," IV (Apr. 12, 1870), 323.
60. "Skating," *Mount Auburn Memorial* 1:25 (Nov. 30, 1859), 197.
61. "Trustees' Records," III (Mar. 4, 1861), 171–75; (Aug. 5, 1861), 212.

EPILOGUE

1. Edward Waldo Emerson, *The Early Years of the Saturday Club, 1855–70* (Freeport, N.Y.: Books for Libraries Press, 1918), 3.
2. Van Wyck Brooks, *New England: Indian Summer* (New York: E. P. Dutton, 1965), 144.
3. Moorfield Storey, quoted in Stow Persons, *The Decline of American Gentility* (New York: Columbia Univ. Press, 1973), 175.
4. Ralph Waldo Emerson, 7. Thoreau, 73–77, 47–48.
5. Horace Bushnell, *The Moral Use of Dark Things* (New York: Scribner, 1868), 76.
6. Van Wyck Brooks, *New England,* 15. T. Jackson Lears, *No Place of Grace: Antimodernism and the Transformation of American Culture* (New York: Pantheon, 1981), 234. Also see Martin Green, *The Problem of Boston: Some Readings in Cultural History* (New York: W. W. Norton, 1966).
7. Van Wyck Brooks, *New England,* 19.
8. Van Tassel, 139. Richard Frothingham, *History of the Siege of Boston, and of the Battles of Lexington, Concord, and Bunker Hill* (Boston: Little, Brown, 1849).
9. Van Tassel, 139. Richard Hildreth, *The History of the United States,* 6 vols. (New York: Harper & Brothers, 1849–56).
10. William Dean Howells, *A Traveller from Altruria: Romance* (New York: Harper, 1894; reprint, New York: Sagamore Press, 1957), 138.
11. Ronald Story, 167.
12. "Trustees' Records," IV (Feb. 6, 1869), 219–20; (Apr. 2, 1870), 312.
13. Bridgman, *Epitaphs,* xv–xix. Shurtleff, 211, 216, 239, and 265.
14. Savage, 20–21. *Historical Sketch . . . Dorchester* 52–56.
15. H. Dearborn, "Report," in T. W. Harris, *Discourse* 65.
16. Mildred McClary Tymeson, *Rural Retrospect: A Parallel History of Worcester and Its Rural Cemetery* (Worcester, Mass.: Albert Rice, 1956), 25. "Report of the Trustees for 1838," in Levi Lincoln, *An Address Delivered on the Consecration of the Worcester Rural Cemetery, Sept. 8, 1838* (Boston: Dutton & Wentworth, 1838), 8–16.
17. *Forest Hills Cemetery: Its Establishment, Progress, Scenery, Monuments, etc.* (Boston: Damrell Moore & George Coolidge, 1858), 78–80. John J. Clarke (Oct. 6, 1846), quoted in Shurtleff, 266–67. "Forest Hills Cemetery," *Mount Auburn Memorial* 1:20 (Oct. 26, 1859), 156.
18. "Trustees' Minutes," II (Jan. 5, 1857), 145.
19. Francis S. Drake, *The Town of Roxbury: Its Memorable Persons and Places* (Boston: Municipal Printing Office, 1905), 231.
20. Putnam, *Address,* 14.
21. Charles T. Jackson, *Final Report on the Geology and Mineralogy of the State of New Hampshire* (Concord: By Order of the Legislature, 1844), 122.
22. *Order of Services at the Consecration of Evergreen Cemetery* (Boston: Tuttle & Dennett, 1850), 12–15.
23. Thomas H. O'Connor, *Fitzpatrick's Boston, 1846–66: John Bernard Fitzpatrick, Third Bishop of Boston* (Boston: Northeastern Univ. Press, 1984), 106–08.
24. "Cambridge Cemetery," *Mount Auburn Memorial* 1:20 (Oct. 26, 1859), 156. John Adams Albro, *An Address Delivered at the Consecration of the Cambridge Cemetery* (Cambridge: Metcalf & Co., 1854). Expansion of the cemetery in 1865, 1885, and 1942 onto low land formerly owned but unusable by Mount Auburn provided space purchased by the less affluent.
25. Van Wyck Brooks, *New England,* 138–43. George Santayana, *The Genteel Tradition* (1931), quoted in Green, *The Problem of Boston,* 46. The remains of William James were deposited in the lot in 1910; and Henry James, Jr., in 1916.
26. A. J. Coolidge (Corporation Secretary) to D. L. Winsor (Superintendent) (Sept. 19, 1864), 175, Letter Book, I, MTA.
27. Charles Sumner to Judge (Joseph) Story (May 14, 1838), in Henry James, *William Wetmore Story and His Friends, from Letters, Diaries, and Recollections* (Boston: Houghton Mifflin, 1903), I:85–86.
28. "Manners and Customs of Ancient Egypt. . . . [and] Annual Report of the Trustees of the Cemetery of Mount Auburn," *North American Review* 93:192 (July 1861): 136. Courcelles, "Silent Cities."
29. Flagg, 35.
30. S[amuel] L. Clemens, *The Adventures of Huckleberry Finn* (1884. Facsimile of 1st ed. San Francisco: Chandler, 1962), 139–40.
31. Edward Bellamy, *Looking Backward* (New York: Viking Penguin, 1982), 44.
32. Van Wyck Brooks, *New England,* 426.
33. *Picturesque,* 208.

Bibliography

MAJOR ARCHIVAL SOURCES

American Antiquarian Society, Worcester, Massachusetts.

Boston Public Library Rare Books Room, Boston.

Harvard University Archives, Cambridge.

Harvard University Countway Library of Medicine, Boston.

Harvard University Houghton Library, Cambridge.

Massachusetts Historical Society, Boston.

Massachusetts Horticultural Society, Boston.

Mount Auburn Cemetery, Offices of the Corporation, Cambridge.

New York Public Library, New York.

REFERENCES

Abdy, Edward Strutt. *Journal of the Residence and Tour in the United States of North America from April 1833, to Oct. 1834*. London: John Murray, 1835.

Abrams, Meyer Howard. *Natural Supernaturalism: Tradition and Revolution in Romantic Literature*. New York: Norton, 1971.

An Account of the Proceedings of the Corporation of the City of New York in Regard to the Existence of Cemeteries in the City. New York: New York Evening Post, 1823.

Ackerknecht, Erwin H. "Anticontagionism between 1821 and 1867." *Bulletin of the History of Medicine* 22 (1948): 567.

Adams, Henry. *Mont-Saint-Michel and Chartres*. New York: American Institute of Architects, 1913.

Adams, John Greenleaf. *Christian Victor; or, Morality and Immorality, Including Happy Death Scenes*. Boston: A. Tomplins, 1851.

Adams, John Quincy. "Death of Children." *Mount Auburn Memorial* 1:39 (Mar. 7, 1860): 310.

Adams, Nehemiah. "Mount Auburn." *American Quarterly Observer* 3 (July 1834): 156–61.

Addison, Agnes. "Early American Gothic." In *Romanticism in America: Papers Contributed to a Symposium at the Baltimore Museum of Art* (May 13–15, 1940). Edited by George Boas. Baltimore: Johns Hopkins Univ. Press, 1940.

Addison, Joseph. *Tatler* 123 (Jan. 21, 1710).

Albro, John Adams. *An Address Delivered at the Consecration of the Cambridge Cemetery*. Cambridge: Metcalf & Co., 1854.

d'Alembert, Jean Le Rond. *Preliminary Discourse to the Encyclopedia of Diderot*. Translated by Richard N. Schwab. Indianapolis: Bobbs-Merrill, 1963.

Alison, Archibald. *Essays on the Nature and the Principles of Taste*. 1790. Reprint. Boston: Cummings & Hilliard, 1812.

Allen, B. Sprague. *Tides in English Taste (1619–1800): A Background for the Study of Literature*. Cambridge: Harvard Univ. Press, 1937.

[Allen, Francis D., comp.] *Documents and Facts, Showing the Fatal Effects of Interments in Populous Cities*. New York: F. D. Allen, 1822.

Ames, Oakes I. "Mount Auburn's Sixscore Years." *Publications of the Cambridge Historical Society* 34 (1951–52): 77–95.

Amory, Cleveland. *The Proper Bostonians*. New York: E. P. Putnam, 1947.

Andrews, Wayne. *Architecture, Ambition, and Americans: A Social History of American Architecture*. New York: Free Press, 1964.

Andrieux, C. "Sépultures." *La Décade Philosophique* 18, an VIII (1800). Paris: n.p., 1800.

"Architecture in the United States." *American Journal of Sciences and Arts* 18:2 (July 1830): 220–29.

Arfwedson, Carl David. *The United States and Canada in 1832*. 1834. Reprint. New York: Johnson Reprint, 1961.

Ariès, Philippe. *Essais sur l'histoire de la mort en Occident du Moyen-Age à nos jours*. Paris: Seuil, 1975.

———. *The Hour of our Death*. Translated by Helen Weaver. New York: Knopf, 1981. (Originally *L'Homme devant la mort*. Paris, 1978.)

———. *Images de l'homme devant la mort*. Paris: Seuil, 1983.

———. "The Reversal of Death: Changes in Attitudes toward Death in Western Societies." *American Quarterly* 26:5 (Dec. 1974): 536–60.

———. *Western Attitudes toward Death from the Middle Ages to the Present*. Translated by Patricia M. Ranum. Baltimore: Johns Hopkins Univ. Press, 1974.

Arnaud, C.-P. *Recueil de tombeaux des quatres cimetières de Paris*. 2 vols. Paris: Arnaud & Germain Mathiot, 1824.

Auzelle, Robert. *Dernières demeures: conception, composition, réalisation du cimetière contemporain*. Paris: n.p., 1965.

[Avril.] *Rapport de l'Administration des travaux publics, sur les cimetières lu au Conseil-Général par le citoyen Avril*. Paris: n.p., n.d. (1793?).

Bacon's Dictionary of Boston. Boston: Houghton Mifflin, 1886.

Baedaeker, Karl. *Paris et ses environs suivis d'excursions diverses: manuel du voyageur*. 3rd ed. Leipzig: Karl Baedaeker, 1872.

Balard, M. *Les Mystères des pompes funèbres de la ville de Paris*. Paris: Emile Allard, 1856.

Ballou, Rev. Hosea. "Address on the Re-Burial of Rev. John Murray" (June 8, 1837). In *The Life of Rev. Hosea Ballou: With Accounts of His Writings*. Edited by Thomas Whittemore. 3 vols. Boston: James M. Usher, 1855.

Ballou, Maturin M. *Biography of Rev. Hosea Ballou.* Boston: Abel Thompkins, 1852.

Baltzell, E. Digby. *Puritan Boston and Quaker Philadelphia: Two Protestant Ethics and the Spirit of Class Authority and Leadership.* New York: Macmillan, 1979.

Bancroft, George. "The Last Moments of Eminent Men." (Jan. 1834.) In *Essays from the North American Review.* Edited by Rice, Allen, and Thorndike. New York: D. Appleton, 1879.

Basil-Hall, Le Capitaine. *Voyage dans les Etats-Unis de l'Amérique du Nord.* Paris: Arthus Bertrand, 1834.

Bate, Walter Jackson. *From Classic to Romantic: Premises of Taste in Eighteenth-Century England.* Cambridge: Harvard Univ. Press, 1946.

[Baudin.] Ministre de l'Intérieur. *Sépultures publiques et particulières.* Paris: Adrien Maréchal, an IX (1801).

Beaumont, Gustave de. *Lettres d'Amérique, 1831–2.* Edited by André Jardin and George W. Pierson. Paris: Presses Univérsitaires de France, 1973.

Belknap, Jeremy. *American Biography: or, An Historical Account of Those Persons who Have Been Distinguished in America, as Adventurers, Statesmen, Philosophers, Divines, Warriors, Authors, and Other Remarkable Characters, Comprehending a Recital of the Events Connected with their Lives and Actions.* Boston: Isaiah Thomas & Ebenezer T. Andrews, 1794–98.

Bellamy, Edward. *Looking Backward.* New York: Viking Penguin, 1982.

Bender, Thomas. "The Rural Cemetery Movement: Urban Travail and the Appeal of Nature." *New England Quarterly* 47 (June 1974): 196–211.

Benes, Peter. *The Masks of Orthodoxy: Folk Gravestone Carving in Plymouth County, Massachusetts, 1689–1805.* Amherst: Univ. of Massachusetts Press, 1977.

Bennett, Steven J. "Chinese Topographical Thinking." *Boston University Journal* (Jan. 1978): 14–27.

Benson, Albert Emerson. *History of the Massachusetts Horticultural Society.* Norwood, Mass.: Plimpton Press, for the Society, 1929.

Bernard, Leon. *The Emerging City: Paris in the Age of Louis XIV.* Durham, N.C.: Duke Univ. Press, 1970.

Bernardin de Saint-Pierre, Jacques-Henri. *Etudes de la nature.* Vol. 5. Paris: Didot jeune, 1792.

———. "Of the Sentiment of Melancholy" and "On the Pleasure of Tombs." In *Studies from Nature.* Translated by Henry Hunter. Worcester, Mass.: J. Nancrede, 1797.

Betts, Edwin M. *Thomas Jefferson's Garden Book.* Philadelphia: American Philosophical Society, 1944.

[Bickham, George, the Younger.] *The Beauties of Stowe, The Gardens of the Right Honourable Richard Lord Viscount Cobham, Addressed to Mr. Pope.* London: L. Gilliver, 1732. Reprinted London: George Bickham, 1750, 1753, and 1756. (The work has also been attributed to Gilbert West.)

Bigelow, Jacob. *An Account of the Sphinx of Mount Auburn.* Boston: By the Corporation, 1872.

———. *Elements of Technology, Taken Chiefly from a Course of Lectures Delivered at Cambridge, on the Application of the Sciences to the Useful Arts.* Boston: Hilliard, Gray, Little, & Wilkins, 1829.

———. "Extract from 'Nature in Disease.'" *Mount Auburn Memorial* 1:2 (Aug. 31, 1859): 90.

———. *Florula Bostoniensis.* Boston: Cummings & Hilliard, 1814.

———. *A History of the Cemetery of Mount Auburn.* Boston and Cambridge: James Munroe, 1860.

———. *Inaugural Address, Delivered in the Chapel at Cambridge, Dec. 11, 1816.* Boston: Wells & Lilly, 1817. Reprinted in *North American Review* 4 (Jan. 1817): 271–83.

———. "On the Burial of the Dead, and Mount Auburn Cemetery." In *Nature in Disease, Illustrated in Various Discourses and Essays to which are Added Miscellaneous Writings, Chiefly on Medical Subjects.* Boston: Ticknor & Fields, 1854. Also in *Modern Inquiries: Classical, Professional, and Miscellaneous.* Boston: Little, Brown, 1867.

———. "On the Limits of Education." In *Modern Inquiries.*

———. *The Useful Arts Considered in Connexion with the Application of Science.* Boston: Marsh, Capen, Lyon, & Webb, 1840.

Billings, Hammatt, "Sketches at Mount Auburn," in Damrell V. Moore and George Coolidge, eds., *The Boston Almanac for the Year 1857,* no. 22 (Boston: John P. Jewett, 1857): 51–2.

Bird, Isabella Lucy. *The Englishwoman in America.* London: John Murray, 1856. Reprint. Madison: Univ. of Wisconsin Press, 1966.

Blair, Robert. *The Grave: A Poem.* 1808. London: Methuen, 1903.

Blake, John Ballard. *Public Health in the Town of Boston, 1630–1822.* Cambridge: Harvard Univ. Press, 1952.

Bledstein, Burton J. *The Culture of Professionalism: The Middle Class and the Development of Higher Education in America.* New York: Norton, 1976.

Boas, George, ed. *Romanticism in America.* Baltimore: Johns Hopkins Univ. Press, 1940.

Bolton, Robert. *Mr. Bolton's Last and Learned Worke of the Foure Last Things, Death, Iudgement, Hell, and Heaven.* London: George Miller, 1633.

Boorstin, Daniel J. *The Image; or, What Happened to the American Dream.* New York: Athenaeum, 1962.

Borromeo, Carlo (Saint). *Arte Sacra: De Fabrica Ecclesiae.* Milan, 1952.

———. *Instructiones Fabricae et Suppelectilis Ecclesiasticae.* Milan, 1577.

Boulton, James T., ed. *Edmund Burke's Philosophical Enquiry into the Origin of Our Ideas of the Sublime and the Beautiful.* South Bend: Univ. of Notre Dame Press, 1968.

Bourde de la Rogerie, Henri. *Le Parlement de Bretagne,*

l'évêque de Rennes et les ifs dans les cimetières, 1636–7. Rennes, 1931.

Bowen, Abel. "Burial in Cities." *Boston News-Letter and City Record* (March 4, 1826): 126–29.

Boyse, Samuel. "The Triumphs of Nature: A Poem." *Gentleman's Magazine* 12 (Aug. 1742).

Braudel, Fernand. *Capitalism and Material Life, 1400–1800.* Translated by Miriam Kochan. New York: Harper & Row, 1973.

______. *The Mediterranean and the Mediterranean World in the Age of Philip II.* Translated by Sian Reynolds. 2 vols. New York: Harper & Row, 1973.

Brayer, J. "The Burial of the Dead." *Christian Examiner* 31 (1842): 137–64, 281–307.

Bridgman, Thomas. *Epitaphs from Copp's Hill Burying Ground, Boston, with Notes.* Boston: James Munroe, 1851.

______. *The Pilgrims of Boston and their Descendants, with Introduction by Edward Everett, also Inscriptions from the Monuments in the Granary Burial Ground.* New York: D. Appleton, 1856.

Bright, Timothy. *A Treatise on Melancholie, containing the Causes thereof, and Reasons of the Strange Effects it Worketh in our Minds and Bodies: With the Physicke Cure, and Spiritual Consolation of Such as Have Hereto Adjoined as Afflicted Conscience.* London: Thomas Vautrollier, 1586.

Brooks, Phillips. "The Episcopal Church."In Justin Winsor, ed. *The Memorial History of Boston, Including Suffolk County, Massachusetts, 1630–1880.* Boston: James R. Osgood, 1881.

Brooks, Van Wyck. *The Flowering of New England, 1815–1865.* New York: E. P. Dutton, 1940.

______. *New England: Indian Summer.* New York: E. P. Dutton, 1965.

Brown, Frederick. *Père Lachaise: Elysium and Real Estate.* New York: Viking, 1973.

B[rown, W. F.] "Crawford's Statue of James Otis." *Boston Daily Courier* (June 17, 1856).

Browne, Mrs. Frances Elizabeth. "Mount Auburn." In *Ruth: A Sacred Drama and Original Lyrical Poems.* New York: Wynkoop & Hallenbeck, 1871.

Browne, Sir Thomas. *Hydriotaphia: Urne-Buriall, or A Discourse of the Sepulchrall Urnes Lately Found in Norfolk.* London: Henry Browne, 1658.

Bryant, William Cullen. *Poems.* Philadelphia: A. Hart, 1851. (See especially "Thanatopsis" [1817] and "A Forest Hymn" [1829].)

______. "Thanatopsis." *North American Review* 11 (Sept. 1817).

Bucke, Charles. *On the Beauties, Harmonies, and Sublimities of Nature: With Occasional Remarks on the Laws, Customs, Manners, and Opinions of Various Nations.* Vol. 1. London: G. & W. B. Whittaker, 1823.

Buckingham, James Silk. *America: Historical, Statistic, and Descriptive.* Vol. 3. London: Fisher, Son, & Co., n.d. (ca. 1840).

______. *The Slave States of America,* Vol. 1. London: Fisher, Son, & Co., 1842. Reprint. New York: Negro Univ. Presses, 1968.

Buckingham, Joseph T. "Mount Auburn." *Mount Auburn Memorial* 2:1 (July 4, 1860). Originally in *Boston Courier* (Sept. 28, 1838).

Bugbee, James M. "Boston Under the Mayors, 1822–1880." In Justin Winsor, ed. *The Memorial History of Boston, Including Suffolk County, Massachusetts, 1630–1880.* Boston: James R. Osgood, 1881.

Bunhill Fields Burial Ground: Proceedings in Reference to its Preservation with Inscriptions on the Tombs. London: Hamilton, Adams, 1867.

Bunting, Bainbridge, and Robert H. Nylander. *Survey of Architectural History in Cambridge: Report Four: Old Cambridge.* Cambridge: Cambridge Historical Commission & MIT Press, 1969.

Bunyan, John. *Pilgrim's Progress.* Edited by J. B. Wharey. 1678. Reprint. Oxford: Oxford Univ. Press, 1928.

Burchard, John, and Albert Bush-Brown. *The Architecture of America: A Social and Cultural History.* Boston: Little, Brown, & Co., 1961.

Burford, Robert. *Description of a View of the Cemetery of Père la Chaise, Including a Distant View of Paris and the Surrounding Country: Now Exhibiting at the Panorama, Leicester Square. Painted by the Proprietor Robert Burford from Drawings taken by Him in the Summer of 1834.* London: G. Nichols, 1834.

"Burial." *North American Review* 93:192 (July 1861): 109–36.

"Burials in Cities." *Boston News-Letter and City Record* (Mar. 4, 1826): 126.

Burke, Edmund. *A Philosophical Inquiry into the Origin of our Ideas of the Sublime and the Beautiful.* 1756. Reprint. Philadelphia: D. Johnson, 1806. Reprint edited by James T. Boulton. South Bend: Univ. of Notre Dame Press, 1968.

______. *On Taste: On the Sublime and the Beautiful.* New York: P. F. Collier, 1909.

Burton, Robert. *The Anatomy of Melancholy, What It Is, With All the Kindes, Causes, Symptomes, Prognostickes, and Several Cures of It.* Oxford: Iohn Lichfield & Iames Short, 1621.

Bushnell, Horace. *The Moral Use of Dark Things.* New York: Scribner, 1868.

Cady, Edwin H. *Literature of the Early Republic.* New York: Holt, Rinehart & Winston, 1967.

Caillot, Antoine. *Voyage réligieux et sentimental aux quatre cimetières de Paris: ouvrage renfermant un grand nombre d'inscriptions funéraires, suivis de réflexions réligieuses et morales.* Paris: L. Haussmann, 1809.

[Calvin, John.] *The Forme of Prayers and Ministrations of the Sacraments, etc., Used in the English Congregation at Geneva; and Approved by the Famous and Godly Learned Man, Iohn Caluyn.* 1556. Reprinted in *The Liturgical Por-*

tions of the Genevan Service Book. Edinburgh and London, 1931.

———. [Jean Calvin.] *Institutes*. Translated by T. Norton. London: n.p., 1611.

C[ambry,] J[acques.] *Rapport sur les sépultures, presenté à l'Administration Centrale du Départment de la Seine*. Paris: n.p., an VII (1799).

Cappon, Leslie J., ed. *Adams-Jefferson Letters*. Chapel Hill: Univ. of North Carolina Press, 1959.

Carrott, Richard G. *The Egyptian Revival: Its Sources, Monuments, and Meaning, 1808–1858*. Berkeley: Univ. of California Press, 1978.

Carver, Robin. *History of Boston*. Boston: Lilly, Wait, Colman, & Holden, 1832.

Cayeux, J. de. *Hubert Robert et les jardins*. Paris: Herscher, 1987.

Cazamian, Louis. "Modern Times (1600–1914)." In Emile Légouis and Louis Cazamian. *A History of English Literature*. Translated by W. D. MacInnes and Louis Cazamian. New York: Macmillan, 1929.

"The Cemeteries and Catacombs of Paris." *Quarterly Review* 21:42 (Apr. 1819): 350–97.

"Cemeteries and Churchyards." *Eclectic Magazine of Foreign Literature, Science, and Art* (Aug. 1844): 449–71.

"Cemetery at Mount Auburn." *New England Farmer* 10:11 (Sept. 28, 1831): 82. (Published originally in *Boston Courier*.)

"The Cemetery of Père-la-Chaise." *New England Farmer* 11:9 (Sept. 12, 1832): 66–68.

Chamberlain, Mellen. *Josiah Quincy: The Great Mayor*. Boston: By the Society, 1889.

Chambers, Sir William. *A Dissertation on Oriental Gardening*. London: W. Griffin, 1772.

Chandler, Peleg W. *The Charter and Ordinances of the City of Boston together with the Acts of the Legislature relating to the City*. Boston: John H. Eastburn, 1850.

[Channing, William Ellery.] "Remarks on National Literature." *Christian Examiner* 7 (1830): 269.

———. "War: Discourses before the Congregational Ministers of Massachusetts." 1816. "Botany." 1818. "Self-Culture." 1828. In *The Works of William Ellery Channing, D.D*. Vol. 3. Boston and New York: American Unitarian Association, 1848.

Charvat, William. *The Origins of American Critical Thought, 1810–35*. Philadelphia: Univ. of Pennsylvania Press, 1936.

Chase, David B. "The Beginnings of the Landscape Tradition in America." *Historic Preservation* 25 (Jan.–Mar. 1973): 41.

Chaumette, Pierre-Gaspard. *Arrêtés du Conseil-Général de la Commune de Paris rélatif aux différents cultes et aux prêtres*. Paris: n.p., le 17 vendémiaire, an II (Oct. 8, 1793).

Cheever, D. W. "Burial Customs." *North American Review* 93 (July 1861): 108–36.

Child, Lydia Maria. *Advice to Mothers*. Boston: Carter & Hendee, 1831.

Chinard, Gilbert. *Volney et l'Amérique d'après des documents et sa correspondance avec Jefferson*. Baltimore: Johns Hopkins Univ. Press, 1923.

City Lands Committee of the Corporation of London. *History of the Bunhill Fields Burying Ground with Some of the Principal Inscriptions*. London: Charles Skipper & East, 1902.

[City of Boston.] *The Charter of the City of Boston and Ordinances Made and Established by the Mayor, Aldermen, and Common Council, with Such Acts of the Legislature of Massachusetts as Relate to the Government of Said City*. Boston: True & Greene, 1827.

[City of Boston.] "An Ordinance to Regulate Interment of the Dead." And "Health." In *The Charter and Ordinances of the City of Boston*. Edited by Thomas Wetmore and Edward G. Prescott. Boston: J. H. Eastburn, 1834.

Clark, Rev. John A., ed. *Christian Keepsake and Missionary Annual*. Philadelphia: William Marshall, 1839.

Clemens, S[amuel] L., *The Adventures of Huckleberry Finn*. 1884. Facsimile ed. San Francisco: Chandler, 1962.

Cleveland, Henry Russell. "American Architecture." *North American Review* 43:93 (Oct. 1836): 378–79.

Coffin, John Gorham. *An Address Delivered before the Contributors of the Boston Dispensary at the Seventeenth Anniversary, October 21, 1813*. Boston: John Eliot, 1813.

[Coffin, John Gorham.] A Fellow of the Massachusetts Medical Society. *Remarks on the Dangers and Duties of Sepulture; or, Security for the Living, with Respect and Repose for the Dead*. Boston: Phelps & Farnham, 1823.

Coke, Edward Thomas. *A Subaltern's Furlough: Descriptive of Scenes in Various Parts of the United States . . . during the Summer and Autumn of 1832*. 2 vols. New York: J. & J. Harper, 1833.

Combe, George. *Notes on the United States of North America during a Phrenological Visit in 1838–9–40*. Philadelphia: Carey & Hart, 1841.

Comité de Salut Public de la Convention Nationale. *Rapport du Conseil de Santé sur la fouille des terres des ci-devant églises*. Paris: n.p., n.d. (1793?).

Cook, Clarence Chatham. *A Description of the New York Central Park*. New York: Huntington, 1869. Reprint. New York: Benjamin Blom, 1972.

Cook, Zebedee, Jr. *An Address Pronounced before the Massachusetts Horticultural Society in Commemoration of its Second Annual Festival, the 10th of Sept. 1830*. Boston: Isaac R. Baits, 1830.

Cooper, Anthony Ashley, Third Earl of Shaftesbury. *Characteristics of Men, Manners, Opinions, Times*. 2 vols. 2d ed. London, 1714. 5th ed. Birmingham: John Baskerville, 1773.

Cooper, James Fenimore. *The Crater*. Cambridge: Belknap Press of Harvard Univ. Press, 1962.

Cooper, William. *A Sermon Concerning the Laying of*

Deaths of Others to Heart, Occasion'd by the Lamented Death of that Ingenious and Religious Gentleman John Gore, who died Nov. 7, 1720. Boston: B. Green for B. Eliot, 1720.

Corbin, Alain. *The Foul and the Fragrant: Odor and the French Social Imagination.* Cambridge: Harvard Univ. Press, 1986.

Cornish, Vaughan. *The Churchyard Yew and Immortality.* London: F. Muller, 1946.

Coupé, J.-M. *De la moralité des sépultures, et de leur police.* Paris: Chez Calixte Vollant, an IX (1801).

Courcelles, Marie T. "Silent Cities." *Cincinnati Daily Enquirer* (Feb. 25, 1877).

Cowell, F. R. *The Garden as Fine Art.* Boston: Houghton Mifflin, 1978.

Creese, Walter L. *The Crowning of the American Landscape.* Princeton: Princeton Univ. Press, 1985.

Cross, Jeremy. *True Masonic Chart or Hieroglyphic Monitor.* New Haven: J. C. Gray, 1819.

"Cultivation of the Willow." *New England Farmer* 11:29 (Jan. 30, 1833): 229.

Curl, James Stevens. *A Celebration of Death: An Introduction to Some of the Buildings, Monuments, and Settings of Funerary Architecture in the Western European Tradition.* New York: Charles Scribner's Sons, 1980.

———. *The Victorian Celebration of Death.* London: Trowbridge, 1972.

Curtis, G[eorge] T[icknor.] "Mount Auburn." *New England Magazine* 7 (Oct. 1834): 316.

Daiches, David, Peter Jones, and Jean Jones, eds. *A Hotbed of Genius: The Scottish Enlightenment, 1730–1790.* Edinburgh: Edinburgh Univ. Press, 1986.

Daly, Cesar. *Architecture funéraire contemporaine: Specimens de tombeaux, chapelles funéraires, mausolées.* Paris: Ducher, 1871.

Dana, Mary S. B. "Mount Auburn." In *The Parted Family and Other Poems.* New York: Dayton & Saxton, 1842.

Dansel, Michel. *Au Père Lachaise: Son histoire, ses sécrets, ses promenades.* Paris: Librairie Arthème Fayard, 1973.

Darnton, Robert. "The Art of Dying." *New York Review of Books* (May 13, 1982): 8–12.

Daubermesnil, François-Antoine. *Rapport fait au nom d'une Commission Spéciale, sur les inhumations.* Corps Législatif, Conseil des Cinq-Cents. Séance du 21 brumaire, an V (1797). Paris: Imprimerie nationale, 1797.

Davies, Horton. *The Worship of the English Puritans.* Westminster: Dacre Press, 1948.

Davis, David Brion. *Antebellum American Culture.* Lexington, Mass.: D.C. Heath, 1979.

Dearborn, Henry A. S. *Address Delivered before the Massachusetts Horticultural Society on the Celebration of their First Anniversary, Sept. 19, 1829.* 2d ed. Boston: J. T. Buckingham, 1833. Published also in *New England Farmer* 8:26 (Jan. 15, 1830): 203.

———. *An Address Delivered before the Massachusetts Society for Promoting Agriculture in Brighton, Oct. 14, 1835.* Boston: George C. Barrett, 1835.

———. "Bunker Hill." *Boston Patriot* (Apr. 1823).

———. "The Cemetery of Père Lachaise." *New England Farmer* 11 (Sept. 12, 1832): 66–67.

———. "Mount Auburn Cemetery: Report of the Massachusetts Horticultural Society upon the Establishment of an Experimental Garden and Rural Cemetery, Boston, 1831." *North American Review* 33 (1831): 399–405.

———. "Proceedings of the Massachusetts Horticultural Society . . . 1831." *New England Farmer* 9:49 (June 22, 1831): 385.

———. "A Treatise on Grecian Architecture." 1828. 2 vols. Manuscript in the Rare Books Room, Boston Public Library.

Dearborn, Nathaniel S. *Dearborn's Guide through Mount Auburn Cemetery . . . for the Benefit of Strangers Desirous of Seeing the Clusters of Monuments with the Least Trouble.* Boston: N. Dearborn, 1847. New editions published annually, with the 12th in 1858.

DeBeer, E. S., ed. *The Diary of John Evelyn.* London: Oxford Univ. Press, 1959.

Defoe, Daniel. *Tour Thro' the Whole Island of Great Britain, Divided into Circuits or Journies* [sic]. 4th ed. London: J. Osborn, 1742.

Delille, Abbé Jacques, "L'Imagination," song 7 (1794). In *Oeuvres.* Paris: Michaud, 1824.

———. *Les Jardins; ou, l'art d'embellir les paysages: Poème.* Paris: Imprimerie de Philippe-Denys Pierres, ca. 1782. Republished as *The Gardens: A Poem.* Translated by Mrs. Montolieu. 2d ed. London: T. Bensley, 1805.

———. "Preface by the Translator." In René-Louis Marquis de Girardin. *An Essay on Landscape; or, on the Means of Improving and Embellishing the Country Around our Habitations.* Translated by the author. London: J. Dodsley, 1793.

Denon, Dominique-Vivant. *Déscription de l'Egypte; ou, Recueil des observations et des recherches qui ont été faites en Egypte pendant l'expédition de l'armée française, publié par les ordres de Sa Majesté, l'empereur Napoléon le Grand.* 21 vols. Paris: Imprimerie nationale, 1809–23.

———. *Voyage dans la Basse et la Haute Egypte pendant les campagnes du général Bonaparte.* 3 vols. Paris: Didot, 1802. Reprint. New York: I. N. Longman & O. Reese, 1803. Reprint. New York: Arno, 1973.

Denvir, Bernard. *The Eighteenth Century: Art, Design, and Society, 1689–1789.* London: Longman, 1983.

Département de la Seine. *Rapport fait au Conseil-Général sur l'instruction publique, le rétablissement des Bourses, le scandale des inhumations actuelles, l'érection de cimetières, la restitution des tombeaux, mausolées, etc.* Paris: Imprimerie nationale, n.d. (ca. 1800).

"The Desolate City." *Columbia Centinel* (Boston) 4011 (Sept. 18, 1822): 2.

Dethlefsen, Edwin, and James Deetz. "Death's Heads, Cherubs, and Willow Trees: Experimental Archaelogy in Colonial Cemeteries." *American Antiquity* 31:4 (1966): 502–10.

Détournelle, Athanase-C[harles.] *Mémoire sur les funérailles et les sépultures*. Paris: n.p., an IX (1801).

Dexter, Henry Martyn. *The Congregationalism of the Last Three Hundred Years*. New York: Harper & Brothers, 1880.

Dickinson, Emily. *Letters*. Edited by Thomas H. Johnson and Theodora Ward. Cambridge: Belknap Press of Harvard Univ. Press, 1958.

[Dix, John Ross.] A Looker-On. *Local Loiterings, and Visits in the Vicinity of Boston*. Boston: Redding, 1845. Reprinted as "An Englishman's Opinion of Mount Auburn." *Mount Auburn Memorial* 2:3 (July 18, 1860): 19.

Doliver, Pierre. *Essai sur les funérailles*. Versailles: Jacob, an IX (1801).

Donnet, Alexis. *Déscription des environs de Paris*. Paris: Treuttel et Wurtz, 1824.

Douglas, Ann. *The Feminization of American Culture*. New York: Knopf, 1977.

Downing, Andrew Jackson. "Domestic Notices" *Horticulturist* 1:4 (Jan. 1847): 328–30; 3:4 (Oct. 1848): 153–8; 4:3 (Sept. 1849): 139.

———. "Foreign Notices: Père le Chaise [*sic*] Cemetery." *Horticulturist* 1:4 (Oct. 1846): 189.

———. *Rural Essays*. Edited by George William Curtis. New York: G. P. Putnam, 1853.

Drake, Francis S. *The Town of Roxbury: Its Memorable Persons and Places*. Boston: Municipal Printing Office, 1905.

Drake, Samuel Adams. *Old Landmarks and Historic Personages of Boston*. Boston: Little, Brown, 1872.

Draper, John W. *The Funeral Elegy and the Rise of English Romanticism*. New York: New York Univ. Press, 1929.

du Boccage, Madame Marie Anne LePage. *Lettres sur l'Angleterre*. 1770. Translated as *Letters Concerning England, Holland, and Italy*. London: Dilly, 1770.

Duffy, John. *A History of Public Health in New York City, 1625–1866*. New York: Russell Sage Foundation, 1968.

Duncan, Mary G. Lundie. *America as I Found It*. London: James Nisbet, 1852. (Especially "The Cemeteries and Firemen," chap. 17.)

Dunlap, William. *History of the Rise and Progress of the Arts of Design in the United States*. New York: Scott, 1834.

Durdent, René-Jean. *Promenades de Paris; ou, Collection de vues pittoresques de ses jardins publiques, accompagnée d'un texte historique*. Paris: M. Guerin & Schwartz, 1812.

Duval, Amaury-Pineu. *Des Sépultures chez les anciens et les modernes*. Paris: Panckoucke, an IX (1801). (Includes "Des Tombeaux," an essay originally published in *La Décade Philosophique* [1793?].)

Dwight, Theodore. *Summer Tours; or, Notes of a Traveler through Some of the Middle and Northern States*. New York: Harper & Brothers, 1847.

Dwight, Timothy. *Travels in New-England and New York:* New Haven: T. Dwight, 1821.

Early, James. *Romanticism and American Architecture*. New York: A. S. Barnes, 1965.

Ehrenpreis, Anne Henry, ed. *Happy Country This America: The Diary of Henry Arthur Bright*. Columbus: Ohio State Univ. Press, 1978.

Eliade, Mircea. *The Sacred and the Profane: The Nature of Religion*. Translated by William R. Trask. New York: Harcourt, Brace, & World, 1957.

Ellis, George E. *Memoir of Dr. Jacob Bigelow*. Cambridge: John Wilson & Son, 1880.

Emerson, Edward Waldo. *The Early Years of the Saturday Club, 1855–70*. Freeport, N.Y.: Books for Libraries Press, 1918.

Emerson, Edward Waldo, and Waldo Forbes Emerson, eds. *Journals of Ralph Waldo Emerson with Annotations*. Boston: Houghton Mifflin, 1910.

Emerson, Ralph Waldo. *Nature*. 1836. In *Ralph Waldo Emerson: Essays and Lectures*. Edited by Joel Porte. New York: Library of America, 1983.

Englizian, H. Crosby. *Brimstone Corner: Park Street Church, Boston*. Chicago: Moody Press, 1968.

Etlin, Richard A. *The Architecture of Death: The Transformation of the Cemetery in Eighteenth-Century Paris*. Cambridge: MIT Press, 1984.

———. "Landscapes of Eternity: Funerary Architecture and the Cemetery, 1793–1881." *Oppositions* 8 (Spring 1977): 14–31.

Evelyn, John. *Silva; or, A Discourse of Forest-Trees, and the Propagation of Timber in His Majesty's Dominions . . . together with an Historical Account of the Sacredness and Use of Standing Groves, with Notes by A. Hunter, M.D.* 4th ed. 2 vol. York, England: Longman, Hurst, Rees, Orme, & Brown, 1812.

Everett, Alexander H. *An Address Delivered before the Massachusetts Horticultural Society at their 5th Annual Festival, Sept. 18, 1833*. Boston: J. T. Buckingham, 1833.

———. "June 7, 1836 Celebration." In *A Memorial of the American Patriots who Fell at the Battle of Bunker Hill, with an Account of the Dedication of the Memorial Tablets*. Boston: By Order of the City Council, 1889.

Everett, Edward. *An Address Delivered at Charlestown, Aug. 1, 1826, in Commemoration of John Adams and Thomas Jefferson*. Boston: William L. Lewis, 1826.

———. "An Oration Pronounced at Cambridge before the Phi Beta Kappa Society, Aug. 27, 1824." *North American Review* 20:11 (1825): 422–23.

———. "The Zodiac of Denderah." *North American Review* 17:41 (1823): 233–42. Also "Hieroglyphics." *North American Review* 32:70 (Jan. 1831): 95–126.

Falip, Edward. *Guide aux sépultures des personnages célè-*

bres inhumés dans les trois grands cimetières de Paris. Paris: Lagrange, 1878.

Fein, Albert. "The American City: The Ideal and the Real." In *The Rise of American Architecture*. Edited by Edgar Kaufman, Jr. New York: Praeger, 1970.

Fessenden, Thomas G. *The American Gardener; Containing Practical Directions on the Culture of Fruits and Vegetables*. Boston: J. B. Russell, 1828.

Finch, I. [John]. *Travels in the United States of America and Canada Containing Some Account of their Scientific Institutions, and . . . An Essay on the Natural Boundaries of Empires*. London: Longman, Rees, Orme, Brown, Green, & Longman, 1833.

Flagg, Wilson. *Mount Auburn: Its Scenes, Its Beauties, and Its Lessons*. Boston: James Munroe, 1861.

Fleming, Laurence, and Alan Gore. *The English Garden*. London: Michael Joseph, 1979.

Foote, Henry Wilder. *Annals of King's Chapel from the Puritan Age of New England to the Present Day*. Boston: Little, Brown, 1882.

Forbes, Harriette M. "Symbolic Cemetery Gates in New England." *Old Time New England* (Bulletin of the Society for the Preservation of New England Antiquities) 24 (Oct. 1933): 46–58.

Forest Hills Cemetery: Its Establishment, Progress, Scenery, Monuments, etc. Boston: Damrell Moore & George Coolidge, 1858.

"Forest Hills Cemetery." *Mount Auburn Memorial* 1:20 (Oct. 26, 1859): 156.

Fourcroy. *Notice sur la vie et les travaux de Lavoisier, lu le 15 thermidor, an IV au Lycée des Arts*. Paris: n.p., 1796. Includes the long, anonymous poem "Stances sur l'immortalité de l'âme." Printed with Mulot, *Discours*. Paris: n.p., 1796.

Frazee, John. "The Statue and Monument to Washington." *North American Review* 5 (Mar. 1835): 350–52.

French, Stanley. "The Cemetery as Cultural Institution: The Establishment of Mount Auburn and the 'Rural Cemetery' Movement." *American Quarterly* 26 (Mar. 1974): 37–59.

Frothingham, Richard. *History of the Siege of Boston, and of the Battles of Lexington, Concord, and Bunker Hill*. Boston: Little, Brown, 1849.

Galignani's New Paris Guide; or, Stranger's Companion through the French Metropolis. Paris: A. & W. Galignani, 1826.

Gauthier-Lachapelle, A. *Des Sépultures*. Paris: DuPont, an IX (1801).

Gay, Peter. *The Enlightenment: The Rise of Modern Paganism*. New York: W. W. Norton, 1966.

"George W. Brimmer." *Boston Daily Advertiser* (Sept. 1838). Also in *Mount Auburn Memorial* 1:44 (Apr. 11, 1860): 345.

Gessner, Salomon. *Idyllen* (1756). Trans. into French by Michel Huber. *Idylles et poèmes champêtres*. Lyon: J. M. Buryset, 1762.

Gilman, Caroline H. "Sweet Auburn: Now Mount Auburn Cemetery." In *Verses of a Life Time*. Boston: James Munroe, 1849.

Gilman, Caroline, and Rev. S. Gilman. *The Poetry of Traveling in the United States*. New York: S. Colman, 1838.

Gilpin, William. *Dialogue upon the Gardens of the Right Honourable the Lord Viscount Cobham at Stowe in Buckinghamshire*. London: B. Seeley, 1748, 1749, and 1751.

Girard, J[oseph] de. *Des Tombeaux, ou de l'influence des institutions funèbres sur les moeurs*. Paris: n.p., an IX (1801).

Girardin, Louis-Stanislas-Cécile-Xavier, Comte de. *Promenade ou itinéraire des jardins d'Ermenonville*. Paris: Chez Mérigot, 1788.

Girardin, René-Louis, Marquis de. *De la composition des paysages sur le terrain, ou, des moyens d'embellir la nature autour des habitations, en joignant l'agréable à l'utile*. Geneva: Chez F. M. Delaguette, 1777. Translated by the author as *An Essay on Landscape; or, on the Means of Improving and Embellishing the Country Around our Habitations*. London: J. Dodsley, 1793.

Goodman, Paul. "Ethics and Enterprise: The Values of a Boston Elite, 1800–1860." *American Quarterly* 18 (Fall 1966): 437–51.

Goodrich, C. A. *The Family Tourist: A Visit to the Principal Cities of the Western Continent*. Hartford: Case, Tiffany, 1848.

"The Grave of a Mother." *Boston Patriot and Daily Mercantile Advertiser* 1720 (Jan. 9, 1823): 2.

Gray, Francis C. "An Address Before the Society of Phi Beta Kappa on Thurs., the 29th of Aug., 1816." *North American Review* 3 (Sept. 1816): 289.

______. "Ancient Cemetery in Naples: Memoria sullo scovrimento di un antico sepolcreto Greco-Romano di Lorenzo Justiniana. In Napoli, 1812." *North American Review* 5 (1817): 119–27.

Gray, John C. *An Address Delivered before the Massachusetts Horticultural Society at the 6th Anniversary, Sept. 17, 1834*. Boston: J. T. Buckingham, 1834.

Gray, Thomas. *An Elegy Written in a Country Churchyard*. London: R. Dodsley, 1751.

Green, Martin. *The Problem of Boston: Some Readings in Cultural History*. New York: W. W. Norton, 1966.

Greenwood, F[rancis] W[illiam] P. *A History of King's Chapel*. Boston: Carter, Hendee & Allen & Ticknor, 1833.

______. "The Miscellaneous Poems of William Wordsworth." *North American Review* n.s. 9 (Apr. 1824): 356–70.

Gregoire, Abbé Henri. *Second rapport sur le vandalisme*. Paris: n.p., 1794.

Greppo, J. G. H. *Essay on the Hieroglyphic System of M. Champollion, Jr., on the Advantages which It Offers to Sacred Criticism*. Translated by Isaac Stuart. Boston: Perkins & Marvin, 1830.

Gridley, A. D. "Cemeteries." *New Englander* 85 (Oct.

1863): 597–619.

———. "Rural Cemeteries." *Horticulturist* 5 (1855): 278–82.

Guillon, C. *Sur le respect du aux tombeaux; et l'indécence des inhumations actuelles.* Paris: n.p., an VIII (1800). (Includes two long poems: "Sépulture" and "Mélancholie" by Legouvré.)

H. "Mount Auburn." *The Christian Examiner* (June 21, 1856).

Habert, Philippe. *The Temple of Death: A Poem.* Translated by John Sheffield Buckingham. London: Daniel Brown, 1701.

Hadfield, Miles. *A History of British Gardening.* Middlesex, England: Penguin, 1985.

Hale, [Dr. Enoch.] "Contagion." *North American Review* 12 (1821): 174–78.

Hale, Nathan. "Mount Auburn." *Boston Daily Advertiser* (1831).

[Hale, Nathan.] *Selections from the Chronicle of Boston and the Book of Retrospections and Anticipations, Compiled in the Last Month of the Last Year of the Town, and the First Month of the First Year of the City.* Boston: [Nathan Hale], 1822.

Hale, Mrs. S[arah] J[osepha.] "Mount Auburn Cemetery." *Godey's Magazine* (1844).

Hall, David. "The Gravestone Image as a Puritan Cultural Code." In *Puritan Gravestone Art: Annual Proceedings (1976) of the Dublin Seminar for New England Folklife.* Boston: Boston University, 1977.

Hampson, Norman. *The Life and Opinions of Maximilien Robespierre.* London: Penguin, 1974.

Harris, Neil. *The Artist in American Society: The Formative Years, 1790–1860.* New York: Simon & Schuster, 1966.

Harris, Thaddeus William. *A Discourse Delivered before the Massachusetts Horticultural Society in Celebration of its Fourth Anniversary, Oct. 3, 1832.* Cambridge: E. W. Metcalf, 1832.

———. *Epitaphs from the Old Burying Ground in Watertown.* Boston: n.p., 1869.

Hawthorne, Nathaniel. "The Lily's Quest." In *The Picturesque Pocket Companion and Visitor's Guide through Mount Auburn.* Boston: Otis, Broaders, 1839.

Helvétius, Claude-Adrien. *De l'esprit; or, Essays on the Mind and Its Several Faculties.* 1758. Translation. London: J. Dodsley, 1759.

Hertz, Robert. *Death and the Right Hand.* Translated by R. and C. Needham. Glencoe, Ill.: Free Press, 1960.

Hildreth, Richard. *The History of the United States.* 6 vols. New York: Harper & Brothers, 1849–56.

Hipple, Walter John. *The Beautiful, the Sublime, and the Picturesque in Eighteenth-Century British Aesthetic Theory.* Carbondale: Southern Illinois Univ. Press, 1957.

"Hiram Powers the Sculptor—Inauguration of Powers' Statue of Webster." *Mount Auburn Memorial* 1:15 (Sept. 21, 1859).

Hirschfeld, Christian Cayus Lorenz. *Theorie der Gartenkunst.* 5 vols. Leipzig: Weidmanns Erben & Reich, 1779–85. Simultaneously published in French as *Théorie de l'art des jardins.* 5 vols. Leipzig: Weidmanns Erben & Reich, 1779. (Especially useful are chapters on "Temples, Chapels, and Ruins" and "Statues, Monuments, and Inscriptions.")

Historical Sketch of the First Burying Ground in Dorchester. Boston: Municipal Printing Office, 1903.

Historical Sketch of the First Burying Place in Roxbury. Boston: Municipal Printing Office, 1904.

Historical Sketch of King's Chapel Burying-Ground. Boston: Municipal Printing Office, 1903.

Historical Sketch and Matters Appertaining to the Granary Burial-Ground. Boston: Municipal Printing Office, 1902.

History of the City Burial Ground in New Haven, together with the Names of the Owners of the Lots therein. New Haven: J. H. Benham, 1863.

Hitchcock, Henry-Russell. *Architecture: Nineteenth and Twentieth Centuries.* Baltimore: Penguin, 1971.

Hodges, Maud de Leigh. *Crossroads on the Charles: A History of Watertown, Massachusetts.* Canaan, N. H.: Phoenix, for the Watertown Free Public Library, 1980.

Homans, Isaac Smith. *Sketches of Boston, Past and Present and of Some Few Places in its Vicinity.* Boston: Phillips, Sampson, & Co., 1851.

Horstein, Edouard de. *Les Sépultures devant l'histoire, l'archéologie, la liturgie, le droit écclesiastique et la législation civile.* Paris: J. Albanel, 1868.

"Horticultural Societies." *Horticulturist* 6:2 (Feb. 1851): 92.

Howe, Daniel Walker. *The Unitarian Conscience: Harvard Moral Philosophy, 1805–1860.* Cambridge: Harvard Univ. Press, 1970.

Howells, William Dean. *A Traveller from Altruria: Romance.* New York: Harper, 1894. Reprint. New York: Sagamore Press, 1957.

Hubbard, William. *General History of New England from the Discovery to MDCLXXX.* Cambridge: Massachusetts Historical Society, 1815.

Hunt, John Dixon. *The Figure in the Landscape: Poetry, Painting, and Gardening during the Eighteenth Century.* Baltimore: Johns Hopkins Univ. Press, 1976.

———. *Garden and Grove: The Italian Renaissance Garden in the English Imagination: 1600–1750.* Princeton: Princeton Univ. Press, 1986.

———. "Pope's Twickenham Revisited." *Eighteenth-Century Life* 8 n.s., 2 (Jan. 1983): 29–32.

Hunt, John Dixon, and Peter Willis, eds. *The Genius of Place: The English Landscape Garden, 1620–1820.* New York: Harper & Row, 1975.

Hussey, Christopher. *English Gardens and Landscapes, 1700–1750.* New York: Funk & Wagnalls, 1967.

Huth, Hans. *Nature and the American: Three Centuries of Changing Attitudes*. Lincoln: Univ. of Nebraska Press, 1957.

Ingenhousz, Jan. *Experiments on Vegetables, Discovering their Great Power of Purifying the Common Air in Sunshine, and of Injuring It in the Shade and at Night, to which is Joined a New Method of Examining the Accurate Degree of the Salubrity of the Atmosphere*. London: P. Elmsley & H. Payne, 1779.

An Interesting Account of the Plague, Yellow Fever, etc., as They Have Prevailed in Different Countries. Boston: At the request of the Boston Board of Health, James Loring, 1820.

Irving, Washington. *The Sketch Book of Geoffrey Crayon, Gent*. 1819–20. Reprint. New York: Dutton, 1963.

Irwin, John T. *American Hieroglyphics: The Symbol of the Egyptian Hieroglyphics in the American Renaissance*. Baltimore: Johns Hopkins Univ. Press, 1980.

Jacques, David. *Georgian Gardens: The Reign of Nature*. London: B. T. Batsford, 1983.

Jaher, Frederic Cople. "The Boston Brahmins in the Age of Industrial Capitalism." In *The Age of Industrialism in America: Essays in Social Structure and Cultural Values*. New York: Free Press, 1968.

———. *The Urban Establishment: Upper Strata in Boston, New York, Charleston, Chicago, and Los Angeles*. Urbana: Univ. of Illinois Press, 1982.

James, Henry. *William Wetmore Story and His Friends, from Letters, Diaries, and Recollections*. Vol. 1. Boston: Houghton Mifflin, 1903.

Jarrett, David. *The English Landscape Garden*. New York: Rizzoli, 1978.

Jarvas, Samuel Farrar. *A Narrative of Events Connected with the Acceptance and Resignation of the Rectorship of St. Paul's Church, Boston*. Boston: n.p., Nov. 1825.

Johnson, Edward. *A History of New England from the English Planting in the Yeare 1628 untill the Yeare 1652*. London: Brooke, 1654.

Jolimont, François-Gabriel-Théodore de. *Les Mausolées français, recueil des tombeaux les plus remarquables par leur structure, leurs épitaphes, ou les cendres qu'ils renferment, érigés dans les nouveaux cimetières de Paris*. Paris: Firmin Didot, 1821.

Jones, Howard Mumford. *American and French Culture, 1750–1848*. Chapel Hill: Univ. of North Carolina Press, 1927.

Jones, Johns Andrews, ed. *Bunhill Memorials: Sacred Reminiscences of 300 Ministers and Other Persons of Note, who are Buried in Bunhill Fields, of every Denomination*. London: J. Paul, 1849.

Judd, Sylvester. *Margaret: A Tale of the Real and the Ideal: Blight and Bloom; Including Sketches of a Place Not Before Described, Called Mons Christi*. Boston: Jordan & Wiley, 1845.

Justitia. "John Hancock." *Mount Auburn Memorial* 1:17 (Oct. 6, 1859): 134.

Kaufman, Polly Welts. *Women Teachers on the Frontier*. New Haven: Yale Univ. Press, 1984. (Includes "The Diary of Arozina Perkins.")

Kean, Robert H. *History of the Graveyard at Monticello*. Charlottesville, Va.: Thomas Jefferson Memorial Foundation, 1972.

Kelly, George Armstrong. *Mortal Politics in Eighteenth-Century France*. In *Historical Reflections* (Canada) 13:1 (Spring, 1986).

[Kemble, Fanny.] *The Journal of Frances Anne Butler, Better Known as Fanny Kemble*. 1835. Reprint. New York: B. Blom, 1970.

Kendall, Edward Augustus. *Travels through the Northern Parts of the United States in the Years of 1807 and 1808*. Vol. 1. New York: I. Riley, 1809.

[King, Moses.] *King's Handbook of Boston Profusely Illustrated*. 4th ed. Cambridge: Moses King, 1883.

———. *Mount Auburn Cemetery, Including also a Brief History and Description of Cambridge, Harvard University, and the Union Railway Company*. Cambridge: Harvard Square, Moses King, 1885.

Koch, Adrienne, and William Peder, eds. *Selected Writings of John and John Quincy Adams*. New York: Knopf, 1964.

Krafft, Jean-Charles. *Plan des plus beaux jardins pittoresques de France, d'Angleterre, et d'Allemagne, et des édifices, monumens, fabriques, etc., qui concourrent à leur embellisement dans tous les genres d'architecture*. 2 vols. Paris: Levrault, 1809 and 1810.

Laborde, Alexandre-Louis-Joseph, Comte de. *Déscription des nouveaux jardins de la France et de ses anciens châteaux, mêlée d'obsérvations sur la vie de la compagne et la composition des jardins, avec déssins par Charles Bourgeois*. Paris: Delance, 1808 [–1815?].

Lafargue. *Motion d'ordre . . . sur la police des cimetières et des inhumations*. Corps Législatif, Conseil des Cinq-Cents. Séance du 14 frimaire, an VII (1799). Paris: n.p., 1799.

Lagarde, André, and Laurent-Michard, eds. *XVIIIe Siècle: Les grands auteurs français du programme*. Paris: Bordas, 1965.

Langley, Batty. *Ancient Architecture Restored and Improved by a Great Variety of Usefull Designs. Entirely New, in the Gothic Mode for the Ornamenting of Buildings and Gardens*. London, 1742.

———. *New Principles of Gardening*. London: Bettesworth, Batley, 1728.

Lassalle, C. *Promenades pittoresques aux cimetières du Père Lachaise, de Montmartre, du Montparnasse et autres, ou choix des principaux monuments élevés dans ces champs du repos*. Paris: A. Fourmage, 1844.

Latrobe, B[enjamin] Henry. "Anniversary Oration Pronounced before the Society of Artists of the United States, by Appointment of the Society, on the eighth of May, 1811." *First Annual Exhibition of the Society of Artists of the United States*. Philadelphia, 1811. Bound with *The Port-folio* n.s. 5:6 (June 1811).

Lawrence, William. *The Life of Amos A. Lawrence*. Boston: Houghton Mifflin, 1888.

______. *A Sermon on the 75th Anniversary of Saint Paul's Church, Boston*. Boston: By the Parish, 1895.

Lawrence, William R., ed. *Extracts from the Diary and Correspondence of the Late Amos Lawrence*. Boston: Gould & Lawrence, 1855.

Lears, T. Jackson. *No Place of Grace: Antimodernism and the Transformation of American Culture*. New York: Pantheon, 1981.

Leclerc, J.-B. *Rapport . . . sur les institutions rélatives à l'état civil des citoyens, Corps Législatif, le 16 brumaire, an VI*. Paris: n.p., 1798.

______. Corps Législatif, Conseil des Cinq-Cents. *Motion d'Ordre . . . sur l'existence et l'utilité d'une réligion civile en France*. Paris: n.p., 9 fructidor, an V (1797).

LeRouge, Georges-Louis. *Cahiers des jardins anglo-chinois à la mode*. Paris: LeRouge, 1776–85.

Levaillant, Maurice. *Les tombes célèbres*. Paris: Hachette, 1926.

Lincoln, Levi. *An Address Delivered on the Consecration of the Worcester Rural Cemetery, Sept. 8, 1838*. Boston: Dutton & Wentworth, 1838.

Linden, Blanche M. G. "Death and the Garden: The Cult of the Melancholy and the 'Rural' Cemetery." Ph.D. diss., Harvard University, 1981.

______. "The Willow Tree and Urn Motif: Changing Ideas about Death and Nature." *Markers* (Journal of the Association for Gravestone Studies) 1 (1979–80): 149–56.

Linden-Ward, Blanche. "Putting the Past under Grass: History as Death and Cemetery Commemoration." *Prospects* (Annual of American Cultural Studies) 10 (1985): 279–314.

______. "Putting the Past in Place: The Making of Mount Auburn Cemetery." *Cambridge Historical Society Proceedings* 44 (1976–79): 171–96.

______. "Strange but Genteel Pleasure Grounds: Tourist and Leisure Uses of Nineteenth-Century Rural Cemeteries." In *Cemeteries and Gravemarkers: Voices of American Culture*. Edited by Richard E. Meyer. Ann Arbor: UMI Research Press, 1989.

Linden-Ward, Blanche, and David C. Sloane. "Spring Grove: The Founding of Cincinnati's Rural Cemetery, 1845–1855." *Queen City Heritage* (Journal of the Cincinnati Historical Society) 43:1 (Spring 1985): 17–32.

Linden-Ward, Blanche, and Alan Ward. "Spring Grove: The Role of the Rural Cemetery in American Landscape Design." *Landscape Architecture* 75:5 (Sept.–Oct. 1985): 126–31, 140.

London City Lands Committee. *History of the Bunhill Fields Burial Ground with Some of the Principal Inscriptions*. London: Charles Skipper & East, 1887.

Longinus, [Dionysius Cassius.] *An Essay on the Sublime*. Translated by Nicolas Boileau-Despreaux. 1674. Oxford: Leon Lichfield, 1698.

Loudon, John Claudius. *On the Laying Out, Planting, and Managing of Cemeteries; and on the Improvement of Churchyards*. London: A. Spottiswoode for the Author. 1843.

Lovejoy, Arthur O. *Essays in the History of Ideas*. Baltimore: Johns Hopkins Univ. Press, 1948. (Especially "The Chinese Origins of a Romanticism" and "The First Gothic Revolution and the Return to Nature.")

Lowell, James Russell. *Letters of James Russell Lowell*. Edited by Charles Eliot Norton. Vol. 2. New York: Harper & Brothers, 1894.

Ludwig, Allan I. "Eros and Agape: Classical and Early Christian Survivals in New England Stonecarving." In *Puritan Gravestone Art: Annual Proceedings* (1976) *of the Dublin Seminar for New England Folklife*. Boston: Boston Univ., 1977.

______. *Graven Images: New England Stonecarving and Its Symbols, 1650–1815*. Middletown, Conn.: Wesleyan Univ. Press, 1966.

Ludwig, Allan I., and David D. Hall. "Aspects of Music, Poetry, Stonecarving, and Death in Early New England." In *Puritan Gravestone Art II: Annual Proceedings* (1978) *of the Dublin Seminar for New England Folklife*. Boston: Boston Univ., 1978.

Lunsford, John. *The Romantic Vision in America*. Dallas: Dallas Museum of Fine Arts, 1971.

Lyell, Sir Charles. *A Second Visit to the United States of North America*. Vol. 1. London: John Murray, 1849.

McCaughey, Robert A. *Josiah Quincy, 1772–1865: The Last Federalist*. Cambridge: Harvard Univ. Press, 1974.

McCloskey, Robert, ed. *The Works of James Wilson*. Cambridge: Harvard Univ. Press, 1967.

MacColl, Malcolm. *Lawlessness, Sacerdotalism, and Ritualism discussed in Six Letters Addressed . . . to the Right Hon. Lord Selbourne*. London: J. T. Hayes, 1875.

Maccubbin, Robert P., and Peter Martin, eds. *Eighteenth-Century Life* 8, n.s., 2 (Jan. 1983): 63–73.

MacDonald, Edward. *Old Copp's Hill and Burial Ground with Historical Sketches*. Boston: By the Author, 1894.

McDowell, Michael McEachern. *American Attitudes toward Death, 1825–1865*. (Ph.D. diss., Brandeis University, Dec. 1977.) Ann Arbor: Univ. Microfilms, 1978.

Mackay, Alexander. *The Western World; or, Travels in the United States in 1846–7*. Vol. 1. Philadelphia: Lea & Blanchard, 1849.

McManners, John. *Death and the Enlightenment: Changing Attitudes to Death among Christians and Unbelievers in Eighteenth-Century France*. Oxford: Clarendon Press of Oxford Univ. Press, 1981.

Malins, Edward. *English Landscaping and Literature, 1660–1840*. London: Oxford Univ. Press, 1966.

Maliphant, George. *Designs for Sepulchral Monuments*. London, n.p., n.d. (ca. 1820).

[Manning, Robert, ed.] *History of the Massachusetts Horticultural Society, 1829–1878*. Boston: Rand, Avery, for the Society, 1880.

Marchant de Beaumont, François-Marie. *Manuel et itinéraire du curieux dans le cimetière du Père la Chaise*. 3d ed. Paris: Emler Frères, 1828.

______. *Le Nouveau conducteur de l'étranger à Paris en 1826*. 13th ed. Paris: Moroval, 1826. (The 6th edition appeared in 1818; the 19th in 1837.)

______. *Vues pittoresque, historiques, et morales du cimetière du Père la Chaise*. Dessinées d'après nature par M. M. Vigneron et Duplat et gravées à l'aqua-tinta par M. Jazet accompagnées de leur déscription topographique, monumentale et morale. Paris: de Plassan, 1821.

Marion, John Francis. *Famous and Curious Cemeteries*. New York: Crown, 1977.

Martin, James Kirby. *Interpreting Colonial America: Selected Readings*. New York: Harper & Row, 1978.

Martineau, Harriet. *Retrospect of Western Travel*. London: Saunders & Otley, 1838.

Marty, Joseph. *Promenades pittoresques au cimetière du Père Lachaise*. Paris: Chaillou, 1835.

Marx, Leo. *The Machine in the Garden: Technology and the Pastoral Ideal in America*. New York: Oxford Univ. Press, 1964.

Mather, Cotton. *Magnalia Christi Americana; or, The Ecclesiastical History of New England from its First Planting in the Year 1620 unto the Year of Our Lord 1698*. New Haven: S. Converse, 1820. Also Hartford: Silus Andrus, Roberts, & Burr, 1820.

Mather, Increase. *Meditations on Death: Delivered in Several Sermons, Wherein is Shewed; I. That Some True Believers on Christ are Afraid of Death, but That They Have No Just Cause to Be So. II. That Good Men as Well as Others May Be Taken Out of the World by a Sudden Death. III. That Not Earth But Heaven is the Christian's Home*. Boston: Timothy Green, 1707.

Mathieu, René. *Ermenonville*. Paris: Nouvelles Editions Latines, 1985.

Maxwell, A. M. *A Run through the United States during the Autumn of 1840*. Vol. 1. London: Henry Colburn, 1841.

May, Henry F. *The Enlightenment in America*. New York: Oxford Univ. Press, 1976.

Mercier, Louis-Sébastien. *Le Tableau de Paris, nouvelle édition, corrigée et augmentée*. Vol. 3. Amsterdam, 1782–88.

Michelet, Jules. *Ma Jeunesse*. 6th ed. Paris: C. Lévy, 1884.

Milton, John. *Il Penseroso*. Oxford: Clarendon Press, 1883.

Moiroux, Jules. *Le Cimetière du Père la Chaise*. Paris: Mercadier, 1909.

Moore, Damrell V., and George Coolidge, eds. *The Boston Almanac for the Year 1857*. No. 22. Boston: John P. Jewett, 1857. (Includes Hammatt Billings, "Mount Auburn.")

Morel, Jean-Marie. *Théorie des jardins, ou l'art des jardins de la nature*. 2 vols. Paris: Panckoucke, an XI (1802).

Morison, Samuel Eliot. *Harrison Gray Otis: 1765–1848: The Urbane Federalist*. Boston: Houghton Mifflin, 1969.

Morison, Samuel Eliot, ed. *The Life and Letters of Harrison Gray Otis*. Boston: Houghton Mifflin, 1946.

[Mount Auburn Cemetery.] *Alphabetical and Numerical Lists of Proprietors of Lots in the Cemetery at Mount Auburn on March 1, 1834, together with the Terms of Subscription and Regulations in Regard to Interments*. Boston: J. T. Buckingham, 1834. (Revised lists of proprietors were published periodically through the remainder of century with varying titles and publishers such as *Catalogue of Proprietors in the Cemetery of Mount Auburn on 1st July, 1835 . . . together with the terms of subscription, regulations concerning visitors and interments, and the Act of the Legislature incorporating the said proprietors*. Boston: Nathan Hale, 1835. Or *Catalogue of Lots Laid Out in the Cemetery of Mount Auburn*. Boston: Nathaniel Dearborn, 1839.)

______. *Annual Report of the Trustees of the Cemetery of Mount Auburn together with the Reports of the Treasurer and Superintendent*. (Published annually for the Corporation from 1836 to the present.)

______. "Proprietors' and Trustees' Records." (Bound manuscript records of Proprietors' annual meetings and Trustees' monthly meetings in the Cambridge office of the Cemetery.) I (Apr. 21, 1835–Oct. 2, 1854). II (Oct. 9, 1854–Feb. 7, 1859). III (Feb. 14, 1859–Jan. 30, 1865). IV (Feb. 6, 1865–May 10, 1870). V (June 8, 1870–Mar. 12, 1875). VI (Apr. 14, 1875–Mar. 13, 1886).

______. "Records of Committees." (Bound manuscript records of occasional meetings of the committees on Lots, on Grounds, and on Interments, in the Cambridge office of the Cemetery.)

"Mount Auburn." *Cyclopoedia of Useful Knowledge* (1835): 9.

"Mount Auburn." *Gleason's Pictorial Drawing Room Companion* (Aug. 13, 1853): 104–5.

"Mount Auburn." *New England Magazine* (Sept. 1831): 236–39.

"Mount Vernon." *New-England Galaxy* 6:276 (Jan. 24, 1823): 1.

Mulot, [Abbé] F[rançois]-V[alentin.] *Discours . . . sur cette question: Quelles sont les cérémonies à faire pour les funérailles et le reglement à adopter pour le lieu de la sépulture?* Paris: n.p., an IX (1801).

______. *Discours sur les funérailles et le respect du aux morts, lu le 15 thermidor, an IV au Lycée des Arts*. Paris: n.p., 1796. (Printed with the essay by Fourcroy.)

______. *Vues d'un citoyen, ancien Deputé de Paris à l'Assemblé Législative sur les sépultures*. Paris: n.p., n.d. (1796?).

Muncey, Raymond Waterville Luke. *A History of the Consecration of Churches and Churchyards*. Cambridge, England: W. Heffer & Sons, 1930.

New Haven. *Proceedings of the City of New Haven in the Removal of Monuments from its Ancient Burying Grounds and in the Opening of a New Ground for Burial*. New Haven: Gray & Hewit, 1822.

Newton, Isaac. *Mathematical Principles of Natural Philosophy*. Edited by Florian Cajori, Berkeley: Univ. of California Press, 1934.

Newton, Norman. *Design on the Land: The Development of Landscape Architecture*. Cambridge: The Belknap Press of Harvard Univ. Press, 1971.

Nicher-Cérisy. *Des Tombeaux*. Paris: n.p., n.d. (ca. 1796).

Norton, Charles Eliot, ed. *Letters of James Russell Lowell*. New York: Harper & Brothers, 1894.

Nylander, Jane C. "Some Print Sources of New England Schoolgirl Art." *Antiques* (Aug. 1976): 292–301.

O'Connor, Thomas H. *Fitzpatrick's Boston, 1846–66: John Bernard Fitzpatrick, Third Bishop of Boston*. Boston: Northeastern Univ. Press, 1984.

Order of Services at the Consecration of Evergreen Cemetery. Boston: Tuttle & Dennett, 1850.

"An Ordinance to Regulate the Interment of the Dead." (Sept. 26, 1822.) In *The Charter and Ordinances of the City of Boston together with the Acts of the Legislature Relating to the City*. Edited by Thomas Wetmore and Edward G. Prescott. Boston: J. H. Eastburn, 1834.

"Ornamental Cemeteries." *Yale Literary Magazine* 21 (Nov. 1855): 45–50.

Orne, Caroline F. *Sweet Auburn and Mount Auburn with Other Poems*. Cambridge: John Owen, 1844.

Panofsky, Erwin. "*Et in Arcadia Ego:* Poussin and the Elegiac Tradition." In *Meaning in the Visual Arts*. Garden City, N.Y.: Doubleday, 1955.

"Paris from Père la Chaise: Recollections of a Solitary Traveller." In *The Atlantic Souvenir*. Philadelphia: H. C. Carey & I. Lea, 1826.

[Parker, Henry M.] *Notes on Mount Auburn, Edited by an Officer of the Corporation; Intended to Serve as a Stranger's Guide Book*. Boston: James Munroe, 1849.

Parrington, Vernon Louis. *Main Currents in American Thought. Vol. 2: 1800: The Romantic Revolution in America*. New York: Harcourt, Brace, & World, 1927.

Pascalis, Felix. *An Exposition of the Dangers of Interment in Cities*. New York: n.p., 1823.

Pattee, Fred Lewis. *The First Century of American Literature, 1770–1870*. New York: D. Appleton-Century, 1935.

Peabody, William B. O. "Margaret." *North American Review* 62:130 (Jan. 1846):102–40.

———. "Mount Auburn Cemetery: Report of the Massachusetts Horticultural Society upon the Establishment of an Experimental Garden and Rural Cemetery." *North American Review* 33 (Oct. 1831): 397–406.

Penny, Nicholas B. *Church Monuments in Romantic England*. New Haven: Yale Univ. Press, 1977.

———. "The Commercial Garden Necropolis of the Early Nineteenth Century and Its Critics." *Garden History* 2 (Summer 1974): 61.

———. "The Macabre Garden at Denbies and its Monuments." *Garden History* 3 (Summer 1975): 58–61.

Pernick, Martin S. "Politics, Parties, and Pestilence: Epidemic Yellow Fever in Philadelphia and the Rise of the First Party System." *William and Mary Quarterly* 29 (1972): 559–86.

Perry, Bliss, ed. *The Heart of Emerson's Journals*. Boston: Houghton Mifflin, 1926.

Persons, Stow. *The Decline of American Gentility*. New York: Columbia Univ. Press, 1973.

Pessen, Edward. *Riches, Class, and Power before the Civil War*. Lexington, Mass.: D. C. Heath, 1973.

Pettigrew, T. J. *The Chronicles of Tombs*. Edinburgh: H. G. Bohn, 1859.

Pevsner, Nicholas. "The Genesis of the Picturesque." *Architectural Review* 96 (1944): 79–102.

Pevsner, Nicholas, ed. *The Picturesque Garden and Its Influence outside the British Isles*. Washington, D.C.: Dumbarton Oaks Trustees for Harvard University, 1974.

Philips, Edith. *Louis Hué Girardin and Nicholas Gouin Dufief and Their Relations with Thomas Jefferson*. Baltimore: Johns Hopkins Univ. Press, 1926.

The Picturesque Pocket Companion and Visitor's Guide through Mount Auburn. Boston: Otis, Broaders, 1839.

Pierpont, John. "The Garden of Graves." In *The Token: A Christmas and New Year's Present*. Edited by S. G. Goodrich. Boston: S.G. Goodrich, 1832. Reprint. Dedham, Mass.: H. Mann, 1841.

———. "Ode Written for the Laying of the Corner Stone of the Bunker Hill Monument, June 17, 1825." In *Airs of Palestine and Other Poems*. Boston: James Munroe, 1840. (Also contains "To My Grave.")

Planta, Edward. *A New Picture of Paris; or, the Strangers' Guide to the French Metropolis*. London: Samuel Leigh, 1819.

Pleasants, J. Hall. *Four Late Eighteenth-Century Anglo-American Landscape Painters*. Worcester, Mass.: American Antiquarian Society, 1943.

Poe, Edgar Allan. "The Domain of Arnheim." First published in *Columbian Magazine* (Mar. 1847). In *Edgar Allan Poe: Selected Prose, Poetry, and Eureka*. Edited by W. H. Auden. New York: Holt, Rinehart, & Winston, 1950.

Pommereul, Général F.-R.-J. *Mémoire sur les funérailles et les sépultures, Question . . . jugée par l'Institut*. Paris: Onfroy; and Tours: Billault, an IX (1801).

Pope, Alexander. *Alexander Pope's Epistles to Several Persons (Moral Essays)*. Edited by James E. Willington. Coral Gables, Fla.: Univ. of Miami Press, 1976.

Poulson, Erastus. "The Grave of Washington." In *Our Country, or the American Parlor Keepsake*. Edited by William H. Ryder. Boston: J. M. Usher, 1854.

Prescott, Edward G., ed. *The Charter and Ordinances of the City of Boston*. Boston: J. H. Eastburn, 1834.

Price, Sir Uvedale. *An Essay on the Picturesque, as Compared with the Sublime and the Beautiful; and, on the Use of*

Studying Pictures, for the Purpose of Improving Real Landscape. 2 vols. London: J. Robson, 1794. Reprint by J. Mawman, 1810.

Prince, William. *A Short Treatise on Horticulture*. New York: T. & J. Swords, 1828. (First original horticultural study published in America, by the head of the Linnaean Botanical Gardens in Flushing, New York.)

Proceedings of the Association of Citizens to Erect a Monument in Honour of Gen. George Washington. Boston: Greenough & Stebbins, 1811.

Pugin, Augustus Charles, and C. Heath. *Paris and Its Environs Displayed in a Series of Picturesque Views*. 2 vols. London: Robert Jennings, 1829.

Pugin, Augustus Welby, and Augustus Charles Pugin. *Examples of Gothic Architecture*. 3 vols. London: H. G. Bohn, 1850.

———. *The True Principles of Pointed or Christian Architecture*. London: H. G. Bohn, 1853.

Putnam, Mrs. C. H. "Letters from Home: Mount Auburn Cemetery." *Young Lady's and Gentleman's Parlor Album* (New York, ca. 1843), 309–12.

Putnam, George. *An Address Delivered before the City Government and Citizens of Roxbury on the Life and Character of the Late Henry A. S. Dearborn, Mayor of the City, Sept. 3rd, 1851*. Roxbury: Norfolk County Journal Press, 1851. Excerpts printed as "Putnam's Address." *Boston Courier* (Sept. 4, 1851); and "Address." *Boston Daily Advertiser* (Sept. 9, 1851).

Quaglia, Ferdinand. *Les cimetières de Paris: Recueil des plus rémarquables monuments funèbres avec leurs inscriptions*. Paris: Levy, n.d. (ca. 1820).

———. *Le Père la Chaise; ou, Recueil de dessins au trait, et dans leurs justes proportions, des principaux monuments de ce cimetière, dessinés et lithographiés par M. Quaglia*. Paris: Ph. Boudon, 1835.

Quatremère de Quincy, Antoine-Chrysostome. "Décoration." In *Encyclopédie Méthodique* 2, pt. 1:179.

———. *Rapport fait au Conseil-Général le 15 thermidor, an VIII, sur l'instruction publique, le rétablissement des Bourses, le scandale des inhumations actuelles, l'érection de cimetières, la restitution des tombeaux, mausolées, etc.* Paris: n.p., an VIII (1800).

Quincy, Edmund. *The Life of Josiah Quincy of Massachusetts*. Boston: Ticknor & Fields, 1868.

Quincy, Josiah. *An Address to the Board of Aldermen, Members of the Common Council of Boston, on the Organization of the City Government at Faneuil Hall, January 1, 1828*. Boston: Commercial Gazette Office, 1828.

———. *An Address to the Citizens of Boston on the XVIIth of Sept., MDCCCXXX. The Close of the Second Century from the First Settlement of the City*. Boston: J. H. Eastburn, 1830.

———. *A Municipal History of the Town and City of Boston during Two Centuries*. Boston: Little, Brown, 1852.

———. "Speech on the Invasion of Canada." (Jan. 5, 1813.) In *Speeches Delivered in the Congress of the United States, 1805–1813*. Boston: Little, Brown, 1874.

R. "Interment of the Dead." *Monthly Anthology* 5 (July 1808): 348.

Ragon, Michel. *The Space of Death: A Study in Funerary Architecture, Decoration, and Urbanism*. Translated by Alan Sheridan. Charlottesville: Univ. of Virginia Press, 1983.

Randall, Henry S. *The Life of Thomas Jefferson*. Vol. 1. New York: Derby & Jackson, 1858.

Reed, Amy Louise. *The Background of Gray's Elegy: A Study in the Taste for Melancholy Poetry, 1700–1751*. New York: Russell & Russell, 1926.

Rees, Ronald. "The Scenery Cult: Changing Landscape Taste over Three Centuries." *Landscape* 19:3 (May 1975): 42.

Rémi, Abbé. *Les Jours, pour servir de correctif et de supplement aux Nuits de Young*. Paris, n.p., 1770.

Report of the Committee Appointed to Inquire into the Condition of the New-Haven Burying Ground and to Propose a Plan for its Improvement. New York: B. L. Hamlen, 1839.

Reps, John W. "Cemeteries, Parks, and Suburbs: Picturesque Planning in the Romantic Style." In *The Making of Urban America: A History of City Planning in the United States*. Princeton: Princeton Univ. Press, 1965.

Riat, Georges. *L'Art des jardins*. Paris: L.-H. May, n.d. (ca. 1810).

Richard, [E. Deb., and Jean-Marie-Vincent Dudin.] *Le Véritable conducteur aux cimetières du Père la Chaise, Montmartre, Montparnasse, et Vaugirard; ou, Guide le plus complet, le plus nouveau et le plus exact, de l'étranger, du curieux, et du promeneur dans ces cimetières*. Paris: Chez Roy-Terry, 1830.

The Rise and Progress of the Present Taste in Planting Parks, Pleasure Grounds, Gardens, etc. . . . in a Poetic Epistle to the Right Honourable Charles Lord Viscount Irwin. London: For C. Moran, 1767.

Roederer, [Pierre-Louis.] *Des Institutions funéraires convenables à une république qui permet tous les cultes et n'en adopte aucun*. Paris: Mathey & Desenne, an II (1793).

Roger-Marx, Claude. "Esthetique des cimetières." *Art sacré* (Paris: Nov.–Dec. 1949): 3–5.

Rogers, Millard F., Jr. *Randolph Rogers: American Sculptor in Rome*. Amherst: Univ. of Massachusetts Press, 1971.

Ronesse, A.-J. *Projet pour les sépultures*. Paris: n.p., an IX (1801).

Rossback, Sarah. *Feng Shui: The Chinese Art of Placement*. New York: E. P. Dutton, 1983.

Rothman, David J. *The Discovery of the Asylum: Social Order and Disorder in the New Republic*. Boston: Little, Brown, 1971.

Rotundo, Barbara. "Mount Auburn Cemetery: A Proper Boston Institution." *Harvard Library Bulletin* 22:3 (July 1974): 268–79.

Rousseau, Jean-Jacques. *Les Rêveries du promeneur solitaire.* Paris: Garnier, 1960.

Russell, Foster William. *Mount Auburn Biographies: A Biographical Listing of Distinguished Persons Interred in Mount Auburn Cemetery.* Cambridge: By the Corporation, 1953.

Russell, Howard S. *A Long, Deep Furrow: Three Centuries of Farming in New England.* Hanover, N.H.: Univ. Press of New England, 1976.

Sacy, Jacques-Silvestre de. *Alexandre-Théodore Brongniart, 1739–1813: Sa vie, son oeuvre.* Paris: Librairie Plon, 1940.

Sagra, D. Ramon de la. *Cinco Meses en los Estados-Unidos de la America del Norte desde el 20 de Abril al 23 de Setiembre de 1835.* Paris: Pablo Renouard, 1836.

Savage, Edward H., comp. *A Brief Mention of the Dates of More than 5000 Events that Transpired in Boston from 1630 to 1880.* Boston: Tolman & White, 1884.

Schlesinger, Arthur, Jr. *The Age of Jackson.* Boston: Little, Brown, 1945.

Schorsch, Anita. "A Key to the Kingdom: The Iconography of the Mourning Picture." *Winterthur Portfolio* 16 (Spring 1979): 41–71.

———. *Mourning Becomes America: Mourning Art in the New Nation.* Clinton, N.J.: Main Street Press, 1975. Exhibition catalogue from the William Penn Memorial Museum and the Albany Institute of History of Art.

Scott, Sir Walter. *The Letters of Sir Walter Scott.* Edited by Sir H[erbert] J[ohn] C[lifford] Grierson. 12 vols. London: Constable, 1932–37.

Scully, Vincent. *The Earth, the Temple, and the Gods: Greek Sacred Architecture.* New York: Praeger, 1969.

Seeley, B. *Description of the Gardens of Lord Viscount Cobham at Stowe in Buckinghamshire.* Northampton: W. Dicey, 1746.

"Sépultures." *Annales Philosophiques, Morales, et Littéraires, ou Suite des Annales Catholiques.* Vol. 1. Paris: Le Clère, 1800.

Shapiro, Henry D. "Putting the Past Under Glass: Preservation and the Idea of History in the Mid-Nineteenth Century." *Prospects* (Annual of American Cultural Studies) 10 (1985): 243–78.

Sharf, Frederic A. "The Garden Cemetery and American Sculpture: Mount Auburn." *American Quarterly* 34 (Spring 1961): 80–88.

Shepard, Odell, ed. *The Journals of Bronson Alcott.* Boston: Little, Brown, & Co., 1938.

Shively, Charles Allen. "A History of the Conception of Death in America, 1650–1860." Ph.D. diss., Harvard University, 1968.

Shurtleff, Nathaniel B. *A Topographical and Historical Description of Boston.* Boston: Rockwell & Churchill, 1891.

Sickels, Eleanor M. *The Gloomy Egoist: Moods and Themes of Melancholy from Gray to Keats.* New York: Octagon, 1969.

Sizer, Theodore, ed. *The Autobiography of Colonel John Trumbull, Patriot-Artist, 1756–1843.* New Haven: Yale Univ. Press, 1953.

"Sketch of the Life of Judge Story." *Mount Auburn Memorial* 1:1 (Aug. 24, 1859): 81.

Skinner, Aaron N. *History of the City Burial Ground of New Haven, together with the Names of the Owners of the Lots Therein.* New Haven: N. Green & J. H. Benham, 1863.

Slater, Peter Gregg. *Children in the New England Mind in Death and in Life.* Hamden, Conn.: Archon, 1977.

Smith, Bradford. *Bradford of Plymouth.* Philadelphia: J. B. Lippincott, 1951.

Snow, Caleb H. *A History of Boston: The Metropolis of Massachusetts.* Boston: Abel Bowen, 1825.

Stannard, David E. "Death and Dying in Puritan New England." *American Historical Review* 78 (1973): 1305–30.

———. *The Puritan Way of Death: A Study in Religion, Culture, and Social Change.* New York: Oxford Univ. Press, 1977.

Stannard, David E., ed. *Death in America.* Philadelphia: Univ. of Pennsylvania Press, 1975. Essays originally published in *American Quarterly* 26 (1974).

[Stevens, Levi Merriam.] *A Handbook for Passengers over the Cambridge Railroad with a Description of Mount Auburn Cemetery,* Boston: William V. Spencer, 1858.

———. *Guide through Mount Auburn: A Handbook for Passengers over the Cambridge Railroad.* Boston: Bricher & Russell, 1860.

Stone, Lawrence. "Death and Its History." *New York Review of Books* 25:15 (Oct. 12, 1978).

———. "Death in New England." *New York Review of Books* 25:16 (Oct. 26, 1978).

———. *The Family, Sex and Marriage in England, 1500–1800.* New York: Harper & Row, 1977.

Story, Joseph. "Lines Written on the Death of a Daughter in May 1831." In *Miscellaneous Writings, Literary, Critical, Juridical, and Political.* Boston: James Munroe, 1835.

Story, Ronald. *The Forging of an Aristocracy: Harvard and the Boston Upper Class, 1800–1870.* Middletown, Conn.: Wesleyan Univ. Press, 1980.

Story, William W[etmore], ed. *Life and Letters of Joseph Story.* 2 vols. Boston: Little, Brown, 1851.

Strang, John. *Necropolis Glasguensis with Observations on Ancient and Modern Tombs and Sculpture.* Glasgow: Atkinson & Co., 1831.

[Strauch, Adolph.] "Monuments." (From *The Report of Spring Grove Cemetery for 1857.*) *Mount Auburn Memorial* 1:28 (Dec. 21, 1859): 218.

Strickland, William. *Tomb of Washington at Mount Vernon.* Philadelphia: Carey & Hart, 1840.

Strong, George Templeton. *Diary.* Edited by Allan Nevins and Milton Halsey Thomas. New York: Macmillan, 1952.

Struik, Dirk. *Yankee Science in the Making.* Boston: Little, Brown, 1948.

"Sweet Auburn." *Mount Auburn Memorial* 1:2 (June 22, 1859): 12.

Switzer, Stephen. *Ichnographia Rustica; or, the Nobleman, Gentleman, and Gardener's Recreation.* London: D. Brown, 1718.

Symes, Michael. "Nature as the Bride of Art: The Design and Structure of Painshill." In Robert P. Maccubbin and Peter Martin, eds. *Eighteenth-Century Life* 8 n.s., 2 (Jan. 1983): 63–73.

T., E. E. "Burial and Burial Places." *Lowell Offering* 2:1 (1840): 154–57.

Tait, A. A. *The Landscape Garden in Scotland, 1735–1835.* Edinburgh: Edinburgh Univ. Press, 1980.

Tashjian, Dickran. "Puritan Attitudes toward Iconoclasm." In *Puritan Gravestone Art II: Annual Proceedings* (1978) *of the Dublin Seminar for New England Folklife.* Boston: Boston Univ., 1978.

Tatum, George Bishop. *Andrew Jackson Downing: Arbiter of American Taste, 1815–52.* Ann Arbor: University Microfilms, 1950.

______. "The Beautiful and the Picturesque." *American Quarterly* 3 (1951): 36–51.

______. "The Emergence of an American School of Landscape Design." *Historic Preservation* 25 (Apr.–June 1973).

Taylor, William R. *Cavalier and Yankee: The Old South and American National Character.* Cambridge: Harvard Univ. Press, 1979.

Thacher, Joseph Stevens Buckminster. "Address at the Commencement . . . 1832." In "Exhibition and Commencement Performances." (1831–32.) Manuscript in the Harvard University Archives.

Thomson, James. *The Seasons.* Newburyport, Mass.: John Mycall, 1790.

Thoreau, Henry David. *Walden.* 1854. Reprint. New York: Thomas Y. Crowell, 1961. Reprint. New York: Harper & Row, 1966.

"Thoughts Connected with Rural Cemeteries." *Christian Review* 13 (Mar. 1848): 22.

Thouret, Michel Augustin. *Rapport sur les exhumations du cimetière de l'église des Saints Innocents: lu dans la séance de la Société Royale de Médicine tenue au Louvre le 3 mars 1789.* Paris: Ph.-Denys Pierres, 1789.

Tocqueville, Alexis de. *Democracy in America.* Edited by Phillips Bradley. 2 vols. New York: Knopf, 1951.

"The Tomb of Spurzheim at Mount Auburn." *Family Magazine* (1853): 404.

"Tombs Under Saint Paul's." *New-England Galaxy* 6:273 (Jan. 3, 1823): 2.

Townshend, Henry Hotchkiss. *The Grove Street Cemetery.* New Haven: The Society, 1848.

Transactions of the Massachusetts Horticultural Society, 1829–1838. Boston: William D. Ticknor, 1847. (Published orations and other proceedings bound together in the library of the Massachusetts Horticultural Society, Boston.)

Trollope, Mrs. Frances. "Letter 22: Père Lachaise." In *Paris and the Parisians in 1835.* New York: Harper & Brothers, 1836.

Tucci, Douglass Shand. *Built in Boston: City and Suburb, 1800–1950.* Boston: New York Graphic Society, 1978.

Tuckerman, Henry. "The Law of Burial and the Sentiment of Death." *Christian Examiner* 26 (1836): 338.

Tudor, Henry. *Narrative of a Tour in North America.* London: James Duncan, 1834.

[Tudor, William.] "Instruction for the Fine Arts." *North American Review* 2 (Jan. 1816): 161.

______. *Letters on the Eastern States.* New York: Kirk & Mercein, 1820.

______. "Monument to Washington." *North American Review* 2:6 (1816): 329–40.

Tyack, David B. *George Ticknor and the Boston Brahmins.* Cambridge: Harvard Univ. Press, 1967.

Tymeson, Mildred McClary. *Rural Retrospect: A Parallel History of Worcester and Its Rural Cemetery.* Worcester, Mass.: Albert Rice, 1956.

Vafflard, Léon. *Notice sur les champs de sépultures anciens et modernes de la ville de Paris.* Paris: Charles de Mougues Frères, 1867.

Van Laar, G. *Magazijn van Tuin-Sieraden; of Verzameling van Modellen van Aanleg en Sieraad, voor Groote en Kleine Lust-Hoven, Voornamelijk van Dezulke die, met Weinig Kosten, Te Maken Zijn.* Rotterdam: Johannes Noman en Zoon, 1802.

Van Tassel, David D. *Recording America's Past: An Interpretation of the Development of Historical Studies in America, 1607–1884.* Chicago: Univ. of Chicago Press, 1960.

Vicq-d'Azyr, Felix. *Essai sur les lieux et les dangers de sépultures.* Paris: n.p., 1778.

Vidler, Alec R. *The Church in the Age of Revolution: 1789 to the Present Day.* New York: Penguin, 1977.

Vidler, Anthony. *The Writing of the Walls: Architectural Theory in the Late Enlightenment.* Princeton: Princeton Architectural Press, 1987.

Vieillard, P. A. "Fouché." In *Nouvelle Biographie Générale.* Edited by Ferdinand Hoefer. Paris: Firmin Didot Frères, 1870.

Viennet. *Promenade philosophique au cimetière du Père-Lachaise.* Paris: Librairie Ponthieu, 1824.

Vinovskis, Maris A. "Angels Heads and Weeping Willows: Death in Early America." *Proceedings of the American Antiquarian Society* 86 (1976): 273–302.

Volney, Constantin-François de Chasseboeuf, Comte de. *Ruins; or, a Survey of the Revolution of Empires.* Albany: S. Shaw, 1822. Translated from the French *Les Ruines, ou Méditations sur les révolutions des empires.* 1791.

Voltaire, François Marie Arouet de. "La Considération due

aux gens de lettres." *Lettres Philosophiques* 12. Paris: Garnier Frères, 1878.

———. "Enterrement." *Oeuvres complètes: Dictionnaire philosophique portatif, ou la raison par alphabet.* Paris: Garnier Frères, 1878.

von Erlach, Johann Bernhard Fischer. *Entwurff einer Historischen Architectur.* Vienna, 1721.

Voss, Frederick S. *John Frazee, 1790–1852: Sculptor.* Washington: Smithsonian; and Boston: Athenaeum, 1986.

Vovelle, Michel. *La Mort et l'Occident de 1300 à nos jours.* Paris: Gallimard & Panthéon, 1983.

W., T. H. "Botanical History of the Yew Tree" *Gentleman's Magazine* 56, pt. 2, no. 5 (Nov. 1786): 941.

Walker, G. A. *Gatherings from Grave-yards; Particularly Those of London: with a Concise History of the Modes of Interment among Different Nations from the Earliest Periods.* London: Longman, 1839.

Walker, Samuel. "Horticultural Societies." *Horticulturist* 6:2 (Feb. 1851): 92.

[Walker, Stephen Duncan.] *Rural Cemetery and Public Walk.* Baltimore: Sands & Neilson, 1835.

Walpole, Horace. *Letters.* Edited by Mrs. P. Toynbee. Oxford: Oxford Univ. Press, 1925.

Walter, Cornelia W. *The Rural Cemeteries of America: Mount Auburn Illustrated in a Series of Views Taken from Drawings Taken on the Spot . . . with Descriptive Notices.* New York: R. Martin, 1847.

Ward, Malthus. *An Address Pronounced before the Massachusetts Horticultural Society in Commemoration of its Third Annual Festival, Sept. 21, 1831.* Boston: J. T. & E. Buckingham, 1831.

Ware, William. "Unitarian Belief." *Unitarian* 1 (Nov. 1827): 17–22.

Warren, F. E. *The Liturgy and Ritual of the Celtic Church.* Oxford: Clarendon Press, 1883.

Warren, George Washington. *The History of the Bunker Hill Monument Association.* Boston: James R. Osgood, 1877.

Warren, John. *An Oration, Delivered July 4, 1783, at the Request of the Inhabitants of Boston in Celebration of the Anniversary of American Independence.* Boston: John Gill, 1783.

Watelet, Claude-Henri. *Essai sur les jardins.* Paris: Chez Perault, 1764.

Watts, Isaac. "The Church-Yard." In *Reliquiae Iuveniles: Miscellaneous Thoughts in Prose and Verse, on Natural, Moral, and Divine Subjects.* London: James Brackstone, 1742.

Webster, Daniel. *An Address Delivered at the Laying of the Cornerstone of the Bunker Hill Monument.* Boston: Cummings and Hilliard, 1825. Reprinted along with "First Settlement of New England." (Dec. 22, 1820.) And "Adams and Jefferson." (1826.) In *The Writings and Speeches of Daniel Webster in 18 Volumes. Vol. I: Memoir and Speeches on Various Occasions.* Boston: Little, Brown, 1903.

"The Weeping Willow." *New England Farmer* 5:43 (May 18, 1827): 338.

Welter, Rush. *The Mind of America: 1820–60.* New York: Columbia Univ. Press, 1975.

Wetmore, Thomas, and Edward G. Prescott, eds. *The Charter and Ordinances of the City of Boston together with the Acts of the Legislature Relating to the City.* Boston: J. H. Eastburn, 1834.

Whately, Thomas. *Observations on Modern Gardening.* London, 1770.

Wheaton, Henry. "Egyptian Antiquities." *North American Review* 30:65 (Oct. 1829): 361–88.

Whistler, Laurence, Michael Gibbon, and George Clarke. *Stowe: A Guide to the Gardens.* London: n.p., 1974.

Whitmore, William H. *The Graveyards of Boston: Vol. I: Copp's Hill Epitaphs.* Albany, N.Y.: Joel Munsell, 1878.

Whitney, Peter. *Weeping and Mourning at the Death of Eminent Persons a National Duty: A Sermon Delivered at Northborough, Feb. 22, 1800, Observed as a Day of National Mourning on Account of the Death of General George Washington.* Brookfield, Mass.: E. Merriam, 1800.

Whittemore, Thomas, ed. *The Life of Rev. Hosea Ballou: With Accounts of His Writings.* Boston: James M. Usher, 1855.

Wiebenson, Dora. *The Picturesque Garden in France.* Princeton: Princeton Univ. Press, 1978.

Wilkes, Charles. *Narrative of the U.S. Exploring Expedition during the Years 1838, 1839, 1840, 1841, 1842.* Philadelphia: Lea & Blanchard, 1848.

Willard, Samuel. "The High Esteem Which God Hath of the Death of His Saints." (Boston, 1685.) In *The Puritans: A Sourcebook of Their Writings.* Edited by Perry Miller and Thomas E. Johnson. New York: Harper & Row, 1963.

Willey, Basil. *The Eighteenth-Century Background: Studies on the Idea of Nature in the Thought of the Period.* London: Chatto & Windus, 1949.

Willis, Peter. *Charles Bridgeman and the English Landscape Garden.* London: A. Zwemmer, 1977.

Willis, Sarah Payson. "Incident at Mount Auburn." In *Fern Leaves from Fanny's Port Folio.* Auburn, N.Y.: Derby & Miller, 1853.

Willsher, Betty, and Doreen Hunter. *Stones: A Guide to Some Remarkable Eighteenth-Century Scottish Gravestones.* New York: Taplinger, 1979.

[Wines, Enoch Cobb.] A Philadelphian. *A Trip to Boston in a Series of Letters to the Editor of the United States Gazette.* Boston: Little, Brown, 1838.

Winsor, Justin, ed. *The Memorial History of Boston, Including Suffolk County, Massachusetts, 1630–1880.* Boston: James R. Osgood, 1881.

Wood, Gordon S. *The Creation of the American Republic, 1776–1787.* Chapel Hill: Univ. of North Carolina Press, 1969.

Woodbridge, Kenneth. *Landscape and Antiquity: Aspects of English Culture at Stourhead, 1718–1838*. Oxford: Clarendon Press, 1970.

———. *The Stourhead Landscape*. London: National Trust, 1982.

Wooley, M. E. "The Development of the Love of Romantic Scenery in America." *American Historical Review* 3 (Oct. 1897): 56–66.

Woolsey, T. D. "Cemeteries and Monuments." *New Englander* 28 (Nov. 1849): 489–501.

Wordsworth, William. "Essay upon Epitaphs." *Friend* 25 (Feb. 1810): 408. Reprinted in *The Excursion: A Poem*. New York: C. S. Francis, 1850.

———. *The Prelude: or, Growth of a Poet's Mind: An Autobiographical Poem*. Book 11 (composed ca. Feb. 1804). New York: Appleton, 1850.

Wortley, Lady Emmeline. *Travel in the United States . . . during 1849–50*. New York: Harper Brothers, 1851.

Wright, C. Conrad. *The Beginnings of Unitarianism in America*. Boston: Beacon, 1955.

Wrighte, William. *Grotesque Architecture; or, Rural Architecture, Consisting of Plans, Elevations, and Sections for Huts, Retreats, Summer and Winter Hermitages, Terminaries, Chinese, Gothic, and Natural Grottos, Cascades, Baths, Mosques, Moresque Pavilions, Grotesque and Rustic Seats, Green Houses, Etc., Many of Which May be Executed with Flints, Irregular Stones, Rude Branches, and Roots of Trees*. London: Henry Webley, 1767.

Young, Rev. Alexander. *A Discourse on the Life and Character of the Hon. Nathaniel Bowditch, LL.D., F.R.S., Delivered in the Church on Church Green, Mar. 25, 1838*. Boston: Little, Brown, 1838.

Young, Edward. *Night Thoughts on Life, Death, and Immortality*. Philadelphia: Benjamin Johnson, 1805.

Zillah. "Mount Auburn." *Lowell Offering* 1:1 (1840): 13–14.

Index

Azalia Path
Azalia Path
SPRUCE AVENUE
Hare-Bell Path
Tulip Path
Trefoil Path
Thistle Path
Pilgrim Path
WALNUT AVENUE
Orange Path
LAUREL HILL
LAUREL AVENUE
Fern Path
MOUNTAIN AVENUE
MOUNT AUBURN
Sumac Path
PINE HILL
Central Square
Ivy Path
Hazel Path
Rose Path
HARVARD HILL
Amaranth Path
Woodbine Path
CEDAR HILL
Hawthorn Path
JUNIPER HILL
TEMPLE HILL
Sweet Briar Path
CHESNUT AVENUE
POPLAR AVENUE
OAK AVENUE
Lotus Path
LOCUS